THE CRISIS OF PARLIAMENTS

ENGLISH HISTORY
1509—1660

CONRAD RUSSELL

Reader in History
Bedford College, London

'This is the crisis of parliaments: we shall
know by this if parliaments live or die.'
SIR BENJAMIN RUDYERD, 1628

OXFORD UNIVERSITY PRESS

Oxford University Press, Walton Street, Oxford OX2 6DP

OXFORD LONDON GLASGOW NEW YORK MELBOURNE WELLINGTON
CAPE TOWN DELHI IBADAN NAIROBI DAR ES SALAAM BOMBAY CALCUTTA
MADRAS KARACHI LAHORE KUALA LUMPUR SINGAPORE JAKARTA HONG KONG TOKYO

ISBN 0 19 913034 5

© OXFORD UNIVERSITY PRESS, 1971

First published 1971
Reprinted (with corrections) 1974, 1977, 1978

Printed in Great Britain by
Richard Clay (The Chaucer Press), Ltd.
Bungay, Suffolk

GENERAL EDITOR'S PREFACE

ONE way in which changes in historical taste and outlook are reflected—
though sometimes slowly—is in the forbidding demands of examiners and
makers of syllabuses. This series is meant to be of practical value to the
students and teachers who have to meet them. But such demands themselves are only reflections of deeper and more important changes in
historical thinking. And that thinking must be reflected directly, as well
as indirectly, in new historical books. *The Short Oxford History of the
Modern World* is consciously designed to take account of the most
important recent historical work. It seems worth while, therefore, to say
what the developments are which have been thought important and how
the principles of design of this series are related to them.

One obvious change in recent historical activity has been a geographical widening of the history we study. Parts of the world hitherto
neglected, or comparatively neglected, by historians bred in the western
tradition of scientific history are now for the first time attracting interest
and attention. In part this is a reflection of our humanitarian and
political concerns: we are coming to realize that we live in one world, and
believe we ought therefore to know more about the parts of it with which
we are unfamiliar. In part, too, it reflects changes in what is available as
source-material. Whatever the source, the impulse is beginning to make
its mark in schools and colleges. They now need books about Latin
America, Africa, or Asia on the scale and at the level of those which in
the past introduced them to European or English history.

This series will include such books, but also others on more familiar
and traditional areas of study. There is, after all, a great need for the
achievements of up-to-date scholarship to be given wide currency in
English and European history. Consequently, this series is tripartite. It
consists of a series of four volumes on modern European history, in
which the British Isles are treated as a part of European society as a
whole. The second group of four volumes is more specialized, being
confined to English history. The third group will be larger and will contain
introductory volumes, covering fairly long periods, on those areas and
countries which are only now beginning to be studied widely. Some of

these are conceived as of continental scope, the projected volume on Latin America, for example. Those on the United States and Russia, on the other hand, limit themselves to a single political entity. In each case, the books in this stream are distinguished by being about a big and important topic for which good introductory manuals are not yet easily available.

The unity which binds these books together, although they will have different levels of detail and scope, is that they all deal with the 'modern world' referred to in the title of the series. This phrase, however, is to be read in a special sense and it is this which makes the series a whole. The subject-matter of *The Short Oxford History of the Modern World* is limited in time, but the chronological limitation is not the same for each book. Conventionally, series of books on the Modern History of different countries line up all their runners at approximately the same starting-gate and get them off together, whether in 1400, 1500, 1600, or any other dramatic, convenient, or merely 'significant' moment. In this series we follow a different scheme. The latest era of world history is here defined thematically, not chronologically. It is the era in which the fundamental institutions of modern European society first take shape and then spread round the world.

Some of these institutions are so widespread that we too readily take them for granted—the national sovereign state, for example. Yet this is even in Europe only a recent innovation and in many parts of the world it did not appear until after 1945. Formally representative political systems (whether real or fictitious) are another of Europe's institutional exports to the world, and there are economic ones, too, such as capitalism, or ideological ones such as Marxist communism or Christianity. In all these instances (and many others could be cited), we have examples of a process by which European gradually became World civilization. Sometimes this has produced new examples of developed 'Western' societies; sometimes it has led to more striking disruptions of tradition and eventually to altogether new institutions and cultural forms. The process, however it ends, defines an era by the break it provides with the past. This era begins at different times in different countries: in roughly 1500 in west European history, in about 1800 in the case of Russia, and at an even later date in the history of China, for example. These are the epochs in the history of different countries and regions in which can be discerned the processes which eventually tie them into the single world in which we live.

Besides moving to different rhythms, it is another consequence of this that not all the books in *The Short Oxford History of the Modern World* will have the same pattern. Differences in presentation are needed to bring out differences of national and regional life. But they will form a coherent series in a methodological sense too. They will have in common a deliberate effort to incorporate recent research and recent thinking which has begun to change the conventional shape of historical writing. This affects both their organization and the proportions of their subject-matter. The core of a good history must be the provision of the essential basic information which is necessary to the exercise of historical imagination and judgement. But lately ideas about what basic information is needed have been changing, for example by a new emphasis on society and its structure at the expense of the traditional political narrative. Historians and their public—which includes even examiners—have begun to think that it may be more revealing to study, say, the growth of cities in nineteenth-century England and its repercussions, than, say, the party struggle. This is only one example of the recent rapid popularizing of the old idea that history is more than past politics. This series attempts to take account of this. Many of its authors are young scholars who, because of their own research interests, are familiar with what is going on at the frontier of current historical work. They and their colleagues will seek to absorb into their accounts the flood of social, cultural, demographic, and many other sorts of monograph which has poured out since 1945 to confuse and muddle the ordinary historical student and the general reader.

The purpose of general books has, of course, always been to reduce to manageable thinking the detailed scholarship of the specialists. But another recent historical tendency has made it all the more important that this should be done. This is the problem, facing teachers of history at all levels, of the crumbling of boundaries which delimited and landmarks which directed their studies. The conventional separation of English and European history is now often an encumbrance to understanding the many processes in which this country was as much involved as any continental state: industrialization is an example. Another would be our changing views of the importance of certain dates. 1917, for example, or 1941, can be defended as much more significant breaks in the continuity of European history than 1914 or 1939. In some places, old guidelines seem almost to have disappeared altogether.

In part these changes arise because much new evidence is becoming available; in part it is because research has addressed itself to old evidence in a new way; in part it is a matter of changing perspective. More fundamentally, it reflects a basic truism about history: that it is theoretically boundless, a continuing debate, and that historians in each generation re-map and re-divide its subject-matter in accordance with their interests and the demands of society.

This series tries to provide a new map. It is bound to be provisional; that is of the nature of general history. But general history can be scholarly in its standards and imaginative in its presentation. Only by combining both qualities can it provide the authoritative guidance which each generation of readers needs if it is to pick its way through the flood of specialized studies now pouring from what has become one of our major cultural industries.

J. M. R.

September 1969

PREFACE

A PREFACE, like a wedding speech, must necessarily be composed largely of thanks. My thanks are due, first, to John Roberts, General Editor of this series, for offering me the commission to write this book, and for never doubting that it would appear. He has been the most helpful General Editor an author could hope for, combining exemplary patience with a remarkable expertise in a period not his own. I have found the commission an education in itself, and for this, too, I owe him my thanks. My thanks are due to the Clarendon Press for more sorts of helpfulness than can well be enumerated. All textbooks are to some extent co-operative efforts, and the preparation of this book has given me a deep sense of gratitude to other scholars working on the period. There has probably been no time since about 1900 when the general standard of work being done on this period was as high as it is today, and the work of several hundred historians has been used to enrich this book. I would like to thank them all. More specifically, I would like to thank the following people, who have read parts of this book in draft, and have made a number of illuminating comments, and saved me from innumerable errors: Patrick Collinson, Robin Du Boulay, Ivor Fishbone, Anthony Fletcher, Tresna Fletcher, Roger Highfield, Peter McCormack, Bob Moore, Wendy Moore, Valerie Pearl, Ian Roy, Bertrand Russell, Horace Sanders, Vivian Sanders, Jack Scarisbrick, Nicola Sutherland, Christopher Thompson, Michael Thompson, Nicholas Tyacke, and Austyn Woolrych. For any errors which remain, I alone am responsible. I would also like to join the long and growing list of historians who have acknowledged the seminar of Sir John Neale and Professor Hurstfield at the Institute of Historical Research. I would like to thank my sister-in-law, Vivian Sanders, for typing the whole work, and for undertaking the highly skilled and very lengthy task of correcting the manuscript to Clarendon Press House Rules. Above all, I would like to thank my wife. She has offered all the traditional form of help. In addition, she is responsible for far more of the reading and research which have gone into this book than is indicated in the footnotes, she has taken a very large share in the formulation of the argument, and she has given expert criticism, historical, literary, and editorial, to the resulting product. Since acknowledgement is insufficient, I would like to ask her to accept the dedication instead.

CONRAD RUSSELL

Bedford College, London
February 1970

CONTENTS

1. TUDOR ENGLAND, 1509–1603

2. HENRY VIII AND THE POPE, 1509–1536

3. STATE OF FLUX, 1536–1570

4. PURITANISM AND FASHION, 1570–1640

5. THE PRICE OF VICTORY, 1570–1618

1. *Tudor England* 1509–1603

I INTRODUCTORY

Many of the king's subjects have no ground to live upon, as they have had before time, and occupations be not always set on work all alike, and therefore the people still increasing, and their livings diminishing, it must needs come to pass that a great part of the people shall be idle, and lack livings, and hunger is a bitter thing to bear.

Discourse of the Common Weal, 1549, p. 48

... for the necessary repressing ... of the inordinate excess daily more and more used in the sumptuous and costly array and apparel accustomably worn in this realm, whereof hath ensued ... such sundry high and notable inconveniences as be to the great manifest and notorious detriment of the common weal, the subversion of good and politic order in knowledge and distinction of people according to their estates preeminences dignities and degrees, and to the utter impoverishment and undoing of many inexpert and light persons inclined to pride mother of all vices ... [no person worth less than £100 a year may wear] any satin damask silk chamlet or taffeta in his gown coat with sleeves or other outermost apparel.

An Act for the Reformation of Excess in Apparel, 24 Henry VIII, c.13

Evidence and its limitations

HISTORIANS may learn much from students of art, architecture, or archaeology. Nevertheless, history is essentially the study of the past by means of written records. Historians are therefore necessarily confined to those subjects on which people have not merely made, but kept, written records. How much the story we tell may be distorted by this process, it is hard to say. If the author of a newsletter reports a violent ambush and attempted murder in Fleet Street, does this prove that such goings-on were normal in Fleet Street, or that the event was recorded because it was so unusual as to be surprising? If six men are brought to trial for saying Anne Boleyn was a bawd, does this prove that such an opinion was general, or that the opinion that she was an honest woman was so common that no one bothered to record its expression? Such questions cannot be answered.

It is easier to see in what ways the subjects discussed by historians must be limited by variation in the making and keeping of records. Some subjects are more readily recorded in writing than others, and some records are more readily preserved than others. Historians are therefore confined to studying those subjects on which records are kept. These are of four main types: the payment of money, litigation, propaganda, and diplomacy. Any historian, whatever efforts he makes, cannot avoid overstressing these themes.

This limitation of records also means that there are some questions which are often asked by the layman to which it is very hard to provide answers. Of these, one of the most persistent is the desire to know the opinions of 'the common people', 'the majority', or 'the nation'. Historians would like to know the answer to this question, but they are necessarily confined to talking about those people who got their opinions recorded. Since this tends to mean those people who got prosecuted for their opinions, this sample necessarily overweights the extremists, and means that general questions must be answered by a string of particular instances. If we are asked the opinion of 'the people' about the Reformation, we can say that a number of people in Yorkshire taverns denied transubstantiation, but the churchwardens of Sheriff Hutton (Yorkshire) kept their Catholic images in storage in Edward's reign, in the hope that they would be able to use them again.[1] This, of course, is not an answer to the question, but we only know even this much because the people in the Yorkshire taverns had the ill luck to speak in the presence of an enemy or an informer, and so were brought to trial, while the churchwardens of Sheriff Hutton recorded in their accounts the cost of shifting the images. It is a necessary part of the historical discipline in the period before public opinion polls that it leads to concentration on the particular, rather than the general. This, however undesirable it may be, is inevitable: mute inglorious Miltons, by definition, leave no records.

'Medieval' and 'modern' history

It is perhaps easier to prevent the historical distortions which happen through the division of periods, and in particular through the notion that there is one point, or one theme, that marks the division between modern and medieval history. It is necessary, for the convenience of students and examiners (and of authors), that history should be divided into periods. It is even necessary, for the general convenience, that there should be an

[1] Dickens, *Lollards and Protestants* (1959), 223–4, 182.

administrative division between early and late history, which may, for want of better words, be called 'medieval' and 'modern'. But it is a false deduction to assume that because we wish to divide our examination papers, history will therefore supply us with a break in continuity at the point where it suits our administrative convenience. Numerous historians, attempting to justify making a division in one place rather than another, have written about supposed divisions between modern and medieval history, but in doing so, they are writing about their own sense of priorities. Different interests and different cultural backgrounds will place the division in different places. Professor Elton, whose definition of 'modernity' is bureaucracy, would place his dividing line in the 1530s.[2] Another, for whom the dividing line is the creation of an uncorrupt civil service insulated from party politics, might place it in the middle of the nineteenth century. A historian for whom the most significant dividing line is the end of the unity of western Christendom might take a date in the 1530s, and another, more concerned with the abandonment of the belief that all public life depends on Christianity, might end the Middle Ages in the nineteenth century on the day Bradlaugh was allowed to take his parliamentary seat as an avowed atheist. A financial historian might place the division in 1694, when the Bank of England was created. Others, with equal logic, might argue a case for the invention of gunpowder, or of printing. Recently, other historians have argued against this disposition to find a sudden break, but perhaps unfortunately, they have done so in terms of arguing that some aspect of English life at a given date was still 'medieval',[3] which leads their readers to look for a sudden break at a later date. It would perhaps be better if historians of the Tudor and Stuart period were to abandon the notion that there is a distinction between modern and medieval history. Any such distinction is a matter of language, not of history, and was unknown in the period. People who quoted fourteenth-century precedents in seventeenth-century Parliaments did not know we would regard them as irrelevant because they were 'medieval' precedents applied to a 'modern' situation.

The rejection of the distinction between medieval and modern history is perfectly compatible with the recognition that the period covered in this volume (like all others) saw very important historical changes. England in 1660 was a very different country from England in 1509. Numerous changes happened during the period which modern readers might be inclined to hail as 'progress'. At the beginning of the period, England was

---

[2] Elton, G. R., *England Under the Tudors* (1962), 184.
[3] e.g. Wolfe, B. P., 'Henry VII's Land Revenues and Chamber Finance', *E.H.R.* (1964), 225–54.

a Catholic country, and believed that its political and social stability depended on the repression of all dissent. At the end of the period, England, if not safe for, was at least so amply populated with Quakers, Catholics, Presbyterians, Arminians, Ranters, Seekers, and Muggletonians that government attempts to suppress dissent were necessarily doomed to failure. At the beginning of the period England was one part of an obscure offshore island, holding such diplomatic importance as it possessed by exploitation of the European balance of power on a shoestring budget. At the end of it, she was a substantial maritime and colonial power, re-exporting colonial produce, and by 1700 almost in a position to hold her own even against Louis XIV's France. At the beginning of the period, England was an agricultural country with one important export industry, the manufacture of woollen cloth. At the end of the period, she had a thriving coal industry, and was exporting the produce of a number of small, but growing, industries based on it. It had not had anything which can strictly be called an industrial revolution, but was well on the way which led to one. At the beginning of the period, sorcery and astrology were widely practised, and science was neglected. At the end of it, the Royal Society was about to be founded, and though Isaac Newton still practised alchemy and wrote treatises on the Book of Revelation, he was also starting on serious research in physics. At the beginning of the period, it was possible to write into an Act of Parliament the words that 'his highness is not minded, for the ease of his subjects, without great, necessary and urgent causes, of long time to call and summon a new Parliament.'[4] At the end of the period, such words were as inconceivable as they had been in Edward III's reign. Instead of having a good chance of living on his own resources, the king was so heavily dependent on the excise and other taxes voted by Parliament, that he could not expect to govern for long in any way it strongly disapproved of.

It is a mistake, however, to assume that all these changes must have happened because somebody wanted them. 'Innovation' was one of the favourite terms of political abuse, and such men as Jewel, an Elizabethan bishop, rebutted the slanderous allegation that Protestantism was new unless 'they think Christ himself to be new'.[5] We are not dealing with a country eager to leave the Middle Ages behind, but with one which was sadly puzzled by change, and often hostile to it.

[4] *Tudor Constitution*, 23–4.
[5] Jewel, John, *Apology of the Church of England* (Parker Soc.), 85.

II THE ECONOMY IN THE SIXTEENTH CENTURY

Prices

Of all the changes, perhaps the one which caused most bewilderment, and certainly the one which most closely defines the beginning of the period of this volume, was the rapid rise in prices, which began about 1510, and continued, at rapid but varying speeds, at least until 1620. To say that this was one of the most important stresses of the period, it is not necessary to say that it was catastrophic; it was only for a few years in the middle of the sixteenth century that prices rose at the speed which the twentieth century has come to accept as normal. Sixteenth-century England, however, unlike twentieth-century Great Britain, was not used to assuming that price rises were normal, and had very little machinery for adjusting them. Those who had the power were quite ready to get away with paying the wages, rents, or taxes their grandfathers had paid, and when they did, it necessarily created difficulties for the recipients, whether they were wage labourers or the Crown.

It is still hard to be dogmatic about how big the price increase was. The recording of prices was random, and they might be subject to considerable local variations. A sudden storm in Shropshire might send the local price of grain, and therefore of bread, far above the level it might reach the same year in another county. Grain prices also varied with the seasons and according to the standard of the year's harvest. Even the prices of industrial goods varied according to the harvest, since the harvest often determined how much potential purchasers had to spend. Political circumstances such as the arrival of the king might affect prices. In 1641, his presence made the market at Malton, Yorkshire, 'very quick',[6] and during the 1640s, the most rapid rise in grain prices was at Oxford. This is probably due, not to variations in Oxfordshire agriculture, but to the arrival of the king's court at Oxford at the beginning of the civil war. This is hardly surprising when James I's household had consumed annually thirteen thousand sheep and lambs, two thousand cattle, nineteen thousand dozen hens and chickens, and presumably corn in proportion. In 1627–30, during an economy campaign, the maximum *waste* permitted daily was 200 loaves, 240 gallons of ale, 24 gallons of wine, and 8 sides of beef, except on Fridays and feast days. The king's average annual bill for diet in the 1630s was £47,000, and it is not surprising that the increased demand in the Oxford market sent up prices. It is hard to tell how much surviving price statistics are affected by the movements of the king or the weather, or by transport costs.

[6] *Agrarian History*, 501.

When overland transport had to be done by horse and cart, the costs of labour and forage could increase prices considerably. On the whole the road system was worse than in Roman times. A normal time for messengers between London and Exeter was a week, while people taking heavy loads north from London would expect, if not attacked by robbers or bogged down, to spend the first night in Hertfordshire. These difficulties in land transport made it hard to shift corn from one district to another in time of famine, and so contributed to regional variations in prices. Water transport, by comparison, was easy and cheap and was sometimes used for improbable journeys. The Sidneys, who owned ironworks in Sussex and coal in Glamorgan, transported the coal to the ironworks by water. One third of London's corn was shipped down river from Henley, and heavy goods from the north-east were normally transported to London by water. This meant that the price of coal, for example, might be within an economic range at Oxford, where the river was navigable by the end of the century, but prohibitively expensive as far away from the river as St. Albans.

However, all the evidence available, though fragmentary, does at least point in the same direction, and, on the whole, coincides with contemporary complaints of rising prices. Perhaps the least inadequate general index of prices is that devised by Professor Phelps Brown and Dr. Hopkins, which is based on the cost of the items in the hypothetical weekly budget of a building labourer in southern England. If prices in 1510 are taken as 100, they had risen by 1521 to 167. The index drops slightly to 150 in the early 1540s, and then rises to over 200 in the later 1540s and to 270 in 1555, 370 in 1556, and 409 in 1557, dropping suddenly to 230 in 1558. Since many people were living on a subsistence level in good years, it is not surprising that the late 1550s produced an exceptionally high death rate and unpopular governments. In 1597, a year of disastrously bad harvests, the index rose 180 points in one year to a peak of 685, and finally settled down in the early seventeenth century in the area above 500.

This index gives some picture of a range of price rises which is likely to have caused considerable dismay after a century during which prices had been more or less stable. Nevertheless it has a number of limitations. In the first place, it deals only with cheaper commodities, and is no guide to the cost of living of the rich merchant or landlord. It also depends, like the modern cost of living index, on a notional average budget, and obscures the fact that some prices rose faster, and others slower, than the index as a whole. If Lord Burghley was approximately accurate in complaining that the cost of war had increased three times from Henry VIII's reign to Elizabeth's, it was probably rising slightly faster than the index as a whole. There are even more interesting variations in the prices of different basic commodities. If prices in about 1500 are taken as 100, by 1650 agricultural prices had increased to 644, timber prices to 524, but industrial products only to 306.[7] The inflation was primarily an inflation of food prices, not of manufactured or imported goods. The differences between the rises in the prices of different agricultural products are even wider. The price of the cheaper grains, such as rye, increased eight times, the price of wheat seven times, of hay and peas six or seven times, of livestock six or seven times, of eggs and milk about five times, of wool four times, and of beef little more than twice. These figures are not quite what might have been expected: the small increase in the price of wool, for example, does not suggest that inflation was responsible for any prolonged pressure to change over from arable to sheep farming. The explanation of these differences, with the possible exception of the price of livestock, appears to be simple: the more heavily the poor depended on any commodity for subsistence, the faster its price rose.

Beef, which was one of the chief staples of the diet of the upper classes, rose remarkably little: it appears that, on the whole, the poor could not afford to eat meat. The price of timber, though partly pushed up by the need of the poor for fuel, was probably exceptionally increased by the demands of naval and mercantile shipbuilding. The index of manufactured goods rose slightly more than that for beef: it included clothes and footwear, which the poor might buy in a good year, but not renew in a bad one. Eggs and milk increased slightly more than wool or manufactured goods: people might go on buying them when they could not afford new clothes, but on the edge of starvation, they would give them up before they would give up bread or beer. Among bread grains, wheat, which was used for the finest bread, rose less than the cheaper grains. Wheaten bread was commonly eaten, but it is possible that the only time the very poor could eat wheaten bread was at the Communion service. It is not surprising that statesmen were perturbed by the 'seditious speeches of the poor in their alehouses', and that a large part of the Privy Council's policy towards industry and agriculture was designed to prevent the riots which famine tended to produce. Nor is it surprising that Henry VIII's Council was alarmed to discover that some people blamed five successive bad harvests on God's displeasure with the king's religious policy: such a belief, if seriously held, could easily provoke rebellion. In 1645–6, one of the many years of bad harvests, the village of Colyton, Devon, lost about a fifth of its population. The parish register ascribes this disaster to 'great

[7] Ibid., 593–695. The Phelps Brown price index is printed in *Economica* (1956), 296–314.

sickness', but it may have been increased by famine.[8] In 1619, a gentleman reported from Lincolnshire that 'our country was never in that want that now it is, and more of money than of corn, for there are many thousands in these parts who have sold all they have even to their bed straw, and cannot get work to earn any money. Dog's flesh is a dainty dish, and found upon search in many houses, also such horse flesh as hath lain long in a ditch for hounds. And the other day one stole a sheep who for mere hunger tore out a leg and did eat it raw.'[9] Such dramatic examples come from the seventeenth century, when the price rise had been under way for some time, but deaths from famine were probably common in years of bad harvests.

Explanations of the price rise

Contemporaries, whose economic theories were confused, usually failed to explain this price rise, and attempts often ended in mutual recrimination. Government statutes showed a tendency to blame profiteering middlemen, or, in 1553, fondness for luxury imports. In some quarters, it was fashionable to blame the idleness and greed of the labouring poor, and Robert Crowley, one of the early Protestant preachers, put the blame on landlords, 'men without conscience. Men utterly void of God's fear. Yea, men that live as though there were no God at all! Men that would have all in their own hands; men that would leave nothing for others; men that would be alone on the earth; men that be never satisfied. Cormorants; greedy gulls.'[10] Enclosures by landlords were always a fashionable scapegoat. In the middle of the century, there was a tendency to blame the successive debasements of the coinage. Merchants tended to blame their foreign customers, and in the 1530s there was a tendency to blame the greed and avarice of the clergy. It is possible that attempts to explain the price rise produced as much social disharmony as the price rise itself, since almost every explanation involved blaming some particular section of society, and most explanations were accompanied by attempts to increase receipts in step with the price rise, while keeping expenditure down to the old figures, together with vigorous attempts to blame everyone else for doing the same.

Attempts to explain the price rise still produce disagreement, but they can now be made within rather better developed economic theories. Prices in general are the product of the relationship between supply and demand,

[8] *Introduction to English Historical Demography*, ed. E. A. Wrigley (1961), 98–9. Laslett, Peter, *The World We Have Lost* (1965), 116.

[9] Wilson, C., *England's Apprenticeship* (1965), 119.

[10] Tawney and Power, iii. 57.

of the proportion between the amount of money available and the amount of goods available for it to buy. The price of an individual commodity is the result of the relationship between the supply of that commodity and the demand for it. If one man has ten apples, and another has ten pennies, the apples may change hands at a penny each, but if the first man has ten apples, and the second has twenty pennies, the apples may change hands at twopence each. If prices go up, either the demand for the goods must have increased, or the supply of goods must have gone down, or both. Reductions in the supply of goods may explain some of the dramatic short-term fluctuations of prices: the peaks in 1597 and the late 1550s, for example, can be explained by bad harvests. But there is no reason, over the century as a whole, to suppose a reduction, either in the amount of food, or in the supply of manufactured goods. The area of cultivated land was somewhat extended by clearings from the waste, and in forests, and the supply of manufactured goods certainly increased. The only commodity for which decrease in the supply can be invoked to explain price increases is timber, and even this is a matter of some dispute.

If the price rises cannot in general be explained by reduction in the supply of goods, they must be explained mainly by increases in the demand. Money, like all other goods, is worth more when it is scarce than when it is plentiful. This is why the only one of the contemporary explanations which is still discussed is the debasement of the coinage in 1526, 1544, 1547, and 1549. The silver content of each coin was decreased, and the supply of coin increased. Most people supposed that the only value of a coin was the intrinsic worth of silver in it, and since people thought the coin was worth less, they naturally demanded more of it in business transactions, and prices rose. Although the debasements in the middle of the century had some immediate effect on prices, they cannot go far towards explaining the price rise as a whole. In the 1540s there were similar price rises in Europe, where there was no debasement, and it is in any case doubtful whether a local English fact can explain events which went on for the whole century and over the whole continent. The increase was under way before the debasements started, and, indeed, probably caused them rather than being caused by them, and neither the earlier debasement of 1465 nor the restoration of the coinage in 1560 seems to have had much effect.

Debasement of the coinage, then, cannot be regarded as having had more than a marginal effect. Another popular explanation is that inflation was due to imports of American silver by Spain. This is at least based on convincing economic theory. Spain did bring into Europe large quantities of American silver, and if silver becomes more plentiful, it must become worth less. This explanation would fit the timing of the rises in prices in the later 1540s, since it was in 1545 that the Spaniards opened the biggest of the New World silver mines, at Potosi in Bolivia. The lull in the price rise in the early 1520s would fit the fact that in that period Spanish silver imports dropped to the exceptionally low figure of 161,000 ducats annually, and the sharp rise in the 1590s would fit the fact that Spanish silver imports reached their peak of 42 million ducats a year in the early 1590s.[11] This explanation must contribute something to the price rise, and in Spain it may be the most important single explanation. But for England it has two major weaknesses. The first is that the price rise had started by 1510, when Spanish silver imports were not yet significant. It could still be argued that the early price increases were due to increased production in the Tyrolean and Bohemian silver mines, but the explanation in terms of silver imports breaks down if it is used to explain the increases in the prices of individual commodities. If it were the main explanation, we would expect the biggest price increases to be in imported goods such as wine, swords, or silks, and to find that other price increases were smaller reflections of these. Increased import prices cannot be used to explain the fact that the biggest rises were in the price of food produced at home, and particularly of cheap grain. It is necessary to find an explanation which fits these variations.

Two other explanations have been suggested.[12] The first is increased government spending. This again is sound economic theory: increases in money supply put up prices when they are used to buy goods, not when they are put away and saved, and today accumulation of a large government surplus is one of the accepted methods of restraining inflation. A government which lives beyond its income increases the amount of money available for spending, and the English price rise begins at about the time when Henry VIII's French wars first made him live seriously beyond his income. But though this explanation is almost certainly true, it is doubtful whether it is significant. Government spending was probably not a sufficiently large part of the national income to produce price rises as dramatic as these.

The second explanation is improvement in credit. This has a similar effect in economic theory, since the object of credit is to enable people to spend more money, and restriction of credit is now a recognized method of checking inflation. Improvements in credit were taking place. In

---

[11] Elliott, J. H., *Imperial Spain* (1963), 174.
[12] Ramsey, Peter, *Tudor Economic Problems* (1963), 118–19.

Europe, banking was developing rapidly and bills of exchange were saving people from the task of carrying bulky loads of coin. This explanation also is certainly true, but it is doubtful whether it is on a large enough scale to be significant.

Population

Few historians now believe the price rise had only one cause, but the most significant cause is commonly thought to have been a rapid increase in population. An increase in the number of people wanting food gives food a scarcity value which sends up its price. This explanation has the great advantage of fitting the variations between one price increase and another: a large underfed population will drive up the price of subsistence foods more than of luxury foods. Our evidence on Tudor and Stuart population is sketchy, but almost all of it suggests a very large increase. In Colyton, Devon, which is almost the only village for which we have full information, the population was rising steadily from the early sixteenth century to 1640, except for two brief intervals in the hard times of the 1550s and 1590s. In the period 1560–1629 55 per cent of married couples in Colyton had over six children, a figure which suddenly dropped to 18 per cent in the period 1647–1719, and then rose again to 60 per cent in the period 1770–1837. Changes of this size are hard to explain, and may be due to the use of some form of primitive contraception.[13] What we know of other places suggests that they may have had similar population increases. The total increase in population from the late fifteenth century to the early seventeenth may have been between 75 and 100 per cent. There are also external signs of the population increase, in the form of land hunger and housing shortage. The entry fines paid to obtain leases of land probably rose more sharply even than grain prices, and pressure on the available supply of rural cottages was met by the building of large numbers of new ones, often illegally. In almost every town, there was a considerable amount of building, and London tried to meet the problem of overcrowding through the Statute of Inmates, an ineffective prohibition of multi-occupation. Historians, with rare unanimity, accept a large population increase as a fact, and if it is a fact, it is probably the most important, though not the only, explanation of the price rise. The explanation of the population increase, on the other hand, is a task which, in the present state of medical knowledge, historians cannot attempt.

New though it is, the study of historical demography has already shed light on a number of questions of social history which are hard to answer

[13] Wrigley, E. A., 'Family Limitations in Pre-Industrial England', *Ec.H.R.* (1966), 82–109.

on a national basis. The latest historian to attempt to work out the numbers of people in different social classes concluded that 'little but uncertainty emerges from these desultory investigations',[14] but it is perfectly possible to answer such questions for one village with a good parish register or local census. We cannot, however, know how typical the answers are. For example, at Colyton, a third of first children were probably conceived outside marriage, and 22 per cent of first children were born in the first six months of marriage. It would be dangerous to quote this picture as typical of the period, since at Clayworth (Notts.) there are hardly any discoverable cases of pregnancy before marriage, and in one of those the couple are known to have been excommunicated by the rector on suspicion of living in sin.[15] Some other conclusions appear to be more generally valid. The proportions of different classes in Clayworth in 1676 may be typical for the sixteenth as well as the seventeenth century. The population of the village was 401, including one clergyman (whose curiosity is the source of our information), 4 gentlemen, 17 yeomen and husbandmen, 22 craftsmen, 18 labourers, and 36 'others', mainly widows, making a total of 98 households. These figures would seem to suggest that the 'extended family', with several related married couples living in one house, is a myth for this period, since 49 per cent of households consisted only of parents and children, and the commonest extra category making up households was servants living in. Although only 4 per cent of the households belonged to gentlemen, 34 per cent of all households had servants. 16 per cent of the population were servants, and 36 per cent children. The craftsmen were the usual ones needed to supply a small rural community: 1 bricklayer, 1 butcher, 1 cooper, 1 'pindar', 4 shepherds, 1 shoemaker, 3 smiths, 2 tailors, 4 weavers, and 3 wrights. The only way in which these figures are likely to be untypical is that by 1676 the proportion of the population classified as 'gentlemen' was much higher than at the beginning of the period. The figures for marriages broken by death are probably also typical: in 1688 there were 67 married couples at Clayworth. Of these, 26 were not first marriages for one or other of the partners: 13 were second marriages, 3 third marriages, 4 fourth, 1 fifth marriage, and 7 unspecified. The proportion of children coming from homes broken by death was 28 per cent, so experience of a broken home was probably commoner than it is today. It appears also to be a myth that the age of marriage was low during this period: it probably was low among

<hr>

[14] Cooper, J. P., 'The Social Distribution of Land and Men in England, 1436–1700', *Ec.H.R.* (1967), 434.

[15] Laslett, Peter, and Harrison, John, 'Clayworth and Cogenhoe', in *Essays Presented to David Ogg*, ed. H. E. Bell and R. L. Ollard (1963), 157–84.

the aristocracy (Lord Burghley was thought eccentric for refusing to arrange marriages for his daughters until they were 16), but in Colyton the average age of women on first marriage was 27, and of men 28. The only explanation so far offered for this late age of marriage is delays in waiting for a house. The stable population, born and dying in the same parish, also appears to be a myth: there was very high mobility, though often within a small geographical range, especially among the lowest income groups, the wage labourers and the servants.

III   SOCIAL CLASSES AND THEIR FORTUNES

Labourers

This mobility may shed some light on how wage labourers survived the price revolution. As a class, they were perhaps hardest hit of all. There was some small increase in money wages, and agricultural wages may have risen to as much as a shilling a day, but in terms of purchasing power, the index of wages fell from 100 at the beginning of the sixteenth century to about 44 for agricultural wages and 39 for building wages by the end of the century. In 1597 the building wage index fell as low as 29. Agricultural workers, in particular, often suffered from very irregular employment.[16] Most of it was seasonal, and if there was no harvest, there was no work. They therefore tended to move to hiring fairs around the country, hoping to go where there was most work. After several failures to find it, they were liable to be classed as vagrants or sturdy beggars, and subjected to a succession of penalties. A very few were still legally villeins (the last villeinage case in England was in 1618, against a man called Pigg, who was found free), but villeinage was as insignificant as it was rare. The main body of labourers who were not free to move were the upper class of labourers, who owned small amounts of land. The economic gulf between labourers who did own land and those who did not was probably one of the biggest in the country, since those who did had a security against temporary periods of unemployment. Perhaps a quarter of labourers owned land. It was often not very much: an Act of 1589 said that no cottage should be leased with less than four acres attached, but the Act was mainly a device to tax those who broke it with fines. Most cottages had less than four acres, and John Pym once let a cottage with ten feet of land attached.[17]

Some labourers might have enough to keep a cow, and would be guaranteed a certain amount of milk, butter, and cheese. Some kept bees

[16] For this and what follows, see *Agrarian History*, 397–465.
[17] Somerset Record Office, DD/BW, Pym MSS., no. 166.

(with sugar at about the same price as today, honey was the main sweetener), and a number kept a pig. A few brewed their own beer, and they might occasionally get meat in the form of a fowl or a rabbit, or occasionally by poaching royal deer. They normally had to buy their grain, but on the whole the position of labourers who owned land does not seem to have been desperate. Their worst shortage was often fuel, and in the Midlands, where timber was scarce, they often had to burn dung. Their worst difficulties seem to have happened when they tried to benefit from rising prices by selling surplus produce, since their ignorance and illiteracy made it easy to defraud them. Some of their occasional attempts to file lawsuits against people who defrauded them produced results which courts must have found hard to follow: 'be it knowen to all men that I Steveyen Greyne doveth kovenleyge me seyevlef to rest yen me haynd the sovem of xviii povend feleymmes moveney, to me George Sparke at the sayem pelayes of ey pch thell he retoveren to bereygges ageyene', i.e. 'doth acknowledge myself to rest in my hand the sum of 18 pound Flemish money to me George Sparke at the same place of Ipswich till his return to Bruges again'. One unfortunate man met a trader in an alehouse, who offered him the great sum of £20 if he would deliver four grains of corn the next Sunday, eight the next Sunday after that, sixteen the next, and so on for a year. The unfortunate man was next heard of in the Court of Requests, pleading for relief from a debt which ran into billions of grains of corn.[18]

Our knowledge of what was happening to labourers is limited by the fact that our chief source of information is inventories of their goods drawn up for probate, and only the richer labourers had inventories made. Four-fifths of labourers who left inventories were not solely dependent on agricultural labour, but had some by-employment. Weaving, knitting, and working on hemp and flax were commonly carried on by labourers and their wives, and their efforts to supplement their wages were one of the chief staples of the cloth industry, and possibly a cause of its expansion. In the area of Birmingham and what was later the Black Country, labourers found extra work as carriers for local manufacturers. To judge from inventories, many of those who had a tenement or a by-employment grew better off during the period. At the beginning of the period, there were many cases in the north and west where the whole family was living in one room and sleeping on straw, but by the end of the period, four-fifths of those who left inventories had three rooms. Some had a little joined furniture, and a few had glass windows. A number were leaving a certain amount of money, and Robert Wood of Nuneaton, who was a

[18] *Agrarian History*, 566–7.

cheese-maker as well as a labourer, left as much as £11. (For comparison, John Hampden's father, who was a moderately, but not exceptionally wealthy gentleman, left goods worth £1,600 and debts worth £3,000, and the Earl of Warwick's annual rental was over £6,000.[19]) Some labourers managed to buy a second tenement, and left it as a jointure for their wives. In this, as in many other fields, it appears to be the successful who leave records, and we know little about the landless labourers. Many seem to have settled in forests, where common rights for grazing a beast were easier to come by. At Deerfold, Herefordshire, many of the local people were afraid they would become a great charge on the rates, and there was a large colony in the Forest of Arden, which many others besides Shakespeare appear to have associated with freedom. It may have been a party of landless labourers, though they are officially described as vagrants, who alarmed a Somerset J.P. by seizing a cartload of cheese and eating it all.

Landlords and tenants

The rising food prices meant that there was prosperity to be gained out of the ownership of land. How these profits were divided between the landlords and the tenants appears to have varied from manor to manor, and from generation to generation, depending on the bargain which was struck at the making of each individual lease. There were two items in the landlord's income from most leases: the entry fine or premium, levied at the signing of the lease and not repeated, and the annual rent. The length of leases could vary sharply: they might be for one life, two lives, three lives (three current lives were calculated by agents as being equivalent to 21 years), or for as much as 99 years or occasionally even more. A tenant who had a 99-year lease in a period of rapid inflation could be certain of a very good bargain during the later part of his lease: someone paying in 1609 no more rent than had been appropriate in 1510 held his land remarkably cheaply. In return for long leases, landlords tended to levy large entry fines, thus increasing their own capital at the expense of their heir's income. On a lease for one life, on the other hand, the benefits of inflation tended to go to the landlord: he could expect a new lease at an increased rent to be a fairly frequent occurrence.

At the beginning of the century, much land was held by copyhold, rather than leasehold, and here too, who got the benefits of inflation depended on the terms of the copyhold. Some copyholds could be inherited from generation to generation, at a fixed rent and fixed entry fines, and on

---

[19] P.R.O. Wards 3.18.2 and 3.19.1. Manchester MSS. Huntingdon R.O. 32/10. These figures all relate to the end of the sixteenth century or the beginning of the seventeenth.

these, if the tenant was not illegally evicted, his position grew better and better. Many other copyholds could only be inherited at a rent and entry fine to be fixed at the discretion of the landlord. On these, the copyholder was liable to be displaced by rents and entry fines which he could not afford, though there is a case on Pym's estate where the copyholder, whose family had been there for several generations, found a rich yeoman who was able to pay the entry fine, and became the yeoman's subtenant.[20] It is hard to make a general answer to the question whether the landlord or the tenant benefited most from inflation, since most leases were a lottery with death. In 1628, one of Pym's tenants was occupying two tenements: one was a copyhold still held at the fixed rent of 1561, and the other was a leasehold for three lives, granted in 1626, which was already void by the death of all three people named in the lease.[21] The best economic prospect for a landlord, if he survived it, may have been an attack of the plague. On the whole, it seems that landlords' rent on new leases rose slightly faster than prices as a whole, but what determined whether the landlord's income kept up with inflation was what proportion of his leases were new. Theories about shifts in economic and political power as a result of inflation seem to be built on very uncertain foundations. What is much clearer is that inflation often caused rapid social mobility within each class, as some got ahead of the price rise, and others fell behind it. Inflation is inimical to the Tudor idea of a stable and co-operative society.

Yeomen and husbandmen

In so far as generalization is possible, it seems that the people who prospered most were often yeomen. The exact status of a yeoman is hard to define, and might vary from county to county. He would probably occupy a moderately substantial farm, held on a fairly long lease. He would have servants, and perhaps sub-tenants, and be able to vote at parliamentary elections or sit on juries, but he would probably not hunt, or drink wine, or indulge in the other expensive habits of gentility. If he was doing well, he might take on leases of other farms, and increase his income. There was no legal control on claims to the title of yeoman, but there was some practical control through the opinion of neighbours. Many people drew up their wills describing themselves as yeomen, but their probate inventories, drawn up by their neighbours, describe them as 'husbandmen'. Whether there was an economic boundary between yeo-

---

[20] Pym MSS., no. 235.
[21] Pym MSS., no. 208. This rapid series of deaths may have been due to the plague of 1625–6.

men and husbandmen is hard to say, since both lived roughly similar lives, but there was certainly a difference in local reputation.

The boundary between the yeomen and the gentlemen, though it was a much more important one, was also very fluid. Perhaps the best evidence for the rise of a number of yeomen is their success in crossing this barrier. In Shropshire in 1433, 48 families claimed the status of gentry, and in 1623 470 families.[22] Officially, the title of 'gentleman' and its superior the title of 'Esquire' were guarded by the College of Arms, but though the College of Arms occasionally held visitations and declared a few people 'base', it was venal, and moreover many people successfully claimed the title of 'gentleman' who had no dealings with the College of Arms. Probably the real test of a claim to gentility was the attitude of the established gentlemen in the county. If a man kept a good table, dressed like a gentleman, hunted with the other gentlemen, and received letters from J.P.s addressed to him as 'gent.', then, for all practical purposes, he was a gentleman. It was an achievement of which people were often very proud: even John Lilburne the Leveller refused to plead when prosecuted under the title of 'John Lilburne, yeoman'.[23] Prosperity was the first step in becoming a gentleman, but the prosperity was not enough without the social acceptance to go with it. Some yeomen may have been richer than a number of the surrounding gentlemen.

The gentry and the peerage

The class of gentry was a wide one. There was a considerable gulf between the retired estate steward living on a small estate recently purchased, and calling himself 'gent.' for the first time, and the established and prosperous gentleman, whose family had enjoyed the title of 'Esquire' for some centuries, and had been knighted two generations out of every three, who was Justice of the Peace and M.P. for the county, and with a daughter married into the peerage. There was no definite gulf separating the higher gentry from the peerage. In economic terms, both had the same relationship to the means of production: they lived off the profits of landownership. In financial terms, though the greatest peers had an income with which no gentleman could compete, many of the poorer peers had smaller incomes than the richest gentlemen. In social terms, they intermarried, dined together, and co-operated in local politics, and by any test which can be devised they must be regarded as being of the same class.

[22] Stone, 67. When Harrington, in the 1630s, discussed shifts in the balance of property he was as interested in increases in the number of the gentry as in increases in their wealth: *Works*, ed. Toland (1700), 34.

[23] Tawney, R. H., 'The Rise of the Gentry', *Ec.H.R.* (1941), 3.

There is no justification for describing gentlemen as 'middle class'. The term 'middle class', and even more the term 'bourgeois', are urban ones, and are very hard to fit into the class structure of rural England, in which people were either gentlemen or not gentlemen.[24] If the term must be used at all, it should perhaps be kept for yeomen and husbandmen, who might employ servants and labourers, but could not move in the same circles as the gentry. But there is no very useful purpose to be served by importing the anachronistic term 'middle class' into English rural history.

Agriculture

Although the profits of agriculture, however they may have been distributed, certainly increased, it is doubtful whether agricultural methods changed as quickly until the end of the century. There was some improvement in agricultural techniques, such as the use of marl and other fertilizers; there was some clearing and cultivation of new land and some marginal changes in products. There was a considerable spread of market gardening, especially in the country outside London, at places like Lambeth, Whitechapel, Stepney, and Fulham. Henry VIII is credited with the introduction of the apricot and gooseberry, and turkeys were first brought in from Mexico in the 1520s. But the main business of cattle, sheep, and corn farming probably did not change very much. Hay was often sufficient to feed large quantities of stock all winter, and it is doubtful whether the grand slaughter of stock at Michaelmas was ever anything more than a myth. Probably the biggest changes were in agricultural marketing.[25] The demands of London and other big centres of food consumption led to the development of much more highly organized markets, and of professional middlemen, who would buy stock as far away as Radnorshire, and bring it to London for sale. The system of bringing cattle down from high ground into the lowlands for fattening was probably extended, and produced a series of large cattle markets along the Welsh border. Much of the government's economic legislation was designed to check sharp practice in marketing.

There is little evidence that the business of agriculture itself grew more 'commercial' before 1560. It was hard to have a more 'commercial' attitude to land management than an efficient medieval monastery. The classical (and often fictional) medieval system of strip farming and common fields had been breaking down long before the sixteenth century. There was probably some consolidation into larger farms during the sixteenth

[24] Hexter, J. H., 'The Myth of the Middle Class in Tudor England', *Reappraisals in History* (1961), 71–116.
[25] On these see the chapter by Alan Everitt, *Agrarian History*, 466–592.

century, but the original process by which strips were put together and enclosed into fields was well under way before the sixteenth century, and in some places, such as Somerset, seems to have been almost complete.

Enclosures

The enclosure which is sometimes supposed to have been the most dramatic change in Tudor agriculture was of a different type. This was large-scale enclosure by landlords, in order to convert arable land to pasture, often for sheep, combined, in the more dramatic cases, with eviction of tenants. Such enclosure certainly happened in the Tudor period, and it certainly produced a large amount of heated literature. But it was not a movement which was in any way peculiar to the sixteenth century, and enclosure of commons, depriving tenants of the right to graze beasts on them, was a more constant complaint in the eighteenth century than in the sixteenth. The comparative rises in wool and grain prices in the sixteenth century do not suggest that many landlords were for any length of time under a powerful incentive to turn over to sheep farming, nor does the drop in real wage rates suggest that the pressure to save labour by converting to sheep farming was often very strong. The real economic incentive for enclosure and conversion to pasture appears to have been confined to a few years, and to a few counties. Though wool prices rose less than grain prices, they appear to have risen earlier, and before 1550 there may have been an economic incentive for enclosure which was lacking later. There also may have been an economic incentive in the midland counties, where London and other big population centres were too remote to make land transport of grain very profitable, and navigable rivers were scarce. Wool was lighter to transport than grain, and those who, like the Spencers of Althorp, bred their sheep mainly for meat might save carriage by sending them to London on the hoof. The largest amount of enclosure appears to have been in Leicestershire, Warwickshire, and Northamptonshire, and to have happened mainly during the reign of Henry VII and before. The amount of land affected may have been about 3 per cent of the total cultivated area of the counties—a significant, but not dramatic figure. These figures, however, are based on the returns of the government commissions to inquire into enclosures, and many of these returns were inaccurate, being, in some cases, sent in by a malicious local jury. Some were successfully disproved in court, and there were certainly other enclosures, such as deer-parks, which the commission never mentioned, so we do not know how much enclosure there really was.[26] But if the amount of enclosure during the sixteenth century

[26] Kerridge, Eric, 'Returns of Inquisitions of Depopulation', *E.H.R.* (1955), 212–28.

was not exceptional, why did the complaints about it become so universal? To many economic pamphleteers it seemed the main cause of the country's economic ills, and it was alleged by rioters to be a motive for some of the century's most serious disturbances. One possible explanation is the invention of printing, which may be why most of the bitterest complaint comes in the 1540s and 1550s, about a generation after the worst enclosures. Many people preferred to have someone identifiable to blame for economic problems, and a landlord evicting his tenants to face starvation could provoke enough feeling to become a very convenient scapegoat. It is also noticeable that though the times of loudest protest against enclosure, such as 1549 and 1597, were not the times of exceptionally rapid enclosure, they were times of exceptionally rapid price rises. Beyond this, the protests belong to the history of ideas, rather than to economic history.

Towns

Enclosure may have done something to increase the number of people officially classified as 'vagrants', but population increase probably did more. Although the tendency of government policy was to blame these people severely for not finding work, many of them may have been looking for it. Many made for the towns, and the Recorder of London sometimes spent the night on the Great North Road at Stoke Newington, arresting them in 'shoals' as they came in. Though the towns were the obvious place to look for work, it is doubtful whether they had enough work to offer. The cloth industry, which was one of the biggest employers, was often moving out into the country, partly to avoid regulation, and partly to employ agricultural workers and their wives wanting extra work. There was money and work in most towns, but it was very unevenly distributed. Two-thirds of the urban population may have been living at or near the poverty line, and many were so poor that they lacked even a tax assessment, 'that sad passport to immortality'.[27] The smaller towns were mainly supply and market centres for the surrounding countryside, and in Oakham the commonest occupation was agriculture. Population was usually small: Aylesbury was around the thousand mark, and the bigger towns, such as Bristol and Norwich, were probably around ten or twelve thousand. In Norwich, cloth-working was the biggest single trade, but there, as elsewhere, the supply trades, such as tailors, butchers, and carpenters, took up a large part of the population. These were trades in which even rigorous apprenticeship systems could not always restrict

[27] Hoskins, W. G., 'English Provincial Towns in the Sixteenth Century,' *T.R.H.S.* (1956), 1–19.

overcrowding, and the 1570 census of the poor at Norwich, showing that many people in work in the supply trades were below the poverty line, suggests that there was not enough work for all the people who had entered these trades. The poor were already often congregated in poor quarters, and few city authorities wanted to crowd them any further. Some towns had local specialities: in Coventry the commonest tradesmen were cappers, and in Northampton shoemakers. The subsidy assessments, even though they normally under-assess the rich, suggest a very uneven distribution of wealth. In Leicester, William Wigston the elder and younger paid nearly a third of the subsidy between them. In Norwich, the assessments show twenty-nine people worth £100 or more owning 40 per cent of the city's wealth.

These small urban oligarchies usually had a secure control of the town government, which was largely conducted by the mayor and aldermen, supported by the rather larger assembly of the Common Council. These town governments, supported by the national government, attempted a more detailed regulation of economic life than has usually been possible since. They supervised the official weights at the town market and made persistent efforts to check shoddy workmanship, which might damage the commercial name of the town. They might regulate wages, and fix hours of work. In 1538, the Common Council of London fixed hours of work in the building industry, which were to start at five in summer and six in winter. At eight in summer and nine in winter the workman was to 'go to his breakfast and tarry thereat but only one quarter of an hour'. He was then 'immediately' to return to work, and stay until dinner at twelve, for which he had an hour 'at the farthest'. He was then to continue till six in winter and seven in summer, 'and in the meantime to have no more than a quarter of an hour for his drinking time'. For these hours, wages were to be 8d. a day.[28]

Some leading merchants made very large fortunes: Thomas Spring of Lavenham, a clothier, was assessed for taxation as the richest commoner in England, and Sir Thomas Gresham, whose money was also largely made in cloth trading, had one of the most ostentatious funerals of the century. But these large mercantile fortunes were very rare, and though they might give their holders wealth equivalent to the richest gentlemen, they never gave them social prestige or political power to match. Gentlemen in the Commons were quite able to despise merchants richer than themselves, and successful merchants usually invested their money in land and set out to become gentlemen. Few successful merchant families stayed in trade more than three generations. In general, urban fortunes

[28] Tawney and Power, i. 115–17.

were not big: increases in the price of manufactured goods were not
enough to encourage large fortunes, and the periodic slumps caused by
bad harvests or the state of foreign trade made trading risky for all but
the few richest. Possibly the safest way of gaining money was moneylending. There were, it is true, acts against usury, but these, according to
the 1545 Act which repealed them, were 'obscure and dark', and produced 'many doubts ambiguities and questions'—in other words they
had been regularly evaded. In the fifteenth century some of the strongest
pressure to evade the Acts had come from the Crown, which needed to
borrow money. The Catholic church did little about usury: Cardinal
Beaufort, in the fifteenth century, had almost certainly taken it, and
church courts very rarely took notice of it. Probably the only significant
change in the taking of interest came in 1545 when the rate was reduced.

IV ENGLAND AND EUROPE

Overseas trade in the first half of the sixteenth century

At the beginning of the century, England had only one substantial
export, undyed woollen cloth. There was a great variety of types of cloth,
and most were well known: merchants could easily recognize the products
of the Norfolk village of Worsted. Almost all these exports were taken to
one place—Antwerp. The country was so dependent on the Antwerp trade
that one foreigner remarked that 'if Englishmen's fathers were hanged in
Antwerp's gate, their children would creep betwixt their legs to come into
the said town'.[29] At Antwerp, there were merchants from Spain, merchants
bringing tropical products, sellers of German metal work, and merchants
providing most other things England might want to import in return for
its cloth. Antwerp also provided elaborate arrangements for credit and
money-lending, and all the facilities for exchange of information resulting from a large gathering of experienced merchants. Almost all this
trade was carried by one company, the Merchant Adventurers. The word
'Adventurer' does not mean that they were adventurous: they were
probably the least adventurous merchants in the whole period. It means
they 'adventured' or invested their money in foreign trade. They were a
closed company with a large entry fee, whose privileges were extended by
Henry VIII, and though there were occasional interlopers, and occasional challenges to their privileges, they had a virtual stranglehold on the
Antwerp trade. Although membership was in theory open to the whole
country, they tended to become a London company, and were continually

[29] Ramsey, Peter, *Tudor Economic Problems* (1963), 9.

denounced by the outports, such as Hull and Southampton, in the name of 'free trade'. Their power had much to do with the rapid expansion of London at the expense of the provincial ports, to the point where London might account for five-sixths of the national customs revenue. Much though their privileges might annoy other merchants, the government normally remained their friend. It was a convenience, when it wanted to know the opinion of 'the merchants', to be able to interview a small and defined body of people.

It could also be argued that their privileges made the trade much less risky. The demands of Antwerp fluctuated violently, and in a bad year a merchant might be left with a large amount of unsold cloth on his hands. For a small merchant, the loss might be ruinous, but a big one, as Gresham demonstrated, might have the resources to carry the loss and sell the cloth the next year. The existence of a large privileged company also helped the Privy Council's policy for the cloth industry. A cottage weaver who could not sell his cloth might be unable to buy bread, and a small town clothier in the same situation might have to dismiss his workmen, producing famine and riot. It was therefore the Privy Council's policy to insist that every year, when the cloth was brought to Blackwell Hall in London, the merchants should buy it, whether they had any sale for it or not. This policy was unpopular with all merchants, and the Merchant Adventurers regularly protested against it, but for a small merchant it was impossible. For a Merchant Adventurer, it was just possible, and they might calculate that the privileges were worth the price. It was alleged that their monopoly had a bad effect on prices, and sometimes the government might turn against them, but in most years their position was secure.

Though the Antwerp trade was the one that mattered at the beginning of the century, others existed. There was a vigorous trade with the Baltic, though English ships were almost entirely excluded from it. The Hanse merchants, from the German and Polish towns on the south coast of the Baltic, had temporarily acquired a virtual monopoly of it. They had played a crucial part in Edward IV's return to the throne in 1471, and in return had won the right to trade at cheaper customs rates than English merchants, as well as numerous privileges for their centre at the Steelyard in London. Henry VII and Henry VIII occasionally tried to nibble at the Hansards' privileges, but there was little success until the second half of the century. Cloth was the main export to the Baltic, and in return there were some imports of grain in a bad year, and also of hemp, pitch, tar, and other naval equipment, of which, at the beginning of the century, the Baltic had a virtual monopoly.

There was a thriving trade from Bristol to Spain until political troubles interfered with it in Elizabeth's reign. A few Englishmen appear to have settled in Seville and taken part in the Spanish-American trade, but at the beginning of the century English trade was almost exclusively European. Spain was the source of the best swords, as well as of oranges and the indispensable sack. In the fifteenth century and at the beginning of the sixteenth, a few traders went on into the Mediterranean, where there was later found to be a market for salted Yarmouth herrings. After 1538, however, the Turkish conquests and the growth of piracy made sailing in the Mediterranean too dangerous. There was a limited trade from Bristol to Iceland, but though Iceland had a hunger for manufactured goods which the Danes, to whom it belonged, failed to satisfy, it was not a sufficient base for an economic boom. Henry VII had usually done his best for English trade, but the beginning of the century was a period of narrowing economic horizons.

Foreign policy

This pattern of trade also had its effect on foreign policy. The need to maintain friendship with the rulers of the Netherlands was so strong that only overwhelming issues, such as Perkin Warbeck for Henry VII or the divorce for Henry VIII, could interfere with it. There was also a strong security concern with the Netherlands. The English east coast is long and flat, and the Netherlands coast is full of harbours. It was a vital English interest to ensure that the Netherlands ports were not occupied by a strong hostile power and it remained so from King John's wars against the French to the defence of Belgium in 1914 and 1940. In 1519, the Netherlands passed under the control of Spain, and became part of the vast empire of Charles V. Charles had succeeded his grandfather in the Holy Roman Empire, and his grandparents Ferdinand and Isabella in Spain. This produced a consolidation of European power. The union of Castile and Aragon, though it still had no institutional basis, now seemed likely to last a generation. The unwieldly collection of German principalities which was called the Holy Roman Empire might be no more solid than it had been, but was likely to benefit from its union with Spanish possessions in Italy. The Mediterranean empire of the Balearic islands, Naples and Sicily was united with the international market of the Netherlands, and with the growing colonial empire of Spain. Charles's titles ended up 'Lord of Asia and Africa'.

Charles V's was not the only important power in Europe. There were three others. The first was the Turks, who controlled the eastern Mediterranean, and in 1526 won an overwhelming victory at Mohacz in Hun-

gary. They made periodic descents on Italy, and once succeeded in saw-
ing in half one of the Pope's cousins. To some, it appeared to be only a
matter of time before they occupied Vienna. The Pope's calls for crusades
against the Turks were probably provoked by more than theology. The
Turks also controlled the North African coast, and Spain, which had only
succeeded in expelling the Moors from Granada in 1492, was very much
aware of being in the Christian front line. The second important power
was Portugal, which had all the wealth of the Portuguese empire in Africa
and the Indies at its disposal. The third, and by far the most important
of the other European powers, was France. The French were the only
European power capable of competing with Charles V on equal terms,
and, believing that they were in danger of encirclement, were usually
ready to do so. They had been fighting the Spaniards in Italy since 1494,
especially for control of the key duchy of Milan, which commanded many
of the Alpine passes. Small pieces of territory along the French–Spanish
border were continually disputed. Francis I of France resented the Spanish
and Portuguese monopoly by papal bull over the New World, saying he
refused to accept it until they produced the will of Adam, making them
his universal heirs. He was quite ready to ally with the Turk, and Charles
V found the cannon used to defend Tunis stamped with the French fleur-
de-lis. Above all, the French exploited the major weakness in the Spanish
empire, its communications. There were two routes from Spain to the
Netherlands. One was by sea, through the Channel, which could easily be
threatened by piracy, official or unofficial. The other was overland, starting in Italy, crossing the Alps, and passing down the Rhine. This could
easily be threatened, either by control of Milan, or by occupying a
fortress on the Rhine. The French had consolidated their own kingdom,
having successfully annexed Brittany in the face of the ineffectual opposition of Henry VII, and both they and the Spaniards seemed to be ready
for a fight to the death.

A large part of Europe had passed under the control of one or other of
these two powers, but there were some other independent forces. In Italy,
the republic of Venice and the Pope were both powerful, and had to enter
into the calculations of the two sides. In the east, the elective kingdom of
Poland was one of the minor prizes, a protection or a gadfly on the eastern
flank of the empire. Switzerland had already established a tradition of
neutrality, and was valuable mainly as a recruiting ground for mercenaries. Denmark and Sweden had little interest in a conflict which was
largely centred on Italy. The same cannot be said of Scotland, which,
though it included an Anglophile party which might occasionally acquire
power, was usually an ally of France. Though Scotland was not a major

power, it was big enough to occupy much of England's attention. It was not only Shakespeare who thought that

> For once the eagle England being in prey,
> To her unguarded nest the weasel Scot
> Comes sneaking.[30]

Henry VII had refused to accept the hostility of Scotland as inevitable, and had arranged an alliance, cemented by the marriage of his daughter Margaret to King James of Scots. But it was a century before this alliance put an end to Anglo-Scottish wars, and meanwhile Scotland remained one of the main areas of competition between England and France.

In the previous century, England had been able to compete with France on equal, or even advantageous terms, and at times an English conquest of France had seemed a serious possibility. In the early sixteenth century, however, England was a minor power. Henry VIII was not conspicuous for modesty, but even he, in writing to Charles V in 1529, described himself as 'a small king in the corner' of Europe.[31] The king of England's revenues were somewhere between £100,000 and £150,000 a year, the French king's about £800,000, and Charles V's £1,100,000. Population is harder to estimate, but the English population cannot have been above four million at the most, while the Spanish may have been eight million, and the French twelve million.[32] Henry VII showed some signs of being interested in a navy: he constructed a dry dock at Portsmouth, and built up a naval arsenal at Woolwich and Greenwich, but he left only five king's ships at his death, and the English war fleet consisted largely of impounded merchantmen. In 1492, Henry VII was afraid even to take these, and, in order not to disrupt trade, hired Spanish warships instead. Ireland, though it was an English possession, was a very insecure one: it was full of Yorkists, and other discontented people, and could do little for an English war effort except provide a base for an enemy, or hold down a few troops who might be needed elsewhere.

There was only one advantage England could exploit, which was its position on the Channel, commanding one of the two key routes between Spain and the Netherlands. This influence could be exerted from both sides of the Channel, since England's one foreign possession (except Ireland) was Calais. Statesmen were much concerned with keeping it, though it cost far more to maintain than the Crown could afford, and had often been a base for political disaffection. In 1524, during a war, its garrison

---

[30] *Henry V*, I. ii. 170–1.

[31] Koebner, R., 'The Imperial Crown of this Realm', *B.I.H.R.* (1953), 37. This letter was written in December 1529, and contained a refusal to help Charles against the Turks.

[32] These figures are taken from Wernham, 12–13. They are necessarily tentative.

consumed 1,000 cartloads of provisions every eight days, and feeding garrison forces on this scale was not a practical proposition for a small power in time of inflation.

On the whole, it could be expected that such influence as this position gave England was likely to be used against France. France was the traditional enemy, and the Hundred Years' War, which had not really finished, had produced a vigorous stream of national propaganda. The English kings still called themselves kings of France, and Henry VIII, at least, may have taken the title seriously, though Burgundy, whose alliance had been necessary to wars with France, had been dismembered and divided between France and Spain. The Channel Islands remained under 'Norman law' long after anyone knew what it was, because if they were once assimilated to English law, the Crown might be held to have abandoned its claim to the Duchy of Normandy. Henry VII had usually tried to keep on good terms with Castile and Aragon (or one of them), and when the united Spain also ruled the Netherlands, the motives for friendship with it were very powerful. On occasion, immediate diplomatic advantage might make the English side with France, but it often went against the grain. The notion that the Spaniards were our 'natural enemies' was one which was not discovered until Mary's reign. It was popularized by the publication of Foxe's *Book of Martyrs* in 1571, and many people did not believe it until long after that.

War and its cost

All through the century, attempts to produce an effective army were among the most serious strains on the Crown's resources. This was the period when gunpowder and artillery were becoming essential and they had a dramatic effect on the cost of war. In the period 1543–5 the French wars cost £1,300,000, excluding the cost of garrisoning and fortifying Boulogne, which may have accounted for another million. On an income little over £100,000 a year, expenses on this scale were not practical politics, but they were a necessity if wars were to be fought at all. Gunpowder was expensive, and so were the casting of cannon and the making of gun carriages. It was then necessary to find horses to pull the gun carriages, and fodder for the horses, and horses to pull the wagons which carried the fodder for the horses. Nor did artillery have the effect of making castles obsolete: it rather produced a demand for heavy expenditure to maintain and fortify them. If a castle or walled town could not defeat an enemy, it might hold him up until more troops arrived or until the campaigning season ran out.

The last private castle in England was built by the Duke of Buckingham early in Henry VIII's reign, but subsequently this and eleven others came to the Crown on Buckingham's attainder. The Crown seems to have been following a deliberate policy of collecting castles, and Henry VII induced Lord Berkeley to surrender his in return for the title of Marquess. In 1534, it was made treason to detain the king's castles—a sure sign that the government took their control seriously. Henry VIII spent considerable sums on building and improving fortifications against the French along the south coast, and these works were a heavy drain on the budget. Abroad, the walled towns of north France might cause even more disastrous expenses, which might become greater if the towns were taken than if they were not, since one of the main effects of gunpowder was an increase in the cost of fortification. Nor did the Crown save any money by giving up obsolete methods of warfare, since almost all through the sixteenth century it was energetically enforcing training in archery.

The extent to which gunpowder changed the art of war is also illustrated by the earnest moral debate which it produced. It was often said to have been invented by the Devil, and a 1489 edition of St. Augustine's *City of God* was printed with two walled cities on the frontispiece, and the Devil's city heavily defended by artillery. Cannon were denounced for the destruction they caused, and also for their socially levelling effects since knights and foot-soldiers were equally vulnerable to them. They were disliked, too, for giving more power in armies to those skilled in ballistics and fortification, and other technical arts. Iago sneered at Cassio as a 'mere arithmetician', and as late as the end of the seventeenth century Louis XIV had difficulty in ensuring that Vauban, being a base engineer, should have unfettered command over sieges. These arguments appear to have discomposed the defenders of gunpowder, but not to have prevented them from justifying its use. The wickedness of the enemy, especially the Turk, was held to be sufficient reason for its use. One man who had destroyed his treatise on artillery, on moral grounds, rewrote and printed it in 1537, when the Turks were advancing. A preacher said that guns were evil, but since the enemy had them, we could snatch them out of mad men's hands to use them against them. It was argued that they were justifiable because of the moral excellence of the purposes for which they were used: a gun cast for Sigismund of Austria was inscribed 'I am named Katrin: beware of what I hold: I punish injustice'. It was commoner to argue, like one of the French Huguenot leaders, that guns were invented by the Devil, but 'man's malice hath made them so necessary that they cannot be spared. To the end therefore to profit by them ...'. Sir Walter Raleigh said that God had not given men teeth or claws, but he had given them intelligence to invent weapons, and therefore they ought to use it. This debate did little to limit the development of artillery, which was checked only by cost and the slow progress of ballistics. The Roman church confined itself to deciding that St. Barbara was the patron saint of gunners.[33]

The other large item in the cost of war was the provision and transport of soldiers' food, and here the government suffered from rising food prices. In 1544, when the army was 40,000, 2,100 people were needed to run the victualling. Some Tudor government servants, such as Wolsey, Paulet, or Bishop Gardiner, who became known as 'Simon Stockfish', grew very skilled in this job, but it stayed thankless. If the work was let out to private contractors, they often cheated the government. If the government did the job itself, it had to bear the discredit of failures. In 1544, it was accused of excluding private competition in order to dispose of its own 'stinking food'. The next year, the commanders of Boulogne sent home a report on the 'corrupt loathesomeness' of a consignment of beef that had been packed in leaky cases among a consignment of coal, and said that much of the meal was also bad. They described, with great satisfaction, how they had managed to conceal the bad by splitting it up among the good consignments. Later in the letter, they recorded that many of the garrison of Boulogne had died. Yet it is doubtful whether the Tudor government was worse than other European governments, and on the whole the system worked tolerably, in spite of occasional crises such as the occasion when an army invading Scotland was left without bread because there were no mills in Berwick, and the Scots controlled the countryside. But it was bound to be expensive when a soldier's daily rations were 1–1½ lb of biscuit, 1 lb of beef, and 1½ *gallons* of beer.[34] The most difficult problem was transport: for Berwick or Calais, where there was water transport and a stable base, it was manageable, but inland it was necessary to requisition innumerable carts. In 1522 and 1523, the transport between Calais and the front line broke down, and in the north, the main reason for the failure to conquer Scotland was a shortage of carts. Sixteenth-century armies frequently withdrew, or began to negotiate for a treaty, at times when the military situation appeared to be in favour of carrying on: this is one reason why many of the century's wars were so inconclusive. On such occasions, the most common reason for withdrawal is that the army had advanced beyond its supply lines, or that the money collected for the campaign had all been spent.

[33] Hale, John, 'War and Public Opinion in the Fifteenth and Sixteenth Centuries', *Past and Present*, no. 23 (1962), 18–32, and 'Gunpowder and the Renaissance', *From the Renaissance to the Counter-Reformation*, ed. Charles H. Carter (1966), 113–63.
[34] Davies, C. S. L., 'Provision for Armies, 1509–50', *Ec.H.R.* (1964–5), 234.

War and society

War also had its effect on the social system at home. Whatever opinion Tudor kings may have held of bastard feudalism, they depended on it for recruiting experienced armies. Feudalism proper was defunct long before the Tudor period, and the feudal host had last been called out in 1385. Feeding and paying a regular royal army would have been far beyond the king's resources, and so they were dependent on lords binding themselves by indenture to bring retainers to the wars. This is one reason why Tudor governments did not have the settled hostility towards either bastard feudalism or the peerage with which they have sometimes been credited.[35] Barons were not all naturally bad, and at times when the monarchy was reasonably strong, its power to grant rewards and patronage could be sufficient incentive to the most fractious peer to serve it loyally. In Henry VII's reign, the Earl of Northumberland was murdered while collecting royal taxes, and in Henry VIII's, the Dukes of Norfolk and Suffolk were among the most consistently trusted servants he had. Strong government meant that the nobility could be secure in their possessions, and although in time of disorder they might try to make more profit out of it than their rivals, they had no natural interest in disorder as such. If nobles could bring bodies of retainers, and even artillery, to serve the king in foreign wars, it was in the king's interest to let them keep them. The existence of statutes against the keeping of retainers meant that the king could either control retaining or increase his income by granting licences for retainers. Not everyone who gained such a licence was a danger: one of the first items in the Elizabethan *State Papers* is a licence to keep liveried retainers, granted to Sir William Cecil.[36] The disorders commonly associated with bastard feudalism had largely been those of a period of weak government. A lord had to show his 'good lordship' to his retainers by helping them, and under Henry VII and VIII the most effective way to do this was not to create riots on their behalf, but to use favour with the king to obtain gifts and appointments for them. Sir Thomas More, who is not a traditional 'over-mighty subject' spent one of the last nights of his life trying to place his retainers with lords who would have a better chance of winning the king's favour than he had himself. Another abuse of bastard feudalism, maintenance, the illegal fostering and financing of other people's lawsuits, had been more profitable in the fifteenth century than it was in the sixteenth, when political influence over lawsuits was often exerted in more subtle ways, but it too had not disappeared.

[35] Dunham, W. H., *Lord Hastings' Indentured Retainers* (1955), *passim*.
[36] Cal., *S. P. Dom.* (1547–80), xv. no. 44.

Though the Crown continued to raise armies through retaining, it had an alternative system, which it was trying to develop. Since 1181, if not longer, there had been a legal obligation on the body of the population to own arms, and to appear with them when summoned for national defence. Early Tudor governments made a number of experiments designed to turn this liability to conscription into an army. At one stage, a crude attempt at a means test provided that anyone whose wife wore a velvet kirtle or a silk petticoat must provide a light horse ready for service. In 1545, Henry VIII kept 120,000 men under arms all summer. This militia was a home guard, designed to repel invasion, and some doubt might be raised whether it was legal to send them abroad. In 1544, the government created a precedent by doing so without any protests, and though the development of the militia was interrupted by attempts in the middle of the century to experiment with foreign mercenaries, it continued more or less steadily into the seventeenth century. However, the problem of training was not seriously tackled until Elizabeth's reign, and until it was, the militia could be no more than an auxiliary force.

V GOVERNMENT FINANCE

Crown lands

The revenues on which the Crown had to tackle these tasks were very little different from what they had been in the fourteenth century, and most of them were badly suited to keep pace with inflation. At the beginning of the century the biggest part of its revenues was income from Crown estates. Edward IV and Henry VII had achieved large increases in the amount of land owned by the Crown, and had produced considerable improvements in administration, but as the century went on, the real income from the Crown estates fell steadily behind the price rise. In Wiltshire, the Herberts' rents on new leases increased sevenfold up to 1640, and the Seymours ninefold, but the rents on new leases of Crown estates only increased threefold. The total Crown estates were yielding £3,765 in 1491, before Henry VII's administration had become effective, £24,000 in 1504, and £88,000 in 1604. These figures are affected by confiscations and sales, but they suggest that though the Crown's rents rose during the sixteenth century, they rose less than prices. There were a number of reasons why this should happen. Land management needed constant supervision, and the Crown owned too much land to have a detailed knowledge of all the woods, fields, and rights of which it was made up. A private landlord might have a physical knowledge of his fields, but the Crown was always having to issue special commissions out of the Exchequer, to impanel a local jury, and inquire on oath whether the Crown had a forgotten right to the tithes of one village, the advowson of another, or a grazing ground outside a third. A verdict was normally returned to suit the local gentry who ran the inquiry. Private landlords might manage on a small paid estate staff, but the Crown had to find a host of small local officials, a steward of the manor of Tottenhall, a keeper of Pickering forest, or a keeper of Hyde Park. It had to be made worth the while of these officials to do their jobs, and the jobs themselves had to be used as part of the very necessary stock of gifts for people the Crown wanted to reward. For example, when the steward of a Crown manor held a manorial court, many small sums might be raised, 3d. from one tenant for absence, 6d. from another for grazing too many sheep on the common, 6d. on a third for not repairing a drainage ditch, and so forth. The government at Westminster could not possibly keep track of all these individual fines, so the steward was often allowed to keep them.

The leases of Crown estates also had to be used as part of the stock of political patronage, which made it difficult to raise a fully commercial revenue from them. In particular, the institution of large entry fines at the beginning of a lease never seems to have taken root on Crown lands. Even if patronage was not involved, it was difficult to transmit the impetus necessary to strike a good bargain with a new tenant all the way from Westminster to an obscure west country manor. Where substantial entry fines did exist, they were often the perquisite of the steward. Natural inertia would often ensure that a Crown manor was leased at a rent very much like the one it had fetched before, so the Crown lost as inflation progressed. Small parts of the Crown's revenue could easily be frittered away without attracting attention. At Castle Donnington, the steward of the manor was found enclosing the king's land to his own use, and pasturing his cattle and sheep in the royal park. Henry VII, whose appetite for details was inexhaustible, found that royal revenue was being reduced by illegal catching of the king's fish in Soham mere, Cambridgeshire. The value of the royal swans was being reduced because keepers were confusing royal swans with their own, so Henry VII decided that only people who did not own swans would be eligible to be keepers. He demanded a list of people who had been illegally killing the king's deer in Pickering Forest, and found it headed by the Archbishop of York, the Bishop of Carlisle, the Abbot of Fountains, the Receiver General of the Duchy of Lancaster, and his own trusted official, Richard Empson. Insisting on points like these took much of Henry VII's time, and won him a good deal of unpopularity, but the rewards are shown by the increase in Crown land revenue during his reign. Crown land revenue would not be sufficient unless managed in this pettifogging spirit. Succeeding rulers who had neither Henry VII's courage nor his energy for detail let the administration of the Crown lands run on as a routine job, and paid the price. In the tug of war between landlords and tenants to gain the profits of inflation, Crown tenants appear to have been among the most fortunate, and though the Crown had its financial loss, it had its political reward. In 1612, a family who bought the manor of Winchcombe from the Crown, attempted to hold a manorial court to fix economic rents and levy new entry fines. They had to abandon the manorial court, and fled before a storm of exclamations, of which 'God save the King' was the most printable. Conversely, if they could survive these initial difficulties, purchasers of Crown land were likely to make a large profit.

The customs

The second most important part of royal income, and by the end of the century the most important part, was the customs revenue. The fact that in 1589 the customs accounted for a third of the king's revenue, and by 1611 for a half, is not so much a mark of the success of customs administration, as of the failure of other sources of income. Customs revenues had at least the advantage of increasing as trade increased, which made them inflation-proof in one way, but they had several disadvantages. Customs were levied in a fixed proportion to quantity on exports of wool and cloth and imports of wine, but at a much lower rate on cloth than on wool. From the fourteenth century onwards, as the English cloth industry expanded, a higher proportion of exports were in the form of cloth, and a lower proportion in the form of wool, and customs revenue was reduced in proportion. This anomaly was altered in 1558, when Mary's government made cloth pay a rate proportionate to wool. This, together with the attacks on the church, was one of the two important changes in the Crown's financial position during the century. Most other commodities paid custom in proportion to their supposed value, at, for example, 1s. or 2s. in the pound. The yield of customs duties therefore depended heavily on the official valuations at which goods were taxed. These valuations were fixed by the Book of Rates, which laid down, for example, that toothpicks were to be taxed as worth 1s. 8d. the gross. Customs raised on a new Book of Rates were more likely to keep up with inflation than customs on an old one, but new Books of Rates were made infrequently. The third difficulty in keeping up the customs revenue was smuggling. There were only two customs posts on the west coast north of Bristol, at the Dee and the Mersey, and customs officers were never able to watch all the small creeks on the Essex coast. The impression given by customs statistics that almost all the country's trade was concentrated at London might mean only that that was the place where customs were most efficiently collected. On tin, which was one of the country's more important exports, the total yield of customs at all the outports was £28.[37] This is obviously not a revealing statistic of the size of the tin trade. Even at London, there was loss of revenue by the corruption of customs officers, who sometimes joined smuggling rings or took money for ignoring them. This is not altogether surprising: royal officials could no more be expected to make no effort to protect themselves against inflation than the Crown could be expected to pay increased salaries to meet the cost of living. In London the tide-waiters in the customs service were paid £4 a year, and the searchers nothing. If there had been no other rewards, no one would have accepted the posts.

Feudal dues

The next important part of the king's revenue was the profits of what has been called 'fiscal feudalism'.[38] Feudalism in the more usual sense, the holding of land in return for military service, was over long before the Tudor period began, but a number of legal obligations which had grown up around feudalism were preserved, and used to raise money, instead of to raise an army. If an estate amounted to a knight's fee, it was not expected to produce a knight. Still less was an estate of a fortieth part of a knight's fee expected to produce a fortieth of a knight, but it was expected, by whatever roundabout means, to produce money. Under feudal theory, each piece of land had been held, either from the king, or from some other person. Each piece of land had been held in return for a specified service: some pieces of land were expected to produce a knight, others to produce a man to guard a castle, some, known as serjeanties, to perform some improbable service like holding the king's head in the boat when he crossed the Channel, and others simply to pay rent. The land which mattered for purposes of fiscal feudalism was that which, several centuries earlier, had been held from the king, and had been expected to produce a knight. On this land, if he could keep track of it, the king had a succession of legal rights, which were zealously preserved long after their justification had expired. The king had once had a legitimate interest in ensuring that the knights of his army were people he trusted, so on the death of a tenant-in-chief (that is of a man who held his land from the king), his heir had to apply to the king to re-grant the land to him. By the sixteenth century there was no question of the king refusing to re-grant the land, but he did charge the heir a payment, called livery, for entering

---

[37] Ramsay, G. D., 'The Smugglers' Trade', *T.R.H.S.* (1952), 152.
[38] See Hurstfield, (1958).

into his inheritance. In effect, the livery charge was a sort of primitive death duty, applying to almost all the landed classes, and it is surprising that it was never exploited to better advantage.

More legal rights arose if a man who held his land by knight service from the king died and left a minor heir. The minor could not perform military service himself, so he and his land passed into the king's wardship until he came of age. If the heir were a daughter, the king, not wanting one of his enemies to win control of the land by marriage, had claimed the right to arrange her marriage, and this right had subsequently been extended to sons. In the sixteenth century, all these rights were without any of their original justification, but they were profitable, and the king could legitimately plead that if he was not to be allowed new financial rights, he ought to be allowed to keep the old ones. It had also been established that if a man held so much as one field of his land by knight service in chief, the king got wardship of it all. The obligation to wardship, then, was attached to particular pieces of land, and fell on anyone who bought that land. The village of Aldermaston (Berkshire) had once been held by knight service, and therefore, although its owner was only a yeoman, his son passed into wardship on his death.[39]

The right to wardship was profitable to the king in two ways: he had the profits of the land during the minority, and the right to arrange the heir's marriage. In the sixteenth century he did not normally exercise these rights himself, but sold them either to the highest bidder or as a favour to someone he wanted to reward. The right to arrange the marriages of heiresses fetched a particularly high price. Wardship, together with the similar right to wardship over lunatics, may have brought in about £5,000 at the beginning of the century, and £15,000 at the end of it. This income, too, rose more slowly than prices. The main reason for this was that wardship revenue was based on the valuations of estates which passed into wardship, and the valuations of estates rose much more slowly than their value. Valuations were officially conducted by a local jury and checked by a local official, but in practice they were often based on little more than the word of the family concerned. The increasing proportion of landlords' income which was in the form of entry fines rather than rents could easily be excluded from valuations. Almost all valuations for taxation increased more slowly than the value of the estates: a valuation might double during the century, when the value of the estate had increased five or ten times. If a man was accurately valued for taxation it was a sign that he was unpopular among his neighbours, and probably, after the Reformation, a Catholic recusant.

[39] P.R.O. Wards 9.590.

The other great disadvantage of this form of revenue, from the Crown's point of view, was that it involved the Herculean task of keeping track of all the land which had once been held from the Crown by feudal military service. In theory, it was necessary to get a licence to sell land which was held by knight service in chief, and the licences were supposed to be a source of revenue. This obligation was often evaded, and it had taken all the energy of Edward IV and Henry VII to produce even an approximate register of land liable to wardship. Once the land had been identified, it was easier to keep track of, but the rate of success was no more than moderate.

Miscellaneous rights

Another right dating from John's reign, which had also outlived its original purpose, was distraint of knighthood. King John had been short of knights to fight the French, and had compelled all those with land worth more than 40s. a year to be knighted. In the sixteenth century it made no difference to the king's army whether a man was called knight, but it was still useful to be able to fine him for not being a knight. There were various other rights of feudal origin which were worth money. The king might call for an aid, which was a direct tax, for ransoming his person, for knighting his eldest son, or for marrying his eldest daughter once. He had a right as overlord to such things as wrecks, whales, sturgeons, and treasure trove. The only one of these of considerable value was the right to all mines containing gold or silver, particularly after the German metallurgist Agricola had argued that this included copper, lead, and iron.[40] In practice, the main source of mining income was the Cornish tin mines, where Henry VII increased the annual rent due to the Crown from a fifteenth to a twelfth of the proceeds. There were various other small fees due to the Crown or its officials, such as fees for recording land conveyances or having grants recorded on the Patent Rolls, but most of these did little more than help to pay the costs of administration. There was some income to be got from sale of licences, to export corn when it was prohibited, to keep retainers, and so forth. The king had the profits of justice, but unless he had the luck to convict a great lord for treason, and confiscate his estates, these were unlikely to be much above the cost of administering the courts. He had some profits from the mint, and some from royal forests. There was more money in the right to receive the incomes of vacant bishoprics which led Henry VII to move bishops from one see to another very frequently.

[40] Stone, 339. Elizabeth obtained the right to copper under this doctrine, and exploited it by starting a mine under the Earl of Derby's windows, but Charles I in 1638 failed to extend his rights to lead.

Purveyance

Only one of the Crown's financial rights was adequately hedged against inflation, and this became one of the most unpopular. This was the right of purveyance, or compulsory purchase of food for the royal household or armies at prices fixed by royal officials. It was commonly alleged that purveyors bought food below the market price, but it has recently been argued that in Henry VIII's reign they paid more or less the current market prices.[41] Even if this was so, the right would be very profitable to the Crown, since it would counteract the tendency of prices to rise whenever the king was buying. It may have done something to check wartime profiteering, and to act as a method of price control. But compulsory purchase in times of scarcity, and even more the right to requisition carts, was necessarily unpopular, and the purveyors often abused their position. One went into partnership with a brother who was trying to levy an illegal market toll, and whenever anyone refused to pay the toll his goods were carried off by the purveyor.[42] Mary started a series of checks on the honesty of purveyors, but by the end of the century purveyance was worth £50,000 to the Crown, and possibly more to purveyors.

These revenues were supposed to be sufficient to support the Crown in all normal times, a belief strengthened by Edward IV's rash assertion to the Commons in 1467 that from then on he was resolved to live of his own, and by the financial talents which enabled him and Henry VII to succeed briefly in doing so. It was often too easy to blame extravagance, rather than inflation, for the fact that their successors could not follow their example, but in many ways kings had to remember that they had to choose between their revenues and their popularity. Kings needed a regular and substantial tax. They came nearer to achieving this from the clergy than from the laity. Convocation, the representative assemblies of the clergy of the provinces of Canterbury and York, being made up of people hoping for promotion from the king, could be induced to vote a tenth, or some other proportion of clerical income, which might bring in £40,000 in a year. This, being an 'extraordinary' tax, could not be made annual, but it could be made frequent.

Parliamentary grants

For expenses beyond this, it was necessary to apply for a grant to a Parliament. The fifteenth and tenth, the old form of parliamentary grant, was fixed by a method which had ossified in 1332, and its yield was falling

[41] Davies, C. S. L., 'Provisions for Armies 1509–1550', *Ec.H.R.* (1964–5), 237.
[42] *Agrarian History*, 503.

fast. Various attempts were made to find a new form of grant. The subsidy, the newer form of parliamentary grant, might be granted generously and might raise a large income at the beginning of the sixteenth century. Henry VIII raised £650,000 in parliamentary subsidies for his French wars in the 1540s. Unfortunately, when Parliament had voted a sum like this, it was impossible to persuade them that it was not big enough. Moreover, subsidies, like wardship assessments, depended for their yield on a valuation by local commissioners of landed income, and therefore failed badly to keep pace with inflation. By the end of the century, subsidy assessments were ridiculous: Lord Burghley, with an income of several thousands, was assessed (by himself) at £133. Mary's government made itself unpopular by making people take an oath to their subsidy valuations, but Elizabeth's government, in 1563, let even the commissioners for collection make their return without taking an oath to their accuracy. It is an interesting comment on the significance of an oath that the returns, which had been dishonest before this change, were much more dishonest after it.[43]

VI   THE CONSTITUTION

Parliament

Parliament, the body which granted this money, held a position in the constitution which could easily become anomalous. It normally had no say in the formation of policy, but it was impossible for the king to finance any active foreign policy if Parliament disapproved either of the policy or of the efficiency of its execution. It is true that there were occasional breaches in the theory that the king could not impose full-scale taxes except by the consent of Parliament. He might occasionally raise a 'forced loan', or what was euphemistically called a 'benevolence'—a tax without parliamentary assent. But benevolences had been declared illegal by a statute of Richard III's reign, and the king could only successfully raise a benevolence if he did not try too often or for too unpopular causes. Similarly, it was current constitutional theory that nothing could have the force of legislation unless it was sanctioned as an Act of Parliament. It is true that between Parliaments the king might issue proclamations commanding people, for example, not to export grain during a famine, but it is and was a matter of dispute what force these proclamations could have, and what courts would enforce them. If the king wanted something to have the indisput-

[43] Miller, Helen, 'Subsidy Assessments of the Peerage in the Sixteenth Century', *B.I.H.R.* (1955), 28. Oaths to subsidy assessments were first introduced by Wolsey in 1523.

able force of law, he had to get it passed by both houses of Parliament and embodied in a statute. Moreover, it was only easy to raise a benevolence or enforce a proclamation in support of a policy which already had the confidence of the politically powerful classes—the sort of policy which Parliament, if summoned, would approve.

But though Parliament had these two indispensable functions, it was not in regular session, and contemporaries spoke of 'a Parliament', rather than 'Parliament'. Its meetings had in the past been very frequent: Edward III had called forty-eight Parliaments in fifty years, and often more than one in a year. Until the Wars of the Roses, it had remained more or less annual, but in recent years its frequency had been sharply reduced. The three longest intervals between Parliaments before Charles I's notorious eleven years were 1504 to 1510, 1515 to 1523, and 1523 to 1529. Later medieval Parliaments had sat for only a few weeks, and sixteenth-century Parliaments rarely sat much longer. Few members had London houses unless they were active in politics outside Parliament, and most wanted to be home for harvest time, to supervise the actions of their stewards. A long stay in London might become expensive, and though many boroughs still paid wages to their members, it is doubtful whether the wages met the rising cost of staying in London. Long sessions of Parliament date from a period after the rise of the town house and the London season, and in 1515 Parliament passed an Act forbidding its members to go home without the written assent of the Speaker and the house, or, if they were Lords, the assent of the house. This Act was often ignored, and its workings provide a list of illnesses of members' wives which were perhaps suspiciously frequent even for the sixteenth century.

Perhaps the functions of Parliament were more like those of a party conference than of any other modern body. Though many of its members might be politically experienced, they were so in virtue of other positions than that of Member of Parliament. Like a party conference, Parliament functioned largely for exchange of information. Members of the Privy Council might want to explain their policy to those who would have to enforce and defend it in the counties, and at the same time Councillors wanted to inform themselves of feeling in the country as a whole. Parliaments, like party conferences, had a great yearning to give advice, and to feel that this advice was being listened to. Some of the advice was about great matters of national policy, but much of the rest was about such local matters as the importation of Irish cattle into Somerset or the state of the harbour works at Plymouth.

Though Parliament did not imagine being in a position to carry out its own advice, it might give advice with great freedom, and often on questions on which the government did not want it. When it did not like the Privy Councillors, it had in the past demanded the right to elect some of the members of the Council. When it thought royal demands for money were due to inefficiency rather than shortage, it had demanded, and obtained, the right to examine royal accounts. It had had a number of unpopular ministers impeached for treason. It had attacked the privileges of the clergy, and discussed the merits of possible alternative foreign policies. The notion that there were certain subjects which Parliament should not discuss, though it seems to have appealed, for obvious reasons, to Richard II and Wolsey, was no part of current constitutional theory: Sir John Neale is right that Parliament did not have a formal privilege of freedom of speech until the sixteenth century, but Professor Roskell is also right in asking, 'what more could the Commons have done, had they enjoyed a formal privilege of free speech, than they were able to do, as it seems, without it?'[44]

Early Tudor Parliaments could still be awkward on occasion, and in 1523 Henry VIII was told by the Commons that the French town of Terouanne had cost him 'more than twenty such ungracious dogholes could be worth',[45] and that it was folly to try to recover an empire in France while Scotland was still independent. However, most of these precedents for parliamentary independence date from a period before 1450, and at the beginning of the sixteenth century, Parliament seems to have been in decline. Professor Roskell argues that in 1422 the Commons had more political initiative than they ever had again until 1640.[46] Certainly under Edward IV and Henry VII Parliament had been meeting less frequently. It appears, if our few records can be trusted, to have been less importunate in offering advice, and the Crown was strengthening its control of procedure. The Speaker, whose eye had to be caught by intending speakers, and who determined the order in which bills were read, had originally been an independent Commons' choice. Sir Peter de la Mare, the first known Speaker (in 1376) had been steward to the Earl of March, one of the lords most hostile to court policy at the time. Other early Speakers seem to have been choices which offended the king, but at some time in the middle of the fifteenth century the Crown appears to have gained control over the selection of the Speaker, and began to pay him a salary. It was not until 1679 that the Commons recovered their original right to

[44] Neale, J. E., 'The Commons' Privilege of Freedom of Speech', in *Tudor Studies*, ed. R. W. Seton-Watson (1924), 257–87. Roskell, J. S., *The Commons and their Speakers in English Parliaments 1376–1523* (1965), 50.

[45] Roskell, op. cit., 327.

[46] Roskell, J. S., *The Commons in Parliament 1422* (1954), 109.

choose a Speaker not nominated by the Crown. If Parliament was declining at the beginning of the sixteenth century, it was following a pattern
which was common in Europe.

Many of the early Speakers whom the Crown had most disliked had
been stewards or followers of great lords, and this raises the question of
the comparative influence of the Commons and the Lords in Parliament.
There had certainly been vigorous quarrels between the houses, but
whether this proves the independence of the Commons, or that minority
Lords had taken more trouble to get their followers returned to the Commons, is not clear. Certainly bastard feudalism had extended into the
competition for parliamentary seats. But this may have given Commons
influence on the Lords who retained them, as well as vice versa.[47] Bastard
feudal retainers were always free to transfer to another lord, and therefore
lords had to satisfy them. Lords, moreover, had councils and took advice,
and an able politician might perhaps even hope to manipulate the policy
of his lord. Many of the Commons were sons and brothers of lords, and it
seems difficult to consider the two houses as if they represented two
separate interests.

Lords' influence over the composition of the Commons lasted all
through the sixteenth century, as well as the fifteenth. Parliament in the
sixteenth century was made up of two members from each county, and
two members each from a number of boroughs, with occasional anomalies
such as Bewdley, which returned one member, and London, which returned four. In the counties, the electorate officially consisted of freeholders worth 40s., but many of these voted as their landlords dictated.
The boroughs had already, early in the fifteenth century, taken to returning considerable numbers of country gentlemen and lawyers, often at the
request of a lord whose favour they wanted. There were more merchants
in the fifteenth-century Commons than the sixteenth, but their numbers
were not large, and their influence smaller. Even London, which had an
organized parliamentary programme, complete with payments to the
Speaker and the Clerk to forward their bills, appears to have had little
success in influencing the house. The Commons were overwhelmingly a
body of country gentlemen, often returned by the interests of the peers,
but by no means subservient to them.

Constitutional ideas and the structure of politics

Since it was difficult for either king or Parliament to dispense with the
other, it is not surprising that the prevailing constitutional theory was of
unity. When Henry VIII addressed Parliament in 1543, and told them that

[47] McFarlane, K. B., 'Parliament and Bastard Feudalism', *T.R.H.S.* (1944), 53–73.

'we at no time stand so highly in our estate royal as in time of Parliament, wherein we as head and you as members are conjoined and knit together into one body politic',[48] he was admitting to the practical facts of the case. The image of head and members, which was constantly used, did not only express the supremacy of the head, but also that it and the members had a common interest. Since king and Parliament needed to co-operate, they stressed their belief in unity. The king also needed to co-operate with the classes whom Parliament represented, the peers and the powerful local gentry. It was occasionally possible for lords and gentry to change their king, but the fifteenth century had cast some doubt on whether the process was expedient. For practical purposes, it was prudent to regard the king as a fixture, however trying his policy might be. But similarly, though the king might promote some people and overthrow others, he had, on the whole, to regard the social framework within which he ruled as a fixture. He had unfettered power to choose his Privy Council and to form policy. But though there were no 'natural councillors', there were few periods during the sixteenth century when the Privy Council did not include at least one representative each from the families of Howard and Herbert. Similarly, the king had to assume some constancy in the local structure of power. However policy might change, Luttrells and Portmans would still be Justices of the Peace in Somerset, and it would not be easy to rule Somerset without their co-operation. Prudent kings took account of the feeling of these people before forming policy, and in their turn, they, if they were prudent, co-operated with royal policy if they could.

The prevailing social and political theory, that of the Great Chain of Being, expressed this interdependence. The other key point of the theory was order. God had created the world in the order which pleased him, each man and each beast in his proper place. This meant that superiors had to be obeyed, and 'the powers that be are ordained of God', but it also meant that superiors had to recognize that they too had superiors above them, and that they were bound together with their inferiors by a tie of common interest in the preservation of the whole order. If order was kept, there was harmony of the sort God had intended. If order was broken, there was chaos. Order did not only demand that inferiors should obey: it could be broken by superiors too. Bishop Ponet wrote while in exile in Mary's reign that 'as the body of man is knit and kept together in due proportion by the sinews, so is every commonwealth kept and maintained in order by obedience. But as if the sinews be too much racked and stretched out, or too much shrinked together, it breedeth marvellous pains and deformities in man's body: so if obedience be too much or too little

[48] *Tudor Constitution*, 270.

in a commonwealth, it causeth much evil and disorder.'[49] This correspondence of the body politic with the human body was drawn constantly. The theory was that one part of God's creation had to correspond to another, like a photograph and its enlargement. And though the head could rule over the body, it could not rule in its own interest, neglecting that of the feet, or else it, as well as the feet, would be hurt. Moreover, the head was not entirely the source of the principles by which it ruled. Princes' supremacy was guaranteed by God's laws, but 'princes are not joined makers hereof with God'.[50]

These theories did not apply only to royalty, but to every other supremacy in the commonwealth, that of fathers, husbands, masters, and landlords, among others. Tyndale reminded children that when their parents were angry with them, God was angry with them. But as always, this theory of supremacy had a reverse side, which Tyndale illustrated in his comments on landlords: 'let Christian landlords be content with their rent and old customs, not raising the rent or fines and bringing up new customs to oppress their tenants, neither letting two or three tenantries to one man. Let them not take in their commons, neither make parks nor pastures of whole parishes. For God gave the earth to men to inhabit, and not to sheep and wild deer. Be as fathers to your tenants: be unto them as Christ was unto us.'[51] This passage is as good an illustration as any other of the difficulties of preserving a theory of rule in the common interest and a stable social order during a period of rapid inflation.

Rulers, whether of a kingdom or of a cottage, might enjoy a divine right to rule, but it was widely held that they ruled subject to the rule of law, and subject to an obligation to rule in the common interest. A ruler who did not respect these obligations was a tyrant, and whatever duties were due to a king might or might not be due to a tyrant. The theoretical question of whether the same duties were due to a tyrant and to a king was always debatable, but the last man who had been widely considered a tyrant was found dead on Bosworth Field. It was not surprising that in 1534 Henry VIII made it treason to call him a tyrant. A tyrant did not necessarily have more power than a king: he was a ruler who used his power for bad purposes. The making of this distinction presupposed that people would agree which purposes were bad, and on the whole, those purposes which were against God's were taken to be bad. This was merely one of the many ways in which political obedience, a stable society, and

[49] Ponet, J., *A Short Treatise of Politike Power* (1556), Sig. C.6. Not all Ponet's views were conventional, but he shared this one with Strafford. Rushworth, *Trial of Strafford* (1680), 182.

[50] Ponet, quoted in Raab, Felix, *The English Face of Machiavelli* (1964), 19.

[51] Tyndale, W., *The Obedience of a Christian Man* (1535) fo. 51.

tolerable rule were held to depend on the fact that the country was united in religion. Paget, one of the most cynical politicians of the century, wrote to the Duke of Somerset in 1549 that 'society in a realm doth consist and is maintained by means of religion and law', and argued that if the unpopularity of the government's religion was combined with a hot summer, it was likely to produce a rebellion.[52] Religion was supposed to be the source of all moral principles, and the only security for the class structure. Before the Reformation, when unity in religion was taken for granted, its need was little stressed. But the last time unity of religion had appeared to be threatened, by the Lollard rising of 1413, Parliament had passed a statute accusing the Lollards of intending 'to annul and subvert the Christian faith and the law of God in the realm, and also to destroy our most sovereign lord the king himself, and all estates [*sc.* classes] within the realm, both spiritual and temporal, and also all polity and the laws of the land finally.'[53]

With these theories of unity, Tudor England was for practical purposes a one-party state. This did not mean that there were no differences of opinion: there were often wide ones. It did mean that it was assumed, even if wrongly, that those who took part in politics were united on a few very broad general principles, and it also meant that differences of opinion worked, not on the government and opposition model, but the way differences of opinion within a party work.[54] When a party is in a healthy state, most offices are open to all shades of opinion within it, and, which is perhaps more important, the key divisions are fluid ones of faction, patronage, and friendship, and cut across ideological divisions. This is why it is not possible in Tudor England to assume that because a man holds a government post, he will, when elected to Parliament, support an individual item of government policy. Nor is it possible to assume that because a man is returned by the interest of a particular lord, he shares all that lord's political views: he may only be the husband of that lord's sister. When the government could not be changed, if a group of people were excluded from office by their opinions, it meant they were permanently excluded or potential rebels, and if a lord collected a following round a particular political programme, he might be suspected of planning a *coup d'état*. So long as groups of faction and patronage cut across divisions on policy, the constitution was working successfully. This is why, at all but a few desperate times, the notion of 'packing' Parliament is an anachronistic one. Individual Councillors might make efforts to find men seats, but

[52] Fletcher, Anthony, *Tudor Rebellions* (1968), 147.

[53] Chrimes, S. B., and Brown, A. L., *Select Documents of English Constitutional History, 1307–1485* (1961), 239.

[54] Williams, Penry, *The Council in the Marches of Wales* (1958), 229.

the men they returned, like the holders of government posts, might be expected to cover all or almost all the range of opinions to be found in the country at large.

The correspondence of a great man, such as Thomas Cromwell or William Cecil, is filled with expressions of humble thanks for his 'favour', and expressions of willingness to do him 'service'. The receipt of large numbers of such letters was an essential part of a minister's or a lord's prestige: it meant that he had a reputation for power. The 'favours' asked for would usually be of some administrative kind: they might involve the grant of a wardship on favourable terms, or a benevolent blind eye during an inquiry into concealed Crown lands. They were more likely to involve influence towards the gift of some government post.

The machinery of government

Administrative posts were not sought for the official salary. The Chancellor of the Exchequer was paid £26. 13s. 4d. (40 marks) per annum, and even the Secretary of State was only paid £100 a year. Posts were sought, partly for the prestige, and for the opportunity they might create to offer the same 'favour' to other people, and partly for the perquisites of office. Most office-holders were paid fees by the public, at the rate, say, of 2s. 6d. for sealing an official document, or perhaps 1d. a line for writing it (this is one reason why official documents grew so long). There were other sources of profit which were less official. It was normal to offer presents to officials, not necessarily as a bribe, but as part of a general relationship of goodwill between them and their clients. Like tipping, the practice could be unobjectionable, but there was a very fine line which divided it from bribery.[55]

The administration itself was undergoing a Parkinsonian proliferation of posts during the century, partly by natural increase, partly by reorganization, and partly by an increase in the number of tasks the government had to undertake. Two departments created during the century, the navy and ordnance offices, represented increases in the range of the Crown's responsibilities. In each of these there were perhaps half a dozen posts which might tempt a gentleman, and many more for clerks, messengers and other functionaries. One of the valuable perquisites of office was the right to appoint to some of these junior posts.

The notion of a 'department' was not normally found. Different sections of the administration were called 'courts' or 'councils', or, if they could not be classified as either, 'offices'. By far the biggest branch of the ad-

[55] On this line, see Hurstfield, J., 'Political Corruption in Early Modern England', *History* (1967), 16–34.

ministration, the Exchequer, had originally had functions which were a confusion of administrative and judicial, but by the sixteenth century the judicial ones had been split off, and it was solely concerned with the task of gathering and auditing the king's revenue. The two offices at the head of it, the Lord Treasurership and, to a lesser extent, the Chancellorship of the Exchequer, were profitable and coveted, and there were many subordinate posts below them. The work of the Exchequer was divided between two functions, one of recording the receipt of revenues, and the other of auditing accounts. It was reasonably efficient at its task, which was that of providing an accurate legal record of what happened to the king's money. Its accounts were not composed to enable historians to discover the size of the royal revenue, but to discover whether obscure local officials owed the Crown three shillings, or not. The Exchequer had a first-rate administrative routine, and could be trusted to chase an overdue debt for up to fifty years, but it was not very good at adjusting to change. It had all a large department's devotion to routine, and would hardly produce new systems of land management.

Under Edward IV and Henry VII, a considerable amount of business had been temporarily removed from the Exchequer, and transferred to the Chamber. This did not mean that the administration literally went on in the king's bed-chamber, but simply that it was outside the existing departmental structure, and could be managed by whatever organizational system the king chose to create. The system was particularly successful for the Crown lands, for which Edward IV created, and Henry VII, after some prompting, continued, a system of trained receivers and surveyors, who, for a while, gave land management the detailed supervision it needed. This period of informally organized administration, like its predecessors under Henry II, John and Edward I, was necessarily short-lived. Chamber financial organization was as subject to Parkinson's law as any other. When one man was given the task of supervising one particular financial task for the Chamber, he collected a staff under him, and if the staff worked well together, they soon became a team, and then an office. For example, in 1503 Sir John Hussey was given the task of administering wardships. He had an office set up to help him, and acquired a subordinate official to track down wardships in each county. By 1505 the accounts were being done by a specialist Receiver of Wards, and by 1528 there was an Attorney of Wards dealing with the legal business arising from wardships. By 1519, the Venetian Ambassador was speaking, slightly prematurely, of a Court of Wards, and part of the informal Chamber administration had developed into a new government office.[56] Other

[56] Bell, H. E., *The Court of Wards and Liveries* (1953), 1–15.

offshoots of the Chamber appeared for a while equally likely to turn into permanent offices, but since they did not survive, they need not be discussed here.

The only branch of the administration which was big enough to rival the Exchequer was the Chancery. This was both a judicial court (in which capacity it will be discussed later), and a government writing office. It was responsible, among other things, for compiling the Patent Rolls, which were a record of royal grants, and for issuing writs necessary to summon people to appear before various courts. The Lord Chancellor, who presided over it, had control of the Great Seal, which was necessary to authenticate royal grants. It kept lists of Justices of the Peace, and compiled the official list of Members of Parliament.

The Household, apart from being an umbrella term to cover the various government operations carried on by the Chamber, was also, in the literal sense, an administration of the royal household. This difficult and expensive task was carried out, at least in name, by the Lord Chamberlain, and by the Treasurer and Comptroller of the Household under him. The household gave rise to a large number of subordinate posts. It employed the purveyors who bought the royal food, and numerous other people such as the Master of the Tents and Revels. A household post, though often discharged by deputy, might mean access to the king's person, and a consequent chance of promotion. It is by the control of the household officers over royal entertainments that the censorship of plays came to be attached to the Lord Chamberlain's office.

One of the more efficient branches of administration was the Duchy of Lancaster, a somewhat anomalous organization which ruled over those Crown estates which had belonged to Henry IV as Duke of Lancaster before he became king. The Duchy of Lancaster, presided over by its Chancellor, had its own court and its own council, and ran a national administration in miniature. It administered its own wardships, and appointed to a large number of local offices. It supervised land revenue, woods, and feudal tenures, and controlled various other things such as a number of castles and vicarages. It was not by any means confined to Lancashire, but was involved in every county in which the Dukes of Lancaster had owned land.

There were more genuinely local councils presiding over Wales and the north, which were too remote to be very easily administered from London. These councils seem to have been first thought of by Edward IV, but the stages of their development were not complete before the middle of Henry VIII's reign. They did not altogether supersede the Westminster administration: wardships and Crown lands from Wales and the north were still handled centrally. They had control of military forces, and administration of royal castles, but their main powers were judicial. They had a succession of commissions giving them most types of jurisdiction, but they were mainly concerned with keeping the peace, and with handling such perennial abuses as robbery and false verdicts by juries.

The English and the Irish

Ireland was administered by a Lord Deputy, who in theory had complete viceregal powers, and a national administration of his own. In fact, neither the Old English settler population nor the native Irish were very securely under the Lord Deputy's control. Racial hostility between the English and the Irish showed no signs of diminishing with the centuries. One Englishman maintained that:

> Wild Irish are as civil as the Russies in their kind,
> Hard choice which is the best of both, each bloody, rude, and blind.

An Irishman, on the other hand, said of the English that 'they are the greatest murderers and the proudest people in all Europe and I am surprised that God tolerates them so long in power—except that he is long-suffering, and his avenging hand is slow but sure, and besides, that the Irish themselves are bad, and that this misfortune is to chastise and correct them. I shall say no more, because I should use up all my ink and paper on this subject.' The English continually failed to make the Irish adopt English law, dress, or language. When it was suggested that the O'Neill should speak English, one of his followers asked, 'thinkest thou that it standeth with Oneile his honour to writhe his mouth in clattering English?'[57] Among the charges against Strafford, a former Lord Deputy of Ireland, one which backfired was the accusation that he had said Ireland was a conquered nation. Strafford told the Lords that he would be doing a great injury to the memory of some of their lordships' noble ancestors if he denied that Ireland was a conquered nation. Ireland, like India later, was a foreign colony, and on the whole it was the less successfully assimilated.

Local government

In England, the period saw considerable development of local, as well as national, administration. The sheriff, who had been the corner-stone of local administration since Anglo-Saxon times, was steadily declining in importance. The only important powers he kept were that of presiding

[57] Quinn, D. B., *The Elizabethans and the Irish* (1966), 12, 23, 88.

over parliamentary elections, which gave some valuable opportunities to exercise 'favour', and that of acting as a postbox for royal writs. The office was expensive, and it is doubtful whether it was often sought for. The escheator, the other important local official of long standing, was also declining in importance. Henry VII took most of the work of administering wardships away from him, and his office was little more than honorary. In his place, Henry VII created the office of feodary, which supervised all the local business of wardships, keeping track of Crown tenures, collecting rents from wards' lands, valuing wards' estates, and conveying information to Westminster. There were three other new county officials connected with the administration of the Crown lands, the receiver, the surveyor, and the woodward. These posts were all moderately profitable, and so long as they were adequately supervised, did something to keep a local check on the Crown lands. The largest amount of local work was done by the Justices of the Peace, whose importance increased as that of the sheriff diminished. They were a fourteenth-century institution, but their powers were considerably extended during the Tudor period. Henry VII gave them the right to take bail, and to act on information, without waiting for a grand jury to produce a formal indictment. They dealt with enforcement of apprenticeship regulations, and organized the repair of local prisons and bridges, and handled the explosive business of licensing alehouses. Major criminal cases they usually left until the royal judges came round on Assizes, but they occasionally dealt with rape and libel, as well as robbery. For criminal business, they met four times a year at Quarter Sessions, but petty administrative business was with them all the year round. The bench was usually made up of the heads of the twenty-five or thirty most important families in the county, and membership was an important mark of local prestige, so the Crown could often express its displeasure with a gentleman simply by leaving him out of the next Commission of the Peace.

The Council

The source of most of the Justices' detailed instructions, and the destination of their reports on local conditions, was the Privy Council, which was the driving force behind the whole administrative machinery, as well as the body which formed policy. The Council varied sharply in size, being as small as twelve under Elizabeth, and above fifty under Mary. On Parkinsonian principles, its importance at any period was in inverse proportion to its size, and it was therefore subjected to periodic reorganizations usually followed by further expansions. Being summoned before the Council was one of the most alarming experiences which might befall a Tudor gentleman, though sometimes appearing was less alarming than not appearing. The Council was always dealing with a large bulk of petty business, as well as with national policy, and sometimes chose to punish offenders simply by keeping them waiting at Westminster running up lodging bills. On one occasion, Wolsey kept De Carteret, who had made an enemy of the governor of Guernsey, waiting in London to appear before Star Chamber for between four and five years.[58]

VII   THE COURTS

Procedure in the Star Chamber and Common Law courts

However, most conciliar jurisdiction was exercised by the Star Chamber. This court had not been invented by Henry VII, but was simply a formalization of the jurisdiction the Council had always had to hear cases. It normally consisted of the Council members and the two Chief Justices, and met regularly at Westminster. It had the advantage that, as Sir Thomas Smith put it, it was possible to overawe an offender by confronting him with the majesty of the whole realm.[59] It was used for government prosecutions, but in the sixteenth century the majority of its business was private suits between party and party, and, to judge from the numbers of suits filed, it appears to have been popular. Officially, it was supposed not to deal with real property cases, which were supposed to be reserved to the Common Law courts, but even Pym's father, who was a Common Law barrister, was prepared to take a real property case to Star Chamber by disguising it as a fraud case.[60] Its chief advantage for litigants who were sure of their ground was the difference between its procedure and that of the Common Law courts.

In the Common Law courts, a criminal prosecution had to begin with a formal indictment, in which every detail had to be correct. It was void if it accused the defendant of committing murder at half past three when in fact he had committed it at three o'clock. A civil suit between two parties was initiated by a series of oral pleadings, which continued, taking up time and money, until issue was joined on a point either of law or of fact. It was not possible to join issue on grounds of both law and fact. A man who was accused of stealing apples might plead, either that they were his apples, or that he had not taken them, but if both were true, he could only plead one or the other. Points of fact in a Common Law court normally had to be proved by independent witnesses. It was not possible

[58] Eagleston, A. J., *The Channel Islands under Tudor Government* (1949), 23–5.
[59] Smith, T., *De Republica Anglorum*, ed. L. Alston (1906), 117.
[60] P.R.O. Sta. Cha. 5 P. 32/34.

to make the defendant go into the witness box and obtain a result by interrogating him.

The procedure in the Star Chamber and other prerogative courts was less fair to the accused, but better designed to find the truth. A suit, whether criminal or civil, was initiated by a written bill, filed by the Attorney-General in a criminal case or the plaintiff in a civil one. The bill gave a general account of what the quarrel was about, but there was no absolute restriction on introducing new matter which had not been in the bill. In reply, the defendant also filed a written bill, giving his version of the story. Each side then prepared a list of questions, and their opponents and any witnesses they chose then had to answer the questions under oath. Both the bill and reply, and these written answers to questions, were before the court when it first heard the case, and they saved much time. If any doubt remained, the court was able to question the parties further under oath. The fines imposed, though on paper they were enormous, were not as crippling as might be supposed, since they were often used as a form of bail for future good behaviour. A man who was fined £5,000 might perhaps pay £500 at once, and then appear before the court each law term to have the outstanding fine reviewed. If he behaved badly, a little more might be levied, and if he had behaved well, the total amount owing might be reduced and, with luck, he would ultimately be pardoned altogether. This is one of the many ways in which the king succeeded in the crucial task of making his favour profitable.

There were three other Westminster courts functioning at the beginning of the period which were not bound by the strict rules of Common Law procedure, Requests, Admiralty, and Chancery. Requests, though its origins are obscure, probably evolved in the late fifteenth century, and was officially designed to give justice to those who were too poor to sue at Common Law. In fact, many litigants in the Court of Requests were probably as prosperous as other litigants, and it probably handled business very similar to the Court of Chancery's, but rather less important. It appears, later in the century, to have handled numerous cases arising out of marketing disputes. The Court of Admiralty dealt with issues involving overseas trade, international mercantile suits, and disputes about prize goods. It did not become particularly important until the crowd of prize disputes during the Elizabethan war with Spain.

The Court of Chancery

By far the most important, and the most popular, of these courts was the Court of Chancery. Chancery had originally been designed to give relief in cases where the strict rules of Common Law produced an unfair result, and administered what was known as equity. This may originally have meant Common Law tempered by the judge's sense of what was fair, but by the end of the fifteenth century Chancery had developed a long string of precedents of its own. Procedure, as in the Star Chamber, was by a written bill followed by written questions, and the defendant had to answer the plaintiff's bill under oath. It dealt with almost all sorts of cases between party and party, but it was necessary for the plaintiff to allege in his bill of complaint that, though he was entitled to redress, 'by the strict rules of common law' he could get no relief. He therefore asked for his opponent to be put under oath, a remedy in which sixteenth-century litigants appear to have had a sublime faith, which was not always quite unjustified. Some of the allegations that relief could not be had by the strict rules of Common Law were somewhat doubtful (Pym once claimed that he could not have relief by the rules of Common Law because he had 'casually lost' the main document in the case),[61] but there was no disposition to question them too closely. The parties often preferred Chancery because it was probably cheaper, and as for the Court itself, all courts wanted to enlarge their jurisdiction, both for prestige, and because it increased the fees due to the court's officers. Chancery had very much increased its jurisdiction during the fifteenth century, partly because, unlike the Common Law courts, it gave protection to uses, which were trusts created for purposes of tax evasion. Before he died, a man would normally make his land over to a collection of trustees, known as his feoffees to uses. These trustees then held the land in trust 'to the use of' the original owner and his heir. When the original owner died, and the Wards officers came to investigate his estate, they found that most of the estate 'belonged' to the trustees, some at least of whom were still alive, and therefore that they were not entitled to take it into wardship. The protection Chancery gave to uses was one of the main reasons for its popularity.

Common Law courts

The Common Law courts at Westminster may have lost a lot of business to Chancery and Star Chamber, and they occasionally adopted some dubious devices to recover it, but the increase in litigation during the century was so rapid, especially in Wales, that the total volume of their business undoubtedly increased. There were three Common Law courts, King's Bench, Common Pleas, and the Court of Exchequer. In theory, King's Bench dealt with criminal prosecutions, Common Pleas with civil suits between parties, and the Exchequer with cases involving the king's revenue, but this division was more honoured in the breach than the ob-

[61] P.R.O. C. 2 Ch. 1 P. 78/57.

servance, and each court grabbed whatever business it could. Each court was staffed by four judges, and for cases of exceptional difficulty, such as ship money, all twelve judges might meet together in what was called the Court of Exchequer Chamber.

The course of a lawsuit

It was possible for a defeated litigant to appeal to Parliament for a writ of error, and in the seventeenth century regular parliamentarians sometimes obtained private Acts of Parliament reversing decrees against them, but there was no normal machinery for appeals. The normal method of dealing with an unsatisfactory verdict was to get the case re-heard, in a slightly different guise, in another court, and if the two courts disagreed, there was no recourse but a hearing in a third court, or a petition to the Privy Council, which might in turn refer the case to a fourth court. In these circumstances, the division of function between different courts remained obscure. A hypothetical case might run roughly as follows: the estate of a Welsh gentleman was entailed, and bound by law to descend to his eldest son, but he, being very fond of his younger son, might attempt to break the entail, and bequeath part of it to his younger son. On his death, the younger son might occupy the property. The elder would take the case to Common Pleas, and obtain a judgement that the entail was valid, and therefore that he was the legal owner of the property. The younger might refuse to move out, whereat the elder would arm his farm labourers, cut down the hedges and march in. After some bloodshed, the younger would bring a case against the elder in the Star Chamber for riot. The Star Chamber, knowing little of the earlier case, would issue an order forbidding the elder to invade the property. The elder might then go back to Common Pleas, and get a writ to the sheriff authorizing him to execute the original judgement giving him the land. The younger might then begin to mobilize influence, and appeal to the Privy Council, whereat both the elder and the sheriff would be thrown into prison for contempt of an order of the Star Chamber. The elder might then mobilize his influence on the Council of Wales, get himself released from prison, and bring a case against the younger in the Council of Wales for fraud. The younger might then get a case brought against the elder for bribing witnesses. At this point, an Exchequer official might discover, with some prompting, that the manor in question was held from the Crown, and had been left to the younger brother without a licence to alienate, so the younger might find himself prosecuted in the Court of Exchequer. At this stage, when the estate was exhausted by legal costs, the brothers might agree to settle out of court.

The Inns of Court

It is not surprising, in these circumstances, that the legal profession was flourishing, nor that a number of gentlemen felt that their sons needed to learn some law at the Inns of Court in London before inheriting their estates. Whether an increasing number of gentlemen were attending the Inns of Court is a harder question, since it was not until Elizabeth's reign that the Inns kept adequate admission registers, and an increase in recorded numbers may only mean an improvement in recording. Most gentlemen who had attended the Inns made themselves out to have a smattering of law, but law was too technical for amateur knowledge to be very easy, and there was no adequate system of tuition at the Inns. It has recently been questioned whether Tudor and Stuart gentlemen really had an amateur working knowledge of the law, as distinct from some ill-digested fragments.[62] However, the Inns of Court certainly provided a social education in the pitfalls of life in London. William Cecil, in his first week at the Inns of Court, lost all his money, bedding, and books at cards. He reacted by constructing a speaking tube into the bedroom of the man who had won the money, and denouncing him at midnight for his sin in 'cozenage and lewdness'. The next morning, the man returned his winnings, and neither ever gambled again.[63] However, if other things than law might be learned at the Inns of Court, there was certainly a regular market for abridgements of statutes and other legal textbooks, and popular legal works accounted for a large part of the output of the early printing press.

Informers

The other group which might profit from litigation was informers. Village constables were not an adequate police system, since the office was often taken on only by those who were not powerful enough to avoid it, and both the collection of royal revenue and criminal prosecutions depended heavily on the work of informers. In criminal cases, the informer was often entitled by statute to half the fine, and in cases of wardship, he might get the wardship at a favourable price. One draft Elizabethan lease was sent up to Burghley with an endorsement by an officer of the court: 'a concealed ward found out by him, to whom my Lord hath granted him [the wardship of] the body, and now he desireth a lease of the lands, if it may so please your lordship.' He got it. Richard Chamberlain, later one

---

[62] Prest, Wilfrid, 'The Legal Education of the Gentry at the Inns of Court', *Past and Present*, no. 38 (1967), 20–40.
[63] Conyers Read, i. 30–31.

of the Wards' most devoted officers, attracted official attention when 'by long suit he discovered a notorious fraud'.[64] Pickings were usually to be found by informing against yeomen, who might have bought land not knowing that it was liable to wardship. One Elizabethan, Paul Rainsford, specialized in this task, and produced some pathetic replies from yeomen who were barely literate, and certainly did not understand the concept of knight service in chief. Once, however, he overreached himself, when he informed against a man at Orpington, who claimed that his land was held by the antiquated Kentish tenure of gavelkind, and therefore that he was not liable to wardship.[65] While the Crown had no effective resources for gathering its own information, procedures such as these were unavoidable.

VIII THE CHURCH BEFORE THE REFORMATION

The Pope

The only one of the country's institutions which was frequently represented at parish level was the church, which may therefore have made more impression on villagers' daily lives than the royal administration did. But though the church was in some senses a national institution, it was also an international one. Whatever might be true in practice, in theory the provinces of Canterbury and York were two separate parts of the western church, united only under the primacy of the Pope. But though there was little dispute about the fact of papal primacy, there was a good deal of quiet doubt about what papal primacy meant. After the Great Schism at the end of the fourteenth century, a number of people had come to believe that the supreme body in the church was a General Council, and that Popes were chief executive officers between sessions of Councils. The fifteenth-century Popes had fought hard against the extremer forms of this theory, but though it had faded into the background, it had not died out. As late as 1516, the Pope issued a bull to say that it was an error to suppose that the General Council was above the Pope. And even if the Pope was the chief officer of the church, there was room for doubt about the right by which he held the position. Popes might believe they were direct successors of St. Peter, holding office by divine authority, but two Catholics as good as Sir Thomas More and Cardinal Pole had believed in youth that the Pope held his office only by human authority, because the church had chosen that form of government. Moreover, kings had a tradition centuries old of arguing that the Pope's authority did not extend to tem-

[64] P.R.O. Wards 12.9 and 12.8.
[65] P.R.O. Wards 15.4.1.

poral matters, and there was always room for dispute about which matters were temporal and which were spiritual.

Nevertheless, a Pope properly handled could on occasion be very useful to a king. Henry VII, in particular, had devoted much of his diplomatic talent to good relations with the Pope, and had found the result rewarding. The crucial point was the king's diplomatic representation at the Vatican. England, being a small country, suffered badly from lack of cardinals, and while there might often be half a dozen French or Spanish cardinals, there was rarely more than one English cardinal, and there had not been one resident in the papal Curia since the fourteenth century. It was therefore necessary to maintain good relations with a number of members of the Curia who could be induced to defend English interests at Rome. The key office was that of Cardinal Protector, who acted as spokesman for the interests of the country he represented. It was usually he who dealt with the legally tangled, but practically simple, business of appointing bishops. When things worked well, the Protector was told whom the king wanted, proposed him to the Pope, and the Pope appointed him. There was still a statute on the books to say that the Pope could not provide to English benefices, but nobody chose to remember this statute while the Pope provided the man the king wanted. This system was so well established that the Pope even appointed Cranmer under it. The Protector also did a good deal of work obtaining for his king various rights and favours which he might want. It used to be thought that this institution was invented by Henry VII, but recent research has shown that, like so many other things, it was invented by Edward IV and perfected by Henry VII.[66] By 1530, every country had its Protector, and there was occasionally trouble with ones who claimed to represent two countries.

Both the Protector and other people who represented the king's interests at Rome did a large amount of work, and their loyalty was essential. It was therefore necessary to pay them, but ecclesiastical funds were available in the form of livings, not of salaries. They were therefore normally appointed to English bishoprics, and though they did not discharge their duties as bishops, they certainly earned their money. Little of the business they handled was strictly theological: of all the correspondence which passed between Henry VII and the Pope, none concerns anything which could strictly be classified as a point of doctrine. Much of it concerns papal confirmation of Henry's title, which he valued highly. When Lambert Simnel's rebels were in the field, Henry immediately reported to the Pope that one of the rebels had uttered Lollard heresy on the battle-

---

[66] Chambers, D. S., *Cardinal Bainbridge and the Court of Rome* (1965), 2 n.

field, whereat he had dropped dead and turned black. The Pope responded
by issuing bulls further confirming Henry's title, and excommunicating
the rebels, and Henry evidently thought the bulls sufficiently valuable to
be translated into English and printed by Caxton for general distribution—one of the earliest cases of the use of printing for government
propaganda.[67] Much correspondence was concerned with dispensations: it
was technically illegal to marry anyone with a common ancestry, *or a
common ancestor by marriage*, within seven generations, and royal families were so intermarried that they were rarely able to marry without a
papal dispensation. There was ordinary diplomatic correspondence about
foreign policy, and mundane correspondence about such matters as the
disturbance of ecclesiastical property rights involved in converting endowments to set up St. George's Chapel, Windsor. There were some exchanges
about administrative matters. Henry persuaded the Pope to issue bulls
restricting the right of sanctuary for criminals. He dealt successfully with
the Pope's claim to tax the English clergy, by saying that although the
Pope had no right to do this, he would tax the English clergy himself, and,
as a matter of goodwill, would pay the proceeds to the Pope. The Pope's
assent was needed, and obtained, for the translations of bishops from see
to see by which Henry created vacancies which increased his revenue.
There was some correspondence about sale of Indulgences to finance the
building of St. Peter's or a Crusade. The only point which produced ill-
will was the papal claim to a monopoly of alum, a commodity used by the
cloth industry for fixing dyes, and the only failure was the negotiations
Henry started for the canonization of Henry VI, and, as a *quid pro quo*,
of St. Anselm, which lapsed, possibly because they were too expensive.[68]
When Englishmen in the next reign spoke of rejecting papal authority,
they probably meant the type of authority the Pope normally exercised,
which was too mundane for it to be easy to remember that he was essential
to the doctrinal unity of western Christendom.

More powerful kings than Henry VII might win larger favours from the
Pope, and in 1501 Alexander VI granted to the Spanish Crown in America
the right to hold office as papal legate, to collect first-fruits and tenths,
rights of patronage in all sees, the right to divide and consolidate dioceses,
the right to prevent any American bishop from returning to Europe without the Viceroy's leave, the right to hold and preside over their own provincial councils, the income from vacant sees, and the right to prevent all

---

[67] I would like to thank my wife for permission to use the results of her research,
on which this section is largely based.

[68] Southern, R. W., *St. Anselm and His Biographer* (1963), 341–2. The negotiations
for the canonization of Henry VI were revived by Henry VIII in 1528.

judicial appeals to Rome.[69] If Alexander VI would make grants like these, kings had no need to denounce his morals, and little temptation to reject papal authority, since most of the advantages of independence were to be had by papal bull. But rewards such as these were only to be obtained by service to the papacy from a great power: they were not to be obtained by bluster at a thousand miles' distance.

What the Pope meant to the public at large is a more difficult question. He did have some important functions: papal decretals were the ultimate source of the canon law by which the church was governed. In theory, there was a right of appeal from English church courts to the papal court of the Rota, but except in very rare politically sensitive cases, it is doubtful whether the right of appeal was very important. The king did not care much if the Pope considered, for example, consanguinity among the burgesses of Hastings,[70] and for many members of the public at large, the cost of a hearing at Rome was so large as to be prohibitive. In practice, appeals to the Pope were normally referred to papal judges delegate in England, with the result that the people who would have heard the case anyway, heard it with papal authority. There was sometimes complaint about money passing out of England to the Pope, but the sums involved were very small. It is doubtful whether people below the rank of bishop or abbot ever had many dealings with the Pope, and it is also doubtful whether anti-papalism was a powerful force in England in the years before the Reformation.

There was certainly a great force of discontent with the church, but there were many targets for criticism which were nearer home, and therefore more provocative, than the Pope. A certain number of avowed heretics made vigorous attacks on the Pope: Tyndale said that he was 'a God on earth, of the kind (I suppose) of Aaron's calf, since he bringeth forth no other fruit but Bulls', and an obscure congregation of Lollards in the Chilterns maintained that he was 'a great beast, and a devil of Hell, and a synagogue',[71] but it seems probable that these people were anti-papal because they held doctrines on other subjects which Popes had already condemned as heretical, rather than because papal authority as such

[69] *Cambridge Modern History* (1902), I. 61. On the powers a Catholic ruler might obtain from the Pope, see also Knecht, R. J., 'The Concordat of 1516: A Reassessment', *University of Birmingham Historical Journal* (1965), 16–32, and Lynch, J., 'Philip II and the Papacy', *T.R.H.S.* (1961), 23–43. The kings of Spain, for example, had no financial inducement to break with Rome. Elliott, J. H., *Imperial Spain* (1963), 89–91.

[70] On appeals, see Mayr-Harting, Henry, 'Henry II and the Papacy', *J.E.H.* (1965), 39–53. The issues changed little in the intervening centuries.

[71] Tyndale, W., *The Obedience of a Christian Man* (1536), fo. 1xv. McFarlane, K. B., *Wycliffe and the Beginnings of English Nonconformity* (1952), 184.

caused them any disturbance. Nor was the Pope one of the real points of enthusiasm for defenders of the traditional church. Robert Parkyn, a devout Yorkshire country priest who kept a diary throughout the Reformation, had much to say about the Mass, and about the images in his church, but he only twice found occasion to mention the Pope. It was only rare characters such as More and Pole, who were used to looking for far-reaching intellectual implications, who, at the last moment, saw the future of western Christendom at stake in the question of papal authority.

Church courts

Some of the most vigorous discontents against the church were directed at the operation of its system of courts. The church might be a religious body, but it was also a legal system and an administration, and in these capacities, failed to command the respect it needed. Church courts handled a number of sensitive issues, and since churchmen had to live and staff an administrative system, they had to raise money from the process. Probate of wills was regarded as a spiritual matter, since a man's last will and testament concerned the fate of his soul. Wills had to be proved in the court of the bishop of the diocese (or occasionally before his representative on local visitation). If land in more than one diocese was involved, the will had to go to London, and be proved by the Prerogative Court of Canterbury. The same system of official fees and perquisites existed here as in dealings with lay administration, and it was met with rather less tolerance. Disputes about tithes were claimed by the church courts, to the professional jealousy of the lay courts, and, since valuable property rights were involved, sometimes to the dismay of the laity. Marriage was a spiritual matter, and all suits concerning it had to go to church courts. This also involved property rights, since marriages, which were normally arranged, were for most people the biggest business transaction of their lives. The cash portion which a bride brought with her might revive a family's fortunes, and the jointure which was settled on the bride to endow her for a possible widowhood might amount to a third of an estate. Jurisdiction over marriage is sensitive enough when a fortune is not involved as well. Cases of defamation and libel were often brought to church courts, on the ground that spiritual matters were involved, and debt and perjury, though often tried in lay courts, were also tried in church courts, on the ground that the church had jurisdiction over the breach of faith involved.

In addition, archdeacons on visitation inquired continually, both into public morals, and into the running of the parish churches. The presentments in the deanery of Bridgwater in 1577–8 are probably a typical selection for any period during the century. A large number of people were presented for not receiving Communion at Easter (an offence as likely to be evidence of sloth or drunkenness as of heresy). A number of church-wardens were presented because their church did not have the largest Bible, and one parish for not having a copy of Erasmus' paraphrases. Some vicars were presented for having two benefices, or for preaching too few sermons. Patrons were presented for allowing the decay of the church, or, in one case, of the vicarage stable. Members of the public were con-tinually presented for fornication or adultery, and frequently for crossing the Bristol Channel to Wales in order to be married without banns. A number were presented for fighting in churchyards, and one for refusing to contribute to the parish rate for the relief of the poor.[72] This is a post-Reformation list, but almost all the items on it are typical of any part of the century. Church court records show little sign that there was a Refor-mation at all. One church court once carried its inquiries into behaviour so far as to excommunicate a woman for 'misbehaving her tongue towards her mother-in-law'.[73] In most cases, either this jurisdiction appeared imperti-nent, or it seemed not to be truly spiritual. Few people like public in-quiries into their sexual behaviour, and it is doubtful whether many believed the safety of their souls was threatened by failure to repair the vicarage stable.

Public cynicism was further provoked by the courts' lack of convincing penalties. In theory, church courts should have been well able to settle disputes between party and party, but they usually failed because, like other Tudor courts, they were plagued by the continual failure of one or other of the parties to appear. In dealing with this, they were deprived of the most useful weapons of secular courts, fine and imprisonment, since, in theory, these, not being spiritual censures, could not be inflicted by a spiritual court. When a party to a suit persistently failed to appear, the court could do nothing but excommunicate him. Similarly, excommunica-tion had to be used as the penalty for a number of prosecutions, and a punishment which in theory threatened a man's hope of salvation had to be used for questions of fees and property whose spiritual content many people found hard to see.[74] As one of the later Puritans put it, 'the spiritual sword comes to be unsheathed about such things as do not at all fall under

---

[72] Somerset Record Office, D/D/Ca, Act Bk. 58. The presentations for not having the Bible or Erasmus' *Paraphrases* could only be post-Reformation.

[73] Hill, C., *Society and Puritanism in Pre-Revolutionary England* (1964), 356.

[74] Bowker, 20–37. Price, F. D., 'Abuses of Excommunication and the Decline of Ecclesiastical Discipline', *E.H.R.* (1942), 106–15. One of these accounts deals with a period before the Reformation, and the other with one after it, but the stories they tell are similar in many respects.

the stroke thereof—many are excommunicated for pigs, apples and nuts and such-like things.'[75] Tyndale and many other early Reformers made some of their bitterest complaints against the abuses of excommunication: 'O ye abominable! Who gave you authority to command God to curse?'[76] The only alternative to excommunication was penance, and here again the church was caught in the dilemma, that its punishments had either to be insignificant or so undignified as to be provocative, or else to face the reproach of being unspiritual. Penances for heresy might involve carrying a faggot and making a submission for the offence in a public place, and for adultery, they might involve standing in the market place in a white sheet with a placard proclaiming the offence. Some church authorities preferred something more useful or less undignified for gentlemen, and would commute the penance in return for, for example, a contribution to the repair of the Fossdyke.[77] But in doing this, they laid themselves open to the charge that they were selling absolution for money, and so committing simony.

Neither did the officials who ran the courts inspire confidence. The apparitors, who were responsible for bringing prosecutions before the courts, were paid in the form of fees from litigants. Since the innocent paid fees as well as the guilty, the apparitors' income depended on bringing the maximum possible number of prosecutions. The other key people in running the diocesan courts, the vicar general, the official principal, the chancellor, and the commissary, also failed to command confidence. They were normally trained civil lawyers, but they had little claim to be spiritual persons. Like modern universities, the church suffered from the fact that its pastoral and learned functions were almost entirely separated from its administrative functions. It was frequently alleged that these administrative powers, backed by the right to impose an oath, were used for no other purpose but to exact money.

Economic problems of the church

The church's own supplies of money were considerable, but they were very badly distributed. Perhaps the greatest of its resources was church land, most of which was owned by bishops, monasteries, or chantries. It had tithe, which was supposed to be a tenth of the produce of each parish, and had originally been designed for the support of the parish clergy. Some parish clergy, the rectors, still received tithe, and, in a period when the

---

[75] Rushworth, III. i. 178.
[76] Tyndale, W., op. cit., fo. cxi.
[77] Bowker, 22. The Fossdyke, when in working order, made Lincoln accessible to water transport. For another unfortunate attempt to finance its repair, see below, p. 207.

value of agricultural produce was increasing, were often doing fairly well. The majority of parish clergy, the vicars, received little or none of the tithes. The tithes of vicarages had been impropriated, either by a monastery or by a layman, and while the impropriators received the benefit from the increase in their value, the vicar was often paid a fixed stipend whose value decreased with inflation. In many cases, moreover, tithe had been commuted in return for a fixed payment which did not keep up with inflation. The result was that many of the parish clergy were very poor indeed. The average net stipend of a vicar in Lincoln diocese in 1526 was £6. 13s. 1½d. a year. In addition to this stipend, clergy were entitled to fees for some of their professional duties. They were entitled to a mortuary fee for conducting a funeral, which was normally supposed to be one of the dead man's two best beasts. It is not surprising that with low salaries during a period of inflation, the clergy often tried to raise their fees, nor that the attempt was often met with indignation.

In order to attract a vicar of any quality into the church, it was often necessary to give him more than one living. Moreover, care of a parish has never been the only ecclesiastical duty. Clerical communities, and some clergy engaged in study or church administration, were necessary, and needed money. There was no separate money available to provide salaries for these posts, whose holders could only be paid by giving them livings in which they were not expected to reside. This happened at all levels. If the President of the Council of Wales was a layman, he could expect to be rewarded with estates, but if he was a clergyman, he could only be rewarded by being given the income from a bishopric. In 1535 Bishop Lee, President of the Council of Wales, said he would accept the king's request to preach the Royal Supremacy, although he had never before been in a pulpit. If he had not, it was because it was not his job. The same problem existed on lower levels. Of the non-residents in Lincoln diocese in 1517, 97 were pluralists, 30 were at the universities, 21 were private chaplains, 14 were canons regular, 10 were diocesan administrators, 2 were on pilgrimage, 8 had parishes which were depopulated, and for 119 the reasons were not discovered. The list included the papal tax collector and the king's doctor. Most of their livings were served by curates, who were even poorer than vicars, and often not of very high quality. The majority of non-residents were in the richer livings.

The system of patronage tended to make it easier for those who were unlikely to reside to get benefices. Advowsons, the power to exercise or sell the right to choose and present the next parson, were legally regarded as real property. They could be bought and sold like estates, and were under the jurisdiction of the lay courts. In Lincoln diocese, out of a sample of

2,760 presentations made at the beginning of the century, monasteries and other religious houses made 1,331, the king 123, the bishop 85, and most of the rest were made by various laymen and by Oxford and Cambridge colleges. People at court and in public life were more likely to attract the attention of owners of advowsons. There was no questioning of the system of advowsons, but some parochial discontent with the results it produced.

Complaints against the church

All these grievances, though they helped to give force to the Reformation, were not reformed by it. Some others were. There was considerable discontent both with confession and with the consequences of the theory of clerical celibacy. These discontents were sometimes linked by the allegations that the confessional was used for the purpose of seduction. Confession also caused financial resentment, because absolution was sometimes expensive. Both had been grounds of discontent for centuries, but there may have been some increase in the complaints during the period shortly before the Reformation: there was certainly a rapid increase in the number of clergy presented for living with women in Lincoln diocese. Whether this represents growing discontent by the parishioners, or increasing clerical disrespect for the ban on marriage, it is hard to tell.

Probably the greatest body of clerical wealth belonged to the monasteries, and many people thought it could be better used. There is no reason to doubt the assertion of Henry VIII's first Act of Dissolution that there were a number of 'great solemn monasteries, where religion is duly observed', but equally it appears probable that there were too many monasteries. There were many with less than twelve monks, and even a man with so little Protestant leaning as Cardinal Wolsey had dissolved a number of what he regarded as superfluous monasteries, though he used the money for other religious purposes. When he fell, dissolution of monasteries appeared in the list of offences of which he was accused.[78] Monastic orders had always tended to expand during their periods of greatest enthusiasm to a larger size than they could easily sustain, and it is interesting that the Carthusians, the order which had most persistently refused to expand, were also the order which was most united in resisting dissolution.[79]

Certainly public enthusiasm for the monasteries would appear to have declined, if the number of benefactions is any guide. Many people left money for education, either in the form of grammar schools, or of university colleges, and a far larger number left money for chantries. The institution of the chantry was an offshoot of the increasing stress on the

---

[78] Coke, Sir Edward, *Fourth Institute* (1679), 91.
[79] I would like to thank Mr. R. I. Moore for this point.

doctrine of Purgatory, and was one of the biggest developments in the later medieval church. It was thought that the offering of Masses for the souls of the dead might help to procure their quicker release from Purgatory, and the result was that large numbers of people left money in their wills to endow the saying of Masses for their souls. These were carried out by a chantry priest, whose sole official duty was often saying in private the requisite number of Masses for his benefactor. Bequests for chantries were perhaps the most individualistic form of religious benefactions possible.

Complaints old and new

Most current complaints against the church were centuries old, and there is no reason to suppose that they were any truer at the beginning of the sixteenth century than at any other time. If the proportion of graduates among the clergy is any guide, which is questionable, its standards may even have been rising. Was there any reason why these long-standing complaints against the church were more powerful or more dangerous than they had been before?

One commonly alleged is growing nationalism. There was certainly intense nationalism in the early sixteenth century, and sometimes, as in the race riots of 1517, it turned into something more serious. But whether there was *growing* nationalism is more doubtful. The Hundred Years' War had produced much nationalism and national propaganda, and in 1363 the Archbishop of York had even proposed that some worship should be in English.[80] It is possible to produce a long list of examples of nationalism from the late fourteenth and early fifteenth centuries, and it is hard to see what type of evidence would prove that nationalism in the early sixteenth century not merely existed, but was growing. If there are more recorded examples of it, this may be only because more documents have survived. Moreover, the only type of discontent with the church which nationalism might explain is anti-papalism, which seems to have been unimportant. It is hard to use nationalism to explain complaints against the archdeacon or the local vicar.

Printing and education

Another possible reason why the discontent may have been more dangerous at the beginning of the sixteenth century is the spread of education and printing. Erasmus, More, and Starkey certainly wanted priests, not merely to go through the patter, but to understand why they did it, and when judged by these higher standards, more priests may have appeared

---

[80] Stubbs, W., *Constitutional History* (1896), ii. 414. See also Galbraith, V. H., 'Nationality and Language in Mediaeval England', *T.R.H.S.* (1941), 113–28.

to fall short.[81] But it is doubtful whether the activities of Erasmus and his friends had as much significance as they have sometimes been credited with. They were a narrow and select intellectual circle, who have attracted attention by their talents rather than by their influence. Some influence they may have had: the Pyms and the Pastons both named a son 'Erasmus' during the 1520s. Nevertheless, these were not the men to head a popular movement, and it is worth remembering that More died for the Church of Rome. The spread of popular education is perhaps more significant: in Lincoln diocese there was certainly an increase in the number of local schools, and some grammar school syllabuses which survive from the 1520s suggest that they used printed textbooks. There certainly seems to have been a rising appetite for knowledge among some of the public. One illiterate picked a book off the village rubbish dump, and hoarded it in the hope that someone would be able to read it to him. When he finally took it to the priest, he discovered that the book was one of Wycliffe's and banned. When Tyndale began to smuggle his translation of the Bible into England in the late 1520s, he found a huge clandestine market, and when, in 1531, he was unofficially approached by Stephen Vaughan with a request to return to England, the sole condition he made was that the king should translate the Bible. He even offered to withdraw his own translation if the king would put out another.[82] Later, in 1546, after Henry had had the Bible translated, and then decided it was only safe reading for gentlemen, one man bought a history book instead, and wrote in the fly-leaf, 'I bout this boke when the Testament was obberagatyd [abrogated] that shepeherdys myght not red hit. I prey God amende that blyndnes. Wryt by Robert Wyllyams keppynge shepe upon Seynbury hill 1546.' A Chelmsford shopkeeper's son described how he and his father's apprentice taught themselves to read and laid the money together to buy the New Testament, how he hid Frith's book on the Sacrament under his bed straw, and how his father threatened to strangle him when he rebuked his mother for worshipping the crucifix.[83] It seems that these people shared the demand of Erasmus and More for a religion which people might not only observe, but understand. This demand for understanding, and for the dispelling of ignorance, which the Reformation never satisfied, and which the Puritans were later to make their own, was probably never a majority demand, and in the early sixteenth century was very rare, but it was enough to cause some alarm.

[81] One vicar was accused by his parishioners simply of not having done any good in the parish. Bowker, 116.
[82] *State Papers* (Henry VIII) vii. 302–3.
[83] Dickens, *Reformation*, 190–1.

Heresy old and new

It was the more significant for the fact that this demand was appearing at a time when the church was threatened by the spread of serious doctrinal heresy, and the heretics were most often ready to satisfy it. There had been a considerable amount of Lollard heresy ever since Wycliffe's time, and there was a steady stream of prosecutions of Lollards. But the Lollards had been an underground movement for over a century, and had received little new intellectual fuel. Many of their doctrines seemed to be subsiding into a general crude irreverence, but this may have done something to prepare the ground for Protestants' increasingly carefully argued objections to much of the formality and ritual of worship. The Lollard objection to the more ritualistic parts of late medieval Catholicism, prayer to saints, fasts, holy water, and pilgrimages, together with the more fundamental objections to Purgatory, transubstantiation, and priestly absolution, were already familiar. The Lollards appear to have sometimes merged with the early Protestants. Some Protestants reprinted Lollard books, leaving them in the original spelling in order to prove their doctrines were respectably old. The Lollard community of Steeple Bumpstead, in Essex, proudly brought their Lollard Bible to show Robert Barnes, the heretic friar. Barnes, to their slight disappointment, replied that he could give them a better Bible, and sent them away with copies of Tyndale's translation.

There was perhaps more alarm about the more polished heresies which were being developed in Cambridge, and, after about 1520, being reinforced by the influence of Luther and other continental reformers. It is hard to measure Luther's influence, but the word 'Lutheran' was occasionally appearing in the accusations of heresy brought in the church courts. Certainly it was Luther who spread the doctrine of justification by faith, which was one of the key points for almost all the early English reformers. The idea that we were justified by our faith and not by our works was commonly attacked by the Roman Catholic church as leading to immorality, but when reformers argue that works do not justify us before God, they do not usually talk of the works that make up a good moral life. They talk of the more complex parts of church ritual, and argue that they contribute nothing to salvation. Tyndale tells the story of a pregnant woman who ate meat on a Friday, 'which thing she durst not confess in the space of seventeen years, and thought all the while she had been damned, and yet sinned she not at all. Is not this a sure burden, that so weigheth down the soul unto the bottom of Hell?' If, he says, 'after thou hast heard so many masses, matins, and evensongs, and after thou hast received holy bread, holy water, and the bishop's blessing, or a cardinal's, or the Pope's, if thou wilt be more kind to thy neighbour, and love him better than before, if thou be more obedient unto thy superiors, more merciful, more ready to forgive wrong done unto thee, more despisest the world, and more thirst after spiritual things, ... then do such things increase grace; if not, it is a lie. Whether it be so or no, I report me to experience.'[84]

The appeal of justification by faith was probably that it made salvation depend much more on a man's belief and understanding, and much less on such mindless works as these. Another appeal was that it made salvation depend less on the goodwill of the priest. A priest could exclude from Mass, or he could say Mass to release a man from Purgatory, but it was harder for him to affect the state of a man's faith. The other constant attack of the reformers, on the doctrine of the Mass, also had the effect of lessening the power of the priest. Many Protestant arguments made the belief of the recipient more important, and priestly consecration less so. A similar attack was made on the other main priestly power, that of absolution. At a time when many of the clergy were unpopular, there was much appeal in a doctrine which made salvation depend much less on their goodwill, or on payments of money to them. Tyndale said that 'the Popes have commanded angels to set divers out of Purgatory. Howbeit, I am not yet certified whether they obeyed or no.'[85]

This doctrinal ferment was not yet widespread or serious, but it could easily become so with a little official encouragement, or even with a slight lifting of the weight of repression. Nor had it yet reached a point where it was impossible for the Roman church to come to terms with it. Justification by faith is a doctrine which has been held by a number of members of the Roman church, and, in a modified form, it once tempted even Cardinal Pole. The denial of the literal doctrine of transubstantiation also had a long history in the Roman church, and many of the reformers' ideas on the Mass could be traced back to Augustine. Indeed, transubstantiation had not been the official Roman doctrine until 1215.[86] Some attempts at doctrinal compromise between Protestants and Catholics were made, and if, as Charles V constantly urged, a Council had been held in the early stages of the dispute, and not postponed till the 1540s, the story might have been very different. Whether the answer to the church's problems was Protestantism or a Council was, and is, a matter of dispute. Whatever

---

[84] Tyndale, W., op. cit., fo. cxxiii.
[85] Tyndale, W., op. cit., fo. cvii.
[86] Dugmore, C. W., *The Mass and the English Reformers* (1958), 152–4.

the answer was, it is hard to argue that it was Henry VIII. Almost every grievance that was being urged against the church in the 1520s was still being urged against it by the Elizabethan Puritans at the end of the century.

Postscript

The question asked on pp. 19–20, why there was so much complaint about enclosure during a period which was not one of exceptionally rapid enclosure, is provisionally answered in Julian Cornwall, *The Revolt of the Peasantry in 1549* (1977). Dr. Cornwall points out that complaints against enclosure are usually accompanied by complaints against engrossing, the combining of several farms or tenements together. Such engrossing, which had been unexceptionable during the period of diminished population after the Black Death, was likely to create protests when population increase led to land hunger. In a period of land hunger, the large enclosed farm is the obvious target for resentment.

2. Henry VIII and the Pope 1509–1536

I THE FRENCH WARS

Would to God you had been at Rome, Master More, when I made you Speaker.

Cardinal Wolsey to Sir Thomas More, 1523[1]

Accession of Henry VIII: instability of the Tudor dynasty

WHEN Henry VII died, in April 1509, his second and only surviving son Henry VIII was proclaimed on the day after his death, and succeeded to the throne without dispute. It should not be supposed that because this event happened, it was necessarily bound to happen. Henry VII was probably one of the ablest kings this country has had, but he left the Tudor dynasty in a much weaker position than is often supposed. His legendary treasure was small, and though he deserves credit for actually leaving a surplus, it is doubtful whether the sum available on his death was more than the cost of one summer's campaigning.[2] Even collecting this small surplus had provoked public indignation. The day after his father's death, Henry VIII arrested Empson and Dudley, the ministers most closely identified with the work of raising revenue. They were subsequently brought to trial for treason, and accused of subverting the laws and impoverishing the king's subjects. In 1503, when Henry VII was ill, the garrison of Calais had discussed possible successors. The claims of Edmund de la Pole and the Duke of Buckingham were canvassed, but no one mentioned the claim of Henry VIII, who was still a minor.

The unpopularity of Henry VII should not be exaggerated, but nor should the stability of his dynasty. He himself had shown that the only indispensable condition for possession of the throne was power, and the

---

[1] J. S. Roskell, *The Commons and their Speakers* (1965), 59.
[2] Wolfe, B. P., 'Henry VII's Land Revenue and Chamber Finance', *E.H.R.* (1964), 251–4.

strong sentiment in favour of the doctrine of hereditary succession which grew during the sixteenth century had only grown far enough to influence the way in which claims to the throne were argued. Perkin Warbeck had been a more real threat than he appears at this distance: Henry VII had taken him seriously enough to cut off the English trade to Antwerp in order to stop the Netherlands supporting him. The intensity of Henry's alarm is shown by his Treasurer of the Chamber's accounts. In these, he recorded his losses at cards, which were usually small. One day the accounts record a loss at cards of £9, with a note: 'this day came Perkin Warbeck.'[3] If Perkin Warbeck could produce such alarm, so could others. The two chief dangers were the de la Poles, a family originally descended from a Hull fish merchant called John Rottenherring, but also descended from Edward IV's sister Elizabeth, and the Duke of Buckingham, probably the most powerful of the descendants of Edward III's numerous younger sons. For most of his reign, Henry VII had been trying to defend his merchants by restricting the trading privileges of the Hanse towns, but in 1504 the Hanse sheltered Edmund de la Pole, and Henry immediately passed an Act of Parliament confirming all their privileges. In Henry VIII's reign, Richard de la Pole, Edmund's younger brother, worried the English by taking service with the French.

The first duty of a king whose title was open to dispute was to prevent the creation of a reversionary interest by marrying and begetting an heir. The first part of this duty Henry VIII discharged speedily, marrying his brother's widow Catherine of Aragon six weeks after his father's death. This marriage involved, at least immediately, alliance with her father Ferdinand of Aragon. Ferdinand, however, was an unstable ally, and much less powerful than he had been before the death of his wife Isabella of Castile. The marriage also involved a papal dispensation to allow Henry to marry his brother's widow.

The other immediate duty of a new king was to get himself crowned. Before discharging this duty, Henry, showing an unusual appetite for paper-work, wrote out a series of amendments to his coronation oath. Instead of swearing to confirm the liberties of holy church, he swore to preserve the liberties *granted to* the holy church by the king, 'not prejudicial to his jurisdiction and dignity royal'. Instead of keeping the peace of the church, he substituted 'to keep unity in his clergy and temporal subjects'. In the promise to keep judgement and justice, he inserted 'according to his conscience'. In the pledge to keep the laws and customs of the realm, he inserted 'approved', and 'not prejudicial to his crown or

[3] Anglo, S., 'The Court Festivals of Henry VII', *Bulletin of the John Rylands Library* (1960–1), 32. I would like to thank my wife for this reference.

imperial sovereignty'.[4] Many of these themes were consistent for the rest of the reign, but they did not, in 1509, appear very important. Henry's conscience, apart from telling him he was the king of France, was otherwise reasonably well behaved. The claim to imperial jurisdiction, though it was to cause trouble later, was not new. It involved the claim, which stretched back to the thirteenth century, that the king had the same legal privileges in his realm as the Holy Roman Emperor had in his. More generally, it meant a freedom to carry on his work without outside interference. How little it might mean is shown by the report sent to Henry before the Reformation by one of his agents that every Irish chieftain had 'imperial jurisdiction' within his own territory.[5] The clauses about the church show that from the beginning of his reign Henry wanted to control his own national church, but this merely shows that he was a sixteenth-century king: it does not show that he was anti-papal. Soon afterwards, he was in close political alliance with the papacy, vehemently denouncing the French because they would 'wantonly destroy the unity of the church',[6] and was awarded the Cap and Sword, a mark of papal favour amounting to choice as Temporal Ruler of the Year. Pope Julius, who was a realist, would probably have been surprised to find any temporal ruler who did not have ambitions to control his own church. The hope that the papacy might allow a ruler to realize some of them was probably one of its chief diplomatic levers.

The Pope and the French war

One of Henry's first diplomatic efforts was designed to win an alliance with the Pope. Bainbridge was sent as resident ambassador to the Court of Rome, and Henry succeeded in obtaining a cardinal's hat for him. In having a permanent resident English cardinal at Rome, Henry VIII had for a few years got a better diplomatic representation at Rome than any king since Edward III. Bainbridge's business was largely foreign policy, and chiefly with English and papal plans against France. Within two months of his accession, Henry was ordering musters, and negotiating with Ferdinand of Aragon and the Pope against France. One of his earliest acts was to commission a translation of a life of Henry V, and he appears to have been ready, both to take his title of king of France seriously, and to appeal to anti-French prejudices in England. On one optimistic occasion, Henry said the king of France would make way for him as King Richard

---

[4] Ellis, H. E., *Original Letters* (1827), i. Frontispiece (my italics). It is possible that these amendments may have been made in the 1530s, and not in 1509.

[5] Quinn, D. B., *The Elizabethans and the Irish*, 34.

[6] Scarisbrick, 29.

did for his father, and the brother of one of his commanders said that if he had a drop of French blood in his body, he would cut himself open to get rid of it.

At the beginning of the reign, Archbishop Warham, Fox, Bishop of Winchester, and Fisher, Bishop of Rochester, were probably the king's most important ministers, and all of them had been trained under Henry VII, who had given the country a rest from French wars. It is unlikely that the decision to start making plans against France was theirs: like most other important decisions of the reign, it was almost certainly Henry's. Henry might have taken warning from the fact that at the same time as he was planning to spend a vast amount of money, the need for popularity was forcing him to abandon some of his methods of taxation, together with Empson and Dudley, who were responsible for them.

In 1511, Henry joined the Holy League, which united the Pope, the Swiss, the Venetians, and Ferdinand of Aragon against France, and in the spring of 1512 he sent the first overseas expedition of his reign to help Ferdinand on the Spanish frontier. The expedition was handicapped by dysentery and mutiny, and even more severely when Ferdinand of Aragon decided to make a separate peace. Nevertheless, Henry was planning an even bigger expedition to France for 1513. The beginning of the war was also, as usual, accompanied by a Parliament. This Parliament obediently voted both a subsidy, a new type of parliamentary tax, and a fifteenth and tenth, the old type. The tax caused some resistance among the poorer taxpayers, and some of it was not collected until 1515. Ultimately, it brought in £62,000, but the campaigns of 1513 have been estimated to have cost £650,000. Since the French, as usual, had made an alliance with Scotland, the English had to fight on two fronts. The Scottish front produced far the bigger success: when the two armies met at Flodden, about 10,000 Scots, including the king, were killed, leaving a new king who was only seventeen months old. Many Scots deduced from Flodden that the Auld Alliance with France was not worth the price, and this fact, together with the regency, gave the English some opportunities to exploit Scottish political divisions. In France, where Henry himself was in command, the results were less dramatic. The king won a skirmish which he dignified with the name of the Battle of the Spurs, and conquered Tournai and Terouanne. In the treaty made the next year, the French also agreed to resume payment of the pension with which they had bought off Edward IV in 1475 and Henry VII in 1492. At the beginning of this war, Pope Julius had prepared a brief transferring the title of king of France, and the French king's title of Most Christian, to Henry, and was even said to have spoken of going to Paris to crown Henry. However, the brief was only to be published if Henry could win France in battle, and the task of persuading the Pope that in 1513 Henry had done so was beyond even the determination of Cardinal Bainbridge. In 1514, Bainbridge suddenly died, and he had no adequate successor as English representative at Rome. Giulio de Medici, later Pope Clement VII, was made English Protector,[7] but there seems to have been little liaison with him. The people who did the day to day work for the English at Rome were either unimportant or unpopular. One of Bainbridge's entourage wrote to Wolsey 'it is necessary for the king's grace to have one, or two if need were, cardinals and residents in the court of Rome both for knowledge of all things that shall succeed here and also for the creation of Popes'.[8] Wolsey appears to have taken no notice of this letter.

Wolsey

It was Wolsey who succeeded to Bainbridge's cardinal's hat, and his rise is probably the most important event in these years. He had been a trusted servant of Henry VII, for whom he had done mainly intelligence work, but it appears to have taken Henry VIII some while to notice his talents. He was willing to pander to Henry's frequent impatience with the details of business, and was prepared to send Henry summaries of treaties 'because it should be painful to your Grace to . . . overread the whole treaty',[9] and yet he always appreciated that the sole source of power was the king's ear. He certainly had a sense of his own importance, and it has been suggested that the reason why there was no adequate English representation at Rome during his rule was that he did not like rivals in ecclesiastical affairs. He was hostile to Parliament, because it tended to interfere in church questions, and only two Parliaments met during his period of power. However, critical verdicts on Wolsey are often based on the assumption that he ought to have behaved in a 'spiritual' way. In fact, he was a politician and administrator of considerable talents who relied on the church as the source of his income. Being of humble birth (a butcher's son), he had no other way to power but through the church, and he took it. As a diplomat, working out the details of a treaty, or as an administrator, helping with the beginnings of the long process by which Tudor governments taught their subjects that it was worth keeping the peace, he was extremely successful, and most hostile verdicts have been based on the assumption that he ought to have behaved in a specially devout way appropriate to a churchman. It was true that he had vanity and ostenta-

---

[7] On the office of Cardinal Protector, see above, p. 56.
[8] Chambers, D. S., *Cardinal Bainbridge and the Court of Rome*, 1.
[9] Scarisbrick, 44.

tion somewhat beyond the ordinary. He liked soft living, and when he was made Bishop of Durham, promptly increased the rent of coal due to the bishop from the Durham mines to a ton per working day.[10] He tried unusually hard to enlarge the jurisdiction of courts over which he presided, and contributed much to the growth of the Court of Chancery. Though he was ambitious, it appears that he had no ambition to be Pope: his aims were for power in England. He made no attempt to build up support, or a body of connections, among the cardinals, and did not even bother to collect his revenue from Rome. He delayed the grant of favours to Campeggio, now English Protector, and so risked the favour of the only cardinal he knew at all well. In 1518, when Campeggio was sent to England as papal legate, Wolsey kept him waiting for several months in the discomfort of Calais, and would not let him into the kingdom until the office of legate was offered to Wolsey as well. At one conclave, his agent thought he did not want to be elected, and at the next, doubt was expressed whether Wolsey would come to Rome if elected. Wolsey said he would come in three months, and that he would bring Henry too![11] Henry's ear was the basis of Wolsey's power, and he meant to stick to it.

Anti-clericalism: the cases of Hunne and Standish

His period of power began with two vigorous anti-clerical agitations. The first was over the case of Hunne, a London tailor, who quarrelled with his vicar over the mortuary fee for a baby of his who had died. The case gave rise to a succession of lawsuits, in which Hunne claimed that excommunication injured his business credit, and finally Hunne brought an action against the vicar for *Praemunire*. The statute of *Praemunire*, of 1393, had originally been designed to stop the Pope translating English bishops to foreign sees, but it also contained some rhetorical passages against diminishing the rights of the Crown, claiming that 'the crown of England had been so free from all time that it has had no earthly sovereign, but is immediately subject to God in all things touching the regality of the said crown'. By Tudor times, the statute had become an anti-clerical jack-of-all-trades, and the common construction of it was to make it illegal to take any case which ought to go to the king's courts to any other courts. Hunne was, then, alleging that the vicar had taken an issue to a church court which ought to have gone to a secular court. The penalty for *Praemunire* was forfeiture of all goods and chattels, and im-

---

[10] Nef, J. U., *The Rise of the British Coal Industry* (1932), i. 138. It is interesting to contrast the criticism of Wolsey with the lack of any similar verdict on Cardinal Beaufort in the previous century, who had been quite as wealthy, and quite as secular in his concerns, as Wolsey ever was.

[11] Chambers, D. S., 'Cardinal Wolsey and the Papal Tiara', *B.I.H.R.* (1965), 20–31.

prisonment during the king's pleasure. When Hunne brought his *Praemunire*, the Bishop of London searched his house and found a Lollard Bible and other heretical books. Hunne was arrested for heresy, and later found dead in prison, and a Coroner's jury returned a verdict of murder against the bishop's Chancellor and the gaoler. The church retaliated by having Hunne posthumously declared a heretic, with the result that all his property was forefeit and his family was left penniless. The common verdict was that Hunne was 'made a heretic for suing a *Praemunire*',[12] and though the case had no practical consequence, it left a large amount of ill-will.

The next case, that of Standish, in 1515, involved more important people, and took place during a meeting of Parliament. It began with Parliament renewing a temporary Act of 1512, which prevented people in minor orders, like sub-deacons, doorkeepers, and acolytes from escaping from the jurisdiction of the secular courts by pleading benefit of clergy. This bill had already been vigorously condemned by the Pope, and the Abbot of Winchcombe preached a sermon at Paul's Cross, which was the easiest place to reach a large popular audience, saying the measure was against the law of God and the liberty of the church. There were then a series of disputations, in which Dr. Standish argued against the official church view. When these had died down, Standish was summoned, as a delinquent, to appear before Convocation. Standish appealed to the king, and there was a further series of disputes, in which the judges accused the whole clergy of *Praemunire*. Henry finally took the case over, said he had no superior on earth, and subsequently made Standish a bishop. But though this case also shows a serious political situation, it would be a mistake to see Standish as a sort of proto-Protestant.

These cases were not followed by any similar explosions. The most important event in the next few years was the birth of Princess Mary, in 1516. She was the first of Catherine's children who lived, and her birth encouraged the hope that there might be a son. Henry was becoming anxious, and in 1519 he called doctors from Spain to examine Catherine, and vowed to go on Crusade if Heaven would send him a son. The situation was not yet hopeless. Nevertheless, anxiety about an heir may have had much to do with the decision in 1521 to execute the Duke of Buckingham, whose father had nearly won the throne in 1483. In 1521, Buckingham was discussing prophecies that he would gain the throne because Henry would have no heir, speaking of killing him, and saying the death of an infant son of Henry's was divine vengeance. Moreover, he could back up these words with twelve castles and an arsenal.

[12] Dickens, *Reformation*, 92.

Some of Wolsey's worst worries during these years were economic. In 1517, major riots against aliens broke out in London and Southampton. The background to the crisis appears to have consisted of poverty and unemployment in London, which one John Lincoln chose to blame largely on the presence of French and Genoese merchants. Having unsuccessfully approached Standish, he succeeded in persuading one Dr. Beale to take the matter up in a sermon. Beale, having spoken at length on poverty, argued 'that this land was given to Englishmen, and as birds would defend their nest, so ought Englishmen to cherish and defend themselves, and to hurt and grieve aliens for the common weal'. Of this sermon, says the chronicler, 'many a light person took courage, and openly spake against strangers'. Then, 'as the devil would have it', a quarrel broke out between a group of merchants and a Frenchman who had seduced an Englishman's wife, and then another with a Frenchman whom the mob supposed to run a gang of criminals. Soon there were mobs of several hundred in the streets, attacking any aliens they could find, and the Lieutenant of the Tower was vainly trying to still the disturbances by bombarding the city with artillery. Wolsey appears to have reacted with great promptitude: he had the streets of the City filled with armed guards, and a Proclamation issued that 'no women should come together to babble and talk, but all men should keep their wives in their houses'. Lincoln and Beale were condemned for high treason, for threatening the king's alliances with foreign princes, Lincoln saying to the last that he had warned people of the mischief caused by strangers, only to be dismissed as a 'busy fellow'.[13] These measures appear to have put a stop to race riots in the City for some time afterwards, and although it has been estimated that the proportion of alien immigrants in London was often up to a sixth, for at least part of the time race relations were peaceful, and there was even a certain amount of intermarriage.

The Imperial election and the second French war

In 1519 international politics were disturbed by the death of the Holy Roman Emperor, and, the title being elective, the major powers investigated the chance of increasing their strength by obtaining it. Charles V, grandson of the previous Emperor, was already ruler of Spain, Naples, and the Netherlands, and the addition of the Empire would make his power the biggest in Europe since Charlemagne. Francis I, king of France, thought that it would be preferable to get himself elected Emperor, and both of them sent in agents, equipped with large sums of cash, to canvass their candidatures. Henry, and possibly the Pope as well, felt that the elec-

[13] Tawney and Power, iii. 82–90.

tion of either of these candidates would upset the European balance of power, and that if they fought each other to a standstill, Henry might have a chance himself. It is hard to say how seriously Henry took this prospect, but he certainly spent money on it.

When Charles V was ultimately elected, Henry's failure seems to have left him at a loose end. A week later he sent off a long letter to the Pope expressing his 'burning zeal' to go on Crusade. However, he soon lost interest in this project, and turned to authorship instead. He had already once written a few pages against Luther, but had not had the persistence to develop them. After the failure of his bid for the Empire, he took them up again, and expanded them into the *Assertio Septem Sacramentorum*, a vehement denunciation of Luther and his theology, and a defence of the papal primacy and the traditional structure of the Catholic church. Whether the book was all Henry's work or not, it served at least one useful purpose: it induced the Pope to give in to Henry's long-standing request for a special title, because the kings of France and Spain had one, and he was made Defender of the Faith. Luther considered the book worth a lengthy reply.

During 1520, attempts to preserve the peace, probably supported by Wolsey, resulted in the organization of a series of summit meetings. Henry met Francis at the Field of the Cloth of Gold, in northern France, an elaborate display of festivity and friendship marred only by the fact that when Henry wrestled against Francis, he made a very bad loser. Charles V was received in great state in England, and met his aunt Catherine of Aragon for the first time. The most obvious result of these meetings was expense, and by 1521, a conference at Calais was negotiating instead the terms of a new Anglo-Imperial alliance. Wolsey, having brought English government to a standstill by taking the Great Seal out of the kingdom, managed the English side of the conference, and spent so much of his own money that the king granted him the abbey of St. Alban's in recompense. The conference produced an agreement to send an English force to invade France, but not until 1523.

When the campaign was about to start, diplomatic attention was diverted to the death of the Pope, and the task of electing his successor. The choice ultimately fell on Cardinal de Medici, who took the title of Clement VII, and on whom the weight of Henry's divorce negotiations fell. He was primarily the Emperor's candidate, but he was a former English Protector, and the English showed every sign of satisfaction with his election. The English forces ultimately landed in France in September, almost at the end of the campaigning season, and achieved a rapid advance which created excited talk in England about the possibility of a

Paris coronation. When they were fifty miles from Paris, the troops got bogged down, came to the end of their supply lines, and had to withdraw with no achievement except the usual expense.

In 1522, the king had raised a forced loan, but he still found it necessary to call a Parliament in 1523 for the beginning of the war. Sir Thomas More, the government choice, was made Speaker (and was the second university man to be Speaker of the Commons), but the Parliament was one of the most awkward Henry had to face. Thomas Cromwell, among many others, drafted a speech to argue that Scotland, rather than France, was the appropriate place to attack, and the Commons showed little eagerness to vote the sums of money needed. Wolsey finally decided to visit the Commons and repeat the request for supply in person. He demanded that the Commons answer in his presence, but More told him that this was contrary to the Commons' liberty of debating in private, and that he could not answer Wolsey's request because of lack of instruction. It was in this Parliament that the Speaker first claimed a formal right of free speech 'in everything incident among us'. The atmosphere of the Parliament is such as to support Professor Roskell's argument that the claim for freedom of speech was not the expression of a growing power in the Commons, but of fear that government pressure might deprive them of rights which they already had.[14] The Commons were finally induced to vote money, though they did so by a vote of only ten or twelve, with all the rest of the House abstaining. The grant was much less than the government wanted, producing £151,000 over four years.

The war made little progress in 1524, and by 1525 the English were thinking of a separate peace. It was at this moment, when the English could not take advantage of an opportunity, that Charles's forces in Italy routed the French at Pavia, and captured Francis himself. Immediately, Henry was filled with eagerness for the French throne, and zealous ambassadors were sent off to persuade the victorious Charles that England was a faithful ally. But if England were to continue the war, money would be needed. Another Parliament was not an inviting prospect, so the government decided to attempt an unparliamentary tax, and settled on one euphemistically called the Amicable Grant, a levy of one sixth on the goods of the laity, and one third on the goods of the clergy. The 1523 subsidy was still being collected, falling, as always, most heavily on the poor. Before the Amicable Grant, taxation was already at a higher level than it had ever been before, and the public, as well as the king, were beginning to feel the weight of the price rise. There was an immediate rising in Kent, opposing the Grant, and saying that the king 'hath not one foot

[14] Roskell, *The Commons and their Speakers* (1965), 51.

of land more in France than his most noble father had, which lacked no wisdom or riches to win the said kingdom of France if he had thought it expedient'. Resistance was widespread, but worst in East Anglia, where there appears to have been widespread unemployment in the clothing industry. The Earl of Essex reported determined resistance from Stanstead, and in Norfolk and Suffolk 20,000 men were in arms against the Grant, and it was doubtful whether the Justices of the Peace would oppose them or join them. Henry sent the Dukes of Norfolk and Suffolk at the head of an army to suppress the rising, but the opposition was stronger than both the Dukes in England could suppress. They advised Henry to watch Buckingham's son, because of his royal blood, and Norfolk explained the difficulty of collecting taxes from the unemployed. Henry, who had initiated the policy for which the money was needed, then withdrew the Grant, pardoned all its opponents, and asked how his commissioners' demands came to be so strict, whereat 'the Cardinal excused himself'.[15] The failure to collect the Amicable Grant should disprove the idea that there was such a thing as 'Tudor Despotism'. Government was a partnership between the king and propertied classes, and if, as in this case, the gentry did not support him, the king had no sufficient force to repress resistance. The poor could always be coerced with co-operation of the gentry, but if the king were to choose to exercise his power in a cause Privy Councillors and Justices of the Peace found offensive, he would be unlikely to succeed.

The breach with Charles V and the succession problem

Having been forced to abandon the Amicable Grant, Henry had no money left to finance any further wars against France, and had to make peace. This enforced peace offended Charles V by depriving him of the English alliance at the moment when it might have been most useful to him. This unwanted breach with Charles confused Henry's foreign policy, and by confusing his foreign policy, also impeded his plans for the succession. Since Catherine was now past childbearing, it seemed clear that Henry's heir would be his daughter Mary. Since she was a woman, it was widely assumed that if she inherited the throne, effective power would pass to her husband. Both prejudice and the Great Chain of Being[16] encouraged strong feelings in favour of male supremacy. Women could hold no other offices, and it was hard to see why the most important office of all should be the only exception. It is doubtful, moreover, whether many of Henry's subjects believed that such a thing as 'Matilda's reign' had ever

[15] Fletcher, A., *Tudor Rebellions* (1968), 17–20, 117.
[16] On the Great Chain of Being, see above, pp. 41–44.

existed.[17] Any rival to Mary's succession could then argue that rule by a woman was unprecedented and intolerable, and might expect a number of people to support him in his objections. If Mary were to succeed without civil war, it would be desirable to find her a husband powerful enough to secure her in possession of the throne.

Henry had been considering this question before 1525, and had selected the most powerful man in Europe—Charles V, father of Mary's future husband. Even if this marriage did not enable Charles and Mary to conquer France and win 'the whole monarchy of Christendom', it would at least unite England and the Netherlands, and secure a powerful occupant for the English throne. It was this plan to marry Mary and Charles V which was ended by England's enforced withdrawal from the war in 1525, since Charles, being deprived of the English alliance, chose to marry Isabella of Portugal instead. Henry was then left to consider alternative plans for Mary's marriage or for the succession. Anyone who quarrelled with Charles was likely to find Francis a good friend, and from 1525, English relations with France began to grow more friendly. By the end of 1526, Henry was discussing plans to marry Mary to Francis. If the most powerful man in Europe was not available, the second most powerful might do instead. At the same time, he appears to have been considering an alternative successor. He had no legitimate sons, but he had one bastard son who had hitherto been kept in obscurity. In 1525, he was created Duke of Richmond and Lord Lieutenant of Ireland and the North, and, which was perhaps more important, he was given official precedence over Mary.

II   THE DIVORCE

As fast as I study to win the Pope, ye study to lose him. Ye, ye have clearly marred all.
Francis I to Bishop Gardiner, 1533[18]

I understand that there is a reformation in religion intended by the parliament; and I wish that several things were reformed; but let me tell you that when you have reformed, that others will come, and refine upon you, and others again upon them; and so proceeding, that at last there will be no religion left, but atheism will spring up. The mysteries of religion are to be let alone; they will not bear an examination.
Ascribed, apocryphally, to Cardinal Wolsey[19]

Neither of these plans for the succession was very convincing, and sometime during this period, perhaps in 1526, Henry began to consider a much

---

[17] Apart from a few months in 1141, 'Matilda's reign' is something of a fiction, and it is arguable that it was contributed to English historiography by nineteenth-century historians.   [18] Scarisbrick, 320.

[19] Aubrey, J., *Brief Lives*, ed. Oliver Lawson Dick (1949), 372. Unfortunately the story is probably false.

more radical solution: the possibility that he might be able to prove that his marriage to Catherine was unlawful, and therefore free himself to beget a son by another wife. Henry later said that his doubts about his marriage to Catherine were suggested to him by the French. This story cannot be proved, but at least a proposal to divorce Charles V's aunt was likely to make Henry quarrel further with Charles, and therefore would be likely to receive French support.

Since divorce, in the modern sense, was not recognized, Henry could only escape from his marriage by proving that it had been null and void from the start. When he had married Catherine, he had been given a papal dispensation permitting the marriage, so if he wanted to prove that the marriage was unlawful, he had to convince the Pope that, for whatever reason, his predecessor's dispensation had been invalid. This task was difficult, but it was by no means impossible. Popes had granted other improbable divorces in recent times. These examples showed the extent of papal power, but, unfortunately for Henry, they tended to show that the Pope had been within his rights in permitting him to marry his brother's widow. In trying to persuade the Pope otherwise, Henry was trying to obtain something which the Pope might have granted, but which he also had every right to refuse.

Persuading him not to refuse was a task which involved foreign policy, negotiation, and canon law. Ideally, strength in all three respects was desirable, but strength in one might to some extent have outweighed weakness in the others. A clear case in canon law might have been accepted by the Pope in any situation. For example, if Henry had been able to show that Catherine was a proven bigamist, no amount of incompetent negotiation or weakness in foreign policy could have stopped him getting his divorce. If, on the other hand, Henry had had the political strength of Charles V, the Pope would have been likely to accept even a weak case in canon law. In a situation where success was in the balance, skilful negotiation and widespread support among the College of Cardinals might have turned the scales in Henry's favour. In fact, Henry's case was weak in all three respects. It was presented when the foreign policy situation was more unfavourable than at any other time in his reign, it was supported by incompetent negotiation, and it was dubious in canon law. For his unfortunate situation in foreign policy, Henry could complain of bad luck, but for his failure in diplomacy and canon law, he had only himself to blame.

Papal foreign policy was dominated by the desire to protect the papal states. This concern was by no means indefensible on spiritual grounds. Temporal rulers were quite capable of attacking the Pope when displeased with him, and, as the story of the divorce showed, Popes could not carry out their spiritual duties in freedom unless they were sure of some temporal protection. When Henry began to negotiate for the divorce, most of the papal states were occupied by the troops of Charles V, who was infuriated with the Pope for making an alliance with Francis. Charles's displeasure was the more alarming since it was backed by power. His troops were steadily gaining ground in Italy, and in May 1527, at the moment when Henry was about to open his negotiations, Charles's troops, without orders, sacked Rome and captured the Pope. He was released in December, and was physically at liberty during most of the divorce negotiations, but he had been badly frightened, and a year later he was telling the English ambassadors that he would be in fear of death if he granted their request.[20] He also had a more realistic fear that Charles might refuse to give back the papal states or might give support to the Protestants in his dominions. Charles was threatening to occupy papal fortresses until the Pope 'carried out his duties' towards Christendom, and he had the power to make his threat effective.[21] Other parts of the papal states were occupied by Venice, and in February 1528, Henry wrote to the Venetians to beseech them to give Ravenna back to the Pope. Henry had no threats or inducements with which to support this request, and it was ineffective. The alliance with Francis was Henry's only asset in the foreign policy of the divorce, but though Francis wrote a personal letter to the Pope asking him to grant the divorce, letters were ineffective unless supported by troops. Casale, one of Henry's representatives at Rome, reported that if the French troops advanced, the Pope would grant his requests, but if not, he would do nothing. The failure of French troops in Italy in 1528–9 was one of Henry's most important reverses, and the only one for which he cannot be blamed.

For the weakness of English diplomatic representation at the Vatican, both Henry and Wolsey could be blamed. Cardinal Campeggio, the English Protector, was the man on whose efforts they had to depend, and Wolsey had persistently offended him. Moreover, Campeggio had always worked in the Curia, not only for Henry, but for Charles V, and while this might have been convenient enough in 1523, in 1527 it was a disaster. Most powers could count on the support of several friendly cardinals in addition to their Protector, but England had for many years not bothered to make friends among the cardinals. There were no English cardinals at Rome, nor even any created in the English interest, and it was not until 1528, when Wolsey's fall was already imminent, that serious attempts were made to get cardinals' hats for sympathetic Italians. Negotiations at

[20] *L. & P.*, iv. 2, 3715.   [21] Brandi, K., *The Emperor Charles V* (1939), 260.

the Vatican depended on knowledge of the complex state of Roman politics, and for many years Wolsey had not bothered to collect this knowledge. In 1527 England had not even any proctors to act as representatives. The sole English ambassador in 1527 was only temporarily in Rome. Even when Henry at last appointed permanent representatives at the Vatican, after the divorce negotiations had been going for some years, he chose no one more influential than the Archdeacon of Dorset and a lay Doctor of Civil Law. He was once sufficiently tactless to send Anne Boleyn's brother on an embassy to the Pope.

Anne Boleyn

Henry's diplomatic position was not strengthened by the fact that, by 1527, he had selected Anne Boleyn as Catherine's successor. Wolsey had hoped that he might marry a French princess, which, as well as ensuring firm French support, would have kept the whole business safely on the unemotional level of matters of state. Henry's obtrusive love for Anne made him look like a middle-aged man asking the Pope to sanction his fling, and may have contributed to the hostility of such influential people as Fisher, Bishop of Rochester, who produced frequent books and sermons against Henry's case. Moreover, Anne's household was a centre of Protestant influence. It is hard to say more about Anne's own religious opinions than that she disliked Wolsey and the Pope, but the religious opinions of the Boleyn chaplains are much clearer. Anne's chaplains included two future Protestant Archbishops, Cranmer and Parker, and her father's chaplain was Thomas Barlow, brother of an Edwardian bishop, and already a known reformer. It was Anne whose patronage brought Shaxton, one of the few known Protestants to be made bishops during the 1530s, to the see of Salisbury.[22] At the least, Anne's elevation would bring Protestants within the patronage structure, though it is typical of the way patronage cut across ideological divisions that Norfolk, who was certainly no Protestant, supported Anne because she was his niece. She had many enemies in England, and though Henry persistently instructed his ambassadors to sing her praises to the Pope, it is unlikely that the Pope regarded her personal qualities as an incentive to grant the divorce.

Anne had the further disadvantage that there was an impediment in canon law to her marriage to Henry, which was uncomfortably similar to the impediment which, so Henry claimed, was so insuperable an obstacle to his marriage with Catherine that no Pope could dispense with it. The alleged impediment to Henry's marriage with Catherine was an impedi-

[22] Dickens, *Reformation*, 169. Brook, V. J. K., *Archbishop Parker* (1962), 15–16. Hembry, P., *The Bishopric of Bath and Wells* (1967), 81.

ment of the first degree of affinity, resulting from the fact that Catherine had been married to Henry's brother Arthur. The impediment of affinity, the obstacle to marrying one's in-laws, resulted from a consummated marriage, but unfortunately for Henry, it also resulted from consummation without marriage. Affinity impeded a man, not only from marrying his wife's relations, but from marrying the relations of any woman with whom he had had an affair, and Henry was known to have had an affair with Anne's sister. Anne underlined the point by banishing her sister from court. All the time he was asking the Pope to say that no Pope could dispense him from an impediment of the first degree of affinity to marry Catherine, he was also asking him for a dispensation from an impediment of the first degree of affinity in order to marry Anne.[23]

Errors in diplomacy and canon law

Henry had to show that the cases were different. There were two ways in which he could have done so. The first way was to find a technical flaw in the original dispensation to marry Catherine. There were several grounds on which Popes might declare their predecessors' bulls of dispensation technically invalid. If Henry proved that the facts alleged in the original dispensation were false, he would have had a good case, as he would have done if he had shown that the Pope had given him a dispensation from the wrong impediment. An argument of this type would have made a tidy diplomatic case without any very far-reaching implications.

Henry, however, conducted his own case, and in so doing illustrated the saying that 'a barrister who conducts his own case has a fool for his client'. Henry's argument was that the obstacle to marriage with a brother's wife was very much stronger than the impediment to marrying any other relations by marriage. He claimed that the Pope, in sanctioning marriage to a dead brother's wife, was acting beyond his powers. He based his case on a text from the Book of Leviticus, that 'if a man shall take his brother's wife, it is an impurity: he hath uncovered his brother's nakedness; they shall be childless'. Henry thought that this curse rested on his marriage, because it was contrary, not merely to the law of the church, but to an explicit command of God, which no Pope could permit him to disobey. It followed that his marriage was, as he wrote to one of his representatives at Rome, 'null, invalid, nefarious, disgraceful, abominable, incestuous, detestable to God and odious to men'.[24] A papal dispensation to marry Catherine, then, had been no more valid than a papal dispensation to commit murder.

[23] For this and what follows, see Scarisbrick, 163–97.
[24] *State Papers*, Henry VIII, vii. 308.

This case had a number of disadvantages. It asked Pope Clement to admit that his predecessor had acted *ultra vires*, and though Popes might be willing to do many things, if suitably persuaded, they were less willing to admit that there were certain things they could never do. If Clement admitted that his predecessor had acted unlawfully, he raised awkward questions about papal authority. Moreover, Henry's text from Leviticus was directly contradicted by another from Deuteronomy. There was a considerable literature on this contradiction, and since Catherine vowed that she 'would live and die in her vocation of matrimony', and employed such able people as Fisher to fight the case for her, it was thoroughly searched, and appeared to tell against Henry's case. It was perhaps more serious that the whole of Henry's case depended on his assertion that Catherine's marriage to Arthur had been consummated, and Catherine, who was in a better position to know, insisted that it had not.

Cardinal Wolsey, considering Catherine's claim that her marriage to Arthur had not been consummated, saw the possibility of constructing a better case. The impediment of affinity, from which Henry had been dispensed, only arose in the case of a consummated marriage. An unconsummated marriage gave rise to a different impediment, from which Henry had received no dispensation. This impediment, the impediment of public honesty, was unimportant. It arose from a marriage ceremony or an engagement, and Popes could easily dispense from it. Nevertheless, it was an impediment, and if Henry had received no dispensation from it, his marriage to Catherine might be invalid, because he had been given the wrong dispensation. Moreover, if Catherine's marriage to Arthur had not been consummated, the Pope's dispensation permitting Henry to marry her had been based on false information, and was void on that ground. This argument would be the more welcome at Rome because it did not blame the papacy, but only Henry VII, who was dead. It was even easy to show that Henry VII had had a motive for misinforming Pope Julius, since at the time when he had been negotiating for the dispensation, the Spaniards had been attempting to make him return the dowry for Catherine's marriage to Arthur, and if the marriage had been consummated, the English had a much better claim to keep the dowry.

This case might not have been strong enough to overcome Henry's disadvantages in diplomacy and foreign policy, but it could only have been an advantage to him to have a strong case in canon law instead of a weak one. Whether it would have been sufficient, we cannot know, since Henry refused to listen to this case. We only know that it was ever put from an abject letter in which Wolsey implored his master to believe that he had not suggested a different case out of deliberate disloyalty. For whatever reason, Henry rejected the strongest argument he could have put to Rome, and, in Professor Scarisbrick's words, 'rarely has pig-headedness, or suspicion, been more harshly rewarded'.[25]

The English began with a bad case, and conducted it clumsily. Henry sent ambassadors to Rome to make friends with the Pope, but at the same time a plan was being considered to gather a body of friendly cardinals at Avignon, declare that the Pope was under duress, and make Wolsey a papal regent. This second plan failed because the Pope was released from captivity in December 1527. The Pope was induced to issue a commission to Wolsey to hear the case in England, but it omitted to authorize Wolsey to give sentence, allowing him only to report to Rome, and was therefore practically useless.

At the beginning of 1528 a more carefully planned campaign was started. In January 1528 Henry, in support of Francis, declared war on Charles without telling the Council or summoning Parliament, hoping that an alliance with France might loosen Charles's hold on the Pope. The Merchant Adventurers were ordered to stop trading to Antwerp and go to Calais instead. The result was widespread unemployment and riots, and in Kent people suggested that Wolsey, who as usual discharged the duty of a good minister to carry the blame, should be put to sea in a leaky boat. Meanwhile, Francis's forces were invading Italy. In February 1528 Henry sent off an elaborate embassy to the papal court at Orvieto. It was headed by Stephen Gardiner, who was an able man, and later to be Bishop of Winchester, and by Edward Fox, the king's almoner. Henry's attempts to have Gardiner made a cardinal were premature. Fox, whatever he may have been in 1528, was certainly a Protestant a few years later. Their instructions included the threat that if their requests were not granted, divine and natural law might compel Henry to cast off his allegiance to the Holy See. They found the Pope friendly, and inclined to be helpful, but extremely indecisive. After they had been ten days with the Pope, Gardiner was threatening that 'if the king could get no more favour at their hands than a common person', he would use domestic remedies. Clement's difficulties were great enough already, before this hectoring and importunate embassy had begun its business. By April, Gardiner was saying 'when we should report what sort of men be here, the favour of that prince who is their only friend should be taken away, and that the Apostolic See should fall to pieces with the consent and applause of everybody'.[26] The difficulty of taking this line with the Pope was that the English could never succeed in frightening him more than Charles could, so all

[25] *State Papers*, i. 195. Scarisbrick, 195.
[26] *L. & P.*, iv. 2. 4120, 4167.

their chances of success depended on favour rather than fear.

The French troops in Italy were doing well, and at last Gardiner got a full decretal commission, authorizing Wolsey and Campeggio to hear the case as papal legates in England. Before starting the case, Campeggio investigated the possibility of persuading Catherine to enter a nunnery, but failed to persuade her. Unfortunately, by the autumn of 1528, plague had broken out in the French army, and when the document finally arrived in England it did not give sufficient authority. A long series of embassies investigated the technical questions involved, and desultorily considered the 'right rare, new and strange' proposal that Henry, like some Old Testament patriarchs whom he cited, should be allowed to commit bigamy. In the middle of these confusions, reports reached England, first that Clement was dead, and then that he was dying. This time, Wolsey, under severe pressure from Henry, did want to be elected Pope: as he wrote to Gardiner, at Rome, it was the last chance of preserving papal authority in England. Meanwhile, Clement's illness was not to be allowed to be an excuse for delay. Wolsey wrote to Gardiner that in 'the king's great and weighty cause of matrimony', Gardiner was 'for no earthly cause to suffer or tolerate delay, in what case soever the Pope's holiness be of amendment or danger of life'.[27] At last, in June 1529, Wolsey and Campeggio began to hear the case at Blackfriars, though Catherine had already petitioned the Pope to revoke the case to Rome. The Blackfriars legatine court produced some high drama, including an implicit comparison by Fisher, who was Catherine's counsel, between Henry and Herod, but it was never likely that it would be able to give sentence before the Pope revoked the case to Rome. Finally, the Pope closed the Blackfriars hearing and revoked the case to Rome. Suffolk exclaimed that 'by the Mass, now I see that the old said saw is true, that there was never legate or cardinal that did good in England',[28] and Henry, angry and impatient after two years' negotiation, was left facing a summons to present his case at Rome.

Reactions to failure

In the summer of 1529, the closing of the Blackfriars legatine court marked the failure of Henry's negotiations with Rome. At the same time, the French troops in Italy were defeated, Francis and Charles made peace, and the foreign policy moves designed to create a more favourable diplomatic situation at Rome had also failed. Henry was defeated, and it was hard to know what to do next. His first step was to sack Wolsey, a move

[27] Muller, J. A., *Stephen Gardiner and the Tudor Reaction* (1926), 29.
[28] Scarisbrick, 227.

which is likely to have pleased Anne. On the last occasion on which Wolsey might have obtained a reconciliation, she prevented the necessary audience by removing the king for a picnic. Sir Thomas More, who succeeded Wolsey as Lord Chancellor, was not a supporter of the divorce, and may have taken office in order to ensure the more effective persecution of heretics.

Henry's next step was to call Parliament for the autumn of 1529. It is hard to know why Henry summoned Parliament. He did not ask it for a subsidy, and did not ask it to consider the divorce until the issue was already settled, four years later. It is doubtful whether Parliament would have supported him: he had already had to forbid crowds to gather outside Catherine's house to demonstrate their support. Instead, Parliament started passing legislation against the English church, dealing with grievances in their own parishes, like probate and mortuary fees, and plurality and non-residence. Henry sympathized with these measures, and, unlike his daughter Elizabeth, refused to accept the argument of Fisher and the bishops that ecclesiastical legislation was no concern of the Commons. These pinpricks against the English clergy are unlikely to have interested the Pope, and, apart from relieving Henry's feelings, it is hard to see that they contributed anything to the issue of the divorce, unless to terrorize the bishops into accepting an eventual English divorce.

Perhaps the best explanation of the purpose for which Henry called Parliament is from a letter Norfolk sent to Rome in 1531 or 1532. He said he wrote as a 'true Catholic man', and warned the Pope of the hostility to the laity, adding that 'notwithstanding the infinite clamours of the temporality here in Parliament against the misusing of the spiritual jurisdiction, yet in his Highness doth remain to stop all such effects, and will do, unless ill and unkind handling enforce him to consent to the same'.[29] In other words, Henry was extending the strategy of blackmail he had used at Orvieto in 1528, and was now threatening to attack the liberties of the English church if the Pope did not give way.

Years of hesitation, 1530–1532

There is no one moment at which Henry VIII 'broke with Rome'. Relations with Rome were growing more strained, and more distant, throughout a long and confused story which lasts from the instructions to the ambassadors to Rome in February 1528 to the Act Against Papal Authority, of 1536. Whether there is any one moment in this story at which either Henry or the Pope realized that they had crossed the Rubi-

[29] Cooper, J. P., 'The Supplication against the Ordinaries Reconsidered', *E.H.R.* (1957), 618.

con, or intended to cross it, is doubtful. Perhaps the most difficult years to interpret are the years 1530 to 1532, when Henry's negotiations with Rome were chiefly aimed at securing the maximum delay, and Parliament was given little more to do than passing laws about vagabonds and malicious prosecutions against alien surgeons. Professor Elton saw these as years of 'bluster and bombast, bankrupt in ideas, without a policy'. Professor Scarisbrick believes that 'beneath the bluster and bluff there was already a hard kernel of conviction',[30] and that Henry was already set on the course leading to the Act of Supremacy, delayed only by the need to secure public support.

Henry's immediate object is clear: it was to prevent the papal lawcourt of the Rota from giving a judgement in favour of Catherine. Henry never seems to have considered the possibility of obtaining a favourable verdict from the Rota, and made no attempt to get one. The Pope's relations with Charles were growing more friendly, and the antics of Henry's ambassadors had not improved his standing in the Curia. Attempts to get cardinals created in the English interest were continuing, but produced persistent failure.

Did Henry have any deeper purpose, beyond preventing a decision at Rome? Professor Scarisbrick has proved that he was already considering rejecting papal jurisdiction, or at least papal jurisdiction over the divorce. Whether Henry ever separated these two ideas in his mind is doubtful. In September 1530 his agents in Rome were instructed to search the Vatican archives to discover whether Henry 'having authority imperial, be under the Pope *in any other matter than heresy*' (my italics). At the same time, Suffolk and Anne's brother were saying the king cared nothing if St. Peter himself should come to life in his realm, 'for the king is absolute emperor and pope in his kingdom'. When a clergyman was accused of heresy for denying the papal primacy, in 1531, Henry had him released on the ground that it was no heresy. He was telling the papal nuncio that 'even if his holiness should do his worst by excommunicating me and so forth, I shall not mind it, for I care not a fig for all his excommunications'.[31] Whether such protestations appear convincing is a matter of opinion, but at least they prove that the idea of rejecting Rome was not a new one suddenly put to Henry in 1532. The idea of rejecting Rome was in Henry's mind before Cromwell could have put it there. It was the king, not his minister, who first thought of rejecting papal authority.

[30] Elton, G. R., 'King or Minister: The man Behind the Henrician Reformation', *History* (1954), 228. Scarisbrick, 289.
[31] Scarisbrick, 290. 'And so forth' presumably refers to the risk that the Pope might depose him.

It is also true that Henry was worried by lack of support for his moves against Catherine and the Pope, and therefore may have been waiting for more support before breaking with Rome. Twice in 1530 he summoned assemblies of notables, which, although hand-picked, failed to declare that Henry was entitled to settle the case in England on his own authority. On this point, Professor Scarisbrick's view has subsequently been supported by Professor Elton's work on the treason laws. All through the period of the Reformation, the government was worried by the threat to its authority carried by seditious speeches. In 1531, a man practising archery said he wished he had the king's body in front of him instead of the butts. A Welsh priest 'wished to have the king upon a mountain in North Wales called the Withvay [*sc.* Y Wyddfa] otherwise called Snowdon hill . . . He would souse the king about the ears till he had his head soft enough.' There were numerous denunciations of Anne as a harlot, and even occasional arguments that 'King Henry VIII is no king of right'.

It was already possible, with luck, to convict people of treason for mere words, usually under the clause of the 1352 Act of compassing the king's death. This clause demanded that the offence be expressed by an overt act, but there were precedents for the judges ruling that speaking words was an overt act. The reasoning behind such decisions was on the lines of the common law doctrine that reasonable men are deemed to intend the natural consequences of their acts. If men say things which they can reasonably foresee are likely to provoke people to kill the king, they are compassing his death.[32] However, prosecutions for words under the 1352 statute were always uncertain, since they allowed a wide discretion to the judges, and Henry's government felt the need for the greater certainty of a new statute. The formula ultimately adopted, in 1534, made it treason to call the king 'heretic, schismatic, tyrant, infidel or usurper of the crown'.[33] When religion, rather than force, had to be relied on as a guarantee of political obligation, any of these allegations might provoke rebellion. It is remarkable that the first draft of a statute on these lines was being prepared as early as the autumn of 1530. This early draft would also have made it treason to take an oath to a foreign prince (i.e. the Pope) against allegiance, or to bring in documents from abroad against the king's jurisdiction. This early draft seems to have been designed to repress opposition in case of a possible breach with Rome. It was originally intended to come into force in March 1531, but it seems that it was not put

[32] Elton, G. R., 'The Law of Treason in the Early Reformation', *H.J.* (1968), 211–36. Professor Elton's interpretation of his discoveries is not in all points the same as that given here. Thornley, I. D., 'Treason by Words in the Fifteenth Century', *E.H.R.* (1917), 556 ff.

[33] *Tudor Constitution*, 61–3.

before Parliament, and remained in draft for four years.

In the light of this evidence, Professor Scarisbrick's argument cannot be disproved. Henry was considering rejecting Rome, and he was worried by lack of support, which might explain his delay. It is then possible to dismiss any other arguments he used as a blind designed to gain time. Nevertheless, much of Henry's output of words was taken up with other arguments. He was experimenting with a theory of the federal structure of Christendom, according to which cases were to be settled in the country in which they arose. He set his agents to do antiquarian research to find support for this argument, which had the advantage of denying Roman jurisdiction over the divorce without denying the papacy altogether.

He was also arguing a case for the 'liberties of England', supported by a copy of Henry II's Constitutions of Clarendon, the Arthurian legends, and the claim to an imperial title, according to which Henry claimed Englishmen could not be cited to appear outside their realm. When Henry claimed that he had no superior on earth, or that he had an imperial crown, he was claiming no more than he had claimed in the Standish case or in his coronation oath, which was a legal, rather than a doctrinal, independence. Throughout the 1530s, Henry's attacks were on Roman jurisdiction, rather than on Roman authority in doctrine. Papal authority in doctrine, the central point of Catholic unity, did not interest Henry, and he was not laying claim to it. The imperial title cannot be regarded as incompatible with membership of the universal Catholic church, since Mary kept it. When Henry made his claims to national independence, did he understand what they implied? Professor Scarisbrick believes that he did: 'informed Englishmen knew what they were doing when they repudiated Rome. They, including the king, made a conscious, explicit choice.' As Professor Scarisbrick says: 'Rome's primacy was a cold, juridical fact',[34] and it was impossible to be unaware of it. But the important word in this statement is 'juridical'. Rome's juridical primacy was obvious enough, but its obvious powers were not the stuff of which the unity of western Christendom was made. The Spanish crown in America possessed (by papal grant) most of the powers which Henry sought, including the right to restrain appeals, but it was still clearly a part of Roman Catholic Christendom. In a long letter to Bishop Tunstal in 1531, Henry claimed to be fully sovereign over his clergy, their courts, and their goods, but argued that these were strictly temporal powers. Tunstal was sufficiently convinced or submissive to write to Pole in 1536 that 'You suppose that the king's grace in taking upon him the title of Supreme Head ... intendeth to separate his church of England from the unity of the

[34] Scarisbrick, 241–2.

whole body of Christendom . . . You do err too far. His full purpose is to
see the laws of Almighty God purely and sincerely kept and observed in
his realm, and not to separate himself or his realm in any wise from the
unity of Christ's Catholic Church.'[35] A very narrow boundary separated
attacks on individual pieces of papal jurisdiction, such as Gallicans, or
Catholics so good as Philip II and Mary were prepared to make, from
total separation from the Roman church. There is one letter in which
Henry showed that he may have appreciated this distinction. In April 1531
he wrote to one of his agents at Rome that if the Pope tried to refer the
case to a neutral place, such as France, 'we shall only reasorte for defence
to the privileagies of our realm' [*sic*], but if the Pope summoned him to
appear at Rome, 'we shall impunge finally his hol poure'.[36]

However, Henry may have had more than one way in mind of attacking Clement's 'hol poure'. He was arguing that Clement's election was
void for simony (an argument he borrowed from Charles V's Chancellor),
and because he was a bastard. For good measure, he also argued that
Charles's election to the Empire was invalid. He was also threatening to
appeal from the Pope to a Council. On one occasion, his agents in Rome
refused to obey instructions to put this argument to the Pope, and sent
Henry papal bulls forbidding appeals from the Pope to a Council. In
March 1532 he told one of his agents in Rome that a General Council,
governed by the Holy Ghost, would produce the Pope's 'no little confusion'.[37]

At the same time, he was arguing that nothing would be done against
the Pope 'provided his holiness had for him the regard he was entitled
to', and persistently trying to persuade the Pope to refer the case back to
papal judges delegate in England. Twice, he argued *in the same letter*,
that Rome had no jurisdiction at all over the case, and that it should
appoint judges delegate to hear the case with papal authority in England.
There are only two consistent threads in Henry's arguments. One is that
they are all self-contradictory, and the other is that they would all, if
successful, end in his getting his divorce.

There is no doubt that he wanted supreme jurisdiction in his church,
and some share of the wealth of the clergy. All princes wanted these
things, though Henry was perhaps less scrupulous than some about his
means of getting them. But he wanted his divorce more, and he would try
any weapon which would help him to get it. If he had any consistent
policy, it may have been to delay the case until Clement's death enabled

[35] Scarisbrick, 276–80. Dawley, P., *Archbishop Whitgift* (1955), 22.
[36] *State Papers*, vii. 298.
[37] Ibid., vii. 358: see also *Spanish Calendar*, iv. ii. 13; Scarisbrick, 261–3.

him to approach a new Pope. Henry's speeches in these years prove that he had already considered the possibility of rejecting the Pope altogether, but they are too self-contradictory to prove that he definitely intended to do so. These years, as Professor Elton argues, are years of 'bluster and bombast, without a policy', but Professor Elton is on weaker ground in arguing that this verdict cannot be applied to Henry's later policy, after Cromwell's rise to power.

From the very beginning, the general theme of Henry's approaches to Rome had been 'give me what I want, or else . . .', and the 'or else . . .' grew more threatening as the years passed. In the autumn of 1529 he brought a charge of *Praemunire* against Wolsey, for exercising a legatine authority independent of the king's. There were some precedents for this type of action, but the king had clearly supported Wolsey's legatine authority. As Gardiner later said of Wolsey's condemnation, 'I . . . take [it] for a law of the realm, because the lawyers so said, but my reason digested it not.'[38] Shortly afterwards, a *Praemunire* charge was brought against all the clergy of England, for holding church courts. The indictment presumably assumed that church courts were only legal if they were the king's courts. In January 1531, Convocation of the province of Canterbury was granted royal pardon in return for a fine of £100,000. If Henry was achieving nothing else, he was improving his finances. Henry allowed the clergy to continue to hold church courts, but refused a request to define the scope of the Statute of *Praemunire*. When the clergy thought the storm was over, Henry demanded that they insert into the preamble of their submission two extra clauses, one calling him 'protector and only supreme head' of the English church, and the other recognizing that the cure of his subjects' souls was committed to him. The clergy, with academic discretion, recognized him as Supreme Head 'in so far as the law of Christ allows', and denied him the cure of his subjects' souls by altering a case in one of his Latin sentences, and with this, for the moment, the king was content. There is nothing to show that Henry attached any precise meaning to these high-sounding claims.

Meanwhile, the attack on the clergy was continued in Parliament, and though Parliament showed its independence by holding up a government bill against evasion of wardship by uses,[39] it was willing to produce a long list of grievances against the clergy, known as the Supplication against the Ordinaries. Most of this document is a long list of small and practical grievances about the working of the church courts, which were mostly unreformed in Elizabethan times. The preamble, however, also included

[38] Muller, J. A., *Stephen Gardiner and the Tudor Reaction* (1926), 35.
[39] Uses were trusts for purposes of tax evasion. See above, p. 52; below, p. 111.

a more far-reaching complaint that the clergy made laws which did not require royal assent. Much of the work on the Supplication was done by Thomas Cromwell, a former servant of Wolsey's who was rapidly becoming one of the most important ministers, but in essence it only repeated the substance of the *Praemunire* charge of 1531. Only the preamble interested Henry. He demanded that the clergy should agree that no future canons should be valid without the royal assent, and that no existing canons should be valid unless they were approved by a body of thirty-two people appointed by the king.

At this point, the clergy began to resist. Archbishop Warham attempted to prosecute the king's protégé Latimer (later Bishop of Worcester) for heresy. Latimer was a Protestant, and a strong favourite of the king's, but it is doubtful whether his favour was due to his Protestantism. It was more probably due to the fact that he was an eloquent preacher, whose favourite theme was the excessive wealth of the clergy. Henry replied by appearing before Parliament with a copy of the bishops' oath to the Pope, claiming that the clergy were 'but half our subjects, yea, and scarce our subjects'. When the king presented his demands for submission, Canterbury Convocation were busy passing reforms of their own, which offered more chance of reforming the church than any of the king's measures. They were trying to restrict non-residence and improve the standard of clerical education, and to limit officials' fees. At first, they resisted the submission vigorously. Warham quoted Thomas Becket, and Henry was even offered quotations from his own *Assertio Septem Sacramentorum*. As time passed, members of Convocation left London, and when the king finally got a submission abandoning the clergy's right of independent legislation, it was signed by no members of the Lower House, and by only three bishops from the Upper House. The 'Submission of the Clergy' was a submission of three people. The next day, Sir Thomas More resigned the Chancellorship.[40]

Anne's pregnancy

Henry's next attack was on taxation paid to Rome. The first Act in Restraint of Annates of 1532 was clearly a bargaining counter measure. It authorized the king to withold some of the taxes paid to Rome, but was not to apply until the king chose. Though taxes paid to Rome were a good propaganda point, they were not financially important. Before the Reformation, the clergy were paying about £4,800 to Rome, and about £12,500 per annum to the king. In the 1540s, they were paying the king about £47,000. As Professor Scarisbrick concludes, 'popery may have been

[40] Kelly, M. J., 'The Submission of the Clergy', *T.R.H.S.* (1965), 97 ff.

superstitious, but it was cheaper. . . . The price of freedom is eternal taxation.'[41]

This quickening of the pace in 1532 may have been due to the rise of Thomas Cromwell. It may also have been due to the fact that Francis was becoming more active, and by the spring of 1532 Henry had arranged to go to France for a formal meeting with him. Francis had recently acquired two new cardinals, one of them the man who was said to have suggested the first doubts about Henry's marriage, and the king clearly hoped that their diplomatic skill might yet get him his divorce from Rome. By this time, the Pope might have realized the desperate consequences of refusal.

The meeting with Francis took place at Boulogne in October, and appears to have been successful. Meanwhile, Archbishop Warham had died in August, and, though Henry left the see vacant for five months he was able to consider choosing a suitable successor for him. All that can be said of the relationship of these events to the most important event of 1532, Anne's pregnancy, is that they preceded it. Whether Anne's pregnancy is a subject for political or sexual explanations is one of the most important, but most unanswerable questions in the whole story. It certainly demanded urgent action, since if Anne should bear Henry an illegitimate elder son followed by a legitimate younger one, this would be a prescription for civil war. It is probable that the pregnancy began in the last weeks of 1532, and was discovered in the first weeks of 1533. In January 1533, when it is likely to have been suspected but not certainly known, Henry chose his new archbishop, Thomas Cranmer, an obscure man from Cambridge who had probably first attracted Henry's attention by suggesting that he appeal to the universities for opinion on his marriage. He had subsequently gained the attention of the Boleyns, who may have been responsible for his preferment. Cranmer's theological position, at this as at other times, is uncertain: he appears to have been unusually capable of honest doubt. He did not deny transubstantiation till much later, but he was interested in justification by faith, doubtful about the papal primacy, and had married illegally very early in his career. The clearest point in his beliefs was his belief in obedience. Since 'the powers that be are ordained of God', he held himself bound to obey the king's commands, however unpleasant, unless the king commanded him to commit sin. Cranmer did not think a command to sin should be violently resisted, but, like all Christians, he believed firmly that it must be disobeyed. For whatever reason, Henry was determined that Cranmer's appointment should be confirmed by Rome in the normal manner, and

[41] Scarisbrick, J. J., 'Clerical Taxation in England 1485–1547', *J.E.H.* (1960), 54.

even advanced money from his own pocket to ensure that all clerical taxes were paid. Rome, having been unwilling or unable to grant him the legal and political favour of a divorce, was willing to grant him the theological favour of providing him with a heretical archbishop, and Cranmer's appointment was proposed by Campeggio, as English Protector, and carried in the normal manner. This is why the Anglican, alone among Protestant churches, has been able to claim that its ministry has a continuous Apostolic Succession from the first years of the church.

Even after the appointment of Cranmer, no final decision had been taken on how to obtain the divorce. Two draft bills were prepared, but there is no evidence that they were submitted to Parliament, so even now it did not consider the divorce. The issue was urgent, since Henry had already married Anne on 25 January 1533. He did put his case before Convocation, and secured a favourable verdict in April. In May, Cranmer declared Henry's marriage to Catherine null by his authority as archbishop. Anne had been calling herself queen before the judgement, and when she was first prayed for in church as queen, some people walked out. Rome could still overrule Cranmer's judgement, and Catherine could be expected to appeal, so Parliament had been asked to pass an Act in Restraint of Appeals to Rome.

The Act of Restraint of Appeals had a magnificent preamble, largely the work of Cromwell, which provided the theoretical defence for a full breach with Rome. It declared that:

Where by divers sundry old authentic histories and chronicles it is manifestly declared and expressed that this realm of England is an empire, and so hath been accepted in the world, governed by one supreme head and king having the dignity and royal estate of the imperial crown of the same, unto whom a body politic, compact of all sorts and degrees of people divided in terms and by names of spiritualty and temporalty, be bounden and owe to bear next to God a natural and humble obedience; he being also institute and furnished by the goodness and sufferance of Almighty God with plenary, whole and entire power, preeminence, authority, prerogative, and jurisdiction to render and yield justice and final determination to all manner of folk resiants or subjects within this realm, in all causes, matters, debates, and contentions happening to occur, insurge or begin within the limits thereof, without restraint or provocation [to] any foreign princes or potentates of the world.[42]

The full justification of the Henrician reformation is here. The clergy and laity, being subjects of one realm, make one body, and one body can only have one head, who can only be the king. To attempt to impose the Pope as a second head on this national body is to bring disunity to it, and dis-

---

[42] *Tudor Constitution*, 344–9. The Act also made it *Praemunire* to bring in any foreign inhibition or excommunication against a judgement within the realm.

unity is unnatural and displeasing to God. The part of the body politic called the spiritualty is 'sufficient and meet of itself' to decide all questions which may come before it without any foreign intervention.

The breach with Rome not complete, 1533–1534

For the moment, this full-blown justification of national independence remained in the realm of political theory, rather than of politics. Early drafts of the Act had forbidden all appeals to Rome, but the final Act did not: it prohibited appeals on wills, tithes, and fees, questions which concerned the property rights of Members of Parliament, and on marriage. It did not prohibit appeals in cases of heresy. This Act was not the 'breach with Rome'. Henry was still negotiating vainly for the creation of cardinals. He was still hoping for results from the meeting which Francis was having with the Pope in October 1533, and when, in the autumn, he heard that the Pope was planning to excommunicate him, he did not announce that he had seceded from the Pope's church, but appealed to a General Council. In the event, Francis, much hindered by the appeal to a Council, was able to defer Henry's excommunication, but was unable to achieve much more. We cannot know what he might have achieved if Henry had been less provocative. In the autumn, the English Privy Council declared that the Bishop of Rome had no more authority outside his province than any other foreign bishop, but it was still appealing to a General Council. It also cited good weather and absence of the plague as evidence of divine approval of the marriage with Anne.

Henry and Cromwell may have been delayed in 1533 by fear of foreign invasion. Francis and Charles were at peace, and therefore free to intervene in England, and though Francis was benevolent, agreeing to stand godfather for the forthcoming child, Henry distrusted him. Cromwell took invasion scares more seriously than Henry, and received a memorandum including a blueprint for a standing army. Foreign policy was not Cromwell's subject, and he never understood the depth of the rivalry of Francis and Charles as well as Henry did. He was not, however, the only Englishman to take the prospect of invasion seriously. At this time, Bishop Fisher appealed to the Emperor to invade England and put a stop to the whole business.

On 7 September 1533, Anne's child was born, and Henry was so disappointed at her sex that he may not have attended her christening. Elizabeth was no better as a candidate for the succession than Mary had been. As yet, however, there was still time for Anne to bear a son.

As the year 1534 went on, Cromwell grew more firmly established in the king's favour, and was appointed to the Secretaryship, bringing to that office greater power than it had had before, or was to have again until the appointment of Cecil in 1558. During the year, a plan was being made to confiscate the lands of the bishops, and put them on fixed salaries. This plan was never put into effect, but the threat of it reduced the bishops' estates by provoking them to offer individual manors, or grants of prebends, to the king, Cromwell, and other leading ministers. When Parliament reassembled in 1534, Cromwell had a full legislative programme ready for it. The Act of Succession settled the succession on Henry's children by Anne, and included the first declaration by Parliament that Henry's marriage to Catherine had been invalid. It included a preamble designed for propaganda, 'calling to our remembrance the great division which in times past hath been in this realm by reason of several titles pretended to the imperial crown of the same, which sometimes and for the most part ensued by reason of ambiguity and doubts then not so perfectly declared but that men might upon froward intents expound them to every man's sinister appetite and affecion after their sense . . . whereof hath ensued great effusion and destruction of man's blood'.[43] All through the mid-Tudor period, the accounts of Sir William Petre, Secretary of State, mark each new succession crisis with a sharp rise in his bills from the armourer. He was not the only man who shared these fears, and the spectre of the Wars of the Roses could be usefully produced to induce people to accept the succession. For further insurance, the Act also demanded an oath of loyalty to the king's marriage and the succession. The priors of King's Langley and Dunstable, when asked to take this oath, also swore to be loyal to any wife whom Henry might marry after Anne's death.

The restraint of Annates was finally confirmed, and the king took to himself the First Fruits of the revenues of newly appointed bishops, and a tenth of all clerical incomes. This, once Cromwell had produced a valuation of all ecclesiastical incomes, increased the royal income by the welcome sum of £40,000 a year. Elizabeth Barton, a Kentish nun who had had visions to the effect that Henry was no longer king in the estimation of Almighty God, was found guilty of treason, and Fisher of misprision of treason for taking her seriously. In the aftermath of her condemnation, the government Treason Act was at last produced and passed. The Act of Supremacy officially incorporated the king's title of Supreme Head into the law of the land, and this was backed up by the prohibition of all appeals to Rome, now including appeals in heresy cases, the prohibition of papal bulls for the consecration of new bishops, and an Act confirming the Submission of the Clergy of 1532, which said that all new

[43] *Tudor Constitution*, 7.

canons were to have the king's assent, and that the validity of old ones was to be decided on by a committee of thirty-two appointed by the king. The king, rather than the Pope, was now the ultimate source of the canon law of the English church. Unfortunately, since the body of thirty-two reported in 1553, and found themselves reporting to Mary, no decision was ever taken on which canons remained in force. The canon law of the English church remained in doubt, and as late as 1641 the Archbishop of York was still proposing that the body of thirty-two demanded by this Act should be revived, to decide which parts of the church's canon law were still valid. For the first time, on Cromwell's instructions, sermons at Paul's Cross, which served a purpose very similar to official broadcasting, were begun without prayers for the Pope, and Protestants were being allowed an increasing share in the preaching of these sermons. The Italian bishops, Ghinucci and Campeggio, were deprived of their sees and replaced by two Protestants, Latimer and Shaxton. Another Act declared that it was no longer heresy to deny the papal primacy. Papal bulls were to be destroyed, and the Pope's name erased from Mass books.

Surely this was the 'breach with Rome'? If so, some people thought it would be temporary. The Abbot of Woburn put his papal bulls into storage, and told his monks not to erase the Pope from Mass books, saying 'it will come again one day'.[44] Henry was being threatened with excommunication, but he had still not been excommunicated. Even if he were, other English kings had quarrelled with the papacy over jurisdiction, and had been excommunicated. Edward I had once even outlawed the whole clergy during a quarrel with the Pope. Henry was trying in his propaganda to place his quarrels in this English royal tradition, and many of his subjects may have believed him. Other quarrels with the Pope had blown over, so why should not this one? One of the year's Acts of Parliament reassured its hearers that it was not to be interpreted as if 'your Grace, your nobles and subjects, intended by the same to decline or vary from the congregation of Christ's church in any things concerning the very articles of the Catholic faith or Christendom'.[45] Though the Act of Supremacy gave the king power to try heresy, it did not say that he had the power to decide what was heresy. The Acts of 1534 said nothing about how it was to be decided what was heresy, and what was not, except that it was not heresy to deny the primacy of the Pope.

It is possible that those who thought the breach would be temporary included Henry. In September 1534, Clement at last died, and Henry, co-operating with the French, warmly welcomed the election of Paul III,

[44] Scarisbrick, 327, n.   [45] *Tudor Constitution*, 354.

and set out to negotiate with him. Charles, some of whose advisers thought the whole question would be amicably settled at a Council, was about to attack Tunis, and was ready to be conciliatory because he did not want the English to attack him while he was away. Unfortunately, shortly before Clement's death, the Rota had at last given a verdict in favour of Catherine, but Henry and Paul seem to have thought that even this obstacle could be overcome. There is no sign that Henry was prepared to give up the Royal Supremacy, and the Imperial Ambassador reported that he would rather take back Catherine than give up all he had taken from the church, but as late as 1536 Pope Paul was prepared to tell him that if he would accept papal authority he could have the same jurisdiction in his realm as Francis and Charles had in theirs.[46] Late in 1534, Henry was offering to resign the title of king of France if Francis could get Rome to give a favourable verdict on his marriage, and in April 1535 Thomas Cromwell was at the old treadmill writing to Casale at Rome for the same purpose.

Henry, however, was as self-contradictory as always. Writing to the French early in 1535, he expressed *in the same letter* his hopes for a favourable papal decision, and objections to the Pope dictating what people should believe and interpreting Scripture.[47] In England events were still moving ahead. Thomas Cromwell was organizing the printing presses for a campaign of justification for government policy. During 1535, a translation was produced of Marsilius of Padua's *Defensor Pacis*, which had placed the church firmly under the lay authority, for the sake of peace, unity, and tranquillity, and declared that the Pope had no more authority than the church chose to give him, giving supreme power to a General Council, which was to be summoned by the 'faithful human legislator'. This work had always been anathema to Popes, but it was useful in 1535. It had one disadvantage, which was that it gave supreme legislative power to the people. Cromwell's editor made a marginal note that 'he speaketh not of the rascal multitude, but of the parliament'.[48] In the same year, Gardiner, who had been in disgrace since his opposition to the Submission of the Clergy, published his justification of the Royal Supremacy. He made a number of vehement attacks on the papacy, and, in the course of his defence of the Royal Supremacy, quoted the fact that the Emperor Justinian had settled points of pure doctrine on his own authority. Gardiner nowhere denies that the Pope has authority over matters of doctrine: his attacks are on papal jurisdiction. But this passage is one of the few which suggest that the king was now being credited with power

[46] *L. & P.*, vii. 1483.   [47] *L. & P.*, viii. 341, 523.
[48] Elton, G. R., 'The Political Creed of Thomas Cromwell', *T.R.H.S.* (1956), 86.

to define doctrine. These works may have annoyed the Pope, but what really destroyed the hope of reconciliation in 1535 was the execution of Fisher and More for refusing to swear to the Royal Supremacy. The execution, which came immediately after the Pope had made Fisher a cardinal, was announced to the Curia by the French cardinals with tears in their eyes, and left Rome thinking of other things than reconciliation.

The breach widens, 1534–1536

Henry's cousin Reginald Pole had at first helped him in his appeal to the universities, but soon afterwards he had withdrawn abroad and took no further part in the proceedings. By 1535, Henry was suspicious of him, and was keeping a watch on his correspondence. Starkey, one of his household who later worked for Cromwell, thanked Cromwell for warning him that the king suspected him, and thereafter regularly reported Pole's doings to Cromwell. Soon other people were interested in Pole, whose academic reputation was very high. In July 1535, a report to one of the cardinals asked him to recommend Pole to the Pope for a cardinal's hat, on the ground that he was 'a relation of the king, but of the white rose', and that it would be a 'Christian and praiseworthy revenge' for the execution of Fisher and More.[49] Pole was appointed cardinal and legate, and by 1536 he had published his book *De Conservanda Ecclesiae Unitate*, which is one of the best presentations of the implications of Henry's breach with Rome. As legate, he urged Francis and Charles to organize a Crusade against England. The causes of the Yorkists and the Catholics were being united.

Even so, the death of Catherine early in 1536, by removing the original cause of the quarrel, created further talks of reconciliation, and even of another mission to England by Campeggio. Like most other events in this comedy of errors, it was mistimed. If Catherine had died before the execution of Fisher and More, or before the legislation of 1534, a reconciliation would have been probable. By now Henry had other worries. In January 1536 Anne miscarried, and Henry, whose interest was already directed elsewhere, decided, first that she had committed adultery with a number of courtiers, including her brother,[50] and second, that his marriage to her was void, because, having had an affair with her sister, he was related to her in the first degree of affinity. The second conclusion was duly registered by Cranmer's court (though Cranmer was much

[49] *L. & P.*, viii. 830, 986.
[50] Charges of adultery are difficult to disprove, and all that can be said of these is that there is no known evidence to support them. Since Henry had decided that his marriage to Anne was incestuous, it might be argued that his accusation against her of adultery with her brother savours of what psychologists call projection.

distressed by the affair), and the first produced a condemnation for treason.

On the day of Anne's execution, Cranmer issued a dispensation from an impediment in the third degree of affinity between Henry and Jane Seymour. With Jane's marriage to Henry, her brother, another man with Protestant sympathies, was brought into favour, and later, as Duke of Somerset, became Protector after Henry's death. The same year, after a long visitation conducted under Cromwell's auspices, a report on monasteries was presented to Parliament, which passed an Act for the dissolution of monasteries with an income of less than £200 a year. The monks were either to be released from their vows and paid gratuities, or else go into larger monasteries. This first dissolution was not an attack on the principle of monasticism: some houses were very sparsely populated, in others the monks either wanted to leave or could be placed elsewhere, and some houses managed to gain exemptions. Cromwell, moreover, had learnt his skill in dissolving monasteries while acting as Wolsey's agent in the foundation of his college at Oxford. The fundamental issues of the dissolution were not raised by the reduction of the number of monasteries in 1536, but by the abolition of monasticism in 1539.

In 1536 Henry was also faced, after numerous false alarms, with a serious rebellion, a collection of risings in the north known collectively as the Pilgrimage of Grace. The first rebels were in Lincolnshire, and provoked Henry to tell the county that it was 'the most brute and beastly in the whole realm'. Their motives seem to have been confused. Some were concerned for church property, others alarmed by rumours of new taxes, some determined to preserve the spire of Louth church, and others to murder the Bishop of Lincoln's chancellor. The Yorkshire rebels, who were the biggest force, appear to have been most concerned about religion, though they were also provoked by the Statute of Uses, by enclosures, and by entry fines. Robert Aske, who became their leader, was certainly primarily concerned about religion, and said that the Royal Supremacy appeared to destroy the unity of the Catholic church. He and many others were concerned for the monasteries, which appear to have had more vitality in Yorkshire than elsewhere. An M.P. for Newcastle, who was one of the rebels, complained that Parliament was not free, because they could not speak of the king's vices, 'but whatsoever Cromwell says is right, and none but that'. Miscellaneous though their grievances were, they do appear to have had some sympathy for the old order, and even for the Pope. This was not unanimous: the second Yorkshire rising was led by Sir Francis Bigod, a Protestant who objected to the Royal

Supremacy. Nevertheless, the rebels created considerable alarm and their power was such that the Duke of Norfolk had to disperse them by false promises instead of by force.[51]

These disturbances happened at a time when the succession was in greater doubt than ever. By declaring his marriage to Anne null, Henry had bastardized Elizabeth, and he was now left with two bastard daughters. His one bastard son, the Duke of Richmond, died at this time when his claim seemed strongest. The new succession Act required by a new marriage refrained from settling the problem, and left Henry to bequeath the crown by will. From this point, the campaign against the papacy was intensified, and a new Act was passed against the 'pretended power and usurped authority of the Bishop of Rome'. It was said that 'imps of the said bishop of Rome' had instilled into 'poor, simple and un-lettered people' a belief in his authority, 'to the great displeasure of Almighty God, the high discontentation of our said most dread sovereign lord, and the interruption of the unity, love, charity, concord, and agree-ment that ought to be in a Christian region and congregation'. After this Act there was no more talk of reconciliation with Rome.

This time, Henry's efforts produced the desired result, and in 1537, Jane Seymour produced a son and died twelve days later. Henry was again a widower, but at least he had a son, who duly succeeded him as Edward VI. Henry had broken with Rome, and he had got a son, but how much the first event was to mean, and how little the second was, yet remained to be discovered.

Postscript

A fully revised version of Professor Elton's views is now available in *Reform and Reformation* (1977). That and his *Policy and Police* (1972) show that this work does not do justice to the constructive contributions made by Cromwell to the growth of English Protestantism after 1534. The account of Cromwell himself in *Reform and Reformation* should be re-garded as definitive. Professor Elton also sketches an exciting new inter-pretation of the Pilgrimage of Grace, in which county faction appears as the reflection of faction at court. On the other hand, I remain unper-suaded, either that Cromwell contributed as much to the original breach with Rome as Professor Elton supposes, or that he made as profound an impression on the ideas and institutions of Tudor England as he has made on the mind of Professor Elton.

[51] Fletcher, A., *Tudor Rebellions* (1968), 20–47, 118–34.

3. *State of Flux* 1536–1570

If we seek but for the truth, that is not to be judged to be always on that side which gets the over hand by power and authority, or suffrages extorted. It is not like wrestling.

Discourse of the Common Weal, 1549[1]

Reactions to the Reformation

How did Henry VIII's subjects react to this remarkable series of changes? Answers to this question must be made up of individual examples collected by the random process of survival. At least it can be said that, apart from the Pilgrims of Grace, many of whom had economic grievances, they submitted to the changes, and were to continue to do so through all the successive turns of Tudor religious policy. How did this come about?

Most of Henry VIII's subjects were not theologians. Men like Norfolk and Shrewsbury, who helped Henry to carry through all the changes of his reign, must be classified as Catholics if they are to be classified at all, but they appear to have seen little of importance involved in the rejection of the Pope. Norfolk once argued that marriage was a temporal matter, and this may have represented his real feeling. A few attacks on the clergy probably appeared to them to be part of the normal stuff of politics, and it is doubtful whether they grasped, or even much cared about, the theological implications. They were conservative in a sense, and expected to be able to continue to hear Mass, to keep images in church, and to preserve all the ritual apparatus of the old religion. Neither they nor their social inferiors had grown up with the assumption that religion was something a man chose: the word heresy meant choosing. Many would have agreed with the Elizabethan gentleman, descended from a family which

[1] *Discourse of the Common Weal*, ed. E. Lamond (1893), 140.

had established itself through a mixture of monastic lands and the favour of a Marian bishop, who said in his will that he believed in the resurrection of the flesh, life everlasting, 'and all other articles of my faith which a Christian man ought to believe'.[2] He made no attempt to define these articles, and may not have cared much whether he was Protestant or Catholic. This unconcern with the whole argument may have existed in a less polished form among the poorer classes. The capper in the *Discourse of the Common Weal* is unfortunately fictional, but his attitude to theologians was probably common:

I would set you to the plough and cart, for the devil a whit the good do ye with your studies, but set men together by the ears. Some with this opinion and some with that, holding this way and some that way, as though the truth must be as they say that have the upper hand in contention. And this contention is not the least cause of these uproars of the people; some holding of the one learning, and some holding of the other. In my mind, it made no matter if there were no learned men at all.[3]

This impatience with controversy would usually produce support for the established order, for several reasons. The first was common prudence. Opposition would probably involve forfeiture of lands, if not execution, and might leave a man's wife and children in poverty, and his servants starving. Sir William Petre, who held office as Secretary from 1544 till Elizabeth's reign (including Lady Jane Grey's reign), was not an unprincipled man, but his chief interest was in his house and his lands, which he had won from his official career. He was fond of his family, and cared for the welfare of his servants. If he had resisted any of the changes of religious policy, his fall would not have concerned only himself: it would have had the same effect on the area of his home that the collapse of a small firm has today. Preachers constantly stressed that gentlemen had duties to their inferiors, and when these duties coincided with self-interest, they may have been the more willingly performed. Moreover, the king was the source of patronage, and a time when he had all the monastic lands available for sale was not the most expedient time to quarrel with him.

Belief in social order and obedience would also lead to conformity. Men who doubted most of the points in dispute would not doubt that social order and obedience to superiors were among the cardinal points of Christian teaching. Many gentlemen agreed with Cranmer that

every degree of people, in their vocation, calling and office, has appointed to them their duty and order. Some are in high degree, some in low; some kings and princes, some inferiors and subjects, priests and laymen, masters and servants, fathers and children, husbands and wives, rich and poor . . . Where there

---

[2] P.C.C. 63 Windebanke: John Colles.
[3] *Discourse of the Common Weal*, op. cit., 21.

is no right order, there reigneth all abuse, carnal liberty, enormity, sin and babylonical confusion. Take away kings, princes, rulers, magistrates, judges, and such states of God's order, no man shall ride or go by the highway un-robbed, no man shall sleep in his own house or bed unkilled, no man shall keep his wife, children and possessions in quietness. All things shall be com-mon, and there must needs follow all mischief and utter destruction.[4]

This same order which gentlemen found so desirable also demanded that they obey the king.

Conformity was also made easier by serious belief in unity. Protestants, as much as Catholics, believed in unity and in the universal church. They had not separated from Rome because they did not believe in unity, but because they did believe in truth, and believed unity could not be had without it. When Cranmer's prosecutors under Mary opened the trial with an oration in praise of unity, Cranmer replied that he 'was very glad to come to an unity, so that it were in Christ, and agreeable to his holy word'.[5] This devotion to unity was not confined to theologians. In Janu-ary 1545 Henry came to Parliament and exhorted them to 'amend one thing which is surely amiss, and far out of order, to the which I most heartily require you, which is that charity and concord is not among you, but discord and dissension beareth rule in every place. Behold then what love and charity is among you, when the one calleth the other heretic and Anabaptist, and he calleth him again papist, hypocrite and pharisee.' This exhortation to people not to disagree with each other does not now sound very impressive, but Petre wrote to Paget that this speech was 'such a joy and marvellous comfort as I reckon this day one of the happiest of my life . . . I saw some, that hear him often enough, water their plants.'[6] An idea which could move such politicians as Petre and Paget to strong emotion must have been very deep-rooted. It is a reminder that we should not necessarily assume that the neutrals of the Reformation had no convictions: some may have had convictions which led them to be neutral.

Protestants would tend to support Henry VIII (though not unani-mously), not because they supposed he was one of themselves, but from mutual self-interest. If they denied transubstantiation, they might be burned, but if they confined themselves to attacking the Pope, Henry and the Council would protect them against the bishops. Even if Henry attacked them, someone such as Cromwell, who had risen to favour

---

[4] *Tudor Constitution*, 15. It is a typical piece of Tudor theology that this passage begins by describing a similar hierarchy among the angels.

[5] *Works of Archbishop Cranmer* (Parker Soc.), I. 392.

[6] Emmison, F. C., *Tudor Secretary* (1961), 59.

during the struggles with Rome, might intervene to protect them. Henry occasionally tried to prove his orthodoxy by onslaughts on Protestants, or by bonfires of heretical books, but he could not afford to make enemies everywhere, and if he had offended all thorough papalists, he would need some moderate Protestants as friends instead. The result was that the weight of repression of heresy became more intermittent, and discussions about doubtful points of doctrine easier to start.

Among Catholics, Fisher, More, and Pole were not the only ones who understood the implications of the breach with Rome. Robert Aske certainly understood what was involved, and so did a man called William Copley, tried under the 1534 Succession Act, who said that 'if there be no Pope, there can be no bishop, and if there be no bishop, there can be no priest, and if there be no priest there can be no saved souls'. Then, descending from the general to the particular, he said that the king's marriage to Anne was invalid because it was not done by the Pope's consent, and 'the Queen's Grace should not be called Queen Anne but Anne the bawd'.[7] Some others appear to have understood the implications later, when questions of doctrine were called in doubt. The Bishop of London and the Abbot of Woburn both later said they wished they had understood the issues well enough to follow Fisher and More. In Mary's reign, Gardiner claimed that he had thought the breach would be temporary, and Bonner that he had acted from fear. In some cases, episcopal claims that they saw the point too late may be true. Six bishops, of whom Tunstal is the most distinguished, survived the whole period from Henry's reign to Elizabeth's, and all of them followed the same course. They all supported Henry, some with varying degrees of reluctance. They all opposed Edward's government, mostly over the issue of transubstantiation: they might abandon the Pope, but they would not abandon the Mass. It may be that the doctrinal changes of Edward's reign led them to a more thorough understanding of the place of the Pope in the Catholic church, for they all supported Mary, but refused all inducements to support Elizabeth. The bishops all feared heresy, and some may have thought that co-operation with the king was the best way to ensure prosecution of heresy. Other bishops were tougher, and had to be terrorized into submission. Nix of Norwich was one of the oldest and the toughest: as early as 1505 he had expressed a desire to curse all maintainers of *Praemunire* 'as heretics and not believers in Christ's church'.[8] In 1532, the Mayor of Thetford complained to Cromwell that Nix had violated the town's liberties by summoning the Mayor before his diocesan court. The normal penalty would have been 6s. 8d., but

---

[7] Elton, G. R., 'The Law of Treason in the Early Reformation', *H.J.* (1968), 225–6.
[8] Kelly, Michael, 'The Submission of the Clergy', *T.R.H.S.* (1965), 108.

Cromwell faced Nix with a *Praemunire* charge and a fine of £10,000, which was sufficient to secure his submission. All of them, however, were in a position much weakened by the fact that they were more interested in their own privileges than in the Pope's.

The hardest group of all to assess are the parish clergy, who are always obscure. The vast majority remained quietly at their posts from the beginning of the Reformation right through to Elizabeth's reign. Robert Parkyn, who was remarkable in leaving a diary, was interested in ministering to his parishioners, rather than determining national policy, and continued to provide them with such sacraments as he could. Others may have been bewildered by the whole affair, or afraid of unemployment if they lost their livings. In most cases, the reasons cannot be discovered, and we can only record that they stayed on.

For most people in this period, liberty meant liberty to do right, and was to be sharply distinguished from licence, which was liberty to do wrong. It was always difficult to preach a doctrine not in official favour and remain unscathed, but most people who felt no call to proclaim their beliefs could expect to remain unmolested a large part of the time.

Administrative reform: the work of Thomas Cromwell

The Reformation was not the only government business of these years, nor was it the only field in which theories about imperial jurisdiction and the supremacy of statute could make a useful contribution to royal policy. The years of Cromwell's power were also years of attacks on liberties and franchises. Previous kings had granted out to various local potentates such portions of their power as the right to nominate Justices of the Peace. In some liberties, including those of the Savoy and Scotland Yard, criminals could take refuge, and neither the king's writ nor the king's officers could follow them. Some holders of liberties also had the power of pardon. Such powers were a great hindrance to the keeping of the peace, and offended Henry's feelings and Cromwell's theories. An Act of 1536 made a more general assault on franchises, and deprived their holders of the right to name J.P.s, and of the power of pardon, which were to be 'united and knit to the imperial crown of this realm, as of good right and equity it appertaineth'. This Act did not abolish franchises. After this Act, however, surviving franchisal powers were of more antiquarian than political interest.

Wales

There is a sense in which the biggest franchise of all was Wales and the Marches, and Tudor policy in Wales is one of their clearest successes.

Scotland remained independent, and Ireland as recalcitrant as ever. Yet though Wales offered a long coast to an invader, and Tudor officials always feared that a foreign invasion would join with a Welsh rising, in the event the worst trouble the Tudors had with Wales was not by any rising against the English, but because many Welshmen became too closely involved in the interplay of London factions in the 1590s. The Spaniards later hoped that Wales might provide a sympathetic base for an invasion of England, but the only time they tried, in 1596, they were routed by the Merioneth trained bands. The moving spirit in the assimilation of Wales with England was certainly Thomas Cromwell. Bishop Rowland Lee, who was appointed President of the Council of Wales in 1534, was Cromwell's protégé, and almost all our knowledge of Welsh affairs in Henry VIII's reign comes from the reports he sent to Cromwell: after Cromwell's fall, almost none of Lee's reports survive. Lee's policy consisted of little more than terror: he was praised for the fact that he was 'not affable to any of the walshrie', and his reports suggest that he regarded hanging as the sovereign remedy for all Welsh ills. He constructed an effective system of informers and spies, and travelled regularly round Wales looking for thieves and punishing juries which returned dishonest verdicts. His chief worry was that at first he had to govern all Wales, including complete military command, on an allowance of £586 a year, and he was not allowed to keep the fines imposed in his court. The Dissolution of the Monasteries, at a time when he was particularly anxious to fortify royal castles against possible rebellion, was a blessing to him, and he used large amounts of monastic stone for repairing royal castles. Meanwhile, Cromwell was working out a more constructive policy.

A series of Acts of Parliament whittled down marcher franchises, and an Act of 1536 introduced the system of Justices of the Peace, which dismayed Lee, because 'there be very few Welshmen in Wales above Brecknock that may dispend ten pound land, and to say truth, their discretion less than their lands'.[9] The policy worked, and competition to be included in the Commission of the Peace became a powerful incentive for securing favour in London. The climax of Cromwell's policy was the Act of Union in 1536 which brought the marcher lordships into the jurisdiction of the shires, gave Wales the right to return M.P.s, empowered the king to divide Wales into shires and hundreds, and fully subjected Wales to English law. There was some initial trouble with the introduction of English law: at Rhayader, in 1544, the Assize judge was murdered, whereat Henry deprived the town of a valuable commodity by shifting the Assizes to Presteigne. The toughest problems with English law appear to have

[9] Williams, Penry, *The Council in the Marches of Wales* (1958), 16, 22.

been over land tenure and the jury system. For a long time, Welsh juries appear to have returned verdicts on their goodwill towards the parties, rather than on the facts of the case. The Court of Wards later thought Radnorshire juries had a conspiracy to find that all tenures in the county were not liable to wardship, and the government often had to use its power to punish juries for their verdicts. There was a good deal of trouble caused by the conflict between Welsh partible inheritance, or common rights, and primogeniture and the more rigorous English freehold doctrine of property, and the crop of Welsh lawsuits may have been as much due to the uncertainties of land tenure as to the use of litigation as a substitute for violence. Perhaps the most important event in assimilating Wales to England was the Dissolution of the Monasteries. This brought the Crown large amounts of Welsh land, which were later granted to important Englishmen. The wealthy Earls of Pembroke and Worcester, and later Leicester and Essex, built up large Welsh estates, and the fact that the most important people in Wales were Englishmen often in favour at court brought Wales into the English patronage network. The complex social rivalry of the Welsh counties came to depend on offices in the gift of Englishmen. The struggle for patronage produced violent rivalries in Wales, but they were rivalries of one Welshman against his neighbour, and of one English lord against another, not of Welshmen against Englishmen. The assimilation of Wales may also have been made easier because the natural trade routes ran down the valleys into England rather than across Wales.

Central administration

This period was also one of reorganization of central administration. The Parkinsonian process by which people administering particular subjects under the Chamber acquired subordinates and a formal organization was accelerated by the increase in government business. In 1535, the new revenue from first fruits and clerical tenths produced a Treasurer of First Fruits and Tenths, whose office was later formalized as a Court of First Fruits and Tenths. The monastic lands produced enough business for a whole office, which was immediately formalized as the Court of Augmentations, with its own seals and its own clerk, usher, messenger, and local receivers. In 1540 the Wards office was formalized under the title of the Court of Wards. Its judicial status was formalized, and it too was given its clerk, usher, and messenger. These changes, and others connected with them, have been ascribed to Thomas Cromwell, given the title of 'The Tudor Revolution in Government', and credited with being the beginning of 'modern government'. Since most of these changes were undone in 1554, when almost all financial business was restored to the Exchequer, it would follow that the sole example of 'modern government' which survived after 1554 was the Court of Wards—a conclusion which is difficult to defend.[10]

It is also questionable how complete Thomas Cromwell's responsibility was. He was certainly the moving spirit, but the Navy Office, which was perhaps more important than any of the others, was formalized after Cromwell's fall, and, as far as can be seen, without any initiative by him. Perhaps the most permanent effect of these changes was an increase in the number of government jobs, with a consequent drain on the Crown's finances, and augmentation of its powers of patronage.

One of Cromwell's acts, for which he receives comparatively little credit, was for the compulsory registering of land conveyances. The complexities of land tenure produced some of the most confused litigation of the period, and an accurate record helped to ease the confusion. It was the same desire for accurate records that led Cromwell to demand the keeping of parish registers of births, marriages, and deaths. When proof of age and disputed marriages were among the regular sources of legal confusion, registers could be very helpful. It was some time before many parishes kept registers, but they were kept in enough places to make Cromwell the patron saint of English demographers.

One of the most important administrative changes, the Statute of Uses, appears to have been largely Henry's doing, rather than Cromwell's. From very early in the Reformation Parliament, the government was trying to pass a bill to put a stop to tax evasion by uses, but the Commons persistently refused to pass it, although Henry told them he was 'greatly wronged' by their opposition to it. Finally, after summoning the judges, Henry got a decision during a current lawsuit to the effect that uses were illegal and landowners could not bequeath their land by will at all. This fearsome judgement threw all land tenure into confusion, and so dismayed the Commons that they were willing to pass the bill Henry put in front of them, simply in order to clarify the situation. This Act caused intense resentment, and it has been called a piece of 'short-sighted political vindictiveness',[11] which, if it had been Cromwell's work, would have been very much better than it was. The measure was too harsh to work, and in 1540 Henry had to retreat to a more sensible compromise. The final compromise increased revenue from wardships, and so did the fact that for the first few years, monastic lands which were sold were to be held by knight service in chief, and so were to be liable to wardship.

[10] Elton, G. R., *The Tudor Revolution in Government* (1953). For criticism of this thesis, see Penry Williams and G. L. Harriss, 'A Revolution in Tudor History?', *Past and Present*, no. 25 (1963), 8 ff.
[11] Ives, E. W., 'The Genesis of the Statute of Uses', *E.H.R.* (1967), 673–97.

II THE ROYAL SUPREMACY

The fight for the king's ear

It was easier to solve the problem of uses than to work out the constitutional and doctrinal implications of the royal supremacy. It was clear that the king was Supreme Head of the church, but what this fact meant in constitutional terms, or what was the doctrine of the church over which he was head, were points in some doubt. The problem which vexed the Elizabethans and the Stuarts, whether the Supremacy was of the king alone, or of the king in Parliament, was never seriously considered under Henry VIII, and there is evidence on both sides. On doctrine, there was doubt, both what the doctrine of the church of England was, and by what authority it existed. Nicholas Harpesfield, later a devoted supporter of Mary, said Henry was 'like one that would throw down a man headlong from the top of a high tower, and bid him stay where he was half-way down'.[12] Between 1525 and 1547 about 800 editions of religious works were printed in English, the majority of them Protestant and many of them printed secretly abroad. There appears to have been a market for them, and there must have been a considerable volume of theological discussion to sustain it. In this situation, guidance was needed for those who wished to be told what to believe, but when it came it was erratic. The king's doctrinal line varied according to the state of foreign policy. When Francis and Charles were at peace, and there were invasion scares, he looked for alliances with German Lutherans, who tended to demand doctrinal concessions, and when Francis and Charles were at war, there might be religious reaction. On other occasions, such as the invasion scare of 1539, he tried to mollify the European powers by giving an impression of doctrinal orthodoxy. His policy also varied according to the rise and fall of different groups who competed for his ear. Gardiner and Norfolk tended to influence him in a conservative direction, and Cranmer and Cromwell, who seem to have formed an effective working partnership, tried to influence him towards a more radical position.

Thomas Cromwell and the Bible

In 1536 Cromwell, the king's vicar-general for ecclesiastical affairs, was in the ascendant, and the Royal Injunctions of that year sharply restricted the number of saints' days, and also introduced the first doctrinal change of the English Reformation, a denial of the efficacy of pilgrimages. People were to be taught that 'they shall please God more by the true exercising of their bodily labour, travail, or occupation, and providing for their

[12] Scarisbrick, 398.

families, than if they went about to the said pilgrimages'.[13] The *Ten Articles* of the same year, issued by Convocation under royal supervision, omitted to mention four of the seven sacraments. Cromwell was also interested in the translation of the Bible, and was discussing it with Coverdale in More's house as early as 1527. Tyndale's translation, being incomplete, needed supplementing. In 1534 Cranmer and Cromwell induced Canterbury Convocation to petition the king for one. In 1535 Coverdale published abroad with an unauthorized dedication to the king, and Cromwell persuaded the king to allow it to be reprinted in England, though with an injunction that people should not dispute its meaning. This was the Bible which was known as the 'breeches Bible', from the unfortunate translation that Adam and Eve took fig-leaves to make themselves breeches. In 1537, another edition by Rogers, chaplain to the Merchant Adventurers at Antwerp, was authorized. By 1539, the various editions had been compared, and Coverdale and others produced a revised edition known as the Great Bible, again largely organized by Cromwell, and supported with £400 of his own money. There was nothing necessarily heretical about translating the Bible, and the hierarchies in other countries were often more sympathetic than the English. In Spain, Cardinal Ximenes produced an official edition.

Nevertheless, it provided the material which enabled people to make their own choices in religion, and in a period of doctrinal flux it was bound to have a large influence. It also had an enormous influence on the speeches, literature, and political thought of England and America, and it is fortunate that it was translated at a time when the standard of language was high. Soon it produced a widespread habit of trying to floor ecclesiastical authority by producing a Biblical text. In the next century, when Prynne opposed Charles I's marriage to a Roman Catholic by quoting a text against marriage to the daughters of the Canaanites or other idolatrous women, some of the arguments of the Catholic bishops against translation were perhaps illustrated. Free translation inevitably led to individual interpretation, however much Protestants might deny it, and individual interpretation inevitably produced some eccentricities at first, and ultimately made unity of religious belief impossible. Early Protestants, who fondly hoped that the meaning of the Bible was so obvious that it could create no disagreements, tried vainly to avoid this danger by pretending that the meaning of the Bible was so plain that 'interpretation' was unnecessary.

[13] Gee and Hardy, *Documents Illustrative of the History of the English Church* (1896), 271. For further condemnation, in 1538, of pilgrimages, relics, and the telling of beads, see ibid., 277–8.

The king's religion

In 1536, translation of the Bible implied no change in the official position. The first comprehensive statement of Henrician doctrine was the Bishops' Book of 1537, a document prepared by the bishops, corrected in detail by the king, and finally re-corrected by Cranmer. The survival of all these stages gives us a uniquely clear picture of Henry's theology, and of the extent to which he was able to impose it on the church.[14] He again attempted to claim a cure of his subjects' souls. He took a strong conservative stand on many questions, defending Purgatory and the celibacy of the clergy (and of former monks and nuns). He attacked the chapter on justification, which went a long way towards the Protestant doctrine of justification by faith alone. His corrections go beyond orthodox Catholicism, and almost to Pelagianism, a heretical doctrine according to which it was possible to perform enough good works to *merit* salvation. Cranmer cut these corrections out, saying they 'may not be put in this place in anywise'. On other points, Henry was more radical: he showed a vigorous dislike of confession, a doubt whether confirmation was a sacrament, and a persistent determination to delete the adjective from references to 'holy orders'. He also produced a number of beliefs which were simply idiosyncratic. He cut out denunciation of wanton attire in women, and of immoderate sleep, and also a statement that kings were bound by their own laws. In a passage on Christian equality, he added 'touching the soul only', and in a passage on the duty of the rich to help the poor he tried to add a condemnation of idle beggars. He cut out a condemnation of astrology, and showed a decided preference for God the Son over God the Father. Finally, he tried to make the Tenth Commandment read 'thou shalt not covet another man's wife without due recompense'. Cranmer replied that 'this addition agreeth not well with the coveting of another man's wife', and Henry withdrew.[15] On this material, it is impossible to classify Henry as either Protestant or Catholic: his theology was a highly individual confusion.

In 1538 Cromwell led him to send out another series of Royal Injunctions. These were published the same year as Henry was negotiating with the German Lutherans, and they included a command that the Bible was to be set up in every church, though people were not to dispute about its meaning. Attempts were made to encourage preaching and the dispelling of ignorance. The injunctions attacked idolatry and relics, and paid off one old score by commanding that the worship of St. Thomas Becket should cease.

[14] For this and what follows, see Scarisbrick, 405–20.
[15] Ridley, Jasper, *Archbishop Cranmer* (1962), 124.

The Six Articles

In 1539, however, Norfolk and Gardiner were gaining Henry's ear, and the process of doctrinal experiment was brought to a temporary halt by the Act of Six Articles, optimistically titled 'An Act for Abolishing Diversity in Opinions'. Although the Bishops' Book had only passed through Convocation, the Six Articles were put through all the panoply of an Act of Parliament. Unfortunately, they shed little light on the question of Parliament's authority in doctrine. Normally, an Act of Parliament specified that it was 'ordained and enacted' by the authority of the king, Lords, and Commons, leaving no doubt that it acquired its authority from Parliament. The penalties for breach of the Six Articles have a normal enacting clause, but the actual articles of doctrine have not: they are merely 'resolved, accorded and agreed' by the *consent* of the king, Lords, and Commons,[16] and thus refrain from asserting that Parliament has any authority to enact doctrine, as distinct from recognizing doctrine which already exists. This position is the more defensible for the fact that the articles themselves are entirely traditional. They affirm transubstantiation (Henry strengthened this article), deny the necessity of communion in both kinds, confirm that clerical celibacy is necessary 'by the law of God' (a stronger position than many Catholics would have taken), and that vows of chastity are to be kept (Henry added 'or widowhood'). They defend private Masses, and affirm that confession is 'expedient and necessary to be retained'. This was the only article which Henry weakened, rudely rejecting an attempt by Gardiner and Tunstal to make the article read that confession was necessary 'by the law of God'. Henry's dislike of confession seems to have been as constant as his devotion to transubstantiation, Purgatory, and the celibacy of the clergy. The only surprising point is the vigour of his objection to communion in both kinds. The demand for communion in both kinds was often an issue of the laity against the clergy, and so strong an anticlerical as Henry might have been expected to sympathize with it, especially since communion in the early medieval church had been in both kinds.

The Six Articles created some dismay among Protestants. Latimer and Shaxton resigned their sees, and Cranmer sent his wife back to her family in Germany. Some time later, when the storm had eased, he recalled her. Though he kept her presence secret, Henry was informed, and Cranmer, to his great alarm, was sent for late at night, but Henry only guffawed heartily, and let the matter drop. This was not the only attempt to ease Cranmer out of the king's favour. Sir John Gostwick, Treasurer of First

[16] *Tudor Constitution*, 389–90.

Fruits and Tenths, once attacked him for heresy in the Commons, only to get a message from the king, 'tell that varlet Gostwick that if he do not acknowledge his fault unto my lord of Canterbury . . . I will sure both make him a poor Gostwick and otherwise punish him, to the example of others'.[17] In 1543 some canons of Canterbury, probably backed from higher quarters, accused Cranmer of heresy. The king allowed the case to come before the Council, but at the last moment gave Cranmer his ring to produce to the Council. When he produced it, the stunned silence in the Council was broken by Lord Russell, saying that they should have known that the king would never let them attack Cranmer. Cranmer's loyalty appears to have got its rewards, and so long as he was in favour, attempts to stamp out Protestantism would not go very far. Persecution under the Six Articles was never very effective. Five hundred were arrested immediately, but all of them were released by a general pardon from the king. In 1544, Cranmer was even able to produce an English litany, which put a severe check on prayer to the saints. During the 1540s Protestantism was probably spreading in the country at large. At Halifax, for example, the proportion of wills which leave out any mention of the Virgin and saints increased sharply during the period. Cromwell's protégé Marshall published a primer containing vehement attacks on prayer to the saints, and although it was banned, a situation in which such views were published by people in high favour, banned, and then published again could only encourage interest in them.

Dissolution of the Monasteries

In 1538, the Pope finally issued a bull deposing Henry, and charged Cardinal Pole with its execution. Henry retaliated by discovering a supposed Yorkist plot, and executing almost all of Cardinal Pole's relations. Early in 1539 there was an invasion scare. English ships were arrested in the Netherlands, and James of Scotland was drawn into the alliance against England. There was much preparation to meet invasion: 40 warships, as well as impounded merchantmen, were ready for action, the militia had been called out, and fortifications were being built along the coast.

As always, war preparations made the king short of money, but in 1539, as in the previous invasion scare of 1536, money came from a monastic dissolution. How closely the two may be connected, it is impossible to say, but much of the monastic stone was certainly used for fortifications. On the other hand, the second Dissolution had been at least contemplated for some time, since a number of the houses concerned had been induced to

[17] Dickens, *Reformation*, 184. The name was presumably pronounced Ghost-wick.

make 'voluntary' surrenders to the king's commissioners. Some abbots who refused found themselves in trouble, and the Abbot of Woburn was executed for treason, because he defended the papal primacy. The monks had foreseen the possibility of dissolution, and for some time they had been letting out their property on long leases, partly as a means of gaining favour, and partly to make their estates less attractive to the king. The second Act of Dissolution contained a clause that all leases made within a year of dissolution were to be void. None the less, most purchasers of monastic property found that it had been so thoroughly leased out that in many cases they had to go on receiving the rents which had been appropriate to the 1530s well into the seventeenth century. One estate subsequently bought by the Hampdens was on a monastic lease which only fell in just in time to help to meet the expenses of the Ship Money trial in 1637. It is an illustration of Tudor sense of family that so many people were eager to buy property on which no substantial return could be expected in their lifetimes.

The second dissolution abolished English monasticism, and thus raised very different issues from the first dissolution. The first, though it was indefensible on the strict ecclesiastical theory that all church property was inalienable for ever, could have been defended as an attempt to prune monasticism and confine it to those monks who had a genuine vocation. The second dissolution removed numerous monks who wanted to stay in their monasteries, and could only be defended on the theory that monasticism of any sort was bad. The Act of Dissolution made no such justification, and only argued that the abbots had surrendered their houses 'of their own free and voluntary minds, good wills and assents'. In some monasteries, this state of affairs could only be brought about by executing the existing abbot and choosing a compliant successor.

For a short while, the monastic lands made a vast addition to the Crown's income, but Henry, and even more Edward's government, lived off their capital and sold the lands to various purchasers. The Crown is perhaps less to be blamed for this than has sometimes been suggested. It acquired the land at the beginning, both of the most expensive of Henry VIII's French wars, and of one of the two worst periods of inflation in the century. It was also a period when the securing of political loyalty was particularly important. It was one of the first duties of the Crown to reward its servants, and the exceptional loyalty of mid-Tudor public servants during the period of religious changes may be connected with the rewards the Crown had to offer. Moreover, though some favoured servants got gifts of monastic land, the large majority of the lands were sold at a good market price, and at valuations which even took some account of entry fines, though the Crown's desire to gain support may account for the fact that from the middle 1540s many of them were sold on tenures which were not liable to wardship. The Crown at first retained an annual rent of a tenth of the value of the property, though by Elizabethan times inflation had made this insignificant. Moreover, the Crown did not sell all the land, and some was still available for purchasers as late as the 1590s. The Crown did make some mistakes. It sold almost all the land between Westminster and the City, which the growth of London later turned into one of the greatest speculative goldmines of the period. In the 1540s, however, urban property was not regarded as a very desirable investment. The Crown's worst mistake was that in addition to selling the lands, it also sold the monastic advowsons, and even, on some occasions, decided on economic grounds to sell advowsons in preference to lands. If the king had retained control of all the monastic livings, he could in a real sense have been Supreme Head of the church. As it was, control of the complexion of the national church passed largely into the hands of those individual gentry who bought the advowsons, and it is doubtful whether the Crown followed any particular policy in the disposal of the advowsons it did keep. The conviction that advowsons were real property was so strong that in Elizabeth's reign, even Catholics who were being harried in innumerable other ways kept control of their advowsons.

Not all the land remained in the hands of the people who first bought it. Wimbledon, a Canterbury manor which Cranmer was induced to surrender, is almost a political history in itself. It was granted in 1536 to Thomas Cromwell, reverted to the Crown at his fall, and was made part of the jointure of Queen Catherine Parr. It reverted to the Crown again on her death, and Mary gave it back to Canterbury. On Mary's death, it was recovered by the Crown, which kept it for some time, and then granted it to the Lord Chancellor, Sir Christopher Hatton. He in turn finally sold it to the eldest son of Lord Burghley, who kept it until the Civil War,[18] when it passed to one of Cromwell's Major-Generals. Most manors had a more stable history than this, and some remained for centuries with their original purchasers. Few of these were in any real sense 'new men'. Most of them were either professional Crown servants who were already building estates, or else established county gentry. There were only two estates built almost entirely of monastic property, those of the Russells Earls of Bedford, and of the Wriothesleys Earls of Southampton. It is also doubtful whether the possession of monastic property made many people feel they had a vested interest in Protestantism. Some families certainly reacted in this way, such as the Russells, the

[18] Du Boulay, F. R. H., *The Lordship of Canterbury* (1966), 325.

Grenvilles, and possibly the Drakes, and some had a sense of insecurity about monastic property. One man purchasing some at second hand in 1550 inserted a clause in the contract that if the Crown seized the property, the seller should return his purchase money.

But this insecurity could lead to other conclusions than Protestantism. One of the biggest monastic estates was built by Sir William Petre, Secretary of State, who, whatever his own religious opinions may have been, certainly left Catholic heirs. Petre was alarmed for his church property in Mary's reign, but his response was to get a private papal bull guaranteeing him in possession. The officers of the Court of Augmentations which administered the monastic lands were mostly Catholics, and some families such as the Earls of Worcester combined large monastic estates with determined Catholicism. It is also doubtful whether the transfer to lay landlords caused particular hardship to the tenants. There is little sign, either that the monasteries had ever been very different landlords from their neighbours, or that their successors much changed the methods of administration. It is even possible that tenants of former monastic property, being protected against inflation by long leases, were among the most economically fortunate people in the country. The dissolution contributed to the increasingly secular atmosphere of English society, but beyond this its effects are open to dispute.

The Statute of Proclamations

There is even more room for dispute about the Statute of Proclamations of 1539. The king had always been able to make Proclamations for matters which could not conveniently wait for Parliament, and people had been expected to obey them. How and by whom they were enforced is still uncertain, and the question how far they had the force of law had been worrying Cromwell for some years. Tudor and Stuart ideas on Proclamations are a subject on which it is hard to be precise. It was generally felt, both that the king had a right to make them and that they should not become an acceptable substitute for Acts of Parliament, but this comfortable ambiguity could only be preserved by moderation and a lack of definition. The 1539 Act is an attempt at definition: it recounts that some people have not been obeying Proclamations, to the dishonour of the king, 'who may full ill bear it', and gives the government statutory authority to punish breaches of Proclamations. We know that the Act was substantially amended during its passage, but we do not know how. Whether this Act is simply designed to clear up ambiguities, or whether it embodies the same principle of delegated legislation, giving statutory authority to Council regulations, which Cromwell had been using for some time, whether it is concerned with enforcement, or whether it is a serious attempt to give the king a legislative power without Parliament, we cannot say. The Act only remained in force till 1547, and its effects are obscure.

Wars and marriages

While these measures were before Parliament, the king was again considering marriage. One son was a doubtful security for the succession, and on Jane Seymour's death the Council advised Henry to face again the 'extreme adventure' of matrimony. For some time the king's ambassadors negotiated, somewhat handicapped by the fact that although Holbein sent back portraits of all the ladies concerned, Henry was unwilling to marry anyone he had not seen. Plans for French and Imperial alliances fell through, and finally, in 1540, a further threat of alliance between Francis and Charles led Henry, with some prompting from Cromwell, to decide on an alliance with the German Protestants. Anne, daughter of the Duke of Cleves, the chosen candidate, was accepted largely on the strength of flattering ambassadors' reports. When Henry saw her, he was dismayed, but Charles V was in Paris on a friendly visit at the time, so he married her. A few weeks later, when the situation had eased, Henry induced Cranmer to give him a nullity for non-consummation, and Anne settled into a comfortable retirement at Hampton Court.

Henry, again a widower, was taking an interest in Norfolk's niece, Catherine Howard. Whether because of Norfolk's increasing influence, or for some other reason still obscure, Henry suddenly decided in the summer of 1540 to get rid of Cromwell. In April 1540 Cromwell was raised to the peerage, but in June he was in the Tower accused of heresy and treason, and before the end of July he was executed, on the same day as Henry married Catherine Howard. A few months later, Henry was telling the French Ambassador that he regretted the whole affair.

He also found cause to regret his marriage, since Catherine certainly committed adultery after her marriage, and may have been secretly married to someone else before it. Henry, though grief-stricken, could find no alternative to having her executed. During these matrimonial misadventures, the alliance between Francis and Charles broke up, and Henry drifted back towards the occupation with which he began his reign—war against France in alliance with Charles V. There was some difficulty about Henry's attempts to induce Charles to recognize him as Supreme Head of the church, which Charles solved by recognizing him as 'Defender of the Faith, etc.'

France, as usual, was in alliance with Scotland. Henry was sufficiently eager to detach the Scots from the French alliance to arrange a visit to

York (the second and last visit by a Tudor to the north), in order to meet James of Scotland. James, however, failed to appear, and in 1542 England was at war with Scotland. An overwhelming victory over the Scots at Solway Moss led Henry to make exorbitant peace demands, but when a treaty was made, in 1543, it did no more than detach Scotland from the French alliance. Henry was thus able to invade France in 1543 without fearing attack from the north, but his campaign in France made little progress until the fall of Boulogne in 1544. At this stage, and when Henry had started another bloodthirsty campaign against Scotland, Francis and Charles made peace. All French resources were turned against England, the French fleet gained control of the Channel, and the English were left expecting imminent invasion. French raiding parties caused some damage in Seaford and the Isle of Wight, but the main invasion was prevented by a fortunate attack of dysentery in the French fleet. When peace was made, in 1546, Henry won French recognition as Supreme Head of the church, and the right to keep Boulogne for eight years. In the long term, these wars had little significance. Their expense provoked two Forced Loans, to which two citizens refused to contribute, and as a result were sent to fight in the front line against the Scots. The wars also contributed to the advancement of Edward Seymour Earl of Hertford, whose victories against the Scots confirmed him in the king's favour.

Catherine Parr

During these wars, Henry made his final marriage, to a twice-widowed woman of 31 called Catherine Parr. This time, he had not merely married a woman with Protestant connections, but one who became a zealous Protestant herself. She patronized clergy, held scripture classes with her ladies-in-waiting, and even published a tract on justification by faith, with a foreword by Cecil. She also had a talent for reconciliation, and Christmas 1543 was the first time all three of Henry's children met under one roof. She was on good terms with the leading Protestant sympathizers at Court, Hertford, Lisle (later Duke of Northumberland), and her brother the Marquis of Northampton.

The existence of such a knot of Protestants around the queen naturally alarmed Norfolk and Gardiner. By this time it was clear that Henry would not live much longer, and whichever faction was in control at the time Henry appointed the Regency Council would have a good chance of eliminating the other. The result is that faction strife on the Council appears to have grown bitterer. In 1543 Cranmer nearly fell, and in 1544 Gardiner's enemies nearly succeeded in removing him. At the last moment Gardiner saved himself, but his nephew and secretary was executed for believing in the Pope. It was then in the name of self-preservation, as well as of true religion, that Gardiner in 1546 tried to sway the faction-fight by attacking Catherine Parr for heresy. He appears to have picked a moment when Henry had grown impatient with Catherine's tendency to discuss theology to warn him that he was nourishing a serpent in his bosom, to complain that although a woman, she was presuming to instruct the Supreme Head, and to offer to draw up articles accusing her of heresy and treason. Henry agreed to sign the bill of articles against her, and plans were started to arrest members of her entourage for questioning. At this stage, Catherine appears to have heard of the charges, and threw herself on Henry's mercy. She prudently picked as the key charge to refute the accusation that she had presumed to instruct the Supreme Head. By the time she had convinced Henry that she had only talked theology to occupy him in his illness, and that she thought it 'preposterous' that a wife should instruct her husband, Henry lost interest in the details of her beliefs, and told her that 'perfect friends we are now again as at any time heretofore'. When Lord Chancellor Wriothesley arrived soon afterwards to begin the arrests, he found himself greeted by the king with shouts of 'knave! arrant knave! beast! and fool!'

The result of the incident was to strengthen Catherine's position, and weaken Gardiner's. Shortly afterwards, Henry decided to arrange an 'exchange' of lands with Gardiner, who acquired the distinction of being the only one of Henry's subjects who ever refused such a request. It is not surprising that Henry left Gardiner out of the Regency Council, nor that when asked whether he had forgotten him, he said, 'I could myself use him, and rule him to all manner of purposes . . . but so will you never do'.[19] During 1546, Norfolk's son Surrey, who had a dubious claim to the throne, very imprudently began to use the royal arms, which gave occasion for a similar attempt to oust Norfolk from the King's favour, which was successful. The whole story of the attack on Norfolk is obscure, and it can only be said that he was saved from execution at the last moment by Henry's death, and thus, by a few hours, became the only one of his servants to serve him from beginning to end of the reformation and survive.

Henry VIII's will

Meanwhile, the Council was sometimes meeting in Hertford's house, and he was assured of a strong position in the Regency Council. Henry probably remembered that when he had been reported to be dying in 1537, the Council had been split between supporters of Edward and Mary. Of all the Councillors, none could be more thoroughly trusted to be loyal

[19] Scarisbrick, 480, 489.

to Edward's succession than Hertford, who was his uncle. This is probably why, when Henry ultimately made his will, in December 1546, he delivered it for safe keeping to Hertford.

The will suggests that he had not developed any sympathy for Protestantism.[20] He commended his soul to the Virgin and saints, and left money for Masses for his soul 'while the world shall endure', and still maintained that a man was justified by works 'if he have leisure'. He asked to be buried with Jane Seymour, and settled the succession on Edward, Mary, and Elizabeth, in that order, regardless of any question about their legitimacy, though with provisos, that Mary and Elizabeth should only succeed if they married with the assent of the Council, and that if he had a daughter by Catherine Parr or any subsequent wife, she should take precedence over both of them. If all three of his children died without heirs, Henry excluded the Scottish line from the succession, and settled it on the Greys, grand-daughters of his sister Mary and the Duke of Suffolk. The Council appointed for the Regency was not entirely Protestant: Cranmer, Hertford, and Lisle, the leading Protestant sympathizers, were balanced by Wriothesley, Tunstal, and Sir Anthony Browne, who were Catholic sympathizers. The majority are hard to identify on either side. What swung the balance, and created the effect of a Protestant Regency Council, was not any decision by Henry, but the fact that in the absence of Norfolk and Gardiner the Protestants were the stronger members, and the key neutrals, Russell and Paget, chose to side with them. England was then left with a Protestant regency council, and a Protestant king as well, since Edward's tutors, who were probably chosen by Catherine Parr, were giving him strong Protestant sympathies. On Henry's death, in January 1547, effective power passed to Edward Seymour, Earl of Hertford, who almost immediately took the titles of Duke of Somerset and Lord Protector.

III THE REIGN OF EDWARD VI, 1547–1553

Weakness of the government

Pole and the Pope reacted to the news of Henry VIII's death by advising Charles V to invade England to put Mary on the throne. Nothing came of this move, and there was no Marian faction on the Council to support it. Nevertheless, both the Edwardian and Marian governments suffered constantly from the fact that their obvious successors were expected to reverse their policies. Such prudent politicians as Paget had to keep an eye to their retreat, and many lesser people might think opposition worth

[20] For the text of his will, see Rymer, *Foedera* xv. 110–16.

continuing if it were the way to favour in the next reign. Edward was aged nine when his father died, and it would be at least seven years before he could be expected to end his minority or beget a son. Plans to unite England and Scotland by marrying him to Mary Queen of Scots, though they were supported by campaigns which the Scots called 'the rough wooing', had come to nothing, and Edward remained unmarried to the end of his reign. Mary Tudor had already shown considerable powers of resistance, and the Council never had any prospect of arranging a marriage for her which they would consider suitable. They spent most of the reign trying to stop her setting a public example to other Catholics by hearing Mass.

The Edwardian government also had all the normal disadvantages of minority rule. The necessity of collective leadership meant a government liable to be indecisive, and policies which might be reversed by intrigues shifting one or two votes on the Council. Faction could also be stimulated by the fact that government patronage was in the hands of those most likely to benefit from it. The Duke of Somerset, and his secretary Thynne, the founder of Longleat, built themselves immense personal fortunes, and for the first time gifts of former church property exceeded sales. Anyone who did not get the share of gifts to which he felt entitled had a standing temptation to help another nobleman to supreme power. It is not surprising that during these two reigns there was considerable extension of bastard feudal retaining. Nor, when every leader wanted to bring his own supporters into the Council, and those who were left out had the power to be troublesome, is it surprising that the Council grew steadily, until by the end of Mary's reign membership was in the region of fifty. Such a body ceased to be an effective decision-making force.

On a lower level, the taking of perquisites by officials increased to a point at which it can certainly be described as corruption. It was also necessary for a minority government to seek popularity with someone. This may be why many of Henry's measures, the Six Articles, the Statute of Proclamations, and the Treason Act, were repealed at the beginning of the reign. A few years later, the government again found it needed the protection of a treason law of the Henrician type. Moreover, few people were prepared to give the respect and submission to a group of noblemen that they would give to the king. When Gardiner chose to argue that the Royal Supremacy could only be exercised by the king in person, and not by a council during a minority, he had picked an argument which, if constitutionally dubious, was at least politically shrewd.

In addition to its inevitable weaknesses, the Edwardian government was accident-prone from the start. It was not the government's fault that it inherited power in the middle of one of the two most dramatic periods of price rises in the century, and at a time when Henry VIII had almost bankrupted the government by his French and Scottish wars. Somerset continued Henry's policy, and though he won a great victory over the Scots at Pinkie in 1547, it remained impossible to conquer Scotland because of shortage of carts. Somerset also continued Henry's method of meeting deficits, by debasing the coinage. Henry had done this in 1526 and in 1544. Somerset repeated the process in 1547 and 1549. The silver content of the coins was sharply reduced, and an element of brass put in instead. Unfortunately for the government, most people believed that coinage, instead of having a nominal value, had only the intrinsic value of the metal in it. Latimer, who had a social conscience, preached against the new coinage before the king, saying he would exchange a shilling of the new coinage for fourpence of the old, and no one could afford to stop him. The only people who could be forced to accept the new coins at their face value were the government. The poor reputation of the new coinage accelerated price rises which had been rapid enough before. As discontent grew, such men as Parkyn in his Yorkshire parish were quite ready to argue that inflation was caused by God's wrath against the government's religious policy.

The period was one of increasing economic agitation. Unemployment was probably growing, and vagrancy and begging certainly were. Though Somerset was believed at the time to have sympathy with the poor, he shared the general horror of vagrants. The most probable cause of increasing vagrancy is population increase in a period when the supply of land and of jobs did not increase in proportion. The common feeling was that if vagabonds and beggars were able-bodied, the reason why they did not work must be that they preferred scrounging. Ridley, now Bishop of London, was capable of some sympathy with vagabonds, but almost the only Englishman of note with whom he shared this distinction was Shakespeare. There were some faint stirrings of the idea later commonly used, of levying a parish rate to finance compulsory work for vagrants, but the commonest reactions were to use whips and stocks. In 1547 Somerset's government passed an Act to the effect that vagabonds should be made slaves for two years. The Act was never enforced, but it testifies to the government's attitude.

The government could not be blamed for vagrancy, which it inherited, nor for the violent attacks of plague in 1550, and of the 'sweating sickness' in 1551. Sweating sickness was an abrupt fever, with which a man could be 'merry at dinner and dead at supper'. It is now thought possible that it may have been a violent form of influenza. These epidemics caused a general tendency to look for scapegoats, for whose sins God might be punishing the kingdom. In a situation of religious division, many blamed these evils on the sins of the other side. Some also blamed the perennial scapegoat of enclosure. The growth of the printing press and of popular preaching made it much easier to arouse public feeling. In 1549, Hales, one of those who put the blame on landlords, was put in charge of a new commission to suppress unlawful enclosures. The commission appears to have aroused public feeling, and produced a number of anticipatory riots against unpopular enclosures, but it had little other effect.

Perhaps the worst of the government's troubles was one due largely to circumstances beyond their control: the crash of Antwerp in 1551. During the early part of the reign, the cloth market in Antwerp had been booming, but in 1551 the market collapsed, probably because it was glutted. Trade fell by 15 per cent the first year, and by another 20 per cent the second, with the result that many merchants went bankrupt, there was widespread unemployment in the clothing districts, and customs revenue dropped sharply. Some blame may be put on the government for manipulating the exchanges in a way which raised the Merchant Adventurers' prices, but in the main, the crash was due to European economic difficulties.

In the long run, the crash may have been good for England, since it produced the beginnings of the search for wider markets, which would not have begun while there was a guaranteed market just across the North Sea. In the same year, Thomas Wyndham made the first recorded voyage to Morocco, and within a few years trades to Guinea, the Levant, and Russia were beginning, and were helped by royal warships. The Russia expedition of Mary's reign, which was designed to find the north-east passage to China, was organized by the government's initiative, and financed by Arundel, Bedford, Pembroke, and Cecil, among others. These were very small beginnings, which did almost nothing to relieve the economic situation before the 1590s, and very little after that, but in the long term they were among the most important things happening at this time.

Religious changes

Such was the background against which the government tried to carry out its religious policy, and it helps to explain why one of the first official acts was the confiscation of the endowments of the chantries. This Act attacked the whole concept of chantries, and justified their dissolution on the ground that they were superstitious. It also raised many complicated questions about schools, hospitals, and other institutions run jointly with chantries. Many schools were refounded, and became King Edward's schools, though for a while there was enough threat to schools to produce a powerful sermon in their defence from Lever at Paul's Cross.[21] The reign was also one of new educational foundations: the desire to promote sound understanding of religion, and thereby to strengthen one's own party, could produce a concern for education. Moreover, it began to attract much of the impulse to charitable benefaction which had previously gone to monasteries or to chantries. The attack on the chantries themselves was carried through successfully, and supplied the government with a much-needed financial windfall, and theologians with an opportunity to attempt the eradication of the doctrine of Purgatory. Some people, who believed their ancestors' or wives' stay in Purgatory could be shortened by Masses in private, may have been bitterly offended by the Dissolution, but their numbers were probably small.

From the beginning of the reign, persecution against most sorts of Protestant was much eased. The result was a large influx of foreign Protestant refugees avoiding persecution in other countries. Many of these, when the situation in their own countries changed, were able to offer reciprocal hospitality to English Protestants in the next reign. This immigration brought great intellectual and economic benefits to England. It provided the beginning of those communities of immigrant clothworkers whose skills kept the English cloth trade alive through the difficult years at the end of the century. It also gave Cranmer the support of some able foreign theologians. Martin Bucer of Strasbourg was made Regius Professor of Divinity at Cambridge, and Peter Martyr, one of the small but select band of Italian Protestants, at Oxford. Both of them contributed much to the new liturgies, and to the job of spreading and refining the new doctrines in the universities. Like many others, they cannot be classified by the convenient labels of 'Lutheran' or 'Calvinist'. Peter Martyr also scandalized some Oxford fellows by bringing his wife to live with him in Christ Church, and Bucer produced a typical mid-Tudor reaction from the Vice-Chancellor of Cambridge, Andrew Perne. In 1550, Perne presided over Bucer's installation as Regius Professor. In the next reign, Mary's government posthumously condemned Bucer, and had his bones dug up and burnt. The ceremonies were presided over by that year's Vice-Chancellor, who was again Perne. In 1560, the Elizabethan government decided to rehabilitate Bucer. His ashes were given ceremonial burial, and the Vice-Chancellor duly presided. By coincidence, he was again Perne. On the other hand, when Archbishop Parker threatened the liberties of

[21] For a recent discussion of this vexed question, see Joan Simon, *Education and Society in Tudor England* (1966), 223–44.

the university by claiming jurisdiction over a university dispute, Perne's was one of the loudest protests raised.

Some of the immigrants were allowed to form their own independent churches, of French, Dutch, or German Protestants. Others travelled about the country preaching. John Knox, who was exiled by the continued Catholicism of Scotland, preached in many places in the north of England. Not for the last time, the government found it could often convert people from popery only by employing clergy who converted them to a Protestantism more extreme than they would have wished. Knox was one of those who helped start the belief, later characteristic of Puritans, that no form of worship was justified unless it was expressly commanded in the Bible. When Bishop Tunstal, still vainly trying to stem the tide, summoned Knox for his attacks on the Mass, Knox replied, 'all service invented by the brain of man in the religion of God, without his express command, is idolatry. The mass is invented by the brain of man without the command of God: therefore it is idolatry.'[22]

The Mass, and the ceremonies attached to it, became one of the key points of argument of Edward's reign. Almost at once the government permitted communion in both kinds, but when the doctrine of transubstantiation was debated among the bishops, in 1548, their opinions produced an almost endless variety. Two very different pictures of the purpose of the service were involved, as well as many views on the question of Christ's presence in the sacrament. In the most old-fashioned view, the key point was the offering of a sacrifice by the priest. He was behind a rood screen, facing the altar with 'his hinder parts to the people', as Protestants put it, and officiated in Latin, which the congregation normally did not understand. Few members of the congregation received the sacrament, as distinct from being present, and if they did, it was only the bread.

In the other view, or collection of views, the separateness and special powers of the priest were diminished, and congregational understanding and participation emphasized. The word 'priest' was dropped by most Protestants, since a priest was one who offered a sacrifice, and they believed that Christ 'by his one oblation of himself once offered' had made a sufficient sacrifice, which could not in any way be repeated. The minister was to officiate in a language 'understanded of the people', facing them, and not behind a rood screen, and the people were to receive communion (in both kinds) as often as possible. For some Protestants, the faith of the recipient, and not the consecrating powers of the priest, were the key to the service. Few English Protestants travelled all the way

---

[22] Dickens, *Reformation*, 235.

down the road to the Zwinglian doctrine of the sacrament, in which Christ was not present in any way, and the service was simply commemorative. On the other hand, few Catholics held a doctrine of transubstantiation as literally material as was suggested by the Zwinglians' favourite question, whether Christ's eyes, nails, and teeth (and sometimes other portions of His anatomy) were separately present in the sacrament. Between these extremes, there were a great variety of views on the nature of Christ's presence in the sacrament, each of them implying a slightly different emphasis in the service.

Some of the early changes were brought about by popular initiative in some parishes. Rood screens were occasionally torn down, and Parkyn's parishioners attacked the keeping of a reserved sacrament with such irreverent words that Parkyn felt that, but that Christ's mercy was so great, he would have expected the earth to swallow them. Attacks on images, candles, and other forms of ceremonial religion, were backed by the government. The separateness of the priesthood was again reduced by the legalization of clerical marriage. In many cases, from the archbishop downwards, this permission regularized a situation which already existed. For some clergy, on the other hand, marriage in middle life created difficulties. Ponet, who gained the bishopric of Winchester when Gardiner was deprived of it, had the misfortune to discover that his 'wife' was already married to a Nottingham butcher, who appeared at his episcopal palace brandishing a meat-axe. Many clergy appear to have been surprisingly willing to discard their wives in the next reign, and Foxe the martyrologist says that this was because they were disillusioned with matrimony. For some of them, the experience may have been very uncomfortable. There are also cases of clergy, and former monks and nuns, who are found remarried in Elizabeth's reign to the people from whom they had been separated under Mary.

The first big change of the reign was the publication of an English Prayer Book in 1549. Stephen Gardiner ingeniously interpreted its version of the communion service as implying transubstantiation, but the whole order and form of the service did not suggest it. The Book was a work of committee theology, and therefore avoided clear statements on many points of doctrine. The significant point was the fact that all parishes were commanded to use a vernacular service, and so far as can be discovered it seems that most of them did. Many Protestants felt that the Book did not go far enough, since, for example, it preserved the word 'altar', and thereby refrained from denying a doctrine of sacrifice in the communion service. On the other hand, for traditionalists, it was the first big change in religion as it appeared in their local parish churches.

Rebellion and Coup d'État

It is unfortunately impossible to give any general picture of reactions to the Prayer Book. It was immediately followed by two rebellions, of which the first, in Devon and Cornwall, was largely directed against religious change, and described the new service as 'like a Christmas game'. The other rebellion, led by Ket, was in Norfolk, and the rebels, whose grievances were economic, thought well enough of the Prayer Book to use it for their camp services. Which of these is the more typical reaction, it is impossible to say.

These rebellions created a serious problem for the government. Lord Russell (with Coverdale, the Biblical translator, as his chaplain) was sent to suppress the western rebellion, and Lord Lisle, now Earl of Warwick, to suppress the Norfolk rebellion. Thus, at a time when his enemies were gaining strength on the Council, Somerset put a large force of foreign mercenary soldiers under the command of his chief rival. Warwick, having quickly suppressed the Norfolk rebellion, planned a *coup d'état*. He complained of a denial of grants and favours to himself, and succeeded in convincing Wriothesley and others that he was rebelling in the Catholic cause: rumours were running around London that he intended to make Mary regent. The attitude of most of the Council was uncertain, and Somerset, at Windsor, had possession of the king. If Russell and Herbert, commanding the troops in the west, had joined him, he might have survived. Somerset, however, broke all the Tudor canons by appealing to the common people for support. Russell and Herbert probably felt the horror they expressed at this action, and for whatever reason, they chose to support Warwick.

Protestantism under Northumberland

Warwick became Duke of Northumberland, and Somerset was executed a year later, when he seemed unwilling to accept the new state of affairs. One young courtier congratulated another on having been sufficiently 'Machiavellist' to foresee Somerset's later opposition.[23] The new government introduced some changes: it ceased war, and abandoned Boulogne to the French. It also abandoned Somerset's apparent championship of the poor, temporarily repealing all the laws against enclosure. But in religion, it soon became apparent that the new government would be more Protestant than its predecessor. Coverdale was sent back to the west as Bishop of Exeter to begin the task of instructing west country papists. Cranmer remained in office, and most of the Henrician Catholic

[23] Conyers Read, i. 72.

bishops who survived went to the Tower. Wriothesley and Northumberland's other Catholic supporters were discarded. In 1550, Ridley, Bishop of London, was allowed to begin the work of replacing altars with communion tables. The communion table, placed in the middle of the church for the parishioner to communicate, was right at the other end of the sacramental spectrum from the altar for the offering of sacrifice, shut away at the east end.

When Hooper, one of the more radical Protestants, was chosen for the bishopric of Gloucester, the Council showed signs of backing him in the resulting dispute with Cranmer and Ridley. Hooper was not willing to wear the full traditional vestments which were still demanded of a bishop, and the resulting dispute with Ridley is worth describing in some detail, since the issue remained a live one until 1642, and was rarely better argued on either side. Ridley's case was not that the vestments were theologically necessary. He thought that the wearing of vestments was a matter theologically indifferent, but that the government had authority to enforce regulations in indifferent matters, and that for the sake of political order, these regulations should be uniformly obeyed. For Ridley, the question was not one of theology, but of political authority. In this, he is the authentic forerunner of the line of Anglican archbishops from Parker down to Laud. Hooper thought the vestments were popish, and that they belonged to an 'Aaronic' idea of the priesthood which he rejected—set apart and magical, rather than teaching and preaching. He thought that indifferent things should only be admitted if it was certain that they were not harmful, which was something he could not say for vestments. In this, as in sacramental doctrine, one of the most explosive points was the nature and position of the priesthood, or ministry.

Hooper finally gave way enough to wear the vestments for consecration, and set about the Herculean task of dispelling ignorance in his diocese. He wrote to Cecil of the people's 'hunger for God's word', but he found that his diocesan clergy were unable to preach it. Of 311 whom he examined, he found that 168 did not know the Ten Commandments. He did an immense amount of work, even presiding in his own diocesan court, but his attempt to grapple with the real problems of the Reformation was unsuccessful. The state of the church's endowments did not permit a real preaching ministry. Some ministers could read the Edwardian *Book of Homilies*, which contained sound Protestant doctrine, and they could leave those of their parishioners who were eager for knowledge to search the Bible on their own. *The Homilies*, however, were over-optimistic in supposing that 'presumption and arrogancy is the mother of all error, and humility needeth to fear no error:... Therefore the humble man may search any truth boldly in Scripture without any danger of error.'[24] Individual interpretation produced individual results, and after Hooper's failure in the few years at his disposal to absorb his type of enthusiasm into the official church structure, it was almost inevitable that hunger for preaching would be met by unofficial endowments, and that unofficial endowments would produce unofficial doctrine.

In official circles, Protestant doctrine was still advancing. In 1552, a new Prayer Book was produced, and supported with a new Act of Uniformity, prescribing penalties for not going to church. It made considerable alterations in the order of the items which made up the Communion service, moving it away from the old doctrine of sacrifice. The new formula for the administration of Communion, 'take and eat this in remembrance that Christ died for thee, and feed on him in thy heart with faith and thanksgiving', did not necessarily imply a denial of Christ's presence, but there was nothing in it with which even a Zwinglian need quarrel. Cranmer was in correspondence with continental Protestant leaders about the possibility of pan-Protestant union, and he was at last occupied with the revision of the canon law demanded by Henry's Act for the Submission of the Clergy. In 1552, he produced the Forty-Two Articles, a comprehensive and thoroughly Protestant statement of doctrine which formed the basis for Elizabeth's Thirty-Nine Articles.

What effect all these changes had on the public at large it is hard to say. Edward's reign was certainly crucial in the growth of popular Protestantism, but since most of our knowledge of popular opinion comes from heresy prosecutions, we cannot trace the spread of doctrines which were not prosecuted. The changes probably strengthened general irreverence for ceremony. The Yorkshire publican who was tried in 1554 for allowing 'evil disposed persons' to gather in his tavern and 'rail against the ... most holy sacrament'[25] may have represented a much more usual attitude in the first year of Mary's reign than in the last year of Henry's. A quarter of all the wills in Marian Yorkshire are cast in a non-traditional form, omitting the Virgin and the saints, and before the Marian persecution grew strong, in 1555, the proportion is higher. Occasionally even a yeoman might make a will involving a lengthy exposition of justification by faith, supported by scriptural quotations. Many wills suggest that their authors were in a theological muddle, but by Edward's death there was certainly a minority of convinced Protestants which, though less strong than, for example, the body of French Protestants, could not be rooted out overnight.

[24] *Sermons or Homilies* (S.P.C.K. 1938), 7.
[25] Dickens, *Lollards and Protestants*, 223.

By the end of 1552 all the Council were becoming worried by the king's health, and Sir William Petre's bills to the armourer were rising sharply. If Mary succeeded to the throne all reform would stop, and many Councillors might be imprisoned. The Duke of Northumberland saw his power drawing to a close and formed an alternative plan. He married his son to Lady Jane Grey, who had a remote claim on the throne as the granddaughter of Henry VIII's sister, and on Edward's death, in 1553, induced the Council to agree to her proclamation as Queen Jane under a document popularly known as 'King Edward VI's testament and the Duke of Northumberland's will'. Some zealous Protestants supported this move. Most of the Council, however, were waiting to see how events turned out, and they turned out with an overwhelming wave of popular enthusiasm for Mary. East Anglia, where she was, was one of the more Protestant areas, but it was so overwhelmingly in her favour that Northumberland, who had gone out to arrest her, gave up and proclaimed her himself. This enthusiasm for Mary was not primarily religious: many known Protestants joined it. Whether it was due to hatred of Northumberland, devotion to the principle of legitimacy, desire to join the bandwagon, or simply to fear of civil war, we will probably never know. Whatever the cause, it was sufficient to bring Northumberland to the scaffold, and Mary to undisputed possession of the throne.

IV THE REIGN OF MARY I, 1553–1558

When Mary succeeded to the throne, in the summer of 1553, she was a single woman of 36 and her heir was a sister widely reputed to be Protestant. In this fact was her sole serious, and ultimately insuperable, disadvantage. To get his divorce, Henry had to bastardize Mary, and so destroyed her prospects of making a suitable marriage. In Edward's reign there was no prospect of agreement about her marriage between her and the Council, and it was not until her accession to the throne that she could be regarded as fully eligible.

All the other difficulties of Mary's reign are normally seen with historical hindsight, and therefore are greatly exaggerated. Historians are often more interested in developments with long-term significance than in those which turned out to have none, and as a result, most of the best research on Mary's reign has been done on the opposition to her policy. It therefore becomes dangerously easy to portray the reign as if it consisted of nothing but opposition. Much discussion of the reign is uncomfortably near the verdict of *1066 and All That*, that the reign was 'a bad thing, since England is bound to be C. of E., so all the executions were wasted'. In 1553, there was every reason to suppose that, given time, Mary would be successful in restoring England to Catholicism. The body of committed English Protestants was much smaller than in France, the southern Netherlands, or Bavaria, and all these were turned by persistent government persecution into Catholic countries, and have remained so to this day. It is true that Mary was starting late, but in Bavaria the eradication of Protestants was not begun till 1570, and yet was successful. As John Stuart Mill said, 'wherever persecution was persisted in, it was successful. In Spain, Italy, Flanders, the Austrian empire, Protestantism was rooted out, and most likely, would have been so in England, had Queen Mary lived, or Queen Elizabeth died.'[26]

Administrative reform

Mary was never subservient to the Pope, and was as ready to defend royal rights against him as any other Catholic sovereign. She refused to abandon the title of the imperial crown, and firmly resisted persistent papal pressure to repeal *Praemunire*. In 1557, when she was faced with a politically hostile Pope, she refused to admit his legate, and kept him waiting at Calais in the old style. She was no more neglectful of the rights of her crown than such rulers as Edward I and Edward III had been.

Much of her government, moreover, was quietly efficient. Lord Treasurer Winchester and Sir Thomas Gresham, the men most responsible for financial policy throughout the mid-Tudor period, stayed on, and had a very successful reign. Some check on administrative corruption seems to have been achieved, and for the Court of Wards, the reign has been described as 'one of the most successful phases of its Tudor history'.[27] A series of commissions investigated the administration of Crown lands, and even began to consider the crucial question of the Crown's entry fines. A new Book of Rates was produced, and the imposition of proper duties on cloth, in 1558, was one of the most important financial achievements of the century. The persistent concern with luxury imports (which enriched the language with the words 'jeans' (Genoa) and 'millinery' (Milan)), produced an Act of restriction in 1553, which may have provided some protection for the home industries which were slowly fostered by Cecil in the next reign. The 1554 Act for repair of the roads was the first attempt to tackle this problem on a national level. After Edward's reign, the impression is of a government in good working order.

The only government institution which is a possible exception is the most important – the Privy Council. Mary seems to have had little idea

[26] Mill, J. S., *On Liberty* (1912), 37.
[27] Hurstfield, J., 'Corruption and Reform under Edward VI and Mary', *E.H.R.* (1953), 29.

whom she could trust, which is perhaps not surprising, and to have imported almost everyone into the Council because she found it hard to prefer one group of people to another. Almost all the old Edwardian Council stayed on, since the queen could not afford their opposition. She also brought in a few members of her household, who had been with her in adversity, and a large number of the old peerage. The two leading factions in the Council were those of Gardiner, who was restored to his bishopric and made Lord Chancellor, and of Paget, who as usual had an eye to the future. Unfortunately, during the two previous reigns, Mary had found that the only people she could really trust were the Imperial ambassadors, and, surrounded as she was by Councillors who had served her father, she found this habit hard to break. Simon Renard, the Imperial ambassador, who was a very able man, told his master that she was 'good, easily influenced, inexpert in worldly matters, and a novice all round',[28] and set out to make the most of the situation. If Mary ever had a chief minister, Renard has the best claim to the title. This, of course, created jealousies among other Councillors, and pushed the French ambassador, de Noailles, into the arms of the opposition. Any plan to impede Mary had a good chance of French support, which was often ably managed. The result was a massive, faction-ridden Council, and continual uncertainty about the control of policy.

Mary began cautiously. Cranmer and Ridley were imprisoned for supporting Lady Jane Grey, but there were few victimizations, and at first even Jane herself was allowed to stay alive – a remarkable piece of clemency. The treason laws were brought back to what they had been before 1534, and her first Parliament showed no objection to repealing the Edwardian legislation and returning to the situation in 1547. Mary had originally wanted to borrow Sir Thomas More's argument that the Royal Supremacy was void because it was contrary to the law of God, but Gardiner persuaded her that she would have to have it repealed by Parliament, thereby unwittingly strengthening Parliament's claim to authority in religion. For the first two years of her reign she left the question of the Royal Supremacy in abeyance, calling herself 'Defender of the Faith, etc.'

The problem of marriage

The most urgent question facing Mary was marriage, which she appears to have intended to settle before provoking any agitation over religion. She had to marry someone, if she did not want her policy to cease with her death, but though she has generally been criticized for

[28] Loades, D. M., *Two Tudor Conspiracies* (1965), 6.

marrying the wrong man, it is hard to see who the right man might have been. She could marry either a subject or a foreigner. In principle, the general opinion was in favour of her marrying a subject, but it is likely that as soon as any individual subject was named, even in rumour, there would have been protests against him. So long as no subject was named, anyone might hope the chosen man would be among his own friends or patrons, but since every subject belonged to some group or faction, his elevation to the post of king could bitterly offend his rivals.

Two subjects were named in speculation, Courtenay and Pole. Both had royal blood, being of Yorkist lines, but neither would have been likely to command much support. Courtenay had spent most of his life in the Tower, and his lack of worldly knowledge and discretion could have been alarming in a king. Pole, though already a cardinal, was only in deacon's orders, and therefore might have been free to marry, but the spectacle of a cardinal as king would have been an open invitation to the forces of anti-clericalism, especially since he had spent much of the past two reigns trying to persuade foreigners to invade England. If she married a foreigner, she would have to choose alliance with either France or Spain, and so would take on enmity with the other, and risk jealousy of foreign influence in the country. Like her sister after her, Mary could expect to find almost universal opinion in favour of her marriage, and almost equally universal protests against any candidate she chose. Neither her sister nor Mary Queen of Scots found the problem of marriage any easier than she did.

It is possible that her mind was already made up when she came to the throne. When her first Parliament asked her to marry within the realm, she interrupted the Speaker, saying that 'to force her to take a husband who was not to her liking would be to cause her death, for if she were married against her will, she would not live three months, and would have no children'. Apart from the imprudent implication that no Englishman could be to her liking, this speech also illustrates that she was less dignified in using a 'poor weak woman' pose than her sister. Elizabeth, faced with a similar petition from the Commons in 1566, replied that 'I thank God I am endowed with such qualities that if I were turned out of the realm in my petticoat, I were able to live in any place in Christendom'[29]—which, though completely irrelevant, probably made a much better impression.

It was soon clear that Mary's choice would be in favour of Philip of Spain, son of Charles V, and heir to his dominions in Spain, Italy, the Netherlands, and America, though not to the Empire. Charles, who was

[29] Neale, *Parliaments*, i. 149; Loades, op. cit., 41.

in the process of abdication, supported the match, and sent his son many helpful pieces of advice about the need to conciliate English nationalism. Gardiner and most of the Council were opposed to the plan, and tried to discourage it, but they could not agree on any alternative. The marriage only had two supporters in high places: one, of course, was Renard, and the other was Paget, who set out to become Philip's chief supporter on the Council. This may not have been pure cynicism, since Paget may have regarded the friendship of the ruler of Antwerp as worth more than any purely sentimental considerations. The debate did not last long: by October 1553, a few months after coming to the throne, Mary had given Renard her formal promise to marry Philip. Over a week later, she told the Council.

Charles V, among others, had been worried by the possible reactions to this marriage. This may help to explain why the English managed to win such improbably favourable terms in the marriage treaty. Philip was not to involve England in his wars against France (which was the chief thing he wanted from the marriage), and he was not to take the jewels, ships, or guns of the kingdom out of the realm without Mary's consent. He was not to be consulted about the filling of English offices, but was to have a 'convenient' number of Englishmen in his own household. He was to be king during Mary's lifetime, but was to have no rights in the kingdom after her death. Philip's son by a previous marriage was to inherit Spain, but a son by Mary would inherit the Netherlands and Franche Comté. This clause might not have been kept, but that Spain should so much as discuss parting with the Netherlands was a portent, and perhaps the brightest prospect for English merchants of the whole century. From the English point of view, the marriage was a good one. It was basically the same scheme as the marriage Henry VIII had been planning between Mary and Philip's father in 1525. Until the revolt of the Netherlands in the next reign, it was still easy to regard Spain as England's natural ally against France, and this was no more likely to provoke xenophobia than any other foreign marriage.

Wyatt's rebellion

It remains to ask why the marriage did provoke xenophobia to the point of producing a major rebellion immediately after the treaty was signed. The rebellion had been carefully planned, to break out simultaneously in Kent, Devon, Herefordshire, and the Midlands. Sir Thomas Wyatt, who led the Kentish rebellion, had been experimenting since 1549 with the attempt to organize a militia, and it may have been this scheme, originally designed for the benefit of a Protestant government, which enabled him to turn out a well-armed force. The old Duke of Norfolk, released from the Tower at the end of Edward's reign, was sent out to suppress his last rebellion, but found that many of his forces deserted to Wyatt, who got as far as Westminster before he could be stopped. At the last moment the citizens of London rallied to Mary, and Wyatt was brought to a halt at the closed gates of the City. The other branches of the conspiracy were muffled by premature detection. The Duke of Suffolk, who was responsible for the Midland plans, was summoned to the Council. He refused to come, saying that if he took refuge among his tenants, no one would dare fetch him. The Council, however, sent the Earl of Huntingdon, his chief rival for local power, who easily suppressed him. The Devon conspirators, most of whom had been prominent in suppressing the 1549 rebellion, produced no effective rising, though Exeter was torn with fearsome rumours about the Spaniards coming to ravish their wives and daughters. The government's alarm was largely because its chief source of information was rumours started by the conspirators. These conspiracies might have raised much more support than they did. When Wyatt was executed, Londoners soaked their handkerchiefs in his blood for relics, and when Sir Nicholas Throckmorton was tried before a London jury, he became one of the few Tudor subjects acquitted of treason charges. It was perhaps more serious that Arundel and Shrewsbury, two of the most powerful peers on the Council, feigned sickness and withdrew from Court, and Elizabeth ignored a summons to Court. The question of Elizabeth's complicity was the one which worried the government most. She was sent to the Tower, and Wyatt was persistently tortured for evidence against her, but he revealed nothing, and her complicity could not be proved.

In fact Elizabeth did know of the rising, though it is doubtful whether she actually supported it. Lord Russell, later second Earl of Bedford, later admitted to carrying Wyatt's letters to her, and in 1566, when exhorted by the Commons to name a successor, Elizabeth gave what is probably the best informed summary of the whole business:

I am sure there was not one of them [the Commons] that ever was a second person, as I have been, and have tasted of the practices against my sister, who I would to God were alive again. I had great occasions to hearken to their motions, of whom some of them are in the Common house. But when friends fall out, truth doth appear, according to the old proverb; and were it not for my honour, their knavery should be known. There were occasions in me at that time. I stood in danger of my life, my sister was so incensed against me: I did differ from her in religion, and so was sought for divers ways. And so shall never be my successor.[30]

[30] Neale, *Parliaments*, i. 148.

It is interesting to discover that Elizabeth thought the rising was essentially about religion, since Dr. Loades, who has made the most thorough recent study of it, has concluded that it was essentially anti-Spanish, and that religion played a very small part in it. It is certainly true that some of the conspirators were Catholic or Catholic sympathizers, and that Wyatt and some of the others had played a prominent part in proclaiming Mary, although they knew she was Catholic. The only change between 1553 and 1554 was the Spanish marriage, which was the main point of the conspirators' propaganda. However, a large number of the conspirators, of whom Suffolk and Throckmorton are the most prominent, also happened to be Protestants, and it is hard to prove that their Protestantism was unconnected with their rebellion. Their long-term interests as Protestants depended on the succession, and at Mary's age, even a year's delay in her marriage might reduce the chance that she would produce an heir. Mary's marriage was also the best chance for Protestants to persuade non-Protestants to join with them in opposition to the regime.

Certainly the official government reactions suggest alarm about religion and the succession. Gardiner began to intensify pressure against heretics, and wanted to bring heresy prosecutions against such makers of irreverent speeches as the man who watched a vicar ceremonially opening a church door with his cross, and asked whether he intended to run at the quintain with God Almighty. Gardiner was also considering proposals for excluding Elizabeth from the succession. Renard deduced that Courtenay and Elizabeth should be executed, and Mendoza reported that Mary could accomplish little while Elizabeth lived. It is also significant that Paget opposed both these reactions, and pleaded for leniency for the rebels. It is a fair measure of future prospects in 1554 that there were two people Paget was unwilling to offend. One was Elizabeth, and the other was Philip. Later, in the 1570s, Elizabeth claimed that Philip had helped her during Mary's reign.[31]

In the summer of 1554, Philip arrived in England and was married to Mary without undue incident. By November, Mary believed herself pregnant. She continued to do so, even preparing the cradle and employing the nurses, until, in July 1555, she finally had to face the fact that her pregnancy was an illusion.

The return to Rome

It was thus while it was believed that Mary would have an heir, and the regime was at its strongest, that the religious policy of the reign was carried through to its conclusion. One of the largest programmes of depriva-

[31] Conyers Read, ii. 169.

tion of parish clergy in the whole period was begun. No theological inquisition into the clergy's beliefs was conducted: the chosen issue was marriage. In Essex, 93 out of 319 parish clergy were deprived, 88 for marriage and 5 for non-residence. By contrast, adulterers were let off with a penance and a fine of ten shillings. It is hard to say why marriage was selected as the issue for deprivation. It may be because, as Dr. Baskerville says, 'the doning or shedding . . . of dogmas is a far simpler matter than the jettisoning of women',[32] and therefore it was easier to prove than heresy. It is unlikely to have been because married clergy were supposed to be necessarily Protestant: of the eighty-eight married clergy in Essex, at least twenty-eight were reappointed elsewhere after dismissing their wives, and only eight can be proved to have had strong objections to Catholicism. It may have been simply because Cardinal Pole was horrified by clerical marriage: at Oxford, he dug up the bones of Peter Martyr's wife and threw them in the ditch. Certainly the whole question of marriage caused dismay to many clergy. One made a will saying that 'I give and bequeath to Eleanor my wife if the law of the realm allow it . . . if not, I give and bequeath to Eleanor Baker'.[33]

Pole had at last come into his own in November 1554, when he arrived as legate from the Pope, to absolve the realm from the sin of schism, and to receive appointment as Archbishop of Canterbury. Acceptance of the Pope proved surprisingly easy, and passed through Parliament with only one dissentient voice. The greatest anxieties of most people had not been about the Pope, but about whether his return would lead to surrender of church lands. The Earl of Bedford probably spoke for many people when, after the question had been discussed, he tore off his rosary and threw it into the fire, 'swearing deeply that he loved his sweet abbey of Woburn more than any fatherly counsel or commands that could come from Rome'. The inhabitants of Woburn itself were by this time mainly Protestant, and were thought to have been seduced to it by the example of Bedford's son.[34] It was one of Mary's greatest disadvantages that she had to enforce her policy through such an equivocal body of Councillors.

The compliance of Parliament up to this time had been as great as Mary could wish. It is hard to say why this should have been so: Mary's attempts to secure the return of men of the 'wise, grave and Catholic sort' had produced little result, though William Cecil, for example, had simply refrained from looking for a seat. He sat again in Mary's fourth Parlia-

[32] Baskerville, G., 'Elections to Convocation in the Diocese of Gloucester under Bishop Hooper', *E.H.R.* (1929), 11.
[33] Grieve, Hilda, 'The Deprived Married Clergy in Essex', *T.R.H.S.* (1940), 160.
[34] Prescott, H. F. M., *Mary Tudor* (1953), 316. Loades, D. M., 'The Enforcement of Reaction 1553–1558', *J.E.H.* (1965), 62.

ment, having noted in his diary shortly before the elections that all hope of the queen's pregnancy had been abandoned. This may explain why the opposition chose this Parliament to make its first stand. They chose as their issues two bills concerning property rights. The first was to renounce the royal revenues from First Fruits and Tenths, a bill which members might expect to lead to increased lay taxation. After a long debate behind locked doors, the bill was carried by 193 to 126. The second bill was to confiscate the property of the Protestant exiles, many of them friends or relations of members who were sitting. On this occasion, Sir Anthony Kingston, one of the most vehement of the Crown's opponents, succeeded in getting hold of the keys, and locked the doors himself. Having presumably done so when the right members were inside, he secured a majority against the bill. He was sent to the Tower, and Cecil was questioned, but suffered no worse fate than being told by Paget that 'you speak like a man of experience'.[35]

At first the government had been eager to encourage its opponents to go abroad, but in 1555 it began the policy of dealing with heretical opposition by burning. The subject is so emotive, and has been so brilliantly described in Foxe's *Book of Martyrs*, that it has become difficult to see it from any but a Protestant point of view. It should be remembered, however, that most of the people who were burned believed in the burning of heretics as firmly as most of the Marian bishops. Even Cranmer, who was renowned for his leniency, had taken part in the burning of heretics. Almost everyone in the country believed that there should be only one religion, and that penalties had to be used to bring this end about. Heretics were burned before Mary's reign, and they were burned after it. The last case of burning in England involved two anti-Trinitarian heretics in 1612, and was carried out by people most of whom were brought up on Foxe's *Book of Martyrs*. Contemporary objections, though common, were not based on the principle that heretics should not be burned: they were based, either on the assumption that the people who were burned were not heretics, or simply on a humanitarian or expedient readiness to ignore principle: the chief opponent of the burnings on the Council was Paget. Only two things were unusual about the persecutions in Mary's reign. One is that the number involved (just under 300) was greater than in other reigns. This was inevitable if the beliefs of the people who had been governing England three years earlier were to be rooted out. The other is that three years later supreme power had passed to the friends and colleagues of the victims: in France, many more heretics were burned than in England, but their executions are not famous.

Many of the martyrs are obscure, but the number also included Hooper,

[35] *Tudor Constitution*, 253.

Ridley, Latimer, and Cranmer. It was Latimer, whose preacher's gift for a phrase did not desert him even in these circumstances, who produced the best-remembered saying of the persecutions: 'be of good cheer, Master Ridley, for we shall this day light a candle which shall never be put out.' Cranmer also remained himself, hesitant to the end. It went against the grain for him to resist authority, and he went through a long series of recantations before he deprived the government of a propaganda victory by recanting all his recantations at the very last moment. The burnings produced many stories of heroism, which made a great impression in an age to which making a good end was so important. They also produced a few remarkable stories of cruelty by the authorities, such as the case of a woman in the Channel Islands who gave birth to a baby at the stake, and the authorities threw the baby into the flames with her. The persecutions also took place during two exceptionally bad summers, which caused harvests bad enough to enable Protestants to talk of God's wrath, and made some of the burnings agonizingly slow. For whatever reason, many executions showed signs of turning into effective anti-government demonstrations, which continued in spite of government proclamations threatening anyone who demonstrated sympathy with the victims. By January 1556, a curfew was being used during executions in London, and by July 1558, Bonner, Bishop of London, was suggesting that they be carried out in secret, to avoid the risk of riot. In 1557, public reaction was strengthened by an attack of the 'sweating sickness' which increased the death rate by about 150 per cent and produced another burst of rapid price rises, and by rumours that Edward VI was still alive. The government found it necessary to prohibit plays, because their use for Protestant propaganda, which went back to the 1520s, had got out of hand.

These were reactions to a dying government. They are no guide to the way England might have reacted to a long period of stable Catholic government. Attention is inevitably concentrated on the repressive part of Mary's policy, because it was the only part she had time to carry out. She had been accused of having no policy but repression, and of failing to discover the Counter-Reformation, or to introduce new spiritual vitality into the English Catholic church. Yet, as Professor Dickens says, 'during those five years of her reign, what materials suitable for use in England were available?'[36] She had, inevitably, to rely on the generation of bishops and church officials who had served her father. For new vitality, a new generation of clergy had to be trained, and the place to look for the vitality of the Marian church is the place which trained them—the universities. Cambridge had been suspect since the 1520s, and the university which

[36] Dickens, *Lollards and Protestants*, 212.

Mary most trusted was Oxford.[37] There were a number of Oxford Protestants, and the exiles included nine Fellows of Magdalen, but on the whole, the university's sympathies were conservative. Mary gave it a large benefaction of former monastic property, which was much needed. Pole was appointed Chancellor, and though some of his measures, such as the attempt to insist on a compulsory lecture system which had been superseded by printing, were failures, much of his university work was successful. The canon law faculty, which had been abolished by Henry VIII, was revived. The Edwardian policy of bringing in distinguished foreign scholars was continued, and one was brought from Padua, where Pole had spent much of his youth, to guide the canon law faculty. Several Councillors and people in government circles made benefactions, and two new colleges were founded. College tuition was becoming more common, and there appears to have been some college control over supplication for degrees. The intellectual resources of Oxford were used for the trials of Cranmer, Ridley, and Latimer, and Cranmer's trial was conducted as a university disputation, with the prosecutor disputing for the degree of Doctor of Divinity. A start was made in directing the university's resources to the task of re-conversion to Catholicism: the M.A. course was temporarily shortened by a year, to meet the need for new parish clergy to replace those who were deprived, and in the divinity faculty a sermon at Paul's Cross, the key point for propaganda, was one of the qualifying exercises commonly quoted in supplications for degrees.

It may be said that these are small measures, compared with the need they had to meet. But it is fair to judge by results. The charge against Mary has been that she did nothing to achieve the standard later set by Cardinal Allen and the brilliant gathering of Elizabethan Catholic exiles. But Allen received his training in Marian Oxford, and so did most of his colleagues in exile. The English Catholics at Louvain in the next reign included thirteen former Fellows of New College, including Harding, who defended the Catholic cause in a memorable disputation with Bishop Jewel. Nicholas Sanders, one of the ablest defenders of the papal monarchy in the next reign, acted as Public Orator in Marian Oxford. What Henrician Cambridge contributed to the Reformation, Marian Oxford contributed to the Counter-Reformation, and if Mary had lived another fifteen years she could have had as brilliant a bench of Catholic bishops as any in the history of the country.

[37] For this and what follows, I would like to thank my wife for permission to use her current research.

The Protestant exiles

Instead, the reign went out with the queen exposing herself to ridicule through another hysterical pregnancy, and involved in another French war, which produced no result but the loss of Calais. Financially, this was a blessing, but it was also a national humiliation, and was said to have produced a sharp reduction in the number of people going to church. The future was with the Protestant opposition, and Paget was in correspondence with Cecil. Though he expressed optimism about the regime's chances, he must have expected the answer he got: 'I fear rather an inundation of the contrary part, so universal a boiling and a bubbling I see.'[38] In this 'boiling and bubbling', the propaganda printed abroad by the Protestant exiles played a large part. Some of the Protestants' propaganda boomeranged against them in the next reign. John Knox, having blown his *First Blast of the Trumpet Against the Monstrous Regiment of Women*, found that he was not allowed to preach in Elizabethan England. Christopher Goodman, at Geneva, argued that government by women was a 'monster in nature, and disorder among men', and pointed out that St. Paul would not allow them to speak in the assembly, 'much less to be ruler of a realm or nation'. Women, he thought, should be in subjection to their husbands. He too was not welcome in the next reign. Knox, Goodman, and Ponet also broke with Protestant tradition by arguing that it was lawful to depose and kill a tyrant. Goodman also argued that a king could not be lawful unless he were elect of God, and produced a doctrine of devolution of divine right. He thought that divine right appertained only to a ruler who did right. If the ruler were a 'wicked Jezebel', divine right devolved to the nobles and councillors, and if they failed to do right, then it devolved to justices, mayors, sheriffs, bailiffs, constables, jailors, and other inferior officers, all of whom were bound to obey God rather than man, and had a divine right to discharge that duty. If all of these failed to do right, God put the sword into the hands of the common people.[39] These writings may have contributed something to the later bad reputation of Puritanism as an enemy of authority, but most of the Protestant exiles were not of this type. Some, mostly among those who went to France, took part in conspiracies, but these were mostly gentlemen of a secular cast of mind, who did not try to justify their proceedings theologically. Most clergy among the exiles were as devoted to the doctrine of non-resistance as Mary could have wished, but they did often imbibe more radical Protestant ideas than were welcome when they returned. They had seen churches

---

[38] Dickens, *Reformation*, 273.
[39] Goodman, C., *How Superior Powers Ought to be Obeyed* (1558), 185, 34–5, 52.

organized with all the simplicity they wanted, and met the ablest of the continental Protestants. Long afterwards there was a tendency among Elizabethan Puritans, both to invoke the practice of the 'best reformed churches', and to write to continental Protestant leaders for advice. At Frankfurt, there was a split among the exiles which was to be significant for the future, between the followers of Cox, who were willing to use the 1552 Prayer Book, and those of John Knox, who thought the 1552 book altogether too ritualistic, and wanted to use a Geneva liturgy.

These people did much to determine the course of the next reign, but it was those who stayed in England who secured Elizabeth's accession. By October 1558, when Mary's death was expected, Elizabeth was taking steps to secure the loyalty of the garrison of Berwick in the event of Mary's death, and by the beginning of November the Spanish ambassador was paying court to her. Finally, Mary herself decided not to follow the example of Northumberland, and named Elizabeth as her successor. After much alarm, Elizabeth's succession was unchallenged when Mary died in 1558.

V THE REIGN OF ELIZABETH TO 1570

For many Protestants, the accession of Elizabeth after the Marian persecution involved a deliverance which they felt was miraculous. Hooker spoke of 'the state of reformed religion, a thing at her coming to the crown even raised as it were by a miracle from the dead: a thing which we so little hoped to see, that even they which beheld it done, scarcely believed their own senses at first beholding'.[40] This sense of miraculous relief raised many hopes which afterwards were sadly disappointed. It is easy for historians, endowed with hindsight, to share some of this illusory sense of a new age beginning in 1558. The 'Elizabethan age', as we think of it, belongs to the second part of the reign, and in 1558 another mid-Tudor ruler was trying to make another mid-Tudor settlement with the aid of the same body of mid-Tudor councillors.

Many of Elizabeth's difficulties were similar to her sister's. She, too, was plagued with male supremacists, whom her sister's reign had done nothing to quieten. Aylmer, trying to answer John Knox's *Blast of the Trumpet*, had no more echoing defence of his sovereign than that her sex was not as dangerous as it might have been, since she ruled in a mixed monarchy, and had to share power with Parliament. Calvin, writing to Cecil, said that the government of women 'was to be ranked no less than slavery among the punishments consequent upon the fall of man'. Nevertheless, he said, there were occasionally some women whose exceptional

[40] Hooker, R., *The Laws of Ecclesiastical Polity*, IV. xiv. 7.

qualities made it appear that they were 'raised up by divine authority: either that God designed by such examples to condemn the inactivity of men, or for the better setting forth of his own glory'.[41] Even Cecil himself never entirely lost his hankering to have a man to deal with, whom he could understand.

Marriage and succession

Elizabeth was also faced with the practical difficulties of a woman ruler—marriage and the succession. Like her sister, she had no direct heir, but she had one advantage her sister had not: since it was not clear who her successor was, it was difficult to construct a reversionary interest. Elizabeth, being better aware than anyone how much a clear reversionary interest had handicapped her sister, remained determined all her reign not to name a successor. The result was serious alarm, not always unjustified. Had she died of the smallpox, as she nearly did a few years after her accession, civil war would almost certainly have followed.

Biologically, her next heir was Mary, Queen of Scots, who was descended from Henry VII's elder daughter Margaret. If Elizabeth was regarded as illegitimate, it was even possible to argue a claim for Mary before her own. Mary, if not as Catholic as she later led people to believe, was certainly no Protestant,[42] and almost all through the reign it remained possible that the accession of Mary would reverse Elizabeth's religious settlement as effectively as she had reversed her sister's. Protestants were therefore painfully aware that their religion depended on the queen's life, and this awareness contributed something to the growth of a vehement devotion to the queen on the part of people who were smarting under the effects of her policies. Many of them, however, were also addicted to discussing the succession whenever they could, and they could find many candidates. In 1566, Elizabeth threatened the Commons that 'if reason did not subdue will in me', she would let them discuss it for her own amusement, and 'some would speak for their master, and some for their mistress, and every man for his friend'.[43]

Mary was not the only Scottish candidate. Those who did not want the union of the kingdoms could argue a case for Henry Darnley (whom, of all people, Mary subsequently married). He was descended from Henry VII's daughter Margaret Tudor by her second marriage. It was also possible to argue for the exclusion of the Scottish line altogether, either on the ground

[41] Neale, J. E., *Queen Elizabeth* I (1934), 71.
[42] On Mary Stuart's religion, see Gordon Donaldson, *Edinburgh History of Scotland*, James V–James VII (1965), 110–13.
[43] Neale, *Parliaments*, i. 149.

that an alien could not succeed, or on the ground that the succession was still governed by Henry VIII's will. By that document, the succession would pass to the descendants of Henry VII's younger daughter Mary, and therefore to Catherine Grey, younger sister of Lady Jane Grey. Catherine Grey had the advantage of being more Protestant than Elizabeth, and Elizabeth kept her imprisoned for most of the reign, for no other offence than being dangerous. In spite of her imprisonment, she succeeded in making a love match with the eldest son of Protector Somerset, and, to add injury to insult, bore two sons. For those who wanted an heir who was neither a woman nor a minor, the obvious candidate was the Earl of Huntingdon, who inherited Buckingham's claim on his father's side, and the Poles' claim on his mother's side. He was the only one of the candidates who had a strong territorial power in England, and he was also one of the most generous patrons of the rising Puritan movement. His claim was good enough for him to be afraid of following Catherine Grey to the Tower, but he finally found favour when Elizabeth wanted a gaoler who could be trusted not to become an ally of Mary Queen of Scots, and he became a loyal public servant. Finally, if the claims of the whole Tudor dynasty were disputed, it was possible to argue a case for Philip of Spain, on the ground that while the Tudors' claim depended on descent from John of Gaunt and his mistress, Philip was descended from Gaunt and his legitimate wife. But little was heard of this claim till the 1580s.

In 1558, Philip's chief interest was in preventing the succession of Mary Queen of Scots. Mary was half-French by birth, was married to the French Dauphin, and, for a short while before her husband's death in 1560, became Queen of France. The union, or even the close alliance, of England, Scotland, and France would be as big a diplomatic coup for France as the accession of Mary Tudor had been for Spain. England was still officially at war with France until the peace of Cateau-Cambrésis was signed in March 1559, and at the beginning of the reign the Catholic menace, for most Elizabethan statesmen, was French. Philip, especially while there was a possibility that Elizabeth might marry a Catholic, or even a Habsburg, husband, was the best friend England had. It was France which pressed the Pope to excommunicate Elizabeth, and Philip who, for twelve years, dissuaded him.

Elizabeth's marriage was the most tempting diplomatic prize in Europe, but was a weapon like a bee's sting, which could only be used once. Both the French and the Habsburgs could hope to bring England into their orbit by marriage, and both could often be frightened by the threat of a marriage to the other. Early in the reign, when the danger was from

France, the leading candidate for marriage was the Archduke Charles, brother of the Holy Roman Emperor. How seriously Elizabeth considered marrying him, and how her subjects would have reacted to a foreign, and Catholic, husband, neither we nor Elizabeth's Councillors can say. Cecil, when asked an envoy's chances, could only reply: 'how he shall speed, God knoweth, and not I.'[44]

The prospect that the queen might marry an English husband seemed to cause no more contentment than that of a foreign husband. In 1559 and 1560 it seemed that the queen might be falling in love with Lord Robert Dudley, Master of the Horse, whom she created Earl of Leicester. Unfortunately, Dudley's family were not popular. His father, the Duke of Northumberland, and his grandfather, Henry VII's minister, had both been executed for treason, and once again, many people found it hard to see why the Dudleys should be raised up above them. Even Cecil, who was as eager for the queen to marry as anyone in the country, was scandalized at the prospect. The Privy Council had to suppress seditious rumours, such as that the queen was with child by Dudley, who was unfortunately married. When, in 1560, his wife was found dead in suspicious circumstances, the rumours became unmanageable. They appear to have been unjustified, since his wife seems to have died of cancer of the breast,[45] but they made it impossible for the queen to marry him. The only result was that he built up a large mushroom empire of patronage, which, though his own religion was unstable, he used mainly for the benefit of Puritans.

It is impossible to say whether Elizabeth ever seriously considered marrying any of these candidates. When her first Parliament, in 1559, petitioned her to marry, she discoursed to them on the virtues of a celibate life, and threatened to live and die a virgin. Most members probably took this for maidenly modesty, but it may have been seriously meant. Certainly, in the same speech, she promised not to marry any husband with whom the realm should have just cause to be discontented. The members did not interpret this as a pledge not to marry, but it is possible that Elizabeth did, and moreover, that if she did, she was right.

The religious settlement

It is arguable that these questions of marriage, the succession, and foreign policy dominated Elizabeth's policy throughout her reign. They certainly dominated much of her thinking about the immediate task of making a religious settlement. There was little likelihood that Spain would intervene as the champion of Catholicism, even if the queen were excom-

[44] Neale, J. E., *Queen Elizabeth I*, 82.
[45] Aird, Ian, 'The Death of Amy Robsart', *E.H.R.* (1956), 69–79. Dudley did not attend his wife's funeral.

municated. Nevertheless, excommunication might be unpleasant with French hostility to support it, and Spanish help was well worth using to prevent it. Elizabeth took some care to make the Spanish ambassador believe that 'she differed very little from us', and that she wanted, if possible, to confine herself to restoring the Royal Supremacy, without altering the form of service. These utterances prove only that this was what she wanted the Spanish ambassador to believe, not that this was all she intended to do. Meanwhile, she was making equally impressive gestures to her radical Protestant subjects, greeting the monks of Mary's revived monastery of Westminster, when they came to her with lighted candles, with the words 'away with those tapers: we can see well enough'. Then, as later, she was gaining all the possible advantages of ambiguity. Whether, as some of her ministers would have said, ambiguity was simply a cover for indecision, it is hard to say. Fortunately, she was able to cloak ambiguity with a superb sense of theatre.

Perhaps the clearest point about government intentions on the settlement is that they wanted to make it possible for all people to attend the same churches. The idea that the Elizabethan government was tolerant in matters of religion is misguided. William Cecil believed that 'the state could never be in safety, where there was toleration of two religions. For there is no enmity so great as that for religion, and they that differ in the service of God can never agree in the service of their country.' The saying that Elizabeth did not like to make windows into men's souls, which is often misquoted to the opposite purpose, is worth quoting. 'Her Majesty, not liking to make windows into men's hearts and secret thoughts, except the abundance of them did overflow into overt and express acts and affirmations, ... in impugning and impeaching advisedly and maliciously her Majesty's supreme power, and maintaining and extolling a foreign jurisdiction.'[46] All this sentence says is that people may hold their beliefs freely if they never express them, and moreover, the words are not the queen's. They are those of an ambitious young man called Francis Bacon, who, on this, as on many other occasions, was pretending to be a government spokesman when he was not.

It is, however, true that Elizabeth's aim was outward conformity, rather than full agreement. This aim was not unprincipled: full agreement had grown hard to come by, and those who conformed outwardly at least committed themselves to the view that the settlement was merely erroneous,

---

[46] Hurstfield, J., 'Church and State; The Task of the Cecils', *Studies in Church History*, ed. G. J. Cuming (1965), 124. This article has finally demolished the myth that the Elizabethan government was tolerant. For Bacon's support for religious repression, see below, pp. 208–9.

and not sinful, and therefore that they were not bound to rebel for religion's sake. One of the key aims of the Elizabethan settlement was to induce Catholics to come to church, on the ground that they would probably be disloyal if they did not. It was a great disappointment to the government when, in 1562, the Pope pronounced that Catholics could not attend Anglican Matins. The government sacrificed much for this aim, but failed to achieve it, and it was against all Tudor presuppositions that the majority of the Catholics, while not going to church, nevertheless remained loyal.

With these presuppositions, Elizabeth is likely to have approached the problem of a settlement in terms of the support she could gather, and her first appointments suggest that she was looking for it in a bewildering variety of directions. Her first appointment was of William Cecil as Secretary of State. This appointment is unlikely to have surprised many people, since Cecil had already been Secretary under Edward, and had pursued the reversionary interest (support of the probable successor against the Crown) with more skill than most. He had obtained appointment as surveyor of Elizabeth's lands in 1550, and had been reputed to be closely allied with her ever since. He was clearly Protestant, but he had been induced to go to Mass in Mary's reign, and might with difficulty be induced to do so again. Elizabeth's charge to him on his appointment may serve for a treatise on Tudor views on the duty of a Councillor: 'this judgement I have of you; that you will not be corrupted by any manner of gift and that you will be faithful to the State; and that without respect of my private will you will give me that counsel which you think best and if you shall know anything necessary to be declared to me of secrecy you shall show it to myself only.' It is necessary to add that when Elizabeth said he would not be corrupted by any manner of gift, she did not expect him not to take gifts. She gave him no specific charge as Secretary, and little of his power ever depended on the office of Secretary. Business still went to the man, not the office, and when Cecil was moved to the Lord Treasurership, most of his business went with him, leaving his successor as Secretary with almost no power. Power depended on the queen's ear, not on offices, and as Dr. Conyers Read said, 'some Tudor Secretaries were little more than clerks, some little less than prime ministers'.[47] Some of her other early appointments to the Council suggested a move in a Protestant direction. Sir Francis Knollys and the Earl of Bedford had both been Marian exiles, and Sir Ambrose Cave, who was given the Duchy of Lancaster, with a large amount of ecclesiastical and parliamentary patronage, was one of 'the hotter sort of Protestants'. On the other hand, many

[47] Conyers Read, i. 119, 121.

of the leading Marian councillors, with the surprising exception of Paget,[48] stayed on, although the Council was sharply reduced in size. Some, such as Shrewsbury, had pronounced Catholic leanings. Elizabeth even made approaches to the Marian bishops: Heath, Archbishop of York, appears to have been offered the chance to continue as Lord Chancellor, and sat on the Council for several weeks. In the event, the only Marian bishops who agreed to serve in her church were Llandaff and Sodor and Man, but whether the settlement would have been different if the Marian bishops had agreed to serve, or whether they would have agreed to serve if the settlement had been different, are matters for conjecture.

Whether the queen had reached any definite decision on the form of her settlement before Parliament met is also a matter for conjecture. She had clearly decided to dispense with the Pope, since she had recalled her envoy from Rome, telling him there was no reason for his staying. The Lord Keeper's opening speech, saying that one of the purposes of the Parliament was 'the making of laws, for the according and uniting of these people of the realm into an uniform order of religion',[49] suggests that she also intended to introduce a new Act of Uniformity and a new service, but when the Parliament met, no such Act was in evidence.

Opinion in Parliament, as usual, had swung sharply towards the new regime, but this time it appears to have swung too far for the queen's liking, especially in the Commons. The dominant influence in the Commons appears to have been a small body of Marian exiles, with about a hundred clear supporters, led by Cecil's father-in-law Sir Anthony Cooke and by Sir Francis Knollys.

By 1559, the evidence is beginning to become plentiful enough to investigate the process by which a change of regime produced a change of opinion in Parliament, and it appears to have happened, not by direct government pressure, but by shifts in the balance of patronage. Some government officers, such as the Chancellor of the Duchy of Lancaster and the Lord Warden of the Cinque Ports, controlled a certain number of seats themselves. In the counties, social prestige determined the returns, and prestige was influenced by favour at court. In the boroughs, a prudent corporation was likely to accept the patronage of a man known to be in favour. Processes such as these might determine the return of a body of members who become the dominant influence, and, as one

[48] Paget's failure to obtain office was not due to lack of desire for it: he petitioned unsuccessfully for the Presidency of Wales. His failure may have been due to ill health, but the surviving evidence indicates possible discontent with the religious settlement, and that he had debts to the queen. *Cal. S.P. Dom.*, xv. no. 35, xii. no. 1, iii. no. 34; Conyers Read, i. 168–9.

[49] D'Ewes, *Journal* (1693), 11.

satirist said, 'as for the rest, they be at devotion; and when they be pressed, they cry "a good motion"'. Returns made through changes in patronage were not in any strict sense government returns: they were returns of Councillors' friends and relations, but already by 1559 it is possible to see the solvent which broke up Tudor and Stuart society. Religion was beginning to be a force which influenced patronage, cutting across neighbourhood and relationship. Four of the greatest Elizabethan patrons, the Earls of Leicester, Warwick, Huntingdon, and Bedford, often used their patronage on religious grounds. Ultimately, such a process might lead to the formation of 'party' groups, for which there was no room within the machinery of a one-party state. Among these, the greatest parliamentary patron appears to have been Bedford, and as Bedford was more Protestant than the queen, so many of his nominees were more Protestant than Bedford. In the Lords, there was less room for swings of opinion, but a number of lords, some of them Catholic, stayed at home and gave their proxies to Privy Councillors, and Bedford arrived with no less than fifteen proxies.[50]

It was clear soon after the Parliament met, if it was not clear before, that it would be impossible to bring the Marian bishops into a new settlement. They unanimously opposed the first major government bill, for restoring the First Fruits and Tenths to the Crown. They also opposed, together with a number of the Commons, a government bill making it possible to enrich the Crown at the expense of the bishoprics by a further series of 'exchanges'. After this, it was to be expected that they would oppose the bill for reviving the Royal Supremacy, which they duly did, together with the Earl of Shrewsbury.[51] The Supremacy Bill appears to have also met trouble in the Commons, though since the chairman of the committee which considered it was Sir Anthony Cooke, it was probably disliked there for not being radical enough. Meanwhile, it was becoming apparent that the queen would have to rely on the Protestant exiles for her bishops, and that she would therefore have to have a church with at least the minimum reforms necessary to enable them to serve. Since only the conservative faction among the exiles would accept anything so moderate as the 1552 Prayer Book, this implied a settlement very different from any the Marian bishops might have supported. These points were certainly clear by the time the Uniformity Bill appeared, after the treaty of Cateau-Cambrésis had removed the risk of war.

When the Supremacy Bill finally emerged, it described the queen as 'supreme governor' and not 'supreme head' of the church. It is hard to

---

[50] D'Ewes, *Journal*, 9. Some of these proxies were held jointly with other lords.
[51] Shrewsbury, who was a Privy Councillor, did not vote against it in its final form.

know how significant this change was, but it may have made it clearer that the queen was not actually claiming to have the cure of her subjects' souls. Nicholas Sanders later said that many Catholics found it more tolerable than the title of Supreme Head. It may also have been intended as a concession to those Protestants who, like Calvin, thought that only Christ could be head of the church. It also contained a clause authorizing the queen to set up commissions, on the lines of the Star Chamber, to try ecclesiastical cases. This clause was not in fact the origin of the Court of High Commission, any more than the 1487 Act had been the origin of Star Chamber, but it did give it legislative sanction, and turned it from an occasional into a permanent institution.

The Prayer Book, when it appeared, was a compromise between the 1549 and 1552 Books. It contained the communion formulae from both books, and to this day there are some Anglican clergy who are only prepared to use one or the other. In some ways it was satisfactory to Protestants. The word 'altar' did not appear anywhere in it, and 'communion table' was used instead. On the other hand, it still retained provision for confession, used the word 'priest', and specifically sanctioned priestly power of absolution. The queen's chief concern appears to have been to preserve the external appearance of parish churches as it had been, and she insisted on the use of all the vestments which had been in use in the second year of Edward VI (whether before or after the Prayer Book of that year was not specified). The doctrine of the settlement, on the other hand, was not worked out until after its bishops were appointed, and the Thirty-Nine Articles, agreed on in Convocation in 1563, gave Protestants much of what they wanted. They were based on Cranmer's Forty-Two Articles of 1552. They roundly denounced Purgatory and the Mass, and fully affirmed justification by faith. Article 17, to all but the ingenious, was a clear affirmation of the doctrine of Predestination, which was coming to be one of the most crucial points of Protestant theology. How it became so may be guessed from the words of the Article itself, which recounted that the doctrine of Predestination was full of 'sweet and unspeakable comfort' to those who felt within themselves the working of God's spirit.

The other constituent of the settlement, the queen's Injunctions of 1559, were a similar mixture. They contained the important concession that the Communion table, though it was to be kept at the east end, was to be brought into the middle of the church at service time. Since it was difficult to move a heavy piece of furniture about the church regularly, this tended to mean that each parish kept it permanently in the place it preferred. On the other hand, they prescribed bowing to the altar, which

was part of the sort of thraldom of superstition from which most Protestants hoped they had been emancipated. Finally, the queen set up a
crucifix in her own chapel, which produced reports in France that she
was not yet resolved of what religion she would be. In the country, the
vestments produced a similar impression, and Lever reported from
Coventry that they led people to believe, either that popish doctrine was
retained, or that it would soon return.

Disappointment of the bishops: the beginnings of Puritanism

This was the settlement in which many of the leading émigrés were
asked to become bishops, and they did not like it. Cox, who became
Bishop of Ely, refused to preach in the queen's chapel, because of the
ornaments. Jewel, who became Bishop of Salisbury, reported to Peter
Martyr that:

so miserably is it ordered, that falsehood is armed, while truth is not only
unarmed, but also frequently offensive. The scenic apparatus of divine worship
is now under agitation; and those very things which you and I have so often
laughed at, are now seriously and solemnly entertained by certain persons (for
we are not consulted) as if the Christian religion could not exist without something tawdry. . . . Others are seeking after a golden, or as it seems to me a
leaden mediocrity, and are crying out that the half is better than the whole.

Sandys, who became Bishop of Worcester, commented on the ornaments
rubric that 'our gloss upon this text, is that we will not be forced to use
them'.[52] In some cases, this was true, and at Loughborough, where the
living belonged to the Earl of Huntingdon, the surplice appears not to
have been used for the whole reign.

Soon Horne, Bishop of Winchester, was reporting to Zürich that 'our
little flock has divided itself into two parties'.[53] But the division was not
between those who were disappointed and those who were not: it was
between those who were willing to swallow their disappointment and
those who could not. When Sandys, as Archbishop of York, made his
will thirty years later, he was still insisting that the surplice was undesirable, but he also insisted that however undesirable it was for him
to enforce it, it was not actually unlawful. Grindal, who later became
Archbishop of Canterbury, decided that true doctrine made it possible
to serve in a settlement which was externally undesirable, and that he
would tolerate the surplice for the sake of obedience to the prince.

Other Protestants whom the queen had hoped to appoint refused. Old
Coverdale, Edwardian Bishop of Exeter, would not serve, and when he
was needed to consecrate Anne Boleyn's former chaplain Parker as

[52] Neale, *Parliaments*, i. 79, 83.
[53] Collinson, P., *The Elizabethan Puritan Movement* (1967), 74.

archbishop, he appeared in an old black gown. Sampson, who was seriously considered for a bishopric, reported to Peter Martyr with the significant distinction that he was prepared to serve as a preacher in the settlement, but he would not take upon himself the government of the church. For the next eight years he contributed, as Dean of Christchurch, to the task of converting a new generation from popery to Puritanism. He also made a complaint which was to become frequent later: there was no machinery for discipline. Dioceses were too large for bishops to govern them, and all the rusty machinery of church government remained unchanged: there was little chance to ensure that a truly Christian life would be a condition for taking communion. An even more radical complaint of Sampson's was that the system of church appointments was unchanged, and clergy and parishioners were to have no share in choosing their ministers.[54]

These men were often the best preachers, and the ones who made the most converts. They also had the sympathy of the most powerful patrons. Gilby, one of the most radical, was a protégé of the Earl of Huntingdon, and was made lecturer at Ashby de la Zouch. As lecturer, he did not have to tolerate the displeasing details of the service, and could confine himself to preaching. There was often more money in these lecturing appointments than in livings, since people would contribute the more willingly to the support of clergy they had chosen themselves. At Sheffield, the parishioners agreed to club together to supplement the income of the living, and as a result, acquired a considerable say in their choice of minister. Much educational, as well as ecclesiastical patronage was in the hands of people who wanted a more radical settlement. Huntingdon, one of the greatest educational benefactors of the period, ensured that his scholars were adequately grounded in the works of Calvin. Once again, as in the medieval church, preaching and enthusiasm, and much of the power of conversion, had been channelled outside the official church machinery, into a body of mobile preachers, whom Foxe the martyrologist (another who refused office) compared to the medieval friars. In 1563, Cecil tried to rectify this situation by introducing a bill to attract able clergy into official livings by taxing either the parishioners or the men who had the impropriations of tithes to ensure more adequate stipends. This bill was rejected: it threatened members' property rights, and though many were willing to pay large sums to support clergy they had chosen, they would not be taxed to pay for clergy of whom they had a low opinion.

[54] *Zurich Letters*, pp. 1–2. This letter was written in December 1558, before any settlement had been made public.

The issues involved were about the dispelling of superstition and ignorance. They were not about church government. Gilby, for example,
had no strong views on how the church should be governed, and was
perfectly willing to accept bishops if they were godly. In the Channel
Islands, even Elizabeth herself accepted a Presbyterian church settlement, with the full machinery of discipline by elected synods and col-
loquies, in which lay elders, as well as ministers, had a part. Horne,
Bishop of Winchester, within whose diocese this settlement existed,
appears to have regarded it with considerable benevolence. Elizabeth
accepted the Channel Islands settlement because she needed preachers
who could preach in French, and therefore had to rely on Presbyterians
from France.[55] For her, as for most of her contemporaries, church government was a means and not an end. Right up to and even after the Civil
War, most people judged church government by whether it produced
clergy and doctrines of the right type. Almost the only people for whom
it was an important issue in its own right were bishops, and because much
history has been seen through their eyes, too much of the religious history
of the period has been written in terms of church government.

The settlement in the Channel Islands suggests that Elizabeth planned
her settlement on grounds of expediency, rather than of any religious
principle. It is possible, however, that her assessment of expediency was
mistaken. It was based on the desire to keep together the mid-Tudor
coalition, to preserve the uneasy compromise which had enabled Cranmer
and Gardiner to sit together on the bench of bishops. But during Edward's
and Mary's reigns both sides had moved on from their old positions:
Tunstal rejected the settlement because it was too radical, and Coverdale
because it was not radical enough, and there was no hope of reviving a
world in which they could both sit together. Even among laymen, Shrewsbury on one side and Bedford on the other had moved too far to share
any middle ground. The first generation of 'Anglicans', men like Hooker,
Bancroft, and Andrewes, to whom the Prayer Book was an object of
affection in its own right, were still in infancy. Since she could not satisfy
the Catholics, Elizabeth might have found it expedient to satisfy a few
of the Protestants.

Money and foreign policy

On other questions, Elizabeth's sense of expediency was surer. She
appreciated the dangers of insolvency, and the connection between insolvency and war. She also appreciated the risk to her popularity involved

[55] On the Channel Islands settlement and its operation, see A. J. Eagleston, *The
Channel Islands Under Tudor Government* (1949), 55–65.

in raising extra revenue, and appears to have made the heroic decision to set out to live within the royal income. At the end of Mary's reign, the Lord Treasurer, Winchester, was investigating ways of increasing revenue from Crown lands, but at the beginning of Elizabeth's he was investigating ways of reducing expenditure by saving on the upkeep of castles. Savings were limited by Winchester's readiness to preserve castles as 'ancient monuments', but the queen's cheeseparing continued. On one occasion she even directed troops involved in a siege to collect cannon balls from under the walls for re-use. Taxpayers benefited, and the chief losers were courtiers. In her first Parliament, the Lord Keeper warned the Houses that the queen could not show that liberality and bountifulness to her servants that she would have been inclined to, and this warning remained in force for the rest of her reign.

Both she and her subjects were helped by the fact that she succeeded at a time when the price rise was temporarily slowing down, and her popularity was much increased by her restoration of the coinage to its former purity. She was, however, prepared to spend money on occasion. From the beginning of her reign she was worried by the lack of a royal armoury, and set Gresham to the task of collecting one. This, together with the development of the militia, brought the Crown to the point where it became the strongest military force in its own kingdom. She was also prepared to take trouble with the navy, and, by enforcing compulsory fish days, to make her subjects keep a merchant fleet ready to serve in war. It still remained difficult, however, for her Councillors to induce her to face the expense of actual campaigns.

Twice, at the beginning of her reign, they succeeded. The first occasion was the outbreak of a rebellion, at least partly Protestant, in Scotland. The rebels looked to England for support, and the government to France. From the English point of view, the real issues were whether Scotland would be dominated by a pro-French or a pro-English party, and whether France might use it as a base for a two-pronged invasion of England. After being faced with a letter of resignation from Cecil, Elizabeth was at last induced to intervene, and was in the main successful. Mary Queen of Scots remained in power, but hedged about with Councillors, and, with religion cutting across the old political loyalties, the risk of effective alliance between Scotland and France was sharply reduced.

The second occasion was the first round of the French religious wars, in 1562. This provided the first opportunity to follow the policy which Cecil described as 'building fires in other men's houses'—a form of keeping enemies away which was much cheaper than a major war. Many of Elizabeth's subjects, including some Councillors, wanted to help the

Huguenots on pan-Protestant grounds, and others hoped that English intervention might lead to the recovery of Calais as the price for withdrawal. The English intervention was a fiasco, and probably strengthened Elizabeth's objection to wars, but the French religious wars continued, with occasional intervals, for most of the rest of the reign. As these wars grew more serious, they sharply altered the balance of European power. It was in Spain's interest to prevent the success of the Huguenots. Spain therefore tended, during periods of war, to make approaches to the ultra-Catholic party in France, whose leaders were the Guise family. Unfortunately for England, this was the family to which Mary Queen of Scots' mother belonged, and the Guises could always count Mary among their allies. There was thus a danger that Philip might come to think of Mary, not as French and therefore hostile, but as belonging to his faction in France, and therefore friendly.

England's relations with Spain were also threatened, from the late 1560s onwards, by the revolt of the Netherlands against Spanish government and the arrival of a large Spanish army to support it. Again many of the rebels were Protestant, and pan-Protestant sentiment produced some reactions like those produced by the Spanish Civil War in this century. Elizabeth was unimpressed by these reactions, and had two main preoccupations. One was that she should remain on friendly terms with whoever controlled the Netherlands market after the revolt was over, and for many years it was not clear who this would be. The other was the long-standing concern of English governments that the territory which is now Belgium should not be occupied by a powerful force capable of invasion. When the Spaniards moved in a large army in 1567, Elizabeth hamstrung it the next year by 'borrowing' the bullion for the soldiers' pay when the ships carrying the bullion were blown into Plymouth by a storm.[56] On the other hand, if the Spaniards were expelled altogether, the people most likely to replace them would be the French, and from the English point of view, the change would not be for the better. For many years, Elizabeth's attitude remained ambiguous.[57]

[56] The story of the bullion is less simple than is often supposed. The ships carrying it had been blown into Plymouth harbour, and a ring of privateers were waiting for them outside. Elizabeth then had three courses open to her: she could let the bullion go to the privateers, she could provide it with an expensive naval escort, or she could keep it. Since the Genoese bankers, whose property it was, were happy to lend it to her instead of Philip, she chose the third course. Wernham, 296.

[57] It was clear enough what Elizabeth would have liked. She wanted to settle the war by mediation, allowing the Netherlands local autonomy under Spanish sovereignty. This solution was always impossible, since Philip would accept no solution which did involve toleration of Protestantism, and the Dutch would accept no settlement which did not. Elizabeth's preferences between the possible alternatives remained obscure. Conyers Read, ii. 187–8.

So did her attitude to incipient trading rivalries with Spain. Occasional Spanish closures of the Antwerp market were usually met by nothing more drastic than the shifting of the cloth trade to Hamburg or Emden. Some of her subjects were beginning to want to trade direct with Spanish overseas territories. Hawkins was developing a flourishing slave trade between West Africa and the Spanish colonies, and some others were beginning to combine Protestantism and profit by raiding Spanish America. Drake, for example, must have found his anti-Spanish feelings reinforced when he passed the time during a calm by colouring in the pictures in Foxe's *Book of Martyrs*. Economically, penetration of the Spanish American markets might be in English interests, but diplomatically, it meant war, and Elizabeth usually cared more about diplomacy than about economics. Her attitude to the whole question is best summed up by her comment when the Spanish Ambassador protested about Drake: 'the gentleman careth not if I should disavow him.'[58]

Mary Queen of Scots

None of these questions caused as much concern as the arrival in England of Mary Queen of Scots, in 1568. She arrived as a refugee, strongly suspected of the murder of her husband, and having been deposed in favour of her infant son James VI. Her arrival put Elizabeth in the worst dilemma she ever faced. The new Scottish regents were ready for English friendship, and willing to try Mary for murder if she were surrendered. This might look like an opportunity to bring about the fall of a rival, but Elizabeth had to consider the reactions of France and Spain. She also had to consider royal trade unionism. The sentiment that rebellion was always sinful was one Elizabeth shared, and which all sixteenth-century rulers had a vested interest in encouraging. As Cecil said, the queen was concerned that 'by this example, none of her own be encouraged', and at one stage she even threatened war to put Mary back on the throne, only to get the reply from one of the Scottish councillors: 'your wars are not unknown to us; you will burn our borders, and we will do the like to yours, and whensoever you invade us, we are sure the French will aid us.'[59] This course was impossible, but it was equally impossible to take the political and diplomatic risks of handing Mary over to the Scottish regency. Keeping her in England carried the risk that she would plot to depose Elizabeth, as she did, but it also had the great merit of sav-

---

[58] Neale, *Queen Elizabeth*, 288.
[59] Conyers Read, i. 385, 387. I regret that Gordon Donaldson, *The First Trial of Mary Queen of Scots* (1970) appeared too late for me to use it.

ing Elizabeth from the need to make a decision, and it was the course which was followed for the next twenty years.

Mary, as probable heir to the throne, now occupied a position like Elizabeth's in the previous reign. Many Councillors therefore tried to establish good relations with her, as many of them had done with Elizabeth in the previous reign. These attempts were mostly made by the more conservative and aristocratic members of the Council, who also hoped to persuade the queen to dismiss Cecil. The episode ended with the imprisonment of Norfolk, and the removal of many of his allies from the Council. From then on, the Council was a more Protestant and less aristocratic body, and the coalition of the mid-Tudor Council had broken up for ever.

In 1569, as in 1536, it was when all was settled in London that the north rose in rebellion. The Earls of Northumberland and Westmoreland, who led the rising, were certainly Catholic, and appealed to Catholicism for their support, but it is hard to know exactly what their purposes were. It is possible that they were driven into rebellion by the belief that they had dabbled too deeply in conspiracy to draw back.[60] The government suppressed the rebellion without difficulty, and Grindal took occasion to remind the Council that the towns which had shown most loyalty were those like Halifax which had good Protestant preachers. The government appears to have taken the hint, and sent Huntingdon, who could at least never be suspected of supporting Mary, to take up the Presidency of the North, where he set up lectureships and made a large contribution to the growth of northern Puritanism.

Fears of foreign involvement in the rising had come to nothing, and Philip was still opposing the excommunication of Elizabeth. However, his influence at Rome was lessened when the papacy passed to Pius V. The Spanish Ambassador at Rome reported that it was impossible to treat him like other Popes, since he knew nothing of reason of state or common prudence, and cared only for the Christian religion. Pius's decision to excommunicate and depose Elizabeth (without complying with the canonical forms) was taken shortly after the rising of the north, and was thus mistimed, like every other event in Anglo-Papal relations during the century. However, it created considerable feeling after the rebellion. Seminaries for Catholic missionaries were already being established in Flanders, and English Catholics, beginning to realize that they had to choose between their country and their religion, were going there in considerable numbers. This bull made every Catholic liable to become a traitor either to his

---

[60] I would like to thank Mr. Anthony Fletcher for allowing me to read a draft paper of his on this subject.

queen or to his Pope—a dilemma which few of them wanted. Many tried to avoid it by retirement, and one Catholic peer excused his not coming to church by claiming that his household was a parish by itself. However, there were inevitably some plots, and they cast suspicion on all Catholics. In 1571, the government secured the law Mary's government had failed to pass, confiscating the property of emigrés. A new treason Act once again made it treason to call the queen a 'heretic, schismatic, tyrant, infidel or usurper of the crown' and (a clause it is surprising the queen allowed) made it treason to say that Parliament could not determine the succession.

4. *Puritanism and Fashion* 1570–1640

I PURITANISM AND ITS BACKGROUND

No, by the faith I bear to God! We will pass nothing before we understand what it is, for that were but to make you Popes. Make you Popes who list, for we will make you none. *Peter Wentworth to Archbishop Parker, 1571*[1]

If I stay here long, you will find me so dull that I shall be taken for Justice Silence or Justice Shallow. *Letter from Gloucestershire, 1594*[2]

THE generation which was coming to maturity after 1570 had been born after the Reformation, and had grown up with the inescapable fact of religious choice. Like many other changes, the change of atmosphere in this period happened, not so much by people changing their ideas, as by the process of birth and death. Francis Hastings, second Earl of Huntingdon, had been able to exploit with equal virtuosity his relationship to the Catholic Poles and to the Protestant Dudleys. His son Henry, who succeeded him in 1560, had been brought up sharing a thorough classical education with Edward VI, and made up his own mind on religious questions by independent study of the works of theologians. The first Earl of Pembroke, perhaps the last illiterate Privy Councillor in English history† was succeeded by a line of patrons of arts and letters, equally ready to commission Vandyck or to receive a dedication of a new edition of St. Augustine or a new play by Massinger. The first Earl of Bedford, whose religion was always that of the government, was succeeded in 1555 by a son who was Protestant and, if his library catalogue is any guide, a scholar. The pliant Sir William Petre was succeeded by a son who, as a firm Catholic, lived in retirement, running a well-built house complete with a set of drains which remained in uninterrupted use until 1952, when the plumber repaired them accord-

[1] Neale, *Parliaments*, i. 205.   [2] Stone, 391.
† Dr. Peter Roberts has suggested that he was literate in Welsh.

ing to a plan of 1566, fetched from the Record Office for the occasion. The descendants of that dedicated climber Sir Richard Rich included a Puritan peer ready to fight a county election against the whole weight of the Privy Council, a seaman whose private fleet made a large contribution to the beginnings of English colonization, and a polished courtier who was one of the closest friends of Queen Henrietta Maria. Of all the families which contributed to Henry VIII's Privy Council, perhaps only the Howards, the Dudleys, and the Seymours were succeeded by men of the same stamp as themselves.

The intellectual and social development of England during this period was encouraged by a long period of internal peace. The war against Spain, though punctuated by occasional Spanish landings, was mostly fought far away on the high seas, and produced rather an enriching variety of new experience than any obstacle to the country's internal development. Many people recognized their debt to this peace, and were inclined to ascribe it to the fact that the government had sufficient control of religion to prevent religious wars. Sandys, Archbishop of York, said: 'what stirs diversity of religion hath raised in nations and king-doms, . . . our times in such sort have told you, that with farther proof I need not trouble your ears. . . . In the meanwhile we sit still under our vine; every man in peace may quietly follow his vocation. God hath not dealt with all nations as he hath dealt with us, the least nation of all.'[3]

Military power: the militia

Though civil wars were avoided, English society was still often violent and coarse, but there are increasing signs of distaste with such an unpolished mode of existence. Bastard feudalism, however, still existed, and in the 1590s showed some brief signs of revival. The Earl of Essex even succeeded in reviving some of his tenants' obligations to do him military service, under a clause in their leases reserving 'other services due and accustomed'. One of the Elizabethan judges, having acquitted a murderer for a bribe, then gave him his livery to protect him from private vengeance. Oliver Cromwell's grandfather appeared at musters at the head of a force of his tenants, and reminded shirkers of the halters and branding irons invading Spaniards would bring with them. It was also in the 1590s that the government at last began to gain real control over bastard feudalism. In 1595, an order was issued that no retainer could be a Justice of the Peace, whereat the Earl of Essex dismissed all his Welsh retainers, claiming that he was confident of their love. In 1601 a similar order was issued for the office of feodary. In 1570, many nobles

[3] Sandys, *Sermons* (Parker Soc., 1841), 47, 61.

still had large armouries. Leicester had Kenilworth fortified for war, and equipped with no less than 100 cannon, but by 1612 Cavendish was pretending to a more ancient lineage than he possessed (he had bought his peerage seven years earlier) by building himself a sham castle at Bolsover. In the crisis of 1588, when Pembroke offered Elizabeth the service of 300 horse and 500 foot, 'of my followers, armed at mine own cost, and with mine own store',⁴ she had the confidence to refuse the offer.

She was able to do this largely because of the development of the militia. During the 1570s, the principle of selection had been introduced into the general musters, which led to the development of a select part of the militia, the trained bands, who, though somewhat ramshackle, had at least experience of drilling and handling weapons. The Lord Lieutenant, a great nobleman in charge of county musters, developed during the reign from an occasional to a permanent appointment, and the work was done by Deputy Lieutenants who were usually the most important J.P.s. Here another piece of patronage was created for the Crown or the Lord Lieutenant and another perquisite for local gentry. It was one which gave some opportunities, especially after the government began to press men for service overseas. In Merioneth, one of the Deputy Lieutenants was said to depend on the office for his living, though it was unpaid. Some hint of how this came about may be gained from Falstaff's claim that, until offered bribes for exemption, he used to press first those whose banns had been called twice. The militia was supported by county and parish armouries, and by a salaried muster preacher. The pill was occasionally sweetened by the issue of free tobacco to the soldiers, and the whole institution was financed by the levy of a local rate which, in effect, enlarged the scope of taxation. More of the cost of the Armada fell on these local rates than on national taxation, and Norfolk had to find over £4,000 in a year. The change from bows to firearms, though by no means complete by the end of Elizabeth's reign, had gone far enough to produce a large increase in cost. The militia meant that many local gentlemen held such military power as they had within a Crown force and subject to Crown patronage. This is one reason why the Civil War, in peculiarly English style, was not an assault on the machinery of central government, but an attempt to take it over. The officers of the militia were the class who sat in Parliament, and in many cases they helped to run the war simply by taking the militia over. Yet the militia remained too underfinanced to be seriously competitive abroad. Before England could again fight France and Spain on equal terms, it needed a major change in the system of public finance, and consequently, in the relations between central and local government. Such a change did not happen before the creation of the New Model Army.

⁴ Stone, 206.

Violence and bawdy

But though England was moving away from the era of private wars, it was moving less quickly away from an atmosphere of riot and murder. Swords were still occasionally drawn in the House of Commons. If the motion for candles in the evening was opposed (to oppose it in effect meant a motion for the closure), the resulting scrimmage might produce a situation in which the Speaker feared for his life. In the Lords, the Earl of Pembroke in 1640 could still break his White Staff of office across the head of a peer who disagreed with him. The fact that Pembroke lost office for this escapade suggests that he had done it too many times before.[5] In Somerset, a dispute about the Pyms' right to build a pew on the site of the old high altar (and thereby to claim to be the first family in the parish) could still be challenged by the employment of a hired cutthroat to lay an ambush in Taunton.[6] Violence could be accompanied by the most luxuriant language, and was not governed by any Queensberry rules. The alehouses were a particular haunt of it, and the *Homilies* could give as a reason for unity of religion that the lack of it led to tavern brawls. Another man who picked his quarrel in a more fashionable spot, outside Westminster Hall, could boast of coming away with a handful of his opponent's beard, and another met an assault by biting out a piece of his opponent's nose, and carrying it away in his pocket. Another told his enemy that 'wheresoever he met him, he would untie his points and whip his etc with a rod, calling him ass, puppy, fool, and boy'.[7] He was never able to carry out this threat, because his intended victim murdered him instead. To a modern audience, Shakespeare appears to have a tendency to end his plays with a large number of bodies on the stage, but compared with his contemporaries, he was remarkably abstemious in this respect. Some of the more fashionable sports, such as bear-baiting, cock-fighting, and attending public executions, involved a certain amount of cruelty. A man being executed who failed to 'make a good end', like Hugh Peters the regicide, produced a reaction from the audience much like that to an actor who has muffed his lines.

With this went some sexual licence. Bastardy cases before the Justices

[5] Pembroke had a bad reputation for this type of behaviour, but the king may have wanted to dismiss him for political reasons.

[6] P.R.O. Sta. Cha. 5 P 10/23.

[7] Stone, 224. It is impossible to offer any quantitative estimate of the amount of violence, but the contemporary impression that it was common may be as important a social fact as its actual extent. It is possible that our sources exaggerate the amount of violence, since a token riot might be the best procedure for starting a lawsuit to try the title to land. Kerridge, Eric, *Agrarian Problems in the Sixteenth Century and After* (1969), 82. I regret that this book appeared too late for me to use it.

were as common as cases of fighting in churchyards before the ecclesiastical courts, though it appears that, where it can be discovered, the bastardy
rate was much the same as in the twentieth century. It may be with sexual
licence as with violence, that the important point is not its frequency,
but the impression it created.[8] Parish church ales did, as Puritans claimed,
produce a noticeable increase in the birth rate nine months later. A story
of Aubrey's about Sir Walter Raleigh and his son illustrates both where
there were inhibitions, and where there were not, and perhaps the process
of change also. Sir Walter had been scolding his son, telling him that he
was such a bear that he was ashamed to go out to dinner with him. The
son made his apologies, and was duly taken:

> He sat next to his father and was very demure at least half dinner time. Then
> said he, 'I this morning, not having the fear of God before my eyes, but by the
> instigation of the devil, went to a whore. I was very eager of her, kissed and
> embraced her, and went to enjoy her, but she thrust me from her, and vowed
> I should not, "for your father lay with me but an hour ago".' Sir Walt, being
> so strangely surprised and put out of his countenance at so great a table, gives
> his son a damned blow over the face; his son, as rude as he was, would not
> strike his father, but strikes over the face of the gentleman that sate next to
> him, and said 'box about, 'twill come to my father anon'.[9]

This story, even if apocryphal, may be more typical of Sir Walter
Raleigh than the more famous apocryphal story of Queen Elizabeth and
the cloak. Stories of this kind are also an essential part of the background
to the rise of Puritanism. Things like the Puritan Sabbath, a sober day
of sermon, discussion of the sermon, and Bible reading, can only be understood against the background of riot in the pub. During the Civil War, a
local ordinance to punish soldiers absent from church decreed that any
soldier 'so tippling' should be fined 12d.[10] The urge to get people to understand their duties as Christians, and to dispel ignorance, has to be seen
against the background of the impulse to draw the sword on a point of
honour. The cult of thrift and sobriety has to be seen against a background of incredible consumption of food and drink. Wine was usually
nobleman's main drink, but they might get through eight pints of beer
a day as well. In 1621, a peer once spent £3,000 on one day's meals. The
Psalm-singers who made up part of the New Model Army have to be

---

[8] For two views on this subject, see Laslett, Peter, *The World We have Lost* (1965),
128–49; Stone, 589–671. Professor Stone may be right that standards at court were
or were thought less strict than elsewhere. They certainly varied widely from village
to village. Ben Jonson, at the centre of fashionable society, congratulated one man on
being able to call his children his own, 'a fortune in this age but rarely known': *To
Penshurst*, lines 63–4.

[9] Aubrey, *Brief Lives* (1949), 319.

[10] Pennington, D. H., and Roots, Ivan, *The Committee at Stafford* (1957), 67.

seen against the background of the officer whose hobby was ravishing, and who would order his troops to do the same while he looked on.

What was Puritanism?

Not all Puritans were 'puritan'. The Earl of Leicester, for example, was notorious for his mistresses, and when he finally married one of them on her husband's death, her father refused to believe in the marriage until it had been repeated in his presence. He was solemnly rebuked for his private life by a junior Puritan factotum, and was sufficiently concerned to reply with a 2,000-word letter of self-justification in his own hand. What then were the distinctive beliefs of Puritanism? This question is not about history: it is about language. 'Puritan', or, more frequently, 'precisian', was a term of abuse used by opponents. Almost the only person to lay claim to the title of 'Puritan' for himself was so improbable a character as John Donne.

There can thus be no agreed definition of 'Puritanism', and any statement about what Puritans believed must be mainly a reflection of the definition chosen. Those to whom the distinctive Puritans are sectaries may say that Puritanism was often anti-hierarchical, but they will not call the Earls of Huntingdon and Bedford Puritans. Those to whom the distinctive Puritans are men like Pym and Hampden may say that Puritanism was socially conservative, but they will not classify Foxe the Quaker or Harrison the Fifth Monarchist as Puritans. Those to whom the distinctive Puritans are men like William Prynne, attacking long hair, the theatre, and the drinking of healths, may say that Puritanism was essentially a movement for sober living, but when they find that the majority of Long Parliament M.P.s could not be induced to attend afternoon sittings because they spent their time at the theatre, the park, or the bowling green,[11] they will have to refrain from classifying them as Puritans. It is only possible to outline the definition used here, which is Basil Hall's, including all those who wanted to reform the church in a Protestant direction, and those who wanted to presbyterianize it from within, but excluding separatists and sectaries.[12] By this definition it is possible to agree with Montague that there could be Puritan bishops. It is a definition which includes about half Elizabeth's Privy Council at one end of the spectrum, and a radical organizer of protests like the presbyterian John Field at the other.

[11] According to D'Ewes. B.M. Harl. MS. 163, fo. 601 r.

[12] Hall, Basil, 'Puritanism: The Problem of Definition', in *Studies in Church History*, ed. G. J. Cuming (1965), ii. 283–96. On the more radical groups excluded from this definition, see below, Ch. 7. They had no political importance in England until after the outbreak of the Civil War.

By this definition, all Puritans were as firm believers in one united national church, regulated by authority, as any bishop. Calamy, a leading presbyterian minister, denounced the doctrine of the independence of the individual congregation on the ground that 'particular congregations are integral parts and members of the church catholic'.[13] They believed they were part of the same universal church, with foreign Protestants, and Prynne attacked Laud on the ground that he would 'unchurch the foreign reformed Protestants beyond seas, and sow division between us and them, who were brethren'.[14] Hardly any of them had any sympathy for toleration: toleration was sinful, and likely to provoke God's wrath. When they claimed liberty, it was 'liberty of the Gospel', and not liberty for error. Their attack on the High Commission, for example, was not because it was repressive, but because it repressed the wrong people. Calamy said that 'the terrible High Commission, that wrack and torture of conscience and conscientious men, . . . was appointed like dogs in the capitol, to scare away thieves, but hath for the most part barked only at honest men'.[15] Calamy was prepared to suffer for his principles: at the Restoration, he asked his fellow-presbyterians not to ask for toleration for themselves, for fear it might be granted to Catholics as well. Many, when claiming liberty of conscience, believed that an erroneous conscience was no conscience.

Predestination

If there is one doctrine which is more characteristic of Puritans by this definition than any other, it is Predestination. It was a belief which they shared with many others, and which they believed to be confirmed by the Thirty-Nine Articles.[16] Calvin, who had worked out the doctrine of Predestination to its fullest extent, had nevertheless believed that only God could know whether a man was predestined to salvation or not. On the other hand, William Perkins, one of the most widely read of the Cambridge Puritans, went so far as to maintain that 'every man to whom the Gospel is revealed, is bound to believe his own election, justification, sanctification and glorification, in, and by, Christ'.[17] A number of Puritan wills suggest that their authors followed Perkins, rather than Calvin. John Hampden's grandfather, for example, began his will with an exposition of justification by faith and certainty of his election: 'I bequeath and give my soul unto that mighty and loving lord, the father, by whom I am

---

[13] Hudson, S., *A Vindication* (1650), foreword.
[14] Prynne, W., *Breviate of the Life of William Laud* (1644), 2.
[15] Calamy, E., *God's Free Mercy* (1642), 6.
[16] For the later disputes about predestination, see below, pp. 210–17.
[17] Perkins, W., *A Discourse of Conscience*, ed. Thomas F. Merrill (1966), 19.

assured it was created, and to the most merciful God the son, by whose bitter death and precious bloodshedding and holy resurrection only and alone the same is redeemed, saved, and justified, and to God the Holy Ghost, by whose holy operation and blessed working in me I know my soul to be sanctified, made holy and prepared fit to reign and live with that holy and blessed Trinity.' He asks to be buried without 'all pompous and glittering shows of worldly toys and vanities', but nevertheless to have a funeral sermon preached to 'some reasonable company of my godly friends' by the local vicar, to encourage others to rise to that place whither his soul by faith should be ascended. Then 'forasmuch as we are commanded by the word of God to render to every man his own', he gets down to a practical discussion of the division of the family jewels. This insistence on justification by faith and Predestination was combined with a strong insistence on the wickedness of man, and on the impossibility of fulfilling God's law. Hampden's grandmother thought that God's image was 'utterly defaced and blotted out in me by my transgression and disobedience', and she therefore expected salvation 'not as the . . . wages of any of my works, but as the free gift of God purchased by the death and obedience of his only son'. From this point, her will continues as a long discussion of the division of her wardrobe between five daughters, including a special bequest to one daughter for composing the differences between two others.[18]

Since no man could merit salvation, God's decree of Predestination to salvation was made at random, and the true and lively faith which justified those who were saved was given to them by the operation of God's providence. When God had chosen a man, he marked him out, not only with faith, but by the marks of God's favour in this life.[19] Since God was omnipotent, everything which happened was a mark of his providence. Calvin thought that not a drop of rain fell without the express command of God. The first reaction of a Puritan faced with an attack of the plague would be to look for those national sins which had caused God's visitation, and to hold a day of fasting and humiliation to avert God's wrath. This doctrine sank so deep that even a worried mother writing to her son at Oxford about his illness, could concentrate on asking him to discover what sins he had committed, so that the Lord should cease to punish him. If a battle was won, it was because the Lord 'went out with our armies'. Beliefs of this sort have tended to produce an identification between Puritanism and prosperity. It is true that petitions might ask

[18] P.C.C. 29 Harrington: Bucks. R.O. W.F. (1594).
[19] Calvin had never quite committed himself to this doctrine, but it was common among his English admirers.

the government to remedy the decay of trade by destroying images, but the real identification between Puritanism and prosperity was not through any particularly commercial Puritan doctrines, but simply the belief, which was not confined to Puritans, though perhaps held most strongly by them, that doctrinal truth was favoured by prosperity. When the Dutch were considering changing their doctrine, in 1619, the English ambassador reported that he could not see why they should not preserve 'that form of doctrine without change or alteration, the fruits whereof appear in their prosperity beyond man's discourse'.[20]

The hunger for preaching is something which is now hard to recapture: Prynne and Marshall both asserted in unguarded moments that sermons were the only means of receiving grace, and one preacher who told his congregation after two hours that he would not weary them any further received the reply 'for God sake, Sir, pray go on, go on'.[21] Certainly some Puritan preaching was heady stuff. Calamy, preaching to the Long Parliament on the Last Judgement, said: 'they that are here cloth'd in silk and velvet shall wish for the mountains to cover them, which yet shall be a poor shelter, for the mountains melt at the presence of the Lord, and the rocks rend asunder when he is angry. . . . O you House of Commons, tremble and sin not . . . we are all in God's hand as a fly in the paw of a roaring lion, as clay in the hands of the potter.'[22] With this preaching went an increasingly literal Bible fundamentalism, sometimes reinforced by a congregation looking up the preacher's texts. Perkins compared a conscience bound by God's word to a man being arrested by a magistrate, and thought that no form of worship was ever permissible except what God had directly commanded: 'for when men set up a devised worship, they set up also a devised God.' This belief in obedience led to an increasingly literal emphasis on the idea that all sins were damnable, since all were rebellion against God's commands. As Calamy told the House of Commons, 'you must repent of your little oaths, and your little sins (as the world calls them, though properly there is no sin little, because there is no little God to sin against)'.[23] Most of their familiar stories were drawn from the Old Testament (which takes up a greater part of the Bible than the New), and stressed continually the withdrawal of the Lord's favour from Israel as a punishment for their idolatry. Another characteristic idea was the godly household. After Whitgift had driven many Puritans out of their livings, they concentrated increasingly on the household as a religious unit.

[20] *Letters of Sir Dudley Carleton*, ed. Hardwicke (1757), 113.
[21] Haller, W., *The Rise of Puritanism* (1938), 55.
[22] Calamy, E., *Englands Looking Glasse* (1642), 4.
[23] Perkins, W., *The Idolatry of the Last Times, Works* (1605), 814. Calamy, E., *Englands Antidote* (1644), 22.

Cawdrey said that however good the laws were 'yet if masters of families do not practice at home catechizing, and discipline in their houses, and join their helping hands to magistrates, ministers', there would be no good result. This was the beginning of the great age of the family Bible and family prayers, and many deserved Cawdrey's commendation for the godly, 'that he hath a church in his house'.[24] He thought that such a household would be rewarded by more obedient wives and children, and more honest and faithful servants.

Society and Puritanism

Did Puritanism involve any particular social philosophy? It has been argued that it can be identified with harsh views on the poor. There was certainly an insistence on serving God in our good and lawful callings, and a fierce denigration of idleness. But these views were characteristic of others besides Puritans. Certainly there were some who had harsh views on the treatment of the poor: among what Mr. Hill calls 'the industrious sort of people',[25] the identification of Puritanism with respectability may have produced this sort of reaction. Yet it is so easy to produce a list to the opposite effect that the point becomes doubtful. The Earl of Bedford was accused by Queen Elizabeth of making all the beggars in England by his charity. During the 1597 famine, Pym's Puritan stepfather wrote to the Lord Keeper to plead for more merciful treatment of the poor,[26] while his father, who left no evidence of Puritanism, treated the poor on his estate harshly. Most Puritan morality was drawn from the Old Testament, which includes numerous denunciations of covetousness, of the use of false weights, of the defrauding of widows and orphans, and other forms of sharp practice. Perhaps the only way in which Puritans may be thought to have encouraged profiteering or capitalism is by their sense of priorities: avoidance of idolatry and false doctrine had such an importance that it might swallow up all the rest. As Marshall once said: 'Such a man was upright with God: the meaning is, all his days he maintained God's worship. And yet let me tell you some of their moralities were no better than they should be. Asa in the text was a choleric passionate man, and covetous in his old age, yet because he went through-stitch in the reformation of religion, Asa's heart was said to be upright with God all his days. With this God useth to cover all their infirmities as it were with a veil.'[27]

On the whole, economic historians are now also beginning to doubt

---

[24] Cawdrey, R., *A Godly Form of Household Government* (1600), Ep. Ded. Sig. A 2 and 3.

[25] Hill, C., *Society and Puritanism in Pre-Revolutionary England* (1965), 124–44.

[26] B.M. Harl. MS. 6995, fo. 127.

[27] Marshall, Stephen, *A Sermon* (1641), 27.

whether there can be any clear identification of Puritanism with any particular economic philosophy. The latest historian of Newcastle has concluded that there 'Puritanism represented no overriding view of national trade'. Dr. Supple has concluded that there were no broad differences of economic outlook between king and Parliament.[28] Occasional fiscal measures were resented for their cost, but the broad principles of state regulation of the economy were accepted on all sides. Puritan M.P.s did not believe in economic *laissez-faire*. Wage-fixing under the Statute of Artificers of 1563, control of entry into apprenticeships, and government regulation of the cloth trade, did not involve any broad disputes of principle. The main economic difference between Crown and Commons was that the Commons had a heavier representation of the outports than of London, while the Privy Council was readier to listen to London merchants, who were on the spot. There was little objection in principle to regulation of trade (except by those who would have preferred it regulated in their favour), and Parliament as well as the Crown upheld the privileges of the Merchant Adventurers. Puritanism was essentially a religious, and not an economic, movement.

II FASHIONABLE SOCIETY

The growth of London

Puritanism was one civilizing force, but it was not the only one. The other was the growth of what may be described as the idea of polite society. In this, the essential prerequisite was the growth of London. It has been estimated that by the end of the seventeenth century the population of London was approaching half a million. Its growth caused frequent protests: in 1604 the customer of Sandwich (who may have been losing business) complained that 'all our creeks seek to one river, all our rivers run to one port, all our ports join to one town, all our towns make but one city, and all our cities and suburbs to one vast and unwieldy and disorderly babel of buildings which the world calls London'.[29] Tudor and Stuart governments shared this prejudice against the growth of London, and persistently tried to discourage it, regularly prosecuting people for illegal building, or for unauthorized entry into crafts, in the 'green belt' round Chancery Lane and High Holborn. The City authorities usually supported these measures, for most of the growth was not in the old City,

[28] Howell, Roger, *Newcastle upon Tyne and the Puritan Revolution* (1967), 339, 343–4. Dr. Howell also concludes that 'attempts to analyse it on a class basis are . . . futile'. Supple, B. E., *Commercial Crisis and Change in England 1600–1642* (1964), 230 ff.

[29] Ramsey, Peter, *Tudor Economic Problems*, 179. This may be an over-estimate of the population of London.

but in the suburbs, where the jurisdiction of the City authorities did not run. If a criminal escaped through the gates of the City, the authorities could not pursue him, but had to fetch a Middlesex or Westminster Justice from his dinner. By the turn of the century, Westminster had grown enough to need a separate Bench of Justices in addition to the Justices for the verge of the Court. The Westminster bench often sounds like a roll-call of fashionable England, and was very hard to get on to. Nevertheless, such old-established Westminster residents as Sir Edward Wardour of Wardour Street, who had succeeded his father as an officer of the Exchequer, complained bitterly of the growth of the Westminster bench.

One of the key forces in the growth of fashionable London was litigation. It was during the law term that London was fullest, and a high proportion of gentry and nobility would be attending because they were taking part in the rapidly increasing number of lawsuits. Whether litigation was in fact growing as an alternative to violence is not clear: violence was often a prelude or background to litigation, which certainly did not exclude it. Nevertheless, by the early seventeenth century, many people were using malicious lawsuits as a means of vexing an enemy. The resources of the law were so great that suits often lasted until victory went to the man with the longer purse. For those who had not the money to travel to London, a malicious lawsuit might compel them to settle out of court. In 1640, the vicar of Bradworthy, in one of the remoter corners of north Devon, was bringing malicious suits against his parishioners in the Devon county court, the consistory court of Exeter, the Star Chamber, the bishop's Court of Audience, and the High Commission all at once. Being unable to attend to plead in all these suits, they had to reach such settlements out of court as the vicar was pleased to accept.[30] For gentry, who could afford it, the prospect of litigation was a strong incentive to strain their purses to buy a town house.

Another of the important reasons for the growth of London was the development of the coach. Coaches had been within the means of such as Sir William Petre since the middle of the sixteenth century, but it was not until about the 1590s that they were within the means of moderately prosperous gentry. Before the development of the coach, journeys to London had normally been undertaken on horseback, and while this might be suitable for gentlemen, whose horses were among their proudest possessions, it was less suitable for their wives, riding side-saddle and exposed to the rain. In a coach, women might get to London with as much comfort as men, and they were often more eager to buy a town house than their husbands were. By 1607, Pym's uncle, the feodary of Somerset, had

[30] *Fourtie Articles* (1642), B.M. E. 132.

a coach, which he described in loving detail when leaving it to his wife, yet the Hampdens, who had a shorter journey from Buckinghamshire, had a town house in Whitehall, but had not, by 1597, afforded a coach. When the Civil War broke out, and king and Parliament were operating rival courts of Wards at Oxford and Westminster, the greater success of the Westminster court appears to have been partly because the feodaries preferred to continue coming to London, which in its turn may have been because their wives found it a better centre of fashion than Oxford.

London life naturally developed to meet this influx. Hyde Park was already becoming a centre for fashionable gatherings, and appears to have been used for the rapidly growing sport of horse-racing: on one occasion, Charles I was attending to watch the races, when he caught sight of Henry Marten, who, though he might count as a Puritan in politics, employed emissaries to find suitable people for him to seduce. Charles said: 'let that ugly rascal be gone out of the Park, that whore-master, or else I will not see the sport.'[31] By 1599, fashions in dress were becoming more elaborate: this was the period of the farthingale and the ruff, accompanied by large displays of jewels. The wardrobe was almost the only thing on which Elizabeth was prepared to be extravagant (though less so than James), and she put others to expense by putting the court back into short cloaks when everyone had just bought long ones. Lord Home, who succeeded to the Wardrobe in James I's reign, is said to have made £60,000 by selling her old dresses. Even Charles I continued the tradition, and in 1626–7 he bought 513 pairs of shoes in twelve months. In 1631, embroidering the bed for the queen's confinement cost £772, and the Duke of Buckingham was thought to spend £3,000 a year on clothes.

The theatre

Though Elizabeth lost her parsimony over the wardrobe, she kept it in face of the rapidly increasing love of gambling. One courtier lost £40 a month to her as an insurance against loss of favour, and Ben Jonson claimed that she played with loaded dice. The Earl of Rutland, whose debts helped to drive him to rebellion in 1601, had been losing £1,500 a year at cards. Yet this world was not only one of ostentation: it was also responsible for one of the most remarkable developments of literature in the country's history. The growth of London, by mixing local dialects, may have given something to the development of the English language. Sir Walter Raleigh is said to have spoken broad Devonshire to his dying day, but Aubrey, writing two generations later, appears to find this fact surprising. London and the court were more important to literature as sources

[31] Aubrey, J., *Brief Lives*, 266.

of patronage and protection from the censorship. Strolling players might easily be confused with vagrants, and the Council of Wales had to ask the help of an Eisteddfod to distinguish between bards and vagabonds. In England, players might protect themselves from vagrancy charges by wearing the livery of a Leicester or an Essex. Authors who attached themselves to one of these lords might therefore have a better chance of having their plays performed.

They would also have a good chance with the censorship. Any comment casting ridicule on the Book of Common Prayer, or any comment on issues of contemporary politics which might cause discontent, could be prohibited. Most plays, being designed for performance within the verge of the Court, were usually censored, not by the normal censorship run by the Archbishop of Canterbury and the Bishop of London and enforced through the Star Chamber, but by the Master of the Revels on behalf of the Lord Chamberlain. If the Master of the Revels received a play in which many people would recognize political comment disguised under fictional names and places, he might be suspicious, but if the Lord Chamberlain happened to be head of his family, and had already approved the play by accepting its dedication, he was unlikely to suppress it. Plays had been encouraged by statesmen for some time, and Cranmer and Cromwell had used plays to spread anti-papal propaganda, but it was with the growth of London that they became really numerous, and that they began to be printed.

Today, it is easy to think of the Elizabethan and Jacobean theatre as meaning Shakespeare, but it did not: Shakespeare was an untypical, and not exceptionally successful, representative of it. It is true that there are some allusions to his popularity. Charles I's prosecutor, in 1649, complained that if Charles had known his Bible as well as he knew his Ben Jonson and his Shakespeare, none of the troubles would have happened. Yet it is the noteworthy point of this speech that it is Jonson who is mentioned first. It was he, and not Shakespeare, who was the real literary lion of the period. Inventories of Royalist libraries seized during the Civil War contain many works of Jonson, but none of Shakespeare. It was the deaths of Jonson and Donne (whom he thought most to be admired for his success in achieving dominance over his passions) which produced elegies from young Lord Falkland. One of the most famous commemorations of Shakespeare, 'what needs my Shakespeare for his honour'd bones', was written, not by any representative of the court, but by Milton. This may perhaps suggest a clue, for Shakespeare, like Milton, was too respectable to be within the main cultural stream of the period. Compared with more typical works, like Webster's *Duchess of Malfi* or Ford's *'Tis Pity She's a*

Whore, Shakespeare's plays look as if Dr. Bowdler had been at them already. Jonson, though much of his verse now appears execrable, had a much lighter touch, demanding less feeling from his audience. He provides more light, satirical pictures of his own society, with hypocritical Puritans called Ananias, and fashionable ladies discussing the respective merits of their lovers and of their dentifrice[32] [*sic*]. It is also possible that he was liked for offering more political comment than Shakespeare. Falkland praised him because his 'ethick comedies' dealt with the tragedies of a tottering state, and Cleveland praised him as a man,

> Who to his fable did his persons fit,
> With all the properties of art and wit,
> And above all (that could be acted), writ.

> Who public follies did to covert drive,
> Which he again could cunningly retrive,
> Leaving them no ground to rest on, and thrive

Literature, art, and building

Poetry, as well as plays, produced some remarkable developments. The writing of verses by men to their beloved had become sufficiently common to worry some of those who had no talent for verse, and Berkenhead, author of the royalist newspaper at Oxford during the Civil War, is said to have made his living for some time by supplying suitable verses to young gentlemen in this predicament.[33] Some of this verse belonged to a world very far distant from the Puritans' England. Sir John Suckling, the inventor of cribbage, wrote:

> Out upon it, I have lov'd,
> Three whole days together,
> And am like to love three more,
> If it prove fair weather.

Other poems, such as Herrick's praise for 'a sweet disorder in the dress', belong to a world in which the simplicity of mid-Tudor society already seems far away:

> An erring lace, which here and there
> Enthralls the crimson stomacher: . . .
> A careless shoestring, in whose tie
> I see a wild civility:
> Do more bewitch me, than when art
> Is too precise in every part.

[32] Jonson, Ben, *Catiline*, II, iii. 145–50.
[33] This story is taken from Aubrey, *Brief Lives*, 129 n. It is queried in P. W. Thomas, *Sir John Berkenhead* (Oxford 1969), 185–6. I regret that this work appeared too late for me to use it.

Much poetry was religious, it is true, and with many of the metaphysicals, as Dorothy Sayers has it, 'you never know whether they mean their mistress or the Established Church'. But the quietism of George Herbert or Henry Vaughan, and even more the elaboration of Crashaw, who introduced incense to his College and was ultimately converted from Arminianism to Rome, belongs to an atmosphere which may have been even harder for Puritans to understand than mere secularism.

Literature was far from the only object of cultural patronage. Family portraits had been collected for some time, and in the early seventeenth century Arundel, Buckingham, and Charles I extended their patronage into making large general collections of pictures. Rubens and Vandyck were knighted by Charles I, and though Laud thought him an extravagance, Vandyck regularly received portrait commissions from members of the English aristocracy. When Cranfield was raised from the City to the Court, he placed a bulk order for sixty unspecified pictures. Inigo Jones was employed by Charles I, and though he was not always paid, he was at least granted a protection to keep his creditors at bay. The queen's palace at Greenwich cost Charles £133,000 at a time when he was very short of funds. This fashion for building spread through almost the whole of society, and produced what has been called 'the great rebuilding'.[34] The price noblemen paid for great houses increased even faster than the price rise: Longleat, in 1570, only cost £8,000, but by the turn of the century, Hatfield cost Robert Cecil £40,000. Lower down the social scale, merchants' town houses and yeomen's farmhouses built at this period are still common. Even labourers' cottages were being more carefully built, with more separate rooms. It has been suggested that better housing and glazing, giving more warmth to children and more privacy to parents, contributed something to the increase in population. Chairs were beginning to be available to more than the head of the household, and cushions were bought even by cottagers. Pym's paternal uncle, though a younger son on an annuity, was equipping his house with silk carpets. It was in this period that Elizabeth's godson Sir John Harrington invented the W.C., though he is better remembered for his verses on treason:

> Treason doth never prosper: what's the reason?
> If it doth prosper, none dare call it treason.

Violence was certainly not abolished in fashionable society, but it was increasingly taking the controlled and polite form of duels, fought by two principals with rapiers and according to rules, rather than indiscriminate

[34] Hoskins, W. G., 'The Rebuilding of Rural England', *Past and Present*, no. 4 (1953), 44–59.

affrays involving servants with bludgeons. Pistols, which could have been a dangerous social leveller, were forbidden to the lower classes, but gentlemen often carried them in addition to swords. James I tried to stop duelling, claiming that 'the qualities of gentlemen are made for society, and not for battery', but he met with little success.[35]

Two cultures?

It is easy to exaggerate the depth and the sharpness of the split between this world and the Puritan world. A number of people lived in both. Milton's 'One talent, which 'tis death to hide' may have been a call to be a Puritan preacher, and *Paradise Lost* and *Samson Agonistes* were selected as subjects out of a list of the same themes as Puritan preachers used in sermons, yet Milton wrote *Comus* for performance as a masque, and perhaps even to dissociate himself from Prynne's attacks on the theatre. John Donne is another who made the combination. He is famed for his love poetry, but he was also Dean of St. Paul's and a famous preacher. He wrote verses about the universal church:

> Show me dear Christ, thy spouse so bright and clear.
> What! is it she, which on the other shore
> Goes richly painted? or which rob'd and tore,
> Laments and mourns in Germany and here?

A copy of his 'Good Friday riding westwards' is preserved among the papers of the Puritan Earl of Warwick. For him, the combination was a matter for some tension. In his later years, he was describing his devotion to his 'profane mistresses' as 'idolatry', worried much about whether he repented, while sadly fearing that he did not. His 'batter my heart, three-person'd God' is a real essay in Puritan theology on justification and election:

> Yet dearly I love you, and would be loved fain,
> But am betroth'd unto your enemy:
> Divorce me, untie or break that knot again;
> Take me to you, imprison me, for I
> Except you enthral me, never shall be free,
> Nor ever chaste, except you ravish me.

For great lords, with large supplies of patronage, the combination might be easier: the fourth Earl of Bedford, rebuilder of Covent Garden and manager of the Long Parliament, had patronage both for Pym and for Inigo Jones, and the Earls of Pembroke appear to have spanned the gulf more successfully than anyone else. Yet even Leicester might have difficulties. When he secured the release of Field the Presbyterian organizer

[35] Stone, 247.

from prison, what should have been Field's letter of thanks consisted largely of denunciations for the grief he caused to the godly by patronizing stage players.

On the whole, however, relations between these cultures were strained. The modern bad reputation of the Puritans is largely due to the theatre's attempts to get its own back. Ben Jonson's stage Puritans were all portrayed as sectaries, money-grabbers, and hypocrites, and even Shakespeare would take the occasional dig at Puritans. Malvolio, in *Twelfth Night*, is his most hostile portrait: 'dost think, that because thou art virtuous, there shall be no more cakes and ale?' His most thorough study of a Puritan is Angelo in *Measure for Measure*, and as the play develops, it emerges that Angelo's insistence on enforcing the letter of the law against sin is not unconnected with the temptations to which he is subject himself. At the end, Angelo continues his error, while redeeming his reputation for consistency, by refusing to ask himself for that mercy which he had denied to others. Perhaps the most sympathetic stage portrait of a Puritan is Cordelia in *Lear*, but even she is perhaps less sympathetically portrayed than modern audiences sometimes suppose: after all, her obstinately literal-minded rejection of a harmless ceremony did lead to a great deal of unhappiness. For some, the separation between the cultures was total. When the Long Parliament proposed to impeach Inigo Jones (for destroying property without a court order to rebuild a church), D'Ewes the antiquarian had to stand up and ask who he was. Fitz-Geffrey, who was Pym's local vicar for part of his youth, was certainly not one of the narrower Puritans: he was a minor (and bad) poet, an admirer of Sidney, Drayton, and Spenser, and had probably read Machiavelli. Yet the Jacobean fashion for women wearing men's clothes and swords shocked him beyond measure: 'I would have our masculine females, our hermophradites [*sic*] in their habit, those daubers of faces, and defacers of God's image, I would have them brought into the house of mourning . . . and there chained awhile to the bed of one that lies a-dying.'[36] Like many cultural splits, this one resulted in the focusing of attention on minor points like dress and length of hair, and it also produced a difference of language and style of conversation which made communication difficult. Probably these differences of style helped to produce the complete failure of communication between such men as Suckling and Calamy, and failure of communication may have helped to bring the disputes of 1640 to the point of Civil War, though it did not seriously divide gentlemen before the death of James.

[36] Fitz-Geffrey, C., *Deaths Sermon Unto the Living* (1622), 24.

Literacy and education

One thing which both these ways of life had in common was that they led to the encouragement of education. At the beginning of the period, there was still a substantial amount of illiteracy. A proposed amendment to an Act of 1547 would have extended benefit of clergy to peers who could not read, and in the remote area of Northumberland, as late as the 1560s, 92 of 146 leading gentlemen could not sign their names. At the end of the period, literacy among gentry was almost universal. The proportion of yeomen who signed their leases instead of making a mark rose sharply, and Kentish petitions to Parliament in 1640 suggest that even some labourers were able to read. By the later 1640s, the propaganda of such as the Levellers depended on the literacy at least of small shopkeepers, if not of labourers. Among gentlemen, education often extended much farther than mere literacy. The laicization of the civil service, though it had begun in the Middle Ages, made rapid progress in the 1530s (as it did in countries which remained Catholic). This contributed something to the laicization of the universities, and the abolition of minor orders in 1550 reduced the proportion of 'clergy' in the universities without changing their population. By the middle of the seventeenth century it was coming to be felt that a university education was an asset even for preferment to the Bench, and university education for gentlemen had really arrived. Gentlemen never entirely took over the universities: many poor people still worked their way through, and the sons of clergy added a new and substantial element to the university population. It is hard to give exact figures or dates for the spread of university education for gentlemen, since they depend on the university matriculation registers, which date from about 1570: an appearance of expansion may simply mean better records. On the other hand, where it is possible to cross-check through the history of an individual family, its first layman known to have gone to university is likely to be found between 1570 and 1590. Of 108 members of the Somerset Bench in Charles I's reign, 80 had been either to a university or one of the Inns of Court, and 36 had been to both. On the other hand, only 20 had taken degrees, of whom 10 were clergymen†

Learning acquired at universities was very far from being confined to the formal syllabus. Many people resided during the vacations, when they might read or listen to lectures on modern languages, cosmography, or geometry. Judging by the material subsequently quoted by university men

---

† The matrimonial debate conducted on this page is concluded in Elizabeth Russell, 'The Influx of the Gentry into Oxford University before 1581: an Optical Illusion?', *E.H.R.* (1977), 721–45.

in the Commons, much of their learning was classical. Aristotle, whom Pym's tutor called 'the dictator in philosophy',[37] was still the groundwork of much of the course. M.P.s usually had at their fingertips a considerable number of quotations from such men as Tacitus, Livy, Cicero, and Ovid, and, particularly if they had been under Puritan influence, they might also have some knowledge of a number of the Fathers, Augustine, Cyprian, or Tertullian, and of some more recent theologians, such as Calvin or Melancthon. Above all, every M.P. knew his Bible well enough to recognize a half-completed or adapted text from almost any part of it. The Book of Exodus says that 'thou shalt not follow a multitude to do evil', and Croke, the first Ship Money judge to decide for Hampden, said he had read that a man should not follow a multitude 'against his conscience', and then proceeded to dissent from the judges who had judged before him. All this material trained members to see issues of high principle in the details of proposals which came before them, probably made their speeches longer, and made it far more improbable that they would meekly submit to proposals put before them. Together with the purchase of town houses, which lessened Members' hurry to go home, this may have done most to change the atmosphere of Parliament.

Science and mathematics

It is still a matter of controversy how much the universities contributed to the growth of science and mathematics, but they certainly contributed something. Much of the scientific advance happened at the college founded in London under the will of Sir Thomas Gresham. But among the distinguished members of Gresham College, Henry Briggs, for example, had had his original training in Cambridge, and ultimately settled in one of the scientific professorships created at Oxford by Sir Henry Savile, Warden of Merton and Provost of Eton. Briggs' greatest contribution was to the development of logarithms: he did not invent them, but discussed them with Napier, the Scotsman who invented them, and published the first logarithm table to be used regularly. He was prepared to consider the practical application of his work, and is said by Aubrey to have had a project for a Kennet–Avon canal. Perhaps one of the most important preliminaries to the growth of mathematics was the development of arabic numerals, as anyone who has tried to do long division in roman numerals will at once appreciate. Even addition in roman numerals regularly defeated officers of the Exchequer. Some people were using arabic numerals fairly early in the period, yet Burghley, for example, did all his work as Lord Treasurer in roman numerals, and even in Charles I's reign, ex-

---

[37] Whear, Digory, *Epistolarum Eucharisticarum Fasciculus* (1628), 42.

chequer officials normally used arabic numerals only for rough jottings, and kept the formal accounts in roman. In the Somerset feodaries' surveys, the earliest arabic numeral is in 1594, to endorse the date on the back of the document, and the first survey mainly in arabic numerals is not till 1640. Others were less conservative than the government, and by Charles I's reign, arabic numerals were common enough to make a reasonable standard of mathematics possible.

Much of the impetus to scientific development seems to have been technological. The most urgent need for mathematics was on the part of seamen, trying to discover their position, and of artillery experts, trying to plot the trajectory of cannon balls. The movement of falling bodies could not be properly understood until some of Aristotle's animistic notions about the 'natural appetite' of bodies to occupy their proper place had been discarded. Most of these were refuted by Galileo, and the process was completed when Newton discovered the law of gravity. The development of mechanics gained much of its impetus from attempts to pump water out of deep mines, which, before the end of the period, were beginning to be successful. Several people were trying to invent steam engines, and the English ambassador was much surprised when a Frenchman engaged in the same attempt was put in a madhouse by Cardinal Richelieu. One optimist even submitted to Charles I's navy office a project for a submarine.

In astronomy, little of the early development was English. Copernicus, Kepler, Tycho Brahe, and Galileo are the key men in the story, and all are continental. Yet their work was much studied, though not always accepted, in England. The point of greatest resistance was not Copernicus' idea that the earth revolved round the sun, but the notion that there were other suns than ours. Francis Bacon, whose claims to scientific fame have been much exaggerated, rejected Copernicus' theory and continued to believe that if man were not the centre of the world, 'the rest would seem to be all astray, without aim or purpose'.[38] New ideas, however, were advancing steadily, and at least one Laudian bishop had Tycho Brahe's *Historia Caelestis* in his library.

In medicine, though the profession was expanding, the general standard of practice remained fairly low. The general standard of Tudor medicine may be illustrated by a remedy for 'weakness of consumption' which Lord Audley once sent to William Cecil:

[38] Lovejoy, A. O., *The Great Chain of Being* (1935), 109, 187. See also Marie Boas Hall, in *New Cambridge Modern History* (1968), iii. 459–62. She stresses the 'essential improbability' of the Copernican theory in the light of the available evidence, and argues that it is surprising that it was so widely accepted.

Take a sow pig of nine days old ... and put him in a stillory with a handful of spearmint, a handful of red fennel, a handful of liverwort, half a handful of red nepe [turnip], a handful of celery, 9 dates clean picked and pared, a handful of grape raisins, and pick out the stones, and a quarter of an ounce of mace, and two sticks of good cinnamon bruised in a mortar; and distill it together with a fair fire, and put it in a glass and set it in the sun nine days, and drink nine spoonfuls of it at once when you list.[39]

Clinical practice depended heavily on purgings and bloodlettings, whose theory was based on Galen's pathology, in which the balance of the body depended on the proportions of the 'humours', of earth, air, fire, and water, whose proportions made a man who was 'plethoric', 'choleric', 'phlegmatic', or 'melancholy'. Galen was still so much respected that Dr. Caius, President of the Royal College of Physicians, could imprison a young doctor for saying that Galen had made mistakes,[40] and Vesalius, who developed the practice of dissection early in the sixteenth century, attributed his failure to confirm Galen's description of the human head to his own lack of skill. Galen's pathology was not fully discarded till the nineteenth century. One big advance was made in England, however, the discovery of the circulation of the blood by William Harvey. According to Aubrey, his discovery made people think him crack-brained, and much reduced his practice, but he had the patronage of Charles I, who employed him before the Civil War, and made him Warden of Merton against the strong opposition of the Fellows.

The development of science during this period was of more significance for the future than for the present. Mathematics were put to some important uses, especially in surveying land, and in actuarial work designed to calculate men's expectation of life in order to assess their entry fines, but science was still too closely involved with magic to make very rapid progress. Napier the inventor of logarithms was devoted to astrology, and even Sir Isaac Newton devoted many of the best years of his life to alchemy. Both of them also wrote theological treatises on the Book of Revelation, and regarded these as having equal importance with their scientific work. All that can really be said before 1640 is that the foundations had been laid from which rapid scientific development could begin.

[39] Conyers Read, i. 92.
[40] Hall, A. R., *The Scientific Revolution* (1962), 38.

III   ECONOMIC CHANGE

Prosperity and poverty

Most of these social changes suggest a steadily rising standard of living. For many people, there certainly was a rising standard of living, but it should be remembered that it is the successful who leave records. Occasional hints suggest that others were not so fortunate. Those whose receipts were running ahead of the price rise, in all classes, might expect to do very well, but most of them probably rose at the expense of others, falling behind the price rise, who were unable to keep their heads above water. Dr. Bowden believes that for the poor, the years 1620–50 were some of the most terrible years this country has passed through,[41] and though this is contradicted by the evidence of labourers' inventories, it should be remembered that it is only the successful who leave inventories, and all inventories can prove is that successful labourers were growing more successful. Certainly, the disastrous harvests of the 1590s and 1620s produced famines which appear to have been as dramatic as any earlier in the century, particularly since the famine at the beginning of the 1620s coincided with the deep depression which followed the ending of the period of rapid price rises, and therefore with widespread unemployment in the clothing industry. Another serious famine in 1630–1 was marked in Somerset by a sharp rise in the proportion of food thefts among cases coming before the Justices. The dramatic price rises of the 1590s, coming when harvest failure had reduced purchasing power, produced numerous bankruptcies among small travelling merchants. Some gentlemen, cursed with tenants on long leases, or numerous daughters needing marriage portions, or simply with extravagance, went bankrupt.

For others, in all classes, the standard certainly rose, and their range of purchases was extended. Wine imports were large, and the farm of the customs on sweet wine was one of the largest items in the Earl of Essex's income. Sugar, though still not available to the poor, was selling by 1600 at about 1s. 8d. the pound, and it has been suggested that it may have been as widely used as wine is today. A certain amount had been refined in England since 1544, but the 1559 Parliament had proposed to prohibit the refining of sugar in England because it was 'counterfeit and unwholesome'. The proposal was not successful, but until the 1560s most English sugar was refined in Antwerp. By the end of the century there were as many as seven English refineries, and the trade was profitable enough to attract the attention of searchers after monopoly. The officers of the Court

[41] *Agrarian History*, 621.

of Wards had sugared wine at eleven, and sugar loaves appear to have
become established on the list of suitable presents for a visiting dignitary.

Tobacco

Tobacco, though it became available later than sugar, appears to have
caught on faster, and to have been available to a much wider range of
classes. It is perhaps a measure of the speed with which the use of tobacco
spread that it provoked such vehement opposition. James I, who disliked
Sir Walter Raleigh, disliked tobacco equally with its importer, and wrote
a vehement *Counterblast* to it, claiming that it injured health and caused
catarrh, and asking, like many of its modern opponents, how one and the
same thing could make it easier, both to wake up and to go to sleep. In
1621, Sir Edwin Sandys, Treasurer of the Virginia Company, rashly moved
a motion in the Commons to protect the Virginia trade by prohibiting the
import of Spanish tobacco, and also proposed to improve the Crown's
finances by levying customs on the re-export of sugar. The proposal on
tobacco let loose a storm of non-smoking indignation. Sir Jerome Horsey,
husband of Hampden's aunt, said that when he was first a Parliament
man, this vile weed was unknown, that thousands had died of this 'vile
weed', that it should be prohibited in alehouses, and that he abhorred it
the more because the king disliked it. He ended by moving to amend
Sandys' motion to make it a ban on all imports of tobacco. He was
answered by a less earnest member, who said he 'loveth tobacco as ill as
any, if ill tobacco', but his motion was carried. This was followed by a
bill against the 'inordinate use of tobacco', which produced an outburst
from another member to the effect that 'tobacco and ale now made inseparable to the base vulgar sort: these accompanied with idleness,
drunkenness, sickness, decay of their estates, etc.'[42] Fortunately this bill
never completed its course, since it would have been one Commons' bill
James would not have vetoed. Glass also became much more common
after Sir Robert Mansel had obtained a monopoly of a process for using
coal for glass-blowing without getting the smoke into the glass. On one
occasion, the Commons' Journals in the first week of January contain an
order to send for the glazier with the utmost speed.

Agriculture and transport

Things such as these were the froth of economic progress, which rested
on a rather solider base. One of the most important gains was the first
large increase for some time in the amount of cultivated land. A large area
of Thames marshes round Plumstead and Erith was drained, and was near

[42] *C.J.*, i. 581, 605.

enough to London to help with the capital's food supply. The biggest gain was through a long series of extensive projects for draining part of the fens. The first fen drainage project of the period had been started by Lord Russell of Thornhaugh in the 1560s, and he had brought over Dutch engineers to make the plans. The Dutch had the greatest experience of drainage works, and the projects of Charles I's reign were mostly carried through by the Dutch engineer Vermuyden. The backing came partly from the king, and partly from a series of peers of whom Bedford was the most conspicuous. With the increase in the supply of land went improvements in its use. Marl, ash, and other artificial fertilizers were becoming more common, and market gardening was being developed. Turnips were common in Norfolk by the middle of the seventeenth century, and cabbages, cauliflowers, and peas were also being grown, though potatoes were unpopular because it was believed they caused wind, and they remained rare until well after the Restoration. With the improvements in agriculture went a series of improvements in transport for its products. Weirs and weeds were cleared, and locks built on a number of rivers. Tolls were used to finance the improvements, and since water was so much cheaper than land transport, the cost still remained within economic reach, for industrial as well as agricultural products. Sheffield steel was being shipped down the Don, Yorkshire cloth down the Aire and the Calder, Cheshire salt and cheese down the Dee, and Lancashire textiles down the Mersey.

From the sea, they could be taken to London by a rapidly growing coasting trade. The demands of the coasting trade, as well as the navy and privateering, stimulated a big increase in shipbuilding. It is hard to produce exact figures, since not all ships were registered, and it is often hard to know whether those which were are English-built or prizes, but total tonnage may have increased between 1615 and 1660 from about 115,000 to 200,000. Many of these were small, but some, particularly some of the ships owned by noblemen with maritime interests, were as big as any in the royal navy. The growth of shipping increased the demand for naval stores from the Baltic, to which, after about 1615, Sheffield knives were exported in exchange. It also caused acute alarm about shortage of timber. It has recently been argued that this alarm was unjustified,[43] but it was almost universal, and at the least there was a shortage of timber suitable for ships in places where it was convenient to transport.

[43] Hammersley, G., 'The Crown Woods and their Exploitation', *B.I.H.R.* (1957), 136–61.

Coal and iron

The belief in a timber crisis did much to encourage the growth of the coal industry, which is perhaps the only development of the period which could possibly be called an industrial revolution. Coal output had been growing for some time, but it was in Elizabeth's reign that development became rapid, and that improved drainage techniques made it possible to work deep mines. At Blyth, the mines stretched under the sea well before the end of the century. Though the Newcastle coalfields were much the most important, they were not the only ones. Mining in South Wales was well developed, and there were a number of coalmines in the Midlands. Coal was quickly adopted for domestic fuel, and produced a series of complaints about the dirt and smell of London. It is probably coal which accounts for the fact that it was the west end of London which became fashionable. As Evelyn said, 'because the winds blowing near three quarters of the year from the west, the dwellings of the west end are so much more free from the fumes, steams and stinks of the whole easterly pile; which when sea coal is burnt is a great matter'.[44] It was also quickly adopted for a variety of industrial processes, and by the end of the period some of it was being exported.

There were only two important restrictions on the growth of the coal industry. The first was transport. It was easy enough to transport coal by sea, and it produced a flourishing coastal trade between Newcastle and London, interrupted only by enemy action or piracy. But its weight was such that a journey of two miles by land might double its price, and its use appears to have been economic only within about fifteen miles of water. Oxford, where the Thames was navigable by the end of the century, used coal, but such places as Watford or St. Albans were outside its range. The other important restriction was that coal, like most early industrial development, was a very risky investment. It demanded a large initial outlay of capital, and it was always possible either that drainage costs would continue to exceed receipts, or that the seam would run out. Even the Earl of Northumberland with a coalfield on the Tyne might find himself making a loss, and when the Court of Wards leased a coalmine at Hemsworth (Yorkshire) they noted: 'memorandum, that there hath not been as yet any profit made of the said coalmine.'[45]

There was some development of the iron industry, but this was held up by inability to adapt it to the use of coal, and by the repeated exhaustion of woods near its sites. Most of the biggest ironworks were in wooded

[44] Wilson, C., *England's Apprenticeship* (1965), 47.
[45] P.R.O. Wards 12.5.

areas, such as the Weald or the Forest of Dean. Nevertheless, a substantial industry was developed, especially in armaments. By 1621 the House of Commons was becoming indignant at the export of cannon to Spain. By the time of the Civil War, armaments manufacturers were a sufficiently recognizable vested interest for Henry Marten to maintain that 'if his majesty should take advice of his gunsmiths and powder-men, he would never have peace'.[46] Lead mining was also developing fast, and the Mendip mines reached a peak of production in the early seventeenth century. Yet these developments, too, were risky to those who invested in them. Leicester made a heavy loss on ironworks at Cleobury Mortimer, and Sir Henry Sidney, Lord Deputy of Ireland, found his steelworks in Sussex broken by Baltic competition. Much of the capital for mining and heavy industry came, not from canny rising capitalists (who usually preferred to stick to the safer trade of moneylending), but from peers rich enough to risk their money, for whom, Professor Stone suggests, industrial or colonial investment might fill much the same function as gambling.[47] A wider circle of people were involved at the craftsman level, and the tanners and nail-makers of Birmingham, the Staffordshire potters, and the pewterers included a number of small men.

Cloth: the new draperies

Though there was enough industry to create a promise for the future, most of it during this period still deserves the verdict that one swallow does not make a summer. It did not create any powerful class, and except for some of the Newcastle coalmerchants, few people had any political or social influence which was based on industrial success. Even those peers who made profits from industry and mining were such as the Earl of Shrewsbury, whose landed wealth was already so great that he could carry a number of losses. The staple English industry was still the old established cloth industry, and the dominant economic influence the inner ring of the Merchant Adventurers, and for them times were growing hard. As early as 1595, Burghley was worrying about economic competition from the Dutch. As the seventeenth century went on it grew more serious, and the cloth trade and the carrying trade were the two places where it was most severely felt. Whenever the effects of Dutch competition were combined with an attack of the plague, disrupting the fairs and markets, or with war, or a bad harvest, a slump would result. The Privy Council's policy towards the clothing industry was largely guided by social, rather than economic motives. During depressions, when clothiers were in danger

[46] Aubrey, J., *Brief Lives* (1962), 266.
[47] Stone, 382–3.

of bankruptcy, the Council was more worried about unemployment and famine riots. It would compel clothiers to keep on men for whom they had no work, and would use the Justices' power to fix wages under the Statute of Artificers of 1563 to increase minimum wages. The only method of cutting costs the clothiers had was to stretch the cloth or otherwise reduce its quality, and this constantly rendered them liable to prosecution.

No adequate substitute was found after the Revolt of the Netherlands caused the disintegration of the Antwerp market, and though the Merchant Adventurers had some good years at Hamburg, the period was dominated by a desire for new markets. Many improbable ones were found, but they were often not suitable. As Sir Edwin Sandys complained, Egypt was too hot for thick English cloth to be a welcome import. Domestic pressure compelled the East India Company to go on exporting woollen cloth until the nineteenth century, but the Indians had little use for it. After 1618, the trade was further handicapped by the Thirty Years' War, which caused a series of abrupt currency manipulations in Germany and the Baltic. These knocked the bottom out of the cloth market, and gave England only the dubious benefit of a cheapening of luxury imports which may have contributed to the growth of court fashion. By the later part of Charles I's reign, the industry was also suffering from crises of confidence due to political instability, and 1640 and 1649 were both years of slumps.

The only part of the cloth trade which was flourishing was what was known as the 'new draperies'. These were lighter, gaudier clothes, designed for a more expensive market and suitable for a warmer climate. They were therefore the more welcome imports in such areas as the Mediterranean, which were not subject to the currency crises of the Thirty Years' War. There was also a market for them in northern Europe, and exports from London to northern Europe rose from just over 3,000 pieces in 1628 to about 13,500 by 1640. There was a parallel expansion in hatting and felt-making. In this growth of the new draperies, England benefited from the Protestant refugees received by Elizabeth. At Halstead, Essex, which was in an area dependent on the old clothing industry, the immigrants were driven out by racial prejudice. As the trade of Halstead decayed, the inhabitants petitioned the immigrants to return, but they refused. Fortunately for the English economy, Elizabeth had no sympathy with these protests against immigrants, and replied that 'they are all welcome. I, at least, will never fail them'.[48] She even allowed them the privilege of having their own churches, organized on lines many Puritans longed to be

[48] Meyer, A. O., *England and the Catholic Church under Queen Elizabeth* (1916), 32.

allowed for themselves. In 1572, she had to stop a bill introduced by a Puritan M.P. to the effect that the services by the French and Dutch churches should be permitted to Englishmen. Archbishop Laud, on the other hand, found their separate churches intolerable, and argued that because they did not conform to the church of England they were a State within a State, and liable to support a foreign invasion. His attempts to rescind their privileges were a threat to the English economy, as well as to Puritanism.

Credit

The expansion of industry and trade, and the survival of gentlemen during the fluctuations of the price rise, was much helped by improvements in credit. The two commonest methods were the mortgage, usually raised on the security of an estate already owned and repaid in a lump sum at the end of the term, and the bond, the system immortalized in *The Merchant of Venice*. Bonds rarely involved anything quite as drastic as Shylock's pound of flesh: the normal bond bound a friend of the debtor to repay something in the region of twice the sum involved if the debtor failed to repay it himself. The courts, not being of the moneylending classes, were often sympathetic to the debtors, and their normal delays also hindered recovery of bonds. One moneylender spent £80 on legal fees in the Court of Common Pleas to recover a debt of £60 from Pym's brother-in-law, and then had to go through another lawsuit before he got the money.[49] After about 1625, Chancery applied the doctrine of equity of redemption of a mortgage, by which the creditor could not foreclose, and seize the estate, if the debtor could continue to pay the interest, or if he could repay the principal late. In spite of the lack of sympathy of the courts, moneylending appears to have been one of the safest professions available, and Cockayne, Cranfield, and Sutton, builders of three of the biggest fortunes in England, all found moneylending one of the best parts of their business. Profits were somewhat lessened when the rate of interest was lowered to 8 per cent, in 1624, but they remained considerable.

Overseas trade: the search for new markets

Improvements in credit and shipbuilding may help to explain the rapid growth after 1580 of overseas trading companies, and the opening out of English trade into areas which had been effectively closed to it for some time. A large share of the Baltic trade was being recovered by the English, and the merchants concerned were incorporated as the Eastland Company in 1579. By 1598, the English were sufficiently securely established in the

[49] P.R.O. C. 2 (Charles I) P. 51/17.

trade to make it possible to close the Hansards' base at the Steelyard in London, but there, as elsewhere, the English suffered continually from the competition of the Dutch. The Russia Company brought back some goods similar to those which came from the Baltic, but though it was established earlier, it never grew very large. The Barbary Company, founded in 1581, was even less successful. Although the Earl of Leicester was one of the chief investors, it found the political difficulties of the Moroccan market too great to make the trade very profitable. It was kept going by the demand for sugar and saltpetre, but it grew little. The West Africa trade had been growing since Edward's reign, and was again based on an incorporated Company. There was some trouble with export cargoes, but the West Africans could usually be induced to accept some English metalwork, and ivory and other cargoes were brought back, in addition to the growing triangular trade in slaves to Spanish America.

One of the most successful markets, though perhaps one of the less significant in the long term, was the Mediterranean. After the Spanish victory at Lepanto in 1571, the threat from the Turks was less, and English ships were becoming strong enough and well enough armed to resist both the Spaniards and the Algiers pirates. Some combined trade with privateering, and one courtier, in 1628, brought back a cargo of pirated marbles. The greatest centre of the Mediterranean was Leghorn, where trade was much helped by the Grand Duke of Tuscany's edict that merchants of all religions might live there without persecution. Trade was a considerable pressure towards religious toleration, and even the Pope once tried to attract trade to Civitavecchia by offering to tolerate heretics there. Aleppo, one of the main trading centres of the Levant Company, became a regular enough market to have a resident English consul, and to provide one of the allusions used by the witches in *Macbeth*, and Turkey also became a trading centre. Currants were one of the main goods brought back, together with indigo and other dyes for cloth, and some of the Levant and Turkey merchants grew very rich. Like almost all other trades except the Eastland trade, it was firmly dominated by London merchants.

The East India Company

Though the Levant was nearer the source for spices and other far eastern products than Antwerp had been, there was still a desire to get them at source in the far east, and in 1591 Lancaster tried a direct voyage to Sumatra. He came back on a French ship, having exhausted his money, but believing the trade had a future. In 1599, a company was formed for trade to the East Indies, with subscriptions from 100 substantial London merchants, and Lancaster led the first voyage. Factors were left behind at Bantam, but the East India Company started too late to secure any firm foothold in what is now Indonesia. By 1598, the Dutch were already sending out 20 ships a year, and after James had lamentably failed to champion the Company when a number of its servants were murdered by the Dutch at Amboyna in 1623, the Company increasingly concentrated its trade on India. Sir Thomas Roe had already been sent on an embassy to the Great Mogul, and though he thought the Mogul's rule was arbitrary, and lacked settled forms of law and government, he was on the whole favourably impressed. The material level of civilization in the two countries was probably much more similar than it became later. Roe thought that forts and wars should be avoided, because they interfered with trade, and it was not until 1639 that the first English fort, Fort St. George at Madras, was built, and even that was put up unofficially by a factor. Indigo, pepper, silk, and saltpetre could be got from India, and English workmen were sent out to teach the Indians to make calico and chintz more to the English liking. But though India had much more to offer England, England had little to offer in return, and the East India Company constantly suffered at home, because, in the face of all current theory, it had occasionally to export bullion. Its biggest profits may have been gained in the flourishing field of re-exports. By 1640, re-exports of overseas produce equalled all other non-textile exports, and though a million pounds of tobacco accounted for much of this, the East India Company had its share. Often they succeeded in using their re-exports to purchase bullion abroad, and so did not have to export it from England. Their trade was also helped by the fact that the price of silver was higher in the East Indies than in Europe. These companies may not have had a significant proportion of total overseas trade, but they did manage to attract a considerable amount of investment from gentlemen and M.P.s. The proportion of M.P.s with investments in overseas trading companies reached 33 per cent in 1621 (though it later fell below 25 per cent), and it is interesting that the majority of them first invested *after* their election to the Commons. The two biggest interests were the East India and Virginia Companies, followed by the Spanish, Irish, Levant, and French, with the Massachusetts Bay Company at the bottom of the list. Some of these gentlemen may have had no more interest in overseas trade than shareholders of Imperial Chemical Industries now have in chemicals, but their money was useful.

The beginnings of colonization: privateering

This expansion of overseas trade was one, but only one, of the influences which led towards the colonization of America. Trading interests tended to be directed towards the West Indies, and though they contributed much to the colonization of Barbados early in the seventeenth century, they contributed less to the northern mainland. Virginia tobacco and Newfoundland cod were the only non-tropical commodities which were as interesting as Barbados sugar. Privateering, though it contributed something to interest in North America, again led rather towards the West Indies. Privateering was largely a hobby for optimists (one privateering ship was called the *Why Not I?*), and it bankrupted many who engaged carelessly in it. Even the Earl of Cumberland, who invested a large fortune and a private fleet in it, was said to have thrown his land into the sea, and when he captured a cargo which might have retrieved his fortunes, it was wrecked in Mount's Bay. Amateur privateers may have done more to relieve domestic disorder than to expand trade, and Sir George Carey's employment of liveried privateers is a fascinating mixture of the old and the new. Many professionals, on the other hand, were much more successful, and in the 1590s privateering was accounting for between 10 and 15 per cent of English imports. The Spanish treasure fleets were never captured, but individual merchantmen often were, and their cargoes may have done something to keep down the price of leather and sugar, and certainly helped to provide capital for investment. Some of Drake's captains had highly successful individual careers. Captain Newport, a former Harwich shipmaster, who combined his privateering with destruction of images and removal of church bells, had many successful voyages, presented a live crocodile to James I's menagerie, and ended up a rich shareholder in the East India and Virginia Companies. Some of the larger City merchants, such as Bayning and Watts, organized their privateering with enough care to have large fortunes to invest in trading companies, or even purchase of land. Raleigh's first unsuccessful Virginia project in 1584 owed something to the desire for a privateering base, but possibly the chief contribution of privateering to colonization was the increased familiarity with the problems of Atlantic navigation.

Motives for colonization

Overpopulation certainly contributed something to the beginnings of colonization, and was frequently given as a reason for colonization both in America and Ireland. Unemployment also contributed to colonization, and it is probably not a coincidence that serious settlement began after the depression of 1620, and that much of it came from clothing counties. But except for the Anglican colony of Virginia, refounded early in James I's reign, religion was probably the most important single motive. The main stream of Puritans, who regarded themselves as members of the

Anglican church and could hold offices, usually wanted to stay in England, at least until Charles I's reign. For members of sects, on the other hand, there was little future in England, and a perceptive royalist wit asked in 1660 'whether that prophecy, the saints shall rule the earth, be not meant of Barbadoes, Jamaica or some *terra incognita*?' The Brownists were one of the most popular targets of late Elizabethan abuse, and in 1597 a company of them petitioned to be allowed to emigrate to Canada, and, with vague geographical sense, expressed the hope that they would also be able to 'annoy that bloody and persecuting Spaniard about the Bay of Mexico'.[50]

The most characteristic doctrine of the Brownists, which later sects took over, was the belief that the church should consist of 'the worthiest, were they never so few'. This was the complete antithesis of Hooker's view that 'there is no man a member of the commonwealth, which is not also a member of the church of England'.[51] Brownist doctrine separated the church from the commonwealth, excluded the magistrate from authority in it, gave power to each individual congregation, and made it impossible to use the church as any guarantee of social order. Although Burghley finally procured Browne's silence by giving him a vicarage, the movement which he started developed further until it produced a proliferation of further sects and groups. Authorities deeply suspected them of preaching social revolution. Certainly they withdrew the generally accepted sanctions for the class structure, and alarm was much increased when Browne was found preaching without a licence at the brick kilns at Islington, whose warmth made them the most popular sleeping place for the unemployed looking for work in London.

Not all who separated from the church were deliberate sectaries. Many other believers in a united church found, after Bancroft's drive against nonconformity in 1604, that they were unable to remain within the national church as it was. When James, at the Hampton Court Conference, threatened that 'I will make them conform themselves, or else I will harry them out of the land', he may not have meant to offer an alternative, but he did. At first, most exiles went to Holland, and the voyage of the *Mayflower*, in 1620, was recruited from an exiled congregation at Leyden. A further big migration to Massachusetts was organized in the 1630s by Winthrop, who had been an attorney practising in the Court of Wards. Unlike Virginia, which was supported by lotteries and collections in churches, Massachusetts was not entirely respectable at

[50] Andrews, K. R., *Elizabethan Privateering* (1964), 197. *Free-Parliament Quaeres* (1660), p. 2 B.M. E. 1019.

[51] Hooker, R., *Ecclesiastical Polity*, VIII. i. 2. For necessary qualification of these points, see Miller, Perry, *Orthodoxy in Massachusetts* (1933).

first, and Heylin, Laud's chaplain, described it as the spleen of the body politic, in which all the ill humours of the kingdom were gathered, and his master was only prevented by the outbreak of Civil War from sending out a bishop to keep the colonists in order. Others were more sympathetic, and in 1636 Lords Saye and Brooke, two of the leading patrons of the main stream of Puritanism, nearly settled in Massachusetts themselves, and only refrained when they found it impossible to persuade the colonists to set up a legislative chamber of 'hereditary gentlemen'. Pym, whose son emigrated, was sympathetic, and ascribed the emigration to 'a spiritual famine of God's word'. Certainly such a famine existed in Pym's own parish, where the churchwardens reported in 1629 that they could not present their vicar for non-residence, because they did not know who he was.[52] In spite of Laud's schemes, the colonists kept their religious liberty, and it is interesting to discover that there was a time when the English government accepted the doctrine of 'no taxation without representation'. In 1621, a bill was introduced into the Commons about the levying of tithes on Newfoundland cod, and Secretary Calvert (later Lord Baltimore, and founder of the Catholic refuge of Maryland) opposed it on the ground that America was not under the jurisdiction of Parliament.[53]

There was some trouble about getting enough women to settle in the colonies, and in 1618 an indignant Somerset J.P. complained to the Council about people who 'pretended a commission to press maidens to be sent to the Bermudas and Virginia',[54] but by the end of the period interest in America had grown sufficiently rapidly to ensure a flow of emigrants large enough to keep the colonies going. When Burghley, at the end of Elizabeth's reign, had drawn up a list of the reign's achievements, he had mentioned nothing happening outside Europe except Drake's voyage round the world, but a generation later the idea of America appealed to Donne enough for him to address his beloved as 'my America, my new found land'. Some emigrants returned to England when the outbreak of the Civil War offered more hope for nonconformists, but there were never enough to threaten the survival of the colonies.

IV STRESSES AND STRAINS:
CONSERVATISM IN A CHANGING WORLD

All these changes, religious and economic, were hard to absorb within a social theory which was based on the notion of a stable social order and unanimity in religious and political purposes. The notion of every man in

[52] Rushworth, III. i. 201: Somerset Record Office, D/D/Ca, Act Book 266.
[53] *C. J.*, i. 626.
[54] *Cal. S. P. Colonial*, 19.

his place was hard to combine with the effect of inflation on the social structure, and the notion that it was a meaningful limitation on the king's power to say that 'the king's prerogative stretcheth not to the doing of any wrong'[55] was hard to preserve when almost every action of the king's was thought wrong by some group of his subjects. Many of the tensions of this period resulted from the incompatibility between social facts and social ideas.

The status-seekers

It was a period of considerable, if not unprecedented, social mobility. Perhaps the best indication of social mobility is the increasing concern with marks of status. The claims of Robert Shallow, Esquire, and of Doll Tearsheet, 'a proper gentlewoman' to their dignities may have been dubious, but they were no more dubious than those of some factual characters. The sale of coats of arms, both by the College of Arms and by bogus heraldic touts, was one of the common abuses of the age, and those who bought coats of arms included the common hangman of London. Competition for seats on the Bench increased as the number of gentlemen rose, and there was even some competition about the order in which gentlemen were listed: one once congratulated himself on being listed fourth after the knights. When knighthoods and titles were for sale in James I's reign, they fetched high prices, and the success of the new Jacobean title of Baronet was partly because the first to become Baronets took precedence on the Commissions of the Peace. Robert Shallow congratulated himself, not only on being a Justice, but on being of the quorum, and this mainly honorary distinction on the Bench was so much sought after that the proportion of members on the quorum rose steadily. Since the increasing number of peers and knights usually had to be on the Commission, it probably grew harder for a mere Esquire to achieve membership. Among the Five Members whom Charles I regarded as leaders of the Long Parliament in 1642, Pym and Strode were not members of the Bench, and Hampden was unable to obtain membership of the quorum. It may have been concern for status which was the main force in the increasing demand for parliamentary seats. Some of this demand was undoubtedly due to political zeal, especially on the part of the Puritans, but many people spent large amounts of time and money on securing election to Parliament, and yet showed little desire to take any active part in the proceedings when they got there. More and more constituencies were finding members willing to serve without wages, and though a few

[55] Finch, Sir Henry, *Law Or A Discourse Thereof* (1627), 85. This sentence is in the middle of an exaltation of the king as a god on earth. I would like to thank Mr. J. P. Cooper for drawing my attention to this treatise.

continued to pay wages after the Restoration, by Charles I's reign the practice was almost extinct. At the same time, the costs of electioneering were rising. They had not reached anything like the dimensions of the eighteenth century, but already by 1640 the second Earl of Salisbury had to spend £350, and disburse 600 gallons of sack, to get his candidate elected for Hertfordshire. Even in Old Sarum, he had to spend £72 on music and drummers, and free meals for the few freeholders. A popular candidate, like Sir Thomas Barrington in Essex, who was the leading local Puritan and backed by the Rich interest, might manage on as little as £42, but the days were past when landlords could always deliver their tenants to any candidate they chose, though they still tried, and often succeeded. At least one lease included an obligation to vote for the landlord's candidate in elections, and in 1614, the Bishop of Bath and Wells promised to deliver his tenants' votes to Sir Robert Phelips, or else they would 'smart for it soundly'.[56] Yet the rising expense is a mark of the growing independence of the yeomanry, and possibly of a decreasing social gap between them and the lesser gentry.

The gentry controversy

For a number of years historians have been arguing that a number of the strains of this period were caused either by the rise or by the decline of the gentry. Tawney believed that the gentry, whom he unfortunately classified as 'bourgeois', were rising, and demanding an increasing share of political power to match their economic power. Professor Trevor Roper, on the other hand, believes that the gentry were declining, and were able to recoup their fortunes only through the law or court office.[57] This controversy has given rise to a variety of detailed research. This has given us a much better understanding of county politics, and of competition for offices, but its only effect on the original argument has been to confirm the verdict of Christopher Hill: 'it is easy to argue that "the gentry" were either "rising" or "declining", if we take samples of the class: for some families were doing the one, and others the other.'[58] It is at least clear, however, that the gentry were not in the position of Sir Henry Wotton's man who was

[56] Hembry, Phyllis, *The Bishops of Bath and Wells* (1967), 213.
[57] For the original controversy, see R. H. Tawney, 'The Rise of the Gentry 1558–1640', ... *Ec.H.R.* (1941), 1–38; H. R. Trevor-Roper, 'The Gentry 1540–1640', *Ec.H.R.* Supplement no. 1, (1953), and J. H. Hexter, 'Storm Over the Gentry', reprinted in *Reappraisals in History* (1961), 117–52. Of the three, Hexter's position has best stood the test of time. Hexter argued that theories about the rise or decline of the gentry could not explain the Civil War, since they were theories designed to explain a deliberate revolution, whereas no deliberate revolution took place.
[58] Christopher Hill, *Puritanism and Revolution* (1958), 8.

... freed from servile bands
Of hope to rise or fear to fall.

Keeping their income ahead of the price rise was, even for those who were successful, often an anxious business leaving them with little fellow-feeling for the Crown's attempts to do the same.

It is hard to give any authoritative verdict on the gentry controversy, since it has made us aware of the extreme difficulty of knowing the size of a gentleman's income. Most figures available are either incomplete, or else designed for taxation purposes, and Tudor and Stuart gentlemen had little to learn about the art of tax evasion. D. C. Coleman has recently remarked that 'the most significant fact about the gentry controversy is that no professional economic historian has ever taken part in it'. Perhaps the subject may be left with the words of the *Agrarian History*: 'the dust has settled sufficiently on the "rise of the gentry".'[59]

Fear of change

Certainly there was a general feeling that order and degree had become too insecure. Lord Chancellor Ellesmere, early in James I's reign, was obsessed by fear of approaching democracy. Although Sir Philip Sidney was one of the very few people Elizabeth ever considered raising to the peerage, when he quarrelled with the Earl of Oxford on the tennis court she was outraged with him for daring, as a mere knight, to quarrel with an Earl. The decision of one of the Howards to marry the son of a London alderman produced an outraged intervention from Lord Burghley. The man replied that he had had no idea 'that your lordship, being hourly busied, and with serious public affairs, would have been acquainted and troubled with such domestical and private matters'. The lady married her merchant, but when she had been widowed and remarried, her second husband never let her live it down. In the 1620s, another bill for restraint of luxury in dress was opposed by an M.P. who said that if it were passed they would not be able to tell their wives from their chamber maids.[60]

These alarms about the stability of the social order were a constant theme after about 1590. Shakespeare thought the times were out of joint, and Donne that ''tis all in pieces, all coherence gone'. Yet it is hard to explain them simply in terms of social mobility. There had always been social mobility, and there had been alarms about men rising above their station ever since the days when chroniclers complained of Henry I

[59] D. C. Coleman, 'The Gentry Controversy and the Aristocracy in Crisis', *History*, 1966, 169. *Agrarian History*, p. 280.
[60] Stone, 630; *C.J.*, i. 584.

'raising vile men from the dust' to make them sheriffs.[61] The social system had always been able to absorb a certain amount of fluidity, and its most zealous defenders had always been those who, like Burghley, had themselves risen from humble origins. Moreover, to any believer in the doctrine of the Great Chain of Being, the social order did not only mean class: it meant obedience to God and the king, and the stability of the estate, the family, and the household as well, and there was concern about all these things, not all of which were likely to be threatened by social mobility.

Family structure

Tudor families were based on formidable theories of patriarchy and male supremacy. Marriage was a business transaction, arranged between the two fathers with the assistance of the family lawyers. The couple, who might not have met before the wedding, were expected to learn to love each other after it, and in those few cases where letters have survived, it appears that they often did. Some were expected to show complete obedience to their fathers. Of course there had always been many cases which were not as strict as this, but by the beginning of the seventeenth century there was a growing fear that the exceptions might become the rule. Roger Manwaring was admittedly a high churchman given to somewhat extravagant utterances, but it is still surprising to find him saying in 1627:

Nothing so much the cause of this neglect and (in a manner) contempt of all dutiful submitting to supreme authority; as the want of that due discipline and correction, wherewith men ought to be framed and smoothed in their minority, and tender age. . . . The coming generation will bring in such a torrent of vice and corruption, as will over-run the world, with rudeness, lewdness and extreme barbarity; and bring upon us that curse, which Isaiah threatens to them, who ought timely to repress such intemperancies. . . . Hence it comes to pass, that the hearts of men (in their tender years) being never subdued with any religious awe, nor acquainted with any reverence or godly fear toward their superiors, do afterward (in their riper times) become so desperate and audacious, as to be so far from honouring the person of their ruler, that they dare, with great boldness, traduce his actions.[62]

As the century went on, the defenders of the extremer form of patriarchy acquired that shrill tone which is characteristic of men who feel the consensus is leaving them behind. Sir Robert Filmer, in 1637, argued that the husband should have power of life and death over his wife for adultery,

---

[61] Southern, R. W., 'The Place of Henry I in English History', *Proceedings of the British Academy*, xlviii. (1962), 129–32.

[62] Manwaring, R., *Religion and Allegiance*, ii. (1627), 5. The irony of this passage is that when the crisis came, the younger generation gave Charles more support than their elders did.

for substituting a child not his own, for habitual drunkenness, and for having duplicate keys. He thought that fathers should have power of life and death over their children on all occasions, and that their natural affection for their children would ensure that their powers were not used 'unnecessarily'.

It is hard to tell how far these complaints corresponded to facts. The *Taming of the Shrew* is evidence only of the history of ideas. But when William Gouge, one of the most popular Puritan lecturers, gave a conventional exposition of the subjection of wives to their husbands during the 1620s, he found his parishioners were complaining that he was a woman-hater. It cannot be proved that love marriages were becoming more common, but concern about them was increasing. Burghley, who had determined not to arrange his daughters' marriages till they were 16, found that both of them made love marriages, one of them disastrous. His later advice was, 'marry thy daughters in haste, lest they marry themselves'. Falkland and the Earl of Berkshire's eldest son were both cast off by their fathers for making love marriages. Sir Edward Coke's daughter refused to marry her father's choice, a relative of Buckingham who was in a lunatic asylum a year later, and she was supported in her refusal by her mother, with such determination that her father needed a battering ram to get at his daughter to take her to the church. In 1621, an M.P. was able to say that 'princes' marriages [are] not drawn on by beauty, etc., as private are'.[63]

Religion and the social order

These changes should not be exaggerated. Love marriages were still sufficiently unusual to provide rich material for gossip. Yet there does appear to be some reason to believe the complaints that social order was being weakened inside families, and here the change cannot be ascribed to developments in the class system. The solvent effects of town life, and particularly the familiarity of love marriages in the theatre, may have had some influence. It is also possible that the stability of authority may, as many feared, have been undermined by differences in religion. All authority, to whatever person it was delegated, was God's authority, and God, as head of the whole order, claimed obedience over and above rulers, fathers, and all his other earthly delegates. In religion, however much such men as Hooker might protest about the dangers of private judgement, choice was a fact too established to be denied. In spite of the censorship, anyone could gain access, with ingenuity, to Catholic as well as Anglican books, and to Puritan and perhaps even sectarian or Ana-

[63] Hurstfield, 143. *C.J.*, i. 655.

baptist ones as well. Even within the official church there were many strands of religion between which choice could be made. And if choice could not be excluded from so important a matter as the means of salvation, it was hard to exclude it from such matters as marriage.

Moreover, religion, instead of binding everyone to their superiors, as it was supposed to do, created many situations in which people had to disobey their superiors in order to obey God, their superiors' superior. Religious difference was no more an excuse for divorce than for rebellion, yet Perkins was able to say that an attempt by a spouse to convert his or her partner to 'idolatry' should be met by Lysistrata tactics. He argued that this was not a breach of the marriage bond, because 'that party is said to depart, in whom the cause of departing is; as in the church, he is a schismatic, in whom the cause of the schism is, and not always he that separates'.[64] In modern language, the attempt to convert a spouse to Roman Catholicism constituted constructive desertion. One of the issues which most exercised the Commons during the 1620s was whether husbands should be made to pay fines for the recusancy of their wives. Inevitably, religious differences between the husband and the wife much weakened the husband's authority, and might lead to tensions. In 1621, Perrott held forth in Parliament on the mischiefs which followed where the husband and wife were of different religions: 'example of one at Acton; where a recusant wife, fearing her husband would train them up in religion [i.e. true religion] killed one or two of her children, with her own hands.'[65] It only remains to add that Perrott had a recusant wife himself. Later, it could be maintained, both that a woman who joined a church without her husband's consent infringed her divine duty of submission, and that one who stayed away from church on her husband's command was failing to recognize that obedience to God came before obedience to earthly authority.

Exactly the same difficulties applied to politics as in the family. The king's authority was weakened whenever people found it impossible both to fear God and to honour the king. It was not a dilemma many people sought: as one Puritan clergyman asked when deprived of his living: 'Is it a pleasure to be in disgrace with the times? Especially of your Majesty, whose favour I do esteem as your person, next unto God's.... Would God your Majesty would believe of us that only the fear of God's displeasure hazardeth us upon your Majesty's, whom if we did not fear less than God, neither should we long fear so much as we ought.'[66] There was little

[64] Perkins, W., *The Idolatry of the Last Times, Works* (1605), 839.
[65] *C.J.*, i. 655.
[66] Barton Babbage, S., *Puritanism and Richard Bancroft* (1962), 382.

questioning of the doctrine of divine right during the early seventeenth century. Peter Wentworth or Pym, as much as any bishop, believed that the king was the image of God, and Laud and Whitgift, as much as any M.P., believed we ought to obey God rather than man. But divine right could not be pleaded against God, and no amount of divine right could bind people to obey a royal command to disobey God. Divine right could come to mean what Sir Edward Coke made it mean, that the king was God's lieutenant and 'therefore must do no wrong', or what Pym made of it, that the king was the head of the body politic, but 'of all diseases, diseases of the brain are the most dangerous'. It could also be used to stress the king's obligations to his subjects. As one Irish M.P. said, the king is the head, and the Commons the feet, but 'the gout is as mortal and dolorous as the headache'.[67] Few M.P.s wanted to reject the doctrine of divine right altogether, since it was the same doctrine which guaranteed their supremacy as fathers, husbands, masters, landlords, and justices, but it was easy enough to use divine right doctrine to reprove the king for disobedience to his own divine superior, or even, like Stephen Marshall preaching to the Long Parliament, to claim the divine right of a prophet to set against the divine right of the king. Peter Wentworth, for example, once told Elizabeth's Privy Council that he was persuaded God had sent him there for the express purpose of persuading them to settle the succession.

Puritan conservatism

It is, and was, fashionable to blame Puritanism for this growing readiness to set up private judgement against the decisions of authority. Such a view contains truth, but it is at least over-simplified. Readiness to dissent from authority extended to other fields than religion and politics. It was no longer possible in 1640 to imprison people for dissenting from Galen, and the obscure country clergyman who discovered in 1609 that bees were ruled by a queen instead of a king was delighted to have found a flaw in Aristotle.[68] Science did something to undermine the accepted world order, of which the order of the heavens had been supposed to be a part, and it seems difficult to prove any further connection between science and Puritanism than that a number of scientists were Puritans. A number of others were not Puritans, and it is hard to prove that in Europe science fared worse in Catholic than in Protestant countries.

Moreover, the main stream of Puritanism, as here defined, was quite

[67] *Commons' Debates in 1621*, ed. Notestein, Relf, and Simpson (1935), ii. 253; Rushworth, III. i. 510; *Captain Audley Mervin's Speech* (1641), 4.
[68] Butler, Charles, *The Feminine Monarchie* (1609).

as intensely conservative and quite as dismayed by the thought of change as the government itself. 'Innovator' was as dangerous a term of abuse among seventeeth-century M.P.s as among sixteenth-century bishops. Few Puritans ever regarded themselves as in any sense 'progressive', and most of them only wished to combine a stable order with respect for truth as they saw it. Pym's tutor, in 1604, lamented, 'alas, what a century we are entering'.[69] Pym's own attitude to change was no more welcoming: he said when impeaching Manwaring in 1629:

The form of government is that which doth actuate and dispose every part and member of a State to the common good; and as those parts give strength and ornament to the whole, so they receive from it again strength and protection in relation to their several degrees. If this mutual relation and intercourse be broken, the whole frame will quickly be dissolved, and fall in pieces, and instead of this concord and interchange of support, whilst one part seeks to uphold the old form of government, and the other part to introduce a new, they will miserably consume and devour one another. Histories are full of the calamities of whole states and nations in such cases. It is true that time must needs bring some alterations, and every alteration is a step and degree towards a dissolution; those things only are eternal which are constant and uniform. Therefore it is observed by the best writers upon this subject that those commonwealths have been most durable and perpetual which have often reformed and recomposed themselves according to their first institution and ordinance; for by this means they repair the breaches and counterwork the ordinary and natural effects of time.[70]

This devotion to the 'first institution' of the commonwealth is the background to the dedicated antiquarianism which learned M.P.s employed in collecting precedents for use in the Commons. There was little difference between the political theory of Puritans and that of bishops. Their one crucial point, that they could not obey a command to sin, they shared with so loyal a man as Cranmer. They had no objection to the Royal Supremacy, and Prynne became one of its chief defenders. They merely thought that the Royal Supremacy did not exempt them from subjection to God, and in this they agreed with everyone except perhaps Hobbes. Hooker thought that no one was so 'brain-sick' as to suppose the Royal Supremacy gave the Crown power against God's will, and even Laud thought that 'if any man think an Act of Parliament is an absolution from the moral law of God, he is much out of the way, and it will be but a poor plea at another bar'.[71]

[69] Whear, Digory, *Epistolarum Eucharisticarum Fasciculus* (1628), 73.
[70] *State Trials*, ed. Cobbett, iii. (1809), 341–2.
[71] Hooker, R., *Ecclesiastical Polity*, VIII. ii. 3; Trevor Roper, H. R., *Archbishop Laud* (1940), 451.

When Puritanism, in its Presbyterian form, was in power, in Scotland and the Channel Islands, it showed no particular revolutionary tendencies. In the Channel Islands the Presbyterian church had excellent relations with the Governor, and the system of lay elders produced a close link between the government of the church and the Bench. In Scotland, by the 1650s, the Kirk had become Charles II's best friends, believing that the king's restoration was the only guarantee for the security of their religion. As they showed no desire to weaken order and authority, so they showed no leaning to religious liberty: godly discipline, and examination before admission to Communion, made Presbyterianism a more effective force for regulating the lives of the laity than Anglican bishops could ever become. Perhaps this is why Presbyterianism was never very popular with the Puritans' lay supporters. In the English counties, Puritan local government showed no sign of disrespect for rank or order. The Knightleys, one of the greatest Puritan dynasties of the period, were indispensable pillars of the Northamptonshire militia, and claimed to be heirs of the early medieval barony of Fitz-Warenne.

Religious choice and political obedience

What was dangerous to the Crown was not Puritanism, but Puritanism in opposition. In France, the Catholic League, when it came to dissent from the government's religious policy, was as subversive as any Puritans ever were, and this suggests that what threatened governments was the existence of a religion contrary to their own, rather than the doctrines of any particular creed. However much they might deplore the fact, Puritans' religious energy and confidence was bound to lead them into religious conflict with the government more often than most of the Crown's other subjects, and the duty of submission to the Lord often became so obsessive for them that it left little room for any intermediate authorities. Total submission of one's will to the Lord may cause pride, as well as humility. Burges, preaching to the Long Parliament, said: 'So a man once married to the Lord by covenant may without arrogancy say: this righteousness is my righteousness, this judgement is my judgement, this loving kindness, these mercies, this faithfulness, which I see in thee, and all that thou hast, is mine, for my comfort . . . direction, salvation, and what not.' Calamy reminded the Long Parliament that unity was not to be had without truth, and told them: 'If I cannot have peace with men, but I must lose my peace with God, farewell peace with men that I may keep my peace with God. One reason why we have so little peace upon earth, is because we seek after it more than after the glory of God.'[72]

[72] Burges, C., *The First Sermon* (1641), 61; Calamy, E., *An Indictment* (1645), 29–30.

'Make you Popes who list, for we will make you none.' Just as the bishops had rejected the Pope because obedience to God took precedence over obedience to man, so Puritans rejected the bishops' arguments for similar reasons. They did not intend, any more than Cranmer had done, to cause confusion, but so long as they vowed: 'no, by the faith I bear to God, we will pass nothing till we understand what it is,' confusion was the inevitable result. Just as the bishops were dismayed when their followers treated them as they had treated the Pope, so Puritans were dismayed when their followers also began to reject their own authority in the name of obedience to God. Denzil Holles, in the Long Parliament, said that 'mechanical men' preaching without licence, 'did very much redound to the scandal and dishonour of this House, as if instead of suppressing Popery we intended to bring in atheism and confusion'.[73] When these un-authorized preachers were brought before the House, the only dispute was whether they should be sent to the Indies or to the bishops. The Puritans, quite as much as the first Protestant bishops, were dismayed by the con-fusion which was the result of their own handiwork.

Crown patronage and its difficulties

As loyalty to the Crown became less intellectually unquestioning, so it may have become less financially attractive. When the Crown did give large rewards, they took forms which provoked resentment among the public. Some of the monastic lands were still being sold in the 1590s, but the majority had gone, and the Crown had acquired no satisfactory new source of patronage to put in their place. As the Crown's resources were weakened by the price rise, so it grew steadily harder for it to reward its servants except in ways which offended its subjects. Queen Elizabeth tried to circumvent some of these problems by not rewarding her servants. The result was a lessening of her popularity at Court, and perhaps increased willingness of officials to take unauthorized rewards from the public, and an excessive readiness to welcome the more liberal ways of James. Shrews-bury said in 1604 that 'she valued every molehill she gave at a mountain . . . which our sovereign now does not'.[74] Appointments as ambassador under Elizabeth were underpaid enough to be feared, and Bedford calcu-lated that he had lost £3,300 on two embassies. When James raised pay-ments to ambassadors, he made appointments more welcome, but ex-hausted the treasury instead. Elizabeth even managed to reverse the posi-tion on occasion, by making her subjects offer gifts to her. The legend that 'Queen Elizabeth slept here' rests on a solid foundation—her readiness to

---

[73] B.M. Harl. MS. 163, fo. 662r.
[74] Stone, 473.

live at other people's expense. Gentlemen who wanted favour had to entertain the queen more lavishly than the gentleman before, and when she left the minimum present for a man who did not want to be suspected of plotting rebellion was £100. The dismay was greater because no one knew when the queen was coming: 'her Majesty threateneth to visit me, and stay in my houses.' Lincoln tried to avoid a visit by shutting up his house in Chelsea, but the queen broke in, and when Nottingham and Cecil had arranged a feast, they sent the bill to Lincoln.

Even Elizabeth had to give patronage to some people, and it usually took the form of delegation of Crown rights which could not be enforced without obloquy. Dyer was given a patent for searching out concealed wardships. The Crown gained little from this, and in effect Dyer was rewarded by being given opportunities for blackmail. Little is known of how he made his money, but when the Pyms successfully concealed a manor from the Court of Wards, Dyer was subsequently leasing a tenement on it.[75] One of Elizabeth's most provocative grants was the grant to Leicester of all concealed royal rights in the Forest of Snowdon. When Leicester had been at work for a few years, it appeared astonishing how many of these rights there were, and particularly how many men's estates were held by defective titles, and were therefore forfeit to the queen and thence to Leicester. Disputes about Leicester's activities normally came before the Council of Wales, where one of the dominant influences was Leicester's steward. Other servants were rewarded by telling bishops to lease lands to them on long leases. Sandys, Archbishop of York, was once bold enough to refuse such a request, but the man who had hoped to get the lease retaliated by sending a woman into his bedroom when he was staying in an inn at Doncaster, discovering him in 'adultery', and trying to blackmail him. Monopolies were another unpopular form of patronage. They were officially supposed to encourage new inventions, but it was hard to see what new invention justified, for example, Sir Walter Raleigh's monopoly of playing cards. The monopolist was rewarded by being able to charge higher prices to the queen's subjects.

Under James, new forms of patronage were used. Some courtiers were rewarded by direct grants of cash, to the great detriment of the Exchequer, others by being allowed to run up large debts to the Crown, which could remain unpaid only during their good behaviour. Others were rewarded by James and Charles making suit for them to rich widows, saying that 'we do not wish to use authority, but will take your compliance as a mark of respect'.[76] The Stuarts' most characteristic form of patronage was titles, which at least cost the Crown nothing. Elizabeth had granted hardly any titles, and there was a large unsatisfied appetite for them. James at first satisfied this free, and once, in the first weeks of his reign, dubbed forty-six knights before breakfast. Later, peerages, knighthoods, and the new title of Baronet, were regularly for sale, and made a large source of income. Yet here again the Crown could only provide patronage by discrediting itself. Sherland said that since honour in the State was a divine thing, the sale of offices or titles was simony. In the end, the Crown had to use pressure, and one Cornish tin merchant was compelled to buy a peerage by a threat of prosecution for usury. He was one of Pym's family circle, and reinforced the opposition in the House of Lords. Even so, he made an enemy of that dedicatedly aristocratic Puritan, Lord Saye and Sele, who complained that now for money a usurer might be made a baron.[77] Others, who preferred money to honour, might be rewarded by being granted the forfeitures of individual Catholic recusants. These grants were often made before the recusants had been convicted, so the grantees were made agents for the prosecution. Such grants were made to the humbler members of the king's household. Some recusants had the good fortune to have their forfeitures granted to friends or relations, who would not exact them, but it is no surprise to discover that when the Gunpowder Plot broke out the forfeiture of one of the plotters was being requested by Lord Saye and Sele.[78] In many other ways, pieces of royal authority were delegated to subjects. When the city of Lincoln wanted to clear the Fossdyke, to bring the city within reach of water transport, they appealed to James to head the subscription list. James had not the money, but granted them the making of three baronets, leaving them to raise the money by selling the titles on the open market. Such measures did nothing to increase respect for the Crown.

Attempts to enforce uniformity: Catholics and Puritans

It was against this background that attempts continued to enforce uniformity of religion in a divided society. Since the attempts were almost invariably unsuccessful, the only result was to produce a collection of oppressed minorities. The Tudor one-party system, in which any normal citizens were assumed to be capable of loyalty, and office was compatible with any opinion, was breaking up, and a growing battery of oaths was used to test the opinions of almost every office-holder. The first sufferers were Catholic recusants. From 1570 onwards, they were excluded from

[77] B.M. Harl. MS. 6424, fo. 78r.
[78] *H.M.C. Salis.* xvii. 451.

Parliament, and from any share in the government of the universities. The powers of the Court of Wards were used to ensure that orphan heirs of noble Catholic families were given a thorough Protestant upbringing. This process often worked so effectively as to produce Puritans, but on one occasion some alarm was caused when an eight-year-old Catholic peer refused to attend prayers in the household of his guardian, Lord Treasurer Burghley, because his mother had told him it was sinful. As time went on, penalties for Roman Catholicism grew more severe. Recusants were made liable to fines of £20 a month, or to forfeitures of two-thirds of their estates, for failure to attend church. Elizabeth occasionally tried to tone down these measures against Catholics, but did little to stop them. Her ministers continued the drive against Catholics, and contributed much to the growing propaganda by which the Pope and the Spaniard were established in the public mind as national enemies. This was the time when the Marian martyrdoms were firmly established in the national mythology. In 1571 Foxe's *Book of Martyrs* was ordered to be placed in churches. In 1584, Sir Walter Mildmay, Chancellor of the Exchequer, reminded the House of the danger of rule by papists, and continued: 'If any doubt what a miserable change this would be, let him but remember the late days of queen Mary, when . . . the Pope's authority was wholly restored, and, for continuance thereof, a strange nation, proud and insolent, brought into this land to be lords over us.' After the beginning of the Armada war, anti-papal language became even more luxuriant. In 1589, Lord Chancellor Hatton, opening Parliament, denounced priests' delight in blood, and the 'atheism' of Cardinal Allen, and 'the unchristian fury, both of the Pope (that wolfish bloodsucker) and of the Spaniard (that insatiable tyrant) in that they never bent themselves with such might and resolution against the very Turk or any other infidel, as they have done against a virgin queen, a famous lady, and a country which embraceth without corruption in doctrine the true and sincere religion of Christ'.[79] If the government was later disturbed by the extravagance of anti-papal feeling, it had only itself to blame. As the seventeenth century went on, the Commons demanded ever severer measures against Catholics. There was a vigorous attack on recusant education, and the Grand Committee on religion conducted an inquisition round the country trying to find recusant schoolmasters. It was sometimes proposed that all Catholic children should be taken from their parents at the age of seven, to ensure that they would have a proper Protestant education. Catholics were excluded from the militia, and Bacon, so far from hesitating to open windows into men's souls, proposed that no one should be so much as allowed to keep a halberd in his house if he

[79] Neale, *Parliaments*, ii. 30, 197.

would not come to Communion.[80] In 1625 there was a national search for
Catholic armour, and Sir Richard Knightley, a Puritan Justice ferreting
round the house of a dowager Catholic peeress, had his nose punched by
her son. In 1624, the Commons proved their sincerity by binding themselves to dismiss recusant servants, on pain of sequestration from the
House. It is not surprising that there were a number of Catholic plots, but
in the main, Catholics were surprisingly patient under this type of treatment.

It was a different story when it began to seem that the government
might attempt similar measures against Puritans. During the Armada war,
most of them had developed the habit of thinking of themselves as the
most loyal citizens the Crown had, which may be one reason why, when
the word 'patriot' first appeared in the English language, it was monopo-
lized by the Crown's opponents. To some extent, moreover, they were
right in feeling that the church was altering away from them. Heylin,
Laud's chaplain, maintained that under Leicester's chancellorship Oxford
had been 'so much altered, that there was little to be seen in it of the
church of England'.[81] To M.P.s to whom the church of England meant the
form of religion they had learnt in Elizabethan Oxford, such doctrines
were offensive. In Elizabeth's reign, Puritans had known that the bishops
were mostly their old friends from the days of the Marian exile, and that
many of the Councillors were their friends and patrons. The increasing
habit of bracketing them with the Catholics as potentially disloyal subjects bewildered, as well as dismayed them. Their position was much
weakened when the generation of the Marian exiles died out, and their
friends began to disappear from the Council and the episcopal bench. By
the end of Elizabeth's reign their patrons, and friends in time of trouble,
were almost all dead. Bedford died in 1585, Leicester in 1589, his brother
Warwick in 1590, and Huntingdon in 1595. Mildmay, Knollys, and Walsingham, their friends on the Council, died at about the same time. Moreover, the Puritan peers had no successors. Leicester and Warwick had no
heirs at all, and the Dudley interest, which had protected radical Protestantism since the 1540s, died out. Huntingdon was succeeded by a collateral of little importance, and Bedford by a minor grandson and a
lawsuit in the Court of Wards. In 1590, Anne Locke, a veteran of the
Reformation and a friend of John Knox, wrote to the Countess of Warwick
lamenting the past halcyon days of liberty of the Gospel, and fearing that
only trials lay ahead. It was not until shortly before the Civil War that the
Puritans again had a body of aristocratic patrons to equal those who died

---

[80] Boynton, L. O. J., *The Elizabethan Militia* (1967), 111.
[81] Heylin, P., *Cyprianus Anglicanus* (1719), 33.

at this time, and the new body of patrons, though they may have had resources equal to the old ones, had access to parliamentary seats, but not to the favour of the Crown. One incident in 1604 after the Hampton Court Conference may serve to mark the change of atmosphere. A group of Puritans led by Huntingdon's younger brother Sir Francis Hastings submitted a set of petitions to James, in which they rashly included the phrase that many of his subjects might be discontented if he did not accept them. Hastings was a pillar of respectability, at the end of a long and honourable career in the Commons and local government. He had been an unofficial candidate for Speaker in the 1604 Parliament, and had written patriotic books during the war about the necessity for loyalty to the Crown, the religion established, and the royal supremacy. He was a zealous Puritan, trying to suppress drunkenness in Somerset, and to ensure that his livings were held by vicars who taught the Gospel to the people. Yet he was no more a rebellious Puritan than his brother had been, and he was a man in whom it was hard to imagine any political disloyalty.

He and his associates were summoned before the Council, and told: 'What danger they had put themselves in by these associations; and that thus combining themselves in a cause, to which the king had showed mislike, both by public act and proclamation, was little less than treason, that the subscribing with so many names were armed prayers, and tended to sedition, as had been manifestly seen heretofore, both in Scotland, France and Flanders in the beginning of those troubles.'[82] They were asked, like rebellious members of a modern political party, to sign a submission, and when they refused they were deprived of their local offices in the Lieutenantcy and the Commission of the Peace. Knightley shortly had to be put back into the Northamptonshire Lieutenancy, because no one else understood the working of the county militia, but the government had already begun to tell some of its most hardworking local agents that they were potential traitors. Ultimately, the government's prophecies were self-fulfilling, though not until Charles and war ended the calm of James's later years.

The rise of Arminianism

Although in many ways the late Elizabethan and Jacobean period was a hard one for Puritans, there was one crucial respect in which they later came to look back on it as a golden age. They might be troubled for their views on church organization, or on ceremonies, but even if Puritans felt that they had to obey God rather than man in these points, they were not the central points of the Gospel. For many Puritan ministers, the call to

[82] Winwood, Sir R., *Memorials* (1725), ii. 49.

preach the Gospel was a doctrinal one, and on the crucial doctrinal issues, especially Predestination, the Puritans of this period believed that theirs was the doctrine established by authority. Grindal had accepted office in the Elizabethan settlement partly because he believed the church's doctrine was pure, and for many later Puritans, their trust in the church's doctrine could be a sufficient compensation for its inadequacy in many other points. It was of this compensation that they were deprived during the twenty years before the Civil War.[83]

Whether the Puritans were right in believing that theirs was the official doctrine of the church is a question into which it is fortunately unnecessary to enter here. The Thirty-Nine Articles were too carefully drafted to commit the Church of England to a Calvinist theology, but they were readily compatible with it, and a high proportion of the Jacobean bench of bishops shared with the Puritans the theology which was derived from Calvin and Perkins. Perhaps the emotive point in this theology (which was derived from Perkins rather than Calvin) was what the Cambridge Heads of Houses in 1595 called 'the comfortable certainty of true faith'[84]—the belief that it was possible for a man to be certain that he was predestined to salvation. The other crucial point which was necessarily involved with this was the Calvinist belief that God's decree that some men should be saved and others damned was unconditional. It was entirely independent of anything the men considered might do, and therefore, once made, was immutable. As the Puritans argued, if salvation were once allowed to depend on what men did, then God's promises were conditional, and could not be certain. They also felt that to make God's decision to save some men and damn others conditional on what men did was to lessen God's power. As Perkins said, 'to make God's will depend on man's will is to put God out of his throne of majesty, and to set the creature in his room'.[85]

In 1595, when some Cambridge theologians had been challenging these points, a number of senior Cambridge dons appealed to Archbishop Whitgift for help. However much Puritans might regard Whitgift as an enemy on other issues, they were prepared to assume he was their natural ally on this one, and in the main their confidence was not misplaced. Whitgift somewhat amended the draft articles sent to him by the Cambridge Puri-

[83] For this and what follows, I am heavily indebted to Dr. N. R. N. Tyacke, 'Arminianism in England in Religion and Politics, 1604 to 1640', Oxford D.Phil. thesis, 1968. I am grateful to Dr. Tyacke for allowing me to read this thesis in draft.
[84] Porter, H. C., *Reformation and Reaction in Tudor Cambridge* (1958), 281. What follows is subject to the modifications made by Dr. Porter. Dr. Porter is undoubtedly right in stressing that there was always a non-Calvinist tradition in the Elizabethan church, but it could be argued that the heir of Bishop Overall's tradition was his admirer Bishop Williams, rather than Laud and the Arminians.
[85] Porter, H. C., op. cit., 295.

tans to allow non-Calvinists to interpret the articles in a sense they could accept, but the final draft which resulted, the Lambeth Articles of 1595, confirmed the Puritan theology more explicitly than the Thirty-Nine Articles had done. The Lambeth Articles were never officially adopted, but they did give some indication of what the Archbishop of Canterbury thought was the doctrine of the church of England, and it was the doctrine which the later Puritans many times petitioned to have confirmed. Archbishop Hutton of York was even more explicit in his agreement with predestinarian doctrine than the Lambeth Articles themselves. The administration of the censorship was on the whole conducted in a way sympathetic to the Puritan case, and it appears that no works directly opposing the Lambeth Articles were licensed for publication until 1624. Bishop Andrewes, one of those who dissented from this theology, was commanded by James to remain silent on one of the points concerned, and Richardson, Regius Professor of Divinity at Cambridge, who was doubtful on another of the crucial points, never attempted to publish his views. The official articles of the Irish church, drafted in 1615 under the influence of Ussher, later Archbishop of Armagh, again explicitly supported the Puritan position. Thus, even if their views were not 'the doctrine established by authority', at least they were the doctrine most commonly favoured by authority.

These views had never had a monopoly in the English church, and between 1595 and 1615 there was a group of people who dissented from them, though as yet hesitantly, and without very coherent alternatives. This situation began to change rapidly after the development of the Arminian controversy in Holland. The Dutch Arminians, followers of a theologian called Arminius, disputed all the crucial points in this theology. They so undermined the doctrine of Predestination as, in effect, to abandon it, abandoning all distinction between those who were elect and those who were not, and believed that no man could be certain of salvation. They believed that salvation partly depended on what men did or felt, and therefore that it was possible for those who were offered grace to resist it, and for those who had received grace to fall from it. Thus the prospect of salvation was always doubtful, and, as one of them put it, man was afloat on an 'ocean of contingency'. For Puritans, such an exaltation of man's power to work out his own salvation was intolerable. As Francis Rous, Pym's step-brother, put it, Arminianism 'maketh the grace of God lackey it after the will of man [and] maketh the sheep to keep the shepherd, that maketh mortal seed of an immortal God'.[86] It came, moreover, perilously close to the heretical position of arguing that men could do

[86] Tyacke, N. R. N., Thesis cit., 1.

enough to deserve salvation, and thus moved back towards those doctrines which the Reformation had been designed to break away from. Indeed, the whole Arminian movement can be seen as a reaction against the Reformation: they have been described as 'a counter-reforming element within the church of England, for whom the Reformation itself was becoming an embarrassment'. One of them, indeed, described it as the 'deformation'. The Arminians were not Roman Catholics (though some of them were later converted to Rome) but they did agree with Rome on the points which men like Perkins had regarded as the crucial distinctions between Catholic and Protestant. Their contemporaries could be forgiven for regarding them, at least, as fellow-travellers.

When the Arminian controversy first started in Holland, however, it appeared that there was no danger of the Arminians gaining power in England, or even gaining a foothold in the English church. King James reacted vigorously, dismissing Arminius as an 'enemy of God', and his ambassador in Holland reported that Arminius' doctrines dissented from those of the Protestant churches of England, Scotland, France, and Germany. One of the most persistent Puritan complaints against Arminianism was that it broke the doctrinal unity of Protestantism. In 1619, when the Dutch succeeded in organizing a synod at Dort to condemn Arminian doctrine, they tried to turn it into a Protestant General Council, and James was among those who responded to their invitation by sending delegates. These delegates on the whole accepted the Calvinist conclusions of the synod, with the approval of King James and both his Archbishops. Here was another semi-official doctrinal formulation for whose confirmation Puritans, and one of the Secretaries of State, were subsequently to petition. In fact, by the time of the Synod of Dort, an Arminian party was already forming in England, and rapidly gaining strength. Neile, Bishop of Durham, was its chief organizer and patron. Many members of his group were in a militant mood, and Montague, for example, was prepared to dismiss many of the bench of bishops as 'Puritans'. In 1624, having found a friendly censor, they raised a test case by publishing a book by Montague, in which he claimed to reduce the points at issue between the church of England and the church of Rome from 47 to 8. Although Montague had apparently not read Arminius, he accepted the full Arminian position.

The question whether such a book was within the bounds permitted by the censorship was crucial, and the House of Commons, among others, reacted vigorously. They did not, on the first occasion, claim to judge Montague's doctrine themselves, but referred it to the Archbishop of Canterbury, in entire (and justified) confidence that he agreed with them. Several other bishops, and the Regius Professor of Divinity at Oxford played a prominent part in the attacks on Montague. In the Commons, only two M.P.s could be found to defend Arminian doctrine during the 1620s. Pembroke, a leading Privy Councillor and Chancellor of Oxford, congratulated the Vice Chancellor on his efforts to prevent Arminian doctrine from gaining a hold in the university. Nevertheless, even with all this weight of official opposition, by the early 1630s Arminianism was for all practical purposes the doctrine of the church of England.

How did this rapid change in the doctrine of the church of England come about? James in 1624 showed some signs of supporting Montague, which were perhaps confirmed by the Commons' attacks on him, but the crucial influences were those of Buckingham and Charles. From 1624, Laud held the post of Buckingham's chaplain and had acquired the nickname of 'the Duke's earwig'. At the end of 1624 Laud was composing for Buckingham a tract attacking 'doctrinal puritanism'—a concept which would have been unintelligible to so vigorous a hammer of the Puritans as Archbishop Whitgift. In 1625 he submitted to Buckingham a list of the clergy marked P. and O. (for 'Puritan' and 'Orthodox'), which was to be used as a basis for preferment. From about 1625 bishops of Calvinist leanings were excluded from episcopal committees. Davenant, Bishop of Salisbury, who had been one of the English delegates to the Synod of Dort, commented: 'why that should now be esteemed puritan doctrine, which those held who have done our church the greatest service in beating down Puritanism, or why men should be restrained from teaching that doctrine hereafter, which hitherto has been generally and publicly maintained, . . . I cannot understand.'[87] In 1626, Buckingham was elected Chancellor of Cambridge, and his appointment was immediately followed by a declaration forbidding the discussion of predestination on the ground that it was 'controversial'. These declarations forbidding controversy were one of the Arminians' main weapons in their rise to power, since their effect was to prohibit as 'controversial' those doctrines which had formerly been publicly and authoritatively taught, and so to make it easier to change them.

Much though Buckingham helped the Arminians, he was unstable, and also had Puritan friends (as well as a semi-Puritan patronage secretary). Their most reliable ally was Charles. In 1623, Wren, one of Charles's chaplains and one of the most dedicated Arminians, was summoned to a conference with Bishops Andrewes, Neile, and Laud, who asked him whether they could expect to do better in the new reign than in the old. Wren replied that they could expect to do much better, since Charles was less inconstant than his father. Charles soon promoted Laud to London, and promised him the succession to Canterbury, thus giving him in turn

[87] Thesis cit., 135.

the two sees which controlled the London censorship. The Cambridge press was already controlled by Arminians, and with Laud's election as Chancellor of Oxford, in 1630, they gained control of the last non-Arminian press in the country. During the 1630s, almost all works licensed for publication were Arminian, except reprints of earlier works, and even those were sometimes refused a licence. 'Thus,' Dr. Tyacke concludes, 'former doctrinal abnormality became the norm.'[88]

Pym's complaint, in 1641, that Laud had used the censorship to publish those things which he ought to have prohibited, had some substance. Indeed, of all those who were offended by this proscription of what had formerly been current doctrine, Pym is one of the most conspicuous, which is curious, since his mother had been a predestinarian who believed she was predestined to damnation. Among the others who were particularly disturbed by these theological changes, many of the parliamentary leaders of 1640 were prominent. Burges, one of the most prominent of the Long Parliament's clerical supporters, and a protégé of the Earl of Bedford, was transformed after a series of attacks on doctrinal Arminianism from a royal chaplain into a vice-moderator of the Westminster Assembly. Rudyerd was conspicuous in the parliamentary attacks on Arminianism during the 1620s, and Saye and Sele and Warwick, two of the most prominent of the Parliamentarian peers, were regarded by Buckingham in 1626 as among the theological opponents who most needed conciliating. Bedford and St. John wrote meditations on Predestination in their commonplace books which suggest that they were probably as shaken by the Arminian triumph as their colleagues.

The theological triumph of the Arminians introduced many other issues into religious controversy. The issue of conformity became more heated, since, in the hands of Arminian bishops, many things became 'nonconformity' which many previous bishops had regarded as orthodoxy. In 1628, a London lecturer was prosecuted for defending the conclusions of the Synod of Dort, which had been confirmed by the English delegates and by King James. It also appears that in England Arminian theology tended to lead to greater emphasis on the sacraments. In Predestinarian theology, there had not been a particularly important place for sacraments: since grace was a free gift of God, without reasons, Perkins had argued that the sacraments could not confer grace, but merely confirm it. For Arminians, who did not believe in this sudden conferring of grace, actions could make much more difference to our ability to take advantage of the grace offered to us. Bishop Morton, arguing against the Arminians in 1626, protested: 'what, will you have the grace of God tied to the

[88] Thesis cit., 264.

Sacraments?'[89] Neile took his emphasis on sacraments so far as to insist on confession before the taking of communion.

With this emphasis on sacraments went a cult of the 'altar'—itself a word unknown to the Elizabethan Prayer Book. Queen Elizabeth's Injunctions had said that the communion table was to be kept at the east end, but carried down into the body of the church at service time. The Arminians held that the altar (a place where sacrifice was offered) should be at the east end and railed in, and only the clergy should be allowed to come within the rails. In the cathedrals of Winchester, Durham, and Gloucester the communion table was moved and turned into an altar, and in 1633, Laud obtained a ruling from the Privy Council that all 'altars' were to be kept permanently at the east end—thus reversing the ruling of Elizabeth's Injunctions. Refusal to bow to the altar (previously rarely prosecuted) became one of the commonest offences in the church courts. Family pews on the site of the pre-Reformation altar (one of which had been cherished by the Pyms)[90] were pulled down. When Sir Nicholas Crispe the customs farmer (one of the men on whom Charles was most heavily dependent) put down a silver flagon on an altar during a consecration service, Laud told him that it had been consecrated, and he would commit sacrilege if he took it home. With Arminian theology came a ceremonial religion of a type which had not been seen since the Reformation, and with this ceremonial religion came an attempt to return to the pre-Reformation emphasis on the dignity and separateness of the clergy. An Arminian vicar maintained that the duty of the laity required a humble distance from God, while the clergy had immediateness of access. Predestinarians, he thought, claimed equality with God. With this emphasis on the dignity of the clergy went a dedicated attempt to recover church property. Laud believed that all those who possessed former monastic land were guilty of sacrilege, and consistently attempted to challenge lay property rights in tithes and impropriations. Pym, whose tithes on one manor had been fixed by a commutation agreement of Henry VIII's reign, found that it was overturned by the bishop with the assistance of the churchwarden, who was his own bailiff.[91]

The Arminians were not Roman Catholics, but it is not surprising that many people thought they were. On almost all points which Protestants had learnt to regard as the distinguishing marks between the church of England and the church of Rome, the Arminians, though Protestant, were

---

[89] Thesis cit., 242. See also Marchant, R. A., *The Puritans and the Church Courts in the Diocese of York* (1960), 52–106.

[90] P.R.O. Sta. Cha. 5 P. 10/23.

[91] P.R.O. C. 2 P. 78/33.

on the Roman side. As Falkland put it in 1641, they intended to 'try how much of a papist might be brought in without popery'.[92] To many whose theological skill was less than Falkland's, Arminianism and popery were indistinguishable. Nor is it surprising that the Arminians' capture of the episcopate led many who had had no objection to godly worship to wonder whether the best way to stop Arminianism was to abolish bishops. D'Ewes the diarist had no objection to the institution of bishops when the Long Parliament met, but after he had listened for a few months to evidence of bishops' attempts to enforce Arminianism, he thought that if bishops were not abolished, 'many of us here must look for very little better safety than the fire'.[93] By comparison with their grievances against Laud, the Puritans' grievances against the Elizabethan and Jacobean church appeared insignificant.

Postscript

My own later work, to be published in *Parliaments and English Politics 1621–9* (Oxford, forthcoming 1979), has convinced me that Jacobean England was much less politically polarized than is here suggested. Jacobean Parliaments were not 'Puritan' bodies, and such prominent members as Coke, Sandys, Digges, Noy and Sir Thomas Wentworth were not Puritans by any possible definition. For my reasons for now rejecting the notion of a 'Parliamentary opposition' see 'Parliamentary History in Perspective 1604–29', *History* (1976), 1–27. I now believe that the picture painted on p. 219 is as correct for the reign of James as it is for the reign of Elizabeth.

[92] Rushworth, III. i. 184–5. Falkland said the Laudians were trying to bring in 'an English, though not a Roman, popery . . . a blind dependence of the people on the clergy'. He said the declarations against controversy had been used to 'tie up one side, and set the other loose . . . and the party to which they gave this licence was that which, though it were not contrary to law, was contrary to custom and for a long time while in this kingdom was no oftener preached than recanted'.

[93] B.M. Harl. MS. 163, fo. 626a.

5. The Price of Victory 1570–1618

I ENGLAND BEFORE THE ARMADA, 1570–1588

I think . . . God be sworn English, there is nothing will prosper against the Queen of England . . . We that have lived in the eyes of all men, choked, as it were, with the blessings of the Lord beyond desert, we, that have lived to see her Majesty's life, so dear to us, pulled out, as it were, even out of the lion's jaws in despite of Hell and Satan, may truly, not indeed in any pride of heart, but in humbleness of soul to our comforts—confess that indeed the Lord hath vowed himself to be English.

Job Throckmorton, M.P., 1587[1]

For these things he thinks that God is angry with the king's treasury.

Thomas Wentworth, M.P., 1610[2]

Parliament

IT has become conventional to say that during the Elizabethan period there was a great increase in the vigour and self-assertiveness of Parliament. It has also become conventional to say that in Parliament the Commons were gaining importance at the expense of the Lords. These propositions appear to be true because we can read Commons' speeches like those quoted at the head of this chapter. We can read Commons' speeches because an increasing number of members were keeping diaries of the proceedings of the Commons, and these diaries, unlike the dry, formal minutes which make up the official *Journals*, give us the cut and thrust of debate. By comparison, we are in almost total ignorance of the debates in the early Tudor Commons, and of the debates in the Lords at any time in the century.

It may well be, then, that the diaries have deceived us into thinking that the Commons were becoming more important, and that a Lords' diary

---

[1] Neale, *Parliaments,* ii. 170.

[2] Gardiner *1610,* 144. The speaker was Peter Wentworth's son Thomas, not Charles I's future minister. The things of which he was complaining were impositions and a tax on alehouses.

or a Commons' diary of an early Tudor Parliament, would have given a very similar impression. We cannot say that the improvement of records itself proves that the Commons were becoming more important, since the bulk of records of all other types increased equally rapidly at the same time. Since this increase in the bulk of records dominates our picture of the period, it is unfortunate that we do not know why it happened. It may have happened, as Francis Bacon suggested, because a sense of rapid change strengthened the desire to make records, or it may have happened for a reason so prosaic as a fall in the price of paper.[3] Whatever the reasons, they are too general to be explained as part of the history of the House of Commons.

It is also easy to misinterpret the Elizabethan Commons by applying to it modern notions of 'government' and 'opposition'. Tudor England was in effect a one-party state, and divisions of opinion were more like those of the wings and groups which make up the sections of a modern political party than those which divide a government from an opposition. One result of this situation was that there was almost always opposition to any controversial item of government policy within the Privy Council itself. Many of the more powerful agitations in the Commons, such as the demand for the execution of Mary Queen of Scots, are not the work of an 'opposition' attacking a 'government', but of back-bench members working in close alliance with a number of Privy Councillors. Even the most loyal members of the government were not above using the Commons in this way. It is hard to know how much of the religious agitation of the Elizabethan Commons represents the attempts of Leicester and Bedford to counteract the influence of the bishops. In 1566, the Commons ended one of their most vigorous agitations of the reign by writing the queen's promise to marry into the preamble of the subsidy bill. The man who performed this act of 'opposition' was no less a member of the government than Secretary Cecil.[4]

It is likely that peers, as well as Privy Councillors, tended to use their friends and sympathizers in the Commons as a method of lobbying the queen. The bishops and Privy Councillors, if they all voted together, could come very near commanding a majority in the Lords, and discontented back-bench lords therefore often found it easier to engineer protests against current policy in the House of Commons than in the House of Lords. A high proportion of the members of the Commons owed their

---

[3] Plucknett, T. F. T., *A Concise History of the Common Law* (1929), 203. For the suggestion about the price of paper, I would like to thank my former pupil Miss Jessica Nichols (now Mrs. John Shepherd).

[4] Conyers Read, i. 367.

seats to the influence of various lords, and while this did not necessarily impose any obligation on them, they often had views like those of their patrons. While the Earl of Huntingdon wanted to put the Puritan case on some issue, it was more useful to leave his brother Sir Francis Hastings to speak in the Commons than to speak in the Lords himself. Such actions did not imply disloyalty. The Commons, like the Councillors, saw their duty as being to give good advice, and if advice was unpalatable to the queen, this did not necessarily mean that it was bad. As Peter Wentworth, one of the most obstreperous and most loyal of back-benchers, put it: 'faithful are the wounds of a lover, saith Solomon, but the kisses of an enemy are deceitful.' Elizabeth's charge to Cecil as a Councillor had been that 'without respect of my private will, you will give me that counsel which you think best'. If, as Peter Wentworth and his friends thought, the position of an M.P. was essentially that of counsellor to the queen, his view of his office was perfectly proper.

Unfortunately, the queen had a quite different view of their function. It was, as the Lord Keeper put it in 1571, that 'they should do well to meddle with no matters of state but such as should be proponed unto them, and to occupy themselves in other matters concerning the commonwealth'.[5] On subjects which the queen classified as 'matters of state', she thought that the Commons should have no independent right to initiate legislation, and that their privilege of freedom of speech simply allowed them to support or oppose the government's bills. If the Commons wanted change in some matter of state, she thought that the correct procedure was for them to offer a petition to her and the Council, and allow them to draft a bill if they saw fit to do so. The Commons, on the other hand, thought that their right of free speech allowed them to initiate bills on any subject they chose. This difference of view accounted for many of the clashes between the queen and the Commons.

Since the queen's notion of 'matters of state' was largely her own invention,[6] the list of topics from which she tried to bar the Commons sheds some light on her own interests. Economic questions, in which she was not particularly interested, she classified as a 'matter concerning the commonwealth', and such major measures as the Statute of Artificers of 1563, setting up procedures for fixing wages and regulating apprenticeship and entry into crafts, originated from private members. On the other hand, religion, foreign policy, marriage, and the succession and the royal administration she classified as 'matters of state'. On the whole, her attempt

[5] Neale, *Parliaments*, i. 320, 189.
[6] Roskell, J. S., *The Commons and their Speakers 1376–1523*, 43–51; Scarisbrick, 250–2; see above, pp. 40, 88.

to exclude the Commons from these subjects was a failure. She was most successful with marriage and the succession, which was so obviously a personal matter that even Councillors in private handled it with caution. After a major quarrel in 1566, the House only once, in 1576, tentatively petitioned the queen to marry, and when Peter Wentworth tried to raise the question of the succession, in 1593, he was discouraged by some of the most active of his fellow-members. On foreign policy, the queen also achieved moderate success. The only important foreign policy debate of the reign was in 1587, on the question whether the queen should accept the offer from the Dutch rebels of the sovereignty of the Low Countries, and this was an occasion when the Councillors and the Commons were in entire agreement. This debate was quoted in the next reign as a precedent to prove that the Commons were entitled to debate foreign policy, but it caused little disturbance at the time.

The queen's two conspicuous failures were over religion and the royal administration. Religion aroused strong feelings, and members could always reply to a prohibition of discussion by saying that they ought to obey God rather than man. On questions concerning the royal administration, the Commons may often have known more than the queen. As members of the public, they were best able to say where the shoe pinched, and since royal administrators were strongly represented in the Commons, they were usually also in a position to hear the departmental view. The Exchequer bill of 1589, for example, was supported by the Chancellor of the Exchequer and by the official whose department it was meant to reform, and yet was stopped by the queen because it dealt with a 'matter of state'. The same issue was still being raised in the Commons fifteen years later.

The queen's failure to exclude the Commons from matters of state was partly brought about by her Councillors. As prudent politicians, they sometimes put the queen's point of view, but they joined with the Commons often enough to show that they had no firm conviction that the Commons should not discuss matters of state. Moreover, on religion, a number of them, and particularly Sir Walter Mildmay and Sir Francis Knollys, were known to sympathize with the Commons rather than the queen. This fact may have made them more persuasive when they urged the Commons to leave an issue alone, but it also made them try to do so more rarely. Even Burghley might occasionally support a religious bill initiated from the floor of the Commons. Above all, it was hard to take the queen's constitutional theories seriously when they were contradicted by the memories of the elder members' lifetimes. Peter Wentworth said that 'I have heard of old Parliament men that the banishment of the Pope and

Popery and the restoring of true religion had their beginning from this House, and not from the bishops'.[7] He was quite right: Henry VIII had wanted nothing better than to see Parliament bring forward bills against the Pope of its own initiative. In her view that there were some subjects on which the Commons should not initiate debates, the queen had only two predecessors: Richard II and Wolsey.

But if the queen's constitutional theories were new, so were many of those which members put up to oppose them. Peter Wentworth's claim to a *de jure* right of free speech, enabling him to say whatever he liked about whatever he liked without fear of punishment, was as unprecedented as the queen's claim to a *de jure* right to prevent discussion of some topics. Henry VIII had taken it for granted that he could punish members if he did not like what they said in Parliament.[8] Perhaps what is really new in Elizabethan Parliaments is the tendency to look for rights, to claim a right of free speech instead of simply speaking. There was no precedent, for example, for the Commons' attempt to ape the Privy Council by claiming a right to secrecy of debate, particularly since the person from whom they wanted to keep individual members' speeches secret was usually the queen herself. It is doubtful whether there was much precedent for the House's attempts to turn itself into a semi-judicial tribunal, with power to imprison its own members, and even to imprison non-members. The privilege of freedom from arrest for themselves and their servants they had possessed before Elizabeth's reign, but it had not then been formalized to the point at which election to the Commons became a reliable protection against an action for debt.

With the formalization of privileges went formalization of procedure. Many Elizabethan members became experienced in the intricacies of committee work, of drafting, or of Parliamentary management. These developments produced an increasingly corporate and effective House of Commons. If they did not produce serious trouble, it was because the Privy Councillors, under increasing difficulty, still retained the confidence both of the queen and of the Commons. However much they might disagree on other issues, when faced with the menace of Spain and the Pope, Crown and Commons were on the same side.

Puritans and bishops

The bishops, almost all of whom had more sympathy with the Puritans than the queen did, occupied a similarly uncomfortable position to that of the Councillors, and during the 1570s they were less successful in dealing

[7] Neale, *Parliaments*, i. 323.
[8] See above, p. 116.

with the strains it created than their lay colleagues were. In the 1560s, there had been little disagreement between the Puritans and the more radical bishops about the changes they wanted in the church. It still had no preaching ministry except in a minority of parishes, it still continued ceremonies which most Protestants regarded as at best misleading, it still had no machinery of discipline except the creaking apparatus of the church courts, it had little effective provision for clerical education, and it had no reliable means of excluding covert papists from membership, and even from vicarages. This last, in the eyes of the queen, was a positive virtue. There was little disagreement between Puritans and their friends among the bishops about whether these things should be reformed, but much disagreement about what should be done if they were not reformed. Bishops such as Horne took the line that they had enough to be going on with, and if they had the essentials of a true church, they should not raise complaints if it was not in all respects a good one. This willing acceptance of a half-loaf did not come easily to most Puritans, especially in the face of the threat from Rome.

Norton, one of the more prominent Puritan M.P.s, said in the Parliament of 1572 that he did not expect to be able to live under a government headed by Mary Queen of Scots, and he and his friends saw the conversion, or suppression, of papists as the only defence against the formation of a Marian fifth column. Men like Norton relied on reformist methods and they would, as a satirist put it, 'act, insist, speak, read, write, in season and out', but they would not cause an upheaval in the church if they did not get their way. Norton was Cranmer's son-in-law, and had no objection to a church governed by bishops: he merely wanted the bishops to enforce the right policy. Norton is typical of the main stream of lay Puritanism, and for him and his colleagues the chosen scene of action was Parliament. In 1563, his friends had failed by one vote to get some of the reforms they wanted through Convocation, and on the whole, their standing there grew less. In Parliament, on the other hand, they could normally command a majority, and they could co-operate with their powerful lay allies on the Council. The ultimate aim of this strategy was that sooner or later the pressure should become powerful enough to induce the queen to make concessions.

This strategy came to be described by its opponents as 'tarrying for the magistrate', and its repeated failures made it seem increasingly inadequate. In 1566, even a bill to confirm the Thirty-Nine Articles, strongly backed by the bishops, had been vetoed by the queen. In the early 1570s, a number of the more radical Puritans, of whom a Cambridge theologian called Cartwright was the most famous, and a silenced London minister called

Field was the most important, were coming to a much more far-reaching conclusion: that the reason why the church was not reformed was that it was governed by bishops. The view had a certain plausibility: even Burghley reacted to some of the bishops by complaining that, 'I fear the places alter the men',[9] but few would join with Field in arguing that hierarchical government of the church was actually a mark of popery. The strength of Field's Presbyterian movement was never very great, though Field's genius as an organizer made it appear greater than it was. The essentials of Presbyterianism were government of the church by assemblies of ministers and lay elders, allowing parishioners a say in choosing their ministers, and 'godly discipline', involving public censure of sinners, and their exclusion from the sacrament, not merely until they had done penance, but until they had actually repented. None of these were particularly congenial to Elizabethans: government by assemblies savoured of the subversive doctrine of equality, and though wherever Presbyterianism existed, J.P.s, in the capacity of elders, acquired a powerful influence, it was easy to brand it, falsely, as democratic and revolutionary. Parishioners' claims to join in the choice of ministers threatened rights of property, and the proposals for excommunication offended that secularism which was perhaps the most powerful force even in Parliamentary Puritanism.

Nevertheless, though Field's movement remained unimportant even within Puritanism, it profoundly affected the terms of debate, not by claiming that church government should be Presbyterian, but by claiming that it should be Presbyterian by the law of God. For most Elizabethans, church government was not a matter of principle, but of expediency: if bishops could produce a godly church there should be government by bishops, but where Presbyterian government was more convenient, it could be adopted. Many might have preferences for episcopal or Presbyterian government, but those who believed church government was only regulated by human law rarely erected their preferences into principles. For this reason, it is difficult to say whether many Elizabethans were Presbyterian or not. Sir Amias Paulet, later keeper of Mary Queen of Scots, held delegated powers (as governor of Jersey) of royal supremacy in a Presbyterian church, and was happy to support Presbyterianism while he was there. When he was at home in Somerset, on the other hand, he was hereditary steward of the manors of the Bishop of Bath and Wells, and was equally happy with government by bishops.[10] The propaganda of

[9] Collinson, 49.
[10] Eagleston, A. J., *The Channel Islands Under Tudor Government*, 55–6. Hembry, Phyllis, *The Bishops of Bath and Wells*, 46–8.

Field and his successors made this uncontroversial position harder to maintain, and ultimately pushed the bishops into retaliation, in the next century, by claiming that episcopal government was necessary by the law of God. On matters of the law of God, compromise was sinful, and these rival assertions weakened what could otherwise have been a promising opportunity for compromise between episcopalian and Presbyterian ministers. Even John Knox had been prepared to accept bishops if their dioceses were small enough to allow them to exercise an actual cure of souls, instead of becoming ecclesiastical administrators. Many bishops were interested in schemes on these lines. Other people, including Hooker and Lord Keeper Bacon, were interested in proposals for bishops to govern their dioceses with the aid of a council, possibly made up of rural deans, thus making their authority less arbitrary. In some parishes, such as Moreton Corbet in Shropshire, the patron had delegated his right of choosing the vicar to the parishioners, apparently without objection from the bishop. Such compromise proposals as these interested neither Field nor bishops who were dedicated to fighting him and his ideas.

The Parliament of 1571

In Parliament, however, the dominant influences were not Field and the bishops, but Norton and Councillors who found him easy to work with. Both the 1571 Treason Act and the 1581 bill for the queen's safety were the product of amicable co-operation between Norton and the Privy Councillors. He did not, like Parliamentary Puritans of 1640, attempt to achieve his aims by legalistic opposition to the government. If the religious disputes of the reign could have been settled between moderate Puritans like Norton and moderate Councillors like Knollys and Mildmay, they would have caused very little trouble.

In the Parliament of 1571, the aims of Norton and his friends were not very different from those of sympathetic bishops. They wanted, with the support of at least one of the bishops, to introduce a bill to make it compulsory to receive Communion, as well as to come to church. This bill involved important issues of principle. Many Roman Catholics who felt that Anglicanism was erroneous, but not damnable, had continued to attend Anglican matins. Under this bill, these 'church-papists' would have been detected and prosecuted. Norton and the Puritans believed than no one who thought Anglican doctrine erroneous could be a loyal subject, but the queen was prepared to trust those who were merely willing to endure the existing church. In this, the event showed that she was right. The bill was ultimately passed by James I, in the aftermath of the Gunpowder Plot, but it had no chance of passing into law under Elizabeth. Norton also wanted official confirmation of the *Reformatio Legum Ecclesiasticarum*, the draft revision of the canon law prepared by his father-in-law, Archbishop Cranmer. Since Henry VIII's reformation had left it in doubt what the canon law of the church was, the adoption of Cranmer's revision seemed a sensible proposal, but the bishops would not support it.[11] The Puritans also wanted a bill to confirm the Thirty-Nine Articles, with a significant exception. Their bill confirmed the articles of doctrine, which the Puritans liked, but it did not confirm the articles of discipline, which were left to depend on the uncertain authority of Convocation. This was the only one of their bills which passed into law. They also wanted to reform some details in the Prayer Book, and to make more attempts to provide a godly preaching ministry. Norton's colleague Strickland introduced these proposals by moving for a conference with the bishops, hoping that reforms could be secured by agreement. The bishops were uncomfortably aware of the queen's settled opposition to all these proposals, and the conference failed. Its failure marks an important stage in the Puritans' loss of confidence in the bishops.

It was after the failure of this conference that Strickland set out to reform the Prayer Book by bill. This bill would have abolished the surplice, kneeling at Communion, and most other ceremonies to which any number of Puritans objected. Sir Francis Knollys, the senior Privy Councillor, must have sympathized with the bill, but warned the House that it was not expedient to pursue it. This warning was not heeded, and Strickland was sequestered from the House. This provocative act was met, not merely with indignation, but with a claim of rights: Carleton, Peter Wentworth's brother-in-law, said that: 'Forasmuch as he was not now a private man, but to supply the room, person or place of a multitude, specially chosen, . . . he thought that neither in regard of the country, which was not to be wronged, nor for the liberty of the House, which was not to be infringed, we should permit him to be detained. . . . He should be sent for to the bar of the House, there to be heard, and there to answer.'[12] The Council gave way to a storm it would have been wiser not to provoke, and allowed Strickland to return to the House.

This Parliament's failure to produce reforms encouraged Field and his fellows to make more radical suggestions, and they marked the beginning of the next Parliament, in 1572, with the *Admonition to Parliament*, a full-

---

[11] On the authority of the canon law after the Reformation, see above, p. 99. This proposal was still being put forward by Bishop Williams and other moderates in 1641.

[12] Neale, *Parliaments,* i. 201. It is typical of the structure of Elizabethan politics that Peter Wentworth's other brother-in-law was Sir Walter Mildmay, the Puritan Chancellor of the Exchequer.

blooded Presbyterian tract arguing that the government of bishops was 'antichristian and devilish and contrary to the scriptures', that the Prayer Book was 'culled and picked out of that popish dunghill, the mass book', and that one of the ecclesiastical courts was 'a petty little stinking ditch that floweth out of that former great puddle, the Archbishop's court'. This tract did not represent 'Puritanism': Norton dismissed it as suffering from 'unreasonableness and unseasonableness', and other prominent Puritans supported him. Even Beza, Calvin's successor at Geneva, expressed his desire 'not to be involved more than I can help in such very indiscreet proceedings'.[13] From 1572 onwards, the Puritan movement was divided between reformists and revolutionaries, and though the reformists were in a large majority it was largely the revolutionaries who dictated official responses to the movement. The 1572 Parliament produced no religious results, though it did have some share in inducing the queen to execute Norfolk for his part in the Ridolfi plot, and in 1573 an episcopal campaign of repression was begun, extending well beyond Field and his circle. Like all such Elizabethan campaigns, it was made haphazard by the operation of personal influence. The Bishop of Peterborough deprived a Presbyterian of the mastership of a hospital, only to receive a letter from Leicester telling the bishop to keep his hands off his 'loving friend' if he wanted his help and good offices in future.[14]

Archbishop Grindal

In December 1575 the flagging hopes of the reformist wing of the Puritan movement were suddenly revived when, on the death of Archbishop Parker, Burghley persuaded the queen to nominate Grindal as his successor. Grindal had accepted office in the settlement in the hope that he would be able to reform it from within, and throughout the intervening years he had succeeded in keeping the confidence of moderate Puritans. If the queen were willing to support him, he had an excellent chance of restoring peace in the church. One of the Councillors advised Grindal that it would be worth preparing proposals before the next meeting of Parliament to remove 'popish dregs' from the church. He added: 'I know it will be hard for you to do that good that you and your brethren desire. Yet (things discreetly ordered) somewhat there may be done. Herein I had rather declare unto your lordship at your repair hither frankly by mouth what I think than to commit the same to letters.'[15] At first, Grindal's chances seemed good. The 1576 Parliament was induced to put forward (by petition) a moderate series of proposals, of which some, such as the reform of excommunication to prevent it from being used as a mere pro-

[13] Collinson, 120–1.   [14] Collinson, 151–2.   [15] Collinson, 161.

cedural device in the church courts, and the granting to parishes of the right to complain (within twenty days) of the clergy supplied by their patrons, might have eased the grievances of the radicals. When the queen referred these petitions to the bishops, action seemed possible. Convocation then put forward a long series of reforming canons dealing with such abuses as ordination of unfit candidates and the lack of education of the inferior clergy. The queen was induced to accept them, though she refused to support Grindal's attempt to make marriages legal during Lent. Grindal then tackled another Puritan grievance by attempting to reform his court of Faculties, which controlled the Archbishop's power of giving dispensations.[16] A number of types of dispensation, such as those which permitted children to hold ecclesiastical livings, were stopped, and Grindal then began plans for reform of the other ecclesiastical courts, and investigations into pluralism and the standards of the clergy. According to Norton, there was a tacit agreement between the Archbishop and the Puritan preachers that they would join together against the papists, the Archbishop refraining from troubling the preachers, and the preachers refraining from breaking the peace of the church. Pamphleteering against the bishops almost stopped, and even Field took to writing against Rome instead.

This promising situation lasted little more than a year. It was brought to a dead halt when the queen commanded Grindal to suppress the exercises known as 'prophesyings'. These, in spite of their name, were not occasions of undisciplined enthusiasm. One bishop, when he first met them in Emden in Mary's reign, said they were like university disputations in Cambridge. They involved a sermon, and a discussion between ministers, often before a lay audience. Many bishops strongly encouraged them because they did something to improve the education and preaching standards of the lower clergy. Bishop Cooper, later notorious as an enemy of the extremer Puritans, even tried to compel clergy to attend them, and some bishops took part in them as moderators. When the queen told Grindal to suppress prophesyings throughout his province, and to limit preachers to three or four for each county, both the whole of Grindal's policy and the freedom of the bishops to govern the church were threatened. Grindal consulted his colleagues, and found that ten out of fifteen were in favour of the prophesyings. Finally Grindal wrote to the queen, refusing to obey her orders because 'I choose rather to offend your earthly majesty, than to offend the heavenly majesty of God'. He told her that she was bound to refer religious questions to her

---

[16] In 1610, Archbishop Bancroft objected to similar proposals on the ground that they would diminish his income. Foster, *1610*, i. 71.

bishops, in the same way as she was bound to refer legal questions to her judges. He added:

remember, madam, that you are a mortal creature. Look not only (as was said to Theodosius) upon the purple and princely array, wherewith ye are apparelled, but consider withal what is that which is covered therewith. Is it not flesh and blood? Is it not dust and ashes? Is it not a corruptible body, which must return to his earth again, God knows how soon? Must you not also one day appear before the fearful judgement-seat of the crucified? . . . And although ye are a mighty prince, yet remember that he which dwelleth in heaven is mightier.[17]

After this letter, Grindal was suspended from office, and all Burghley's skill could not ease him back in favour. The peace of the church was broken. The *Admonition to Parliament* was reprinted, and on the episcopal side authority passed to Aylmer, Bishop of London, who threatened to deal with Puritans by sending them to 'Lancashire, Shropshire, Staffordshire, and such like barbarous places'. Together with his backer Sir Christopher Hatton, Aylmer was consistently ready to influence the queen against Puritanism. Secretary Walsingham, instead of pressing for reforms, warned one of his juniors: 'if you knew with what difficulty we retain that we have, and the seeking of more might hazard (according to man's understanding) that which we already have, ye would then, Mr. Davison, deal warily in this time when policy carrieth more sway than zeal.'[18]

Foreign affairs and the succession

For Walsingham, Leicester, and many of Grindal's other supporters, their religious aims went with desire for a more aggressive, anti-Spanish foreign policy, and on this issue too, events appeared to be moving against them during the 1570s. In 1570 the first tentative moves were being made towards hostility between England and Spain, but to older Elizabethans it did not come naturally. Even as late as 1589, Burghley said that 'the state of the world is marvellously changed, when we true Englishmen have cause, for our own quietness, to wish good success to a French king and a king of Scots'.[19] Nor was it easy to form a settled foreign policy in the changeable state of Europe in 1570. The rivalry between France and Spain was still a settled fact, and so was Spain's determination to

---

[17] Strype, Grindal, 572. The case of Theodosius, to which Grindal referred, had been the standard precedent used by Popes to prove that rulers could be excommunicated.

[18] Collinson, 194. On Davison's failure to heed this warning, see below, pp. 241–2.

[19] Conyers Read, ii. 456.

suppress the revolt of the Netherlands, but the attitude of England to these facts was uncertain. In France and Scotland, internal dissension made policy unpredictable, and changes in their policy might still drive England into alliance with Spain against them. From the English point of view the key questions were the queen's marriage, Mary Queen of Scots, and the Netherlands. In 1570, the Duke of Alba's army appeared to be suppressing the revolt of the Netherlands, and both the English and the French were anxious about what it might do either as a result of victory, or in order to bring it about. If Philip of Spain chose to execute the papal bull deposing Elizabeth, a victorious army in the Netherlands would be in a good position to invade England. Alternatively, if Alba failed to suppress the Netherlands, he might choose to blame his failure on the rebels' ability to escape across the frontier to France or across the sea to England before preparing a new raid. Dutch privateers based in England were a menace to Spanish shipping. Both for England and for France, there were two possible ways of meeting the Spaniards' threat of retaliation: they might conciliate Spain, in order to make the Spaniards less willing to carry it out, or they might harass them to make them less able to carry it out. In France in 1571 political influence was passing to the Huguenot Admiral Coligny, who favoured the second course. England's attitude, as always, was unpredictable, but if Coligny wanted open war with Spain, he would find an English alliance worth working for.

The unfamiliar prospect of alliance between England and France necessarily raised the question of Scotland. The faction who were ruling Scotland in the name of the infant James VI were friendly to England, but Mary Queen of Scots still had partisans in arms in Scotland, and if they were successful they would be likely to turn Scotland into an open enemy of England. And unless Elizabeth married and had children, Mary Queen of Scots, as probable heir to the English throne, was a tempting ally to anyone who might be likely to quarrel with England. If France were to make friends with Elizabeth, Mary would be tempted to make friends with Spain instead. De Spes, the Spanish ambassador in England, was eager to make common cause with Mary against Elizabeth. He had been in treasonable communication with the northern rebels and with the Duke of Norfolk, and no one knew how much more support he might find for Catholic plots against Elizabeth. These dangers created a strong case for the queen's marriage, and an even stronger one for finding some friends, and when the French, late in 1570, began tentative negotiations for a marriage between Elizabeth and the French king's brother the Duke of Anjou, they found a sympathetic response. The more Protestant of the queen's advisers disliked the idea of marriage with a Catholic, and the negotiations centred largely on Anjou's right to practise his religion in England. The queen's attitude to the marriage is hard to discover, but Burghley was in favour of it, largely because it might prevent the growth of a reversionary interest round Mary Queen of Scots. He said that if the queen married, even if she did not have children, 'there would long be the possibility of children, the people would still cling to the hope that the crown would remain in the line of king Henry VIII, and the curious and dangerous question of the succession would in the minds of quiet subjects, be, as it were, buried—a happy funeral for all England'.[20]

The danger of an uncertain succession was made more obvious by the discovery, late in 1571, of the Ridolfi plot. Ridolfi's plan appears to have been to depose Elizabeth and to put Mary on the throne. His plans certainly involved Norfolk and Mary's ambassador, and possibly the Spanish ambassador as well. Norfolk's support could have made the conspiracy really dangerous. To underline the danger, Elizabeth fell seriously ill, and Leicester and Burghley watched for three nights by her bedside. To English Protestants, it was uncomfortable to leave Mary alive and plotting only a heartbeat, or a pistol-shot, from the throne, but Elizabeth was reluctant to take any action against her. Sir Thomas Smith, Elizabeth's ambassador in France, commented, 'God preserve her majesty long to reign over us by some unlooked-for miracle, for I cannot see by natural reason that her highness goeth about to provide for it.'[21] On the other hand, since Mary was half-French, it would have been difficult to execute her and negotiate for a French alliance at the same time.

In the spring of 1572, possibly as a result of protests from the north German Hanse towns, Elizabeth expelled the Dutch pirates from England. The result was that they seized Flushing and Brill, on the Netherlands coast, while the Spanish troops were away guarding the French frontier, and the revolt of the Netherlands took on a new lease of life, creating promising opportunities for intervention, and reviving English fears of French power in the Netherlands. During the summer, a large body of English volunteers went to the Netherlands, with the sympathy of Burghley, if not of the queen. The French marriage negotiations had already lapsed by St. Bartholomew's Day, when a large number of French Huguenots, including Coligny, were massacred in Paris. This revived most of the traditional English distrust of France, and Alba took the opportunity to restore England's interest in good relations with Spain, while France was again distracted by civil war. In 1573, amity with Spain was

---

[20] Conyers Read, ii. 32. I would like to thank my colleague Dr. N. M. Sutherland for some very helpful discussions of the Anjou marriage project.

[21] Neale, *Parliaments*, i. 242.

formally restored, both sides promised not to help each other's exiles, trade was reopened, and the first crisis between England and Spain was peacefully ended.

The supporters of a more energetic policy scored occasional points, of which the most famous is Drake's voyage round the world, financed on a joint stock basis by the queen and some Privy Councillors. Having made a profit of £160,000 (perhaps six months' revenue) out of the enterprise, the queen then approved it by knighting Drake. On the main issue of the Netherlands, however, nothing was done except the financing of occasional small loans to the rebels, and the war continued to drift on its inconclusive course. On some occasions, the queen even seemed willing to encourage the French to intervene rather than herself, but these occasions were mostly ones when a Spanish victory seemed imminent. In 1578, when the French king's brother, the Duke of Alençon, appeared to be offering the rebels serious support, the queen responded, not by outbidding him, but by distracting him with suggestions that she might marry him. But though the Alençon marriage negotiations served an obvious diversionary purpose, they may also have been seriously meant. The queen was now forty-six, and though her doctors earnestly assured Burghley that she was still capable of having children, she would not remain so much longer.

Opposition to a stable dynasty with an heir was usually politically unwise, but opposition on behalf of the heir to the throne might be very productive, as Burghley and others who had befriended Elizabeth in Mary's reign had cause to remember. Catholic opposition was already alarming. In England, a remarkably able series of missionaries, trained in exile at Douai and Louvain, were coming back and strengthening the resistance of English Catholics. They maintained that they were not traitors because, among other reasons, they came unarmed, to which Burghley replied that Judas also came unarmed, but so long as it was supposed to be an article of Catholic faith that Elizabeth ought not to be queen, the government found it hard to take so detached an attitude. In Ireland, an open rebellion received the Pope's support, materially in money, and spiritually through Nicholas Sanders, one of the ablest of all the Catholic missionaries. Ireland cost money, and there was not enough for effective help to the Netherlands as well. As the Earl of Sussex commented, 'for the queen to be the head of the war is more, I fear, than she can go through withal or the realm will maintain'.[22] On the other hand, Spain in unfettered control of the Netherlands coast would be in a position to browbeat England with trade embargoes or any other more alarm-

[22] Wernham, 336.

ing weapons she chose. In these circumstances, the case for a French alliance was strong. If it were rejected, and the marriage with it, the rest of the reign would be one long struggle for the succession. Burghley, who supported the marriage, gloomily listed the effects of the crisis which he expected to follow its rejection: increased efforts to repress Catholics, increased need for military force, and increased taxation to pay for it. The majority of the Councillors, however, were opposed to it, largely because Alençon was a Catholic, and the queen finally decided against it, remarking sadly that 'her own servants and favourites professed to love her for her good parts, Alençon for her person and the Scots for her crown . . . but they all ended in the same thing, namely, asking her for money'.[23] The Council reacted by recommending an embargo on the making, selling, or firing of pistols within two miles of the queen. In the next Parliament, they, together with Norton, sponsored a bill which, in its final form, made it treason to withdraw the queen's subjects from their allegiance, or *for that intent* to convert them to Rome. Fines for non-attendance at church were raised to £20 a month, and hearing Mass was made punishable with a fine of 100 marks (£66. 13s. 4d.). This Act remained the basis of the law against recusancy for the next sixty years. The oaths of allegiance and supremacy were demanded for more and more positions, including membership of the militia. Recusants had been excluded from the House of Commons since 1570, and Burghley proposed that they should also be excluded from the medical profession and the Inns of Court. Though Campion and a number of priests were executed for treason, repression remained haphazard, and Sir James Croft, who may have been a Catholic, remained on the Privy Council.

When the Throckmorton plot, another Catholic plot against the queen's life involving Mary and the Spanish ambassador, was detected, concern for the queen's safety became more intense. On the initiative of some of the Councillors, most of the leading gentlemen swore loyalty to the Bond of Association, a document which bound them to pursue to the death anyone *on whose behalf* the queen might be assassinated. Burghley prepared a draft bill for the Parliament of 1584, under which, in the event of the queen's assassination, supreme power (including the right to try the queen's murderers, appoint a new Council, and determine the succession) would have rested with Parliament during the interregnum. Nothing came of the bill, but it is another illustration of the fact that her leading servants did not share her views on the position of Parliament. Other Councillors were attempting to ingratiate themselves with possible successors. Lord Hunsdon was hoping to marry his daughter to Mary's son

[23] Conyers Read, ii. 283.

James. Leicester was trying to marry his son to the other Stuart claimant Arabella Stuart (who was descended from Henry VII's daughter Margaret by her second marriage, and had the advantage over James and Mary of having been born in England),[24] but the plan was frustrated by his son's death. Since Leicester had an arsenal of 100 cannon, and his brother-in-law Huntingdon controlled the Scottish borders as President of the North, he might, if he had survived the queen, have been in a good position to place his own candidate on the throne.

The drift to war and its effect on English politics

Meanwhile, other events were hardening Spain's attitude to England. Spanish imports of silver were rising to their peak, and since many Spanish Councillors blamed the covert sympathy of England for their failure to suppress the Netherlands, it seemed tempting to use this money for an invasion of England. The Turks' preoccupation with war against the Persians left the Spaniards free to divert resources from the Mediterranean to the Atlantic. One of the most important issues for Spain was the Portuguese succession, which fell vacant in 1580. Portugal controlled a considerable fleet, and an empire as large as Spain's, and Philip had the best claim to the succession. On the other hand, Catherine de Medici had a claim on behalf of France, and many Portuguese supported a bastard pretender, Don Antonio. Philip gained control of Portugal, but the Azores, which lay across the route of the treasure fleets, declared for Don Antonio. The English, fearing the increase in Spanish power which control of Portugal might bring about, decided to support Don Antonio, who became a welcome source of commissions to English privateers.

Neither Elizabeth nor Philip of Spain wanted war, and they moved towards it slowly and hesitantly. So long as France was powerful, England and Spain still had an interest in reviving their old alliance against France. For England, there was little interest in precipitating a war against a vastly superior enemy: after the conquest of Portugal, the Spanish navy amounted to between 250,000 and 300,000 tons, the Dutch to 232,000, and the English only to 42,000. For the Spaniards, preoccupied as they were with the Netherlands and with their ancient rivalry with France, there was little sense in adding unnecessarily to the number of their enemies. Philip had already faced two bankruptcies during his reign, and there was a case for avoiding a third.

This situation began to change rapidly after 1584. Parma, the new

---

[24] Arabella Stuart's claim to the throne depended on the argument, which might become popular if sufficiently encouraged, that James VI could not succeed because he was an alien.

Spanish governor in the Netherlands, was winning what looked likely to be decisive victories, and when the Dutch leader William of Orange, who had co-ordinated the whole revolt, was assassinated, the Spaniards' victory seemed almost assured. It was at this point that the death of the Duke of Alençon deprived the Dutch of their last hope of effective help from France, and left France, like England, facing a succession crisis. In the strict biological sense, the heir to the French throne was now Henry of Navarre, who was a Protestant. To his enemies, this prospect appeared intolerable, and they began to organize to prevent his succession. Philip of Spain first reacted by offering subsidies to Henry of Navarre if he would create civil war in France, but soon moved into alliance with Navarre's enemies, who also had power to create civil war, and moreover were also Philip's co-religionists. From Elizabeth's point of view it was equally important that Navarre's leading enemies, the house of Guise, were Mary Queen of Scots' family, and Mary thus became one of Philip's allies. If Philip could place Guise supporters on the thrones of France and England, his strength would be immeasurably increased. Mary's French connections were no longer likely to restrain Philip from giving her whole-hearted support. Since a Spanish intervention on behalf of Mary would be more likely to be supported by an English fifth column than a Spanish intervention on behalf of Philip, the case for executing Mary was much strengthened.

The division of France into two sides, one supported by the Spaniards and the other by the English, destroyed the European balance of power. In this changed situation, English policy became more aggressive. Elizabeth's attitude to colonies had always been hesitant, and in 1574, she had revoked a colonizing patent to Sir Richard Grenville, for *terra Australis*, after he had sailed, in order to satisfy the Spanish ambassador. In 1584, on the other hand, she sanctioned a voyage by Raleigh on the first attempt to found an English colony in Virginia. She sanctioned another expedition by Drake (Burghley advised Drake to sail quickly before the queen changed her mind), and refrained from checking the increasing amount of privateering. These expeditions cost the Spaniards considerable dislocation, and considerable expense in protection, in addition to the privateers' actual captures. The Spanish governor of La Margarita reported that the pearl fisheries had been brought to a standstill, and added: 'since your Majesty cannot prevent this, because your majesty is far away, then may Jesus Christ remedy the situation.'[25] The most provocative of the English actions was that the queen in 1585 at last sanctioned open intervention in the Netherlands, and sent in an army under the command of Leicester. It was budgeted to cost £126,000 a year, more than a third of her annual in-

[25] Andrews, K. R., *Elizabethan Privateering* (1964), 172.

come, and in fact cost a good deal more. The expedition's success was limited, but once again it prevented the Spaniards from finally suppressing the revolt. Philip retaliated by ordering the seizure of all English ships in Spanish harbours, and achieved a large haul of prizes, in which two London merchants lost as much as £37,000. This act did not stop the Spanish trade, but it drove many merchants to recoup their losses by privateering.

This heated pre-war atmosphere in turn affected the domestic political situation in England. There were two ways in which the risk of war might alter reactions to religious troubles in England. The first, favoured by Leicester and Walsingham, and, during the period of crisis, by Burghley, involved suspending hostilities against Puritans at least until the danger was over. However they might behave on other issues, their loyalty against Spain was impeccable, and their energy and organizing ability often considerable. Few people were better qualified, for example, to write anti-papal propaganda. Leicester took two of the most committed Presbyterian ministers to the Netherlands as his chaplains, and even extended his patronage to the Presbyterian leaders Cartwright and Field. As for the more moderate Puritan gentlemen, most of them could be relied on to busy themselves in the organization of their county militia. The counterpart of this policy would have been more effective persecution of Catholics, and the execution of Mary Queen of Scots.

The arguments for this policy were largely domestic, but the arguments which moved the queen were usually diplomatic. She was interested in the possible attitudes of Scotland and France, and of the Pope. At this moment, the Scottish Presbyterians were in disgrace, and many of their leaders were in exile in England, receiving a warm welcome from Walsingham and others. At a time when the Spaniards were threatening to make an alliance with Scotland, Elizabeth was not eager to welcome James's refugees. Neither the French nor the Scots could react favourably (at least in public) to the execution of Mary Queen of Scots, and though Elizabeth allowed her Council to issue periodic orders for the disarming of Catholic recusants (which one man implemented by arresting his grandmother), she did not want to make it impossible for Catholics to remain loyal. Moreover, a great deal depended on Philip's attempts to induce the Pope to finance his projected Armada. When first approached, in 1583, the Pope was understandably doubtful, both whether the Armada would actually sail, and also whether Philip was concerned for the interests of the Catholic church, or only for those of the house of Habsburg. It was at this time that the Pope was led, by means of which we know nothing, to believe first that Elizabeth was considering conversion to Catholicism, and later that as a ruler she had not an equal in Europe.

Finally, when Philip did succeed in obtaining papal support for the Armada, it was only on a basis of payment by results.[26]

Archbishop Whitgift and the origins of Puritan legalism

Since the suspension of Grindal, the see of Canterbury had been in commission. In 1583, Grindal died and was succeeded by John Whitgift. If the queen had been trying to impress the Pope with her hostility to Puritanism, she could not have made a better choice. She may have chosen him for diplomatic reasons, or she may have chosen him for the only thing he had in common with Grindal—they were both bachelors. For whatever reason he may have been appointed, it was soon apparent that he would have the support of the queen for a vigorous campaign against Puritans of all sorts. His first move was a demand for general clerical subscription to three articles. The first, accepting the royal supremacy, the Puritans regarded as unexceptionable. The third, approving the Thirty-Nine Articles, most of them could accept if it were interpreted according to the 1571 statute, as covering only the articles of doctrine, but not if it were meant to cover the articles of discipline as well. The most difficult article was the second, which asked them, not merely to approve the use of the Prayer Book but also to make the sweeping declaration that it contained *nothing* contrary to the word of God. Many ministers who used the Prayer Book (or most of it), and were prepared to avoid any attacks on it, could not subscribe to a formula as far-reaching as this. Most Puritan clergy, not wishing to make trouble or to lose their livings, responded by offering various forms of limited or conditional subscription. For a while, it seemed likely that Whitgift would not accept them. He accepted a formula submitted by 300 ministers in Leicestershire, possibly with the support of the Earl of Huntingdon, but he suspended sixty ministers each in Norfolk and Suffolk. A campaign on this scale reached far beyond the limits of any form of extremism, and threatened to drive out of the church many ministers who were no more Puritan than most of the Privy Council.

It was to the Privy Council that the ministers petitioned for relief, and the Council, with the single exception of Sir Christopher Hatton, was willing to support them, and summoned Whitgift to appear to answer the petitions. Among all the people who were dismayed by Whitgift's doings, one of the very few who welcomed them was Field, who believed that Whitgift had much strengthened the support for total abolition of bishops. Norton, on the other hand, urged Whitgift to tolerate those ministers who

[26] On these negotiations, see Lynch, J., 'Philip II and the Papacy', *T.R.H.S.* (1961), 23–42.

were prepared to keep a 'peaceable silence'[27] on controversial issues. One of the points which seemed particularly bitter to the Puritans and their sympathizers was that Whitgift appeared to have little interest in any faults among the clergy except Puritanism. For years, Puritans had been asking for an end to pluralism and non-residence, and for a preaching ministry, only to be met with the reply that there were not enough learned ministers. In these circumstances, they felt that it did not make sense to silence most of the preaching ministers there were, while leaving idle incompetent and dissolute clergy to stay on in peace. As one of them said, 'to go about to put out thirty or forty in a shire, and then to say, where shall we have preachers, is an odd kind of question'. It was with this point in mind that the Puritans began to undertake surveys of the clergy, showing both the shortage of preachers, and what sort of clergy Whitgift had not deprived. In Essex, they found that the vicar of Much Baddow had had a child by his sister, as well as being a former popish priest still suspected of popery, and a number of others who had been convicted of incontinence or drunkenness, as well as being unable to preach. Both the Council and the 1584 and 1586 Parliaments strongly sympathized with the argument that these were the sort of clergy who should have been first deprived.

Nevertheless, a number of ministers wished 'that a reconciliation should be offered to the bishops, that since we profess one God and preach one doctrine we may join together with a better consent to build up the church',[28] and Burghley and Walsingham finally succeeded in working out a compromise acceptable to both sides. The majority of suspended ministers were restored to their cures, to the disappointment of Field. Whitgift, however, promptly started a new round. This time, he chose to proceed through the Court of High Commission. This body had originally been a series of ad hoc commissions to exercise ecclesiastical jurisdiction under the Royal Supremacy, but by 1584 it had developed into a regular ecclesiastical prerogative court, distinguished from other ecclesiastical courts by its power to fine and imprison. There was little room to dispute the legality of the court, since it had been sanctioned, though not created, by the Act of Supremacy of 1559; but there was room to dispute its power to fine and imprison, which had been granted to it only by the queen's letters patent. Common lawyers were able to question whether it was possible to give a court the power to fine and imprison without the backing of an Act of Parliament. There was also room for legal objections to its procedure under the ex officio oath. This oath, administered by the judges of the court (usually the bishops, reinforced with some civil lawyers and some Privy Councillors), bound the party to swear to tell the truth in

27 Collinson, 257.   28 Collinson, 247, 261.

answer to any question he might be asked. Whitgift was thus able to ask Puritan ministers, under oath, whether they were guilty of each of the normal Puritan nonconforming practices (and opinions). If they were guilty of any of these offences, they were bound to confess to them if they did not want to go to Hell for perjury. If they refused to take the oath, they could be sent to prison for contempt of court.

This procedure was not only used against known nonconformists. When Burghley recommended two Cambridge graduates to Whitgift for preferment, Whitgift, instead of preferring them, tendered them the *ex officio* oath, and administered a set of twenty-four articles for them to answer. Apart from being a provocative act, this was a gross slight to Burghley, who told Whitgift that this was a proceeding 'savouring of the Roman inquisition, and is rather a device to seek for offenders than to reform any'.[29] Even Burghley's protection was no help to the unfortunate victims.

Whitgift was creating a situation in which there was a wide divergence between the secular law, based on Acts of Parliament, and the ecclesiastical law, based on episcopal canons and injunctions. There was no secular law, for example, that bound people to subscribe to those of the Thirty-Nine Articles which dealt with discipline and ceremonies. Many common lawyers were already worried by the shift of business (and fees) to ecclesiastical courts, and it was natural for them and the Puritans to make common cause. It was the response to Whitgift which produced the identification, frequent for the next few years, between Puritanism and legalistic objections to the prerogative. Two Puritan lawyers and government officials, Robert Beale, clerk of the Council, and James Morice, Attorney of the Court of Wards, were peculiarly responsible for this development. Their objections to the *ex officio* oath started the legal tradition which led to the American Fifth Amendment, whereby no person can be compelled to incriminate himself, and they also resurrected the clause of Magna Carta saying that no one could be tried except by the legal judgement of his peers or by the law of the land. As they interpreted this clause, the law of the land meant common law or statute, and the High Commission's power to fine and imprison, being authorized only by the queen's prerogative, was no part of the law of the land.[30] In Cawdry's case, Morice, Cawdry's counsel, argued that a minister's benefice was his freehold property, and therefore that he could not be deprived of it without the sanction of statute or common law. The judges rejected this argument (though it was later accepted by Chief Justice Coke in Fuller's case) but

[29] Conyers Read, ii. 295.

[30] On the legal issues involved in the fight against the High Commission see Thompson, Faith, *Magna Carta* (1948), 197–230.

the Puritan lawyers did score some remarkable successes. The High Commission claimed, as part of its power to imprison, the right to hold suspects in custody pending trial. In 1590, they sent a messenger to arrest one Simpson in Northamptonshire, and Simpson barricaded himself into his house, and shot the messenger dead. At his trial, he pleaded that since the High Commission had no right to imprison, the messenger had been committing an assault, and he had acted in legitimate self-defence. His plea was accepted by the Assizes, and he was found guilty only of manslaughter.[31] The common law courts also had the power to issue prohibitions, to prevent a court from hearing cases over which it had no jurisdiction, and they soon began to issue prohibitions to the High Commission in accordance with the interpretation of the Puritan lawyers. Ultimately, prohibitions grew so frequent that Laud threatened to arrest the next man who brought a prohibition into court, whereat a Puritan brought one into court and threw it at him. From the appointment of Whitgift, this running legal battle continued until the Civil War, and though Beale and Morice, who were devoted government servants, cannot be classified as members of 'the opposition', some of their successors perhaps can be. As Professor Collinson says of Whitgift, 'for the sake of what was surely an unattainable degree of uniformity, he made it more difficult to deal effectively with the hard core of extremists, and placed his own episcopal order in grave danger. In the long run, the Whitgiftian policy, continued in their generations by Bancroft and the Laudians, was as much responsible as any Puritan excess for destroying the comprehensiveness of the church of England and its fully national character.'[32]

Mary Queen of Scots

For the Puritan Councillors, concern for the Protestant religion involved concern for the queen's safety, and they believed that the queen's safety demanded the execution of Mary Queen of Scots. On this issue they had the support of more cautious Councillors such as Burghley, and they were successful. In 1585, Secretary Walsingham allowed Mary to establish what she supposed was a secret method of communication with the outer world. She at once took advantage of it to enter into yet another plot involving plans for the death and deposition of Elizabeth, and Walsingham was able to read the details of the plot as they developed. With this evidence, together with a full confession from Babington, the chief conspirator, the Council were at last able to induce the queen to bring Mary to trial. She was tried by a commission including the Councillors and two of the most

[31] Prynne, W., *Breviate of the Prelates' Intolerable Usurpations,* etc. (1637), 152.
[32] Collinson, 246–7.

notorious Catholic peers in the country. The evidence was too plain to allow any verdict but guilty.

The Councillors then had to find a means of persuading the queen to allow the sentence to be carried out. In this, their obvious ally was Parliament. Burghley wrote to Walsingham that 'we stick upon Parliament, which her Majesty misliketh, but we all persist, to make the burden better borne, and the world abroad better satisfied'.[33] Parliament pressed strongly for Mary's execution, and voted a subsidy with alacrity.

However, though this was in the short term the most important business of the 1586–7 Parliament, the business which has caught the attention of later historians was the attempt to introduce a bill for a Presbyterian church settlement. In the short term, this was a storm in a teacup, involving only six members, who were easily outmanoeuvred by the Puritan Councillors. However, the incident did produce a storm about the queen's right to imprison members, and another protest about freedom of speech from Peter Wentworth, who claimed that M.P.s could 'freely and without controlment of any person or danger of law, by bill or speech . . . utter any . . . griefs touching the service of God, the safety of the prince, and this noble realm'. He also asked, ominously, 'whether the prince and state can . . . be maintained without this Council of Parliament, not altering the government of the state?'[34] What put into Peter Wentworth's head the idea that the Crown might dispense with Parliament altogether, and introduce a new type of 'constitution', it is impossible to say. As an anticipation of the seventeenth century, this speech is fascinating, but in the short term, it was no more than an interlude in the story.

The French and the Scots were still pressing Elizabeth not to carry out the sentence against Mary. Elizabeth suggested to Mary's keeper, Sir Amias Paulet, that he should privately put Mary to death under his oath to the Bond of Association. Paulet replied: 'God forbid that I should make so foul a shipwreck of my conscience.'[35] Having sworn to the Bond of Association, he was guilty of perjury in refusing, but later events suggest that he was very prudent. At last Elizabeth was induced to sign the warrant, and left it in the hands of Secretary Davison, who appears to have believed that she had authorized him to send it off. In the case of the Duke of Norfolk, the queen had recalled a death warrant she had already signed, and the Council agreed to send the warrant off at once, and not to tell the queen 'before the execution were past'. Robert Beale, clerk of the Council, was sent off to supervise the execution, and soon reported that it had been done, adding that 'she demanded to speak with her priest, which

[33] Conyers Read, ii. 361.   [34] Neale, *Parliaments,* ii. 155.
[35] Neale, *Queen Elizabeth,* 279.

was denied unto her the rather for that she came with a superstitious pair of beads and a crucifix'.[36]

When the queen learnt of the execution, she sent Secretary Davison to the Tower, and dismissed Lord Treasurer Burghley from court. James, who had privately assured Leicester that he would not object to the execution, whatever he might say in public, announced that he believed the queen's story that Davison had sent the warrant off without authorization. Davison never recovered the queen's favour, though he continued to receive his salary, and Burghley was not allowed into her presence for four months. He spent those months sending her long and humble letters, quoting from the Book of Job, which are preserved among his papers, endorsed 'not received'. In these letters, he humbled himself in every possible way but one: he never admitted that he had done wrong. Whether the queen's apparent anger represents her real feeling about the execution of Mary, or whether it was simply designed to impress the Scots and the French, we do not know. Neither did Burghley.

II WAR FINANCE, 1588–1603

While in disgrace, Burghley was still busy with the almost impossible task of finding the money to meet the Spanish Armada, and also with the last negotiations for peace. These negotiations had little chance of success, but they shed some light on the crucial issues. The English commissioners were to press for (but not insist on) toleration for Dutch Protestants, which was an indispensable condition of any settlement in the Netherlands. They were to insist that the Spaniards should repay English loans to the Dutch, which the English could not afford to do without. They were to demand freedom from the Inquisition for English merchants in Spain. In return, they were to be prepared to abandon support for the Portuguese pretender Don Antonio, and to renounce the right to trade with the Spanish colonies, provided the terms only applied to territory which Spain actually occupied. These terms suggest that in return for protection of their interests in Europe, the English were prepared to sacrifice their interests in the Atlantic.

Neither the Spaniards nor most of the English Council had their hearts in these negotiations, and more importance attached to the war preparations. These were given an extra year by Drake's success, in 1587, in 'singeing the king of Spain's beard' by burning the Spanish fleet in Cadiz harbour, and perhaps more important, destroying all the staves for the Armada's water casks. The navy was in reasonably good shape, thanks to

[36] Conyers Read, ii. 369.

Sir John Hawkins, for whom Burghley had obtained the post of Treasurer of the Navy in 1578. He was a seaman, not a civil servant, and succeeded in reducing the annual peace-time cost of the navy from £10,000 to £6,000, by cutting down on what he regarded as corruption. Even in the patriotic atmosphere of 1587, he had to face bitter feuds with officials objecting to the loss of what they regarded as legitimate perquisites. At least, however, the ships were seaworthy and adequately armed.

The real problem was money. Seamen's wages had been raised in 1585 from 6s. 8d. to 10s. a month, which sheds some light on the fact that in January 1588 the queen decided to reduce the crews to half strength. Nevertheless, in the summer of 1588 the navy was still costing an emergency figure of £13,000 a month. In 1587, the crown's total expenditure had risen from a normal level of about £150,000 to £367,000,[37] and Burghley's estimates for the summer of 1588 were even more alarming. In addition to the cost of the navy, he planned to conscript merchant ships for the period of the campaign (this was not a precedent for Charles I's Ship Money, since it was a levy of ships, and not of money). He estimated that these, together with other ships which might be pressed into service, would cost £27,000 for food and wages, and another £5,000 for powder. The annual cost of the forces in the Netherlands was running at about £130,000. Ireland, which was already costing about £25,000 a year, he thought would cost an extra £7,000. He estimated £12,000 for stationing a force of 3,000 men on the Scottish borders to guard against a possible alliance between Spain and Scotland, and £6,000 for armies to defend the coasts and the queen. The total was over a quarter of a million. These figures excluded much of the cost of training and drilling the militia, which was borne by the counties on local military rates assessed on the same basis as the subsidy. The forces which were mustered at Tilbury to meet the Armada were left in the counties until the last possible moment, in order to postpone as long as possible the moment when their cost had to be shifted to the Exchequer, and Elizabeth's famous speech to the troops at Tilbury was made (though she did not know it) the day after the Armada had passed. More money was available through these local rates than in the Exchequer, which even had to reduce the queen's bodyguard because it could not afford to pay them.

The local military rates, together with a forced loan of £75,000 and a Parliamentary subsidy which was in arrears, created a burden of taxation to which Burghley was afraid many people would object. Norfolk had to

---

[37] These figures are taken from Conyers Read, ii. 410 ff., and their original source is Lord Treasurer Burghley. They are therefore, even if inaccurate, the figures on which the government was working.

find over £4,000 in military rates alone, and though many people were eager to pay, even in 1588 many people were more concerned with evading taxes than with financing the war. Many people who lived in two places tried to evade payment in each on the ground that they were paying in the other, and a number of people in Hertfordshire protested, possibly rightly, that the military rates were illegal. Herefordshire complained that once servants were trained as soldiers they would be unruly, and unwilling to serve their masters. In Hampshire, a number of people expressed fears that their emergency contributions might be permanent. Parliament, though willing to vote subsidies, turned a determinedly deaf ear to complaints about the gross inadequacy of their asesssment. Even Lord Treasurer Burghley, often though he complained of the dishonesty of subsidy assessments, never raised his own assessment at an income of £133. 6s. 8d., though his income ran into thousands. If even 1588 produced no better reactions than this, there was little hope for success at the time, not far off, when the whole of the royal financial system would need fundamental reform.

The Armada war

Fortunately, the Armada arrived before the English ran out of money to feed the fleet, and even more fortunately, it refrained from taking an opportunity to catch the English fleet before it had got out of Plymouth Sound. Philip's instructions were not to engage the English until the Armada had joined up with Parma's army in the Netherlands, and before they could do that they were harried by the English, and then scattered by a storm which left most of their ships wrecked round the coasts of Scotland and Ireland. The English summary, that 'the Lord blew, and they were scattered' is a more accurate summary of the course of the fighting than some of the legends which succeeded it. 1588, however, was not the end of the struggle: it was the beginning. Spanish silver imports were still at a peak, and Spain was not willing to accept defeat. The cost of the war was soon increased, when it merged into the war for the French succession between Henry of Navarre and the Guise faction. Subsidies and troops to help Henry of Navarre were added to the English budget, and the risk of invasion was greatly increased in 1590, when the Spaniards occupied Brittany. Large sums of money were used up on overseas voyages, which, except for one raid on Cadiz by the Earl of Essex, were usually unsuccessful. Invasion scares continued, and many gentry moved out of coastal areas. In 1597 and 1599, the Spaniards sent Armadas as large as that of 1588, and both times they came much nearer to success. In 1597 there was no English fleet ready, and in 1599 the land defences had broken down, and the alarm from Plymouth reached Hampshire and London at the same time. Both times, the Spanish fleet was again dispersed by gales. Fortunately, the effectiveness of the English militia was never put to the test except in small skirmishes. At Mousehole, the trained bands ran away from a Spanish landing, but at Cawsand Bay a raiding party was turned back by one man defending his cottage with a caliver. The cost continued at the same exorbitant level, and Parliamentary subsidies were inadequate to meet it. The 1589 Parliament voted two subsidies, which brought in £280,000, but from 1589 to 1593 the war cost over £1,000,000. Even including the subsidy, this came perilously near the whole of the queen's annual income for the period.

The cost could only be met, partly by borrowing and partly by sales of Crown lands, both of which threatened future income. In 1588 the queen sold Crown lands worth £126,000, and in 1599–1601, when an army had to be raised to suppress a major rebellion in Ireland, she sold lands worth £213,000.[38] The war thus left heavy debts to be met out of a reduced income. The sales of Crown lands, together with the even larger sales at the beginning of the reign to pay for the war in Scotland, probably reduced the Crown's income by about £24,000 a year, a sum which it would cost much unpopularity to replace out of the normal methods of taxation. The Crown often sold advowsons in preference to lands (on economic grounds), thus weakening its power to control the clergy with one hand, while it tried to strengthen it with the other. The figures looked likely to confirm the verdict of one of the members of Leicester's council in the Netherlands, who said that 'these three hundred years and more never any king [of England] was able to continue wars beyond sea above one year'.[39] The wars did continue, but the Crown was never out of debt at any time in the next fifty years.

Parliament, Puritanism, and the need for financial reform

Most fundamental improvements in this situation would involve the assent of the political community in Parliament. In 1593 and 1597 Parliament helped the situation by voting the unprecedented sum of three subsidies, and in 1597 one member even proposed that they should vote the queen an annual grant. In 1601, when Spanish troops had actually landed in Ireland, Parliament voted four subsidies. But though in 1601 they got as far as debating improvements in the method of their assessment, they did nothing. Parliament was ready to be ordinarily helpful, but it was not ready to consider any general alterations in the financial system. Nor were

[38] These figures are taken from *Agrarian History*, 265–7.
[39] Wernham, 379.

they willing, particularly when voting such large sums, to abandon agitation about their usual financial and administrative grievances. In 1589, immediately after the Armada, the House of Commons gave their support to a bill against Purveyance, a long-standing grievance which was also necessary to the provisioning of armies.[40] The bill was introduced by Hare, clerk of the Court of Wards, who was later to be on the receiving end of similar agitations. If the Crown was to be denied even some of the revenues it already had, its chances of achieving solvency would become negligible. On this occasion, the situation was saved by the statesmanship of Burghley and Knollys. Burghley already wanted to replace the random raids of purveyors with fixed compositions on a county basis. His scheme was introduced with the co-operation of the Commons, and worked well enough till it was out-dated by inflation in the 1620s.

Knollys, who persuaded the queen and Commons to accept this compromise, was the oldest member of an ageing Council. He had first sat in Parliament in 1534, and though he survived to sit in one more Parliament, both his age and his increasing resentment of the clericalism of Archbishop Whitgift were beginning to limit his usefulness. Throughout the queen's reign, the political unity necessary to the peaceful functioning of Parliament had been secured by the queen's moderately Puritan Councillors. They had kept channels of communication open between the Puritans and the government, preventing them from feeling that they were beyond the political pale. They had kept enough of the confidence of back-benchers to be able to explain to them some of the complexities of the administrative point of view, and they had usually been able to steer necessary business through the House. On the other hand, they had frequently taken a more independent view of their position than the queen found palatable. In 1584, when the Commons' petitions on religion had been supported by Knollys and Mildmay, the queen had said: 'we understand they be countenanced by some of our Council, which we will redress or else uncouncil some of them.'[41] She did not uncouncil them, but when they died they were not succeeded by men like themselves. Beale, though he sometimes did the work of Secretary of State during the illnesses of his brother-in-law Walsingham, was never raised to full membership of the Council. The new men appointed to the Council in the last years of Elizabeth's reign could be relied on to do what the queen wanted, but the price of this obedience was that they could not be relied on to persuade the House. Many of them were second-rate men: Mr. Secretary Herbert

---

[40] On purveyance and the complaints against it, see above, p. 37 and below, pp. 266, 277.
[41] Neale, *Parliaments*, ii. 69.

became known in James's reign as 'Mr. Secondary Herbert', and Sir John Fortescue, Chancellor of the Exchequer, is famous only for being the victim in a constitutional test case in 1604. No one could query the ability of Whitgift, the first clergyman to sit on Elizabeth's Council, but he did not sit in the Commons, and could not have persuaded them of anything if he had. The Earl of Worcester, appointed in 1592, not only to the Council, but also to an ecclesiastical commission, was an open Catholic, and though his acceptance of membership was a vindication of the queen's consistent attitude to the Catholics, it could not be used as a means of keeping the loyalty of Puritans. By 1601, it is doubtful whether there was a single Councillor who had any sympathy for Puritans.

None of these changes had, as yet, produced any serious effects. There was little explosive Puritan discontent in the Parliaments of the 1590s. In 1593, there was widespread support for a bill introduced by Morice to abolish the *ex officio* oath, but on the whole the reforming Puritans in the House of Commons were weakened by lack of patrons, and perhaps inclined to wait for the new reign. The extreme, Presbyterian, wing of the Puritan movement was never the same after the death of Field, in 1588. His successors achieved a brief success with a series of satirical pamphlets under the name of 'Martin Marprelate'. These were the nearest thing the century produced to *Private Eye*, and the Earl of Essex, for example, found the tracts so amusing that he carried one of them about in his pocket. The search for Martin Marprelate's presses, conducted with great detective skill by Bancroft, who was chaplain in turn to Whitgift and to Hatton, also uncovered many of the private papers of the Presbyterians. These were used for a lengthy prosecution of the leading Presbyterian ministers in Star Chamber, during which Burghley had to rely on the defendants to learn what was happening. After this trial, and the deaths of the great Puritan patrons, both wings of the Puritan movement were leaderless, though not diminished in numbers. But though Puritan discontents did not impair normal good relations with the Commons, they may have prevented the exceptional goodwill necessary to fundamental financial reforms. The extraordinary subsidies were voted strictly on a basis of emergency, and the task of persuading the Commons that emergencies arose so easily because the normal financial system was outdated would have been thankless, if it had been seriously attempted. It would also have required a degree of far-sightedness and imagination among the Crown's ministers which most of them did not possess.

Inflation, office-holders, and patronage

These financial troubles coincided with one of the two most rapid periods of price increases of the century, and with an even more rapid increase in the cost of living in London, which Crown officials had to meet. They also coincided with economic troubles. A long series of bad harvests threatened most people's sources of income and, in 1597, produced a riot against enclosures in Oxfordshire. It is a mark of the government's alarm that Sir Edward Coke, the Attorney General, set out to construct a case for arguing that riots designed to change the law were treason. His doctrine was constructed in such a form as to carry the implication that any combination to obtain higher wages was also treason.[42] This alarm about the reactions of the lower classes should perhaps be seen in the light of the complaint, made in the Parliament of 1601, that they were having to sell their pots and pans to pay the subsidy. The poor, however, were not the only people who were reluctant to part with more money in the hard economic circumstances of the 1590s.

Among all the sums of money the public had to pay, those which caused most discontent seem to have been those which went to support office-holders. At the same time, the office-holders, like everyone else, felt the pressure to increase their income to keep pace with inflation, and since most of them had to live in London, they may have felt it more than many others. Offices were regarded as the office-holder's property, and if owners of estates were allowed to increase the income from their property, office-holders found it hard to see why they should not do the same. Many of the methods they found were liable to cause resentment. In the Council of Wales, one of the members had the power, as a member, to decide whether to sanction bills to initiate a lawsuit, but also the right, as clerk of the signet to the Council, to receive a fee for each bill sanctioned. He clearly had an interest in increasing the amount of litigation before the Council. Pembroke, who was appointed President of the Council of Wales in 1586, set out to attack increases in fees taken by officials for drafting or sealing documents, and met a very hostile reaction from officials, one of whom remarked that, 'I perceive there shall few men's estates here be unsearched.'[43] Since Pembroke was worried about the loyalty of the Welsh in 1588, there was a strong case for acting as he did. On the other hand, fees were a normal part of an official's income, and it was hard to see why they should not increase to keep pace with inflation, like other people's incomes. As President, Pembroke had occasion to appreciate the

---

[42] Coke, *Third Institute,* 9–10.
[43] Williams, Penry, *The Council in the Marches of Wales* (1958), 278.

other side of the argument. The official allowance from the Exchequer for maintenance of the Council had not been increased since 1553, and was grossly inadequate. It was supposed to be supplemented out of the fines the Council imposed on offenders, but these were insufficient, and often were hard to levy. In the 1580s and 1590s, the Exchequer could not consider paying more. Pembroke's predecessor had spent £782 of his own money on the Council, and it was reasonable to assume that office-holders should not need to subsidize their offices. The Council of Wales reacted by sharply increasing the fines it imposed on offenders. This made the Council solvent, but it produced a very hostile public reaction. It was shortly after the increase in fines that local gentry joined with common lawyers in attempting to claim that the court's jurisdiction was illegal, and their arguments proved unfortunately popular. There is no reason to suppose that this story is exceptional.

Increases in official fees cannot be classified as corruption, since the fee applied uniformly to all clients, and was simply a piecework rate of payment. Payments for official favour, on the other hand, were somewhat more dubious. The giving and receiving of presents was a normal part of official life, and there was little future for anyone who tried to dispense with it. On a small scale, it could simply be a normal part of good relations. But in a period of rapid inflation, when salaries did not increase, and attempts to increase fees might be met with official disapproval, gifts might be the only part of an official's livelihood which could be regarded as inflation-proof. An interesting sidelight on Leicester's income is shed by the man who offered him a gift of £20 together with a petition to get him on to the Denbighshire bench. It transpired that Leicester had already supported so many such requests that he had promised the queen not to forward any more for two months. By the end of the two months, Leicester was dead. Unfortunately, we do not know whether other candidates for the Welsh bench had offered him similar sums. A present of £20 may have been within normal limits, but when Robert Cecil sold the wardship of John Hampden to his mother in return for a gift of £500, which was more than twice the official price, he was perhaps stretching the limits of official behaviour.[44] It is unfortunately impossible to say whether the taking of official gifts increased, since officials did not normally keep records of their gifts, but public resentment certainly increased. Some people clearly tried to increase their profits from office, but it was hard to make fortunes anywhere near the level of those which had been made during the Dissolution of the Monasteries.

[44] Hurstfield, J., *The Queen's Wards* (1958), 78, 127, 264. Behind this story there was a vicious internal feud in the Hampden family. P.R.O. Wards 3.18.2.

Normally, officials of any standing might hope to find good service rewarded by grants from the Crown. In the 1590s, however, such rewards as the queen had to give mostly had to be paid for by assuming the odium of collecting some of the more unpopular parts of the Crown's revenue. Parts of the customs, for example, were farmed out to Walsingham and Essex. Walsingham earned his grant by the use he made of the customs for intelligence work, and the Crown received a guaranteed annual income as rent. The Earl of Essex's farm of the customs on the sweet wines, on the other hand, brought him immense profits for little very obvious service. It is not surprising, that members of the House of Commons, faced with unprecedented requests for taxation, focused their resentment, not on the money going to fight the war, but on the money going to reward those, as they thought, more fortunate among their number who had won an official grant or concession. The issue over which this feeling came to the surface was monopolies, granted to favoured people to reward them with the right to charge the public a higher price. In the 1601 Parliament, an agitation against monopolies broke out immediately after a debate on the extraordinary burden of the subsidy. The indignation of the House appeared to be almost unanimous. The member for Warwick called them 'the whirlpool of the prince's profit', and complained of the corrupt activities of the monopolists' agents, taking bribes to refrain from prosecuting those who infringed their patent. Another member complained that monopolies produced poor quality goods, saying: 'and to what purpose is it to do any thing by Act of Parliament, when the queen will undo the same by her prerogative?' The mover was also one of the earliest M.P.s to use the argument current in the next reign, that since the queen, like God, could do no wrong, anyone who had done wrong could not plead the queen's grant to excuse them.[45]

On this occasion, the queen saved the situation with what was known as her 'golden speech'. She called a deputation from the Commons before her, and promised them redress. She expressed sorrow and indignation that her grants should have been abused to oppress her subjects, and said:

I do assure you there is no prince that loves his subjects better, or whose love can countervail our love. There is no jewel, be it of never so rich a price, which I set before this jewel: I mean your love. For I do esteem it more than any treasure or riches: for that we know how to prize, but love and thanks I count unvaluable. And though God hath raised me high, yet this I count the glory of my crown, that I have reigned with your loves. . . . That my grants should be grievous to my people, and oppressions privileged under

[45] For this debate, see D'Ewes, *Journals,* 644–6.

colour of our patents, our kingly dignity shall not suffer it. Yea, when I heard it, I could give no rest unto my thoughts until I had reformed it.[46]

This speech, with its studied alternation of 'we' and 'I', was a superb rhetorical performance, and the more effective because it was also true. Though the situation was saved, the underlying strains which had produced the monopolies were still there, and were to produce more monopolies in the next reign. So was public discontent: Robert Cecil overheard people in the streets, saying, 'God prosper those that further the overthrow of these monopolies. God send the prerogative touch not our liberty.'[47]

Essex and the Cecils

For these frustrations, the House of Commons was the natural forum, but most of the frustrations of the 1590s were gathered together outside Parliament under the banner of one man, Robert Devereux, Earl of Essex. Unfortunately, psychological interpretations in history are rarely possible. Apart from the lack of crucial personal evidence, few psychiatrists would pronounce confidently on the condition of people they had not seen. Were such interpretations possible, Essex might be a very interesting candidate for them. His father had died when he was eleven, and his mother had subsequently married her lover, the Earl of Leicester. On his father's death, Essex had become a royal ward, and had been brought up as a son of the house in Burghley's household. He had shown all the airs and skills appropriate to a successful position at court. Unfortunately, it became increasingly apparent that Burghley's political heir would be his younger son Robert Cecil, who, as his father grew older, discharged many of his duties jointly with him. Robert Cecil was a small, hunchbacked, unprepossessing young man, with none of the personal glamour which recommended Essex. He also had a much better mind than Essex, but it is not clear that Essex appreciated this point. It was at a time when Robert Cecil's position was becoming increasingly apparent that Essex inherited the patronage network of his stepfather, Burghley's chief rival, the Earl of Leicester. At the same time, he obtained Leicester's old office of Master of the Horse, and much of Leicester's personal influence with the queen. The combination of the queen's ear and substantial estates in Wales and Staffordshire gave Essex considerable powers of patronage, which he exercised indiscriminately. He was largely responsible for a considerable revival of bastard feudalism. He was reputed to be a generous

[46] Neale, *Parliaments,* ii. 389–90.
[47] Neale, *Parliaments,* ii. 386.

patron, and one man is recorded to have offered his steward £100 for the right to wear his livery. He appealed to the frustrations left by a long period of peace, and when he was appointed to the Council, in 1593, he set out to make himself the spokesman of the military men against the statesmen. He had many adventurous military plans, and appears to have had talent as a strategist and military organizer. Unfortunately, his plans were often too grandiose for the Elizabethan Exchequer, and in the field he developed an unfortunate habit of losing his battles. On at least one occasion, he quite unjustly laid the blame on Lord Treasurer Burghley for failing to provide him with adequate support.

Essex appealed to the desire for honours, which had been disappointed for many years by the frugality of the queen. One of the rights of a commander in the field was to create knights, and this right Essex exercised with remarkable generosity. The queen was not creating more than about 10 knights a year, but Essex created 21 after his defeat at Rouen in 1591, 68 after his victory at Cadiz in 1596, and, against the queen's orders, 81 in Ireland in 1599. A courtier remarked that he would 'huddle them up by half hundreds'.[48] One optimist believed that Essex's powers extended further than this, and offered £1,000 to a lady he thought could influence Essex to influence the queen to give him a peerage. He had interests in privateering, and was not particular in choosing where to give his support. Sir Anthony Sherley, one of the most feckless privateers of the decade, financed both his privateering and an unofficial 'diplomatic' mission to Persia on Essex's already overstretched credit. Essex occupied himself with the Welsh bench, and once thanked the Lord Keeper for 'continually' satisfying his requests to have more men added to it. He collected players, authors, and other miscellaneous people, including Shakespeare, who in return offered him some gratuitous advertisement in the theatre. He listened to Francis Hastings' invitation to take over his stepfather Leicester's Puritan patronage and influence, and patronized a number of Puritan ministers. He also, however, set out to make friends with Archbishop Whitgift, and completed the spectrum by extending his patronage to a number of Catholic recusants, including many of the later leaders of the Gunpowder Plot.

There was nothing new about patronage, and even the reckless comprehensiveness of Essex's use of it need have threatened nothing except his credit. Unfortunately, Essex saw patronage as a struggle against the Cecils, in which Robert Cecil was to some extent forced to compete. Except for the perennial influence of the houses of Howard and Herbert, most other patronage was swallowed up in the rival networks of Essex

---

[48] Stone, 73, 100.

and Cecil, gathered in hostile array against each other. One of Essex's followers caught the spirit by promising him 'never to be so base as to be a neuter'.[49] It was also unfortunate that Essex was determined to extend his patronage network into control of the major political offices, which the queen, though she might listen to recommendations, preferred to fill on grounds of merit rather than of faction. Essex began this course with the Attorney Generalship, which he demanded for Francis Bacon, who was at that stage his follower. Bacon was an able enough man, but he had little or no legal experience, and the obvious man for the post was Sir Edward Coke, Solicitor General. Robert Cecil tried to persuade Essex that it would be more expedient to press for the office of Solicitor General for Bacon, which 'might be of easier digestion to her Majesty'. Essex replied: 'digest me no digestions, for the Attorneyship for Francis is that I must have; and in that I will spend all my power, might, authority and amity, and with tooth and nail defend and procure the same for him against whomsoever; and whosoever getteth this office out of my hands for any other, before he have it, it shall cost him the coming by.'[50] When Coke was made Attorney General, Essex set about the queen to win the Solicitorship for Bacon, in such a spirit that the queen told him to go to bed if he could talk of nothing else. After a year and a half, the queen gave the office to Serjeant Fleming, who had a reputation as a lawyer. Unfortunately, the number of major offices which fell vacant in the 1590s was exceptionally large, and almost all of them were contested in this spirit. The queen preferred, whenever possible, to have offices open to more than one faction, and through more than one channel of patronage. She did not want to deliver all power to the Cecils, but equally, she could not easily give way to requests which, in effect, dared her to refuse. She was thus left with no recourse but to keep offices vacant. The Chancellorship of the Duchy of Lancaster was twice put into commission, and on one occasion Sir John Fortescue was appointed to the office for ten days. Towards the end of her reign, in 1590, the Secretaryship passed back to the overburdened Burghley, who had been relieved of it over twenty years earlier on the ground of old age. His son Robert did most of the work, and finally obtained the office in 1596, when Essex was abroad on campaign. When Burghley at last died, in 1598, the Mastership of the Wards was kept vacant for nearly a year, bringing all the business of the court to a standstill, and thereby depriving the queen of much revenue at a time when it could not easily be spared. Robert Cecil finally obtained the office in 1599, once again when Essex was away on campaign.

For Essex, these reverses were disastrous. The whole of his motley

[49] Stone, 211. [50] Neale, *Elizabeth*, 334.

following had been held together only by the belief that he could obtain rewards from the queen, and without that belief they had nothing in common but their debts, which for many of them were bigger than they could ever hope to pay. In 1599, a major rebellion in Ireland left Essex with a last chance to win military glory and recover his fortunes. Whether his failure in Ireland was his own fault or not, it was complete. After secret and possibly treasonable negotiations with Tyrone, the rebel leader, he returned to England in desperation, celebrating his return by invading the queen's bedchamber (fully armed) while she was dressing. The confusion he had left behind in Ireland, if nothing else, would have forced the queen to withdraw her favour from him. Finally, he was refused renewal of his farm of the sweet wines, and with it his last chance of ever paying his creditors, who were becoming importunate. At some time during this period, Essex began to contemplate rebellion. It is hard to say what his aims in rebellion were. He was certainly in correspondence with James VI, and may have hoped to restore his fortunes by being the king-maker who had James declared heir to the English throne. He also claimed that his misfortunes were entirely due to the hostility of Cecil, Raleigh, and other people at court, and may have hoped to remove them. He kept, even for rebellion, the support of a number of heavily indebted peers, of a number of minor gentry, of several Puritan preachers, and many of the future leaders of the Gunpowder Plot. Not all of this miscellaneous crew were happy with the enterprise, and the Earl of Southampton had to nerve himself to rebellion by reading Aristotle's *Politics*. When the rebellion came, in February 1601, it turned out to be no more than an armed parade through the streets of London, to which the only possible conclusion was Essex's execution for treason. Though Essex died, all the frustrations which had given him a following survived, and remained without any means of political expression. His son became the leading Parliamentarian general in the Civil War.

All through this crisis, Robert Cecil, hindered by a vicious propaganda campaign against his character and his deformity, was trying to carry on the normal business of government. As Master of the Wards, he was the first minister since Lord Treasurer Winchester in Mary's reign to make a serious attempt to tackle the failure of the Crown's income to keep up with inflation. His father had allowed the Wards to run on unchanged, bringing in about the same income at the end of the reign as at the beginning. In the financial situation of 1599, this was not enough. Robert Cecil decided that the main reason for the failure of receipts to increase was the low valuation of wards' lands, and decided that if this could not be increased, he would raise the normal prices charged for wardships.

His father had normally sold wardships at a price around one and a quarter times the official valuation of the ward's lands. Robert Cecil decided to raise this to three times the official valuation, claiming, probably truly, that this was still less than the real annual value. He began this policy at once. He was faced by a number of grants countersigned by his father, which had not been complete at his father's death. On a number of these, he crossed out his father's price and inserted an increased one of his own. On one lease, he increased the entry fine from two years' rent to three, adding a note: 'two years' fine increased by me.'[51] One of the reasons why official valuations were low was that they tended to exclude entry fines, and Robert Cecil issued an instruction to his feodaries that they should hold manorial courts on wards' estates, and receive the entry fines themselves.[52] This instruction remained a dead letter. Had it been implemented, it would have provoked an explosion, but if carried through, it might have produced an immense increase in revenue. As it was, Cecil produced an increase of revenue of rather more than £2,000 a year. In this, as in so many other things, however, it was necessary to ask whether the money was worth the price. As in the Council of Wales, an increase in the revenue raised was followed by an outcry for the court's abolition. By 1604, Nicholas Fuller, a Puritan lawyer who may have previously practised in the Court of Wards,[53] was arguing that wardship should be abolished because it was contrary to natural law, and was finding vocal support in the House of Commons. On most issues, the gentry tended to want to keep the constitution as it had always been. On most issues, this conservatism was buttressed by a large amount of contemporary theory. On financial issues, it was so popular as to be dangerous, and Elizabeth's successor would be committed, from the start of his reign, either to changing this attitude, or to fighting it, or to letting sleeping dogs lie.

The succession

By 1601 it was becoming increasingly clear that the queen's successor would be James of Scotland. Some of the reasons for this were in the state of foreign affairs. Since Mary Queen of Scots' death, the hopes of those who wanted a Catholic *coup d'état* on Elizabeth's death were necessarily pinned on Spain, since Philip III of Spain was now the only Catholic claimant left in the field. Philip was prepared to press his claim, which in 1601 he transferred to his daughter, but Spain's hopes of making

[51] Hurstfield, 312–16; Russell, 'Robert Cecil and His Father's Wardship Leases', *Notes and Queries* (January 1969), 33.
[52] P.R.O. Wards 9.526, 12 February 41 Elizabeth.
[53] P.R.O. Wards 15.6.1. shows 'Fuller' pleading on behalf of Paul Rainsford the informer. The identification is uncertain.

an effective claim to England had always depended on the weakness of France. By this time, Henry of Navarre was securely established on the French throne, and had fought his war with Spain to a successful conclusion. He had also, by becoming a Catholic, opened a wide breach between the Pope, who was willing to accept his conversion, and the Spaniards, who were not. The result was that the Pope was not eager to support a Spanish conquest of England, and one Spaniard remarked that 'no woman was more careful not to arouse suspicion in her husband than was the Pope as regards the French king'.[54] The English Catholics, too, were split between the faction of the Jesuits, which was willing to fight to the death, and that of the secular priests, who hoped for some form of compromise with the English government. The Grey line and Arabella Stuart, though attractive candidates to some, lacked the power to make their claims effective. James, on the other hand, being a king already, could raise troops to support his claim against any Catholic invasion.

In these circumstances, competition in England was tending to centre, not on who should be king, but on who should be king-maker. In spite of the attempts of Essex, and of Parsons the Jesuit, to persuade James that Cecil really supported the Spanish Infanta, it was Cecil who won this competition, keeping up a long running correspondence with James, and sending him, a few days before Elizabeth's death, a draft of the proclamation which was to announce his succession. Finally, on her deathbed in March 1603, the queen at last broke her silence on the subject, and named James as her successor. The Council proclaimed him at once, and Sir Robert Carey, who had his horses ready along the route, got the news to Edinburgh in three days. The whole issue was settled before any other candidate had time to raise a disturbance, and, to the astonishment and relief of those who had been stockpiling arms against the queen's death, the succession crisis passed off in complete peace.

III   THE PRICE OF VICTORY: THE REIGN OF JAMES I TO 1618

New wine in old bottles

For James, however, his difficulties were only just beginning. All those hopes and frustrations which had been focused on Essex were now turned to him, and since an alien king in a new kingdom, still with many potential rivals, needed friends, he would have to satisfy some of them. Puritans were still hoping for reform of the church, and had pinned many of their

[54] Hurstfield, J., 'The Succession Struggle in Late Elizabethan England', in *Essays Presented to Sir John Neale* (1961), 378.

hopes on the new king. Indeed, as some of them told James in 1604, they had passed over many grievances in the last years of the queen's reign 'in regard of her sex and age', as they politely put it, and 'much more' for fear of disturbing the succession.[55] In other words, knowing they would get no redress from Elizabeth, they had pinned all their hopes on James. On the other hand, many Catholics were hoping for some easing of their burdens, and, if not for complete toleration, for lower fines, less investigation, and more hope of access to patronage. Many bishops were hoping for an end to the system of stripping their estates by long leases to reward courtiers, while courtiers, on the other hand, were hoping for rewards less frugal than those the queen had given them. Merchants with interests in the Spanish trade hoped for peace, while those who were interested in privateering and colonies wanted more vigorous support than Elizabeth had ever given to overseas expansion. Many others hoped for the easing of the burden of war taxation, and at least one member of the Commons remembered the occasion, in 1588, when the Commons had first been asked for two subsidies, and had been induced to vote them on a promise that 'the like should never more be heard of. But how this promise hath been kept, you all know as well as I.'[56] This feeling may have been stronger in the humbler classes, on whom taxation fell most heavily. Many members of Parliament protested that they were restrained from voting higher taxes by fear of reactions in their constituencies. Such protestations were of course convenient to them, but they may have been sincere. The growing independence of yeomen voters, reflected in the higher cost of electioneering, suggests that members may have had a genuine need to take account of other opinions than those of the gentry. Ministers, looking at the desperate state of the royal finances, and at a House of Commons in which members might wear clothes worth £100 apiece 'and for some of them the very panes of their breeches were nothing else but laces embroidered with gold',[57] felt that the Crown should tap a higher proportion of the national wealth. Between these miscellaneous hopes, James, even if he were a statesman of genius, would be doomed to disappoint the majority.

King James was no doubt unfortunate in the unsolved problems he inherited, but listing his difficulties cannot justify the way he handled them. There is no reason to dispute Professor Notestein's verdict that 'few kings

---

[55] *The Apology of the Commons* (1604), in Tanner, J. R., *Constitutional Documents of the Reign of James I* (1960), 22. The passage about the queen's sex and age is no more than polite fiction. In the monopolies debate, where they had some hopes of success members were not in the least inhibited.

[56] Gardiner, *1610*, 47.

[57] Foster, *1610*, ii. 127.

have been so fitted by nature to call forth an opposition'.[58] Many of the reasons for this were personal. It was hard for a monarchy to work effectively without some respect for the person of the monarch, and James, though he was always exhorting people to respect him, did not help them to succeed. Early in his reign, when he was inspecting the Isle of Wight militia, James showed such obvious alarm at the military exercises that one of the Deputy Lieutenants rashly put on paper the opinion that he was 'the most cowardly man that ever I knew'.[59] He also noted that James was much more interested in watching the boy cadets than in watching the soldiers. Though James was married, and had children, there was little doubt that he was homosexual by inclination, and though this caused less moral indignation than it might do today, it did create considerable feeling about the grounds on which patronage and preferment might be awarded. He had a poor head for drink, and frequently failed to make sufficient allowance for it. He showed an undignified curiosity on unsuitable occasions. For example, the day after his daughter's marriage the couple were not allowed to get up until the king had visited them and heard a detailed description of the night from the bridegroom. In business, he was lazy, and frequently absent at crucial times, and yet was not good at delegating responsibility to ministers who were doing the work. His speeches, which were too frequent, were verbose, plaintive, and pompous. Remarks like 'I will not be content that my power be disputed upon',[60] which Elizabeth might have made impressive, in James's mouth were merely petulant. He was continually talking about his kingly dignity, and yet was not dignified. It is true that he was often unreasonably treated, but he was the sort of leader who provokes unreasonable behaviour in his followers. Moreover, he was often so vacillating in his decisions that it was hard to know how to avoid opposing him.

Prejudice against Scots

His worst disadvantage, however, was in no sense his fault. This was that he was a Scot: an alien, and a member of a race of aliens against whom the English had a long-standing and vocal prejudice. One M.P. said that Scots traders should be called pedlars, rather than merchants, another that the union of England with Scotland was as natural as the union of a prisoner with his judge. On this occasion, a message from the king, blaming the Commons for allowing the speech, provoked the House

[58] Notestein, W., *The Winning of the Initiative by the House of Commons* (1924), 33.
[59] L. O. J. Boynton, *The Elizabethan Militia*, 209.
[60] C. H. MacIlwain, *The Political Works of James I* (1918), 310.

to send him briefly to the Tower, but others continued to say the same things. Nicholas Fuller, the Puritan lawyer, opposed the naturalization of Scots born since James's accession to England on the ground that God had made some people apt to live in one climate, and some in another. He compared the admission of Scots to England to the tearing down of a hedge round a rich pasture, allowing the cattle from the neighbouring barren pasture to trample all over it, and claimed that the shortage of good jobs, the shortage of places in the universities, and the overcrowding of London lodgings, left no room for them. The Stuarts never succeeded in diminishing this hostility to Scots. In 1640, a Kentish preacher maintained that if a Scotsman ever went to Heaven, the devil would go too, and in 1649 a journalist maintained:

> A Scotch man enters Hell at's birth,
> And 'scapes it when he goes to earth
> Assured no worse a Hell can come
> Than that which he enjoys at home.
> . . . .
>
> A Scot an English earldom fits
> As purple doth your marmuzets
> Suits like Noll Cromwell with the crown,
> Or Bradshaw with his scarlet gown.[61]

The influx of 'hungry Scots' was never on the scale English propagandists suggested, but there was no escape from the fact that the most conspicuous Scottish immigrant was the king, and these continual onslaughts on the Scots did not increase his goodwill towards his English subjects.

Royal extravagance and the thirst for patronage

James was also culpably generous and extravagant. Whoever succeeded Elizabeth would have had to be more generous than she was: the pent-up hunger for titles and for grants could not be contained for ever. An alien king in a new kingdom had to dispense patronage. But when James, on his way south to London, created forty-six knights before breakfast, he was perhaps carrying generosity to excess. The distribution of peerages was also overdue but excessive. But the grant of titles was less serious than the grant of cash: pensions, annuities, and lump sums became a favourite way of rewarding royal servants. Nor did James compensate for his generosity to his servants by personal frugality. Some of the increases in expenditure were no fault of the king's. After so much anxiety about the succession, he could not be blamed for having a wife and children, though

---

[61] *C.J.*, i. 334–6; Nedham, Marchamont, *Digitus Dei* (1649). B.M.E. 550. 29. Nedham is perhaps the only Englishman of the time who could be described without anachronism as a 'journalist'. See below, p. 365.

their households were expensive. He could not be blamed for the fact that the Wardrobe had to be re-equipped for a new, and male, monarch, though he could perhaps be blamed for the fact that the £60,000 said to have been made by the sale of the queen's dresses was left as a perquisite to Lord Home, a Scottish immigrant who became keeper of the Wardrobe. He could not be blamed for the increases in prices, nor for the fact that he increased payments to ambassadors, who had come to be so poorly paid that the appointment was dreaded.

When all these points are listed, they do not explain all the increases in royal expenditure. Elizabeth's ordinary expenditure had remained well within an income of little over £300,000, but James's rose almost at once over £400,000, reaching a peak of £522,000 in 1614. The immediate increases show up clearly in individual departments: the cost of the Household, covering the court's daily living expenses, rose by £40,000, to almost twice what it had been under Elizabeth. The cost of the Jewel House rose by over £9,000, of the Office of Works by £21,000, and of fees and annuities by £50,000.[62] James's deficits were of a different type from Elizabeth's, as well as being bigger. Current financial theory was based on the distinction between ordinary and extraordinary revenue and expenditure. Ordinary revenue, the receipts of the Crown lands, the customs, and so forth, were supposed to cover all ordinary expenditure, such as the Household, royal patronage, the costs of administration, and so forth. It was only for extraordinary expenditure, such as war, a coronation, or a royal funeral that the king was supposed to be able to ask for help from Parliament. As Sir Edward Coke put it in 1625, 'ordinary charges the king should bear alone, but where there is a common danger, common help: in extraordinary he may require relief'.[63] But this relief, a subsidy, was only designed to contribute *towards* extraordinary expenditure, not to pay the whole of it. Queen Elizabeth worked on this financial theory, achieving a regular surplus on her ordinary account, and falling into debt only through the extraordinary expenses of war. James, on the other hand, was invariably in deficit on his ordinary account, and Parliament was being asked to provide extraordinary income to subsidize ordinary deficits: to subsidize James in living beyond his income. Such a situation had been bound to arise sooner or later, and Elizabeth had only avoided it by a degree of parsimony which could not have lasted. At some time, Parliament would have to understand that these financial theories were outdated, and the king's ordinary income would have to be increased. In

[62] These figures are taken from Ashton, R., 'Deficit Finance in the Reign of James I', *Ec.H.R.* (1957), 15–24.
[63] Ashton, R., *The Crown and the Money Market* (1960), 39.

1603, this time could not have been postponed long. But it did not help that these points had to be explained to Parliament under a king who was conspicuous for his extravagance. James's insolvency was not only due to his extravagance, but his extravagance was so conspicuous that it was not easy to persuade Parliament of this point. One of the commonest images of the parliamentary speeches of the reign compares the Exchequer to a leaky cistern, which there is no point in filling until the leaks have been stopped. One M.P. complained that the Commons 'find the Exchequer to be like the ocean, whereunto, though all rivers pay tribute, yet it is never satisfied'.[64] He told the story of one of the Roman emperors, who, finding his finances under strain, restored them by 'discharging an unnecessary train of such as lived idle at his court, withdrawing from them their pensions and salaries, saying there was not a thing more ignoble, nay more cruel, than that they should be suffered to consume the riches of the commonwealth, who with their true labour brought no profit thereunto'. Such complaints were over-simplified, but they appeared too convincing to be easily answered by one of the king's ministers claiming that he was 'free from banqueting and surfeiting'.[65] The best answer to these charges about lavish giving was the one James made: most members of both Houses had either received some of it, or asked to do so.

The Hampton Court Conference

James also found it the harder to secure exceptional goodwill in the House of Commons for his failure to come to terms with Puritanism. In 1603, there was no reason to assume that James had any quarrel with the moderate Puritans, and the more disciplinarian bishops were alarmed about his possible intentions. One of James's Scottish chaplains had established close relations with a number of Puritan leaders, and led them to believe that moderate demands might be met with concessions. It was thus with semi-official encouragement that the Puritan leaders submitted a list of their desires to King James in the Millennary Petition, so called because it was said to represent the views of a thousand ministers. The demands of the petition were all old and studiously moderate. They asked for the surplice 'not to be urged', and the *ex officio* oath to be 'more sparingly used', for restrictions on pluralism and non-residence and the provision of a preaching ministry; for the use of impropriations to sustain preachers, the removal of such terms as 'priest' and 'absolution' from the Prayer Book, and examination of parishioners before they took Communion. One of their requests, for the abolition of the use of the sign of the

---

[64] Foster, *1610*, ii. 402.
[65] Gardiner, *1610*, 17.

cross in baptism, was supported by a number of bishops. Two demands, for further uniformity of doctrine, and for enforcement of the sabbath, represented the newer preoccupations of the Puritan movement.

These requests were in the Grindal tradition, and any of them might have been granted. The king arranged a conference to discuss them at Hampton Court. Those attending were selected by the Council, and were neither extremists nor sharply divided into two parties. Two of the Puritan spokesmen have been described as 'so near the middle of the road as scarcely to merit the name of Puritan'.[66] The other two were Presbyterian by preference, but they accepted episcopal government, and had no intention of pressing for Presbyterianism. Reynolds, the chief Puritan spokesman, believed, like his pupil Hooker, in a Grindalian system of moderate episcopacy, assisted by a council of ministers. Four of the bishops selected to attend opposed some of the ceremonies, and were perhaps more in sympathy with the Puritan ministers than with Bancroft, their chief episcopal colleague. The conference remained amicable almost throughout, and though James once grew annoyed when Reynolds, in the course of asking for the prophesyings back, used the word 'presbyter', his anger was mild and brief. Reynolds had, after all, referred to 'a bishop and his presbyters', and the system of limited episcopacy he was discussing was one to which James had no particular objection, since he introduced it in Scotland two years later, with considerable success. A number of small reforms were agreed on during the conference, and were incorporated in a revised edition of the Prayer Book. It was also at the Hampton Court Conference that the decision was taken to produce the Authorized Version of the Bible. James's conclusion from Hampton Court seems to have been, not that Puritanism was a menace, but that it was too mild to be taken very seriously. 'If these be the greatest matters you be grieved with,' he said, 'I need not have been troubled with such importunities and complaints as have been made unto me.' Whitgift, Bancroft, and the high church bishops were perhaps as offended by the decisions at Hampton Court as the Puritans, and failed to implement some of them.[67]

Archbishop Bancroft

The decision from which the Puritans suffered most was taken a few weeks after the conference. When Archbishop Whitgift died, praying that

[66] Collinson, 455.

[67] For recent accounts of the Millennary Petition and the Hampton Court Conference, see Collinson, 448–467; Tyacke, N.R.N., Thesis cit., 11–35; Curtis, Mark, 'The Hampton Court Conference and its Aftermath', *History* (1961), 1–16; Babbage, S. Barton, *Puritanism and Richard Bancroft* (1962), 43–73.

he would not live to see another Parliament, James chose Bancroft as his successor. Bancroft had been Whitgift's chief lieutenant in all his campaigns against the Puritans, and had won his reputation primarily as an ecclesiastical detective. His understanding of Puritanism was not as deep as his knowledge, and, like many of his successors, he suspected all Puritans of tending, either to Presbyterianism or to separatism. But though Bancroft was a dedicated enemy of Puritans, James's own hostility to them should not be exaggerated. Even in appointing Bancroft, he was doing no more than continuing the policy which Elizabeth had followed since the fall of Grindal, and throughout his reign, Grindalians continued to receive a fair share of episcopal appointments. At least until the 1620s, Puritans found James no worse than his predecessor, and on occasion perhaps slightly better. If it was growing slightly harder for a Puritan to be a member of the political establishment than it had been in Sir Francis Walsingham's days, this was not because there were any new grievances, but because, for fifty years, attempts to reform the existing grievances by normal political means had persistently ended in failure. As some of the Commons reminded James in 1604, his reign had produced a general hope of reform, and it was necessary to remind him, as it had been necessary to remind his predecessor, 'what great alienation of men's hearts the defeating of great hopes doth usually breed'.[68]

These hopes were further disappointed when Bancroft began his rule with a campaign for subscription which revived the crisis atmosphere of 1584. He obtained the passage through his first convocation of a series of canons threatening excommunication *ipso facto* for those who said the Prayer Book contained anything contrary to scripture, for those who dissented from any of the Thirty-Nine Articles (not only those to which subscription could be demanded by Act of Parliament) and for those who impugned any rites and ceremonies. This last canon, if applied with the full rigour of law, should have led to the excommunication of at least two of the bishops. The canons also included a few merely irritating clericalist points such as the prohibition of musters in churchyards. Bancroft's campaign for subscription to these canons was less drastic than for a while it seemed likely to be, but it did lead to the silencing of about ninety ministers, on whose behalf Parliament continued to petition for some time. The first petitioners on their behalf, who included Sir Francis Hastings and the brother of the dean of the Chapel Royal, were surprisingly greeted with the accusation that they had committed treason,[69] but this threat did not deter others from following them.

[68] Tanner, *The Apology of the Commons* (1604), 220.
[69] See above, p. 210.

The Gunpowder Plot

Most unfortunately, the hostile reception of this petition coincided with a rumour, current for about a week, that James intended to become a Catholic. This rumour, which originated from negotiations in which James hoped to induce the Pope to renounce his claim to depose kings, appears to have been believed in the Roman Curia, as well as in England. It followed a period of vacillation in the enforcement of recusancy fines which had confused everyone. From November 1604, the fines were again thoroughly enforced, with the full support of Robert Cecil, who told the Archbishop of York: 'I love not to yield to any toleration; a matter which I well know no creature living dare propound to our religious sovereign. I will be much less than I am, or rather nothing at all, before I shall ever become an instrument of such a miserable change.'[70] The main variations in enforcement of the fines were caused by the use of recusants' forfeitures as a form of patronage, but since they were often granted to the king's humbler servants before the recusants' conviction, this measure gave a number of private individuals an interest in securing the conviction of recusants.

In some Catholics, this 'defeating of great hopes' produced more hostile reactions than it did in most Puritans. Their first reaction was to look for help to Spain. But in 1604 King James brought the long war with Spain to an end, maintaining that as king of Scotland he had never been at war with Spain. This peace was beneficial to English trade, and to the royal finances, but it threw the English Catholics back on their own resources. Catesby, a former follower of Essex, appears to have been the first to think of blowing up Parliament during the state opening. The plan marks a recognition by the conspirators that Parliament was the real enemy, and in addition to destroying Parliament they planned to seize the king's children. Since the members of the Privy Council would be at the state opening, they could hope to destroy all authority in the State, and, with the aid of a small body of armed men, might hope to seize power. Catesby succeeded in obtaining the support of Tresham, one of the richest and most heavily fined of Catholic gentlemen, of Thomas Percy, the Earl of Northumberland's steward, who was able to gain the use of one of the cellars of Parliament, and of a Yorkshireman called Guy Fawkes, after whom the conspiracy came to be known. By November the fifth, 1605, when the second session of James's first Parliament was due to open, the conspirators were ready to act. The majority of them were gathered in the Midlands, ready to seize the king's children, and Guy Fawkes was left in

[70] Gardiner, *History*, i. 226.

London with a store of barrels of gunpowder under the Houses of Parliament. Robert Cecil, on the other hand, was also ready to act. He already suspected a plot, and had been keeping a very close eye on the movements of Catholic suspects, and at the last moment he was warned of the plot by Lord Mounteagle, a Catholic peer whose connection with the conspirators is still obscure. After this, Guy Fawkes was easily discovered beside his barrels of gunpowder, and the other conspirators in the Midlands were overcome after a brief resistance.[71]

For Puritan M.P.s who were in the Commons that day, this was confirmation of all that they had ever said about the menace of popery. Though at first the House reacted with remarkable calm, they were soon moving bills for the repression of popery, and for public thanksgiving for their deliverance. An Act was quickly passed for special prayers in honour of their deliverance from 'the Babylonish and antichristian sect of them which say of Jerusalem "down with it, down with it" . . . whose religion is rebellion, whose faith is faction, whose practice is murdering of souls and bodies'.[72] Every fifth of November, these special prayers were said, and accompanied by a special sermon which was usually a flower of seventeenth-century invective. In 1640, the Gunpowder Plot was ranked beside the defeat of the Spanish Armada as one of the two deliverances for which thanks were given in the daily prayer of the House of Commons. A number of members who were in the House that day were still sitting in 1640, and many others were sons or nephews of men who had sat in 1605. It is not surprising that when these men and their children later heard rumours of Catholic plots, they were willing to believe them.

King James reacted as strongly as the Commons, and for some time he cushioned his bedroom with feather beds, as a protection against blast. The result of this unanimity between the king and his Parliament was a new law against recusants, in which the fines were once again increased, and churchwardens were encouraged to present those who did not come to church by a fine of £1 for every failure to inform, and a reward of £2 for every conviction obtained through their information. Recusants were to be made to take an oath that the Pope could not depose kings. The king also granted the measure for which the Commons and the low church bishops had been pressing since 1571, compelling attendance at Communion, as well as at matins. Recusants were forbidden to appear at court or within

[71] See Gardiner, S. R., *The Gunpowder Plot* (1897) for the detailed story. I am grateful to Professor J. Hurstfield for the opportunity to discuss the conspiracy with him, and for much other help on matters to do with Robert Cecil.

[72] Prynne, W., *Canterburies Doome* (1645), 246. The Act did not specify the wording of the prayers, which were subsequently altered by Laud, to the indignation and alarm of Puritans.

ten miles of London, unless in a recognized trade. They were forbidden to practise at the bar or as doctors, or to be trustees or executors, and Justices of the Peace were empowered to search their houses for arms. To the great grief of many members of the House of Commons, enforcement of this Act was never more than sporadic. English Catholicism survived, and so did the terror which it inspired.

The Parliament of 1604

The tortuous story of James's dealings with recusants was still in progress when his first Parliament met, in the spring of 1604. Bancroft's campaign against the Puritan ministers was in full swing, and the king's extravagance was beginning to become apparent. It was also appearing that he would have to exploit some of his existing sources of revenue more thoroughly than his predecessors had done. One error for which he suffered in the 1604 Parliament was his generosity in the granting of titles. By 1604 almost every member of the Council had a peerage, and the king was represented in the Commons only by Mr. 'Secondary' Herbert, and by Sir John Stanhope. Neither of them had any skill as a Parliamentarian, and government business appears to have been managed mainly by Sir Francis Bacon, who, though he still held no office, appears to have acted as a self-appointed government spokesman. The Crown's other instrument for managing the Commons was the Speaker, and the 1604 Commons produced the portent of a contested election for the Speakership. When Herbert proposed Sir Edward Phelips, others 'muttered' the names of Sir Francis Hastings, Sir Francis Bacon, and others. Phelips was finally elected, and proved helpful, but sometimes too much so for the dignity of his office. On one occasion, when the House was attacking purveyance, he succeeded in deferring the passage of a bill until the next day, and reported when the next day came that he could not arrive on time 'for that having taken pills overnight which did not work as expected, he had not been well all night'. It was said that 'the opinion of the House and the ordinary speech was that he had taken a pill from the purveyors'.[73] Robert Cecil also made great efforts to manage the Commons by means of regular conferences with the Lords, but neither conferences nor a friendly Speaker were any substitute for a spokesman on the floor of the House.

On the first full business day, the first three speakers were private members.† One spoke for Robert Cecil. Another was Peter Wentworth's son Thomas, member for Oxford City, who complained of a royal charter al-

[73] *Stuart Constitution*, 33.

† N.R.N. Tyacke, 'Sir Robert Wroth and the Parliament of 1604', *B.I.H.R.* (1977)

lowing the universities to return members for the first time, and raised the issue of the Buckinghamshire election, the first business which the House turned to consider.

Sir John Fortescue, Chancellor of the Exchequer, who should have been the third Privy Councillor in the House, had lost the election to Sir Francis Goodwin, a local gentleman from a moderately Puritan family. The Council had then considered whether there might be some legal way of voiding Goodwin's election. Having discovered that Goodwin could be technically outlawed, they got the election quashed, and Fortescue was elected at a second election. The Commons reacted by at once declaring Goodwin elected, and having him sworn in as a member.

In doing so, they had raised what became a constitutional issue of some importance—the question who was to be judge of disputed election returns. The Commons, perfectly correctly, claimed that they had been judges of disputed election returns until 1406. The king, equally correctly, claimed that Chancery had judged disputed election returns since 1406. This issue had been raised twice before, in 1586 and in 1593. In 1586, both the Commons and Chancery had considered the disputed return in question, and fortunately they had come to the same conclusion, so no dispute over jurisdiction had arisen. In 1593, Coke, who had been an ultra-royalist Speaker of the Commons, had persuaded the Commons not to prosecute their claim.

The important question in 1604 is why both sides considered the issue worth a serious dispute. The Commons claimed that if the returns were left to Chancery, when fit members had been chosen 'the Lord Chancellor, or the sheriffs, might displace them and send out new writs, until some were chosen to their liking'[74]—in other words, the Council might attempt to pack Parliament. They added, in tones which were to become increasingly familiar during the Stuart period, that the integrity of the then Lord Chancellor was such that they had no such fears at present, but that the precedent was a dangerous one for future generations. The Commons' approach to this case suggests a distrust of the Council, and a readiness to see it as having an interest contrary to that of the Commons, which were completely new. It is also one of the earliest appearances of a type of argument which remained current for the rest of the century: if the king could decide an election, enforce a proclamation, or raise a tax, once, then he might do it all the time, and liberty would be gone. As one of the judges said in 1606, this was like arguing that it was not safe to allow the king a right to pardon criminals, since if he could pardon one, he could legally pardon them all. It is a type of argument which suggests both legalism

[74] *C.J.*, i. 163.

and profound distrust, but it is hard to show how this distrust was implanted.

This temper was perhaps encouraged by James's unlucky claim, during the dispute, that the Commons only held their privileges by his grace. To people of this distrustful temper, such a claim suggested that James intended to take their privileges away, and they met it by arguing that their privileges were of right, and no king could ever take them away. The issue in this argument about the Commons' privileges was an important one—whether the Commons were a necessary part of the constitution. Behind this argument, which continued for the rest of the reign, there is perhaps the fear expressed by Peter Wentworth in 1587, and expressed frequently in the 1620s, that the Crown might decide to dispense with Parliament altogether, and set up an 'arbitrary government', or unparliamentary constitution. The claim which the Commons advanced against this threat, that they were an indispensable part of the constitution, was supported by a rapidly growing amount of antiquarian research on the early history of Parliament. On many occasions, such as this one, the precedents they quoted were correct. There were many powers which Parliament had had in the fourteenth and fifteenth centuries which had lapsed under the Yorkists and the Tudors. They were less accurate, however, in developing, with the assistance of Sir Edward Coke, a doctrine of the 'ancient constitution', according to which the English constitution had remained unchanged from time immemorial. William the Conqueror and the Saxons, it was said, had merely confirmed it, and Parliaments could be traced back to the days of the Romans. If Parliament had always existed, the king could not have a sovereign power to rule without it, and, indeed, in this 'ancient constitution' in which no one part was supreme over any other, sovereign power could not exist at all. As Coke put it, 'Magna Carta is such a fellow, that he will have no sovereign.' The Commons never claimed sovereignty: they claimed, like Hobbes after them, that 'the name of tyranny signifieth nothing more nor less than the name of sovereignty'.[75]

In 1604, these developments were only just beginning, and the distrust which appeared in the Goodwin *v.* Fortescue case is only a faint sign of the distrust which was to develop later. One of the most crucial, and one of the most difficult, questions of the early Stuart period is why this distrust developed. It has been fashionable to blame James's tendency to

---

[75] Poocock, J. G. A., *The Ancient Constitution and the Feudal Law* (1957), 30–69; Rushworth, J., *Historical Collections*, i. 562; Hobbes, *Leviathan*, ed. Oakeshott, 463. Hobbes's view of sovereignty is the same as that held by most of his contemporaries. He differs from them in saying that since men could not agree to limit power in terms of the fundamental law or the will of God, sovereignty, however undesirable, was nevertheless necessary.

theorize about the doctrine of divine right, but if King James's speeches are compared with those made by members, it is hard to see how the doctrine of divine right could be at fault, since the members shared it.[76] They did not, it is true, agree with James that his divine right gave him an immunity from having his decisions questioned, but it was soon apparent that James could not escape from having his decisions questioned. He did, after all, give way over the Goodwin *v.* Fortescue case, and in so doing, showed that some of the fears which the Commons expressed about him could equally well have been expressed by him about the Commons. The Commons' committee of privileges sometimes decided disputed elections in a partisan spirit, and claimed a power to restore old boroughs which had once returned members. When a popular Parliamentarian like Sir Robert Phelips discovered, after several years' historical research, that his home borough of Ilchester had returned members in Edward I's reign, he had no difficulty in persuading the House to supply him with a pocket borough.

Some of James's Councillors distrusted the intentions of the Commons to a point which might justly have made the Commons suspicious. Lord Chancellor Ellesmere, in 1610, thought that if they were allowed to 'usurp and encroach too far upon the regality', their power, if not restrained soon enough, would 'break out into democracy'. Northampton, Lord Privy Seal, maintained in 1610 that 'I think nothing so hurtful to the commonwealth as the multitude of free schools', because people went from there to the universities, where they had too easy a life and came out discontented, to 'go up and down breeding new opinions'.[77] Northampton was widely reputed to be hostile to the existence of Parliament, but to explain the Commons' suspicions by the attitudes of ministers is to create a hen and egg problem, for it is almost impossible to determine whether the Commons were reacting to Northampton and Ellesmere, or they to the Commons.

Some clues may be gained from the *Apology of the Commons*, a document drawn up at the end of the session to justify the House's proceedings, and called, in typically Stuart fashion, 'A Form of Apology and Satisfaction'. It is hard to tell exactly whose views this document represents. It was drawn up, as S. R. Gardiner said, *in the name of* the Commons,[78] but

---

[76] I hope to substantiate this argument in detail elsewhere.

[77] Foster, *1610*, i. 276. i. 235. Another version of this speech reports him as complaining of 'scum . . . sent out of the University.' i. 79.

[78] Gardiner, *History*, i. 180 (my italics). On the *Apology*, as on the Hampton Court Conference, Gardiner's actual position was much closer to the conclusions of recent research than is often supposed. For a recent discussion of the *Apology*, see Elton, G. R., 'A High Road to Civil War?' in *Essays in Honour of Garrett Mattingley*, ed. Carter, Charles H. (1966), 325 ff.

it never finished the process of passing through the House, and it cannot be shown that it represents the views of more than a majority of the members of the committee which drew it up. The chairman of the committee was a former follower of Essex. Perhaps the most significant thing about this laborious self-justification is that it was drawn up at all. Its preamble expresses dismay at the growth of 'jealousy and diffidence', or fear and distrust, between the king and his Commons. From 1604 to 1642, this lament of disunity grew more and more frequent. M.P.s were quite right that the constitution could not work without some unity between the king and Parliament. Yet both sides continued to think, like the authors of the *Apology*, that unity would return automatically if mischief-makers were removed, and so increasingly desperate attempts to restore unity became the cause of further disunity. The authors of the *Apology* justified their fear for the future of Parliament by putting it into a European context: 'What cause we your poor Commons have to watch over our privileges is manifest in itself to all men. The prerogatives of princes may easily and do daily grow; the privileges of the subject are for the most part at an everlasting stand. They may be by good providence and care preserved, but being once lost are not recovered but with much disquiet.'[79] Whatever may be said for this interpretation of English history, in a European context it was largely true. In France, the 1614 meeting of the Estates General was the last before the Revolution, and in Spain, though Pym, for example, still regarded it as a constitutional monarchy (or rather collection of monarchies) the powers of the king were increasing, and those of the Cortes declining. By the eighteenth century, the decline of representative institutions had gone so far that Charles James Fox was able to claim that there were only two constitutions in Europe, that of Britain and that of Württemberg.[80] M.P.s were certainly right in seeing the decline of Parliaments as a contemporary trend.

The authors of the *Apology* were also right in their diagnosis of the two principal causes of distrust: religion and money. There was certainly coming to be a settled hostility between Parliament and some of the clergy. This is perhaps not surprising, since in trying to gain power for Parliament in religious matters, the Puritans persistently appealed to the long-standing anti-clericalism of the laity. The continuing attacks on the High Commission, for example, appealed, not only to the desire of Puritans to be allowed to preach, but to the desire of laity not to be controlled by the clergy. The Commons' response to Bancroft's canons of 1604 was to claim that no canons under which the laity might lose life, liberty, or goods

[79] Tanner, op. cit., 222.
[80] Carsten, F. L., *Princes and Parliaments in Germany* (1959), 5.

should be valid unless confirmed by Parliament: that laymen should not
be punished except by laws drawn up by other laymen. This argument
was justified by appeals to Henry VIII's reign, and particularly to the Act
for the Submission of the Clergy. These appeals were wrong in the letter,
since Henry VIII had only insisted on canons being confirmed by the king,
not by Parliament. Yet they were right in spirit: the seventeenth-century
parliamentarians, as much as their predecessors, were concerned to attack
the legislative independence of the clergy. It was no comfort to them if the
king confirmed the clergy's canons: their fear was the same as that of
Lord Chancellor Audley in Henry VIII's reign, that 'you bishops would
enter in with the king and by means of his supremacy order the laity as
ye listed'. Bancroft was right in complaining that 'Henry VIII and the
state misliked the clergy. The king that now is, loveth his clergy as ever
any. It is hard if the clergy now be as much misliked as then.'[81] It is not to
be wondered at if Bancroft and some of the other clergy began to dislike
Parliament.

Though these were to be among the most explosive issues of the next
reign, in 1604, and for most of James's reign, the issue which caused most
ill feeling was money. The authors of the *Apology* were right in complaining of the king trying to raise more. The increase in the cost of the
Household was enough to explain why purveyors should have 'rummaged
and ransacked since your majesty's coming-in far more than under any of
your majesty's royal progenitors'. They were right in complaining that
much of the king's revenue fell into the hands of 'devouring promoters'.

One of their most interesting claims was that they did not dare to impose such charges on the people without their consent to them. Fear of
mob violence was never far from the minds of many gentlemen, and it
may be the most significant fact about the Goodwin *v.* Fortescue election
that Goodwin, the private gentleman, had been elected in spite of the
unanimous support of the Justice of the Peace for Fortescue, the Privy
Councillor. Justices were bound to be alarmed by a situation in which their
candidate could be rejected by their own tenants.

Financial expedients, 1604–1610

The 1604 session of Parliament also was not asked to vote a subsidy, on
the ground that the four subsidies voted in 1601 were still being collected.
It is true that four subsidies was an unprecedentedly large vote of taxation
and part of the reluctance of the Jacobean Commons to vote subsidies was
not that they wanted to vote less than previous Parliaments, but that they
objected to being asked for more. James's demands for subsidies in peace-

[81] *Tudor Constitution*, 25; Foster, *1610*, i. 221.

time were as heavy as Elizabeth's in wartime. On the other hand, James had inherited a debt of £400,000 from Elizabeth. He had to pay for her funeral and for his coronation, and he was living consistently beyond his income. He might well have answered the *Apology* by saying that the wealth of subjects might easily and did daily grow, but the revenues of the king were at an everlasting stand. James had to do something to raise money. He had to find ways of increasing his revenue which did not depend on Parliament. His necessities produced the beginnings of a long-overdue overhaul of the royal financial system to bring it up to date with inflation.

Attention was given first to the customs, which were the part of the royal revenue most easily made proof against inflation. The difficulties in collection of customs were the usual administrative ones: since the officials had no appreciable salary, and there was not enough detailed supervision to give much impetus to the collectors, much of the money did not reach the Exchequer. Elizabethan experiments with farming parts of the customs collection suggested that the system was worth extending. In 1604 the government set up the Great Farm of the customs, by which the collection of the main body of the customs was leased to three business-men for seven years in return for a fixed rent of £112,000 a year. This system gave the Crown a guaranteed and predictable income, hedged against slumps and trade embargoes. It gave the farmers, who were able to supervise the system with an attention the government could not give, an interest in collecting as much customs revenue as possible. At the end of each lease, the government could negotiate a new one to keep up with inflation. In practice, they were able to negotiate new leases during the existing ones, since the farmers appreciated that the government's favour was essential to renewals of their lease. In 1606, in response to the growth of trade caused by the peace with Spain, their rent was raised to £120,000, in 1611 to £136,000, and in 1614 to £140,000.[82] Though the system brought profit to the government, it was attacked on the ground that it also brought immense profits to the farmers. This was undoubtedly true. It is also true that the Crown could have made a bigger profit if it were able to pay proper salaries to its officials and stop corruption. But to say that the Crown would be richer if it could pay its officials salaries and stop them taking perquisites was simply to say that it would have been richer if it were richer. About 200 senior posts in the administration as a whole would have been involved, not including any junior posts, and the cost of living in London and keeping a coach could not be estimated at much less than £1,000. Salaries of less than £2,000 would not have been practical, and

[82] Ashton, 88–97.

salaries of £2,000 for 200 officials would have cost the Crown £400,000 a year—almost the whole of its annual expenditure. Professor Aylmer has estimated the cost to the country of official fees in the 1630s at about £300,000, and this figure excludes all the money which officials made from gifts and gratuities.[83] A realistic figure for putting the civil service on a salaried basis might be nearer £600,000 than £400,000 *per annum*. Such a proposal could only be taken seriously if it could be shown how the king might double his income, and achieve the supervision necessary to make attacks on corruption effective. The question of official salaries is only one of the ways in which the king was not rich enough to afford economies. So long as he could not pay his civil servants, he had to allow them opportunities for private profit.

The customs farmers at least made some return for their profits in the form of loans, which were becoming an increasingly essential part of the king's finances. With the rate of interest at 10 per cent, loans were an expensive way of managing deficits, and even the simplest form of credit, that of leaving royal tradesmen's bills unpaid, tended to be met by higher prices. The size of the loans the king was demanding were far beyond the resources of the London money market, and only the customs farmers, the Corporation of London, and a very few rich merchants and speculators were able to provide them. Failure to repay loans from the Corporation of London might have political repercussions, so the customs farmers were a very welcome source of relief. If, as sometimes happened, they could not be repaid, they might be given various concessions or perquisites: titles, export licences, or government contracts. The system appears to have suited both parties, and some of the farmers continued to help the king during the Civil War, long after arguments of self-interest are likely to have ceased to be an effective inducement.

The Farm of the customs and the improvement of trade, however, were not enough to prevent the debt from increasing. By 1606, the debt had reached £735,000, and the annual deficit was running at £81,000. In that year, Parliament was induced to vote three subsidies and other grants, which together added up to £453,000 over four years. This was a welcome relief, but it was not enough to pay the debt, and it did nothing to meet the annual deficit. Even this sum was only brought in after Robert Cecil had written brusque letters to stir some of the collectors into activity.

It was at this stage that the government was presented with a welcome and unexpected opportunity: the opportunity to free the customs, by far the biggest branch of taxation, from parliamentary control. This oppor-

---

[83] Stone, 450; Aylmer, 248–9. These figures are necessarily tentative, but they are as likely to be under-estimates as over-estimates.

tunity was presented by the judgement in Bate's case, in 1606. Bate was a member of the Levant Company, importing currants from Turkey, and he refused to pay import duty on his currants because it had not been imposed by parliamentary assent. The original dispute was perhaps more to do with the privileges of the Levant Company, which was undertaking a new and sometimes risky trade, and needed a considerable amount of political support, than with general questions of taxation. The original case perhaps belongs, not to the history of the struggle against arbitrary taxation, but to the history of the struggle against the trading powers of regulated companies. Unfortunately, however, the case led to a general legal discussion of the right to impose customs duties.

The judges found two lines of precedents bearing on the case, and, as in most other Stuart revenue cases, the issue turned on the question which was the relevant line. According to one line of precedents, mostly Tudor, the king could impose duties for the purpose of regulating trade: he might impose embargoes as a weapon of foreign policy, or put on duties as a retaliation against hostile duties in other countries. This was part of the king's power to direct foreign policy, which neither was nor could be controlled by settled rules of law. It was part of the king's prerogative, and he had to be trusted to exercise it for the common good. The other line of precedents, mostly from the fourteenth and fifteenth centuries, showed that the king could not raise taxes in general or customs duties in particular without the assent of Parliament. In particular, a statute of 1340 clearly and specifically prohibited the raising of customs duties not sanctioned by Parliament. It was as clear that the king's power to raise revenue was restricted by Parliament as that his power to control foreign policy was not. The issue thus became one of the purpose for which the king was raising the imposition on currants, and the judges, not being professional clairvoyants, could not give judgement on the king's purposes, but only on his actions. They thus had to assume that the king's purposes were what he said they were, and give judgement for him. The Commons, though they gave some support to Bate, showed no sign of making a major issue of the case. At this time, the only unparliamentary customs impositions involved were the duty on currants, which was part of a trade war with Venice, and a duty of 6s. 8d. a pound by which James showed his disapproval of tobacco, and it was easy to believe that both of these were designed for the regulation of trade.

This was the situation in the spring of 1608, when Robert Cecil, now Earl of Salisbury, was made Lord Treasurer. He was faced by a debt which was now nearly a million pounds, and by disturbances in Ulster which cost the Crown £98,000 in a year. There was little prospect of reducing the king's expenditure, so the only alternative was increased income. Salisbury appreciated that the logic of the judgement in Bate's case could be extended to any customs duties which the king was prepared to claim were designed for the regulation of trade. He therefore introduced additional customs duties, subsequently known as the Impositions, which, when combined with a new Book of Rates, brought in about £70,000 a year. The alarm which this caused in the Commons can be appreciated. In the light of the king's need for money, their usual argument that what the king did once he might do regularly was for once sound: many further impositions were introduced before the Civil War, until, by the late 1630s, they were bringing in £218,000 a year. It was largely in answer to the impositions that the Commons laid steadily greater stress on their claim that subjects' property could in no circumstances be taken without their consent. Hakewill, in 1610, argued, in attacking the judgement in Bate's case, that the king could not even be allowed to levy taxes without consent in time of sudden war. He asked: 'Who shall judge between the king and his people of this occasion? Can it be tried by any legal course in our law? It cannot. If then the king himself must be the sole judge in this case, will it not follow that the king may levy a tax at his own pleasure, seeing his pleasure cannot be bounded by law?'[84]

These were not Salisbury's only measures to restore solvency. Most parts of the royal revenue could be increased by those who were prepared to do enough work and face enough unpopularity. The more unpopular tasks, such as finding those whose titles to their estates were defective, discovering concealed Crown lands or recovering old debts to the Crown, were often farmed out to commissions, but the unpopularity of the commissioners often rebounded on the Crown. It is hard to estimate what was made from sources of this type, but Salisbury claimed in 1610 that the calling in of old debts since 1578 had brought in £200,000. This search after old debts also gave the Crown a new means of patronage: those who kept its favour might be excused payment of their debts for so long as their favour lasted. The possibilities, and the dangers, involved in stretching the smaller items of Crown revenue are illustrated by a rejected proposal put up to Salisbury by Sir John Swinnerton, an unsuccessful bidder for the Great Farm of the customs. Swinnerton offered to take over the Alienations Office at a rent double or treble the income it was bringing in to the king, and to pay a heavy entry fine for the privilege. Since the fees paid to the Alienations Office for licence to sell manors held of the Crown were assessed on the valuations of estates, there was ample scope for in-

---

[84] Tanner, op. cit., 252. This speech shows that Hakewill understood the concept of sovereignty, and rejected it.

crease, but these increases could only be obtained by commercial methods of exploitation which were politically intolerable. Salisbury said that Swinnerton could only make this sum by administering the office like a grocer, and rejected the proposal, although Swinnerton had offered him a gift of £60,000 to support it.[85]

Salisbury tried to increase the receipts of the Crown lands, which, together with the customs, provided most of the king's income.[86] In 1603 the Crown lands were bringing in £88,000 a year, and there was considerable scope for increases. Salisbury introduced surveyors, who found that many estates were grossly undervalued. One block of estates in Yorkshire, which was bringing in £3,291, brought in £11,449 after it had been re-valued. The introduction of more nearly economic rents, combined with substantial entry fines, might do much for the king's revenue. The amount of work involved, however, was formidable. Each estate, and each field, needed to be re-valued, and an effective bargain struck for it. It was also necessary to undertake detailed investigations into the amounts retained by receivers, stewards, bailiffs, and other local officials. Sir Julius Caesar, Chancellor of the Exchequer, continued some of this work after Salisbury's death, and by 1619 the costs of administration had been reduced from £18,000 to £9,000. The amount of work involved in raising each pound of this money was too great to be really productive. This was even truer of Salisbury's attempts to improve the administration of the Crown woods. At first, he found such confusion, according to his contemporary biographer, 'as his Lordship . . . thought himself in a wood indeed'.[87] It was easy enough to introduce entry fines for leases of Crown woods, but it was much harder to keep any check on trees taken by keepers as perquisites. Salisbury decided that the Crown could only keep track of the trees by having each tree numbered. It is typical of the state of the Crown's revenue that the Lord Treasurer should have to meet an acute financial crisis by ensuring the numbering of individual trees. The work was of course prohibitively unproductive, but if the Crown could have been made solvent at all without threatening the position of Parliament, it would have been by measures such as these. After two years, it was clear that the attempt to improve Crown land revenue, however well managed, would not be sufficiently productive. Sales of Crown lands to pay the king's debts decreased receipts faster than Salisbury could increase them, and economic administration was incompatible with the use

[85] Foster, *1610*, i. 204. Salisbury said he would as soon farm his daughter's virginity.

[86] On Salisbury and the Crown Lands, see *Agrarian History*, 268–74.

[87] Cope, Sir Walter, *An Apology for the Late Lord Treasurer*, in Gutch, J., *Collectanea Curiosa* (1781), i. 123.

of Crown estates for patronage. Nor could even the greatest success guarantee the impetus necessary to keep up the improvement. In fact, the revenue of the Crown lands collapsed after Salisbury's death, and by 1628, after further substantial sales, the net profits of the Crown lands, after the costs of administration had been met, had fallen to £10,000.

The Great Contract and the parliamentary session of 1610

By 1610, the subsidy and sales of Crown lands, together with all the other measures, had reduced the debt to £280,000, of which £120,000 was an Elizabethan Forced Loan which had not yet been repaid. The deficits, however, were still continuing, and it was clear that Salisbury was fighting a losing battle. In the spring of 1610, when James's first Parliament assembled for its fourth session, Salisbury put forward the most statesmanlike and far-reaching financial proposal of the reign, the proposal known as the Great Contract. Under this proposal, Parliament would vote the king an annual grant of £200,000, in return for which the king would abandon many of his more unpopular revenues. Wardship, together with a number of the charges which went with it, was to be abolished, and so was purveyance of food, though not, to the dismay of the Commons, the compulsory requisitioning of carts. The enforcement of royal rights through informers was to be abandoned. The Crown was to sell its right to debts due to it from the period from Henry VII's reign to Mary's (which Salisbury estimated at £700,000). In return for all these concessions, the Commons were also to make an immediate grant of £600,000 to pay off the king's debts. Financially, this proposal might have benefited both king and subjects. The king would have gained a revenue about £100,000 bigger than what he abandoned, and the subjects would have saved a host of fees and other payments to officials. Salisbury estimated that the fees for holding *Inquisitions Post Mortem* (to value the estates of those who died holding land from the king) alone cost the subjects more than £100,000 a year, and none of this money came to the Crown.[88] At a later stage of the Contract, a proposal was discussed to pay compensation to the leading officials involved. This proposal was unpopular in the Commons, but it was not over-generous. The whole scheme resembled the financial settlement which was ultimately made at the Restoration, in 1660.

If the proposal was such a good one, it remains to ask why it was not accepted. One possible reason is the sheer novelty and radicalism of the proposal, which did not fit the constitutional conservatism of both M.P.s

[88] Foster, *1610*, i. 59. This estimate cannot be checked.

and Councillors. With alarm at the novelty of the proposal went considerable anxiety and uncertainty about its effects, shown up in a series of contradictory objections. Sir Julius Caesar, Chancellor of the Exchequer, thought it did not grant the king enough money, because it was not inflation-proof. In fact, the inflation which had lasted the whole of the previous century was to slow down considerably within the next ten years, but neither Caesar nor Salisbury could know this. In the Commons, one M.P. thought it would give the king so much money that he would never want to call Parliament again, while another thought it would not give the king enough to make him solvent, and they would be burdened with a series of further demands. Nicholas Fuller thought the Commons should not grant the Contract without some concessions to Puritans, nor until the king had abandoned impositions, because the Commons could make no gift until they were certain what was lawfully their own. Other M.P.s thought they could not vote the Contract unless they could present some substantial concessions to their constituents. Otherwise, as one of them said, their constituents 'would say, we have been all this while like children in catching butterflies'.[89] At court, Bacon, who disliked Salisbury, was warning James not to haggle with his subjects as if he were a merchant, and James was very doubtful whether his dignity permitted him to abandon the principle of feudal tenures.

The Contract was not passed because there was not enough trust, and not enough goodwill, between the king and Parliament. Both sides were left to face Salisbury's warning that if the Contract were not passed, the king would have to exact all he could from the revenues he had, and that this would be much more than it had ever been before, 'but when a king extendeth his uttermost authority, he loseth his power'.[90] What effect the Contract would have had if it had been passed, it is hard to say. It would have left the king with rather less revenue than his son had in the 1630s, and therefore would not have enabled him to fight wars without the help of Parliament. On the other hand, it would have given James a surplus on the current expenditure of 1610. Perhaps it might have enabled the constitution to operate without further change for another generation. Whether it would also have removed the financial distrust which was the chief obstacle to improvement is more doubtful.

The list of grievances produced by the Commons in 1610, which James complained was as long as a tapestry, contributed to the mutual distrust. The financial, and possibly the constitutional, complaints might have been eased by the passage of the Contract, but the religious complaints would

[89] Notestein, *Winning of the Initiative*, 43.
[90] Foster, *1610*, i. 70.

not. Many of the religious grievances of 1610 were very old ones, and there is no reason to suppose that they were more explosive in 1610 than they had been before, but fifty years of failure to obtain reforms may have been enough to make many members feel unhelpful. The complaints against the High Commission went back to the days of Beale and Morice, and were supplemented only by a complaint against the Commission's granting of alimonies to separated wives 'to the great encouragement of wives to be disobedient and contemptuous against their husbands'.[91] The complaints against Bancroft's deprivations of Puritan clergy, and against canons not confirmed by Parliament, went back to 1604. The surprising point about these complaints is that the Puritans should still have hoped to remedy them by reformist methods.

Some of the constitutional grievances were newer. The Commons complained against a legal dictionary published by Cowell, Regius Professor of Civil Law at Cambridge, which claimed that the king had the power to legislate or raise taxes without the assent of Parliament. James agreed with the Commons in condemning the book and ordering its suppression, but the next year he appointed Cowell to membership of the High Commission. The Commons also complained of James's use of Proclamations, expressing a fear 'that proclamations will by degrees grow up and increase to the strength and nature of laws ... and may also in time bring in a new form of arbitrary government upon the realm'. Proclamations had been in regular use for many years, and it is hard to tell what made the Commons begin to fear that they might supersede Acts of Parliament. Even in 1641, Pym was prepared to admit that they had a legitimate use between Parliaments, and they do not seem to have caused as much dismay in other Parliaments as in 1610. It is true that James had issued many more proclamations than his predecessors, and had recently published a book of proclamations, but this was probably the result of verbosity rather than of any deliberate desire for despotism. Probably the root of the alarm in 1610 was the fear that shortage of money would drive the king into arbitrary methods of government. As Salisbury said, the M.P. who compared him to Empson and Dudley showed want of charity, but if the king were to be solvent, the methods of Empson and Dudley were needed.

The 1610 Commons also set out to attack two of the king's servants, and claimed the right to punish them. Both of the men concerned were involved in revenue farming. One was a commissioner for concealed debts, and for the collection of fines for various offences, and was accused of doing his work too well. The other was a commissioner for the collection of fines from recusants, and was accused of not doing his work well

[91] Foster, *1610*, ii. 265.

enough. In addition to raising all these issues, the House listened to proposals for a petition to exclude all Scots from court. It was perhaps not
until 1626 that the Crown again had to face such a hostile and suspicious
House of Commons. It had redeemed itself only by voting what was now
the insignificant sum of one subsidy.

At the end of 1610, too late to affect the atmosphere of the Parliament,
the death of Bancroft presented James with the chance of choosing a new
Archbishop, and he chose Abbot, Bishop of London. Abbot was an Archbishop in the Grindal tradition, and until the rise of the Arminians began
to weaken his hold on the king's favour, relations between the Crown and
the Puritans were very much easier than they had been under Bancroft or
Whitgift. Abbot's views on doctrine were, from the Puritan point of view,
impeccable, and he also shared their views on such issues of growing concern as the enforcement of the sabbath. He was not an enthusiast for ceremony, and there was no grand campaign during his archiepiscopate for
the exclusion of Puritan ministers from the church, nor any grand campaign by Puritan ministers or M.P.s against the bishops. He was perhaps
on more friendly terms with the House of Commons than any other Archbishop since Cranmer. His own chapel at Lambeth, though to the ceremonial eye of his successor Laud it appeared to be set out 'more
undecently than is fit to express',[92] was organized in a way which was
reasonably unprovocative to the Commons. He did not achieve any very
drastic reforms in the church, but he did achieve peace—an achievement
not made by any other Anglican Archbishop before the eighteenth century.

Political drift

Salisbury, now very ill and suffering from overwork, was left to wrestle
with the king's regular deficit. A Forced Loan of £116,000 was raised in
1611, of which only £4,000 had been repaid by 1618, and one new source
of revenue was invented—the sale of titles. The order of baronets was invented simply for the purpose of selling them, originally at a price of
£1,095. The innovation caused a good deal of indignation, but a number
of people, including some of the Parliamentary leaders, were willing to
buy titles. The aristocratic prejudices of the Earl Marshal's court were
offended, and they consoled themselves for their inability to degrade a
Shrewsbury draper from his baronetcy by pronouncing him no gentleman
instead. However, the only financial danger to the scheme was the flood-
ing of the market, which lowered the price to £220 by 1622. The government responded by creating new orders of Baronets of Ireland and

---

[92] Laud, *Works* (1847), iv. 198.

Baronets of Nova Scotia, and by extending the policy of sales of peerages, English, Scottish, and Irish. Earldoms at £10,000 each did much to help the Exchequer. Once again, however, the market was flooded. One unfortunate man who bought an Irish Earldom found such a shortage of places of which there was not already an Earl that when the government at last found him a vacant town he felt compelled to send his own emissary to confirm that it actually existed.[93] The sale of titles was useful, but its potentialities were limited. By 1613, the annual deficit was up to £160,000, and by 1618 the debt was up again to £900,000. Continental monarchies might run regularly with debts on this scale, but their total resources were much larger, and a king who did not have to ask anyone's consent to raise taxes might have better credit than the king of England. After the death of Salisbury, in 1612, the Treasury was put into commission, and James acted as his own secretary, or claimed to do so. The years from 1612 to 1618 are in the main years of political drift.

In 1613, the king had to face two other extraordinary expenses which also had important political consequences—the marriage of his daughter, costing £60,000, and the funeral of his eldest son, costing £16,000. His son Prince Henry, who probably died of typhoid fever, had been a strong Protestant, interested in overseas exploration, and an admirer of Sir Walter Raleigh, who had been in the Tower since 1603 under suspended sentence of death for a supposed plot in favour of Arabella Stuart. The heir was now James's younger son Prince Charles, who, unlike his brother, would be willing to marry a Catholic if there were an argument of foreign policy in favour of doing so. James's daughter Princess Elizabeth, who was and remained extremely popular, married the Elector Palatine, the most vigorously Protestant of the German princes. The marriage was popular, but it had political consequences which could not be foreseen at the time.[94]

At the same time, a long and complicated court scandal was beginning, which, though of no great importance in itself, probably helped to damage the reputation of the court in the eyes of Puritans. The central character in the scandal was the king's homosexual favourite, Robert Carr, a Scotsman whom James made Earl of Somerset. Somerset had not a very profound influence on policy, but he had a large share in James's bounty. In 1613 Somerset fell in love with the Countess of Essex. After the public washing of a good deal of dirty linen, Lady Essex finally obtained a divorce from her husband, and married Somerset, in spite of the opposi-

[93] Mayes, Charles R., 'The Early Stuarts and the Irish Peerage', *E.H.R.* (1958), 24.

[94] See below, pp. 290–2.

tion of Archbishop Abbot. Unfortunately, one of Somerset's followers, Sir Thomas Overbury, probably had some information which might have impeded the divorce, and he appears to have been poisoned on the instigation of Lady Essex. Two years later, in 1615, the murder was discovered. Somerset appears to have tried to defend himself by threatening to make revelations about the king, presumably about his homosexual relations with him. Somerset and his wife, though publicly tried and convicted, were pardoned, and the only immediate result was to leave the way open for a new favourite.

It was between the first and second rounds of this scandal, in 1614, that the king decided to risk summoning another Parliament. This Parliament only sat for a few weeks, and passed no legislation whatsoever, wherefore it came to be known as the Addled Parliament. The issue which caused most heat appears to have been impositions, which provoked one of the Commons' earlier incursions into speculative political theory. This was started by the attempt of a member who had diplomatic experience abroad to argue that hereditary kings could impose, but elective ones could not. Sir Edwin Sandys replied by attempting to argue that the English monarchy was contractual, and Peter Wentworth's son Thomas by finding precedents in the Books of Daniel and Ezekiel. Sir Dudley Digges restored the debate to firmer ground by arguing that the central point was that they did not want to change the laws of England. The desire to keep the constitution unchanged in a changing world, buttressed by the study of law and English history, probably represents the consistent position of the majority of the Commons throughout the early Stuart period. The Addled Parliament did, however, produce one constitutional innovation, on the suggestion of their most vociferous hothead, Sir Roger Owen, who was described as 'the gentleman whose brains flew up and down in his head as a bird flies in the air'. Owen moved that the luckless Bacon, who had at last been made Attorney General, should be excluded from the House, and added that Privy Councillors only sat at all by courtesy of the House. Remarkably, Owen managed to win a majority for this doctrine, and the House, though allowing Bacon to sit for that Parliament, resolved that the Attorney General could not be a member in future. In this atmosphere, the few Privy Councillors in the House could not provide any leadership, and the Commons had not yet produced their own effective leaders. The result was an exceptionally confused House, and one member who complained that the House was growing like a cockpit was told that he assumed 'too much regularity to himself'.[95] The House was also disturbed by an outburst of indignation against Bishop Neile, who argued in

[95] Moir, T. L., *The Addled Parliament* (1958), 85, 100.

the Lords that they should not hold a conference with the Commons because they were undutiful and seditious, and by a long agitation about what James later called 'a strange kind of beast called undertakers'.[96] The undertakers, who were supposed to have undertaken to manage the elections to produce a House to the king's satisfaction, appear to have been largely mythical. Both then and now, it has been widely suspected, though not proved, that much of the disorder in this Parliament was produced at the instigation of Northampton and the Howards, who represented a group on the Council which wanted to persuade James that it was not worth calling Parliament. When the Commons decided that they would not vote any money until impositions were removed, James dissolved them, and imposed an arbitrary levy of 2d. a barrel on beer instead. He relieved his feelings to the Spanish Ambassador, saying that: 'The House of Commons is a body without a head. The members give their opinions in a disorderly manner. At their meetings nothing is heard but cries, shouts, and confusion. I am surprised that my ancestors should ever have permitted such an institution to come into existence. I am a stranger, and found it here when I arrived, so that I am obliged to put up with what I cannot get rid of.'[97] Like many of James's most famous statements, this one should perhaps not be taken to represent more than the mood of the moment.

Shortly after the Parliament, James tried out one of the most famous, and most unfortunate, of his revenue projects. Alderman Cockayne, who prepared the project, and after whom it is known, was a rich merchant, moneylender, and Crown creditor.[98] Like many others, he was concerned about the fact that most English cloth was exported undyed to be dyed by the rising cloth industry of the Dutch, thus leaving to them much of the profit of the finished product. Cockayne's scheme involved setting up an English dyeing industry, and forbidding the export of undyed cloth. In return for providing the kingdom with this great benefit, Cockayne was to take over the position of the Merchant Adventurers as sole controller of the export trade in English cloth. The government was to gain an extra £40,000 annual revenue, from increased customs on the export of more valuable cloth, and on the import of dyestuffs. In December 1614, after

[96] Gardiner, *History*, iv. 26. On the elections to this Parliament, which in fact were perfectly normal, see Moir, 30–55.

[97] Gardiner, *History*, ii. 251. On Gondomar, see Carter, Charles H., 'Gondomar: Ambassador to James I', *H.J.* (1964), 189–208. A full reassessment of Gondomar's influence on James must await the publication of Professor Carter's forthcoming book.

[98] For the latest assessment of the Cockayne project, see Supple, B. E., *Commercial Crisis and Change in England 1603–1642* (1964), 33 ff. It remains an open question whether Cockayne's project was a failure or a fraud.

the failure of the Parliament, James gave Cockayne his way, suspended the charter of the Merchant Adventurers, and handed over the control of the trade to Cockayne. Cockayne's new company was to take over the obligation of the Merchant Adventurers to buy cloth as it came up to London from the country, and hold it until they had a market for it. Cockayne, having failed to get financial support from most of the Merchant Adventurers, conspicuously failed to do this. By 1616, Gloucestershire clothiers were complaining that they had £400,000 worth of unsold cloth on their hands, and unemployment in some of the clothing districts was rising to proportions which threatened riot. Cockayne meanwhile was making money by using his privileged position to gain licences to export undyed cloth. It is even possible that this was his original intention. After two years, the project had patently failed, and the trade was handed back to the Merchant Adventurers. Though Cockayne's project probably contributed little to the great depression of 1620, it may have contributed more to the resentment of clothiers at government economic interference. James was left to think of new measures, and to do so with a new favourite, and in a new political and economic situation.

Postscript

The judgements on James I made on pp. 257–8 are superseded by R. C. Munden in *Faction and Parliament 1604–29*, Ed. K. M. Sharpe (Oxford, 1978), and in chapter II of my *Parliaments and English Politics 1621–9* (Oxford, forthcoming 1979). In Mr. Munden's phrase, most criticisms of James I depend on the belief that James's problems had solutions, which James should have found. Since James did not entirely share this confidence, he often preferred to let sleeping dogs lie. The account of the Goodwin v. Fortescue case on p. 267 is also superseded by R. C. Munden in *E.H.R.* [forthcoming]. Mr. Munden believes the dispute has more to do with rival court factions than with electoral opposition.

6. The Reigns of Buckingham and Charles 1618–1642

I BUCKINGHAM AND JAMES, 1618–1625

... George, Duke, Marquis and Earl of Buckingham, Earl of Coventry, Viscount Villiers, Baron of Whaddon, Great Admiral of the kingdoms of England and Ireland, and of the principality of Wales, ... general governor of the seas and ships of the said kingdom, lieutenant-general, Admiral, Captain-General and Governor of his Majesty's royal fleet and army lately set forth, Master of the Horse of our Sovereign Lord the King, Lord Warden, Chancellor and Admiral of the Cinque Ports, and of the members thereof, Constable of Dover Castle, Justice in Eyre of the forests and chases on this side the river Trent, Constable of the castle of Windsor, Gentleman of His Majesty's bedchamber, one of his Majesty's most honourable Privy Council in his realms both in England, Scotland and Ireland, and knight of the most honourable order of the Garter.[1]

*From the Commons' Articles of Impeachment
of the Duke of Buckingham, 1626*

Buckingham and reactions to him

IN 1615 a brewer was sent to prison for refusing to give James I beer on credit. At a time when the terms 'credit' and 'reputation' were interchangeable, this was an alarming development for the king as well as for the brewer, but it may be that the brewer's commercial judgement was as sound as his political judgement was unsound. After the Dissolution of the Addled Parliament, the king's debts were rising steadily, and even the City of London was beginning to share the brewer's doubts about the king's credit. In 1617, he succeeded in raising a loan of £96,000 through the Corporation of London, but some citizens were reluctant to contribute. James dealt with one of them by exercising his undoubted right to command his subjects to attend him in the uncharitable form of making the man walk behind the royal progress from London to Carlisle.

[1] Rushworth, I. 303. One of the charges against Buckingham was the engrossing of offices.

Power at court after the dissolution of the Addled Parliament and the fall of Somerset rested mainly with the large tribe of the Howards, who were unlikely to take any effective action to ease the royal deficit. A number of the king's servants were hoping to produce reforms, including Sir Edward Coke, who at this time divided the debts into 'eating debts, such as were taken up at interest, the second, crying debts, due to soldiers, mariners, tradesmen, and such as live on labour, the third, pressing debts, but named them not, nor explained not his meaning therein'.[2] The pressing debts probably meant debts to people whom the king could not, politically, afford to leave unpaid. Such worries do not seem to have much concerned the Howards, and least of all Suffolk, now effective head of the family and Lord Treasurer. For him, the royal debts represented an effective source of private income, since he often had the valuable power to decide which should be paid first. The Howards, moreover, were suspect to many people on grounds of religion and foreign policy. They were thought to be pro-Spanish, and for many of them, the extent of their inclination towards Roman Catholicism is as hard for historians to discover as it was for their contemporaries.

Many of James's ministers who wanted a lever against the Howards were thus inclined to welcome the appearance of a new favourite. George Villiers was a young and obscure country gentleman, handsome and agreeable, eager to please everyone, but not exceptionally well endowed with brains. In April 1615, some of the Howards' enemies succeeded in inducing the queen to petition James to give him office (it was one of James's psychological peculiarities that he would only adopt a new favourite if his wife could be induced to recommend the man). Villiers was appointed a Gentleman of the Bedchamber (a new department created by James, and staffed mainly on grounds of favour) and given a pension of £1,000 a year. Thus it is that George Villiers, Duke of Buckingham, one of the most corrupt ministers the Crown has ever had, came into power with the backing of a group which was working for administrative reform. The Howards saw the threat to their position and attempted to prepare a rival favourite by washing his face every morning with sour milk. The Howards were unsuccessful, and though it was not until 1619 that Suffolk was dismissed from the Lord Treasurership, their power fell steadily as Buckingham's rose.

Clarendon's comment on Buckingham is that no man 'rose, in so short a time, to so much greatness of honour, fame and fortune, upon no other advantage or recommendation, than the beauty and gracefulness of his person'.[3] Buckingham must have had talents: no man without talent could

---

[2] Ashton, 34.   [3] Clarendon, *History of the Rebellion* (1702). i. 9.

have succeeded in descending as favourite from father to son. But talent for devising policies or conducting administration was not among Buckingham's abilities. In spite of this fact, he quickly gained such standing with the king that no political decision, and no choice for promotion, could be made without his agreement. He undertook the work of patronage with a dedication which had been given to it by no other man since the death of Essex, and he achieved that complete control over all, including the highest, offices, for which Essex had worked in vain. Like Essex, moreover, he was grossly extravagant. His *official* income in 1623 was over £15,000, and his income in the form of gifts from the Crown and the sale of offices may have exceeded this, but nevertheless he was capable of falling heavily in debt. He had the further disadvantage, which Essex had not had, of being endowed with a vast tribe of friends and relations who had to be provided for. Marriage to one of Buckingham's female relations was often a necessary condition of office, and Court perquisites had to be provided for his male relations as well as for himself.

It is, however, a mistake to think of an entity called 'the Parliamentary opposition' arrayed in unyielding hostility to Buckingham. For at least the first half of his reign Buckingham shared with Essex a willingness to extend his patronage indiscriminately to people of all political persuasions. Before 1624, no one was necessarily cast into opposition for his opinion, so the machinery of the one-party state in which unity was preserved, and preferment open to all shades of opinion, was not broken down. On Buckingham's own opinions before 1624, it is hard to pass judgement. Laud subsequently claimed to have rescued him on the threshold of conversion to Rome, but on the other hand he had ample favour for John Preston, one of the leading Puritan lecturers, who seems for a while to have had considerable influence on him. Packer, his patronage secretary, was a low churchman who had parliamentarian leanings in the Civil War. Perhaps the most accurate verdict would be that Buckingham's opinions were neither very stable nor very deep-rooted. He was certainly always open to new influences from anyone who was friendly to him. Those who received his patronage included Laud the Arminian, Sir John Eliot the M.P., and Lionel Cranfield the devotee of administrative reform and reduction of the king's expenditure. Powerful Puritan peers like Lincoln or Warwick, who could afford Buckingham's favour, did not need to feel that all was lost, or that their policies could not be heard in the king's counsels.

Even lower down the social scale, reactions to the rule of Buckingham might be ambivalent. In the winter of 1620, John Hampden's mother, finding that 'here is multitudes of lords a-making' reacted by wanting her son to get a peerage, in order that he should not be behind so many new creations.[4] Some people's reactions changed during the 1620s. In 1620, an obscure official in the Crown land administration called John Pym was corresponding with his tutor about whether it was proper to desire honour in the State, and, at about the same time, submitting a memorandum suggesting improvements in the administration of the Crown lands.[5] He expressed doubt whether honour was worth the price, and we may doubt whether he was able to pay it. It is possible that he believed (truly) that most of those who received preferment in the Exchequer were much less able financiers than he was. If he felt any resentment, his tutor, who had been dismayed by the corruption of literary patronage since 1604, was well able to encourage it. By 1626, Pym probably agreed that the sale of office was 'an offence unnatural against the law of nature',[6] and that since honour in the State was a divine thing, sale of office was simony.

The most widespread grievances against Buckingham were not for his political outlook but for his extravagance and his incompetence. While Buckingham was spending a sum in the region of £3,000 a year on clothes, it was hard for him to convince the Commons that the king was genuinely short of money, and easy for the Commons to claim that the shortage of money was because too much was spent on Buckingham and his friends. His direction of policy was erratic, and the Dutch envoys were not alone in concluding that the Duke of Buckingham did not know much about the affairs of Germany. Seymour was making a plausible claim in 1628, when he said that if they voted any more, 'all that we give will be cast into a bottomless bag'.[7] The allusion in the minds of his hearers is likely to have been to Sir James Bagg, one of the most corrupt of Buckingham's agents. It was at this period and in response to the seeming incompetence of Buckingham's administration, that the legend of the great and glorious days of Queen Elizabeth began to gain wide currency. Two M.P.s played a large part in popularizing it. One was Sir Edward Coke, reminiscing of the days of his youth, and commenting on the incompetence of the navy administration that in Queen Elizabeth's days the Admiralty had not been used to dance a pavan.[8] The other was John Pym, a new and as yet unimportant M.P., whose picture of the Elizabethan age may have been influenced by the fact that his stepfather had been one of Sir Francis Drake's executors. For such men as Coke, distrust of Buckingham combined with their own personal failure (Coke had lost the Lord Treasurer-

---

[4] B.M. Harl. MS. 4712, fo. 397v.

[5] Whear, D., *Epistolarum Eucharisticarum Fasciculus* (1628), 42. B.M. Add. MS. 12,504, fo. 169v. I would like to thank my wife for this reference.

[6] Rushworth, I. 336.   [7] Rushworth, I. 519.

[8] A pavan was a highly formalized type of dance.

ship in 1620 to a rival who was willing to pay £20,000) and the combination produced a sense of national humiliation reinforced by military defeats. This could produce dangerous opposition, but nothing in it was irreconcilable. There was rarely malice in Buckingham, and he had much more ability to maintain a working relationship with his enemies than Charles I was to show later. There was still a group of Privy Councillors, led by Pembroke and Archbishop Abbot, whose sympathies were largely with Parliament, and those hardy perennials, the families of Howard and Herbert, still controlled a small amount of patronage which Buckingham did not manage.

Cranfield

The first of Buckingham's protégés to be given a chance to show his talents was Lionel Cranfield, the only merchant to rise to high government office in the early Stuart period. He was of humble birth (which was continually quoted against him by his critics), and had begun his career by marrying his master's daughter when he was an apprentice. Fortunately for his career, she died in time for him to marry one of Buckingham's relations when he wanted to move from a very profitable career in the cloth trade to high political office. He brought business principles to the king's finances, and so offended many people. He was probably the man in Sherland's mind when he quoted Aristotle to the effect that merchants should not hold office in the State unless they had been out of trade for ten years.[9] Cranfield made some successful attempts to increase the king's income. When the Great Farm of the Customs was due for renewal, he obtained a higher rent for it by creating a fictitious 'ghost' syndicate largely run by himself to bid against the existing syndicate and force up their price. He increased the rates of customs on aliens (who were not represented in the House of Commons). His main efforts, however, were directed to reducing royal expenditure. His first target was the royal household, always one of the most expensive departments. He determind to end the system by which the king paid inflated prices in return for long credit, saying, 'the king shall pay no more than other men do, and he shall pay ready money; and if we cannot have it in one place, we will have it in another'.[10] In effect, household contracts were to be put to competitive tender. He also set out to investigate the money spent in the household, which came in 1617 to £77,000 as against £48,000 in the last years of Elizabeth's reign. After long and laborious calculations, he discovered that a large proportion of the

[9] Colin G. C. Tite, *Impeachment and Parliamentary Judicature in Early Stuart England* (1974), 198 n.
[10] Ashton, 34, n.

oxen purchased for the household were remaining in the hands of the household officials, and put a temporary stop to this large-scale fraud. He set out to stop allowances for meals to absent officials, to cut down the number of courses allowed to Councillors, and to stop the practice of replacing used candles before they had been burned to the end. These economies saved the king £18,000 a year and earned Cranfield a reputation for ungentlemanly concern with trivia, but they were by their very nature the type of economies which could not be continued without constant supervision over a long period of time.

Cranfield was also the moving spirit in a commission which investigated the Navy Office, where he found similar abuses. Buckingham supported these reforming efforts for a while because the navy was in the hands of Nottingham, who was a Howard, but when Buckingham was made Lord Admiral to preside over these onslaughts on corruption the appointment created a sharp contrast between the Lord Admiral's standards and those which were expected of his juniors. A similar onslaught on the Ordnance office reduced expenditure from £34,000 to £14,000. Cranfield's prize case, however, was the administration of the Wardrobe, a purchasing department to which his business skill was well suited. His predecessor, Lord Hay, one of the most extravagant of Jacobean courtiers, had been running the Wardrobe for about £42,000 a year. Under heavy pressure, he agreed that it might be run for £28,000 a year. Cranfield offered to run it on £20,000 a year if he were allowed to keep any saving within that figure. He kept the king's costs down to £20,000, and made a profit for himself which may have been as much as £7,000. In achieving this saving, however, he started a major political dispute by depriving the Wardrobe clerks of their poundage, a percentage per pound passing through their hands which they had previously been allowed to take. The clerks' poundage was not corruption: it was a legitimate part of their income, much like taxi-drivers' tips. The Wardrobe clerks reacted like taxi-drivers deprived of their tips, and were still pursuing Cranfield for the money long after his fall from power. This example illustrates that in trying to cut administrative costs, Cranfield may have shown too much indifference to what is now called the principle of social cost: he may have been too indifferent to the political loss which was the price of his financial gain.

The Thirty Years' War

For a short time it looked as if the attack on the deficit might be successful, but in 1618 the European situation became so threatening that many of the new savings had to go on rearmament. The Twelve Years' Truce between Spain and the Dutch was to expire in 1621, but the centre of the

European crisis was James's son-in-law, Frederick, Elector Palatine. The Holy Roman Emperor was elected by seven Electors, of whom three were Catholic bishops, and three Protestant princes. The seventh Elector was the king of Bohemia, who was normally the head of the House of Habsburg. In 1618, however, there was a powerful movement in Prague against Habsburg rule, and the Bohemian estates claimed that they had the right to elect their king. The man they chose was Frederick, Elector Palatine. If he were successful, there would be a Protestant majority among the Electors to the Holy Roman Empire. When Frederick accepted the Bohemian Crown a crisis began which threatened to involve all Europe. The Spaniards were likely to help the Austrian Habsburgs, the French either to oppose them or to help their opponents. Some of the German princes might resist the extension of the power of the Emperor, and the Swedes and the Danes might be expected to intervene in Germany, and the Dutch take advantage of Spanish involvement to capture Spanish colonies in the Pacific. Above all, England could be expected to enter the war, both for dynastic reasons and because in parliamentary circles both pan-Protestantism and personal affection made Frederick's wife Elizabeth far the most popular of James's children. Hampden's mother thought that 'all true hearted England hearts' were deeply involved in supporting Elizabeth and her husband.[11] The wife of another Puritan M.P., eagerly followed the course of the war in Dutch newspapers, whose circulation at this time contributed to introducing the idea of the newspaper to the English. On the other hand, if M.P.s were to support a war they would have to trust Buckingham with the administration of it, and they trusted neither his purposes nor his skill. Sir Robert Phelips, a prominent M.P., kept a whole volume of papers on the Bohemian crisis in his study, but he was remarkably unhelpful in Parliament when asked to vote money to meet the crisis.

To some extent, Phelips' distrust was justified. James did not like the notion of elective monarchies, and took the line that his son-in-law was a usurper in Bohemia. Instead of supporting him wholeheartedly, he offered to send ambassadors to mediate and pacify the continent. The crisis also strengthened, instead of weakened, a long-cherished project of James's to marry his son to a Spanish princess, and to base a European pacification on an alliance between England and Spain. Gondomar, the Spanish ambassador, who had acquired a considerable influence over James, warmly supported this project. So did such men as Cranfield, to whom the dowry of a Spanish princess seemed a welcome relief. English hostility to Spain had grown during a period when French power had been negligible. The restoration of French power, as it restored the early Elizabethan balance

[11] B.M. Harl. MS. 4712, fo. 397v.

of power, also restored the early Elizabethan arguments for some measure of friendship with Spain. However, there were many arguments on the other side. James himself, in a book he dedicated to his eldest son in the 1590s, had argued that marriages between Catholics and Protestants were always sinful, and many supported his early opinion against his later one. Some M.P.s and others had developed interests in overseas expansion and privateering, which would be threatened by friendship with Spain. Others were strong believers in friendship with France. Moreover, the Spaniards were known to want substantial concessions to the English Catholics as part of the marriage treaty, and many who had reacted strongly to the Gunpowder Plot feared the effect of such concessions. Both James and the House of Commons shared one illusion: both thought that by their dealings with Spain they could affect the policy of the Emperor in the Palatinate and Bohemia. James thought that if he reached a settlement with Spain, the Spaniards could induce the Emperor to withdraw from the Palatinate. A number of M.P.s thought that a sea war against Spain in the West Indies, as well as bringing opportunities for profit, could divert the Emperor from his war in Germany. Though the Spanish and Austrian Habsburgs were closely allied, they were not so inseparable that either would give up their vital interests at the request of the other. However, since Shakespeare was wrong in supposing Bohemia to have sea-coasts, it was hard to see what other policy was open to England.

The Parliament of 1621

James, however, did agree to send a small force when Frederick's own Electorate of the Palatinate was invaded by Habsburg troops. Shortly after this, in the spring of 1621, James and Buckingham agreed to summon a Parliament. This Parliament met in the middle of a severe economic depression, which had caused the bottom to fall out of the cloth industry, and caused widespread unemployment. The depression was later accompanied by severe harvest failure and famine. In these circumstances, the king was unwise to say in his opening speech that none of his subjects were in poverty except through their own fault, and, having no policy to meet the depression, he might expect Parliament to try and supply one.

The Parliament of 1621 was the beginning of a determined attempt by James and Buckingham to come to terms with Parliament. It was allowed to continue sitting without fear of dissolution for longer than any other Parliament of the period, and is also unusually well documented. It thus provides a good chance to judge the temper and aims of Parliament at work. It received uncertain leadership from the Crown: the Speaker, Serjeant Richardson, had never before been a member, and had not the control of procedure an experienced Speaker could have exercised. The Commons included the exceptionally large number of nine Councillors, who covered as wide a range of the political spectrum as the Elizabethan Councillors had done. However, they were much occupied in feuds with each other, and could not use their diversity to advantage while advising a king incapable of firm decisions. Moreover, only one of them was a first-rate parliamentarian, and that was Sir Edward Coke. Coke had already quarrelled with the king when he was sacked from the Chief Justiceship in 1616, but he had continued to give reasonably loyal service until he failed to gain the Lord Treasurership in 1620. In 1621, he was preoccupied with rivalry with Bacon and some other Councillors. He had acquired an unrivalled legal reputation, largely through his law reports, published during the early years of James's reign, and when the Commons found him ready to lead attacks on maladministration, and to support them all with precedents, they regarded him as a legal oracle. One commented bitterly: 'this is the first Parliament that ever I saw Councillors of State to have such a care of the State',[12] and compared his progress to that of a great Parliament man in Queen Elizabeth's time. The other two M.P.s with most influence in the Commons were Sir Edwin Sandys and Sir Robert Phelips. Both of them were far more experienced in parliamentary procedure than most Councillors, and their careers show the House beginning to evolve an effective leadership of its own, independent of the Privy Councillors. Neither, however, was in any sense a revolutionary. Sandys was the son of a bishop, and certainly no Puritan, and his chief interests were in trade, reversing the decision on Impositions, and administering the Virginia Company. Sir Robert Phelips was the son of the Speaker of 1604, and one of two substantial gentlemen who were competing for control of county politics in Somerset.[13]

Like Sir Thomas Wentworth, later Earl of Strafford (one of the younger members who made his mark in the 1620s) Phelips saw national politics chiefly as a means to the control of his own county. He was a moderate Puritan, but no more so than many courtiers, and on at least one issue, the attempt to suppress Somerset church-ales in the 1630s, he sided with the court against the Puritans. His was a type of career which had always been common, and was easy enough in a time of political unity. In the 1620s it was becoming increasingly difficult. Power in the county depended on two sources: one was the favour of the Crown, expressed through success in appeals to the Privy Council, and the possibility of Council

[12] Gardiner, *History*, iv. 41.
[13] On Phelips' career in local government, see Barnes, T. G., *Somerset 1625–1640* (1961), 281–98.

support in local feuds. It was also expressed through appointment to local commissions, of which Phelips was an indefatigable member. He was Justice of the Peace, Deputy Lieutenant, Commissioner of Sewers, Commissioner for making the river navigable between Bridgwater and Taunton, and Commissioner for Swans. Membership of these commissions was an essential part of Phelips' power, and in 1626 exclusion from the Commission of the Peace produced a brief but zealous exhibition of conformity. On the other hand, power in the county also depended on the support of the county community, the gentlemen and yeomen who could make or unmake knights of the shire, the community whose support gave him his claim to be heard by the Crown. If he was to retain the confidence of these people, Phelips would have to resist royal claims to taxation, and protest vigorously at those workings of the royal administration which caused resentment in the county. The unfortunate Sir Robert Phelips was in the position of a man trying to ride two horses whose paths were likely to diverge. Whenever his type of career became impossible, civil war would be hard to avoid. As yet, however, his opposition was not so irreversible that it would have been impossible for him to use his immense capacity for hard work as a member of the Privy Council. Other equally obstreperous members made the transition to government service, such as Noy and Hakewill the lawyers, and Wentworth, later Earl of Strafford.

Phelips spent much of his time in 1621 attacking the import of Irish cattle into Somerset, and diaries of the Commons' proceedings show that much of their time was not spent on great matters of state, but on the reform of small administrative or legal abuses which had not been or could not be reformed by prerogative. The king had offered a number of bills of grace which met this mood, but the House also produced numerous others. They tried to revive the cloth industry by bills against the wearing of silk and other expensive materials by those who were not gentlemen, and members for the provincial ports tried to persuade the House that the depression would be best met by rescinding the trading privileges of the London-based Merchant Adventurers. They also involved themselves in such questions as the making of sub-standard salt, the abolition of trial by battle, repair of roads, and preventing brewers from being Justices of the Peace.

They voted two subsidies early in the session, and then concentrated on grievances. They introduced some bills on religious subjects, such as keeping the sabbath, punishment of drunkenness and swearing, and the repression of Catholic recusants, but in all they spent less time on religion than any other Parliament of the century. In this lack of involvement in religious grievances, it is perhaps possible to see the effect of ten years of

Abbot's administration of the church. Two general themes recur constantly among their grievances. One is an onslaught on increases in official fees, in which they showed themselves quite indifferent to the case Bacon had put against a similar onslaught in 1606, that gentlemen had raised their rents, and merchants their prices, and it was unreasonable if only officials could not increase their fees. The other constant theme is resentment at the granting, and even more at the enforcement, of monopolies. In chasing these grievances the House showed an increasing willingness to act in an executive and judicial capacity, calling people before them for questioning, and issuing executive orders—in short, assuming much the same sort of authority as most of them enjoyed in their own counties as members of the Bench. In questioning monopolies, they took this authority a stage further, by bringing some of the offenders to a formal trial.

Among the monopolies they attacked, two led to particular dispute. These were a monopoly for the manufacture of gold and silver thread, which involved extortion from workmen, and appeared to affect the supply of bullion, and a monopoly of the always sensitive subject of licensing of inns and alehouses. Apart from extortion, and the opportunity for corruption involved, there was also legal doubt about the authority by which the monopolists had fined infringers of their monopoly, calling the body which did so a 'court'. The Commons' investigations led them to Sir Giles Mompesson, a remote kinsman of Buckingham. Behind Mompesson, as the House knew, were two of Buckingham's brothers who drew much of the profit from the monopoly. Buckingham appears to have decided that it was wise to refrain from obstructing the investigation, and the House refrained from pressing the charge against his brothers. The House of Commons were told by Hakewill, the veteran of 1610, that he could find no precedents for the House trying a man for an offence committed out of Parliament which was not directly against the House, so they decided to call in the Lords to condemn Mompesson. These debates did much to encourage the steadily growing antiquarian and historical interest current among gentlemen of the time, and Sir Robert Cotton, owner of the best historical library available, found his services widely in request.

The reference of Mompesson's case to the Lords was the first step towards the revival of the procedure known as impeachment, whereby the Commons acted as prosecutors, and the Lords as judges. In this, as in a number of other cases, the Commons had cited many of their medieval precedents correctly. Their objectivity was not always unquestionable, but since there genuinely had been a time when Parliament had been much more important than it was in the early seventeenth century, the precedents were usually there to be found. Mompesson was disgraced, fined, banished from court, made incapable of giving evidence in a lawsuit, and given other miscellaneous punishments.

Having condemned Mompesson, the Commons found themselves in a difficult situation. They wanted to condemn the making of the grant to Mompesson, as well as its execution. They could not attack the king, but they hoped to attack some of the king's servants who had helped to pass the grant. But what were they to do if the men concerned pleaded that there was no law against giving the king bad advice, or, more serious, that they had merely obeyed the king's command? The king could do no wrong: this was a legal maxim too firmly established to be questioned: but did this mean that if the king gave a wrong command, his servant was punished for obeying him? There were some medieval precedents to suggest that it did. Coke seems to have been ready to grasp this nettle, using divine right theory to support him. He said that: 'every grant against the liberty of the subject is void . . . for the king is lieutenant of God, and as God cannot do wrong neither in law can the king.'[14] James, however, had the power of dissolution, and would not allow the Commons to enter on this ground. It was in a sense fortunate for the Commons that at this stage one of their members made a complaint against one of the referees, Lord Chancellor Bacon, that he had taken a bribe, from himself, and had not acted on it. If Bacon had taken bribes in lawsuits, this was an act the king had not commanded him to perform, and an offence which could be tried without raising dangerous political issues. Lord Chancellor Bacon was therefore impeached for corruption, decided not to risk defending himself before the Lords, and was fined and degraded from his office. The Lords and Commons had recovered their power, not used since the fifteenth century, to remove those of the king's ministers who did not command their confidence. Since 'corruption' could be alleged against any minister out of favour, they could count on being able to exercise this power on any occasion when the king chose not to dissolve them. When the king finally did dissolve the 1621 Parliament, it was not over impeachments, but over their attempt, in the second session, to fill an obvious void by debating foreign policy on the prompting of Buckingham. James told them they had no right to debate foreign policy, and though one member quoted the precedent of 1587, James was adamant, and dissolved the House, which had still only voted its initial two subsidies. This Parliament is an interesting interlude in the story. It showed none of the constitutional

---

[14] Roberts, Clayton, *The Growth of Responsible Government in Stuart England* (1966), 35.

See also Judson, M. A., *The Crisis of the Constitution* (1949), 22. This book is by far the best general account of constitutional ideas in the early seventeenth century.

panic, that the king might abolish Parliament, which was current in 1610 or in 1629. It showed no sign of attempting to overturn the constitution itself: after all, there could not be parliamentary government until a majority of members were willing and able to live most of the year in London. On the other hand, it clearly intended to reform what it thought amiss in the administration without reference to the government's wishes, if any.

The trip to Madrid, 1623

James followed the end of the session by imprisoning a number of unco-operative members, unwisely including in the number John Pym, an obscure new member whose apparent martyrdom may have helped towards his nomination to the Committee of Privileges in the next Parliament, and his rise to eventual primacy in the House. After the dissolution, the Spanish dowry appeared a more tempting prospect than ever, and negotiations continued, though at a slow pace, since the Spaniards' main object was to keep James out of the war as long as possible. Finally Charles, Prince of Wales, whose imagination appears to have been captured by dreams of his hypothetical beloved, grew impatient, and he and Buckingham set out on one of the most madcap of political adventures— the trip to Madrid in 1623. This, apart from being an undignified escapade (complete with false beards) and a gross breach of diplomatic protocol, was also dangerous. It involved riding across France in disguise, giving a golden opportunity to anyone interested in holding the Prince of Wales to ransom, and offered the Spaniards what might have become an opportunity to dictate terms. It also created numerous rumours, both in England and in Spain, that Charles meant to announce his conversion to Rome. Perhaps the greatest importance of the trip to Madrid, however, is that it seems to mark the moment at which Buckingham began to swap horses, and to become the favourite of the Prince of Wales instead of the king. For Buckingham, the trip to Madrid provided the two achievements of attaching Charles to himself, and of preventing him from marrying a wife who might have become Buckingham's rival.

In 1623 Charles, Prince of Wales, was almost an unknown quantity. He was twenty-three, but all his childhood he had been overshadowed by his elder brother and sister, both adventurous people of great spirit. He had had a serious speech impediment, and appears to have felt a fastidious distaste for the standards of his father's court, leading a remarkably isolated existence. At Madrid, for the first time, he thought he was free and independent, doing what he chose, and from this time onwards, Buckingham's hold over the son was as strong as over the father. The fact that the trip to Madrid was a fiasco appears not to have affected this point. The Spaniards, though infinitely courteous, would make no commitment, and when Charles finally climbed a garden wall in the evening in order to behold his beloved, they were dismayed. The only practical achievement of the trip was that the cost to the Spaniards finally defeated an economy campaign which was in progress at the Spanish court. After much confusion, Charles and Buckingham returned to England bitterly offended with the Spaniards. Charles's return, alive, a Protestant, and a bachelor, was greeted with massive rejoicings involving 108 bonfires between St. Paul's and London Bridge.

The Parliament of 1624

Since Buckingham now shared Parliament's attitude to Spain, he could attempt a reconciliation with it. A Parliament was summoned for 1624, in order to vote supplies for a war with Spain. Cranfield, now Lord Treasurer, was dismayed by the probable cost of war, and offered Buckingham gloomy figures about the debts. More rashly, he tried to groom his cousin as a homosexual favourite who might replace Buckingham. In return, he was offered to the Commons, where he had many enemies, for impeachment as proof of Buckingham's desire to make friends with them. James observed that all good treasurers were unpopular, but did nothing to discourage the prosecution. Cranfield was tried (again mainly for corruption), convicted, degraded, fined, and made to make over his favourite house at Chelsea to Buckingham. This Parliament also achieved some reforming legislation. Informers were at last excluded from the courts at Westminster, and left to practice only where the opinion of their neighbours could be used to check their activities. The rate of interest was lowered to 8 per cent: a measure favourable to debtors, including both the king and many members. An Act was passed to declare monopolies illegal. Unfortunately, monopolists could evade this Act by turning themselves into corporations. There were, however, some tensions even in this Parliament. Some M.P.s wanted a sea war, and were unhappy about plans for a land war. There was some distrust about whether Buckingham and Charles really intended to go to war with Spain. There was also some tension about the subsidy. The government chose to ask for the necessary, but unprecedented, sum of six subsidies. Even some of its own Councillors warned them that they could not get so much, because 'the sound indeed of six subsidies is fearful'. The sum produced the expected reaction. One member said that the queen had only asked for two subsidies in 1588, and that ought to be enough. Another, again using divine right imagery against the king, said: 'he would have us follow his Majesty, as Peter followed Christ, afar off.'[15] Finally, the government accepted the advice of those Councillors who urged them to ask only for three subsidies, and they got this sum, which, though generous from the Commons' point of view, was inadequate from the government's. Even then, the subsidies were to be spent only on the war, and to be administered by a committee chosen by the Commons. Perhaps the most ominous dispute was the revival of serious religious grievances, over a book written by Montague, which had been allowed to pass the censorship, and challenged a number of crucial points of current Protestant theology.[16] Pym, among other members, at once saw the significance of this issue, and started the Commons' attacks on Arminianism. The issue was new to many members, and one thought Montague had been accused of Arianism. Such blissful ignorance would not last long; Archbishop Abbot had fallen out of favour, and the period of religious peace over which he had presided was over.

II BUCKINGHAM AND CHARLES, 1625–1629

The state is inclining to a consumption, yet not incurable.
Sir Edward Coke, M.P., 1628

This is the crisis of Parliaments; we shall know by this if Parliaments live or die. . . . Men and brethren, what shall we do? Is there no balm in Gilead? If the king draw one way, the Parliament another, we must all sink.
Sir Benjamin Rudyerd, M.P., 1628[17]

King Charles I succeeded his father in March 1625, as the centre for almost as many contradictory aspirations as his father had been in 1603. The Arminian clergy had been more securely in James's favour for the last year of his life than they had ever been before, but with Charles they could hope for a constancy of favour which they had never obtained from his father. Parliamentary Puritans, on the other hand, now had a king who, as Rudyerd said, was 'bred in Parliaments', and who might be better able to trust their good intentions than his father had been. As Rudyerd said, 'the disagreement betwixt the king (who is with God) and his people begun and continued by mutual distrusts in Parliament have been the cause of almost all that we can call amiss in this state'.[18] Perhaps, if the distrust had been largely personal, a new king might remove it. For those who wanted a forward foreign policy, Charles inherited the throne already committed to war, and with a mercenary army already on its way towards the Palatinate. The army was a mangy crew, and never got further than the

[15] Willson, *Privy Councillors*, 280–1.
[16] On the theological issues involved in this case, see above, pp. 210–17.
[17] Rushworth, I. 501.   [18] Gardiner, *1625*, 9, 10.

Dutch coast, but at least it was a start. On the other hand, those who hoped for favour to Catholics might take comfort from the fact that, after his breach with Spain, Charles inherited the throne committed to a French marriage, and though the terms were secret, it might be suspected that they included some concessions to Catholics. His wife, Henrietta Maria, had little importance during Buckingham's lifetime, but after the death of her rival she became the second person ever to win Charles's friendship. She was lively, amusing, and gay, but unfortunately she had a poor head for politics, and did not know it. It was perhaps even more unfortunate that she was a devout Catholic, and when, after Buckingham's death, she began to bear Charles sons, fears were expressed about her influence on them. In 1633 a Northamptonshire clergyman was brought to trial for praying 'that the prince be not brought up in popery, whereof there is great cause to fear'.[19] The reign of James II shows that his fears were not misplaced. The opening of Charles's reign was also marked by the worst attack of the plague in the first half of the century, which caused 35,000 deaths in London, closed Bartholomew and Stourbridge fairs, ended the law term, and made many foreign ports refuse to receive English ships. Apart from the general dislocation, the plague was serious both for its effect on customs revenue and because such attacks were normally interpreted as signs of divine displeasure. In these circumstances, Charles was faced with the usual strains of war finance: £360,000 as a subsidy to the king of Denmark, £240,000 to Mansfeld's mercenaries, and £100,000 to the troops in the Low Countries.

The Parliament of 1625

In these circumstances, the opening Parliament of the reign was of more than usual importance. It voted two subsidies, which was generous enough by Elizabethan standards, but pitifully inadequate in 1625, and showed some dismay at being told this was not enough. In other issues, it proved less helpful. One of the duties of the first Parliament of a reign was, so the king thought, to vote him Tonnage and Poundage (the main body of the customs dues) for life. Since the fifteenth century, every king had been voted Tonnage and Poundage for life, and Charles regarded it as Parliament's duty to vote it to him. Many M.P.s, however, were still alarmed about impositions, and felt it as urgent as ever to assert that customs revenue was under parliamentary control. They therefore voted Charles Tonnage and Poundage for one year only. The members involved in this move included Coke, Phelips, and Rolle, a London merchant conspicuous in the resistance to arbitrary customs dues. It was an unwise move, since,

[19] Gardiner, *History*, x. 225.

when the year expired without any settlement, the king was inevitably provoked into collecting Tonnage and Poundage without parliamentary authority, and therefore had to assert his right to do so. Since his biggest single item of revenue was at stake, he had no choice. It was almost inevitable that the king's ministers were provoked into making threats that the king might, if enough provoked, do without Parliament. It was easy to cast envious eyes across the Channel at monarchies which were not so hamstrung, and to threaten Parliament with the adoption of continental practice in England. In reply, the Commons dug in their heels: Phelips claimed that 'we are the last monarchy in Christendom that yet retain our ancient rights and liberties'.[20] Members of the Commons were showing an increasing willingness to question the king's choice of counsellors, and Phelips' precedent of the impeachment of the Duke of Suffolk for acquiring undue influence over the king in Henry VI's reign aimed uncomfortably closely at the Duke of Buckingham. Sir Robert Cotton the antiquary supplied members with a set of precedents for parliamentary choice of the king's counsellors, but they did not quote them, confining themselves to asking the king to choose a good Council, and to listen to it. They conducted an inquest into the spending of the subsidy they had appropriated to the war in the previous Parliament, and a committee under Pym and Sandys produced a thorough scheme for the reform of the old grievance of impropriations. Needless to say, no reform resulted: many laymen were unwilling to reform impropriations, and neither Puritans nor bishops were prepared to reform them in order to allow patronage to fall into the hands of the other side. By 1625, the words 'the other side' were becoming ominously applicable in religion: Buckingham was now relying chiefly for his religious advice on William Laud, Bishop of Bath and Wells, and other Arminian clergy. The dispute between Puritans and Arminians was on a different scale from the dispute between Puritans and bishops like Whitgift: the losers would be branded, not merely as schismatics, but as heretics, and the Puritans were certain that it was the Arminians, and not they, who were heretical. The stakes were high when this dispute was again fought out over the issue of Montague, who had defended his position in another book. There was unlikely to be room in the Church of England for the losers, and neither side believed there was room for any church in England except the Church of England. The Commons' case against Montague was presented with great theological skill by Pym, and supported by Archbishop Abbot. The Commons seemed to be making progress when Charles announced that he had made Montague one of his chaplains, and commanded them to leave the case alone. They did not do

[20] Faith Thompson, *Magna Carta,* 320.

so, but if they were doing battle with the king himself, the prospects were gloomy. The Parliament was dissolved for its attack on Buckingham, and a Forced Loan was raised. Whatever members may have felt, they still helped to work the machinery of local government, and Sir Walter Earle, one of the members responsible for limiting the vote of Tonnage and Poundage to one year, and later conspicuous for his resistance to Forced Loans, acted as a commissioner for collection of the loan in his home county.[21] It is part of the politics of the early Stuart period that the Crown's opponents at Westminster were also, as an essential part of their social status, its devoted servants in their own districts. Again, perhaps, it is relevant to compare a seventeenth-century Parliament to a modern party conference, rather than to a modern Parliament.

The Parliament of 1626: the attack on Buckingham

Charles was then forced to maintain his war by borrowing on the security of the Crown jewels, but since the Dutch, from whom he was raising the money, doubted whether he could part with the Crown jewels without the authority of Parliament, he had to use Buckingham's jewels as collateral security. Even so, the fleet which was sent out against Cadiz in the autumn included one ship with sails which had seen service against the Armada. The commander then landed the troops and the wine in one place, and the food in another, and the fleet returned in a bedraggled and inglorious state. In 1626, when the king again met Parliament, at the time-limit of the previous vote of Tonnage and Poundage, the tension was higher than in the previous Parliament. The Venetian Ambassador reported that 'in order to fortify the king's authority, they speak of bringing the troops from the fleet to the Tower and its neighbourhood. This would be a very violent innovation, very ill-adapted to the humour of the country.'[22]

In turn, many of the parliamentary leaders seem to have been determined to attack the Duke of Buckingham. It may or may not be a coincidence that their determination to attack him begins at the same time as his conversion to the support of Arminianism began to be generally appreciated. Certainly the Commons were becoming more and more deeply involved in the case of Montague, and feeling that their case needed to reach a wider public. Sir Nathaniel Rich, a relation and political ally of the Earl of Warwick, suggested that when Pym put the case to the Lords he should do so at the Lords' bar and not at a conference, in order to achieve greater publicity. In these atttacks on Montague, Pym felt that he

[21] P.R.O. Exchequer 401/2586, 274.
[22] Willson, *Privy Councillors*, 50.

spoke as defender of the orthodox Church of England. He was defending the same doctrine which his stepfather and his tutor had taught him in his youth, and he was doing so out of the Thirty-Nine Articles, the *Homilies* and the works of James I, all of which he believed contradicted Montague's doctrine. He thought that Montague's doctrine tended to sedition, by setting the king against the people, and the people against each other: in short, that there was not room for two religions in one State. He also felt, as to some extent Montague did himself, that Montague's book removed many of the distinguishing marks between England and Rome. Under Pym's leadership, the Commons' Grand Committee on religion was attempting to search out recusants, and in the process developing powers very much like those of a modern American Senate Committee. He claimed the power to search recent government records, in order to detect pardons to priests, and conducted an inquisition into Catholic schoolmasters up and down the country. His importance in the House, and that of others among the less experienced members, was increased by the fact that Charles, who always believed that the agitation in his Parliaments was the work of a few subversive activists, had attempted to exclude a number of the senior opposition leaders by pricking them as sheriffs, who, being returning officers, could not legally be returned to Parliament. He was successful in every case except that of Coke, who, typically, appeared at Westminster bearing a sheaf of precedents to show that a sheriff could be a member.[23]

The new leaders who replaced the sheriffs were not very different from the old ones. Pym was purposeful, and Rudyerd, a political ally of the Earl of Pembroke, though he was anxious for an accommodation, shared his patron's distrust of Buckingham, and Savile said: 'no man will be willing to give his money into a bottomless gulf'. In spite of these fears, the House passed a vote of four subsidies, but left the subsidy bill in committee while they proceeded to an attempt to impeach Buckingham. In so far as they had leaders in doing so, they were Sir Dudley Digges and Sir John Eliot, a fiery speaker from Cornwall, who had been Buckingham's protégé until very recently, but said that he had been disgusted by the effects of Buckingham's incompetence, particularly on the navy. The articles of impeachment accused Buckingham of engrossing offices, of corruption, and of wasting the king's estate. Charles could not abandon his favourite, and he dissolved Parliament, giving up hope of the four subsidies which were still in the pipeline.

---

[23] *C.J.*, I. 817, 825. The House was dissolved before it had decided whether to allow Coke to take his seat.

War finance: the Forced Loan and the Five Knights

Shortly after the breach with Parliament, Buckingham's diplomacy led England into a war with France, based largely on a dispute about the rights of neutral ships to carry enemy goods, and fanned by Buckingham's vanity about English sovereignty of the seas. Thus, for the only time in two centuries, England was faced with the nightmare of war with Spain and France at once, with the hostility of both the major continental powers, either of which England would have found it difficult to fight alone. There can be no more striking example of Buckingham's diplomatic incompetence. The war did, however, help Buckingham by straining relations between Charles and his French wife, who might have been a powerful rival for the king's affection. Fortunately, however, Spain and France both had too many other difficulties to take the hostility of England as seriously as they might have done. The Spaniards landed and burned houses on the Cornish coast, but that was the worst fate England had to suffer. Buckingham's expedition, in 1627, to Rhé, to help the French Huguenots against the French Crown, was a fiasco on an even grander scale than the Cadiz expedition of 1625.

During this period the king was spending about £103,000 a year on the navy, and the results suggested that it was doubtful whether he was getting value for money. The war also imposed strains on the militia. Since 1624, the government had been planning to organize what it called an 'exact militia', and in 1626, in addition to preparation to meet an invasion scare unprecedented since the last Spanish war, the counties also had to raise the money to pay professional sergeants who were sent to train the militia. Cheshire, which helped the sergeants, spent £4,000 out of military rates on training under them, but other counties were more obstructive. Since 1613 the legal questionings which had been applied to civilian taxation were coming to be applied to military taxation as well. The 1628 Parliament, not wanting to be obstructive on the point, thought of passing a bill to give the militia a secure legal basis, but defaulters were not so eager to clarify the law. Troops also had to be billeted while waiting for shipment abroad, or simply waiting, and here again the legal basis for compulsory billeting was dubious. The billeting could be a real strain. In Sussex, there was little trouble, but in the Isle of Wight many of the troops were unpaid, and the Privy Council decided it was safe to leave them unpaid for a little longer, since they were too naked to be seen marching in public. Some of them were Highlanders, and aroused the racial feelings of some of the inhabitants, who thought they were 'as barbarous in nature as their clothes'. They rioted from time to time, and when they left the

Isle of Wight the troops left behind them seventy known bastards. Those who had had troops billeted on them were supposed to be paid a billeting rate of 3s. 6d. a week, but in 1635 half the money owing to the Isle of Wight was still unpaid. One of the Deputy Lieutenants commented that they should oppose future attempts at billeting at the risk of their lives.[24]

All these military preparations cost money. Many of Charles's regular lenders came to help, and Burlamachi, the greatest of them, lent £70,000, although, as Charles said, 'we have no constant or apparent means to give satisfaction'.[25] In 1633, Burlamachi finally went bankrupt. An enormous amount of Crown land was made over for sale to the City of London in return for debts of £349,000, some of them dating from 1617. Other loans were repaid by raising new ones. But somehow a tax had to be raised from the king's subjects, and Charles set out to raise a Forced Loan equivalent to five subsidies.* Laud wrote to the local clergy instructing them to preach in favour of the loan, and two, Sibthorp and Manwaring, replied with such enthusiasm as to suggest that taxes, by whatever authority they were imposed, were due to the king by divine right. Manwaring also suggested such extravagances as that kings participated in God's omnipotence, and that there could be no justice between king and subjects because they were too unequal. Abbot was shocked by these effusions: he refused to licence Sibthorp's sermon for printing, and later told Manwaring that his divinity was largely wrong. However, the sermons were printed in spite of the Archbishop's opposition. A number of various M.P.s, however, refused to pay the loan. Sir Thomas Wentworth, later Earl of Strafford, joined the number of those imprisoned for refusal, together with John Hampden's uncle and a number of others. It was at this stage that the word 'patriot', which was coming into regular use in many countries, became in England the property of the opposition.

Some of those who were imprisoned decided to test the legality of their imprisonment, by suing a Habeas Corpus. The object of this Habeas Corpus was not to test the legality of the loan, but to obtain release on bail pending a trial at which the legality of the loan might be tested. The return to the Habeas Corpus was that they were imprisoned 'by the king's special command', and the issue which was brought to trial in the Five Knights' case was not the forced loan, but whether the king's special command was a sufficient justification for the imprisonment. The issues were

[24] Boynton, *The Elizabethan Militia,* 244 ff., and 'Billeting: The Example of the Isle of Wight', *E.H.R.* (1959), 23–40. I would like to thank Mr. Anthony Fletcher for information about Sussex.

[25] Ashton, 41. * Charles also revived the practice, unused since 1563, of making collectors and taxpayers take an oath to the accuracy of their valuation. Birmingham Reference Library, Coventry MSS, Commissions for the loan of money, 1.

the typical ones of an early Stuart constitutional lawsuit. It was argued for the Five Knights that if the king could imprison one man by his 'special command', then he could so imprison anyone he chose, and that, as they charitably put it, under some other less trustworthy king, this power might be dangerous. Therefore, they argued, the king's power must be limited in all cases by certain and known rules of law, and as Magna Carta said, he could only imprison by the law of the land. Attorney General Heath, for the Crown, argued that the king had to be able to imprison before he could bring a formal accusation in some political cases: after all, there had at first been no other justification for imprisoning the Gunpowder Plotters. On the argument that because the king could do it in one case, he might do it in all cases, he argued that a certain modicum of trust was necessary to the running of the government. After all, he pointed out, because the king could pardon a traitor or a felon, legally he might pardon them all: 'but shall any say, the king cannot do this? No, we may only say, he will not do this.' The real point of the case, which could not be argued in law, was that an emergency power designed to deal with conspirators or potential rebels was being used against respectable citizens, who did not like it. The judges, however, could only go by the precedents, which said that there had been many previous cases of imprisonment by the king's special command, and they found for the king. As the judges said, if they were given no reason for the imprisonment, 'it is to be presumed to be for matters of state, which we cannot take notice of'.[26] Judges could not try politics, nor could they prescribe remedies for the lack of trust between the government and so many of its subjects.

At the same time, Charles was rapidly bringing the Arminians to supreme power in the church. Laud had probably already been promised Canterbury, and his friends on the episcopal bench were promoted, and even Montague was given a bishopric. Non-Arminian bishops were left off episcopal committees and excluded from crucial decisions. Already some Arminian writers were beginning to branch out from their basic points of pure theology to defend a highly ceremonial, ordered religion. Dr. Cosin, archdeacon of Durham, published a book of *Devotions* involving set hours of prayer, and a thoroughly ritualistic approach to religion. Prynne replied to it with a book called *Dr. Cosins his Cozening Devotions*, but already opponents of Arminianism, and of the high-flown ceremony which often went with it, were beginning to find it hard to pass the censorship. It was in these unpropitious circumstances that Charles once again tried to meet Parliament.

[26] *Stuart Constitution*, 109.

The Parliament of 1628–1629

The Parliament of 1628 was more suspicious of the Crown's intentions than its predecessors. Its members were in a constant state of alarm about the possibility that the king might put an end to all parliamentary institutions. This alarm was not eased by rumours that the Council had resolved that if Parliament did not vote taxes, the king would be justified in imposing them on his own authority, and using a force of foreign mercenaries to collect them. The Commons, like several of its recent predecessors, began by petitioning for a public fast in humiliation for sins which made 'a wall of separation between God and us'. The choice of Laud to preach the opening sermon is not likely to have eased their fears that the country's religion was about to be altered, and a fast, apart from its theological uses, might also be an occasion for a show of solidarity. They also set about attacking arbitrary imprisonment, arbitrary taxation, billeting, and martial law. The military grievances were obvious to all who had recent experience of soldiers, and the other two were designed to prevent repetition of the Forced Loan and the Five Knights' case. Under the surface, distrust of Buckingham was as powerful as ever, though before the session the parliamentary leaders may have agreed not to attack Buckingham, as the price of being allowed to remain in session. The moving spirits in the Commons were mostly familiar: Coke, Phelips, Eliot, Seymour, Rudyerd, Pym. One man was more prominent than he had been before: Sir Thomas Wentworth, later the king's servant and Earl of Strafford. He was particularly heated about the billeting of soldiers on subjects who opposed the government. It was he also who was responsible for getting a vote of five subsidies, a substantial sum, passed through the House, and held up in committee while the House proceeded with its grievances. On these, they appear to have found considerable sympathy among the Lords. The four main grievances—arbitrary imprisonment, arbitrary taxation, billeting, and martial law—were finally presented to Charles in the form of a Petition of Right, tying him to settled rules of law in all these subjects. Charles was at last induced to give his assent to it. He subsequently maintained, however, both that it was a private petition and did not bind him, and that since it only asked for confirmation of existing law, it did not bind him to abandon practices which were permitted by existing law. At the time, however, the Commons trusted the Petition of Right as securing for them what they asked. The five subsidies were reported from committee, and Charles was able to raise loans while he waited for them to come in.

Having received his five subsidies, Charles decided to hold another session of this Parliament in 1629. Before it met, the situation had been transformed: Buckingham was murdered by an embittered soldier aggrieved by the mismanagement of his last expedition. Charles, having lost his only friend, had to listen to his subjects noisily rejoicing outside his windows. This event perhaps did more to produce a coldness between Charles and his subjects than any other. Politically, the most disastrous consequence of Buckingham's assassination was that Charles fell in love with his wife, whose political ideas were much more purposeful than Buckingham's, and from the parliamentary point of view, more dangerous. The immediate result, however, was that Charles took two of the Commons' leaders, Wentworth and Noy, into his service. As usual, Charles did not take on new advisers with any intention of changing his policy, but simply in order to win more men to the support of existing policies. For Wentworth, no sacrifice of principle was involved in taking office. His chief devotion was to unity between Crown and Parliament, and his chief grievance was Buckingham. With Buckingham dead, a servant of the Crown might promote unity and good government.

On the other hand, Wandesford, his political ally, was still prominent in the Commons' attacks on what old Sir Miles Fleetwood, Receiver of the Wards, called 'Arminian sectaries'. Wandesford complained of pardons to Sibthorp and Manwaring, and to Cosin, a theological Arminian, who had been attacked by the Commons, and said: 'this grieves us, when his majesty's grace goes so swiftly to these malignant persons, and so slowly towards his best subjects, who have as good an interest.' Old Sir Robert Phelips, sitting in his last Parliament, complained of the rapidly widening scope of the term 'Puritan': 'to be an honest man is now to be a Puritan.'[27] For the first time since the 1580s, the Commons in this session were as preoccupied with religion as with money, and Pym was collecting a steadily growing list of official and semi-official formularies of faith which contradicted Arminian doctrine. For Pym, unlike Wentworth, it was impossible, on grounds of principle, to take office under an Arminian government. In the next eleven years, as men realized the implications of the religious change which was taking place, he was to be joined by many others.

Members in this session also had a major financial grievance: the collection of Tonnage and Poundage dues, which still had not been voted by Parliament, and the imprisonment of merchants who refused to pay them. From this time on, Charles's attempts to discover sources of finance independent of Parliament were closely linked in many members' minds with his attempts to change the country's religion. If he were introducing Arminianism, he would get no supply from Parliament, so he would have

[27] *Commons' Debates for 1629*, Ed. Notestein, W., and Relf, F. H. (1921), 176–8.

to find independent sources of finance. If he were altering the religion by law established, he would have to emancipate himself from the control of law, and therefore of Parliament. If he were protecting a faction which might expect to be imprisoned by Parliament, they might be expected to advise him against calling Parliament. Moreover, it was axiomatic for most members that a legal, constitutional rule was only possible between people who shared the same common assumptions : it was not possible to exercise constitutional government over those who could expect to be objects of religious persecution. If a time was coming when most leaders of the Commons could expect to be objects of religious persecution, Charles would have to find arbitrary methods of ruling which did not leave him dependent on Parliament. Thus fears about Arminianism and about un-parliamentary taxation continually reacted on each other, and were built up into a picture in which both the country's religion and its government were thought likely to be altered to something most members would find intolerable. When Prynne later maintained that Ship Money was wanted for setting up idolatry, he was doing no more than parody widely current fears.[28]

Charles soon tired of the House in this mood and resolved to adjourn it. Some of the more hot-headed members chose the occasion of the adjournment for a demonstration. Eliot was deeply involved in it, and the moving spirits also included two who were to be among the Five Members thirteen years later, William Strode, a minor gentleman from Somerset,[29] and Denzil Holles, son of a disappointed office-seeker, and the sort of moderate Puritan for whom office was rapidly becoming impossible. When the Speaker tried to rise, he found that the seats next to the chair, which should have belonged to Privy Councillors, had been occupied by Holles and one of his friends, who told him to sit until they had passed three resolutions, condemning Arminianism and Tonnage and Poundage not voted by Parliament. When he tried to say that the king had commanded him to rise, he was told that the House had the right to decide for itself when it would adjourn. Holles, exclaiming, 'zounds, you shall sit as long as the House pleases' led a group of members in forcibly holding the Speaker in his chair while the resolutions were read and carried.[30] These riotous scenes, in which the abler politicians among the parliamentary

[28] Prynne, W., *Hidden Workes of Darkenes* (1645), 196.

[29] Strode, though a member of the Somerset Commission of Sewers, never became a J.P.

[30] This demonstration was undoubtedly prearranged. See I. H. C. Fraser, 'The Agitation in the Commons, March 1629', *B.I.H.R.* (1957), 86–95. The question at issue, whether the Speaker could rise without the consent of the House, had been raised prophetically by Peter Wentworth in 1587. Neale, *Parliaments,* ii. 155.

leaders took no part, did much to lower the reputation of Parliament, and were still being quoted against it eight years later by so sympathetic a critic as Justice Hutton in the Ship Money trial. They may have played a crucial part in leading Charles to decide that he would have enough support to be able to make members' fears come true, and do without Parliament. He dissolved the Parliament, and justified his proceedings in a long declaration, claiming that the object of the parliamentary leaders was 'that all things may be overwhelmed with anarchy and confusion'.[31] The leaders of the tumult were tried and imprisoned, and when Eliot died in the Tower, Charles even refused to release his body for burial. Charles did not meet Parliament again until he was in a state of desperation.

III RULE WITHOUT PARLIAMENT, 1629–1640

The most serene, quiet and halcyon days that could possibly be imagined.
                                    Lord Falkland, M.P., 1641[32]

It might have been thought that the death of Buckingham would have reconciled many of the Crown's critics, particularly since it was followed by a period of government more efficient than any since the death of Robert Cecil. For many, this was the case. Two of the managers of Buckingham's impeachment later accepted office under the Crown. For many others, on the other hand, efficiency was not enough, since they distrusted the purposes for which efficiency was exercised. For them, efficiency could mean the transformation of irritation at the government's activities into fear. Only one among Charles's advisers was a man who commanded much confidence in the parliamentary leaders: the Earl of Pembroke. Unfortunately, the fourth Earl of Pembroke, who succeeded his brother in 1630, was much less able than his predecessor, and his usefulness to the government was limited by a long running feud with Laud. Sir John Coke, the aged Secretary of State, was another who might have been trusted. He was firmly anti-Arminian, and, as Clarendon put it, 'loved the church well enough as it was twenty years before'.[33] He, however, was one of those government servants who do much of the work, but form little of the policy. Among the bishops, two, Laud and Neile, had been named by the Commons in 1628 as being untrustworthy for Arminianism, and it was these two whom Charles raised, first to the Privy Council, and then to the Archbishoprics of Canterbury and York. Perhaps

[31] Rushworth, I. Appendix, 10.
[32] Rushworth, III. i. 86.
[33] Clarendon, *History of the Rebellion*, i. 122.

the gravest point of suspicion, for many parliamentarians, was the number of Catholics or crypto-Catholics in the king's confidence. The Earl of Arundel, who shared with Charles a common enthusiasm for art, was in his confidence for much of the 1630s. For Arundel, as for most of the Howards, it is hard to pronounce with confidence on his attitude to Catholicism, but in 1641, when an official looking for recusants called at Arundel's town house off the Strand, his doorman threatened to assault the official if he presented anyone in that house as a recusant.[34] Arundel was alarmed enough by this incident to waive all claim of parliamentary privilege on behalf of his doorman when the case came to be investigated. Lord Treasurer Weston, a man who demonstrated that efficiency and corruption were compatible, had been denounced as a Catholic by Sir John Eliot in 1629. Though Eliot could not have known it, he was right: Weston announced his Catholicism on his deathbed. Cottington, Chancellor of the Exchequer and later Master of the Wards, was said to have announced that he was a Catholic when he was ill, and reverted to Protestantism on his recovery. Cottington is perhaps the most underrated man of Charles I's unparliamentary government: he has commonly been seen through the eyes of Laud and Wentworth, who detested him for his habit of pulling their legs, among other failings. Cottington was certainly a cynic, but the work he did for the government was well done, and he did as much to increase the king's income as any of them.[35] In fact, Charles enforced recusancy fines on Catholics with more strictness than James, but this little knot of Catholics, aided as they were by the queen, did nothing to ease the fears of those who already thought he intended to change the country's religion. In fact, though the public did not know it, the main enemy of these Catholics at court was Laud, who thereby incurred the bitter dislike of the queen. When, in 1636, Charles caused dismay by accepting a resident papal agent at court, it was Laud who protested in the Council against the wave of conversions which followed. The agent himself, reporting that he could buy the Council to Rome for 20,000 crowns, excepted only Laud. Though Charles gave Laud consistent support in the management of the church of England, in other issues he trusted him less than is often supposed. Wentworth, even more than Laud, never gained the control over policy which many people credited him with possessing. He formed a working alliance with Laud, but he made few other friends at court. He realized his life's ambition by being sent to govern Yorkshire as Lord President of the North, and thereafter was sent

[34] *Journal of Sir Symonds D'Ewes*, Ed. Notestein (1923), i. 133, 137.
[35] The story of his Catholicism is disputed in Martin J. Havran, *Cardine Courtier: The Life of Lord Cottington* (1973).

to try his abilities (and his temper) in governing the Irish. Wentworth was still a believer in unity between king and Parliament, but his impatience could sometimes make him appear more despotic in inclination than he was. On one occasion, after dissolving an Irish Parliament, he threatened to pass every Act they had rejected by proclamation: 'it being necessary that these people should see that his Majesty will without more ado be obeyed.'[36] Wentworth had a knack for getting things done, and a knack for making enemies and for making a personal fortune, but not for winning the confidence of Charles.

For a while, this government was tried by issues left over from the 1620s. Richard Chambers, a London merchant, was called before the Council for refusing to pay Tonnage and Poundage, and exclaimed: 'the merchants are in no part of the world so screwed and wrung as in England: in Turkey they have more encouragement.'[37] He was called into Star Chamber for attempting to make a division between the king and the people, and to make the king's subjects dislike him. He was asked to sign a submission, the usual gesture of restoration of unity, which he rejected, offering nine scriptural quotations to justify his refusal. Laud remarked that 'if the king had many such Chambers, he might want a chamber for himself', and Chambers went back to prison, from which he emerged just in time to return there for refusing to pay Ship Money.[38] Other merchants soon concluded that it was not worth abandoning their trade over Tonnage and Poundage, and began to pay it without dispute. Michael Sparke, Prynne's printer, raised another dispute by claiming that the Star Chamber decree on which censorship rested had no legal basis, since it was based neither on Common Law nor on Act of Parliament. In the movement towards freedom of ideas, printers deserve a credit which they have not normally received. Prynne, like most other authors, who attacked the government, was not interested in freedom, but in truth: he was as much concerned that the government permitted what it should have prohibited, as that it prohibited what it should have permitted. Printers, on the other hand, were the only trade which had a vested interest in freedom of expression.

If Charles were to rule without Parliament, he needed peace. This was not only for the obvious reason that he could never afford war without a Parliament, but also because a state of sullen ill-will among his subjects would be much more dangerous in wartime, when their active services were needed, than in peacetime, when the king merely needed them to continue with their lawful occupations. In the autumn of 1630, the war with Spain was ended by a treaty which in effect restored the terms of 1604.

[36] Wedgwood, C. V., *Thomas Wentworth: A Revaluation* (1961), 163.
[37] Rushworth, I. 670.   [38] Laud, *Works* (1847), iv. 75.

The Palatinate still roused strong feelings among Charles's subjects, many of whom regarded the whole of the Thirty Years' War as a fight to the death between Catholics and Protestants, but in renouncing Parliament, Charles had in effect renounced his right to a foreign policy, and could do nothing.

In 1630 and 1631, the government was also faced by two bad harvests, a rapid rise in the price of wheat and a major famine. In Somerset quarter sessions, thefts of food rose above all other types of theft. The government responded with the Book of Orders, which was not only a programme for famine relief and to check profiteering, but also a major general reform of local government. Supervision of the poor law was made much tighter and masters were to be compelled with more vigour to take apprentices whom the justices sent to them. This measure produced the unfortunate effect that some masters used cruelty as a means of getting rid of unwanted apprentices. Supervision of alehouses, and of highway repair, was made stricter, and the petty sessions, frequent meetings of justices in a small part of the county, were formalized. Members of each tier of local government were bound to send detailed reports to the stage above. For a while, before the scheme foundered against the weight of human inertia and the distractions of collecting Charles's unparliamentary taxes, it worked well. Even when it was at its best, however, some government servants were prepared to ignore it on occasion. Wentworth proposed to take advantage of famine prices in London to make a larger profit than usual on his corn, and when the famine ended, before he had put his scheme into practice, he noted that: 'God be praised, gains there will be none.'[39] There is no sign that the Book of Orders created any division between 'paternalists' and 'capitalists'. Wentworth's ambivalent attitude was common, while Fitz-Geffrey, vicar of the parish in which Pym had been brought up, gave his wholehearted support to the Book of Orders.

The church under Archbishop Laud, 1633–1640

The bitterest issues of the 1630s were religious. In 1633, Laud at last obtained Canterbury on the death of Abbot, and, together with Neile at York, was able to deliver complete control of the church into the hands of the Arminians. Preferment was rarely open except to those of Arminian persuasion, and one future Restoration bishop, when asked what the Arminians held, replied: 'all the best bishoprics and deaneries in England.'[40] Almost all the opponents of the Arminians on the episcopal bench had been appointed before 1624. Under cover of declarations for-

[39] Wedgwood, *Thomas Wentworth*, 99.
[40] Clarendon, *Life* (1827), I. 56.

bidding controversy, Laud and his followers tried to root out the Predestinarian theology which had previously been common. In order to do
this they had to call in many doctrinal compilations which had previously
been regarded as orthodox. For example, the Irish Articles of Religion of
1615, which had unambiguously conceded to the Predestinarians what
they asked, were replaced with the English Thirty-Nine Articles, whose
greater ambiguity gave the Arminians more scope. Foxe's *Book of
Martyrs* and Jewel's *Apology of the Church of England*, both semi-official
Elizabethan compilations, were frequently quoted against the Arminians,
and both were refused a licence for reprinting in 1637. Many of Laud's
followers were more extreme than he was. Dr. Cosin, at Durham, called
his Communion services 'Mass' and the Reformation a 'Deformation'.
Montague, who was promoted from the bishopric of Chichester to Norwich, regretted the dissolution of the monasteries, and believed in purgatory and the use of relics. One of Laud's minor followers maintained that
Confession was necessary to salvation. It is perhaps not surprising that
some Puritans found it hard to see the difference between such people
and Roman Catholics. The vicar of Chigwell defended prayer to the
saints and provided Puritans with one of their rare successes in their
attempts to identify high church theology with an immoral life. The vicar
was found by a parishioner in a tavern with a woman on each arm, and
being asked whether these were the saints he prayed to, answered 'yes'.[41]

The commonest point of dispute, however, was still ceremonies. This
was not because either side regarded ceremonies as the most important
issue, but because they were more readily enforced, and therefore provided a more natural point of nonconformity, than theological opinions.
Moreover, the key point of ceremony, the altar, provided an issue with
profound theological implications. Laud claimed that 'a greater reverence
is due to the body than to the word of the Lord'[42]—a highly questionable
assertion which committed him to a long battle with the Puritans on
whether preaching or the Sacraments was the centre of religion. In 1633,
soon after his appointment to Canterbury, Laud brought the issue of the
altar (the very name was an innovation) to a head. The test case was over
the church of St. Gregory's, a small parish church next to St. Paul's. The
case should have been heard in the ecclesiastical Court of Arches, where
it should have been tried by Sir Henry Marten, a low churchman appointed
by Abbot, who had said in Parliament in 1628: 'let us wrestle with the
king in duty and in love, and not let him go in this Parliament till he
comply with us.'[43] Marten was prepared to give a judgement repeating

---

[41] B.M. Harl. MS. 163, fo. 578v.
[42] Laud, *Works,* iv. 284.   [43] Rushworth, I. 521.

Queen Elizabeth's Injunction of 1559, that the communion table should be kept at the east end and brought down into the body of the church at service time. He was not prepared to judge that the altar should always be kept at the east end. In law, Marten's position was sound, but Laud sacked him, and took the case to the Privy Council, which gave the judgement he wanted. This attempt to set up altars was carried into other places, and met considerable resistance, which was enough for so cautious a man as Williams, Bishop of Lincoln, to write an anonymous pamphlet: *The Holy Table, Name and Thing*, against Laud's policy. At Grantham, in Williams's diocese, the vicar found when he tried to move the altar to the east end that he had a tug of war with his parishioners. Williams observed smugly that no ceremony was as important as Christian charity: a remark which Laud probably found uncharitable. The vicar of Grantham also bowed and genuflected before the altar so extravagantly that he once fell flat on his face in the aisle, to the great delight of some of his parishioners. Bowing had been commanded in Elizabeth's Injunctions, but it had never been a central point of episcopal policy, as it was under Laud. An increasing number of presentations to church courts were for not bowing to the altar or at the name of Jesus. To Puritans, who valued their emancipation from superstition, this represented exactly the type of thraldom from which they hoped they had escaped. To Laud, on the other hand, it was a necessary remedy against profanity: 'tis superstition nowadays for any man to come with more reverence into a church than a tinker and his bitch to come into an alehouse. The comparison is homely, but my just indignation at the profaneness of the times makes me speak it.'[44] It is true that some Puritans protested too much about their freedom from superstition, and one man felt compelled to demonstrate it by pissing in Canterbury cathedral. It may be doubted, however, whether compulsory bowing to the altar was the remedy for this type of irreverence. When they had set up altars at the east end, the Laudians often railed them in. Laud said the motive for this was 'to prevent dogs from pissing on them, or worse', but to Puritans it savoured of magic territory closed for the priest—in short, of superstition. Parishioners, instead of receiving communion in their places, were asked to come up to the rails to receive it. This again became a flashpoint in the church courts, because, when ordinary parishioners were told to perform a definite action, they were thereby given an opportunity to refuse.

Another issue on which an opportunity to refuse was created was the Book of Sports. This was in its original form a document of 1618, saying what sports and games were lawful on Sunday. Under James, there had

---

[44] Laud, *Works*, VI. i. 55, iv. 254.

been occasional disputes about it. In 1633, it was reissued, and a vigorous campaign was started to induce clergy to read it from their pulpits. To those who regarded Sunday as a repetition of the Jewish Sabbath, or to those who, like Prynne, could say: 'so many paces in the dance: so many paces to hell', this was of course impossible, and a number of the deprivations of clergy of the period were for not reading the Book of Sports. A similar opportunity for resistance was offered at Shepton Mallet, where the bishop tried to force the parish church to buy an organ. They objected, not only because they disliked organs but also because they thought the bishop had no right to enforce a rate on them to pay for the organ.

Issues concerning church economics and church property also provided much of the battleground during Laud's administration of the church. The clergy were beginning to fight back against the persistent denigration and impoverishment they had suffered from laity for the past century. Most of the Laudians shared the willingness to denigrate Henry VIII which was becoming fashionable in clerical circles, believing that all church property was inalienable, and that Henry had committed sacrilege in taking it away. This doctrine was a direct challenge to all holders of monastic land, a challenge which some of Laud's sympathizers occasionally tried to make effective in Scotland and Ireland, and it did much to increase the number of Laud's enemies. The Laudians felt even more strongly about spoliation of bishoprics, and when Montague was made Bishop of Norwich he reported that 'Henry VIII stole the sheep, and gave not so much as the trotters for God's sake'.[45] They did what they could to rectify this situation by trying to shorten the length of leases of church property, and to stop the use of long leases to reward patrons. Here they were doing the same thing which many Puritans in the Elizabethan Commons had tried to do, and fell foul of the same lay feeling as the Elizabethan Puritans had done. They were also, like the Puritans, worried about impropriations, but both Puritans and Laudians preferred to see impropriations remain as they were rather than be delivered to the other side. Laud overthrew a Puritan organization called the Feoffees for Impropriations, which was designed to buy up impropriations and use them for the support of the type of clergy they thought godly, and Laud thought factious. He also tried to force holders of impropriations to pay higher maintenance to their vicars, and in some cases he succeeded. He also made numerous attempts to ensure that tithes kept pace with inflation, and in some cases succeeded. He made no attempt, however, to attack the solid control of advowsons, and therefore of the complexion of the parish clergy, by laymen. So long as Warwick, Bedford, Pembroke, and their like controlled most of the

[45] Prynne, W., *Canterburies Doome* (1645), 555.

livings, Laud could not produce a fully Laudian parish clergy, and when the crisis came, in the 1640s, it emerged that most of the future Presbyterian leaders had held livings in the Laudian church. Laud did, however, attack what one of his bishops called 'the ratsbane of lecturing'. Endowments which allowed clergy to preach without holding a living or saying the liturgy were an easy opening for nonconformists, and Laud tried to ensure that no one was ordained unless to a living where he would have to say the service. None of this added up to Roman Catholicism, but Puritans were not the only people who thought it did. In 1633, Laud was offered a cardinal's hat, and replied that he could not accept it 'till Rome were other than it is'.[46]

Financial expedients, 1629–1637

In financing his government, Charles was greatly helped by the fact that the long inflation of the past century was coming to an end, and in increasing his revenue, he could have some hope of catching up with inflation. On the whole, his attempts to increase his income were very successful. Thanks to the expansion of trade, the impositions dating from 1607 were bringing in £119,000 by 1636, and Charles took further advantage of the judgement to impose a further set of new impositions, bringing in £60,000 a year. In all, over £200,000 a year of his income thus depended on the judgement of Bate's case. A further set of impositions on the coal trade brought in another £18,000 a year. A highly profitable monopoly in soap was bringing in £29,000 a year by 1636. This caused intense indignation partly because the monopoly company included a number of papists, and thus produced an agitation against 'popish soap', and partly because the soap was said to be inferior in quality. The government organized a trial before a body of peeresses and laundresses, in which it was pronounced that the monopolists' soap washed whiter than independent soap, but few were convinced. Pym later complained that the Star Chamber (where offenders against the monopoly were prosecuted) 'hath been used to set a face of public good on things pernicious, as soap'.[47] It would be a mistake, however, to see an issue of economic philosophy behind the soap monopoly: the independent soap-boilers, who made most of the protests of principle against the monopoly, later took it over by offering a higher price than the original holders. Charles did, however, cause some irritation among merchants by his frequent ham-handed interventions, and those who had no objection to intervention might object to ham-handedness, or to sheer provocation.

Another of Lord Treasurer Weston's schemes was the large-scale use of

[46] Prynne, op. cit., 432.   [47] Rushworth, III. i. 23.

fines for not being knighted. This was an example of the government's talent for antiquarian finance, which they might justify by arguing that if they were not allowed new revenue, they must be allowed to keep old ones. It is also an example of the government's habit of using laws for purposes contradictory to those for which they were made. The original purpose of the law on knighthood had been to compel people worth more than £5 a year to be knighted, in order that the king should have enough knights. The last thing Charles wanted, however, was for people to be knighted: he wanted to fine them for not being knighted. This is illustrated by the story of a Yorkshireman called James Mauleverer.[48] He lived 180 miles (four days' journey, on his estimate) from London, and on 30 January a proclamation was posted in his village commanding him and others of his income to be at Whitehall on 31 January to be knighted. As Mauleverer pointed out, this was impossible, and he asked the judges to agree to let him be knighted, instead of paying his fine. The judges were not convinced, and he had to be fined for his failure to be knighted. This was an old source of income, but it had never been fully exploited, and for a while it brought in over £100,000 a year.

Another smaller source of income, but perhaps a more provocative one, was the use of the Forest Laws. This was suggested by Attorney General Noy, who was using for Charles the same antiquarian legal scholarship he had once used for Parliament, having, according to Clarendon, been flattered into showing his skill by 'making that law, which all men else thought not to be so'.[49] According to strict Forest Law, all buildings, and all ironworks, agriculture, and similar activities were illegal within the bounds of what was legally forest. Finch made these ideas effective, obtaining from local juries verdicts extending the boundaries of the royal forests, after threats to keep them locked up over the weekend in one case, and to send them to Star Chamber in another, and the king was then authorized to fine everyone within the new forest bounds. Once again, however, the last thing he wanted was for them actually to obey the law and get out of the forest: if they did, he could never again fine them for being in it. The same policy determined the activities of Charles's commissions against enclosures. Laud may have wanted to have some enclosures actually thrown open, but the general preference was for fining enclosers and leaving the enclosures, so that they could be fined again on the next commission. Similarly, a ban on new building near London was transformed into a tax on it. This system of compounding for nuisances, as it

---

[48] The case of Mauleverer became one of the articles in the impeachment of the judges in 1641.

[49] Clarendon, *History of the Rebellion*, i. 73.

was called, much annoyed Pym, who said that if the thing men paid for was a nuisance, they should be made to remove it, and if it was not a nuisance, they should not be fined for it. Nevertheless, Pym was using exactly the same system on his own estates, and for the same reason—to bring his income up to date with inflation and to pay his debts.

By the second half of the decade, these and similar measures had brought the king's income to the immense figure of £899,000. During the past 120 years, the Crown's income had risen from between £100,000 and £150,000. Prices, during this period, had risen from a base figure of 100 to somewhere under 600. In other words, the Crown's income had now increased faster than the price rise, and it should have been in a better position than it was in 1510. Nevertheless, it was not solvent. It is true that Charles balanced his accounts, but he only did so by anticipating his revenues, that is, by spending them before he had got them. He began the 1630s with a war debt of £277,000, which he had reduced to £204,000 by 1633. By 1637, the debt was up again to £315,000, and one small branch of the revenue had been spent ahead until 1651. Charles may have been more successful than his predecessors, but he still did not live within his income. But if his income had increased faster than the price rise, this fact cannot be explained by the smallness of his income. The financial history of the 1630s needs more investigation, but it appears that the explanation is the size of royal expenditure. Why Charles's expenditure was so high, it is as yet hard to say: he did not throw his money around in gifts with anything like the lavishness of James, and he undertook no wars during the 1630s. His household was certainly expensive, but until it is investigated in more detail we do not know why. He certainly spent a large amount of money on building and paintings: the bill for the queen's palace at Greenwich was £133,000 and Laud was known to think that Vandyck was an extravagance. It should also be remembered that the range of the government's responsibilities, and the size of its civil service, had increased in this, as in most other centuries. This expansion was not all wasteful. The £75,000 a year which Charles received from the Court of Wards justified the cost of a department, and whatever might be said of the efficiency of the Navy and Ordnance offices, the government could no longer renounce responsibility for the fields which they represented. The relationship between the government's expenditure and the range of its responsibilities still needs further investigation. Charles attempted to combine increases in his income with administrative reform, and attempts to cut down official fees. He achieved some temporary economies in the household, and sentenced some officials for increasing their fees, but he had no hope of being able to pay full official salaries, and no administrative reform short of that was likely to be very effective.

The situation in 1637: Ship Money

Until 1637, it looked as if Charles was going to succeed. He was no more insolvent than rulers usually were, and in the absence of Parliament, there was little focus for opposition. Charles was certainly isolated. In 1627, the proportion of peers exchanging a New Year's gift with the king had been 75 per cent, and during the 1630s it fell to between a half and a third. As Professor Stone says, 'Charles, Henrietta Maria, and Laud had thus contrived to restrict the court to a narrower circle than had been seen for over a century.'[50] But if peers had no armies, Charles did not need to worry if they sulked in their tents. The machinery of local government was still working, whatever those who ran it may have felt about government policy, and the king still had control of preferment. He did, however, have to face occasional demonstrations. In 1637, Prynne, Burton, and Bastwick, three Puritan pamphleteers, were brought to trial for attacking the bishops, mainly for altering the religion of the church of England. Their only possible defence was to claim that what they said was true. This was ruled to be a repetition of the libel which constituted the original offence, and they were held to have confessed themselves guilty, and were sentenced to have their ears cut off. At the pillory, the crowd gathered round them and soaked their handkerchiefs in their blood. The author of the account in the *State Papers*, who was in the process of conversion to Catholicism, commented: 'you may see how nature leads men to respect the relics of martyrs.'[51] Along the route to his imprisonment at Caernarvon, Prynne was cheered and fêted, and at Chester, the bishop found 1,000 pictures of Prynne distributed round the town. Wentworth, in Ireland, shrewdly remarked that 'a prince that loseth the force and example of his punishments, loseth the greatest part of his dominion'.[52] Cases of this type contributed to the growing unpopularity of the Star Chamber, which, being staffed with Privy Councillors, could be used much more readily than the Common Law courts to enforce a policy. The objection, however, was not so much to the Star Chamber as to the policies enforced in it. The cult of a martyr of the government, however, was no more than a means of keeping up the opposition's spirits, and it seems possible that at this time many of the leaders of the opposition were contemplating following the example of other Puritans, and emigrating

[50] Stone, 464.
[51] Cal. S.P. Dom. (1637), 332.
[52] Wedgwood, C. V., *Strafford* (1935), 206.

to America. In 1636 they received a patent for a colony in New England at Saybrooke, so called after Lords Saye and Sele and Brooke. Saye and Brooke themselves finally refused to go because the New Englanders refused to set up a legislative chamber of 'hereditary gentlemen'. How many others may have considered going with them, we do not know, but during 1637 Pym and Hampden both made their wills and settled their estates on closely interlocking groups of trustees. Most of the opposition leaders had been closely connected for some time through the Providence Company, a company for colonizing a West Indian island which was also used as a front for opposition political meetings.

It was at this stage, however, that the tide began to turn. In 1637, Charles chose to take John Hampden to court for refusal to pay Ship Money. Richard Chambers and Lord Saye and Sele had been trying for some time to be taken to court over Ship Money, and Charles's choice of John Hampden for the test case raised him to an importance he might otherwise never have acquired. Ship Money was by far the most profitable of Charles's financial expedients, bringing in up to £200,000 a year. The Crown defended Ship Money, like impositions, by creating a confusion between two lines of legal precedents. Charles claimed that the relevant precedents were not those which said the king could not raise taxes without the consent of Parliament, but the equally valid precedents which said he could, in an emergency, conscript ships and men for purposes of national defence. He might also compel people to contribute financially to the conscription of a ship. But when he did this, the ship which was conscripted, did not become the Crown's property: it reverted to its original owners as soon as the campaign for which it was conscripted was over. This was the form in which Ship Money worked in the City of London: the Londoners collected the money to hire a ship, which served with the royal fleet for six months, and then reverted to the City of London. In this form, Ship Money was unquestionably legal. This was the form in which Charles professed to be using it in other counties: the Ship Money writs commanded Buckinghamshire to provide a ship at Portsmouth (presumably hiring it): they did not command citizens of Buckinghamshire to finance the regular upkeep of the royal navy. Finance for the royal navy, however, was what Charles wanted, and he was not legally entitled to raise it without the assent of Parliament. He therefore had to pretend that instead of raising a tax for the navy, he was conscripting ships. These powers of naval conscription, moreover, only existed in time of emergency and some people were rather doubtful whether there was really an 'emergency' every year from 1634 to 1640. However, when the case came to trial, the judges were not able to decide whether there had been an emergency, 'they being', as

Falkland later put it, 'judges, and neither philosophers nor politicians'.[53] If the king said there was an emergency, they had to believe him.

The king had already obtained extrajudicial opinions from the judges justifying Ship Money as a form of naval conscription. Therefore some of the possible issues were closed in the Ship Money trial. Oliver St. John, counsel for Hampden, advanced his arguments against unparliamentary taxation, and Attorney General Bankes, for the king, advanced his arguments for powers of conscription in an emergency. Both argued well, and both were right. The problem, as in Bate's case, was to decide which was the relevant line of argument. There were twelve judges, and seven would give a majority. When the first five had all judged for the king, it looked as if the case was closed. Then came the turn of Justice Croke, a long-standing friend of the Hampden family. He chose to resist the pressure the Crown had brought to bear on the judges, and delivered a thunderous judgement for Hampden. In the Inns of Court, men said the king had Ship Money by hook but not by Croke. He was followed by two other judges on the same side. None of these, however, tackled the central issue, which line of precedents was relevant. The king's judges assumed that Ship Money was not a tax, and Hampden's assumed that it was. The only judgements which tackled this issue were two masterly ones by Bramston and Davenport, which showed, by a careful examination of the terms of the writ, that the money could not be paid anywhere but to Westminster, and if it were paid to Westminster, it was a tax. Their judgements, concentrating as they did on procedural points, saved them from having to give a general verdict on the uncomfortably large issue of prerogative versus law, and enabled them to avoid some of the far-reaching *obiter dicta* produced by the other judges.[54] Finally the king won the case by the narrowest possible margin of seven to five. Hampden, having had a judgement that Ship Money was legal, duly paid it, but the judgements of Hutton and Croke for Hampden had gravely damaged the king's case in the eyes of the public, and people who previously had only complained of their assessments began a massive campaign of tax refusal, until by 1640 only a third of Ship Money was coming to the Treasurer of the Navy, and sheriffs, threatened with having to pay the deficit out of their own pockets, were distracted by the persistent failure of their attempts to collect it. In political terms, the winner of the case was Hampden.

[53] Rushworth, III. i. 86.
[54] Russell, 'The Ship Money Judgments of Bramston and Davenport', *E.H.R.* (1962), 312–18. Russell, 'Justice Croke and the Hampdens', *Notes and Queries,* (Oct. 1968), 367.

IV THE DRIFT TO WAR, 1637–1642

This ... Parliament, which hath sat so long, hath all this time while but beaten the air, and striven against the stream.

Denzil Holles, M.P., May 1641

A gloom of the king's brow would disperse this feeble people for anything yet we see, if the terror of God and us [sc. the Scots] afrayed not their enemies, if help from God and us did not continue their courage.

Robert Baillie, Secretary to the Scottish Commissioners in London,
December 1640[55]

Scotland

The name of John Hampden is better known in the history of English liberties than the names of Lord Rothes, Lord Loudoun, and Lord Balmerino, but it does not deserve to be: King Charles's government did not fall by any mistakes in its dealings with the English opposition, but through overconfidence in its handling of the poor and despised kingdom of Scotland. By 1637, if the opinions of the gentry in 1640 are any guide, Charles probably had few friends. He had had to remove a number of Justices from the Bench for unhelpfulness over the collection of Ship Money, and those who remained were desperately and thanklessly overworked. Among the peerage, he had few fast friends, and some dubious allies even on his own Privy Council. Even the bench of bishops were not all his friends: George Coke, Bishop of Hereford, one of the few non-Arminian bishops, was almost in disgrace: Morton, Bishop of Durham, another pre-Arminian, was being reported on by a spy appointed by Archbishop Laud. Williams of Lincoln, the leader of Laud's opponents on the episcopal bench, was in prison for subornation of perjury. But though Charles had few friends, his enemies were powerless: by refusing to pay Ship Money, they might increase the amount of work facing the government, but few could face the repetition of such necessarily unsuccessful demonstrations. Most preferred to pay their Ship Money and keep out of trouble. There was no rival candidate for the throne to provide a focus for opposition, and though some lords might perhaps still be able to raise small bands, the government's control of military force was too secure for rebellions of the Essex type to be regarded as practical politics. The fast which the Puritans held to avert God's wrath as manifested in the severe plague of 1636 was turned into an occasion for demonstration, but Laud prohibited the fast for fear it might spread the infection. So many Puritan preachers and lecturers had been silenced that the survivors were unable to

---

[55] Baillie, R., *Letters and Journals* (1841), i. 283. Rushworth, III. i. 243.

use their pulpits as a focus for opposition. Some of the greatest Puritan preachers, such as Burges, Calamy, Marshall, and Simeon Ashe, survived, but only because they were under the patronage, respectively of Bedford, Warwick, and Brooke. The peers who were their patrons had all the responsibility of outlook which goes with great possessions, and though Warwick protested vehemently at Charles's attempt to declare almost all Essex legally forest, most of them co-operated when they honestly could. Bedford rebuilt Covent Garden and worked with Charles in draining the fens, and Warwick turned his energies to the West Indies, while Brooke, who was among the more irreconcilable, could think of nothing better than emigration. If King Charles were to start a war, and needed the help of Parliament, these men might be able to make conditions for their support, but as long as Charles was at peace, they were powerless.

The kingdom of Scotland was a different matter. Like the Spanish kingdom of Catalonia, which also rose in revolt in 1640, it had all the characteristics of a neglected frontier kingdom.[56] Many Scots resented both the fact that the English had a near-monopoly of the king's presence, with all the opportunities for influence and profit which it created, and their exclusion from England's growing overseas trade, and the fact that they had no say in the formation of English foreign policy. Unlike the English, they felt that Scots did not get a large enough share in the profitable English offices, or enough say in the filling of Scottish offices. Charles had offended a number of Scottish nobles by his attacks on the inheritance of offices, and he also suffered from the same financial problems as in England. By the 1630s, guests at royal banquets were being asked to bring their own food. After successful manipulation of several Scottish Parliaments, Charles succeeded in acquiring a new regular tax on annual rents, which was called 'the greatest taxation that ever was granted in Scotland heretofore in any age'.[57] He had caused great alarm in 1625 by trying to revoke all Crown grants of ecclesiastical (including monastic) property since 1540. This attempt was almost totally fruitless, but since similar attempts were being made in Ireland, there were some doubts whether this might not represent a settled policy, to be resumed whenever possible.

However, though an archbishop refused his place at Charles's coronation rather than wear a surplice, and though Rothes and Balmerino, two of the most powerful opposition lords, challenged the legality of Charles's manipulation of the 1633 Scottish Parliament, the Scottish opposition, like the English, seemed to be powerless. They were handicapped by the

[56] For this parallel, see Elliott, J. H., 'The King and the Catalans', *Cambridge Historical Journal* (1953), 253.
[57] Donaldson, Gordon, *Edinburgh History of Scotland* (1965), 302.

fact that the two greatest forces in Scottish politics, the peers and the Puritan ministers, did not work easily together. Scottish Presbyterian ministers tended to be as clericalist as any bishop, and the anticlericalism of the Scottish peers was as strong as that of the English.

Charles provided these two groups with a common cause by his attempt to introduce a new Prayer Book into Scotland. For some time, Roman Catholics had been asking how one Supreme Head could be head of three religions in three kingdoms, and Charles wanted uniformity of religion between England and Scotland. Charles seems at first to have wanted to introduce the English Prayer Book, but was persuaded to agree to something more definitely Scottish. Between 1634 and 1637, a three-sided correspondence was conducted about this book between the king, Laud, and the Scottish bishops. Out of this there emerged a number of concessions to Scottish views, such as the deletion of the word 'priest'. But though Charles and Laud seem to have been willing to be at least moderately conciliatory, some of the rising party of Arminians among the Scottish bishops, who also saw the book, were not. The most provocative decision was over the communion formula. Instead of the Elizabethan compromise with two alternative formulae, the book included only the formula from the 1549 Prayer Book, leaving out the 'commemorative' formula of the 1552 Prayer Book. This decision was taken on the advice of Wedderburn, Bishop of Dunblane.[58]

But the most inflammatory thing about the book was not its contents, but the manner of its imposition. King Charles never showed it to a Scottish Parliament or church assembly, but simply commanded the Scots to use it by proclamation. If Charles could introduce a new liturgy simply by proclamation, then he could introduce a new religion, or a new tax, or anything he chose, by proclamation. All pretence at constitutional government, at least in religion, had been abandoned. The introduction of the book, in the summer of 1637, was met with a serious riot in St. Giles's kirk at Edinburgh, and by a protest from Montrose (later one of Charles's most devoted supporters) that it represented 'the brood of the bowels of the whore of Babel'.[59] The Scottish Council felt that the book should be withdrawn, but Charles, in the name of decency, order, and reverence, refused to give in to riots. The result was that the Bishop of Brechin, in the name of decency, order, and reverence, had to read the service to his congregation while glowering at them over a pair of loaded pistols.

In February 1638 the Scottish opposition drew up a Covenant, binding

---

[58] On this, see Donaldson, Gordon, *The Making of the Scottish Prayer Book of 1637* (1954), 41 ff.
[59] Donaldson, *Prayer Book*, 73.

them to oppose these innovations. Many of the drafters of the Covenant were clear Presbyterians, but not all: according to Professor Donaldson, at this stage 'it was obviously the intention to revert to the moderate episcopalian regime which had existed during most of the period between the Reformation and King Charles's innovations'. Though Rothes, for example, tried to stick to this position, the ministers soon led the movement on to demands for a strict Presbyterian discipline, while their lay colleagues set out to buy arms on the Continent, and Loudoun investigated the possibility of help from France. Presbyterianism, when unofficially introduced, 'proved admirably adapted to be an instrument of the aristocracy and gentry', and Charles was faced by a movement too well organized to be suppressed by any Scottish resources.

The Bishops' Wars and the Short Parliament, 1637–1640

King Charles, then, had two courses open to him: he could withdraw the Book, which would be a sacrifice of conscience, and might be interpreted as renouncing his power to order his Scottish subjects, or else he could raise an army in England or Ireland to suppress the Scots. Typically, Charles chose both courses. He withdrew the Book, which was already withdrawn because no one dared read it, and sent Hamilton, one of the few Scots in his confidence in England, to negotiate. His instructions were to 'flatter them with what hopes you please . . . until I be ready to suppress them'.[60] Finally, in the summer of 1639, Charles succeeded in creating an army, drawn largely from the English militia, and financed by loans and gifts from Catholics, office-holders, and various people dependent on the regime. Whether the array was fit or willing to fight, however, was another question. This question was never put to the test, since the English army looked at the Scots outside Berwick, and decided to make peace. The king agreed to a new Scottish Parliament and church assembly, but no settlement was possible when one side would not agree to abolish bishops, and the other would not agree to keep them. While he was negotiating, Charles summoned Wentworth from Ireland. It was only at this stage that Wentworth, who was now raised to the Earldom of Strafford, came into the centre of English politics. For him, the issue was simple: the Scots were rebels, and rebellion ought to be put down. He may not have been the king's ablest minister, but he was the most determined. He was not an Arminian, but he was a believer in obedience, and it was typical of him that he once complained that Puritans had no more joints in their knees than an elephant. However, though he sank most of his large personal

---

[60] Donaldson, *Scotland,* 314, 321, 317.

fortune in the task, he could not raise an army without money, and there is much truth in his comment: 'never came man to so mightily lost a business.'[61] The Scottish church assembly abolished bishops, and enacted that every adult male in Scotland should be made to take the Covenant, so Charles's determination to fight remained as large as his means were small. Finally, in April 1640, he summoned Parliament to raise money to fight the Scots.

As seventeenth-century politicians always said, their system demanded unity: if the king formed foreign policy, and Parliament financed it, there was deadlock if they were not united. The Short Parliament of April and May 1640 is a classic example of such deadlock. Strafford had hoped that the old racial hostility against the Scots might come to the king's rescue (Laud annotated one of their papers: 'not worth three of their lice'),[62] but many members of Parliament sympathized with the Scots, and even those who did not were more interested in Ship Money than in helping the king to suppress them. In eleven years a number of grievances had accumulated, and they were not going to help the king off Laud's hook without reforming them first. Charles, whose stubbornness was equalled only by his weakness, decided Parliament had nothing to offer him, and dissolved it. Convocation, however, remained in session, passing canons about such provocative subjects as the altar and the power of kings. It also decided to detect Presbyterian sympathizers by imposing, on its own authority, a new oath of loyalty to the government of the church by 'archbishops, bishops, archdeacons, deans, etcetera'. Many who were not committed to Presbyterianism objected to being asked to swear to renounce it for the future, and the oath became merely a new centre of opposition. Many chose to suppose that 'etcetera' meant the Pope, and on one occasion Dr. Duck, Chancellor of the diocese of London, was only saved from serious injury when trying to impose the oath because someone broke up the gathering by shouting 'a mad bull!' At the same time there was an acute slump in the cloth trade, and a financial crisis provoked by lack of business confidence. Even the City Aldermen, who, unlike many less senior people in the City, were mostly Charles's friends, were so unhelpful that Strafford advised the king to hang some of them. In July, Charles induced the Merchant Adventurers to lend £40,000 rather than let him seize bullion which had been deposited for security in the Tower. At the same time, Strafford was negotiating for help from Spain, a negotiation which was worse than useless, since not only did it fall through, but a copy of Strafford's letter landed on Pym's desk. How it arrived there we cannot tell,

[61] Wedgwood, *Thomas Wentworth*, 296.
[62] *Notes of the Treaty at Ripon*, Ed. J. Bruce, (1869).

but in general the parliamentarians' intelligence was one of their strongest weapons. The trustees of Pym's estate included John Graunt, a member of the opposition organization of the Providence Company and the man who ran the royal messenger service. One of Oliver St. John's household was John Thurloe, who later, under Cromwell, became one of the greatest intelligence experts in English history.[63]

Charles did not only have to face the gentry: he had to face a mixture of extreme Puritanism, social radicalism, and reactions to unemployment among the lower classes. In May 1640 a party of apprentices, glovers, tanners, sailors, and dockhands marched on Lambeth to hunt 'Laud the fox' for breaking the Parliament. Laud had escaped, but the government were worried enough to have the leaders convicted of treason, and to make the last use of the rack in England for extorting confessions. Some of these popular protests were on behalf of causes very different from those of the peers and gentry who formed the backbone of the parliamentarian cause. John Lilburne the Leveller, who was involved in some of these early demonstrations, stood for a very different cause from Saye and Sele, who, under the Protectorate, refused to take a seat in Cromwell's Upper House because he would not sit with brewers and draymen. The Separatist congregation in Southwark who maintained that there was no church but where the faithful were, that the king could make no law because he was not perfectly regenerate, and that he was to be obeyed only in civil matters, stood for a very different cause from Denzil Holles, maintaining that 'mechanical men' preaching without licence made it seem 'as if we would bring in all atheism and confusion, instead of godly discipline'.[64] A few of the parliamentarians, such as Saye and Brooke, may possibly have believed in separation from the church of England, but the majority were as firm believers in a united national church and in the existing class system as the king himself. Their alliance with the popular radicals, to whom they gave their opportunity, was an uneasy one, even in 1640.

At last, Charles managed to raise enough loans to start a new war against the Scots. The customs farmers, if no one else, were still giving him wholehearted support, and they were the best source of loans in the kingdom. He managed to gather a somewhat disorderly army, which straggled north, rioting on the way, and severely diminished by desertion. The Scots this time took the initiative, and crossed the Tweed on 20 August 1640. The English army met them at Newburn, on the Tyne, but was routed, leaving the Scots to occupy Newcastle unopposed. Once again, it was clear

---

[63] *H.M.C. Portland*, i. 3–4; Pym MSS. no. 237. Thurloe was one of the witnesses to this document.
[64] B.M. Harl. MS. 6424, fo. 6r; B.M. Harl. MS. 163, fo. 279.

that Charles's army could not, or would not, fight, and once again he had to negotiate. A temporary settlement was patched up, leaving the Scots occupying England at the king's cost until they received satisfactory terms. Charles was thus bound to pay the Scots £850 a day, and though he tried to obtain money from a Council of Peers, it was clear that nobody would give him such a sum of money except Parliament. Charles had to concede all the Scots' demands, submit to a Scottish occupation of London, or else call Parliament. He chose to call Parliament, but with what aims, or what hopes, it is hard to tell.

The Long Parliament and the outbreak of the war

When the Long Parliament met at Westminster, on 3 November 1640, it met under the protection of the Scottish army. When the Scottish commissioners arrived in London to negotiate a treaty, Warwick was among those who called on them their first night in town. For the parliamentary leaders, their relations with the Scots were crucial: as they told Baillie, the commissioners' secretary, if the Scots made terms with the king and went home, they were undone. The situation, then, was a three-sided one between the king, the Parliament, and the Scots. An alliance of any two of these could defeat the third. If the parliamentary leaders made terms with the king, they could buy the terms by voting him enough money to defeat the Scots. If the king made terms with the Scots, he could dissolve the Parliament and carry on as before. Perhaps the weakest possible alliance was that with which the Long Parliament opened, between the parliamentary leaders and the Scots. The Scots appear to have agreed with the English leaders to delay concluding the treaty until Parliament had got what it wanted from the king. There were three major weaknesses in this scheme. In the first place, it was easy enough to make it expedient for Charles to settle with the parliamentary leaders, but it was impossible to make Charles believe in taking the expedient action. If Charles were to choose to be pig-headed, the situation could only deteriorate. In the second place, the scheme was likely to founder on the problem of bishops: the Scots' price for delaying the treaty was £300,000 'Brotherly Assistance' and the abolition of bishops in England. On the other hand, part of the price of a settlement with Charles would necessarily be the retention of bishops. It is not surprising that the parliamentary leaders were constantly apologizing to the Scots for not introducing a measure to abolish bishops, nor that the Scots were occasionally a little suspicious of these delays. The third defect of this scheme was that it cost £850 a day to pay the Scottish armies, and since discontent with taxation was probably one of the main reasons for popular support for the Parliament, the imposition of such heavy additional taxation risked riots and demonstrations against the Parliament.

What were the aims of the parliamentary leaders, which were to be achieved by this process? It is easy enough to summarize their legislative programme: abolition of Ship Money, reversal of the judgement in Bate's case giving the king power to levy customs duties without parliamentary assent, abolition of Arminianism, an end to the High Commission and the Star Chamber, triennial Parliaments, exclusion of bishops from the House of Lords, and so forth. This programme, except for Bishops' Exclusion, they carried through, and yet, in June 1641, they were still desperately trying to delay the treaty with the Scots, reporting rumours of plots, and apparently as unsatisfied as they had ever been. What more did they want?

The answer is some share in executive power. Their dilemma is well illustrated by the drafting of the bill for Triennial Parliaments, one of their earliest measures. They had learnt from their experience over the Petition of Right that it was no use merely passing laws while Charles kept the power to interpret them in the opposite way from that their drafters intended, and even to claim that they were not laws at all. If they simply passed a law for triennial Parliaments, Charles could safely ignore it, as his son did in 1684. When Strode introduced the bill in the Commons, it therefore included a clause to say that if the king did not issue the writs, the sheriffs and constables should proceed to hold elections as if they had received writs. The Lords inserted clauses giving power to the Lord Keeper, or to twelve peers, to summon a Parliament if the king did not, but left in the clause saying that the sheriffs and constables could hold elections if their superiors did not act. Charles's reaction to this bill is also typical of him. While it was still passing through the houses he told them that he would not have his authority given to sheriffs and constables, and he would never pass it. When, in spite of this warning, it was presented to him, he said he would take time to think about it. Finally, some weeks later, he passed it, having convinced many people that he did not mean to observe it. Thus, as usual, he got the worst of both worlds.

The parliamentary leaders needed some share in executive power. It seems very improbable, however, that they meant to do this by setting up such a thing as 'parliamentary government'. The notion was an alien one to the period, and moreover, it was hard to have parliamentary government when the majority of members did not have town houses. By May and June 1641, large numbers of members were eager to go home. Sir Robert Harley, though he was one of the wealthier members, was living in lodgings, and was constantly bombarded with letters from his wife regretting his absence from home. Even Pym presumably did not want to live for ever in lodgings in the King's Fishyard in St. Margaret's West-minster. Though 'lodgings' were often on a more comfortable scale than the name suggests, they were expensive for members who did not regularly come to London, and as late as William III's reign, Halifax thought that lodgings difficulties made it hard to keep Parliament in regular session. Regular session of Parliament also raised the level of Westminster rents. A much more practical scheme, which was constantly discussed, was for the opposition leaders to be given the key offices of state. Bedford was to be Lord Treasurer, and his protégé Pym to be his deputy as Chancellor of the Exchequer. Saye and Sele was to be Master of the Wards, and Holles or Lord Mandeville, eldest son of the Earl of Manchester (Lord Privy Seal) to be Secretary of State. Other opposition leaders were to be given places on the Privy Council. There were many medieval precedents (which the parliamentary leaders had at their finger-tips) for Parliament forcing the king to accept new Councillors. In 1388, which was one of their favourite precedents, and in 1258, the king had had enough sense of expediency to make the necessary concessions. Charles, it is true, did appoint Saye and Sele to the Wards and to membership of a large Treasury commission, and did put Essex, Bedford, Saye, Mandeville, Warwick, and Strafford's old enemy Lord Savile on to the Privy Council. He also made Bedford's protégé Oliver St. John Solicitor General. But Charles appears to have thought that he could win men by giving them profit and position but not power, and he never showed any sign of giving these men any share in the formulation of policy.

So long as policy was formed by Cottington or the queen, Denzil Holles could truly protest that 'we have but beaten the air, and striven against the stream'. One possible reason for the failure of these schemes is that a necessary part of the bargain would be for Parliament to vote Charles an adequate revenue. According to Clarendon, Pym found that he could not carry any such measure through the Commons, and that he had more power to do the king hurt than to help him, whereat he is said to have fallen into a great melancholy. There is no way of checking the truth of this story, but it is probable enough.

Another disagreement was about whether Strafford's life should be spared. Strafford was in an uncompromising mood which made him a likely obstacle to any settlement, and the parliamentary leaders may have believed, as they said they did, that he had a settled plan to introduce an arbitrary and tyrannical government in which the king would rule without Parliament. The parliamentary leaders impeached him for high treason for making a division between the king and the people, a doctrine of treason which, though it had precedents, was capable of dangerous extension, and, as some of the parliamentary leaders were to discover, could boomerang against those who used it. It appears to have been part of Charles's price for a settlement that Strafford's life should be spared, even if he was convicted. Saye and Savile tried, at least in public, to keep to this part of the bargain, but it was hard to convince either their colleagues or the Scots. Moreover, since Strafford actually was planning, shortly before his execution, to escape from the Tower and lead an army against the Parliament,[65] there was bound to be some suspicion of Charles's motives in wanting to spare his life. Charles consistently spoiled the effect of his concessions by allowing it to be believed that he would like to use force against those who had extorted them. Another possible reason for the failure of these schemes is that Bedford, who of all the parliamentary leaders was probably the most able to conduct them, died in May 1641. Though the Commons adjourned their committees for his funeral, they had no other equally diplomatic leader. If Clarendon is right that Saye, who was perhaps the most obvious Puritan among the parliamentary leaders, took over the task of negotiating with the king, it is not surprising that the negotiations were unsuccessful, since an acute personal antipathy grew up between Saye and the king.

It is doubtful whether the question of the abolition of bishops was a stumbling block in any other way than because of the Scots' commitment to it. Many of the leaders had no firm commitment either way on the question. Sir Robert Harley, chairman of the Committee for Abolishing Superstition, who was ultimately one of the movers of the bill to abolish bishops, had been described by the non-Arminian Bishop of Hereford a few years earlier as one of his best friends in the shire.[66] Bedford's protégé, Dr. Burgess, one of the most important of the clerical members of the leadership, was suspected by the Scots of being willing to tolerate bishops. Warwick's chaplain Gauden was an episcopalian, and Warwick probably was. Some of the clergy among the parliamentary leadership, such as Calamy, were committed Presbyterians, but among the laity there was little more enthusiasm for Presbyterian than for episcopal clericalism.

If these men were to reach a moderate settlement with the king, there was a large party of moderate episcopalians of the Grindalian school waiting to benefit from it. It was this group who were called to assist the Lords' committee on innovation in religion, and the parliamentary leaders made a number of attempts to conciliate them. Bedford made at least one helpful gesture to Williams, Bishop of Lincoln.

[65] This allegation was proved by Gardiner, S. R., 'Plan of Charles I for the Deliverance of Strafford', *E.H.R.* (1897), 114–16. Strafford offered the Lieutenant of the Tower £22,000 to bring about his escape. B.M. Harl. MS. 163, fo. 676r.

[66] *H.M.C. Cowper (Coke)*, ii. 173.

The leaders also had to take account of a group of members to the left of them, of which the most conspicuous members were Marten, Haselrig, and Alderman Pennington of London, the first two later regicides. It was Pennington who organized a massive London petition for the abolition of bishops in December 1640, and there may be significance in the fact that Pennington tried to establish good relations with the Scottish commissioners: he may have had good reason to suspect that the leaders were less willing to help the Scots to abolish bishops than he was. It may have been Pennington, rather than Pym, who was able to call out apprentices on demonstrations, and the relations between the two groups were not always harmonious. Strode once caused a minor storm by comparing Pennington to the sons of Zeruiah, Biblical characters notorious for their impatience. On at least one occasion, the change from impeachment to attainder against Strafford, the leadership lost control of the House of Commons to this group, which, unlike Pym and his friends, was not prepared to give any effort to preserving good relations with the Lords.[67]

The greatest difficulty in leading was that Parliament did not recognize the concept of leadership. There is at least one recorded occasion on which Stephen Marshall, one of the parliamentarian clergy, tried to act as an unofficial whip,[68] but in general, whipping was impossible. In any division, the dominant body would be a large number of rather crusty, angry country gentlemen, unwilling to take instructions from anyone, and swayed by the mood of the moment. Most of these members objected to the same things as the parliamentary leaders. They wanted to restore a working partnership between the king and the gentry, and to remove those things, such as Ship Money, attempts to increase tithes or to set up altars, which impeded it. With them often voted a body of future royalists, Hyde, Falkland, Digby, Culpeper, and others. Most of these future royalists were as deeply opposed to the king in 1640 as his long-standing opponents from the Providence Company. They too wanted to remove Catholics from high office, to impeach Lord Keeper Finch and Archbishop Laud, to have triennial Parliaments, and to restore government according to the rule of law. Where they parted company from the Providence Company men was not in what they wanted, but in the fact that they would not go to the same lengths to get it.

This division, which was essentially one of temperament, began to become apparent over the attainder of Strafford. Under the influence of

---

[67] The change was opposed by Rudyerd and Hampden, both of whom can be seen as spokesmen for the leadership. Verney, *Notes on the Long Parliament* (Camden Series), 49–50.

[68] B.M. Harl. MS. 164, fo. 1013v. The attempt created considerable resentment.

Marten and Haselrig and the radicals, the Commons abandoned the formal process of trial by impeachment, whose delays had once caused Marten to threaten a Commons' strike, and changed over to Bill of Attainder, simply declaring, as an act of legislation, that Strafford was a traitor. This did begin to look, as one M.P. said, as if 'we had condemned him because we would condemn him',[69] and a number of members began to feel that it was inconsistent to impeach Strafford for threatening the rule of law, and then break the rule of law to condemn him. St. John, for the leadership, was quite prepared to face this contradiction: he said that 'we give law to hares and deer, because they be beasts of chase, but it was never accounted foul play to knock wolves and foxes on the head as they can be found, because they be beasts of prey'.[70] Indeed, if Strafford was planning to use force against Parliament, respect for the rule of law might lead only to the abolition of law. The issues on this, as on many later occasions, were whether it was permissible to act illegally to preserve the rule of law, and whether, in the last resort, members would trust the king or not. In the Commons, fifty-nine members voted in favour of Strafford. In the Lords, he had more sympathizers, and the attainder bill only gained a majority after some skilful teamwork by the opposition peers had caused the bishops to withdraw from the trial, a major riot outside the House had sharply re- duced the number of peers attending, and Pym had announced news of a plot in the army against the Parliament a few minutes before Warwick brought in the attainder bill. Strafford was executed, and at the same time a bill was passed to prevent the king from dissolving Parliament without its own consent. One reason for this bill was to give security to people who had lent money against future parliamentary subsidies, but it was not the only reason: when the king came to the Parliament a few days before this bill was introduced, a number of members of the Commons thought he had come to dissolve them.[71] However, fears of an abrupt dissolution did not stop: if Charles had an army, a mere Act would not restrain him from dismissing Parliament. Cottington was said to have considered asking for foreign help, and the queen was believed to have done so. In the early weeks of May 1641, war was very near. There were wild rumours of an impending French invasion in support of the king, and parliamentary representatives were sent hurrying off to secure Portsmouth, and to mobilize the trained bands in some of their home counties.

The parliamentary leaders, sincerely or not, fostered these rumours of plots. The king had still not conceded power to them, and though they

---

[69] Gardiner, *History*, ix. 338 n.

[70] Rushworth, J., *Trial of Strafford*, 703. As St. John said, 'errors in great things, as war and marriage, they allow no time for repentance; it would have been too late to make a law, when there had been no law'.   [71] B.M. Harl. MS. 163, fo. 512r.

were as frightened of the 'rascal multitude' as the king was, they may have hoped to show him that if he did not settle with them, he could expect something a good deal worse, which was true. The result was an atmosphere of panic in the Commons. When a member sat on a board in the gallery, which cracked, members cried out that they smelt gunpowder, and went running into the streets, even though old Sir Robert Mansel the monopolist drew his sword and bade them stand like true-born English men.[72] The alarm spread to the City, and the City trained bands had marched as far as Covent Garden before they realized their help was not needed. Meanwhile, the Scots were becoming impatient, and the task of delaying the treaty was becoming desperate. It was all the more difficult for the fact that many members wanted to go home, and the leaders, if they valued their influence in the Commons, could not afford to appear to delay the treaty. Ironically enough, the members who were most help to them were those who were coming to be royalists, the episcopalians Falkland, Hyde, and Culpeper, who fought tooth and nail against the clause of the treaty for religious conformity between the two kingdoms.

The other big obstacle to the conclusion of the treaty was money: a bill was introduced, possibly on Scottish prompting, to raise the money by confiscating the lands of deans and chapters. If it passed, this bill would satisfy the Scots, and at least it could be relied on to keep members talking. In the event, it produced a debate on whether money employed to keep up cathedrals as centres of clerical learning, rather than to provide preaching in the parishes, was 'usefully' employed. This debate was a classic of its kind, and occupied the House for some time. With each month which ended, more money was needed, and the opportunities for delay were increased. On one occasion, however, the leaders only avoided having enough money to pay off the Scots by a superb exercise in parliamentary tactics by Pym and Holles. The customs farmers were threatened with impeachment, and told Pym that if they were let off impeachment, they would provide enough money to pay off the Scots. Others were certain to hear of this offer, and the House was certain to be unsympathetic to anyone who opposed it. Pym therefore came to the Commons and moved that this disastrous offer be accepted. Holles, who had been chairman of the committee preparing the impeachment of the customs farmers, then got up and said that they should first report the votes of his committee. After this exchange had been repeated a number of times, with apparently growing indignation, a back-bencher proposed[73] that the House should adjourn for

[72] B.M. Harl. MS. 163, fo. 588b
[73] B.M. Harl. MS. 163, fo. 616–17. See Russell (ed.), *The Origins of the English Civil War* (1973), pp. 113–5.

dinner, which it did. Soon afterwards, the parliamentary leaders introduced the bill for the abolition of bishops, which again kept members talking, and for which the Scots were probably unwilling to wait longer.

In introducing this bill, the leaders were much weakening their chances of a settlement with the king, and as time passed the king was much improving his chances of a settlement with the Scots, after which he could dispose of Parliament as he pleased. To add to the general alarm, 1641 produced a long, hot summer, and the plague broke out in London. During July and August, little progress was made, and on one occasion, the Commons even broke their principles by sitting on a Sunday. Long debates were producing fatigue, and on one occasion, when important new business was introduced late in the afternoon, the Speaker, who had no deputy, protested that it was very late, and he had sat very late the night before, and he could not hold out to sit seven or eight hours a day. Pym, who was careful of good relations with the Speaker, moved that the House adjourn. Sooner or later the House would have to have a recess, or it might be unable to do business for lack of a quorum. Popular discontent was growing, and the Venetian Ambassador complained that common people, and even women, were setting up to preach. The censorship had broken down, though a parliamentary committee laboured valiantly to reimpose it, and a stream of pamphlets of various styles was coming off the press. Large numbers of scurrilous verses were produced, such as *Lambeth Fair, Or the Sale of the Bishops' Trinkets*.[74] Members were printing their speeches, though the leaders struggled to preserve the principle that speeches could not be printed without the consent of the House. All this publication was producing a general ferment which was growing harder to suppress. The first regular English newspapers appeared during this period, to the dismay of many respectable citizens.

Rumours were still spreading about the king's intentions of calling in foreign help. The queen was discussing going to Holland, possibly to raise troops, and some of the parliamentary leaders may possibly have been discussing plans to seize the queen.[75] The parliamentary leaders were struggling in vain to ensure that when the armies were disbanded, the English army should be disbanded before the Scottish army. Perhaps most alarming, the king started threatening to go to Scotland. The Venetian Ambassador reported that when he did, the foreign ambassadors would move with the queen to Bristol, in order to be out of danger if the king

---

[74] On Richard Overton, the author of this pamphlet, see below, pp. 347–8.

[75] B.M. Harl. MS. 6424, fo. 94r. Sir John Clotworthy, who appears to be the original source of this story, was the leadership's spokesman on Irish affairs. He was well informed, but not necessarily reliable.

came back to London at the head of a Scottish or English army. Warwick tried to persuade the king not to go, but at the end of August he went. The treaty was concluded on 7 September 1641, and Parliament was left without protection. So long as the king was in Scotland, they were safe, and they decided on a recess during his absence. During the recess, they left a standing committee in session at Westminster (which was charged, in addition to urgent business, with the task of setting up a West India Company), and they sent another committee, headed by John Hampden, to keep an eye on the king in Scotland. In Scotland, the king conceded all the Scots' demands, and so accepted the terms which, if he had taken them in 1639, would have saved him from ever having to call Parliament at all. Exactly what happened in Scotland is obscure, but the king did not secure the Scots' agreement to help him against Parliament, and when he came back, late in November 1641, it was without an army.

Before he came back, the political situation had again been transformed, and he had again been uncomfortably reminded that he ruled over three kingdoms. Towards the end of 1641 a massive rebellion broke out in Ireland, and once again Charles could not suppress it unless the English Parliament would vote him the money. Parliament, though much distressed by reports of massacres of Protestants in Ireland, was not going to vote the king money to cut their own throats. Part of the Scottish army was sent to Ireland, and for the rest, Pym proposed that Parliament should vote the king the money to suppress the Irish rebellion if he would appoint such great officers as Parliament should be willing to trust. This proposal produced one of the characteristic debates of the second session. Waller the poet, one of the uncomfortable hesitators of the Civil War, said that this was as much constitutional innovation as what Strafford had done. Pym replied that if he were guilty of the same offence as Strafford, he should suffer the same penalty, and if not, Waller should be made to withdraw. After Waller had been sent outside while the question was debated, the House made him withdraw. After this unpromising beginning, Hyde argued the case against Pym's proposal: that the right to appoint great officers was a hereditary flower of the Crown, and that if the House had any respect for the constitution, it should not take the power from him. Pym finally had to modify his proposal, and won the division by 151 to 110. Once again the division was between those who would bend the constitution in order to preserve it and those who would not, and between those who were willing to trust the king and those who could not.

This issue was soon joined by another: attitude to the public at large. During November the House was debating the Grand Remonstrance, a long, comprehensive indictment of Charles's government ever since 1625, accusing him of setting up arbitrary government and relying on the support of a 'popish and malignant' party. The only possible aim of this document was to appeal to the people at large by making propaganda against Charles, and when, in the small hours, a number of members attempted to enter their protestations against the decision to print it, the House nearly broke up in riot. The Remonstrance itself was only carried by eleven votes.

The situation was one of deadlock. Parliament had failed to get its way out of the king, and would have to face steadily more violent courses if it was to go on trying. If the leaders took this course, stripping Charles of more and more of his powers, and raising popular agitation against him, they would make enemies in the House, and possibly lose their majority. This, perhaps, was what Charles hoped would happen. He, meanwhile, would not concede what was wanted, and lacked either the will or the resources to use force against the Parliament. At the end of December 1641, it seemed that he was at last plucking up courage to follow the advice of those who urged him to use force. He changed the Lieutenant of the Tower, and sent troops to guard the Surrey magazine at Kingston. The City, where the parliamentarians were winning control from the king's sympathizers among the aldermen,[76] suffered a major panic, and barricades were put up in Cheapside, while women prepared boiling cauldrons to pour on the heads of marauding cavaliers. The Commons, meanwhile, read a bill sponsored by Haselrig to transfer control of the militia to people nominated by Parliament: if Charles was to raise force, so would they. At last all Charles's preparations brought forth an attempt to accuse five members of the Commons, Pym, Hampden, Haselrig, Holles, and Strode, and one Lord, Mandeville,[77] of high treason. The attempt was incompetently carried out, and though Strode attempted to stay and face his accusers, the five members had taken refuge in the City. The members were also incompetently selected: St. John, for example, was omitted, and the inclusion of Holles and Strode, who had helped to hold the Speaker down in his chair in 1629, probably reflected Charles's belief that he was dealing with a long-standing conspiracy by a few people. The fact that Charles had actually come to the House with armed men at his back brought alarm to fever pitch, and the Commons withdrew to meet at the Guildhall, under the protection of the City. Hyde, Falkland, and Culpeper, who were beginning to lead the king towards constitutional courses, and

[76] On the issues involved in city politics during this period, see Pearl, Valerie, *London and the Puritan Revolution*, 107–59.

[77] Mandeville is sometimes known by his other title of Kimbolton, or by the title of Manchester, which he inherited from his father in 1642.

trying to win him a majority in the House, were in despair. At last, the king decided that the atmosphere in London was too uncomfortable, and withdrew, first to Hampton Court, and then to Windsor. He and his Parliament never met again in the same place until he was put on trial for his life by the vote of twenty-six members six years later.

The Civil War was another seven months in gestation from this occasion, but it was hard to see any way of avoiding it after the king's withdrawal from London. Both sides issued lengthy Remonstrances and collections of Propositions, appealing for support and attempting to show that the breach of unity was all the other side's fault. The propaganda of these months, however, is more a contest about the placing of the blame than any genuine attempt at a reconciliation. It seems that neither side really wanted the war, but both were too frightened of the other's intentions to trust any settlement. Both were too frightened to avoid making military preparations, and each could point to the other side's military preparations as proving the necessity of their own. In Professor Aylmer's words, 'the orthodox maxim of *si vis pacem, para bellum*, carried the day, and was followed by its usual consequences'.[78] The key issue of these months was control of the magazine at Hull, where the king might have landed foreign troops. Parliament sent Sir John Hotham down to take control of Hull, and war grew appreciably nearer when Hotham refused to open the gates to let in the king. In March, the king withdrew to York, and one by one the royalists members slipped away to join him, but it was not until August that the king raised his standard at Nottingham, and a state of war was legally begun.[79]

Any attempt to analyse the causes of this war must take account of the way it began. Hypotheses which attempt to explain why people might have wanted to fight a civil war are valueless for explaining a situation in which they did not want to fight one. Attempts to explain a deliberate revolution are inappropriate to a situation in which no deliberate revolution took place. It is also important to distinguish between leaders and followers. Far-reaching social explanations may be appropriate to the careers of radicals like John Lilburne. But these were not the men who made the revolution: they were the men who, later, would raise a revolution against the men who made the revolution. For the political leaders who made the war, there seems to be only one explanation: sheer fear of the intentions of the other side. Behind this fear is a profound depth of misunderstanding of the other side: the misunderstanding is appropriate

[78] Aylmer, 382.
[79] The unfurling of the king's banners legally created a state of war. Keen, Maurice, 'Treason Trials under the Law of Arms', *T.R.H.S.* (1962), 102.

matter for deep explanations, but they will not be explanations of a war: they will be explanations of personal and ideological distrust, and of the breakdown of a system of government which the parliamentarians desperately wanted to preserve, but which could not keep up with inflation or with division in religion. The argument of 1641 was not about how to replace this system of government: it was about whom to blame for its failure to work efficiently and to the general satisfaction. That the system itself might have become inoperable was a prospect which only a few temperamental extremists, Haselrig and Marten on one side, and perhaps a few of the queen's circle on the other, could face. When the wheel came full circle, in 1660, the same men started the same scheme for the king to fill the great offices with men Parliament trusted. Once again the scheme misfired, though once again Saye and Sele got high office.[80]

Those who made the war were a small number of people in Parliament. Those who took sides in it were a large number of people all over the country. This distinction should be remembered in attempts to make social analyses of the allegiance of the public. The motives which might impel a man to choose between sides which already existed were very different from those which might impel a man to make a side. Many, for example, chose the side which controlled the area of their estates, the side from which they might hope to win military contracts, or simply the side they expected to win. It is hard to see deep social cleavages in the choice of sides. The gentry, many of whom were engaged, were split fairly evenly, with a slight majority for the Parliament. The peers were mostly engaged, with a slight majority for the king. Some merchants, most of whom were Puritans, were deeply engaged, but the majority of merchants were not: war, after all, is bad for trade. In some towns, the split seems to have been between an inner ring of merchants who had won concessions as customs farmers or monopolists, and an outer ring which objected to the privileges of the inner ring. This should not necessarily be seen as a split of principle, since some members of outer rings were happy to be as exclusive as their predecessors when in power. The fact that Puritan sympathies tended to be concentrated in towns might have a social significance, but it might not: Puritanism was spread through books and sermons, both of which were more easily organized in towns than in the country. Nor should too much be made of the geographical distribution of support, since every area included its royalists and parliamentarians: there were even royalist sympathizers in London. In the last resort, geographical distribution of support was determined by the fluctuating movements of armies more than by any social principle. Only two recurrent divisions

[80] Charles II, with possibly deliberate humour, made him Lord Privy Seal.

emerge from analyses of allegiance. One is religious: Puritans were on one side, and Catholics and Arminians on the other. The other is of age: both in Parliament and in the Civil Service, royalists were on average ten years younger than parliamentarians. One possible explanation of this mystifying fact is suggested by Dr. Tyacke's discovery that a large majority of the members who were conspicuous opponents of Arminianism in the 1620s had completed their education before 1600. In religion, at least, it is the parliamentarians who were the conservatives, defending the doctrines they had learnt when young. On both sides, the Civil War was a last desperate attempt to ensure that there should be only one religion in England. It was also the failure of a system of taxation. The two failures were closely connected.

Postscript

The account of the appropriation of supply in 1624 and of the dissolution in 1625 are superseded in my *Parliaments and English Politics*. It now appears that the appropriation of supply in 1624 was largely the work of James himself. There is no sufficient reason for believing that the Parliament of 1625 intended to impeach the Duke, since it lacked the noble and conciliar leadership which was so essential to the impeachment of 1626. The outbreak of the French war of 1627 may owe as much to the state of French domestic politics as to any errors by the Duke. Some of the judgements made on Queen Henrietta Maria in this chapter are justly criticized by R. M. Smuts, 'The Puritan Followers of Henrietta Maria in the 1630s', *E.H.R.* (1978). The Queen's French loyalties always cut across her Catholic loyalties.

7. England's new chains discovered
1642–1660

Our posterity will say that to deliver them from the yoke of the king we have subjected them to that of the common people. If we do this, the finger of scorn will be pointed at us and so I am determined to devote my life to repressing the audacity of the people.

Earl of Essex, Parliamentary Commander in Chief, 1644[1]

I could not, riding alone about my business, but smile out to God in praises, in assurance of victory because God would, by things that are not, bring to naught things that are. Of which I had great assurance; and God did it.

Oliver Cromwell, Parliamentary Lieutenant-General,
recalling the evening before the battle of Naseby, 1645[2]

In the autumn of 1642 the majority of England's leading citizens appear to have been surprised, not to say dismayed and incredulous, to find themselves at war. Even in the king's camp at Nottingham there was a strong body of feeling in favour of negotiation rather than war. At Westminster, the aim had never been to start a war, but to use the threat of war to force Charles to come to a political settlement which would enable them to avoid fighting. It took a long time for many members to appreciate that their mere appearance in arms would not be sufficient to convince Charles that they meant business, and to bring about satisfactory negotiations. At worst, many hoped that winning one battle might be sufficient, and even as late as the summer of 1643, one prominent M.P. wanted to end the war with one formal set piece battle on Hampstead Heath. In many of the counties, hesitation was even greater than among the leaders. In Yorkshire, a number of gentry hoped to keep the war out of their county, and in Kent

[1] Brailsford, H. T. N., *The Levellers* (1961), 35.
[2] Woolrych, *Battles*, 125.

there was little sign of war until the arrival of a force from Westminster at the end of the year. Kent is a good example of the misleading nature of the maps which show some parts of the country for the king, and others for the Parliament. It is true that Parliament retained military control of Kent throughout the war, but this is primarily because the king never succeeded in sending any troops there. There was some royalism, and much neutralism, among the Kentish gentry, and Kent was 'Parliamentarian' only in the sense that it was under parliamentary control. Civil War maps are also misleading because they conceal the extent to which the war was a matter of local feuds, often dating from long before the war. In Oxford, the university was for the king, while the town was parliamentarian. In many counties, royalist and parliamentarian families had been on opposite sides ever since the Wars of the Roses.

There is little sign that the two sides in 1642 represented any profound social divisions. In the towns, there was some tendency for the war to become a contest of an outer ring against a privileged (and royalist) inner ring, but these contests do not seem to have covered any very profound differences of economic approach or social class. In London, Dr. Pearl has concluded that the new aldermen 'frequently adopted commercial policies . . . and policies in regard to municipal affairs, which were very similar to those of their predecessors'.[3] In Staffordshire, a detailed investigation has shown no clear social or economic division between the two sides.

The clearest division between the two sides seems to be religious and cultural. It is almost universally true that Puritans fought for the Parliament, and high churchmen and Catholics for the king. This does not mean that either side was composed of zealots: many of the M.P.s who fought for Parliament were no more Puritan than Archbishop Grindal had been, and were perfectly willing to accept Puritan bishops like Archbishop Ussher of Armagh. It appeared, however, that under Laud there was no room in the national church for people of this stamp, and neither they nor Laud were able or willing to imagine a world in which men could live in safety outside the national church of their country. Their object was not to destroy the national church, but to prevent the bishops from driving them out of it. Baxter, a moderate Puritan clergyman, complained that the bishops were the greatest sect-makers in England, adding: 'to persecute men, and then call them to charity, is like whipping children to make them give over crying.'[4] Together with the religious division went a division between a Puritan civilization, cultivating the virtues of sobriety, thrift, and hard work, and a courtly and fashionable civilization. During the war

---

[3] Pearl, Valerie, *London and the Puritan Revolution* (1961), 245.
[4] Nuttall, G. F., *Visible Saints* (1957), 7 n.

in Yorkshire, the royalist commander challenged Fairfax, the parliamentarian commander, who was trying to mask the disadvantages of inferior numbers by a skilful use of fortified towns, to come out and put it to the issue of one pitched battle. Fairfax replied that he did not choose to fight wars according to the rules of Amadis de Gaule or the Knight of the Sun. Hyde's friend Chillingworth, preaching before the king at Oxford, produced one of the most effective summaries of the war when he said that all the scribes and pharisees were on one side, and all the publicans and sinners on the other. It is easy to exaggerate this division: most of the parliamentarian commanders, including Fairfax and Cromwell, had long hair, and there were plenty of parliamentarians whose lives provided material for scandalous gossip, but as a summary of the driving force behind the two sides, Chillingworth's verdict may be allowed to stand.[5]

More fundamental issues were involved in the allegiances of the American and West Indian colonies. Barbados reacted like many English counties, by wanting to preserve its neutrality, and was successful: anyone calling another man 'Roundhead' or 'Cavalier' was forced to buy a dinner for everyone who heard him do so. Other colonies were more enthusiastic. In Virginia, where attempts were made to exclude all non-Anglicans from the colony, government was on the whole in the hands of gentlemen, and the settlers were already beginning to import Negro servants to cultivate the tobacco plantations. In Virginia, royalism was aimed at preserving both church and gentry. The Catholic colony of Maryland had little choice but to be royalist. In Massachusetts, on the other hand, the English institution of the gentry had never really taken root, and political power was in the hands, not of gentlemen, but of an oligarchy of members of Puritan churches. The colony was populated largely by emigration of English Puritans, who, though not in the strictest sense separatists, organized their churches on lines which had nothing to do with the Church of England. Power in Massachusetts was usually in the hands of the whole body of the faithful congregation of each church. They regarded themselves as a 'saving remnant' of the faithful, having escaped from England, as Lot had escaped from Sodom, before the wrath to come, and they were ready to expel from the colony anyone whose Puritanism

---

[5] A speech by Cromwell is commonly quoted against this view, in which he said that 'religion was not the thing first contested for, but God brought it to that issue at last': Carlyle, *Cromwell's Letters and Speeches* (1849), iv. 106–7. This speech needs to be interpreted in the light of the fact that in seventeenth-century usage, 'religion' normally means 'true religion'. See above p. 201 and Woodhouse, A. S. P., *Puritanism and Liberty* (1938), 153–4. In the context of this speech it is clear that by 'religion' Cromwell meant liberty of conscience, which, as he said, was not the thing contested for at the beginning of the war.

did not satisfy them, saying that Massachusetts was no place for such as they. Massachusetts was strongly parliamentarian, and in the later years of the war many of its inhabitants, feeling that England was now safe for them, came back, and played a large part in English preaching and politics. Together with them came a large number of Puritan refugees from Holland, whose radicalism deeply shocked many of the M.P.s for whom they were fighting. For some of these people, godliness, and not gentility, was the test of qualification to hold political power, a doctrine which parliamentary Puritan gentlemen rightly regarded as subversive.

Some of these returning exiles brought with them some radical political ideas. Holland was a republic, and a constant reminder that a nation could run successfully without a king. One minister back from Holland believed that kings only acquired divine right by the choice of the people, and another man back from Massachusetts believed that the only way any government could normally acquire divine right was by democratic election. Such doctrines, though they preserved the belief that divine right was the only way in which any government could be legitimate, were hard to combine with the old hierarchical doctrines of the Great Chain of Being.

Parliament's war aims

These ideas, however, were in sharp contrast to the political ideas current in Parliament, where there was little attempt to justify resistance to the king, because many of the members maintained throughout the war that they were not fighting against the king, but for him, to rescue him from the evil counsellors who surrounded him. Parliamentary commissions were issued in the name of king and Parliament, and this fiction was sustained by a distinction between the public and private capacities of the king. Taxpayers in East Anglia were asked in 1643 to subscribe to a formula that the orders of Parliament were to be obeyed as much as those of former Parliaments, 'and that because the king's authority and power is there, though his person be not'. The parliamentary Vice-Admiral, changing sides after the war was over, said he had supposed all this time that he was fighting to bring the king to his Parliament. The arguments of the parliamentarians were not expressed in terms of parliamentary sovereignty, but in terms of unity. As Pym said, 'the king and his people are obliged to one another in the nearest relations . . . he is the head, they are the body: there is such an incorporation, as cannot be dissolved, without the destruction of both'.[6] Lord Saye and Sele, defending a theory with a long history, believed that England was a mixed monarchy,

[6] Rushworth, *Trial of Strafford*, 666. *Stuart Constitution*, 285.

in which the supreme power was king, Lords and Commons, and that they were fighting to preserve the existence of Parliament, which was one part of the supreme power of the kingdom. Saye was thus able to combine fighting for Parliament with maintaining that it was never lawful to take up arms to change the laws of the kingdom.

The parliamentarians were not fighting for parliamentary sovereignty. They believed, with some justification in fact, if not in law, that the government of England had been a working partnership between the king and the gentry, and they felt that they needed to prevent the king from dissolving this partnership and ruling without any attempt to co-operate with the gentry. In their pleas for restoration of unity, they must be taken to be sincere: they did not want a divorce between king and Parliament, but a restitution of conjugal rights.

For most of them, the guarantee of co-operation between the king and the gentry, and the terms on which it took place, was the rule of law. One of the most popular beliefs among the parliamentarians was the belief in 'fundamental law', though, as Hobbes later complained, 'I could never see in any author, what a fundamental law signifieth.' Fundamental laws, on the whole, were those laws which determined that the type of constitution in England should not change: that the king would continue to work in partnership with the gentry, or, as Parliament would have it, with the 'people'. Denzil Holles, one of the most conservative of the parliamentarians, could only explain the war by saying that 'It pleased God in his just judgement, for the punishment of our sins, to set a spirit of division between the king and the people.'[7] These people were not rebelling against the social hierarchy. Saye, according to Clarendon, was as proud of his title as any man alive, and thought that the peers were essential to preserving a balance of power between the king and the people. Such men were not natural revolutionaries: if they were to win a victory, they were likely to be embarrassed by it, and if the king were still to refuse to negotiate a settlement with them, they were unlikely to have much idea what to do next. They were, in Professor Kenyon's phrase, 'sturdy reactionaries', who wanted, not a brave new world, but a return to the old world of Grindal, Leicester, and Walsingham.

Division between Parliament and its radical supporters

This social conservatism is illustrated in the first list of parliamentary colonels. Out of twenty, ten were peers, and four were knights or baronets. The Commander in Chief was the Earl of Essex, a moderate and gentlemanly Puritan who, in Hexter's phrase, 'embodied everything that stood

---

[7] *Memorials* (1699), 4. Holles was writing in 1648.

for respectability and conservatism'.[8] It was soon apparent, however, that Parliament would have to rely on supporters whose outlook was very different from their own. Puritanism in the hands of a real social radical could mean something very different from what it meant in the hands of the Earl of Essex, and once Parliament had started the habit of using the Bible or Coke's *Institutes* as a touchstone to try whether the actions of authority were in accord with the law of God or the law of the land, they could not be too surprised if some of their followers applied the principle against themselves. For example, the second in command of Lord Brooke's regiment was John Lilburne, who four years later was telling the House of Lords: 'All you intended when you set us a-fighting was merely to unhorse and dismount our old riders and tyrants, that so you might get up and ride us in their stead. And therefore my Lords . . . if you shall be so unworthy as to persevere . . . in the destruction of the fundamental laws and liberties of England . . . I will venture my life and heart's blood against you with as much zeal and courage as ever I did against any of the king's party.'[9] The fact that in the circumstances of 1642 Lord Brooke and Lilburne worked harmoniously together is a testimony to the character of both men, as well as to the power of Puritanism to create strange bedfellows in the fight against the king, but the parliamentary conservatives were entitled to wonder whether in the end they might not find their allies more dangerous enemies than the king.

The variety of pamphlets released by the collapse of censorship already showed that the enforcement of Puritan orthodoxy under the control of the gentry was going to be very difficult indeed. Overton, later Lilburne's colleague in the Leveller movement, was already showing his power as a satirist, and he was exactly the sort of person who worried the parliamentary leaders. He was a printer by trade, and had been in exile in Holland, where he had belonged to a Baptist congregation. But Overton did not only represent religious radicalism: he also represented a tough secularism which in the end would be much harder for Puritan authorities to deal with. He published a pamphlet in 1643 expressing doubts about the immortality of the soul, and in his pamphlets he showed a satirical anti-clericalism in the tradition of Martin Marprelate. He was not content with making fun of bishops, but showed himself equally ready to satirize Puritan orthodoxy by parodying the demand that Cheapside Cross should be pulled down as a monument to idolatry. Overton believed the State should have no power to enforce religion at all, and could be relied on to muster all his wit against any body of clergy who looked likely to gain

---

[8] Hexter, J. H., *The Reign of King Pym* (1941), 113.
[9] Brailsford, op. cit., 93.

control. Many obscure religious radicals were hoping that at last they would be free from the threat of persecution, and the Parliament was in the difficult position of having to rely on their support while hoping to be able to disappoint them afterwards.

Moreover, some of Parliament's supporters who were not gentry showed an alarming vigour in prosecuting the war. The gentry, on the whole, tended to fight in the style of people who expected to have to sit together on the Bench after the war was over. They would fight hard enough in a battle, but safe-conducts, paroles, and truces were usually faithfully observed, and outside armies they would continue to treat each other with courtesy. There was a very different spirit in the small town of Birmingham, where the metal-workers at once set out to produce 15,000 sword-blades for Essex's army. According to Clarendon, they were 'so generally wicked' that they used to seize on any party of royalists they could find in the neighbourhood, and send them to Coventry, which was the site of the nearest parliamentary garrison. This appears to be the origin of the phrase 'sending to Coventry'. Birmingham is unlikely to have become more moderate when punished for its 'wickedness' by a vicious sack from the royalist commander Prince Rupert.

Divisions in Parliament

The reaction of many members of Parliament to their own supporters could be summed up in Wellington's words about his troops: 'I don't know whether they frighten the enemy, but by God, they frighten me.' As early as 1643, one of the parliamentary supporters gave it as his reason for changing sides that Parliament were promoting too many officers who were not gentlemen.* These tensions produced something of a split among the members of Parliament. The split was not about whether they sympathized with the radicalism of some of their supporters: they did not. The split was about whether they regarded their radical supporters or the king as their worst enemies. Most misleadingly, these two groups in Parliament have come to be known by the names of 'Presbyterian' and 'Independent'. As usual, theories of church government have provided convenient labels for classification, without providing much of the real ground for dispute. There were some genuine Presbyterians and Independents, and there were some people, especially among the clergy, for whom this difference was a genuine ground of dispute, but it was not the basis of the political groups in Parliament.

Roughly, the division between genuine Presbyterians and Independents

* The real reason appears to be that his garrison had not been paid. East Riding R. O. Hotham MSS, 1/10.

was between those who looked to Scotland, and those who looked to New England for an example of how to run a Puritan church. The Scottish Presbyterian system provided an efficient means for running a disciplined national church. Each parish was governed by the minister, with the aid of lay elders, and the parishes were united by the authority of a system of assemblies leading up to a national synod. In Scotland, Presbyterianism tended to mean clerical supremacy, but in England, most Presbyterians insisted, to the dismay of the Scots, that synods should be firmly under the control of Parliament, and that a much higher proportion of power than the Scots would tolerate should be given to lay elders. Since lay elders, in practice, tended to mean the J.P.s, Presbyterianism on the English model, whatever Charles II might say to the contrary, was a suitable religion for gentlemen. Even the list of offences for which excommunication was allowed was to be fixed by Parliament, to guard against clerical tyranny. Most of the English Presbyterians objected vehemently to toleration, wanted one united national church, with no dissent permitted, and wanted to preserve the supremacy of the gentry.

The true Independents, on the other hand, were Congregationalists, who, though they might allow the existence of elders, believed that ultimate authority rested with the whole body of the congregation. They also believed that the church consisted, not of the whole nation, but of the Elect, the Saints, who were voluntary members of a church. They might, and in Massachusetts did, rely on the power of the State to repress dangerous doctrines, but they had no machinery equivalent to that of the Presbyterians for enforcing unity between different congregations. For most M.P.s the difference between Presbyterian and Independent church government was not a matter of fundamental principle, and it has been hard to take the division between 'Presbyterians' and 'Independents' literally since J. H. Hexter discovered that a higher proportion of political 'Independents' than of 'Presbyterians' served as Presbyterian elders.[10]

However, the Presbyterian–Independent divide became a convenient peg for two much more fundamental and closely related divisions. The first was between those who did, and those who did not, think it vital that the country should remain united in one national church, and the second was about whether England should or should not remain under the political control of the gentry. Since religion had always been held to be one of the main guarantees of the existing social order, these issues became more and more closely involved during the 1640s. It is easy to exaggerate the sup-

---

[10] Hexter, J. H., 'The Problem of the Presbyterian Independents', *American Hist. Rev.* (1938–9), 29–49. See also Underdown, D. E., 'The Independents Reconsidered', *Journal of British Studies* (1964), 57–85.

port of Independent clergy for toleration, yet for believers in toleration, as for social radicals, the Independents were clearly the better horse to back.

The issue of Presbyterians against Independents in any case did not become acute until after Parliament had won the Civil War, and during the Civil War, the different groups in Parliament are better known by the names of the peace and war parties. The peace party regretted the war, and were looking for the first convenient means of getting out of it. They were consistently in favour of negotiations with the king, not unduly punctilious about obtaining any real guarantees for a settlement, and consistently against measures for the more vigorous management of the war. One of them once opposed fortifying a town which was threatened by the king on the ground that to fortify it would be illegal. The war party, on the other hand, were inclined to distrust Charles, to be suspicious of negotiations, and to support measures for raising more money or more troops. The peace party, on the whole, tended to see the war ending in a settlement, and the war party to see it ending in a victory. Unlike royalists and parliamentarians, these two groups on the parliamentary side were separated by some social division. The peace party had a large majority among the peers, and in the Commons it tended to gather those gentry with the largest incomes.

In the Commons, the two groups were roughly evenly balanced, and power tended to rest in the hands of a small middle group, dominated by Pym, who, with the declining importance of the parliamentary peers, was for the first time approaching real leadership in Parliament. Pym shared all the conservatism of the peace party, but at the same time, he appreciated that there was no point in fighting a war without trying to win it. The effect of this position was that Pym and his friends would support proposals for negotiation, while trying to carry measures for the more vigorous prosecution of the war, in case the negotiations should fail. Yet, while they wanted to make their military force effective, Pym and his friends were determined to keep it in reliable hands, and were consistent supporters of Essex as commander in chief, even when Essex's military failures made it increasingly clear that he was not a good general.

War finance and administration

'An army,' as Harrington later said, 'is a beast that hath a great belly, and must be fed.' Winning the war was largely a matter of financial organization and resources: an army with no ammunition could not fight, and an army with no food usually would not fight. Probably Pym's greatest achievement was the creation of a financial and administrative machine which, in the long run, would enable Parliament to win the war. It has been said that 'the civil war was won by committees',[11] and it is one of the distinctions of the parliamentarians that they turned the committee into an efficient instrument of business. In London, the indefatigable energy of Prynne was harnessed to running a Committee for the Accounts of the Kingdom, while in each county parliamentary taxes were collected, and local forces organized, under the authority of a County Committee which was dominated by the leading parliamentarian M.P.s in the county. The advantage of these County Committees was that they knew each other and had an established authority in their own area. Their disadvantage was their determined localism. They tended to insist that their forces were raised for the defence of the county, and to refuse to pay them if they were sent on a campaign anywhere else. The troops themselves were usually glad enough of the excuse to go home. To almost as great an extent, this was also true of the associations of neighbouring counties which were formed during the war. In 1645, the committee of the Eastern Association strongly opposed the proposal to create the New Model Army, which was to be a national army. When a gentleman from Hertfordshire objected that the proposal was for the safety of the kingdom, they answered that the safety of the kingdom was no concern of theirs, since they had met as a committee of the Eastern Association. Parliament had almost as much difficulty as Charles I in establishing a firm control over county authorities.

Yet, though the taxes often stayed in the county, they were collected, in sums which, by pre-war standards, were quite incredible. Suffolk, for example, paid £337,000 in the years from 1642 to 1648. Much of the war was paid for by loans on the security of the Public Faith, and by sequestering the estates of royalists, but a number of new taxes were also created. The most important of these was the Excise, which was Pym's own invention, and was carried through by him against powerful opposition in Parliament. This was a sales tax on such popular commodities as beer and tobacco, which brought in over £300,000 a year. It was highly unpopular among the poor, and among people who ran small businesses. Yet it was too useful to be abolished, and even survived the Restoration. The other main parliamentary tax, the Weekly Assessment, was ironically modelled on Ship Money, and brought in over £600,000 a year. Taxes on this scale provoked widespread public resentment. It was only possible to vote them because the voting of taxes no longer needed agreement between king and Parliament, and only possible to collect them because soldiers could be used to enforce payment.

By contrast, the king had a less effective system for raising money.

[11] Pennington, D. H., 'The Committee for the Accounts of the Kingdom', in *Essays Presented to R. H. Tawney*, Ed. F. J. Fisher (1961), 182.

He finally introduced an Excise of his own, but too late to be very effective. In the main, the king relied on contributions from his richer supporters, a weekly assessment, and sequestration of his opponents' estates. If the war could be brought to a quick conclusion, Charles might have a finanical advantage, but he had not the financial and administrative machinery to stand up to Parliament in a long-drawn-out struggle.

Paradoxically, Charles's character meant that what should have been the royalists' advantage of having a single central command became one of their main disadvantages. Charles could have imposed one clear policy on his followers, but he did not: he had a Council of War, but he was always reversing its decisions behind its back, often without telling its members. He continued with his old weakness of following two contradictory policies at once: he often combined negotiations with Parliament for a settlement with attempts to persuade the Dutch, the Danes, or any other allies he could find to send foreign troops to suppress his rebellious subjects. Since his letters to foreign powers were often intercepted at crucial moments, and his own ministers rarely knew whether he was supporting the policies he had asked them to carry out, he tended to get the worst of both worlds.

A crucial obstacle to his attempts to get foreign help was Parliament's control of the navy, established at the very beginning of the war. The fleet also helped to sustain parliamentary garrisons at Hull and Plymouth, and could be used regularly to relieve sieges of ports, or to move food and artillery. The Earl of Warwick, who commanded the fleet on Parliament's behalf, was an experienced sailor, and popular with his men, and it is arguable that he contributed as much to Parliament's ultimate victory as any land commander.

Charles too suffered some division among his supporters. The division, roughly, was between those whose loyalty was based on the concessions of 1641, most of whom hoped to settle the war by negotiation, and the queen's friends, who had no interest in constitutional concessions, and hoped to win the war by calling in foreign or Irish troops. Many of his supporters took no line on these issues: for them the king was king, and that was 'all ye know, and all ye need to know'. They took seriously the belief on which almost all Englishmen had been brought up, and to which even the parliamentarians continued to pay lip-service, that rebellion was a sin, and 'they that resist shall receive to themselves damnation'. For them, it was the same principle of obedience which guaranteed the supremacy of their own class, and they tended to see a threat to the position of the gentry inherent in the parliamentarians' cause long before it was there. Much of the evidence to suggest that parliamentarians wanted to challenge the peerage, for example, is taken from the words of alarmed royalists like the Marquis of Newcastle. This evidence, though it tells us nothing about the parliamentarians, tells us a good deal about Newcastle. If the king had won, these divisions among his supporters might have become crucial, but in the event, they were all merged in defeat.

II THE CIVIL WAR, 1642–1645

You often hear us called the Popish army, but you see we trust not in our good works.

> *Marquis of Newcastle, on finding his siege trenches at Hull flooded*
> *by the parliamentarians, 1643*[12]

The opening rounds, 1642–1643

When Charles had gathered an army, the obvious thing for him to do was to attempt to recover control of his capital, which was the seat of most of the administration, and a valuable source of funds. By the middle of September 1642, Charles had gathered a substantial army at Shrewsbury. He had found, as he was to continue to do for the rest of the war, that Wales was one of his best recruiting grounds for foot-soldiers, a fact which gave rise to much anti-Welsh propaganda in London. He had also been joined by his nephew Prince Rupert, son of Elizabeth of Bohemia, who, though not his commander in chief, rapidly became his ablest general. Having resumed the sale of titles, Charles managed to raise enough money for a campaign, and set out for London. At the end of the first day's march, he spoke to his troops at Wellington, telling them that they had few enemies to meet but Brownists, Anabaptists, and atheists. This may have been good stuff to give the troops (though it is unlikely to have convinced those with neighbours or brothers on the other side), but the tragedy of the speech is that Charles may have actually believed it.

On 23 October 1642, Charles found the parliamentarian army under Essex approaching him from the rear, and the two armies, each about 14,000 strong, met in battle at Edgehill. As the armies prepared for battle, one of the senior royalist commanders stopped for a brief prayer: 'O Lord, thou knowest how busy I must be this day. If I forget thee, do not thou forget me . . . March on, boys!'[13] When the battle started, Rupert's cavalry routed the forces opposite them, and, not for the last time, charged off in hot pursuit and took no further part in the battle. In the rest of the battle, Parliament had a slight advantage. Unfortunately for those who hoped the war could be settled by one battle, the result could only be

---

[12] Gardiner, *GCW*, i. 242.   [13] Gardiner, *GCW*, i. 44.

described as a draw, and a draw involving considerable bloodshed at that. Charles continued his march on London, and Essex drew off his army in good order to defend it.

By November, Charles had reached Brentford. As he drew nearer, the peace party in London grew stronger, and negotiations were opened. Charles had two possible courses: he could put his heart into the negotiations, or into the attack on London. Typically, he chose both courses, and in the middle of the negotiations, when many parliamentarians thought there was a cease-fire, Holles and Brooke's regiments at Brentford found Rupert's cavalry bursting on them out of the mist at a few yards' distance. Heroic fighting by Lilburne, who was taken prisoner, enabled them to withdraw in good order. Charles's troops were now only eight miles from London, and in the City, women from the Lady Mayoress to Billingsgate fishwives were digging trenches and putting chains across the streets to stop cavalry charges. The City trained bands marched out to join Essex's army in defending their homes. On 13 November, the two armies were drawn up facing each other on Turnham Green: about 12,000 troops under Rupert, against about 24,000, half of them raw levies with no experience of fighting. Rupert's troops were handicapped by the fact that the ground was unsuitable for a cavalry charge. The City troops were accompanied by a vast crowd of their wives and families, waiting on the sidelines to see what would happen. If Rupert had won, the war would probably have been over. As it was, he spent the whole day watching the parliamentarian troops, to the accompaniment of loud noises from the crowd whenever any movement was seen in his army. In the evening, he withdrew without fighting, and the City wives brought out their husbands' dinners on to the field.

After Turnham Green, Charles withdrew to set up headquarters at Oxford, and both sides settled down to a long war. In 1643, Charles had three armies: a northern army under Newcastle, a western army under Hopton, and Charles's own army from Oxford. Victories by Newcastle at Adwalton Moor, outside Bradford, and by Hopton at Roundway Down, near Devizes, gave Charles control of most of the north and west, and tipped the military balance sharply in his favour. However, the parliamentarian garrisons of Hull, Plymouth, and Gloucester still held out, and the royalist troops were reluctant to leave them in their rear. Hull and Plymouth were sustained by sea, and Essex succeeded in inducing the London trained bands to march out to relieve Gloucester, fighting another drawn battle at Newbury on the way home.

Return of the Scots, 1643

Though the parliamentarians held out through 1643, their morale was poor. A number of their supporters joined the king, believing they had backed the wrong horse, and London was filled with the usual recriminations of a side which fears it may be losing the war. There were demonstrations for peace, and for the more vigorous conduct of the war, and caballing for and against Essex as commander in chief. A royalist plot to kidnap the parliamentary leaders, run by an M.P. still at Westminster, added to the general suspicion. The morale of the City was lower for the fact that they had gone through the whole winter without coal. The king controlled the Newcastle and Durham coalfields, and though he would have sent coal to London, the taxes on it would have enabled him to finance the hiring of foreign mercenaries. In asking them to go without coal, Parliament put a considerable strain on the loyalty of its supporters. A man who claimed to have invented a substitute for coal said that: 'Some fine-nosed City dames used to tell their husbands: "O husband! We shall never be well, we nor our children, whilst we live in the smell of this City's seacoal smoke: pray, a country house for our health, that we may get out of this stinking seacoal smell." But how many of these fine nosed dames now cry "would to God we had seacoal, O the want of fire undoes us, O the sweet seacoal fire we used to have".[14]

Pym and his friends could only see one way to change the situation without handing over control of the army to people radical enough to drive some of their supporters over to the king, and that was to induce the Scots to come to England as their allies. The Scots were conservative enough not to wish to make any dangerous use of victory, and their presence in England could sharply tilt the balance of the war.

The Scots' price, as always, was twofold: money to pay their troops, and the imposition of Presbyterianism on England. These terms were difficult for Pym to satisfy: to raise the money, he had to get his new taxes supported by a movement which had largely been designed to resist Charles's much lighter taxation, and to get agreement for the Scots' Presbyterianism, he had to overcome opposition from many of the later 'Presbyterians', such as Holles and Essex, who wanted to keep open the option of returning to government by bishops, and resented the notion of throwing out one clerical domination, only to accept another. However, the negotiations were at last successful. A Solemn League and Covenant was signed with the Scots at Edinburgh, in which Sir Henry Vane, the

[14] Howell, Roger, *Newcastle upon Tyne and the Puritan Revolution* (1967), 154. Coal was commonly known as 'seacoal' because it had originally been gathered in the form of lumps scattered on the seashore.

most radical of the English negotiators, succeeded in achieving a loophole by making it bind the English to reform their church according to the example of the best reformed churches *and according to the word of God*. It was thus possible for soldiers like Cromwell to take the Covenant without believing that the word of God coincided at all points with practice at Edinburgh. The reform of the church was referred to the Westminster Assembly, a body of thirty laymen, a few Scots observers, and 125 ministers, mainly Presbyterian. It drew up a Directory of Worship, a catechism, and a Confession of Faith which was used by American Presbyterians until the 1960s, but its schemes for church government hung fire for some time.

The Scots' entry into the war was counteracted by an armistice between Charles and the Irish rebels, enabling him to bring over some English regiments from Ireland, and creating a panic about the prospect of an invasion by the 'barbarous Irish'. It was also counter-balanced by the death of Pym, Hampden, and Brooke. Pym's death at the end of the year seriously weakened the middle group in Parliament, in spite of gallant attempts by St. John to keep it going. Parliament was left more and more divided into factions, with fluctuating majorities and without coherent leadership. The other two deaths were perhaps as serious. Hampden, who was killed in a cavalry skirmish against Prince Rupert, had been developing into a popular and successful soldier. If he had lived, he might have prevented the army leadership from passing into the hands of people who were too radical to get on with Parliament. Lord Brooke, who was shot by a sniper at Lichfield, might have made a valuable contribution to a settlement because, in addition to his priceless ability to get on with Lilburne, he was the only one of the parliamentary leaders who had any sympathy for the principle of toleration.

Marston Moor, 1644

The Scots' army was everything men like Holles wanted: it enforced Puritan discipline, punishing swearers with acts of public repentance and loss of pay, and even punished irreverent speech against the king as high treason! Their presence soon tilted the balance of the war by making the king's northern army turn round to face them, and by reopening London's coal trade. Their first major contribution to the fighting was at the battle of Marston Moor, on 2 July 1644, the biggest battle of the war. Marston Moor also marked the first major contribution of the man who was later to become the Scots' greatest enemy, Oliver Cromwell, commander of the cavalry of the Eastern Association. He was a Puritan gentleman from Huntingdonshire, who was acquiring a partly undeserved reputation for radicalism as a result of his determination to win the war at all costs.

The battle began, for reasons which are not entirely clear, unexpectedly at 7.30 in the evening, while Newcastle was quietly smoking his after-dinner pipe. On the parliamentary right, the Yorkshire army was caught between musket fire from the hedges and a fierce cavalry charge, and was thoroughly beaten. In the centre, the Scottish foot held their ground, though having much the worst of the fighting. The key to the battle was on the parliamentary left, where, for the only time in the war, the two greatest cavalry commanders, Cromwell and Rupert, met face to face. At first, the advantage appeared to be with Rupert, and Cromwell was wounded in the neck, but he was reinforced by a body of Scots at the crucial moment and for the only time in the war, Rupert's cavalry broke and fled. Cromwell then succeeded in re-grouping his cavalry and his arrival in the centre changed the course of the rest of the battle. Most of the royalists broke and fled, and as Cromwell reported, 'God made them as stubble to our swords.' The winners, having no water, were left to drink puddles and sleep on the battlefield. On the royalist side 4,000 were dead, 6,000 withdrew in good order under Rupert, and the rest were either taken prisoner or fled in disorder. Newcastle escaped to the continent, and Parliament captured 'enough colours to make surplices for all the cathedrals in England, were they white'.[15]

Marston Moor gave Parliament control of the north, but it did not settle the war. In Scotland, a Highland army under Montrose began to win victories over the Covenanters, distracting the Scots from the war in England. In the west, Essex marched down into Cornwall, and allowed his army to be surrounded at Lostwithiel. Essex escaped and left his infantry to surrender, provoking jokes from royalist newspapers about the fact that, though the army had vowed to 'live and die with the Earl of Essex', Essex would not live and die with them. In the autumn, another indecisive battle was fought at Newbury, and at the end of 1644 the war seemed no nearer a conclusion than at the beginning.

The New Model Army, 1645

The second battle of Newbury brought to a head a smouldering quarrel between Colonel Cromwell and the Earl of Manchester, his commanding officer. In an argument about whether to continue the battle of Newbury for a second day's fighting, both men summed up their position in an exchange which has become deservedly famous. Manchester said that 'if we beat the king ninety and nine times, yet he is king still, and so will all his posterity be after him, but if the king beat us once we shall all be

[15] Gardiner, *GCW*, i. 382, ii. 2.

hanged, and our posterity made slaves'. Cromwell replied: 'my Lord, if this be so, why did we ever take up arms at first?' Cromwell's charge against Manchester was simply that he did not want to win the war. This may well be true, and it is probable that by this time he regretted ever having joined the war at all. The counter-charges against Cromwell were more various, and involved the two key issues of toleration and the supremacy of the gentry. He was accused of promoting officers who were not gentlemen, and of promoting an officer who was an Anabaptist, to which he replied: 'admit he be so, shall that render him incapable to serve the public?' He was also accused of calling the Westminster Assembly persecutors, and of commenting on the Scots' attempt to enforce Presbyterianism: 'in the way they now carry themselves, pressing for their discipline, I could as soon draw my sword against them as against any in the king's army.' Cromwell later said that 'I had rather be overrun by a Cavalierish interest than by a Scotch interest',[16] and his letter reporting Marston Moor conspicuously fails to give any credit to the Scots. It is true, however, that the triumph of Scottish discipline would have resulted in the imprisonment of many of Cromwell's soldiers, and possibly of Cromwell himself for lack of orthodoxy. Cromwell, perfectly reasonably, regarded this as a poor return for victory. Lieutenant-Colonel Lilburne, who had his own quarrel with Manchester, supported Cromwell, and Essex, Holles, and the Scots supported Manchester.

The quarrel finally produced a motion, moved by Cromwell, for a self-denying ordinance, by which all members of Parliament would lay down their commands. This motion would have got rid of Essex and Manchester, but it would also have got rid of Cromwell himself, a prospect Cromwell seems to have been perfectly willing to accept. He owed the continuation of his career, ironically, to the Lords, who refused to pass the self-denying ordinance until it had been amended to make it possible to re-appoint serving members of Parliament.

At the same time, plans were started for the organization of a New Model Army, which was to be a national army, controlled and paid from Westminster, and not by the counties. It would thus be able to move around the country uncontrolled by the localism of county committees. The command of the New Model Army was given to Sir Thomas Fairfax, commander of Parliament's Yorkshire army, who, then as later, had no identifiable line on any of the political questions which divided the parliamentarians. The post of commander of the foot was given to Major-General Skippon, a veteran officer with mild Presbyterian sympathies. Fairfax succeeded in obtaining the post of Lieutenant-General

[16] Gardiner, *GCW*, ii. 59, i. 312, ii. 23; *C & P*, i. 25.

in command of the horse for Cromwell on a temporary basis.

The New Model Army provoked great contempt among the royalists, who dismissed it as a rabble, and called it the 'New Noddle'. It also provoked great alarm among the more respectable parliamentarians, as a hotbed of radicalism and sectarianism, and in the Lords, an attempt to purge Fairfax's list of officers was only defeated by one vote. In fact, the New Model Army at the beginning was a less radical force than is often supposed. Many of its foot were recruited by press-gang, or by offering royalist prisoners the opportunity of enlistment instead of imprisonment. Its officers, especially the cavalry officers, some of whom came from Cromwell's original troop, were perhaps more radical, but even among the colonels, only seven of the first thirty-seven were not gentlemen. There was certainly something in the way of eccentric religious opinion in the New Model Army from the beginning, but there was also a considerable amount of plain ignorance and crudeness. The Governor of Newport Pagnell, admittedly a devout Presbyterian, reported that 'I think these New Modellers knead their dough with ale, for I never see so many drunk in my life in so short a time.' He called them 'an ungodly crew, grown so wild since they came near the enemy that devout Christians cannot abide them'. Baxter, a mild Presbyterian who acted briefly as an army chaplain, was shocked by the numbers of heresies in the army, but he also said that the majority, especially of the foot, were 'ignorant men of little religion'. Perhaps more alarming, he found many soldiers willing to kill the king, saying 'they thought it folly to irritate him either by wars or contradictions in Parliament, if so be they must needs take him for their king, and trust him with their lives when they had thus displeased him'. Some also asked: 'what were the Lords, but William the Conqueror's colonels?,'[17] a question of which much more was to be heard when it was taken over by the Levellers. Many, Baxter reported, believed that the civil government had no powers in religion at all. This common man's scepticism is perhaps more characteristic of the New Model Army than extreme Puritanism, and it probably owed more of its prowess as a fighting force to regular pay than to religious enthusiasm. When not paid, it mutinied like any other army. However, it was mainly the extremer Puritans who did the work of preaching to the army, and sects and heresies spread in it as the years passed.

Naseby, Langport, and Philiphaugh, 1645

The New Model's first major battle was at Naseby, near Leicester, in June 1645. They had a superiority in numbers of almost two to one, but

[17] Woolrych, *Battles*, 114; Gardiner, *GCW*, ii. 328–9.

many of them were inexperienced, and they were not the formidable fighting force they became later. The battle of Naseby was remarkably close. Rupert, in spite of having to charge through the cross-fire of a company of dragoons whom Cromwell had posted behind a hedge, as usual routed the forces opposite him and charged off the field in pursuit. In the centre, the parliamentary foot were losing, though not conclusively beaten. The battle was settled because Cromwell, on the other wing, once again succeeded in re-forming his horse after routing the forces opposite him, and returning to the main battle. His arrival turned its course, and almost all the king's foot, to the number of about 5,000, were taken prisoner. Cromwell, reporting the battle to the Speaker, concluded his letter, 'honest men served you faithfully in this action. Sir, they are trusty: I beseech you in the name of God not to discourage them . . . He that ventures his life for the liberty of his country, I wish he trust God for the liberty of his conscience, and you for the liberty he fights for.'[18] Before the Commons sent the letter to the press, they cut this passage out. Such actions contributed to the soldiers' growing doubt whether they could trust Parliament to make a settlement on their behalf once the war was over.

The war was not ended by Naseby, which need not have been more decisive than Marston Moor. The king's cavalry was still intact, he could easily recruit more foot in Wales, and he still had a full army in the west. It was this army which the New Model next went to fight. They met it at Langport, in Somerset, on 2 July 1645, and in spite of the disadvantage of having to conduct a cavalry charge through a ford and uphill along a narrow lane, they won another victory as overwhelming as Naseby. Both Charles's field armies had now been cut to pieces, and his recruitment was handicapped by unwillingness to join a losing cause. Rupert, recognizing the inevitable, advised Charles to make peace. Charles's last hope, Montrose, was beaten at Philiphaugh, and Covenanter control of Scotland was once again secure. If Charles had believed in political expediency he would have taken the advice of Rupert and the queen and negotiated the best terms with Parliament he could get. However, Charles did not believe in expediency: he believed in right action regardless of circumstances. He told Rupert:

I confess that, speaking as a mere soldier or statesman, there is no probability but of my ruin; yet, as a Christian, I must tell you that God will not suffer rebels and traitors to prosper, nor this cause to be overthrown; and whatever personal punishment it shall please him to inflict on me, must not make me repine, much less give over this quarrel; and there is as little question

[18] Gardiner, *GCW*, ii. 252.

that a composition with them at this time is nothing else but a submission, which, by the grace of God, I am resolved against, whatever it cost me; . . . Indeed I cannot flatter myself with expectation of good success more than this, to end my days with honour and a good conscience.[19]

The last royalist garrison, at Harlech, did not surrender until 1647, but from 1645 onwards, Parliament's main worries were about what to do with a victory won by an army they did not trust against a king who would concede nothing. Many of them, having no more sense of expediency than Charles, were unwilling to accept the fact that there was no solution to this problem.

III POST-WAR ENGLAND, 1645–1660

You are a free people, and are not to be pressed or enforced to serve in wars like horses or brute beasts, but are to use the understanding God hath given you, in judging of the cause, for defence whereof they desire you to fight.

William Walwyn the Leveller, 1648[20]

Notions will hurt none but those that have them. But when they come to such practices as telling us, for instance, that liberty and property are not the badges of the kingdom of Christ . . . this is worthy of every magistrate's consideration.

Oliver Cromwell on the Fifth Monarchists, 1654[21]

One of the most interesting facts about this period is that for the first time it is possible to discover something about the opinions of members of the middle and working classes: for the first time it became possible to write a history of England which is neither a history of the gentry nor a series of statistical abstractions. Yet even in this period it is not possible to generalize about the opinions of 'the people'. We know a good deal about the opinions of some people and groups who wished to get their opinions into print. But it is rash in any period to assume that those who go into print are typical of the people as a whole. Many people were concerned to win for men below the rank of gentleman some share in political power, but even Overton the Leveller thought that only a minority were behind these attempts: he thought that 'the spirits of this people (naturally of themselves noble and free) are even vassalaged, and drawn into an inconsiderate dislike of their own primitive, natural and national rights, freedoms and immunities'. He thought the majority of them were

---

[19] Gardiner, *GCW*, ii. 287.

[20] Walwyn, W., *The Bloody Project*, in *Leveller Tracts*, Ed. W. Haller and Godfrey Davies (1944), 142. Walwyn was writing immediately before the outbreak of the second Civil War.

[21] *Cromwell's Letters and Speeches*, Ed. Carlyle (1846), iv. 35.

'bestialized in their understandings', and had become 'contented slaves' to the Lords.[22] Of these 'contented slaves', we know little: it was, on the whole, the radicals who went into print.

Anti-religious reaction

We can learn something of the activities and opinions of those who did not write books from the activities of a Presbyterian minister called Thomas Edwards, the 'shallow Edwards' of Milton's sonnet on toleration. He, in order to show the dangers of toleration and a free press, set out, with the co-operation of a number of other Presbyterian ministers, to collect and record every error or scandal he could find, including such things as the conversation of his boatman. His list of errors does not altogether give the picture which Edwards meant it to give, of an outburst of wild religious enthusiasm, but rather of a tough common man's scepticism, often taking the form of a reaction against the rigours of conventional religion, or even against religion itself. He quotes, for example, a man who said there was no God, or if there was one, the Devil was a god, and another who proposed to sell his Bible, saying he could make as good a book himself. One of the most consistent themes in Edwards's list of errors is a reaction against the terror of Hell: 'there is no Hell but in this life, and that's the legal terrors and fears which men have in their consciences.' With this went a vigorous reaction against the Puritan orthodoxy of Predestination: 'that it could not stand with the goodness of God to damn his own creatures eternally', and 'God hath not decreed all the actions of men, because men doing what God decreed, do not sin'.[23] This reaction against Predestination was characteristic of much of the left wing of Puritanism. Walwyn, or the early Quakers, for example, could not believe that there were some men whom God had predestined to damnation, and to whom his grace was simply not accessible. Thus, ironically, it came about that the theology of some of the most radical Puritans resembled the Arminianism of the Laudian bishops.

The reaction against the terrors of Hell and sin also took the form of what was known as Antinomianism, the doctrine that 'to the pure, all things are pure', and that 'if a man by the spirit know himself to be in the state of grace, though he did commit murder or drunkenness, God did see no sin in him'. Saltmarsh, one of the chaplains in the New Model Army, has given us an unusual description of the process which led him to an Antinomian position. He was so obsessed by the terror of his own sinfulness that he used to contemplate suicide, and could repent only for fear of

[22] Overton, R., *A Defiance . . . to the House of Lords* (1646), 1–2.
[23] Edwards, T., *Gangraena* (1645–6), i. 27, 35, 20.

damnation, as he put it, with 'legal sorrow'. He finally relieved some of his anxieties by convincing himself that even those who were truly sanctified might fall back into sin, but that Christ, being merciful, did not reject them for these sins: 'to whom he is once merciful, he is ever merciful', and therefore 'no sin can make one less beloved of God, or less in Christ'.[24] In the hands of others, Antinomianism was a much cruder doctrine than it was for a serious preacher like Saltmarsh, and for orthodox Presbyterians, the appearance of Antinomianism simply proved how right they had been to insist on strict Predestinarian orthodoxy and the denial of all toleration. There was a good deal of cynicism about the scriptures: many maintained that they provided no certain guide, sometimes falling back on visions and revelations as a substitute, and one cynic said that 'to read Scripture in English to a mixed congregation without present expounding it, is dangerous, and worse than to read it in Latin: for in Latin, as it doth not good, so it doth no harm'.[25] Anticlericalism was as live a force as it had ever been: Lilburne's onslaughts on the 'black-coats' reached as sympathetic an audience as attacks on 'bald-pates' had ever done before the Reformation. One man put the spirit of English laicism in a nutshell by maintaining that the congregation should receive the Lord's supper with their hats on, and the ministers should administer it with their hats off.

The extremest example of this anti-religious reaction was the group known as the Ranters, who, though they were commonly classified as a religious sect, appear to have been rather an anti-religious sect. They appear to have denied that there were such things as sin or Hell, and they were repeatedly accused of believing in free love. They used religious language largely for purposes of parody: one of them 'let a great fart, and, as it gave report, he muttered these words, let every thing that hath breath praise the Lord'. A Ranter song, which the reporter said he had printed because it was the least obscene he could find, ran as follows:

> The slavish terror that men have,
> And thoughts of Hell to fear
> Is unto us a laughing stock,
> We give to it no ear.
>
> . . . .
>
> Which we enjoy with sweet content
> A short life and a merry
> Is all the heaven that we expect,
> Let's drink off our Canary.

[24] Saltmarsh, J., *Free Grace* (1645), 79.
[25] Edwards, op. cit., i. 19.

> The fellow-creature which sits next
> Is more delight to me
> Than any that I else can find,
> For that she's always free.[26]

Puritanism and revolution

Most of the revolutionary force of the 1650s was secular in inspiration, and largely concerned with class interests. The one genuinely revolutionary thing in Puritanism was the demand for the right to preach. By 1649, this had in the main been won, and Puritanism was beginning to lose some of its heat. Yet, though there was nothing very revolutionary about the essence of Puritanism, and in Scotland and Massachusetts it proved itself a much more effective religion for the support of authority than Anglicanism had ever been, nevertheless, it could be harnessed to give very powerful support to a radicalism based on other grounds.

There are several ways in which this was true. The first of these was simply that it could encourage people to ask 'why?', and to a man with a barrack-room lawyer spirit, a text of scripture could be a very effective weapon, since it involved an appeal to a higher authority than that which was being challenged. For example, two servants who conceived a child and married each other were reminded by their master of a covenant not to marry during their period of service, and replied that it was a 'devilish covenant'. For some, such as those who maintained that 'children are not bound to obey their parents at all, if they be ungodly',[27] Puritanism was a convenient excuse, and perhaps some aid to their courage in challenging the established order.

Other radical uses of Puritanism deserve to be taken more seriously. One followed from the doctrine, which could be traced back to Perkins, that it was possible to know who were the Elect. This doctrine, which had formerly been part of Puritan orthodoxy, was listed by Edwards as an error, when its possible implications had begun to become apparent. From this followed the Independent doctrine, that the church should be composed of 'visible saints', who should separate from communion with the unregenerate, a doctrine which was applied with such rigour by the Independent minister at Acton that he reduced his congregation to two women. Such a doctrine might have been harmless enough: it was, after all, a Christian cliché that a man's chances of salvation had nothing to do with his worldly status. But the idea of visible saints, preached to people who had been brought up on the exact identification of church and state, and who in any case were no longer willing to accept the gentry's monopoly of

---

[26] *The Ranters Ranting* (1650), B.M. E. 618. 'Canary' is canary wine.
[27] Edwards, op. cit., i. 34.

power, could have revolutionary implications. Edwards, thorough as usual, succeeded in finding this doctrine expressed in its most revolutionary form: 'all the earth is the saints', and 'there ought to be a community of goods, and the saints should share in the lands and estates of gentlemen and rich men'.[28] Very few Puritans were as crude as this, but the notion of the Fifth Monarchists, that the country was about to enter the millennium, in which Christ would reign with the saints for a thousand years, was recognized by Cromwell as essentially a threat to the position of the gentry, and it was only an extension of the argument used by some of the regicides, that Charles I was unfit to rule, because he was 'a stranger to the work of grace and the spirit of God'.[29] If claims to political power were to be based on sanctity, the gentlemen had no better chance of being regarded as saints than anyone else, and at last a principle had been found which offered a serious challenge to the notion of their natural superiority.

The Fifth Monarchists, who carried this doctrine through to its conclusion, deserve more sympathetic study than they have yet received. The bad press they have had ever since their own day is largely based on a few reports on their activities, printed in the *Calendar of State Papers*, compiled by Marchamont Nedham for the Council of State. Marchamont Nedham was a brilliant journalist, somewhat in the style of Lord Beaverbrook, but he was a cynic, and as one royalist said, he was like a cat: whichever way you threw him, he would always land on his feet. At the time, he was the official government journalist, and his reports on the Fifth Monarchists are evidence of what the Council of State, which largely consisted of gentlemen, wanted to hear.

The Fifth Monarchists were a group who gathered round 1650 out of a variety of other sects. Their distinctive doctrine was belief in the millennium, the Fifth Monarchy, when political power would be taken over by Christ. They were therefore against all human power, and in a sense, they were anarchists. Yet, like many anarchists, they were more against existing government than against all government, and much of their head of steam seems to have been secular in inspiration. Their characteristic concerns were with issues like law reform, tithes, and advowsons, issues in which the position of the gentry was at stake. They were strongly in favour of war with the Dutch, and though Christopher Feake, one of their leading preachers, said this was because the Dutch tolerated Arminianism, and allowed Henrietta Maria to import arms to England during the Civil War, it also suited the economic interest of small traders and craftsmen. They

[28] Edwards, op. cit., i. 34.
[29] *State Trials*, Ed. Howell, i. 960. Draft speech of Cook, the prosecutor. Charles's refusal to plead deprived Cook of the opportunity to deliver this speech.

maintained that, since the legislative power was Christ's prerogative and not man's, the laws should be based on the law of Moses. Many have followed Cromwell in regarding this as proof of their wild impracticality, but they seem to have attached a coherent meaning to the proposal. Like many radicals since their time, they thought the English common law was too severe on offences against property, and wanted, for example, to abolish the death penalty for theft. One of them also suggested that there were 'no customs or excise in the days of the Messiah'. On the other hand, they wanted the law to be more severe on moral offences, and wanted the death penalty for several things prohibited in the Book of Leviticus, such as adultery (which was in fact punishable by death during the 1650s, though few juries ever convicted) or for having intercourse with a woman during her period. Aspinwall, who had returned from Massachusetts, thought the laws of New England were a near enough approximation to the laws of Moses, and it is possible to suspect that one of the chief attractions of the laws of Moses was that they were not the laws of gentlemen. Aspinwall wanted the community's officers elected from the lower ranks of men, and Feake maintained that aristocracy and monarchy had an enmity to Christ, omitting to mention democracy. Their millennarian prophecies contributed to raising the courage to challenge the rights of property, and Cromwell made it quite clear that it was this, and not the idea of the Fifth Monarchy, with which he sympathized, which made him regard them as subversive. As Christopher Feake said, 'many wise men after the flesh have been (and now are) much offended, that a company of illiterate men, and silly women, should pretend to any skill in dark prophecies, and to a foresight of future events which the most learned rabbis, and the most knowing politicians, have not presumed to hope for'.[30]

Muggletonians and Quakers

If any sect deserves the reputation for religious enthusiasm which has commonly been pinned on the Fifth Monarchists, it is the Muggletonians. Muggleton believed that Cain's parents were Eve and the Devil, while Abel's parents were Eve and God. This enabled Muggleton to build up a schizophrenic confusion of identities. God, he thought, had desired to have a generation of children of the serpent so that he could destroy them. He also believed that Reason was the Beast in the Book of Revelation. Muggleton's other distinctive doctrine was that he was one of the two heavenly messengers foretold in the Book of Revelation, the last prophet who would come before the end of the world, and the man to whom God

[30] Feake, C., Preface to Mary Rande, *The Little Horn's Doom and Downfall* (1651).

had delegated the power to decide who would be saved and who would be damned. Muggleton once wrote to a Quaker with whom he had quarrelled: 'I do pronounce you cursed and damned soul and body from the presence of God, elect men and angels to eternity; neither shall that light within you, nor any God deliver you from this curse, but according to my word it shall be upon you, because you shall know that God hath given power to man to curse you to eternity, and that there is a prophet of the Lord in the land.'

Two Quakers replied to this pamphlet, addressing Muggleton as 'friend: for so we can call thee, as Christ did Judas', and saying that: 'thou hast polluted thyself, thou hast defiled thyself, thou hast made thyself unclean, and thou art unclean, and art in the highest state of Ranters from the holy body, in the polluted body, and where ever thou hast an entrance thou wilt defile.'[31] The mildness which has since become characteristic of the Quaker movement was not characteristic of it in its early days in the 1650s. Rightly or wrongly, gentlemen tended to be much more alarmed by the subversive notions of the Quakers than of any other religious group. Quakers tended to base authority on revelation, and their founder, George Fox, recorded, for example, that 'the Lord opened to me that being bred at Oxford or Cambridge was not enough to make a man fit to be a minister of Christ'.[32] The Quakers rejected the doctrine of a formal ministry, and organized, as they still do, meetings for worship which were conducted without any formal service, and in which the speaking was done by private members of the congregation. They denied a large proportion of the ideas which were used to sanction existing social order: for example, they refused to take off their hats in the presence of anyone, a gesture whose significance is much like that of a modern private soldier refusing to salute his commanding officer. They refused to take oaths, regarded as the only sanction for legal proceedings, on the ground of the Biblical injunction to 'swear not at all'. Most of them were pacifists, though they appear to have done some recruitment among serving navy captains. They would refuse what other people thought harmless formalities, such as addressing J.P.s as 'worshipful', on the ground that 'them that are right, deny all worships, and worship God'.[33] They seem to have been the only sect growing out of the revolution which totally denied the divine right of civil authority.

[31] Muggleton, Lodowick, *The Neck of the Quakers Broken* (1663), 6–7.
[32] *Journal of George Fox*, Ed. Pickard (1902), 7.
[33] Farnworth, R., *Several Petitions Answered* (1653), B.M. E. 703, 3.

Truth and unity: the Protestant dilemma

Alarm about the Quaker movement appears to have been much exaggerated, as was the alarm about most of the radical sects. However, there was another way in which Puritanism might create difficulties for an authority which believed in uniformity of religion. In this, Puritans were facing a dilemma which had faced all Protestants since the Reformation. Protestants had rejected the authority of the Pope on grounds of truth, but in so doing, they did not want to destroy the unity of the church: why, after all, should truth be incompatible with unity? Yet, as they rejected authority on grounds of truth, they created an opening for those of their followers who did not agree with them to do the same thing. The text that 'we ought to obey God rather than man' was, it is true, a Christian cliché, but if too many people acted on it in contradictory senses, the church could not remain united. As one of the Independents saw, the Presbyterians, in trying to enforce the unity of the church, were trying to defend ground which had been indefensible since the Reformation: 'Little do men know how much they contribute towards keeping of the Pope in his chair, by pleading as much as they do for such a universal visible church, subject to government: for if there be such a church of divine institution, then it will necessarily follow, that there must be a universal ordinary pastor of that church, and then the Papists will thank them.'[34] As Saltmarsh, for example, pointed out, all the same arguments which had justified the Presbyterians in resisting the authority of the bishops could be used to justify the Independents in resisting the authority of the Presbyterians. For the Presbyterians, however, there was one crucial difference: their doctrines, they thought, were true, and the Independents' were false. However, as Walwyn the Leveller said, even this was a familiar story: Pope, bishops, Presbyterians, and Independents had each in turn claimed that their word was God's, and attempted to enforce it, though they were 'no more infallibly certain of the truth they raise from Scriptures than any of those they so much condemn'. What was really subversive here was not Puritanism, but the doctrine of religious unity, enforced in a period of religious division. As Walwyn said, if the government would once protect people without taking account of their differences in religion, it would have a much better chance of receiving their loyalty in return. Walwyn anticipated Mill in arguing that the principle of civil authority should be that 'every man ought to be protected in the use of that, wherein he doth not actually hurt another',[35] rather than that one doctrine ought to be

[34] Nuttall, G. F., *Visible Saints* (1957), 66.
[35] Walwyn, W., *The Vanity of the Present Churches* and *Walwyn's Just Defence*, in *Leveller Tracts*, 257, 392.

enforced because it was truth. This position was highly unusual, and Walwyn was only able to make it defensible because he had his own theory of political obligation, and did not have to depend on notions of divine right to secure an obligation to obey the government. For Walwyn the ground of obligation was consent, and the ground of consent was a shared desire for protection in material things.

In the great debate on toleration and the freedom of the press which raged throughout the later 1640s, very few cut through the argument as successfully as Walwyn. Milton put all his literary talent into his sonnet on freedom of conscience, or into his plea for freedom of the press in *Areopagitica* (a work which appears to have been quite unnoticed by his contemporaries),[36] yet Milton never achieved the scepticism about our authority for claiming that we know the truth, without which it was hard to make a tolerationist position coherent. Hobbes, who did achieve this scepticism, nevertheless kept the assumption of his youth that a society could not be held together unless it was based on one agreed religion. He therefore argued that, since we could never know infallibly whether our religion or our opponents' was true, we had always to assume, rightly or wrongly, that the government's religion was true. Hobbes therefore believed, not in toleration, but that we should obey the sovereign even if he commanded us to turn Mohammedan.

It is easy to exaggerate the extent to which many leading Independents were in favour of toleration. Their position tends to be that 'I'm in favour of toleration, but . . .', and their general statements in favour of toleration tend to except papists and prelatists, Quakers and Ranters, and a number of other people. In abandoning the theory of a national church, they had abandoned many of the purely ecclesiastical arguments for persecution, and made it possible for them to argue for a much wider range of religious liberty than the Presbyterians would ever accept. However, they had often not abandoned two of the crucial arguments for religious unity. One was the belief that divine right, however it might be acquired, was in the last resort the only guarantee of obedience to authority, and therefore that some really subversive doctrines ought to be prohibited. The other was the belief that where we were absolutely certain that something was an error, and yet permitted it, we were guilty of 'countenancing' it, or being acces-

---

[36] Ironically, the only work of Milton's which attracted much attention was his *Doctrine and Discipline of Divorce*, which was commonly quoted, together with Roger Williams' *Bloody Tenent of Persecution*, as the sort of work which illustrated the need for censorship. Edwards tells the story of a woman who was attracted by the *Doctrine and Discipline of Divorce* because she wanted to get rid of her husband on the ground that he was 'unsanctified'; Edwards, op. cit., ii. 11.

sories after the fact. When pushed, leading Independents tended to ask awkward practical questions along these lines. In 1648, when the Levellers offered a proposal that Parliament should be allowed no authority in religion whatever, Ireton, Cromwell's son-in-law, asked whether they really wanted to allow liberty 'to practice idolatry, to practice atheism, and anything that is against the light of God'. A leading Independent minister observed that there were dangerous consequences in the doctrine that the civil authority had no power over men's consciences, 'for a man may make conscience of some things that are contrary to common morality'. He cited the case of a man whose conscience demanded that he commit bigamy.[37] It was not until the nineteenth century that Walwyn's position even began to gain wide acceptance.

Secular radicalism: the Levellers and law reform

Perhaps the most powerful union of religious and secular radicalism was in the Leveller movement. The Levellers were something of a portent, being the first secular party in English history. For each individual Leveller leader, his religion was a powerful part of the force behind his politics, but their religion had little in common. Lilburne was an old-fashioned orthodox Puritan, a strict Predestinarian, and a regular reader of such familiar Puritan literature as Foxe's *Book of Martyrs* or the works of Calvin and Perkins. He was peculiarly certain of his own rightness, and in the habit of appealing to his 'old and faithful counsellor the Lord Jehovah' at crucial moments of his career. Walwyn was sceptical and detached in his approach and Arminian in his theology, and his favourite reading was classical authors such as Thucydides and Plutarch. Overton was a straightforward secular anti-clerical, and, like Lilburne, had some talent as a barrack-room lawyer. He liked using the phrase that 'an Englishman's home is his castle'.[38]

The force binding these people together was secular, and essentially one of class. They were not Levellers in any literal sense: the title was pinned on them by their opponents, and they persistently disowned it. Nor did they represent 'the poor': Lilburne and Overton were professional printers, and Walwyn a merchant. Their followers claimed that most of them had given up farms and trades to fight in the war, and it appears that on the whole they represent yeomen, small businessmen, craftsmen, and the rank and file of the New Model Army, rather than the real poor. They were, however, in favour of a very wide extension of the franchise, to all

[37] Woodhouse, A. S. P., *Puritanism and Liberty* (1950), 143–6.
[38] Overton, *A Defiance . . . of the House of Lords* (1646), 11.

who had not forfeited their 'birthright' of independence from others, that is, in effect, to all except servants and beggars. One of their most interesting theories was that of the 'Norman Yoke'. They thought the existing ruling class, and the existing law and property structure, had been imposed on the country by William the Conqueror, and therefore that their position was sanctioned by nothing except force. This position was capable of considerable extension, and in 1653, a group of Kentish labourers petitioned Barebone's Parliament to exclude all landowners from political power on the ground that they were inheritors of the 'Norman Yoke'.

The Leveller programme was less far-reaching than this. They wanted to abolish the House of Lords and the Monarchy, and to turn England into a republic with a wide, perhaps a democratic, franchise. They wanted to abolish the Excise, which pressed very heavily on the poor and on small businessmen. When Lilburne once tried to set up as a soap-boiler, he became peculiarly indignant that he had to pay the excise twice, both on his raw materials and on the finished product. They wanted the rate of interest lowered to 6 per cent, and they carried on a vigorous assault against the privileges of trading companies, in the name of an almost Cobdenite theory of 'free trade'. They were the first of many radicals to mount a campaign for the abolition of tithes, which was to become one of the most explosive issues of the period. Gentlemen, on the whole, wanted to maintain tithes. Many received them as impropriators, and they were part of their rights of property. Others found it hard to see why they should pay to maintain gentlemen. But the issue of tithes remained explosive when they were paid to the minister. They had been arranged in a society whose members all belonged to one church, and it was hard to see why a Baptist should be forced to pay tithes for the maintenance of a Presbyterian, or even more, in cases where a radical gentleman had control of the presentation, or it had passed to the congregation, why an Anglican should be forced to pay tithes for the maintenance of an Independent. Many of the Independent ministers, being appointed to livings maintained by tithes, became supporters of them. Moreover, as they asked, how was it possible to defend the abolition of tithes when no other way for supporting ministers could be worked out? Some of the extreme radicals thought that ministers should maintain themselves by working during the week, to which Prynne replied with a lengthy treatise maintaining that Christ had never worked with his hands. Others believed in voluntary offerings to the clergy, but it was very doubtful whether these would be big enough. It was thus hard to justify either the retention of tithes or their abolition, and the issue remained a cause of dispute right through to the Restoration.

Much of the Levellers' energy, like that of many of their successors in the 1650s, was devoted to the issue of law reform. This, too, became largely a dispute between gentlemen and non-gentlemen. The technicality and detail of a common law based on precedents was little threat to gentlemen who, even if they had not learnt much at the Inns of Court, could afford to brief a good counsel. An ordinary man, on the other hand, might find that a perfectly just complaint against a gentleman was defeated by a maze of legal technicalities he did not understand. One of the key demands in the move to make the law intelligible was that English should be used in the courts instead of law French, and this was carried into law in 1650. Law French, by this time, had become a thoroughly dead language, often unintelligible except to professional lawyers: Sir Edward Coke, for example, once recorded that on being libelled, 'Job, que fuit le mirour de patience, ... devient quodammodo impatient.'[39] The other big advantage gentlemen had in legal proceedings was their cost, and reduction of costs was always one of the key issues in the law reform campaign. Most reformers wanted to decentralize legal proceedings, and have a far higher proportion of them in the counties and not at Westminster, thus saving those who did not own town houses from the costs of waiting in London for their case to be heard. Overton followed this up with a proposal for the J.P.s to be popularly elected, and Walwyn, one of the inventors of the belief that trial by jury is a bastion of English liberties, wanted to go back to the system of the Saxon hundred courts, before the imposition of the Norman Yoke, when a man's judges had been the whole body of his neighbours. One of the reformers' main targets was the Court of Chancery, and here much of their grievance seems to have been the familiar complaint against the system of fees and perquisites by which officials were paid. These complaints dated back to the 1590s, and most of the reformers of the 1650s were no more ready to offer any alternative method of paying officials than the Jacobean Commons had been.[40] The only exception was Hugh Peters, an Independent minister who proposed to turn the legal profession into a salaried National Legal Service on much the same lines as the present National Health Service. If any body of opinion in England represents 'the rise of the middle classes' or 'the bourgeois revolution', it is the Levellers, but it must be remembered that the Leveller movement failed. If there was a 'bourgeois revolution' in seventeenth-century England, it was a failure. The people who ultimately benefited from the revolution were the Whig aristocracy, the great magnates who dominated the politics of the eighteenth century. The middle classes had to wait until the nineteenth, or

---

[39] Coke, *Reports*, 5, 125b. I regret that Donald Veall, *The Popular Movement for Law Reform, 1640–1660* (1970), appeared too late for me to use it.

[40] On the issues involved in the question of fees, see above, pp. 248–51, 272–3.

perhaps even the twentieth, century before they secured a substantial share in political power.

Hugh Peters

But though the Leveller movement was in the main crushed by 1650, some of its demands were carried on, with almost equal lack of success, by other social reformers. Occasionally agitation passed lower down the social scale, and the Newcastle keelmen once organized a strike for higher wages. The most persuasive defender of social reform during the 1650s was perhaps Hugh Peters, another of the returning exiles from Holland and New England. He had a remarkable readiness to recommend financing public services out of government funds. He wanted, for example, to solve one of the most thorny economic problems of the period, the inability of agricultural labourers to find any reliable way of marketing their produce, by setting up a system of government buying at guaranteed support prices much like that which is used at present.[41] * Like Overton, he thought it was the government's duty to provide hospitals, adding that Amsterdam was 'far advanced herein'. He wanted to abolish patronage and purchase for army commissions, and base them solely on merit and length of service, to set up a national bank, to consolidate most taxes in the form of one income tax, to have a licensing tax on coaches, to reduce the transport cost of food by spending public money on building canals, and to provide a system of state insurance for merchants trading overseas. He wanted to allow unrestricted immigration, to have an official registry of land conveyances, to set up publicly maintained houses for bringing up orphans, to set up county courts, and to replace imprisonment for debt with attachment of earnings. He wanted to pull down timber buildings in London, and to improve the City's water supply, for fear of a great fire. Perhaps the most remarkable fact about him is the comparatively low importance he gave to religion, compared with social reform. He said that 'many commonwealths subsist without true religion, and much mercy, but without justice, no commonwealth can long subsist'.[42] Such a remark would have been unthinkable in any pre-war Puritan, and it is a sharp illustration of the increasingly secular atmosphere of the politics of the 1650s.

Like many others in the period, Hugh Peters was both a strong believer in education and a leader in attacks on the universities. Like many other university reformers, he wanted to abolish gowns on the ground that they were 'monuments of idolatry', and to turn the universities into more strictly

[41] On the difficulties this proposal was designed to remedy, see above, p. 14.
[42] Peters, Hugh, *Good Work for a Good Magistrate* (1650), 28.
* Written 1969.

'useful' places, concentrating on vocational training, not so much general centres of learning as preachers' training colleges. In this approach, he had strong sympathy from the Fifth Monarchists and many others. As a result of this spirit, the period saw a good deal of founding of new schools, and one attempt to set up a new university at Durham. Oxford commented that by creating too many universities, the main end of universities would be quite destroyed, and though the body was created, it was never given the power to confer degrees.

The royalists

In the face of this outburst of radical feeling, the gentry had the great disadvantage of being divided by the original issues of the Civil War. A number, including some former royalists, rallied to Cromwell, greeting him, in Waller's words, as:

> One whose extraction from an ancient line
> Gives hope again that well-born men may shine.

In the long run, however, many found that the only solid body to which they could rally was the royalists, who had remained a remarkably coherent and unchanging group throughout the 1650s. But what had the royalists to offer the lower classes? The answer seems to be that the only thing they had to offer was wit, bawdy, and the appeal to a gay life. This appeal the royalist newspapers exploited with great skill throughout the 1650s. They advertised a performing baboon, or said that a dancer:

> Doth in best judgement, as far exceed the Turks,
> As Shakespeare Heywood in his comic works,

while carrying, as one royalist poet put it:

> . . . not one syllable of State,
> Amidst our pleasant mirth.[43]

This was of course a sound way of avoiding the censorship, which Cromwell was trying to reimpose, but it was also good propaganda. Bawdy became almost a signature tune of the royalist newspapers, and in a world which was growing increasingly tired of religion and politics, many people came to feel that the loss of freedom of speech was a price worth paying for a gay life.

This should not be taken to imply that Puritanism was quite as Puritanical as is sometimes supposed: the popular picture of Puritan killjoys is one which the royalist newspapers during the 1650s had a large share in creating. Cromwell himself dismayed Puritanical citizens by allowing

[43] *Mercurius Fumigiosus* or *The Smoking Nocturnall*, no. 13, Aug. 22–30 (1654), 118. B.M. E. 809. Heath, Robert, *Occasional Poems* (1651), 22.

'mixed and lascivious dancing' at his daughter's wedding, and attempts to enforce public morals were always sporadic. In 1650, a bill against immodest dress was thrown out by Parliament. It is true that the theatre, maypoles, and celebration of Christmas were prohibited for most of the period of Puritan rule, and continued only in a clandestine form, but the Cromwellian government was persuaded by Charles I's former poet laureate to revive plays by the ingenious argument that the decline of the London season lessened the profits of city tradesmen. There was a vigorous attack on bear-baiting (and Colonel Pride killed the bears in the Southwark bear-garden with his own hands) and in the middle 1650s the fact that race-meetings and cock-fights were used for meetings of royalist plotters enabled the Puritanical members of the government to muster enough support to prohibit them. Such attempts were never more than sporadic. The royalists were the more successful in attacking them for the fact that they could appeal to sympathizers even within government circles.

Ultimately, the main legacy of this period may have been the growth of scepticism and secularism in place of idealism and religion. By 1660, there was a widespread desire to avoid trouble by not meddling in matters of state. George Wither the poet said in 1660 that his principle was 'really and sincerely to submit to every power whereunto God by his grace or permission shall be pleased to subject him without an intention either directly or indirectly to be active in innovating or changing the same'.[44] With this approach went a growing doubt about our means of knowledge about religious questions. It had been amply demonstrated that scripture could be interpreted in various ways, and visions had been discredited by the frequency with which they were claimed. Hobbes remarked that if a man claimed that God spoke to him in a dream, 'this proveth no more than that he dreamed God spake to him, which is not of force to win belief of any man'. One of the prominent figures of the 1650s, and one who was more typical than is often supposed, is Anthony Ashley Cooper, later Earl of Shaftesbury, whose political career began in Barebone's Parliament in 1653. His religion has been described as 'at best, deistic',[45] and it was he and his contemporaries who first worshipped the God of the Age of Reason, 'a being whom all must acknowledge incomprehensible'. Charles II caught the spirit of his new subjects when he remarked after the Restoration that the only 'visible church' he knew was the hilltop church at Harrow. Puritan idealism was replaced by Restoration wit. In 1660, Waller presented Charles II with a panegyric when he landed at Dover,

[44] Carlson, Norman E., 'George Wither and the Statute Office', *Notes and Queries*, March 1969, 99.

[45] Haley, K. H. D., *Shaftesbury* (1968), 66.

and Charles told him it was not as good as the panegyric he had written for Cromwell. Waller promptly replied: 'poets, Sire, succeed better in fiction than in truth.'[46]

For those who still cared about ideas, and particularly for the Quakers, the Restoration meant the return of full-scale censorship, the postponement of the reforms for which they had been working for two, or even three, centuries, and the beginning of a period of repression as ruthless as any this country has ever known. The Fifth Monarchists vainly attempted a rebellion, and stood up to persecution in small groups until about 1670. The Quakers, by an unparalleled display of passive obstinacy, somehow managed to survive, but most of the tougher Puritans went abroad. It was left to Milton to speak the swan-song of Puritan England:

If their absolute determination be to enthral us, before so long a Lent of servitude, they may permit us a little shroving-time first, wherein to speak freely, and take our leave of liberty.[47]

IV THE SEARCH FOR A SETTLEMENT, 1645–1653

Parliament ... may not tolerate erring consciences, nor false doctrines, any more than they may suffer idolatry.

> *The Scottish Dove (Scots' newspaper in England)*, 11 March 1645[48]

You who have conquered the kingdom, done all this service, and now when you have done all this, might expect your arrears [of pay], look to enjoy your liberties, yea and expect preferments, good places as you have well deserved, it may be, you shall be cast into a stinking prison.

> *Hugh Peters, preaching to the Army*, 1646[49]

Contending groups, 1645–1649

It was never likely that any agreed settlement could be made after the end of the Civil War, because the negotiations involved too many different parties pursuing incompatible objects. Even with real political skill on all sides, a settlement would have been very difficult to achieve. Yet it could only be made harder by the astonishingly unpolitical method in which most of the parties concerned pursued it. Fear and idealism made a bad mixture, and it could only make the situation more difficult that most of

---

[46] Aubrey, J., *Brief Lives*, Ed. Dick (1949), 359.
[47] Milton, J., *The Ready and Easy Way to Establish a Free Commonwealth* (1660), in *Prose Writings*, Ed. K. M. Burton (1958), 220.
[48] B.M. E. 327.
[49] Edwards, op. cit., iii. 27.

the parties concerned had an uncompromising determination to achieve things which could not possibly be. Charles I, Denzil Holles, the Scots' leaders, and John Lilburne all belonged to that school of thought which holds that the proposition that politics is the art of the possible is not merely open to abuse, but actually sinful. The only one of the participants in the search for a settlement who was willing to take account of the limits of possibility was Oliver Cromwell, second in command to the army after Fairfax. Since Fairfax was non-political, and Major-General Skippon Presbyterian, he tended to take the lead when political questions came up in the Army Council. Cromwell thought that 'it is our duty, as Christians and men, to consider consequences'.[50] His philosophy as a Christian strengthened him in this belief: he took literally the Calvinist doctrine of Providence, according to which each event came about because God had caused it to happen. The way to discover God's will was therefore not so much to study scripture, or to rely on visions (which Cromwell distrusted), but to examine God's Providence as shown in events. Thus, to adapt a phrase which was later used of Gladstone, if Cromwell found the ace of trumps up his sleeve, he genuinely believed that God had put it there, and had no hesitation in playing it. This philosophy gave Cromwell two disadvantages. The first was that he was unduly vulnerable to reverses, since they led him to believe that he had sinned, and acted against God's will. The second was that he was very slow and indecisive when he could not decide what God's will was. On the other hand, once he had reached a decision, he was capable of swift and decisive action without any qualms of conscience.

For Charles I, on the other hand, there was little room for manoeuvre. He believed that it was sinful to yield any important part of the power he held before the war, or to concede anything of substance at the expense of the Anglican church. Since this belief was not based on any calculation of expediency, the fact that he had lost the war made no difference to his position. Like many of his contemporaries, he took seriously the notion that disasters were a punishment inflicted by God for our sins, and he thought the sin for which he was punished was his consent to Strafford's execution. His philosophy thus led him to a conclusion directly opposite to any calculation of political expediency: that God would punish him further if he made any further concessions. On the other hand, Charles did not believe it was sinful to trick and mislead rebels by dishonest negotiations, and such room for manoeuvre as he might have depended on his powers of deception, and other people's willingness for self-deception.

[50] Gardiner, *GCW*, iii. 384.

Among the Presbyterians, there was as much willingness for self-deception as Charles could wish. Moreover, they were sharply divided among themselves. The Scots, and the majority of the Westminster Assembly, wanted to impose full clerical Presbyterianism on England. When people protested that such a proposal was tyrannical, the Westminster Assembly asked 'how can that power be called arbitrary, which is not according to the will of man, but the will of Christ?'[51] Parliament, on the other hand, were firmly convinced that the church should be under the control of the laity, and when the Westminster Assembly voted that ecclesiastical jurisdiction was vested in the church by divine right, Parliament voted them guilty of a breach of privilege.

The Presbyterians all wanted to keep the king on the throne, but as Spittlehouse the Fifth Monarchist later said, they were only 'demi-royalists' who wanted the king restored so that they could 'ride upon his back'. That Charles might be unwilling to surrender his power, or that he might be unwilling to persecute adherents of his own religion, were possibilities they never considered, and since they did not consider them, they could not evolve any policy to meet them.

The Presbyterian M.P.s were equally unpolitical in their attitude to the army. For Holles, for example, the army were 'the meanest of men, the basest and vilest of the nation, the lowest of the people',[52] and he was too frightened of them to consider the possibility that they might have legitimate grievances: to give concessions to such dangerous revolutionaries was only to encourage them. In fact, the army's demands at first were extremely moderate. The first essential for them was their arrears of pay: 1647–9 were years of a serious slump, drastic price rises, and heavy unemployment, and to be turned loose penniless and without a job was an uninviting prospect. In March 1647, the pay of the foot was 18 weeks in arrears, and of the horse 43 weeks in arrears, amounting to a sum of £331,000. Parliament was entitled to say that such a sum was difficult to raise, but it became distressingly clear to the army that they found it much easier to raise the money for regiments influenced by Presbyterian commanders than for the more radical regiments. Since they were not paid, the army were forced to live at free quarter, and thus Parliament could force them to make themselves more unpopular. The other essential, for many of the army, was toleration: the issue for which many had fought was the right to worship as they pleased, without fear of arrest, and when a parliamentary ordinance of September 1646 decreed the death penalty for denying the Trinity or the Incarnation, and imprisonment for life for

[51] Gardiner, *GCW*, iii. 6.
[52] Holles, *Memorials* (1648), 1.

denying Presbyterianism or infant baptism, many were alarmed. This ordinance was not enforced, but few soldiers were willing to disband the army and give Parliament power to enforce it. It is hard to say for how many of the army the issue of toleration was crucial: it may be that if the army had been paid, those who insisted on toleration might have been too few to cause trouble.

After the spring of 1647, there was the added danger of a split between the army rank and file and its leaders. In April 1647, Parliament offered the army six weeks' arrears on disbanding, and proposed to send those who were not disbanded to suppress the continuing revolt in Ireland. In Ireland, they would be safely out of the way while a settlement was negotiated, and the officers were to be purged before they went. At that time, the private soldiers appointed Agitators, rank and file soldiers from each regiment who were to represent their colleagues. Their functions were much like those of shop stewards.

Some of the Agitators became part of a rapidly improving Leveller organization in the army, and popular riots against the excise helped to give the Levellers a large body of support in London. A series of debates at Putney between the officers and the Leveller leaders only helped to show what a profound gulf there was between Cromwell and Ireton, who believed in the rights of property and a limited franchise, and their semi-democratic opponents. Cromwell began to express fears of 'confusion' in tones almost reminiscent of Holles, while the *Agreement of the People*, the main Leveller manifesto, is thought to have achieved the fantastic sale of 20,000 copies. But the Levellers, who wanted a new Parliament elected on their franchise, were just another group who wanted impossible things. It was impossible to have a republic based on free elections in a predominantly royalist country, in which the king's accession day was still greeted with spontaneous public celebrations. Free elections on the Leveller franchise would have produced a government ready to reject every proposal for which the Levellers fought.

Parliament, army, and king, 1647–1649

When the war ended, Charles first surrendered to the Scots, believing, as he told his wife, that they had no sincere attachment to Presbyterianism, and only wanted a share of the bishops' lands. The Scots found they could reach no settlement with the king, and handed him over to the English Parliament and went home. Parliament then had the chance to try to reach a settlement with the king, based on the Propositions of Newcastle, which would have set up a Presbyterian church, and given Parliament control over the militia for twenty years. These attempts were also unsuccessful.

By the spring of 1647, it looked as if the situation was one of deadlock, and Parliament was increasingly turning its mind to the task of suppressing the army. One of the survivors of the 1641 leadership said that 'it's now come to this, that they must sink us, or we sink them'.[53] Parliament, being uncomfortably aware of its lack of military force, was considering plans to raise a Presbyterian army out of the City militia and old soldiers who had been dismissed when the New Model Army was formed. These plans ultimately came to nothing, but they created some alarm. Cromwell, not wishing to make trouble, was considering going to Germany and taking service as a mercenary with the Elector Palatine. Meanwhile, the army and the parliamentary leaders were exchanging declarations in a paper war uncomfortably reminiscent of the one which had preceded the original war. All the arguments for limitation of the power of the executive which were used in Parliament against the king, were now used by the army against Parliament, which proved as unwilling to listen to them as the king had been.

This situation was transformed in June 1647, when a junior officer, Cornet Joyce, captured the king and brought him into the control of the army. Whether this move had the prior approval of Lieutenant-General Cromwell or any other senior officers, we will probably never know. Charles I, by this time, had a position much like that of a king at chess: he had virtually no power of his own, but control of him tended to confer control of the board. The army officers opened negotiations with Charles on the basis of the Heads of the Proposals, an interesting document drawn up by Cromwell's son-in-law Ireton. On religion, this document anticipated the settlement of 1689, by which the king was to be allowed his own church, including bishops, but the bishops were to have no right to persecute those who were outside the church. The army's arrears were to be paid, and some of the minor Leveller proposals on law reform were to be enacted. There was to be a mild extension of the franchise, a new election, and a limit of two years to the length of time a Parliament could sit. Parliament was to control the militia for ten years, and the excise was to be abolished. Cromwell and Fairfax aroused profound suspicion among the radicals by these negotiations, and a Leveller Colonel proposed that Cromwell be impeached. However, the king took the line that 'you will fall to ruin if I do not sustain you',[54] and held out for better terms. There was a limit to the power of Cromwell and Fairfax to carry the army in a settlement, and the negotiations broke down.

Charles was the more ready to see the negotiations break down because

[53] Gardiner, *GCW*, iii. 274.
[54] Gardiner, *GCW*, iii. 340–1.

he was opening other negotiations with the Scots to start a new war on his behalf. Parliament, by this time, had been faced with an uncomfortable situation by the army's occupation of London. In July 1647, Parliament had made brief attempts to conciliate the army, whereat they had been faced with a riot by city conservatives. Speaker Lenthall was held in his chair while a resolution was passed inviting the king to London. After this, 57 M.P.s and 8 peers fled to the army. These have been classified as 'Independents', and some of them were, but it is worth realizing that they included the Earl of Manchester, who was frightened of mobs even if they were Presbyterian, as well as a number of political realists. It was to restore these members to their seats that the army occupied London at the beginning of August 1647. Some of the leading Presbyterian members were impeached or fled abroad, and for the next fifteen months, parliament and army continued an uneasy truce. A motion moved by Marten, for no more negotiations with the king, was defeated by 84–34, with Cromwell one of the tellers against it.

The king, meanwhile, was completing negotiations with the Scots, and hoping that many of the parliamentary Presbyterians would support him. In December 1647, his negotiations were completed. Presbyterianism was to be enforced, and the Scots were to have freedom of trade with England and some posts on the English Privy Council. To the great disappointment of the devout party in Scotland, Charles was not forced to take the Covenant. It is possible that at this time Cromwell and St. John were considering replacing Charles I with Charles II, a scheme which had been started by some of Charles I's own commanders in 1645.[55]

For the moment, however, Cromwell's task was to fight a second civil war against the new alliance of Scots and royalists, which began in the spring of 1648. The Scots were supported by a variety of royalist risings. The fleet declared for the king, objecting to their new commander on the ground that it was 'most reasonable that that man should hold no command, who openly professed himself to be a *Leveller*'.[56] The latent royalism of Kent at last burst into the open, reinforced by dislike of the petty tyrant who ran the county committee, and there were royalist risings in Essex and south Wales, among other places.

In political terms, the support for the king in the second Civil War should have been powerful enough to ensure victory, but it was the support of largely untrained troops fighting what was by this time probably

[55] Such schemes proved impossible because neither Charles II nor any other members of the royal family would co-operate in them. The lack of suitable pretenders is one of the facts which distinguish the Civil War, both from earlier crises, and from the crisis of 1688.

[56] Kennedy, D. E., 'The English Naval Revolt of 1648', *E.H.R.* (1962), 255.

the best army in Europe. Fairfax routed the royalists in Kent, and captured Colchester after a long and bitter siege. Cromwell succeeded in capturing Pembroke after some delay caused by having his artillery wrecked in the Severn, and then turned to face the Scots. He reacted vehemently when he found his men had not been provided with any shoes, but after he had got the shoes, he marched north into Yorkshire at high speed. He then found the Scots had taken the Lancashire route, and, having crossed the Pennines by another forced march, caught them unawares, and cut their army to pieces in detail at Preston.

To Cromwell, the second Civil War was something of a landmark. He was bitterly angry at what he thought quite unnecessary bloodshed, and because Charles had tried 'to vassalize us to a foreign nation'. It also meant that Charles was resisting the judgement of Providence, by which he had lost the first war. The fact that he had also lost the second encouraged Cromwell to share the increasingly prevalent army view of Charles as a 'man against whom the Lord hath witnessed'. He followed up the battle of Preston with an early use of transportation to the colonies as a punishment, and turned his mind back to the task of dealing with the king.

However, the crucial decisions about the fate of the king seem to have been taken by Ireton and the other army officers, while Cromwell was away suppressing the royalist garrison of Pontefract. Parliament, meanwhile, was opening another negotiation with the king, at Newport, according to which Parliament were to have the power to appoint the great officers, and the control of the militia for ten years. Presbyterianism was to be set up for three years, and toleration was to be allowed outside it. The army distrusted these negotiations, and they were right: Charles was saying in private that he was only offering these concessions to facilitate his escape. On 6 December 1648, when M.P.s arrived at Westminster, they found the door guarded by a force of soldiers under Colonel Pride, a former brewer's drayman. Pride arrested forty-five members on a list he had with him, and turned back ninety-six others. The survivors continued to meet under the name of the House of Commons, and were known from then on as the Rump.

The trial of the king, 1649

On 28 December 1648 the Rump passed an ordinance for the trial of the king. As Gardiner says ,'Charles was to be brought to trial mainly because, as long as he lived, England could have no peace.' However, though it might be for the good of England to have Charles dead, it was impossible to bring him to a legal trial. Oliver St. John, now Chief Justice, seems to have been perfectly happy afterwards to have the king dead, but he was unwilling to pretend he had a legal right to try him. All courts were the king's courts, and all law was the king's law, and the High Court of Justice, a sort of parliamentary Star Chamber which the Rump ultimately set up, had no claim to be a court at all. The 'Act' by which it was set up, had not the royal assent, nor the assent of the Lords, who were abolished for opposing the trial of the king. Nor was the claim of the Rump to be the House of Commons, representing the people of England, very easy to defend. As Algernon Sidney inconveniently pointed out: 'first, the king can be tried by no court; secondly, no man can be tried by this court.'[57]

In the court, Bradshaw, an obscure lawyer who had been given the presidency, and Henry Marten, the republican M.P., had probably as much influence as Cromwell. They defended their position in arguments many of which were later borrowed by Locke, according to which the ultimate authority was in the people, and the king held office as their trustee, and so long as he ruled according to law and for the common good. Locke himself was at this time a seventeen-year-old schoolboy at Westminster, and since the school was only a few yards from the place of execution, the boys were locked in for the day. Locke spent the day arguing out the rights and wrongs of the case with a fellow-schoolboy called John Dryden.

Charles found there was nothing he could do but achieve the aim he had set himself in 1645, of ending his days with honour and a good conscience. But the constitution of the court enabled him to get much the better of the trial. He refused to plead, on the ground that he did not recognize the legality of the court, and turned his defence into a defence of the whole principle of the rule of law. He said many forms of force could acquire power, like a robber with a pistol on Shooter's Hill, but that if anyone who obtained power could claim to be a legal court, the rule of law was at an end. Veteran parliamentarian clergy like Burges and Marshall preached vehemently against his execution. When he was at last executed, on 30 January 1649, he made the classic good end: when the executioner held up his head with the customary words: 'behold the head of a traitor', the crowd reacted with a deep groan. Charles I was not a successful man, let alone a successful king, but he was a very successful martyr.

The rule of the Rump, 1649–1653

Republican England started unprepared: it was some months before they passed an Act declaring England a commonwealth, and resolving that 'the people were under God', the origin of all just power. When this

[57] Gardiner, *GCW*, iv. 291, 296.

Act was being passed, a member asked how it was possible to say England was being restored to its 'ancient state' of a commonwealth when it had never been one. Henry Marten, who, from the start, was one of the dominant influences in the Rump, got up, with every appearance of great solemnity, and asked the member to explain to him a text of scripture which described how a man who had been blind from birth had had his sight restored to him. The member subsided.

The Rump might claim that 'the people' were the origin of power, but their own claims to represent the people were highly dubious. They had been elected nine years earlier, but they were a small minority of Parliament, owing their presence simply to the fact that they had not been on the lists supplied to Colonel Pride for his purge. They were extremely unpopular in the country at large, and never dared to face an election. They had, like pre-war civil servants, to live in London almost full-time without salaries, and, as a result, soon fell foul of all the old complaints of administrative corruption. Some of them did very well for themselves, and Sir Arthur Haselrig succeeded to so much of the wealth of the former bishops of Durham that a royalist wit once asked whether the Covenant did not bind people to turn him out, because it bound them to abolish all the dregs and relics of episcopacy. However, as in all the arguments about administrative corruption during this period, there were two sides, and the Rump had to live.

Unfortunately, as yet, we still know very little about the Rump. They were mostly gentlemen, even if some of them had radical sympathies. Many of the most influential members were serious republicans, often of an oligarchic type, getting their inspiration from Venice, Holland, or ancient Rome. They have been classified as 'Independents', and some of them were, but they also included political realists like Oliver St. John, and a number, like Marten, who were simply secular in outlook. They were reasonably tolerant in religion, but, apart from the abolition of law French, they did very little to further the cause of reform. The Levellers detested them, and felt they had been sold out.

We know most about their foreign and commercial policy, but we do not know enough about them to say with any confidence how far it represents their economic interests as a group. They paid a great deal of attention to the fleet. They increased its size, and put Colonel Pride in charge of the most efficient victualling service it had ever had. With its aid, they suppressed the royalist colonies, and reached settlements with them which conceded the principle of 'no taxation without representation'. On the other hand, with the Navigation Act of 1651, they started the policy which ultimately led to the revolt of the American colonies, of insisting that they trade only with England, and in English ships. This was one of the few Acts of the Interregnum which were continued unchanged at the Restoration. The Navigation Act was largely aimed at the Dutch, whose carrying trade was undercutting everyone else in Europe, and, in the face of Cromwell's opposition, the Rump started a war with the Dutch in the spring of 1652. The war was largely for commercial rivalry, and produced a clear English victory. Cromwell, when he became Protector in the autumn of 1653, ended the war on reasonably advantageous terms.

The Rump's greatest difficulties resulted from the fact that the Scots and the Irish were still holding out for Charles II. As Gardiner said, the struggle between king and Parliament was broadening out into a struggle between England and the rest for supremacy over the British Isles.

Wales was comparatively easily dealt with. During the war, it had been royalist, and parliamentarians were worried by the lack of hold religion had in Wales. One asked: 'where more ignorance, where more hatred to the people of God, where the word saint more scorned ... than in Merionethshire?'[58] In 1650, Parliament appointed a Committee for the Propagation of the Gospel in Wales, which, in addition to making provision for public education, went to great trouble to provide Welsh Bibles, to augment livings, and to provide Welsh-speaking preachers. To the dismay of Presbyterians, Welsh-speaking Puritans tended to be unduly radical. However, the Commission was successful, and Welsh nonconformity is perhaps the most enduring result of the Puritan revolution.

Ireland was a tougher case. There was a temporary alliance between the Catholic, anti-English rebels who had been under arms since 1641, and the royalist forces under Ormonde. The two overwhelmingly outnumbered the parliamentarian forces in Ireland, and Charles II might find Ireland a suitable base for the invasion of England. In 1649, a large force under Cromwell was sent over to Ireland. Before going, he had to suppress a mutiny organized by the Levellers, who thought this was a revival of the old scheme to get them out of the way in Ireland while the gentlemen settled the kingdom behind their backs. However, he succeeded in getting away. He had no difficulty in defeating the Irish, but accompanied his victory with large-scale massacres after the sieges of Drogheda and Wexford. The only surprising thing about these massacres is that Cromwell thought he needed to justify them: most Englishmen agreed with him that the Irish were 'barbarous wretches' not entitled to the protection of rules of civilized warfare. It was one of the most shocking facts about Walwyn

[58] Hill, C., 'Propagating the Gospel', in *Essays Presented to David Ogg*, Ed. H. E. Bell and R. L. Ollard (1963), 40 n.

and Overton, the Levellers, that they said that the Irish, like the English, were only fighting for liberty and freedom of conscience. The majority of the deaths were due to a deliberate policy of crop-burning and starvation followed by Ireton after Cromwell returned to England. It has been estimated that the deaths amounted to about 600,000 in a total population of 1,400,000. It is not surprising that when these campaigns were followed by a new plantation scheme, displacing a number of Irishmen for English settlers and sending them to infertile land in the west, the result was a bitterness some of which still survives. However, this may not be the whole story. Ireton found that his greatest worry as commander was the number of his troops who married Irish girls who professed to be converted to Protestantism.

Cromwell was soon recalled to England to lead a campaign against the Scots. Fairfax had resigned the post of commander in chief rather than serve against the Scots, and thus, in 1650, Cromwell for the first time acquired command of the English army. After a long campaign, he defeated the Scots at Dunbar, but was unable to follow up his victory because of the skill of Leslie, the Scottish general, in selecting defensive positions. Finally, he allowed the Scots, accompanied by Charles II, an open road to invade England, and they took it. In 1651, the combined Scottish and royalist force was routed at Worcester. Charles II escaped in disguise, attending the celebrations of a report of his capture, and telling a blacksmith who shod his horse that the trouble was all the fault of that rogue Charles Stuart for bringing in the Scots. Next time, he came without the Scots.

After Worcester, the commonwealth's enemies were defeated, but it was no nearer a settlement at home. The Rump was on increasingly bad terms with the army, and was more and more firmly refusing to dissolve itself and hold elections. Finally, the army induced Cromwell, who had 'sought the Lord day and night, that he would rather slay me than put me upon the doing of this work',[59] to dissolve the Rump. Cromwell turned them out in style, and people in the City celebrated their departure by roasting rump steaks in the streets. The Rump were generally unlamented, but the search for a settlement had to begin again from the beginning.

A much more complex account of the Rump and its dissolution is offered in Blair Worden, *The Rump Parliament* (1974).

[59] Gardiner, *C & P*, ii. 263.

V CROMWELLIAN ENGLAND, 1653–1660

I am as much for government by consent as any man, but where shall we find that consent?

Oliver Cromwell, 1656[60]

Your experience tells you how unsettled things must be, till I am restored to that which belongs to me, which would restore peace to the nation, and you are master of too good a fortune not to desire that security.

Charles II to Anthony Ashley Cooper, 1655[61]

Contending groups, 1653

Cromwell's decision to dissolve the Rump appears to have been taken on the spur of the moment, and he had not even time to put on his outdoor clothes, let alone to make any plans for the future government of England. As in 1649, republican England was caught unprepared. Then, the problem had been postponed by the continuation of the Rump, but in 1653, it could be postponed no longer. Of the institutions of 1641, the monarchy and the Lords had been abolished, and now the Commons had been abolished too. Cromwell as commander in chief was, as he bitterly complained, the only constituted authority left in the kingdom.

Moreover, the list of the regime's irreconcilable opponents had been increased by the addition of the members of the Rump, devout republicans and many of them able politicians, who were painfully aware of their own claim to be the sole legitimate authority. For Ludlow, one of the Rump's members, the Rump stood for the principle that the kingdom should be governed by its own consent, which he said was the cause for which the war had been fought. Bradshaw, President of the court which had condemned Charles I, said he would rather be ruled by Charles II than by Cromwell. The Levellers, too, had for some time been showing signs of moving towards the royalists, and Lilburne said that if England must have a king, he would as soon have Charles II as any other. The Levellers were by this time insignificant, but Cromwell's alarm about them does not seem to have been much eased.

A few royalists and Presbyterians came in to support the government during the 1650s, but the majority remained irreconcilable. Prominent Presbyterians like Manchester remained in retirement, but at any moment they might enter into active alliance with Charles II, with incalculable consequences. Moves which satisfied radical social reformers might well tip them into Charles II's camp.

In this confused situation, there were two sources of power, in almost

---

[60] Gardiner, *C & P*, iv. 263.
[61] Haley, K. H. D., *Shaftesbury*, 89. Cooper did not respond to this invitation, and only committed himself to Charles II in 1660, with a few weeks to spare.

constant opposition to each other. One was that part of the gentry which was still active in politics. Their hold on local government was unshaken, and though a number of minor gentlemen had reached the Bench because of the displacement of their seniors, the Bench was still a collection of gentlemen. Most Puritan gentlemen wanted civilian control over the army, the rule of law, no taxes without parliamentary consent, and a settled constitution under which they would know what the government could do and what it could not.

The army high command had much more various aims. Some, such as Major-General Harrison the Fifth Monarchist, had considerable sympathy with the radicals. All wanted to ensure that the army should have regular pay and reasonable control of its own affairs. Many had made themselves considerable fortunes, and Major-General Lambert, for example, now owned that familiar political weathercock, the manor of Wimbledon.[62] Above all, the army had acquired since 1645 a general suspicion of civilian hostility towards them, and wanted a supreme authority which would protect them against it.

The basis of Cromwell's power in the 1650s was that he was the only man who could command the support of both these conflicting interests. He was both commander in chief of the army and a gentleman by birth. He had won the confidence of his men by persistent concern for their welfare, but above all, because when they were under his command, they won their battles. He could always be trusted to secure them toleration and arrears of pay, and showed, for example, a concern to provide pensions for wounded soldiers, or sailors' widows, which no other government of the century could match. He was prepared to sympathize with those of the radicals' aims which alleviated their position without threatening the power of the gentry, such as reform of imprisonment for debt.

On the other hand, Cromwell's concern for the welfare of his men was essentially the paternalist concern of a good officer. He wanted the gentry to use their political power for the benefit of their inferiors, but he was never prepared to compromise their hold on it. He spoke in 1654 of 'the authority in the nation:—to the magistracy, to the ranks and orders of man—whereby England hath been known for hundreds of years. A nobleman, a gentleman, a yeoman: the distinction of these: that is a good interest of the nation, and a great one. The natural magistracy of the nation, was it not almost trampled under foot, under despite and contempt, by men of Levelling principles?'[63] Beneath his confused English, gentle-

---

[62] On the previous history of the manor of Wimbledon, see above, p. 118.
[63] Carlyle, *Cromwell's Letters and Speeches*, iv. 28. The grammatical confusion is characteristic of Cromwell's attempts to think aloud.

men could easily recognize Cromwell as one of themselves, as a fitting leader, not for the English Revolution, but for the English Counter-Revolution.

Barebone's Parliament, 1653

This speech, however, was made after the failure of an attempt to come to terms with the radicals. When the Rump was dissolved, Cromwell listened to advice from two factions in the Council of Officers. One, headed by Lambert, wanted to vest power in a small executive Council of State, while Harrison wanted a nominated assembly of the saints, to usher in the Fifth Monarchist millennium. The proposal he ultimately adopted was balanced between these two: it was for a nominated assembly of 140 members, selected by the Council of Officers. Harrison and his friends on the Council of Officers nominated some real radicals, but other officers nominated men like Ashley Cooper, who, whatever he might be, never claimed to be a saint. For the only time in English history, the government accepted responsibility for providing lodgings for the members.

Cromwell appears to have expected this body to act as a constituent assembly, to set up a permanent constitution, but when they met, they decided to call themselves a Parliament, resolved, like the Rump before them, that they were the supreme authority in the nation, and set out on a programme of reforming legislation. They came to be known as Barebone's Parliament, after Praise-God Barebone, a London leather-seller and a Baptist, whose writ was used as a specimen writ of summons.

Barebone's Parliament, like the Fifth Monarchists, has suffered consistently from a bad press, and perhaps for the same reason, not that it was fanatical, but that it threatened too many vested interests. It was on the whole an assembly of gentlemen: of 144 members nominated or co-opted, 115 were J.P.s, and though it had a rather higher representation of minor gentry than was normal, it was a body of moderately substantial citizens. It was on the whole a civilian assembly, and though it contained a number of men who had once served in the army, the original nominees included only four serving soldiers. For the first time, it contained representatives of Scotland and Ireland, as well as England and Wales. It appears to have included about 40 radical members, and about the same number of conservatives and a floating vote which gave the victory in divisions to each side in turn.[64]

[64] Much of this information is derived from a paper delivered by Professor A. H. Woolrych to the Anglo-American Conference of Historians in 1966. I am grateful to Professor Woolrych for permission to read this paper in draft, and to quote from it.

Cromwell subsequently alleged that the Parliament was run by the Fifth Monarchists. It included between 11 and 14 committed Fifth Monarchists, who, it is true, had a programme for the Parliament on which it proceeded to act. But this was a perfectly practical programme, which commanded support, not because it was managed by a Fifth Monarchist lobby, but because it included the points for which radicals in general had been pressing for years. They hoped to codify the law, and to reduce it 'into the bigness of a pocket-book, as it is proportionable in New England and elsewhere', to abolish the Court of Chancery and tithes, and to abolish gentlemen's right of presentation to livings. As one of the radicals said, a gentleman might use his right of presentation to present 'one that being beholden to him, shall be sure to serve him, and to forbear his lusts, or else marry his kinswoman or his wife's gentlewoman or chambermaid in consideration of being presented to be settled there'.[65] For the gentry, on the other hand, their powers of presentation were a right of property, and an attack on them was an attack on property in general. Barebone's Parliament succeeded in carrying some reforming legislation, such as a reduction of legal fees, an Act for the relief of poor prisoners, and an Act allowing civil marriages before a J.P. On the other hand, they were not radical enough to show much sympathy for a petition from John Lilburne, appealing against a sentence of banishment imposed on him under the Rump.

Finally, the moderate members became too alarmed by these attempts on their position, and one morning when they had a majority, they voted their own dissolution. A small group of radicals sat on. When the colonel who came to clear the House asked what they were doing, they said, 'we are seeking the Lord', to which the colonel replied, 'then you may go elsewhere, for to my certain knowledge he has not been here these twelve years.'[66]

The Protectorate, 1653–1659

Barebone's Parliament was the radicals' last chance. On its dissolution, Cromwell turned to Lambert and his friends, who had already drawn up a new constitution. It was by this constitution, the Instrument of Government of 1653, that Cromwell acquired the office of Lord Protector and a settled constitutional position. On the other hand, real power under the Instrument was given, not to Cromwell alone, but to Cromwell and a

---

[65] L.D. *An Exact Relation*, in *Somers Tracts*, vi. 278, 279. The proposal for the codification of the law was not new. It had been put forward in 1641 by the Earl of Berkshire, who was told that it was 'rather to be wished, than expected': B.M. Harl. MS. 6424, fo. 18v.

[66] Roots, Ivan, *The Great Rebellion* (1966), 169.

Council of State, whose first members were nominated by the Instrument itself. Their successors were to be chosen by a complicated method of indirect election involving Parliament, the Council, and the Protector. The Instrument thus marked the abandonment of the notion of parliamentary sovereignty held by the Rump, and a return to the constitutional tradition of the pre-war parliamentarians, in which the essential check on the executive was to be provided by control over the composition of the Council. In this concern to control membership of the Council, the Instrument is in the main tradition of English constitutional development, which stretches back to Simon de Montfort, and forward to Sir Robert Walpole. The Instrument guaranteed toleration for all who worshipped Christ (that is, all but Socinians and Unitarians), except papists and prelatists and those who were 'licentious' (probably the Ranters). In practice, Cromwell did all he could to give *de facto* toleration to papists and prelatists as well.

The Instrument marks a return to the constitutional ideas of 1641, and with it, a number of the men of 1641 came back towards the centre of power. The motion for the dissolution of Barebone's Parliament had been moved by Saye and Sele's son-in-law and helped through from the Speaker's chair by Pym's step-brother; Oliver St. John, a long-standing friend of Cromwell's, also worked with him, and St. John's former servant Thurloe became Secretary of State. Nathaniel Fiennes became one of the Commissioners of the Great Seal, and the Clerk of the Council of State was Jessop, former Secretary of the Providence Company. Cromwell resumed many of the ceremonies of the court: he knighted the Lord Mayor of London, had Lambert carry the sword of state before him at the opening of Parliament, and regularly retired on Friday evening to Hampton Court, giving rise to the claim that he can be called the inventor of the English week-end. He once absent-mindedly addressed Henry Marten as 'Sir Henry', to which Marten gravely replied, 'I thank your Majesty.'[67]

The beginning of the Protectorate produced little change in economic policy; the government of the Protectorate was as ready to regulate the economy as any other, and defended such traditional things as the apprenticeship system and the privileges of borough corporations. It has been argued that in economic policy Cromwell was 'the heir of Burghley, and even of Charles I'.[68] In religion, the Cromwellian government showed sympathy to Puritans of all sorts except the Fifth Monarchists and the

[67] Roberts, Michael, 'Cromwell and the Baltic', *E.H.R.* (1961), 411. Aubrey, J., *Brief Lives*, Ed. Dick (1949), 266.

[68] Ramsay, G. D., 'Industrial Laissez-Faire and the Policy of Cromwell', *Ec.H.R.* (1946), 108. This position is supported in a forthcoming article by Mr. J. P. Cooper in the *Transactions of the Royal Historical Society*. I am grateful to Mr. Cooper for allowing me to read this article before publication.

Quakers, some of whom were imprisoned on the ground that they were subversive. Gentlemen kept their rights of presentation, and their nominees were approved by a body of 'Triers', a collection of Puritans of all sorts from Presbyterians to Baptists, who examined candidates for livings to decide whether their abilities were sufficient, but did not attempt to impose any uniformity of doctrine or church government. Discipline over errant clergy was exercised by similar local bodies of Ejectors. For the first time, there was a practical working union between Puritans of almost all sorts.

In foreign policy, Cromwell's government was less certain. His foreign policy has received a disproportionately large part of the attention of historians, because it is easily isolated as a subject for examination purposes. It is doubtful whether it received nearly so much of Cromwell's attention. Many members of the government were handicapped by the poor standard of their Latin, and the Swedish ambassador reported that 'blind Miltonius has to translate from English anything they want done, and you can easily imagine how slowly it goes'.[69] There has been much argument about whether Cromwell's foreign policy was based on religious or commercial grounds. This argument is on the whole misplaced, since there seems to be no evidence that Cromwell saw any conflict between England's religious and commercial interests. There is no such thing as a foreign policy which suited the interests of a mythical body called 'the merchants': the merchants' economic interests varied according to the country they traded with. East India merchants tended to want to fight the Dutch, while West Indian merchants tended to want to fight the Spaniards. Merchants trading to Bordeaux tended to want friendship with France. Merchants trading to the Baltic tended to be against the Danes, who had the power to close the Sound and were temporarily in alliance with the Dutch. They may have been worried by Cromwell's readiness to import naval stores from America instead of the Baltic.

Cromwell was inclined to friendship with the Dutch. This was not particularly on Protestant grounds: the Dutch had recently driven out the Stuarts' old allies the House of Orange, and Cromwell, whose foreign policy was much influenced by the need to prevent a Stuart restoration, had a strong interest of security in making sure the House of Orange did not return to power. He was also interested in colonial development. He prohibited the growing of tobacco in England in order to guarantee a market for colonial produce. His one major war, undertaken in 1655, was against Spain in the West Indies. It led to the conquest of Jamaica, which

---

[69] Roberts, Michael, 'Cromwell and the Baltic', *E.H.R.* (1961), 411. This was John Milton the poet, who held the post of Latin Secretary.

Cromwell made vigorous efforts to colonize. He regularly used transportation as a punishment, thus increasing the colonial population. He was also much interested in the Mediterranean: he at last took effective action against the North African pirates who had provided Charles I with his excuse for levying Ship Money, and considered an attack on Gibraltar on the ground that it would be both a help to English trade and an annoyance to the Spaniards. On the other hand, he also regarded Spain as a natural enemy on religious grounds, and thought that the peace with Spain in 1604 was the worst mistake James I had made.

Neither foreign policy nor anything else could attract enough support to Cromwell's regime to save him from constitutional problems which plagued every government of the period. His first Parliament, called in September 1654, took over much of the desire to restrict the executive which had characterized early Stuart Parliaments. Cromwell insisted on regarding it as a Parliament under a settled constitution, not a constituent assembly. Parliament, however, did not see what right Major-General Lambert had to impose a constitution on them and insisted on regarding the Instrument as subject to parliamentary revision. Cromwell finally gave way, after insisting on four 'fundamentals': that power should be shared between a single person and a Parliament, that there should be liberty of conscience, that Parliament and the Protector should share control of the militia, and that Parliaments should not make themselves perpetual. Even on these terms, he had to exclude a large number of members who were devout republicans and mostly former members of the Rump. These men were continually re-elected to Parliament throughout the Protectorate, and it proved continually impossible to reach any working arrangement with them. The republicans, along with the royalists, the radicals, and most of the Presbyterians, had to be added to the list of irreconcilable opponents of the regime.

The royalists remained a closed clique, marrying almost entirely within their own group, as if, Cromwell complained, 'they meant to entail their quarrel, and prevent the means to reconcile posterity'.[70] They were also making plans for a large-scale rising in 1655. This was never likely to succeed, because Secretary Thurloe, a master of intelligence, was always too well informed of their plans. He had control of the Post Office, and an agent who could recognize all the leading royalists' hands. This agent sorted *all* the post in London every evening, reading all the letters which seemed likely to interest him. When the rising came, in 1655, only a few men led by Penruddock, in Wiltshire, succeeded in starting a campaign. But Penruddock's rising could easily have been much more dangerous than

[70] Firth, C. H., 'The Royalists under the Protectorate', *E.H.R.* (1937), 641.

it was. In Yorkshire, Nottinghamshire, Shropshire, and many other places, small groups of royalists turned out in arms, and one initial success might have enabled them to raise concerted risings.

Penruddock's rising was the crisis of the Protectorate. In Somerset, 3,000 private citizens turned out in arms to oppose Penruddock. It looked as if the Protectorate could now count on the support of that crucial uncommitted body of opinion which wanted to defend established government, as if Cromwell, like the Tudors, could count on the support of those who wanted peace and quiet, or simply to back the winner.

Stresses and strains, 1655–1658

However, the government appears to have panicked at the extent of the royalist conspiracy. Cromwell, speaking to his second Protectorate Parliament, expressed intense alarm, particularly about the insignificant attempts to produce an alliance between royalists and Levellers. In this alarm, shortage of money played a crucial part. At about the same time as the rising, he had lost a test case in the courts over customs dues which was uncomfortably similar to many cases under the Stuarts, and like the Stuarts he had continued to levy the sums in question. Parliament had all the readiness to restrict the government's income it had had under the Stuarts, and though the government had an income which was fantastic by pre-war standards, the cost of the army and navy ensured that it was not solvent. The monthly assessments were bringing in £919,000, customs and excise £700,000, and miscellaneous income £101,000, making a total of £1,720,000 *per annum*. England's power in European politics under Cromwell was largely because, for the first time, the English paid taxes on a scale similar to the French or the Spaniards. On the other hand, these figures shed a sharp light on the protests of the Levellers and the Fifth Monarchists against the excise. Expenditure was on an even greater scale: the army was costing £1,057,000, the navy £768,000, and other expenses £214,000 *per annum*, leaving a deficit of £230,000 *per annum*. Shortly after Penruddock's rising, Cromwell's lifeguards, who had not been paid, broke into his kitchen and took his dinner. Cromwell merely told his servants to give them any further provisions they needed.

It was in this situation, in which the government needed more troops, but could not pay those it already had, that Cromwell decided to institute the rule of the Major-Generals. The original purpose of the Major-Generals was for each of them to organize a citizen militia within a limited area: their functions were to be like those of the old Lords Lieutenant. The Major-Generals were also to enforce a punitive decimation tax against royalists. The Council, however, appears to have found the opportunity offered by the division of England into eleven districts, each under a Major-General, irresistible. A long series of additional instructions were issued, directing the Major-Generals to supervise almost everything from prosecution of robbers to executing the laws for the benefit of the poor. They were to license alehouses, purge the J.P.s, suppress horse-racing, and in general to 'promote virtue'. With these powers, and the army to support them, the Major-Generals rapidly became the most unpopular men in England.

The Major-Generals finally drove a wedge between Cromwell's civilian and military supporters. When the second Protectorate Parliament was called, in the autumn of 1656, the elections were dominated by the cry of 'no courtiers, no swordsmen', and Parliament assembled in a thoroughly awkward mood. They first took up the case of James Nayler, a Quaker who was supposed to have claimed to be Christ.[71] In addition to the horror caused by Nayler himself, the case involved two other crucial issues: the authority of the Instrument of Government, and the issue of parliamentary supremacy. The Cromwellian councillors in the House could only defend Nayler by delaying tactics, which, though very skilfully used, ultimately failed. Nayler was given a variety of savage punishments, and Cromwell could only save his life.

Parliament then refused to renew the decimation tax, and offered Cromwell a new constitution, called the Humble Petition and Advice, whose crucial point was to get him to take the title of king. One reason for this proposal was that Cromwell was now 58, and had just escaped an assassination plot, so Parliament feared a succession crisis. If he became king, his eldest son Richard Cromwell would succeed without question. But the main point of the proposal, as St. John argued in an eloquent speech in favour of it, was not to increase Cromwell's power, but to reduce it. As St. John said, they knew what a king could do, but not what a Protector could do, and the restoration of kingship could mean the restoration of the rule of law. As Hexter says, 'one does not usually try to please an autocrat by prescribing a limitation of his power, but St. John, better than most men, knew his Cromwell'.[72] For St. John and his friends, a Puritan monarchy under Cromwell would have meant the achievement of everything they had wanted ever since 1641. The army, on the other hand,

---

[71] The accusation that Nayler had claimed to be Christ may have rested on a misunderstanding of the Quaker doctrine of the Light within, according to which there was something of Christ in each of us. See Nuttall, G. F., *James Nayler: A Fresh Approach*, *Journal of the Friends' Historical Society* (1954), supplement no. 26.

[72] Hexter, J. H., *The Reign of King Pym* (1941), 170. This speech is only recorded as being by 'the chief justice', and the speaker may have been the other Chief Justice, Glyn, another veteran of 1641.

were strongly against this proposal: many of them were sincere republicans, and moreover, they recognized that the proposal was essentially aimed against them. Major-General John Lambert, the army's favoured candidate for the succession, said the issue was not just whether it should be Richard or John, but whether England should be a monarchy or a republic.

For whatever reason, Cromwell refused the crown, and accepted the Humble Petition and Advice in a revised form which set up an Upper House, or, as they called it, an 'other House', of Parliament, and allowed Cromwell to nominate his successor, but did not make Cromwell king. Nothing, however, could restore the co-operation between Cromwell's military and civilian supporters. After a few more unhappy months of power, Cromwell died in September 1658.

The return to kingship, 1658–1660

The succession crisis appeared at first to have passed off calmly, and Richard Cromwell was recognized as Protector. However, Richard Cromwell was neither ambitious nor a skilled politician, and had none of his father's hold on the loyalties of the army. His accession was greeted by a campaign led by the veterans of the Rump for the 'good old cause' of republican government, in which they enlisted the sympathy of so many junior officers that the army high command fell in with them. Richard Cromwell resigned, and the army recalled the Rump. The Rump turned out to be as high-handed as ever; Haselrig told Lambert 'you are only at the mercy of the Parliament', to which Lambert replied: 'I know not why they should not be at our mercy.'[73] The post of commander in chief had passed to Fleetwood, Cromwell's son-in-law, who was married to Ireton's widow, and he was unequal to the post. In October 1659, the Rump declared illegal all acts and ordinances since they had been dissolved, cashiered Lambert, and put the army command into commission. For the army, this was too much, and they dissolved the Rump, and set up a Committee of Safety. Once again, there was no basis for co-operation between the Rump and the army.

Finally, General Monk, commander of the English forces in Scotland, started a march on London. Nobody knew what Monk intended to do, but as commander of the last paid and disciplined force left, he could do what he liked. Meanwhile, the army had once again re-summoned the Rump. All attempts to achieve a settled government were equally failures, and there was only one possible solution: the return of the king. Yet it took time to reach this solution. Monk began by recalling all the members who

[73] Roots, Ivan, *The Great Rebellion* (1966), 243.

had been secluded from the Long Parliament. They made one final attempt to impose Presbyterianism on England, and at last dissolved themselves. According to the Act of 1641, the Long Parliament had been dissolved with its own consent. Charles, meanwhile, had issued a declaration from Breda, offering an indemnity, and suggesting that he might allow liberty of conscience.

The Long Parliament had ordered the issue of writs for a free Parliament, for which, for the first time, everyone, including former royalists, could vote. The resulting House of Commons included sixteen members of the Rump, a number of Presbyterians, but almost no one associated with the army. There was a large majority in favour of restoring the king. With them came back the House of Lords, and the two Houses had little difficulty in resolving that by the fundamental laws, the government should be in the hands of king, Lords, and Commons. The conservatism of the English gentry had triumphed. On 25 May 1660, Charles II landed at Dover. He came to take over the constitution of 1641, the ancient constitution the parliamentarian gentry had always wanted to preserve. The army was paid off in full and disbanded before the question of toleration was settled against them by the Cavalier Parliament, in 1662. King and gentry resumed their partnership, and resumed the attempt to secure an unattainable unity in religion, and to work an outdated constitution.

ABBREVIATIONS AND SELECT BIBLIOGRAPHY

Agrarian History. *Agrarian History of England and Wales* Vol IV, ed. Joan Thirsk (Cambridge, 1967).

Ashton. Robert Ashton, *The Crown and the Money Market* (Oxford, 1960).

Aylmer. G. E. Aylmer, *The King's Servants* (London, 1961).

Bowker. Margaret Bowker, *The Secular Clergy in the Diocese of Lincoln* (Cambridge, 1968).

C.J. *Commons' Journals.*

Cal. S. P. Dom. *Calendar of State Papers, Domestic.*

Collinson. P. Collinson, *The Elizabethan Puritan Movement* (London, 1966).

Conyers Read i, ii. Conyers Read, *Mr. Secretary Cecil* Vol. 1, *Lord Burghley* Vol. II (London, 1955–60).

Dickens, *Lollards and Protestants.* A. G. Dickens, *Lollards and Protestants in the Diocese of York* (Oxford, 1959).

Dickens, *Reformation.* A. G. Dickens, *The English Reformation* (London, 1964).

Donaldson, *Prayer Book.* Gordon Donaldson, *The Making of the Scottish Prayer Book of 1637* (Edinburgh, 1954).

Donaldson, *Scotland.* Gordon Donaldson, *Edinburgh History of Scotland* Vol 3 (1965).

Edwards. T. Edwards, *Gangraena* (London, 1646).

Foster, *1610.* Elizabeth Read Foster, *Parliamentary Debates in 1610* (Yale, 1966).

Gardiner, *History.* S. R. Gardiner, *History of England 1603–1642* 10 vols (London, 1893).

Gardiner, *1610.* S. R. Gardiner (ed.), *Commons' Debates in 1610* (Camden Series, 1861).

Gardiner, *1625.* S. R. Gardiner (ed.), *Commons' Debates in 1625* (Camden Series, 1873).

Gardiner, *GCW.* S. R. Gardiner, *The Great Civil War* 4 vols (London, 1894).

Gardiner. *C. & P.* S. R. Gardiner, *The Commonwealth and Protectorate* 4 vols (London, 1903).

Hurstfield. J. Hurstfield, *The Queen's Wards* (London, 1958).

L. & P. *Letters and Papers of Henry VIII* ed. J. S. Brewer (London, 1920–32).

Neale, *Parliaments.* Sir John Neale, *Queen Elizabeth I and Her Parliaments* 2 vols (London, 1953–7).

Rushworth. J. Rushworth, *Historical Collections* (London, 1659).

Scarisbrick.　J. J. Scarisbrick, *Henry VIII* (London, 1968).

Stone.　Lawrence Stone, *The Crisis of the Aristocracy* (Oxford, 1965).

Stuart Constitution.　J. P. Kenyon (ed.), *The Stuart Constitution* (Cambridge, 1966).

Tawney and Power.　R. H. Tawney and Eileen Power (eds.), *Tudor Economic Documents* (London, 1924).

Tudor Constitution.　G. R. Elton (ed.), *The Tudor Constitution* (Cambridge, 1960).

Tyacke.　N. R. N. Tyacke, 'Arminianism in England: Religion and Politics' (Oxford D.Phil. thesis, 1968). To be published shortly by the Clarendon Press.

Wernham.　R. B. Wernham, *Before the Armada* (London, 1966).

Willson, *Privy Councillors.*　D. H. Willson, *The Privy Councillors in Parliament 1603–1629* (Minneapolis, 1940).

Woolrych, *Battles.*　A. H. Woolrych, *Battles of the Civil War* (London, 1961).

OTHER ABBREVIATIONS

B.I.H.R.　*Bulletin of the Institute of Historical Research.*

B.M.　British Museum.

B.M.E.　British Museum: Thomason Tracts.

B.M. Harl. M.S.　British Museum: Harleian manuscripts.

E.H.R.　*English Historical Review.*

Ec.H.R.　*Economic History Review.*

H.J.　*Historical Journal.*

H.M.C.　Historical Manuscripts Commission, Reports.

J.E.H.　*Journal of Ecclesiastical History.*

P.C.C.　Prerogative Court of Canterbury (Wills formerly at Somerset House).

P.R.O.　Public Record Office.

P.R.O. Sta. Cha.　Public Record Office, Star Chamber.

R.O.　Record Office.

T.R.H.S.　*Transactions of the Royal Historical Society.*

FURTHER BIBLIOGRAPHY

I regret that the following books appeared too late for me to use them:

Claire Cross, *The Royal Supremacy in the Elizabethan Church* (1969). This book shows the extent to which the Elizabethan Church was dominated by powerful local influences.

F. R. H. Du Boulay, *An Age of Ambition* (1970). The best general description of the fifteenth-century background.

Peter Heath, *The English Parish Clergy on the Eve of the Reformation* (1969). Dr. Heath's conclusions confirm those of Mrs. Bowker, which have been used here.

C. Hill, *Oliver Cromwell and the English Revolution* (1970).

Roger Howell and David E. Brewster, 'Reconsidering the Levellers: the Evidence of *The Moderate*', in *Past and Present*, no. 46 (February, 1970). This article modifies what is said on pp. 370–1 of the Levellers' views on the franchise. It shows that the Leveller newspaper *The Moderate*, was committed to universal suffrage, and asks whether we have any reason to suppose that the Levellers as a body shared any common view on how far the franchise should be extended.

W. J. Jones, *The Elizabethan Court of Chancery* (Oxford, 1967). This book shows that there was a considerable centralization of litigation in London in the 1590s, which clearly contributed to the growth of London. It also suggests that in Chancery the growth in the 1590s of a tribe of administrative projectors, holding patents of monopoly for various pieces of administrative work, was largely due to defects in the existing administrative machinery. The increase in the volume of business created a need for new posts, which the existing Chancery officials were reluctant to satisfy, for fear of diminishing their fees and privileges.

Eric Kerridge, *The Agricultural Revolution* (1967). Dr. Kerridge argues that the supposed 'agricultural revolution' of the eighteenth century was a myth, and that the most important changes in agriculture were introduced between 1560 and 1670. These changes are similar to those described on pp. 185–6, but Dr. Kerridge suggests that their scale and significance was much greater than had previously been thought. These conclusions, if confirmed, would show that by the middle of the seventeenth century the diet of the poor was much better than is suggested here, and would provide an explanation for the slowing down of price increases after 1620.

W. Lamont, *Godly Rule, 1603–1660* (1969).

S. E. Lehmberg, *The Reformation Parliament* (Cambridge, 1970). Dr. Lehmberg's evidence suggests the possibility of a revision of the story of Henry

VIII's divorce. He shows conclusively that the Reformation Parliament was not meant to provide Henry with his divorce, and, indeed, quotes Henry as forbidding Parliament to discuss the divorce on the ground that it was a 'spiritual matter'. He stresses the crucial part of Convocation in granting the king his divorce, and reminds us that a number of deaths among the episcopate produced a considerable change in the complexion of Convocation during the early years of the Reformation Parliament. He shows that the king was attempting to get his divorce from the English clergy as early as February 1532, but was obstructed by the opposition of Archbishop Warham. This makes it possible to see an intelligible motive for the otherwise rather purposeless attacks on the English clergy during the opening years of the Reformation Parliament. They may have been designed to terrorize, not the Pope, but the English clergy, into granting Henry his divorce. This would imply that Professor Scarisbrick was right in arguing that Henry already intended to reject the Papacy by 1529 or 1530, and that the delay was caused by the need to terrorize the English clergy into compliance, and above all to wait for the death of Archbishop Warham. However, there is no reason to suppose that, if the Pope had offered Henry his divorce during this period, he would not have accepted it. It looks increasingly doubtful whether a definitive account of these years can ever be written.

Ida Macalpine, John Brooke, and Abe Goldberg, *Porphyria: a Royal Malady* (1968). The authors argue that James I, as well as George III, suffered from a rare metabolic disorder called porphyria, and that some of their supposed character defects should be ascribed to attacks of intense pain.

Wallace MacCaffrey, *The Shaping of the Elizabethan Regime* (1969).

Alan Macfarlane, *Witchcraft in Tudor and Stuart England* (1970). This book is a detailed sociological study, which for the first time makes possible a proper account of the subject of witchcraft. The peak of witchcraft prosecutions appears to have been between 1570 and 1600. Belief in witchcraft appears to have been extremely widespread, and in Essex, the worst-affected county, witchcraft produced the second largest number of Assize prosecutions after theft. Essex witches appear not to have used broomsticks, cauldrons, or any of the other more dramatic appurtenances associated with their trade, and Dr. Macfarlane concludes that, by comparison with their African counterparts, they lived 'austere and blameless lives'. The majority of witches appear to have been both older and poorer than their accusers, and, in sharp contrast to the African evidence, it appears that it was usually the accuser, and not the witch, who was guilty of anti-social conduct. The majority of witches seem to have bewitched their victims in anger at being refused some neighbourly service, usually the gift of some small amount of food, such as butter, milk, or beer, but sometimes something such as credit at the local shop. The witch in *Macbeth*, who was accused of witchcraft by a prosperous 'rump-fed' sailor's wife, because she had asked for, and been refused, a gift of some chestnuts, appears to be a typical case; but the dramatic cauldron session later held by the witches in *Macbeth* appears to be quite untypical, and possibly taken from James I's book on the subject. Dr. Macfarlane suggests that an accusation of witchcraft was a device for projecting the guilt for unneighbourly conduct on to the supposed witch, who suffered from it. The witchcraft cult, then, appears to have been a reaction to the decline in hospitality and good neighbourliness described by Mr. Hill in *Society and Puritanism* (1965), pp. 259–97. Whether Mr. Hill is right in connecting the growth of this individual-istic attitude with Puritanism remains an open question. Dr. Macfarlane has found no correlation between Puritanism and witchcraft prosecutions, and, indeed, has found Puritans who said that being bewitched was a just punish-ment for anti-social conduct. His own evidence would suggest that inflation, food shortage, and perhaps changes in agriculture, contributed more to the breakdown of good neighbourliness than any religious doctrines. His picture of Essex villagers constantly resorting to 'wise women' or witch doctors to be cured of witchcraft shows a county which was more pagan than Christian, and we must hesitate before ascribing its ideas to Christian doctrine.

J. H. Plumb, *The Growth of Political Stability in England* (1967). Professor Plumb's argument that the electorate was growing in size dovetails with the argument, suggested in Chapter V, that it was growing in importance.

Violet A. Rowe, *Sir Henry Vane the Younger* (1970).

Paul Seaver, *The Puritan Lectureships* (Oxford, 1970).

P. W. Thomas, *Sir John Berkenhead* (Oxford, 1969). This book makes pos-sible a more thorough analysis of the Royalist press and propaganda than is attempted here.

Donald Veall, *The Popular Movement for Law Reform, 1640–1660* (Ox-ford, 1969). Makes possible a more detailed account of the subject than has been attempted here.

Charles Wilson, *Queen Elizabeth I and the Revolt of the Netherlands* (1970).

B. P. Wolfe, *The Crown Lands, 1461–1563* (1969). Dr. Wolfe shows that the idea that the king should live off his own has a much less lengthy medieval history than its seventeenth-century exponents supposed.

Perez Zagorin, *The Court and the Country* (1969).

November 1970

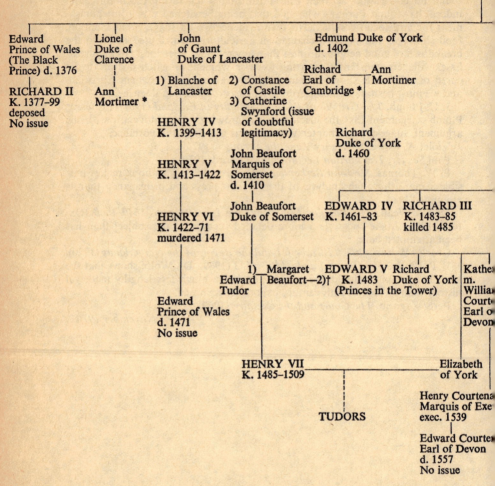

Edward
Prince of Wales
(The Black
Prince) d. 1376

RICHARD II
K. 1377–99
deposed
No issue

Lionel
Duke of
Clarence

Ann
Mortimer *

John
of Gaunt
Duke of Lancaster

1) Blanche of
Lancaster

HENRY IV
K. 1399–1413

HENRY V
K. 1413–1422

HENRY VI
K. 1422–71
murdered 1471

2) Constance
of Castile
3) Catherine
Swynford (issue
of doubtful
legitimacy)

John Beaufort
Marquis of
Somerset
d. 1410

John Beaufort
Duke of Somerset

Edmund Duke of York
d. 1402

Richard   Ann
Earl of   Mortimer
Cambridge *

Richard
Duke of York
d. 1460

EDWARD IV   RICHARD III
K. 1461–83   K. 1483–85
             killed 1485

1) Margaret   EDWARD V Richard   Kathe
Edward Beaufort—2)† K. 1483   Duke of York   m.
Tudor   (Princes in the Tower)   Willia
                                        Court
Edward   Earl o
Prince of Wales   Devon
d. 1471
No issue

HENRY VII   Elizabeth
K. 1485–1509   of York

TUDORS

Henry Courtena
Marquis of Exe
exec. 1539

Edward Courte
Earl of Devon
d. 1557
No issue

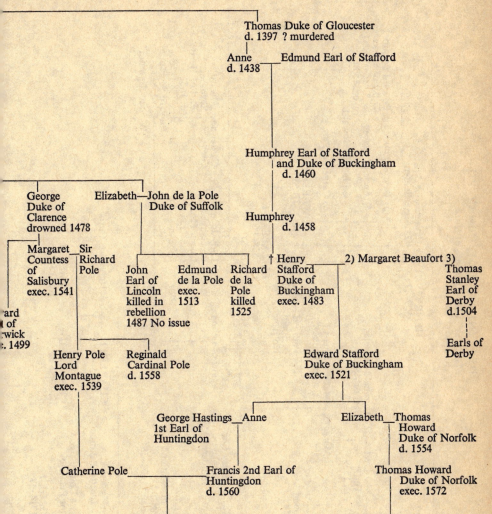

Thomas Duke of Gloucester
d. 1397 ? murdered

Anne   Edmund Earl of Stafford
d. 1438

Humphrey Earl of Stafford
and Duke of Buckingham
d. 1460

George   Elizabeth—John de la Pole
Duke of   Duke of Suffolk
Clarence   Humphrey
drowned 1478   d. 1458

Margaret Sir
Countess Richard
of   Pole   John   Edmund   Richard   † Henry   2) Margaret Beaufort 3)
Salisbury   Earl of   de la Pole de la   Stafford   Thomas
exec. 1541   Lincoln   exec.   Pole   Duke of   Stanley
                      killed in 1513   killed   Buckingham   Earl of
ard   rebellion   1525   exec. 1483   Derby
 of   1487 No issue   d.1504
wick
. 1499   Earls of
                      Henry Pole Reginald   Edward Stafford   Derby
                      Lord   Cardinal Pole   Duke of Buckingham
                      Montague   d. 1558   exec. 1521
                      exec. 1539

                           George Hastings Anne   Elizabeth Thomas
                           1st Earl of   Howard
                           Huntingdon   Duke of Norfolk
                                                                    d. 1554

          Catherine Pole   Francis 2nd Earl of   Thomas Howard
                                     Huntingdon   Duke of Norfolk
                                     d. 1560   exec. 1572

          Henry 3rd Earl of Huntingdon   Howards

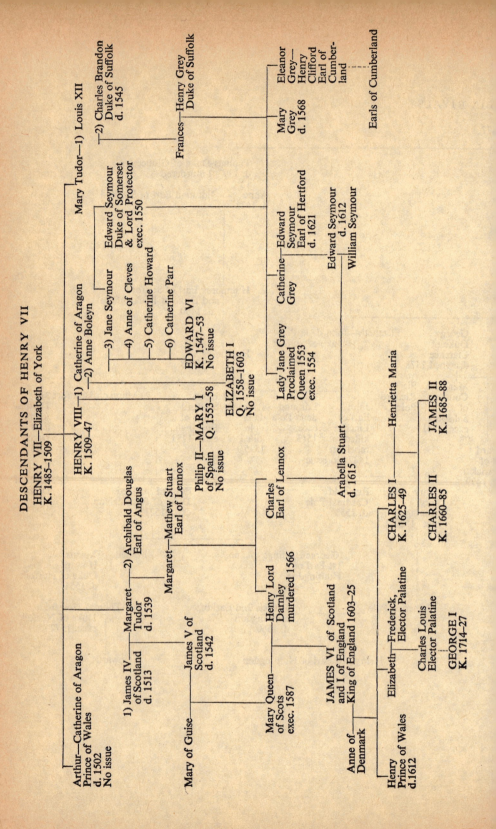

DESCENDANTS OF HENRY VII

HENRY VII—Elizabeth of York
K. 1485–1509

Arthur—Catherine of Aragon
Prince of Wales
d. 1502
No issue

HENRY VIII—1) Catherine of Aragon
K. 1509–47
2) Anne Boleyn
3) Jane Seymour
4) Anne of Cleves
5) Catherine Howard
6) Catherine Parr

Mary Tudor—1) Louis XII
2) Charles Brandon
Duke of Suffolk
d. 1545

EDWARD VI
K. 1547–53
No issue

Philip II—MARY I
of Spain   Q. 1553–58
No issue

ELIZABETH I
Q. 1558–1603
No issue

Margaret—Mathew Stuart
Earl of Lennox

Edward Seymour
Duke of Somerset
& Lord Protector
exec. 1550

Catherine—Edward
Grey   Seymour
Earl of Hertford
d. 1621

Lady Jane Grey
Proclaimed
Queen 1553
exec. 1554

Frances—Henry Grey
Duke of Suffolk

Mary Grey
d. 1568

Eleanor
Grey—
Henry
Clifford
Earl of
Cumber-
land

Earls of Cumberland

Edward Seymour
d. 1612
William Seymour

1) James IV
of Scotland
d. 1513

Margaret
Tudor
d. 1539

2) Archibald Douglas
Earl of Angus

James V of
Scotland
d. 1542

Charles
Earl of Lennox

Arabella Stuart
d. 1615

Mary of Guise

Henry Lord
Darnley
murdered 1566

Mary Queen
of Scots
exec. 1587

JAMES VI of Scotland
and I of England
King of England 1603–25

Elizabeth—Frederick,
Elector Palatine

Henrietta Maria

CHARLES I
K. 1625–49

CHARLES II
K. 1660–85

JAMES II
K. 1685–88

Anne of
Denmark

Henry
Prince of Wales
d.1612

Charles Louis
Elector Palatine

GEORGE I
K. 1714–27

TABLE OF EVENTS

1509 Accession of Henry VIII: Marriage to Catherine of Aragon. Parliament 1509–10.
1510 Execution of Empson and Dudley. Price and Wages indices *c*. 100.
1511 Henry joins Holy League against France. Parliament, 1511–12.
1512 War against France and Scotland.
1513 Battle of Flodden and Battle of the Spurs.
1514 Peace with France. Hunne case. Parliament, 1514–15.
1515 Wolsey made Chancellor. Standish case.
1516 Birth of Princess Mary.
1517 Race riots in London and Southampton.
1519 Charles V elected Holy Roman Emperor.
1520 Price index 137, wages index 73.
1521 Execution of the Duke of Buckingham. Henry published *Assertio Septem Sacramentorum,* and was made Defender of the Faith.
1522 French war.
1523 Parliament. Campaign in France.
1525 Failure to collect the Amicable Grant. Charles V captured Francis I at Pavia. Peace with France.
1526 Henry began to consider divorce from Catherine of Aragon. Debasement of the coinage.
1527 Sack of Rome by Charles V.
1528 Embassy to the Pope at Orvieto. First threats to renounce the papacy. War against Charles V in alliance with France. Epidemic of the 'sweating sickness'.
1529 Legatine court considered the divorce at Blackfriars. Henry summoned to Rome. Fall of Wolsey. Meeting of Parliament (till 1536).
1530 Price index 169, wages index 59.
1531 *Praemunire* charge against the clergy. Clergy acknowledged Henry as Supreme Head of the Church 'in so far as the law of Christ allows'.
1532 Submission of the clergy. First Act in Restraint of Annates. Death of Archbishop Warham (August). Meeting with Francis I at Boulogne (October). Pregnancy of Anne Boleyn (December).
1533 Appointment of Archbishop Cranmer. Cranmer married Henry to Anne (January) and granted him his divorce from Catherine (May). Act in Restraint of Appeals. Birth of Princess Elizabeth.
1534 Act of Supremacy. Treasons Act. First Protestant bishops appointed. Death of Pope Clement VII. Fresh negotiations with Rome.
1535 Execution of Fisher and More.
1536 Reginald Pole made Papal Legate. Death of Catherine of Aragon.

Fresh negotiations with Rome. First dissolution of the Monasteries. Execution of Anne Boleyn. Henry's marriage to Jane Seymour. Pilgrimage of Grace. Act against Papal Authority. Statute of Uses.

1536 Union of England and Wales.

1537 Birth of Prince Edward. Death of Jane Seymour.

1539 Great Bible published. Parliament. Act of Six Articles. Second Dissolution of the Monasteries. Statute of Proclamations.

1540 Price index 158. Henry married to and divorced from Anne of Cleves. Execution of Thomas Cromwell. Henry's marriage to Catherine Howard. Execution of Catherine Howard.

1541 Parliament, 1541–4.

1542 War with Scotland. Battle of Solway Moss.

1543 War with France. Henry's marriage to Catherine Parr.

1544 Debasement of coinage.

1545 Parliament.

1546 Peace with France. Fall of Norfolk. Price index 248.

1547 Death of Henry VIII. Succession of Edward VI. Hertford (Edward Seymour) becomes Duke of Somerset and Lord Protector. Parliament. Debasement of the coinage. War with France and Scotland. Battle of Pinkie. Dissolution of the chantries. Clerical marriage permitted.

1548 Communion in both kinds permitted.

1549 Debasement of the coinage. First English Prayer Book. Rebellions in Norfolk and the West Country. Fall of Somerset. Northumberland takes power.

1550 Plague epidemic. Peace with France. Price index 262.

1551 Epidemic of the 'sweating sickness'. Crash of Antwerp.

1552 Parliament 1552–3. Second English Prayer Book.

1553 Death of Edward VI. Northumberland fails to place Lady Jane Grey on the throne. Accession of Mary. Execution of Northumberland. Parliament.

1554 Two Parliaments. Mary's marriage to Philip of Spain. Restoration of Catholicism.

1555 Mary's first hysterical pregnancy. Parliament. Religious persecutions begin.

1556 Epidemic of the 'sweating sickness,' 1556–7. Price index 370.

1557 Price index 409. Queen's second hysterical pregnancy. War with France.

1558 Reform of the customs systems. Loss of Calais. Death of Mary. Accession of Elizabeth. Price index 230.

1559 Peace with France. Religious settlement. Protestant rising in Scotland successful with English support.

1560 Restoration of the coinage. Price index 265.

1562 First French Civil War. English intervention on Protestant side.

1563 Parliament.

1566 Revolt of the Netherlands. Parliament.

1568 Mary Queen of Scots took refuge in England.

1569 Rebellion of the North.

1570 Papal bull excommunicating and deposing Elizabeth. Price index 300.

1571 Parliament. Ridolfi Plot.

1572 Parliament. Execution of Norfolk.

1575 Appointment of Archbishop Grindal.
1576 Parliament.
1577 Suspension of Archbishop Grindal.
1580 Spanish conquest of Portugal. Price index 342, wages index 58.
1581 Parliament. Act against Roman Catholics.
1583 Appointment of Archbishop Whitgift.
1584 Parliament. Throckmorton Plot. Henry of Navarre becomes heir to the French throne. Assassination of William of Orange. Raleigh's voyage to Virginia.
1585 Treaty of Joinville between Philip II of Spain and the Guise family. English intervention in the Netherlands. Babington plot.
1586 Parliament, 1586–7.
1587 Execution of Mary Queen of Scots. Price index 491, wages index 41.
1589 Parliament.
1590 Price index 396, wages index 51.
1593 Parliament.
1597 Parliament. Price index 685, wages index 29. Rebellion in Oxfordshire.
1600 Price index 459, wages index 44.
1601 Essex Rebellion. Parliament.
1603 Death of Queen Elizabeth. Accession of James I (James VI of Scotland).
1604 Peace with Spain. Hampton Court Conference. Appointment of Archbishop Bancroft. Great Farm of the Customs. Parliament, 1604–10.
1605 Gunpowder Plot.
1610 Failure of proposal for the Great Contract. Appointment of Archbishop Abbot. Price index 503, wages index 40.
1612 Death of Robert Cecil, Earl of Salisbury.
1614 Addled Parliament. Cockayne Project.
1618 Outbreak of the Thirty Years' War.
1620 Price index 485, wages index 41. Beginning of economic depression: severe unemployment in clothing industry.
1621 Parliament. Impeachment of Lord Keeper Bacon and others.
1623 Prince Charles and Buckingham travel to Madrid.
1624 Parliament. Impeachment of Cranfield. Decision for war with Spain. First parliamentary attacks on Arminianism.
1625 Death of James I. Accession of Charles I. Plague epidemic. Parliament. Marriage of Charles to Henrietta Maria of France.
1626 Parliament. Attempted impeachment of Buckingham. War with France while war with Spain still continued.
1627 The Five Knights' Case.
1628 Parliament 1628–9. Petition of Right. Assassination of Buckingham.
1629 Tumult in the House. Beginning of eleven year's unparliamentary government.
1630 Peace with France and Spain. Price index 595.
1631 Famine. Price index 682.
1633 Appointment of Archbishop Laud.
1634 First levy of Ship Money.
1636 Plague epidemic.
1637 Case of Burton, Bastwick, and Prynne. King wins Ship Money case by

7 judges to 5. Attempt to enforce new Prayer Book on Scotland. Armed resistance.

1638 Scottish National Covenant.

1639 First Bishops' War.

1640 Short Parliament. Second Bishops' War. Long Parliament, 1640–53.

1642 Outbreak of Civil War. Battle of Edgehill. Royalists advance to Turnham Green.

1643 Solemn League and Covenant. Scots enter the war. Meeting of Westminster Assembly. Excise introduced.

1644 Battle of Marston Moor. Cromwell's quarrel with Manchester.

1645 Self-denying Ordinance. New Model Army formed. Battles of Naseby and Langport.

1646 Parliament passes Blasphemy Ordinance. King surrenders to Scots, who surrender him to Parliament. Propositions of Newcastle (Parliament's peace proposals).

1647 King captured by the army. The Heads of the Proposals (the army's peace proposals). Growth of Leveller movement in the army: appointment of Agitators. Price index 667.

1648 Second Civil War: army defeats Scots and royalists. Pride's Purge. Price index 770.

1649 Execution of Charles I. England declared commonwealth: supreme power for the Rump Parliament. Cromwell's campaigns in Ireland. Price index 821.

1650 Army defeats Charles II and the Scots at Dunbar. Price index 839.

1651 Army defeats Charles II and the Scots at Worcester.

1652 War with the Dutch.

1653 Cromwell dissolves the Rump. Barebone's Parliament. Instrument of Government. Cromwell Lord Protector. Peace with the Dutch.

1654 First Protectorate Parliament.

1655 Conquest of Jamaica. War with Spain. Penruddock's rising. Price index 531.

1656 Rule of the Major Generals. Second Protectorate Parliament.

1657 Humble Petition and Advice: new constitution. Cromwell refuses the crown.

1658 Death of Cromwell. Richard Cromwell Protector.

1659 Resignation of Richard Cromwell. Recall of Rump. Army dismiss and again recall the Rump. Booth's rising. General Monk, from Scotland, marches on London.

1660 Monk recalls secluded members of the Long Parliament. Long Parliament dissolves itself legally, and issues writs for a convention Parliament. Convention Parliament recalls Charles II. Restoration of the Monarchy.

GLOSSARY

Advowson. The right to choose the clergyman to occupy a living, or to sell the right of choosing him to some third party.

Alchemy. The attempt, by pseudo-scientific methods, to convert other substances into gold.

Arminians. Originally the followers of a Dutch theologian called Arminius, alias Hermandszoon. In general, those who wished to deny or diminish the force of the doctrine of Predestination. See pp. 210–17.

Assizes. Periodic sessions of visiting royal judges on circuit, to hear cases in a county.

Astrology. The attempt to predict the future through the study of the stars.

Attainder. Act of Parliament declaring a man a traitor, without formal trial.

Bail. Security given for the release of a prisoner before or during his trial.

Bastard Feudalism. See *Feudalism.*

Benefit of clergy. Ability to escape from the jurisdiction of the secular courts by pleading 'clergy', i.e. ability to read. In 1547 an attempt was made to extend benefit of clergy to peers who could not read. The number of offences to which it was applied was steadily reduced during the sixteenth century.

Book of rates. Official valuations of goods for customs duty. Most goods paid a fixed percentage of their nominal value for customs duty, and the Books of Rates fixed the values on which duty was paid.

Canonization. Official procedure of the Roman Catholic church for declaring a person a saint.

Canon law. Law by which the church was governed. Its ultimate authority was papal decretals (before the Reformation) and canons issued by bishops (after the Reformation).

Cardinal protector. Cardinal acting as a country's permanent representative at the papal court.

Chantry. Institution designed for the saying of Masses in perpetuity, in order to release the soul of its founder from Purgatory.

Cinque ports. Five ports with traditional privileges and liabilities for providing ships in time of war: Dover, Hastings, Sandwich, Romney, and Hythe.

Civil law. Roman Law, as opposed to English common law. *Also,* law regulating lawsuits between party and party, as opposed to criminal prosecutions. *Also,* secular law, as opposed to ecclesiastical law.

Convocation. Representative assembly of the clergy, either of the province of Canterbury or of the province of York. There was no national convocation.

Common law. English law, as opposed to Roman law, law of nations, law merchant, etc. *Also,* law based on precedents, as opposed to law based on parliamentary statute.

Communion in both kinds. The granting to the laity of the communion wine as well as the communion bread.

Consistory court. Bishop's court for hearing civil lawsuits between party and party, or prosecutions brought on behalf of the bishop.

Cooper. A maker or repairer of barrels.

The elect. Those who were thought to be predestined to salvation. Also referred to as 'the saints'.

Enclosure. Fencing off of previously open land: (*a*) by evicting tenants and substituting sheep farming for arable or common grazing rights, or (*b*) in order to consolidate previously scattered agricultural smallholdings. See pp. 19–20.

Entail. Legal device by which a man could leave land to his heir, subject to the restriction that the heir could not sell it, but must in turn leave it to his heir.

Entry fine. Premium paid by tenant to landlord on signature of a new lease.

Episcopalians. Those who believed the church should be governed by bishops.

Equity. Ground of proceedings in the Court of Chancery. See pp. 51–2.

Excommunication. Exclusion from the communion of a church. Punishment commonly used by ecclesiastical authorities.

Ex officio oath. A proceeding *ex officio* in the church courts was a prosecution brought by the church authorities. The oath bound the accused person to answer truly any question he might be asked, including the question whether he was guilty.

Farm (of a source of revenue). System by which a source of revenue was leased to contractors, who paid a fixed rent, and kept any surplus above their rent.

Feodary. County representative of the Court of Wards.

Feudalism. A system of tenure of land in return for military service. Extinct long before this period began, but certain legal obligations connected with it survived. See *Wardship.* Also used by Marxists to describe the existence of a powerful landholding aristocracy. This usage is not generally recognized by non-Marxist historians.

Bastard feudalism. A contractual system under which lords obtained followers, and gave them patronage in return for service, often military. Distinguished from feudalism proper by the fact that it had no connection with land tenure, and by the fact that a retainer could change his lord.

Knight's fee. Amount of property which, when feudal military service survived, had been bound to supply one knight.

First fruits. The year's revenues of a newly appointed bishop. Paid as a tax, first to the Pope, and then to the king.

Gentlemen. In theory, those whose right to a coat of arms was recognized by the College of Heralds. In practice, those who were so regarded by their neighbours. See pp. 17–18.

Hanse. A federation of north German and Baltic trading towns. *Hansard.* A man from the Hanse.

High commission. A court to hear ecclesiastical cases, set up under what became a permanent commission from the Crown. The only church court allowed to impose fines or imprisonment.

Husbandman. Small farmer of status similar to, but less substantial than, a yeoman (q.v.). See pp. 16–17.

Huguenots. French Protestants.

Idolatry. The worship of statues or pictures. Also used by Puritans to mean the worship of anything other than God (e.g. saints).

Independent (after 1642). Strictly a Congregationalist, believing in the autonomy of individual congregations. Also used of a political group sympathetic to the army and to the ideal of toleration.

Indulgences. Documents available in the late mediaeval Catholic church, whereby remission of the temporal penalty for sins was granted, usually in return for a sum of money.

Indictment. Formal written accusation beginning a prosecution at common law.

Inquisition post mortem. See *Wardship*.

Impeachment. From French *empêcher*, to hinder or obstruct. Strictly a trial in Parliament, with the Commons acting as prosecutors and the Lords as judges. Used more loosely of any trial or accusation in Parliament (e.g. the 'impeachment' of the Five Members). Also used in its original French meaning.

Impropriations. See *Tithes*.

Jointure. Portion of estate settled on a bride as endowment for a possible widowhood. Sometimes forfeited on remarriage.

Knight's Fee. See *Feudalism*.

Liturgy. Officially prescribed text of a church service.

Lollards. A late mediaeval sect with some points of resemblance to Protestantism. Founded by Wycliffe and others during the reign of Richard II. See p. 66.

Mass. Service of Communion in the Roman Catholic church.

Matins. Service of morning prayer, without communion.

Militia. County force of private citizens, organized on a home guard basis by local gentlemen as representatives of the Crown. *Trained bands.* A select part of the militia given special training.

Mortuary fee. Fee paid to a clergyman for conducting a funeral.

Ordinance. Decree claiming the force of law, passed (1642–9) by both Houses of Parliament without the royal assent. Also measures enacted by Cromwell as Lord Protector without the consent of Parliament.

Outports. Ports other than London

Papist. Abusive name for member of Roman Catholic church.

Patent. Short for letters patent—literally, an open letter. A document making a grant from the king to a subject, bearing the Great Seal. Used particularly of patents of monopoly.

Pluralism. The holding by a clergyman of more than one living with care of souls.

Praemunire. Statute of the fourteenth century, making it illegal to take cases to any other courts which ought to go to the king's courts. Commonly used to attack clerical claims to independence from the Crown.

Prelatist. Abusive name for one who believed the church should be governed by bishops.

Prerogative. King's discretionary power to act without being bound by rules of law.

Prerogative court. Court acquiring all or some of its powers by exercise of the royal prerogative, and not by Act of Parliament or immemorial tradition.

Presbyterians. Those who believed in a united national church to be governed without bishops. Also used (after 1642) to mean a political group opposed to toleration, and sympathetic to the Scots and to the supremacy of the gentry.

Probate. Legal recognition of the validity of a will.

Proclamation. Decree issued by the king or king and Council, without consulting Parliament.

Puritan. A member of the church of England who believed that it was insufficiently reformed: one of the 'hotter sort of Protestants'.

Purveyance. Compulsory purchase of food at fixed prices by the Crown, to feed armies or the royal household. Also used of money collected in place of this right.

Purveyor. Official engaged in the system of purveyance.

Recusant. One who refused to go to church. Often short for Catholic recusant.

Sanctuary. Right of criminals to take refuge in a church, or in an area from which law enforcement officers were excluded (e.g. Scotland Yard). Also name given to the place in which criminals took such refuge.

Sheriff. Originally the king's chief official in a county. In this period mainly involved in serving writs and other petty business. Also the returning officer in parliamentary elections.

Simony. The purchase of a church living, or other spiritual benefit, for money. Called after its original practitioner, Simon Magus: Book of Acts, 8 : 18.

Socinianism. A collection of heretical doctrines on the Trinity and other subjects.

Seisin. Legal term meaning possession, rather than ownership.

Schism. Separation from the church.

Statute. Law enacted by both Houses of Parliament, with the royal assent.

Synod. National church assembly.

Transubstantiation. The belief that during the Roman Catholic Mass, the bread and wine literally become the body and blood of Christ.

Trained bands. See *Militia.*

Tithes. In theory, a tenth of the produce of the parish, paid to support the local clergyman. In practice, often commuted for a fixed sum, and often impropriated, i.e. taken over by someone other than the parish clergyman, who in turn paid him a fixed sum. See pp. 61–2.

Use. A trust for the ownership of land, designed to keep the land out of wardship. See p. 52. *Feoffee to uses.* A trustee in a use.

Vagrant. A person poor, unemployed, and of no fixed address.

Villein. Obsolete legal status. Originally a countryman legally unfree to move or to own property.

Wardship. Rights held by the king over land which had once been held from him by feudal military service. If any such land was inherited by a minor heir, the king gained custody of the land and the heir, and the right to arrange the heir's marriage. A few lords also still kept rights of wardship over their tenants. See pp. 34–6. *Inquisition* post mortem. Inquest held after the death of a Crown tenant, to discover what land he held, what it was worth, and whether it was liable to wardship.

Yeoman. Moderately substantial farmer with no claim to be a gentleman. See pp. 16–17.

INDEX

Italic figures indicate main entries

accused of playing with loaded dice, 174

on immigration, 189–90

'slept here', 205–6

granted out her unpopular rights as patronage, 206

and Parliament, *220–2, 250–1*

and Earl of Essex, *251–4*

died (1603), 256

other refs., 136, 220, 243

Ellesmere, Earl of. *See* Egerton, Thomas

Emden (Germany), 159

Empson, Richard (exec. 1510), servant of Henry VII, 32, 69, 279

Enclosures, *19–20,* 126, 318

Entails, 53

Erasmus of Rotterdam (d. 1536), publicist, 60, 64–5

Essex, Frances Howard, third Countess of, later Countess of Somerset, 281–2

Essex, Robert Devereux, second Earl of (exec. 1601), 110, 163, 184, 244, 250, *251–4*

Essex, Robert Devereux, third Earl of (d. 1646), Parliamentarian general, 281–2, 331, 342, 346–7, 350, 353, 354, 355, 357, 358

Etcetera Oath, the (1640), 327

Evelyn, John, diarist, 187

Exchequer, the, *45–6,* 110–11, 221

Excise, the, 351, 366, 371, 379, 380, 394

Excommunication, 60–1

Exeter (Devon), 6, 138

Fairfax, Sir Thomas (d. 1671), Parliamentarian general, 344, 358, 377, 380, 382, 386

Falkland, Lucius Carey, second Viscount (of the peerage of Scotland; killed 1643), M.P., 175–6, 200, 217 and n., 310, 321–2, 333, 335, 338

Falstaff, Sir John, Shakespearean character, 164

Famine, 7–8, 23, 38, 171, 184, 248, 313

Fawkes, Guy, 264–5

Feake, Christopher, Fifth Monarchist, 365–6

Fees, official, 45, 59, 248–9, *272–3,* 319–20, 372

Fen drainage, 186

Feodaries (county representatives of Court of Wards), 49, 163, 255

Ferdinand, King of Aragon, 24, 70, 71, 72

Field, John (d. 1588), Presbyterian, 178–9, *223–5,* 226–7, 228, 237, 247

Field of the Cloth of Gold, the (1520), 77

Fiennes, Nathaniel (d. 1669), M.P., 391

Fiennes. *See* Saye and Sele, Viscount and Baron

Fifth Monarchists, 361, *365–6,* 376, *390,* 391–2

Filmer, Sir Robert, political theorist, 199–200

Finch, Sir Henry, lawyer, 196 and n.

Finch, Sir John, first Lord Finch of Fordwich, Chief Justice of the Common Pleas and Lord Keeper, went into exile (1640), 318

Fisher, John (exec. 1535), Cardinal, Bishop of Rochester, 72, 85, 87, 88, 97, 98, 101

Fitzalan, Henry. *See* Arundel, Earl of

Fitz-Geffrey, Charles (d. 1638), clergyman, 179, 313

Five Knights' Case, the (1627), *305–6*

Five Members, so-called impeachment of (1642), 338

Fleet Street, 1

Fleetwood, Major-General William, Cromwell's son-in-law, 396

Fleetwood, Sir Miles, Receiver of the Wards, M.P., 308

Fleming, Serjeant, Solicitor General, 253

Flodden, battle of (1513), 72

Forest laws, 318

Fortescue, Sir John, Chancellor of the Exchequer, 247, 253. *See also* Goodwin v. *Fortescue*

Fossdyke, the (Lincs.), 61, 207

Fox, Edward (d. 1538), Bishop of Hereford, 86

Fox, George, Quaker, 367

Fox, Richard (d. 1528), Bishop of Winchester, 72

Foxe, John, martyrologist, 27, 129, 141, 208, 314

Francis I, King of France (1515–1547), 25, 76–7, 78, 80, 82, 86, 87, 95, 97, 100, 120

Frankfurt am Main (Germany), 145

Frederick, Elector Palatine, 281, 291

Free Speech, right of, in Parliament, 40, 78, 88, *220–2,* 296

Fulham (Middx.), 18

Fuller, Nicholas, M.P., Puritan lawyer, 255, 259, 278